GREY ART GALLERY & STUDY CENTER
CENTRO AFFARI E PROMOZIONI - AREZZO

OUT OF THE OPULENT PAST

ITALIAN TREASURES
FROM THE ETRUSCAN AGE TO THE RENAISSANCE

GREY ART GALLERY AND STUDY CENTER
NEW YORK UNIVERSITY
June 16 - August 1, 1992

1992 DISCOVERY OF ITALY

THIS EVENT IS PART OF 1992: DISCOVERY OF ITALY,
PROMOTED BY ITALIAN TRADE COMMISSION (I.C.E.)

AUTHORITIES' COMMITTEE

Presidenza del Consiglio dei Ministri
Ministero per i Beni Culturali e Ambientali

SPONSORING COMMITTEE

Regione Toscana
Istituto Nazionale per il Commercio Estero
Comune di Arezzo
Provincia di Arezzo
Camera di Commercio di Arezzo
Centro Affari e Promozioni - Arezzo

In collaboration with:

Associazione Orafa Valenzana
Ente Fiera di Vicenza
Monte dei Paschi di Siena
Consorzio Produttori Orafi Aretini

HONORARY COMMITTEE

L. Jay Oliva *President New York University*
John Brademas *President-Emeritus New York University*
Naomi Levine *Senior Vice-President for External Affairs New York University*
Leslie Berlowitz *Vice-President for Institutional Advancement Director, The Humanities Council New York University*
Thomas Sokolowski *Director Grey Art Gallery & Study Center New York University*

Vannino Chiti *Presidente della Regione Toscana*
Marcello Inghilesi *Presidente dell'Istituto Nazionale per il Commercio Estero*
Francesco Sisinni *Direttore Generale del Ministero dei Beni Culturali e Ambientali*
Valdo Vannucci *Sindaco di Arezzo*
Mauro Tarchi *Presidente della Provincia di Arezzo*
Bianco Bianconi *Presidente della Camera di Commercio di Arezzo e del Centro Affari e Promozioni*
Anna Maria Maetzke *Soprintendente ai Beni A.A.A.S. di Arezzo*
Francesco Nicosia *Soprintendente Archeologico per la Toscana*
Antonio Paolucci *Soprintendente per i Beni A.S. di Firenze*
Bruno Santi *Soprintendente per i Beni A.S. di Siena*

ORGANIZING COMMITTEE

Grey Art Gallery & Study Center - New York University
Istituto Nazionale per il Commercio Estero
Centro Affari e Promozioni di Arezzo
Soprintendenza Archeologica per la Toscana
Soprintendenza ai Beni Ambientali, Architettonici, Artistici e Storici di Arezzo
Soprintendenza ai Beni Artistici e Storici di Firenze
Soprintendenza ai Beni Artistici e Storici di Siena

SCIENTIFIC COMMITTEE

Anna Maria Maetzke
Francesco Nicosia
Cecilia Alessi
Alessandro Bagnoli
Dario Bartoli
Stefano Casciu
Gabriele Cateni
Giuliano Centrodi
Giuseppina Carlotta Cianferoni
Mario Cygielman
Gianni De Tommaso
Mario Iozzo
Kirsten Piacenti
Laura Speranza
Luigi Tondo
Franca Maria Vanni
Paola Zamarchi Grassi

MUSEUMS

Museo Archeologico di Firenze
Museo Archeologico "Gaio Cilnio Mecenate" di Arezzo
Museo degli Argenti di Firenze
Museo del Duomo di Arezzo
Museo Guarnacci di Volterra
Museo Statale d'Arte Medievale e Moderna di Arezzo
Museo della Collegiata di Montevarchi
Museo Civico di Sansepolcro
Capitolo della Cattedrale di Arezzo
Chiesa di S. Agostino di Castiglion Fiorentino
Chiesa del Suffragio di Monte San Savino
Chiesa di S. Giovanni a Cerreto di Castelnuovo Berardenga
Chiesa di S. Martino a Cispiano di Castellina in Chianti
Convento della Verna
Palazzo Vescovile di Arezzo
Pieve di S. Giovanni Battista di Cavriglia
Pieve di S. Maria Novella di Radda in Chianti
Pinacoteca Comunale di Castiglion Fiorentino
Collezione privata di Arezzo

ORGANIZING PROJECT

Istituto Nazionale per il Commercio Estero
Grey Art Gallery & Study Center - New York University
Centro Affari e Promozioni di Arezzo

The showing at the GREY ART GALLERY AND STUDY CENTER at NEW YORK UNIVERSITY, has been made possible, in part, with funds provided by the ABBY WEED GREY TRUST and the FRIENDS OF GREY ART GALLERY.

GENERAL CO-ORDINATION

Thomas Sokolowski
Franco Fani
Daniel Virtuoso

OPERATIONAL COMMITTEE

Frank Poueymirou
Michele M. Wong
Wendell Walker

Alessandra Carlomagno
Paola Cavigli
Elisabetta Trombettoni

CATALOGUE

Publishing co-ordination
Paola Cavigli
Giuliano Centrodi
Daniel Virtuoso

Editing
Giuseppina Carlotta Cianferoni
Mario Iozzo

Texts
Cecilia Alessi - C.A.
Dario Bartoli - D.B.
Stefano Bruni - S.B.
Gabriele Cateni - Ga.C.
Giuliano Centrodi - G.C.
Giuseppina Carlotta Cianferoni - G.C.C.
Maryo Cygielman - M.C.
Maria Giovanna Cutini Gheri - M.G.C.G.
Anna Maria Esposito - A.M.E.
Daniela Galoppi Nappini - D.G.N.
Pamela Gambogi - P.G.
Anna Maria Maetzke - A.M.M.
Laura Martini - L.M.
Anna Maria Massinelli - An.M.M.
Maurizio Michelucci - M.M.
Emanuela Paribeni - E.P.
Gabriella Poggesi - P.G.
Anna Rastrelli - A.R.
Giovanni Romanelli - G.R.
Luigi Tondo - L.T.
Fiorenza Vannel Toderi - F.V.T.
Franca Maria Vanni - F.M.V.
Paola Zamarchi Grassi - P.Z.G.

Translations
English Express - Arezzo
Anna Jezler - Firenze
Vox Service - Firenze
Claire O'Connor - Arezzo
Claire Pinks - Arezzo

Photographs
Le Fotografie sono state realizzate da Daniel Virtuoso e Andrea Sarno ad eccezione delle seguenti:
nn. 245 - 249 - 250 - 252 Marcello Bertoni
nn. 177 - 181 - 182 - 183 Luigi Miccinesi
nn. 132 - 138 - 163 Paolo Tosi

Photolithography
Studio Lito 69 - Firenze

Printing
Nuova Grafica Fiorentina

EXHIBITION DESIGN BY

Remo Buti
Guido Venturini

EXHIBITION DESIGNER ASSISTANT

Elena Danti

Execution
A.B.B. di Bruschini - Arezzo

Forwarding Agent
SPED-IN - Arezzo

PRESS OFFICE

Mass Media - Roma

PACKING AND FORWARDING AGENT

Bortolus - Firenze

ACKNOWLEDGEMENTS

We would like to thank: Il Direttore Generale del Ministero dei Beni Culturali e Ambientali Dr. Francesco Sisinni, il Vescovo di Arezzo Mons. Giovanni D'Ascenzi, il Vescovo di Fiesole Mons. Luciano Giovannetti, l'Arcivescovo di Siena Mons. Gaetano Bonicelli, l'Assesore all'Industria, Artigianato e Commercio della Regione Toscana Dr. Luigi Badiali, il Dipartimento Attività Produttive della Regione Toscana, i funzionari ed il personale della sede ICE di Roma e di New York.

and also: Padre Eugenio Barelli, Maria Grazia Benini, Paolo Bini, Gabriele Bolognesi, Paolo Caiani, Stefano Cipolli Scali, Francesco Comanducci, Don Pasquale Corsi, Francesca Delli, Don Giovanni De Robertis, Piero Fusi, Don Gino Giannini, Paola Goldoni, Mario Guidotti, Don Walter Iacomoni, Don Ermanno Martini, Bruno Michelucci, Don Ilio Pagni, Lamberto Parigi, Don Silvano Pieri, Adelaide Poggiali, Giovanni Raspini, Luca Raspini, Don Aldo Romoli, Don Avo Tani, Giuseppe Venturini

We would also like to thank Abet laminati for their help in setting up the floor of the exhibition with "Parqcolor" produced by their associated company PL SPA (Vertemate, Como - Italia)

Bianchi & Bruni- Collezione mobili imbottiti (Pistoia, Italia)

This exhibition pays tribute to the history and tradition of the Tuscan goldsmiths, and in particular those from Arezzo.
The works on display are testimony of both the search for the origin and the continuation of this tradition through time: Relics of sacred and profane art found amongst the acheological finds dating from the Etruscan era moving through to the Roman and Midieval periods to the later Renaissance.
Noteworthy, besides the precious metals, are the most skilled techniques of workmanship: Ranging from «granulation» to «filligree», from «embossing» to «chiselling».
With «Out of the Opulent Past: Italian Treasures from the Etruscan Age to the Renaissance», the Italian Trade Commission gives meaning to «1992: Discovery of Italy» slogan heading the comprehensive programme of events celebrating the discovery of America. Waiting to be discovered is the strength behind the «Italian System» in a global context: Modern, rational, and open, but at the same time rich in cultural traditions that testify to its past, making most of the present, while looking towards the future.
Our aim is to reaffirm the «made in Italy» image and to promote sales of Italian products abroad. With this in mind we consider our association with the «J.A.» exhibition to be integral to our programme of activities: That of juxtaposing a cultural message with both the realties of productivity and the trade of gold and silver creations.

Marcello Inghilesi
President
Italian Trade Commission

Further to the customary economical events Centro Affari e Promozioni of Arezzo, since its foundation, has also contributed enormously to the development of cultural events in Italy and abroad with the co-operation of Public Bodies, Trade Associations, Credit Institutes and private citizens.
This meeting has given significant results and year after year, thanks to the valuable commitment on behalf of the organizing and scientific committees, we have been able to propose important cultural events.
This year, in collaboration with the Soprintendenza Archeologica of Tuscany, the Soprintendenza ai Beni Ambientali, Architettonici, Artistici e Storici of Arezzo, the Soprintendenza ai Beni Artistici e Storici of Florence, the Soprintendenza ai Beni Artistici e Storici of Siena, we propose a vast historical and cultural itinerary on goldware from Ancient Times to the Baroque period.
This represents a great opportunity for American visitors to compare two-hundred and fifty precious works of art, each of which find a special place in history.
The exhibition shall be arranged in the precious Grey Art Gallery in New York thanks to the commitment and collaboration of the Istituto Nazionale per il Commercio Estero [Italian Trade Commission] which has introduced this exhibition in the program: «Discovery of Italy 1992».
We would like to express our most sincere thanks to the New York University, to Grey Art Gallery, to the Regione Toscana, to the Italian Trade Commission, to the Promoting and Organizing Committees and to all those who have contributed to the realization of the Exhibition.

Bianco Bianconi
Chairman
Centro Affari e Promozioni - Arezzo

The Grey Art Gallery & Study Center, New York University is pleased to participate in «1992 Discovery of Italy», through its presentation of *Out of the Opulent Past: Italian Treasures from the Etruscan Age to the Renaissance*. From the earliest time, the Italian penisula has been host to numerous civilizations, each of which has contributed to the rich amalgam that is Italy today. In no other part of the globe, do pagan and christian, republican and imperial, pacific and militaristic eras so neatly conjoin — each building on the other, the successor often employing the symbols of his predecessor for his own edification. In sum, the Italy of 1992 is one great palimpsest whose richness is incalculable. The present exhibition gathers together some 250 objects of various types and styles ranging from Etruscan gold fibulae to gem-encrusted Medieval reliquaries which enshrine and protect the even-more-precious bodily fragments of Christian saints. When looking at these objects, it is difficult, nay impossible, to separate the finesse of the craftsmanship from the inherent beauty of the materials used from the ultimate use to which the art work will be put. All these elements come together in an irresistible melange of opulence and splendour. While it would be all to easy to relish the glittery opulence alone, the value of these objects is contained in the collective strength which they express about the ideals or individuals which they glorify. Given the comparable wealth of intellectual disciplines found within the academic community of New York University, this exhibition will provide our scholars with many cultural artifacts to study. I am most grateful for the help of the Italian Trade Commission here in New York City; and Centro Affari e Promozioni of Arezzo. Without their financial assistance and guidance, this event would not have been possible.

Thomas W. Sokolowski
Director
Grey Art Gallery & Study Center, New York University

The significant moment in history which is the present, characterised by an increasingly urgent search for peace and understanding between nations, is reflected in this exhibition, which aims to make better known in the United States certain distinctive aspects of the Italian, and specifically Tuscan, cultural heritage.
The aim has been to bring together an important group of art works and archeological finds and through them present a general picture of the Etruscan and Roman civilisations. These civilisations may be evaluated through their precious artifacts which exemplify the stage of culture and technology characteristic of the different cultural periods that Tuscany has passed through in its long history.
The history of personal ornament, one of the major themes of the exhibition, allows us to follow without difficulty the evolution of taste from the Orientalising period (at the end of the 8th century B.C.) in a society which while maintaining continuity, was subject to constant change according to the frequent cultural, and sometimes even ethnic, influxes and confluences in the region.
But fundamental to this natural and constant change there is an ever-present technological evolution in which, in its most significant form, and developing with each successive period, we can observe in the most precious artifacts, such as those intended as ornament. It is in this technological evolution — in gold-working and in metal-working in general, as in the carving, engraving and the making of gems and glassware — that later production of similar objects in the West is deeply rooted, continuing up to the present day.
It is in this regard that specifically precious finds, «precious» because made from precious metals, and which go back to the earliest recorded period of Etruscan civilisation, are placed alongside votive bronzes, and carved bone and ivory. Together they help to give a clear idea of the nature of the collections not only in the Museo Archeologico in Florence but also in some of the other important museums in Tuscany, like the Guarnacci museum in Volterra or the Arezzo museum named after Caius Cilnius Mecenate, the close friend of the Emperor Augustus.
The character of the Tuscan museums was founded upon the great collections of aristocratic families, and in their formation the greatest representatives of the Tuscan nobility were personally involved, in collaboration with their scholarly contemporaries. It is appropriate, then, that a significant part of this exhibition is devoted to a remarkable group of gems (cameos and intaglios) belonging to the Museo Archeologico in Florence, to which they came at the end of the last century (that is at the time of the museum's foundation), having long been part of the Medici and Lorena collections.
We hope, therefore, that this exhibition will contribute to the spreading and deepening of mutual awareness and will encourage an ever greater interest in understanding our culture from its remotest origins.

Francesco Nicosia
Superintendent
Soprintendenza Archeologica della Toscana

This exhibition, which will be in New York, represents a cultural event of great importance exhibiting fine examples of goldware created in Etruria and Tuscany from Ancient Times to more recent times. It is probably the first time that these precious and refined examples of art are being presented in the United States.
The exhibition covers many centuries allowing visitors to compare different cultures, ways of life, social activities, sensitivity and spirituality. These creations are fruit of goldsmiths' ability, patience and gifted workmanship who have been able to create exquisite works of art from jewels to objects of cult and objects tied to the image of royalty.
Probably, in the United States, this aspect of our artistic activity is less known than the masterpieces created by the most famous Italian artists of the Renaissance Period: from Masaccio to Piero della Francesca, from Raffaello to the divine Michelangelo whose masterpieces arouse enthusiasm and emotions all over the world. It is, in fact, this lesser known art form that becomes very complementary to the message transmitted by our major arts. The American public will undoubtedly find amongst these works, even if so different in conception, importance and workmanship compared to their recent values, a common spiritual motivation in seeking expression of the greatest values in life through human abilities.

Anna Maria Maetzke
Superintendent
Soprintendenza ai Beni Ambientali
Architettonici Artistici e Storici di Arezzo

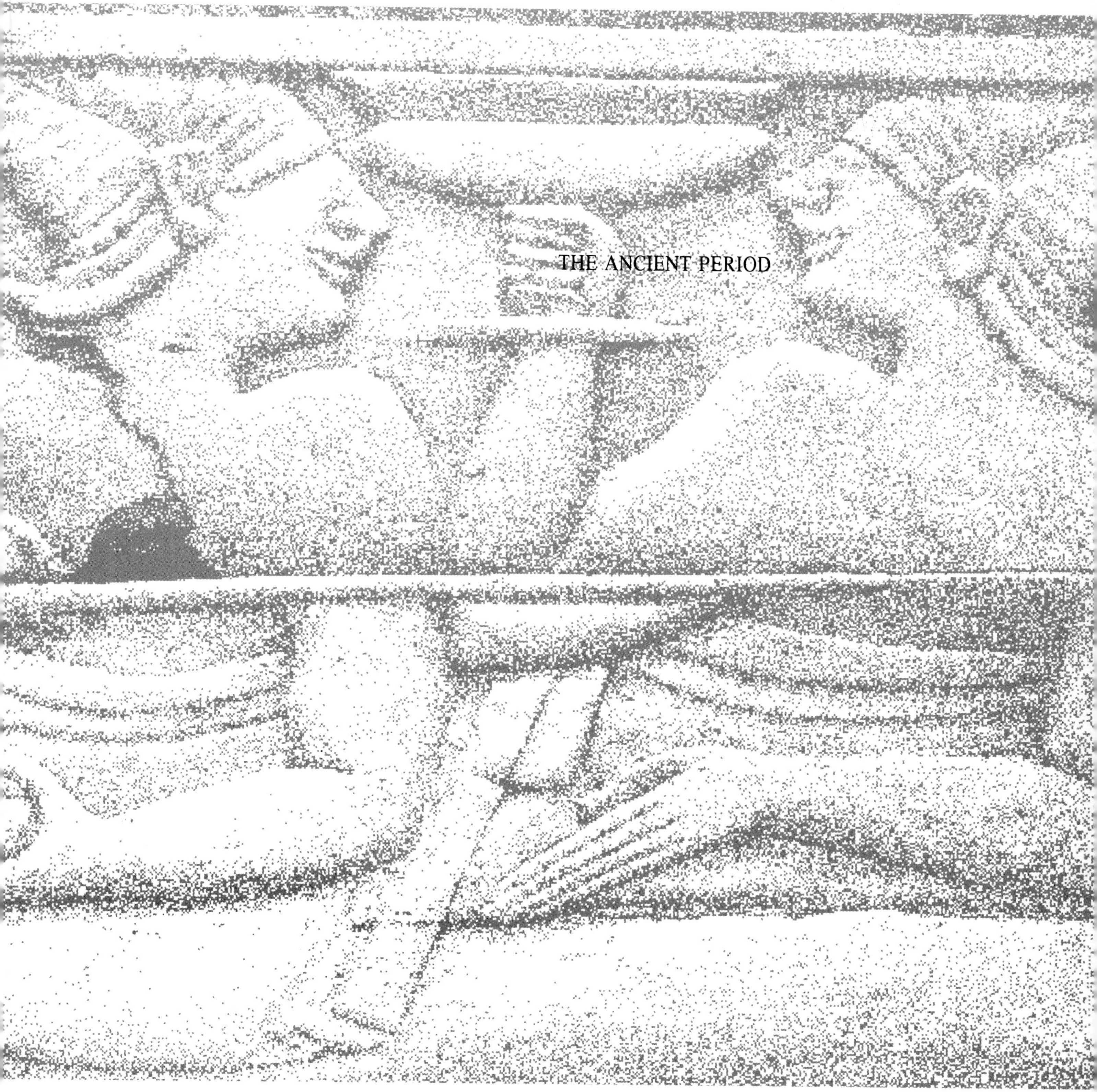

THE ANCIENT PERIOD

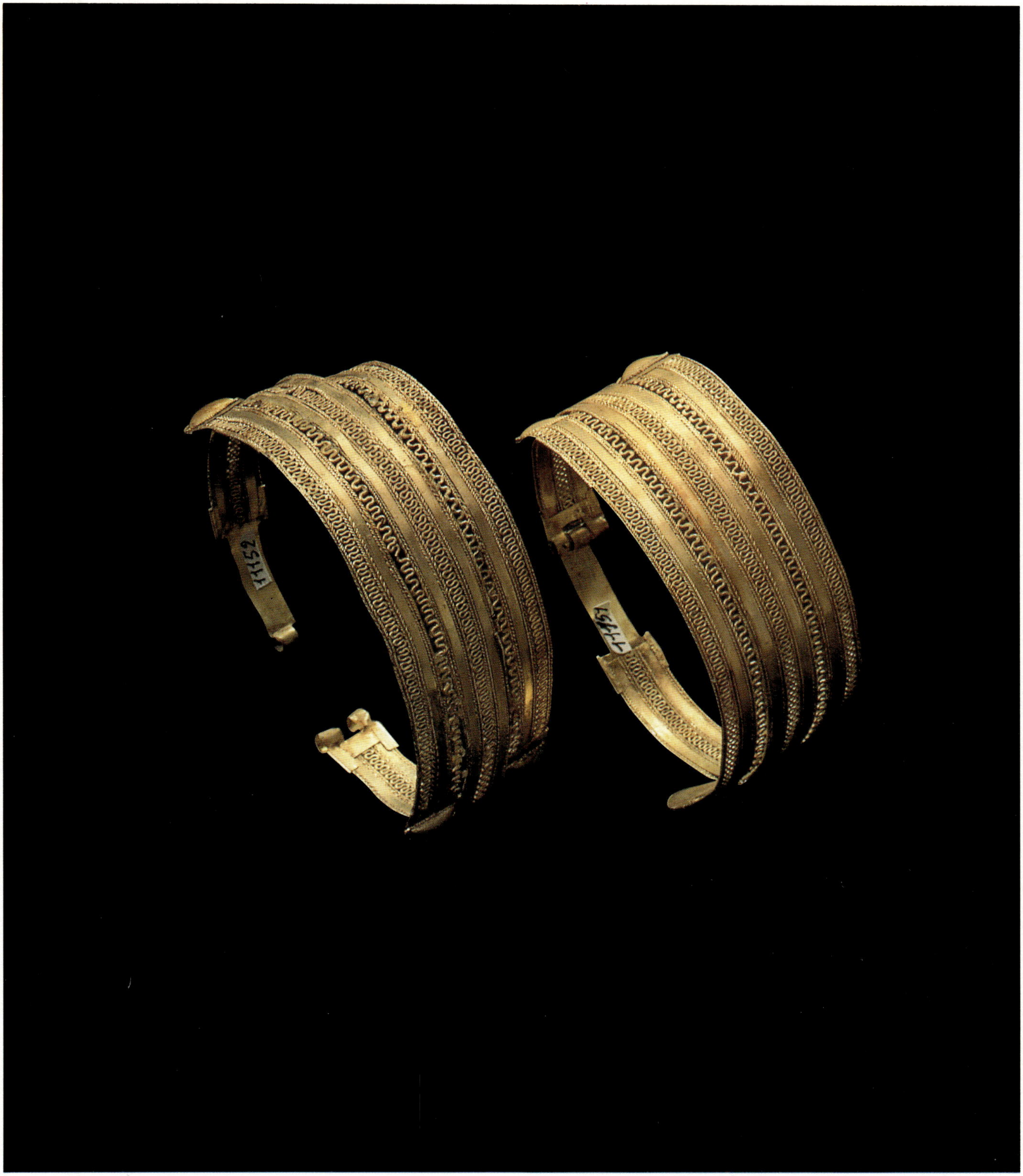

1

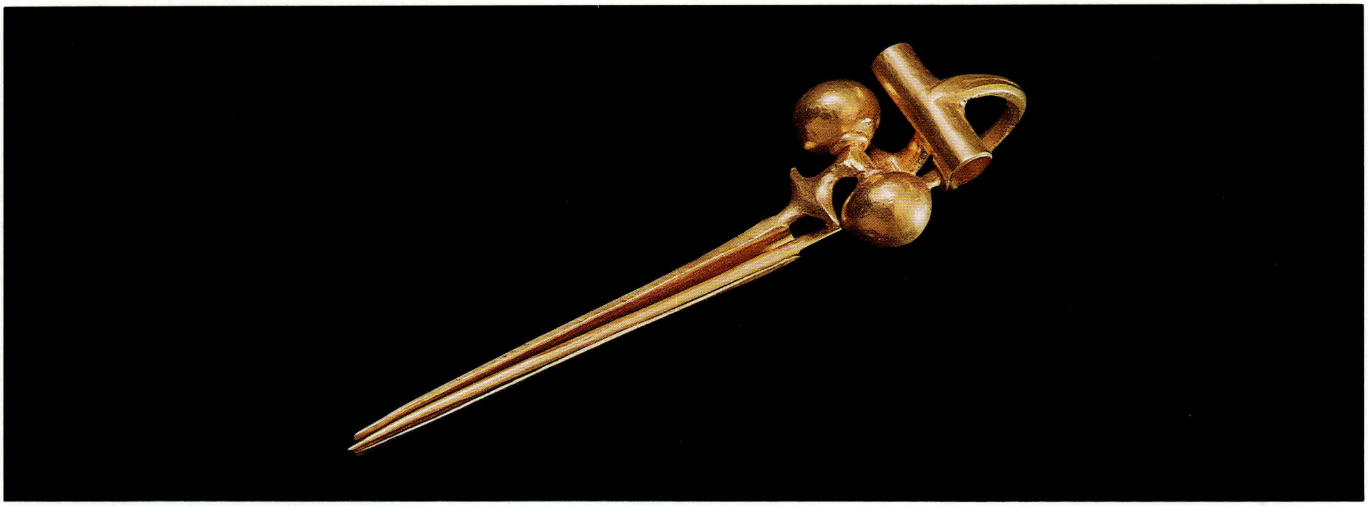

2

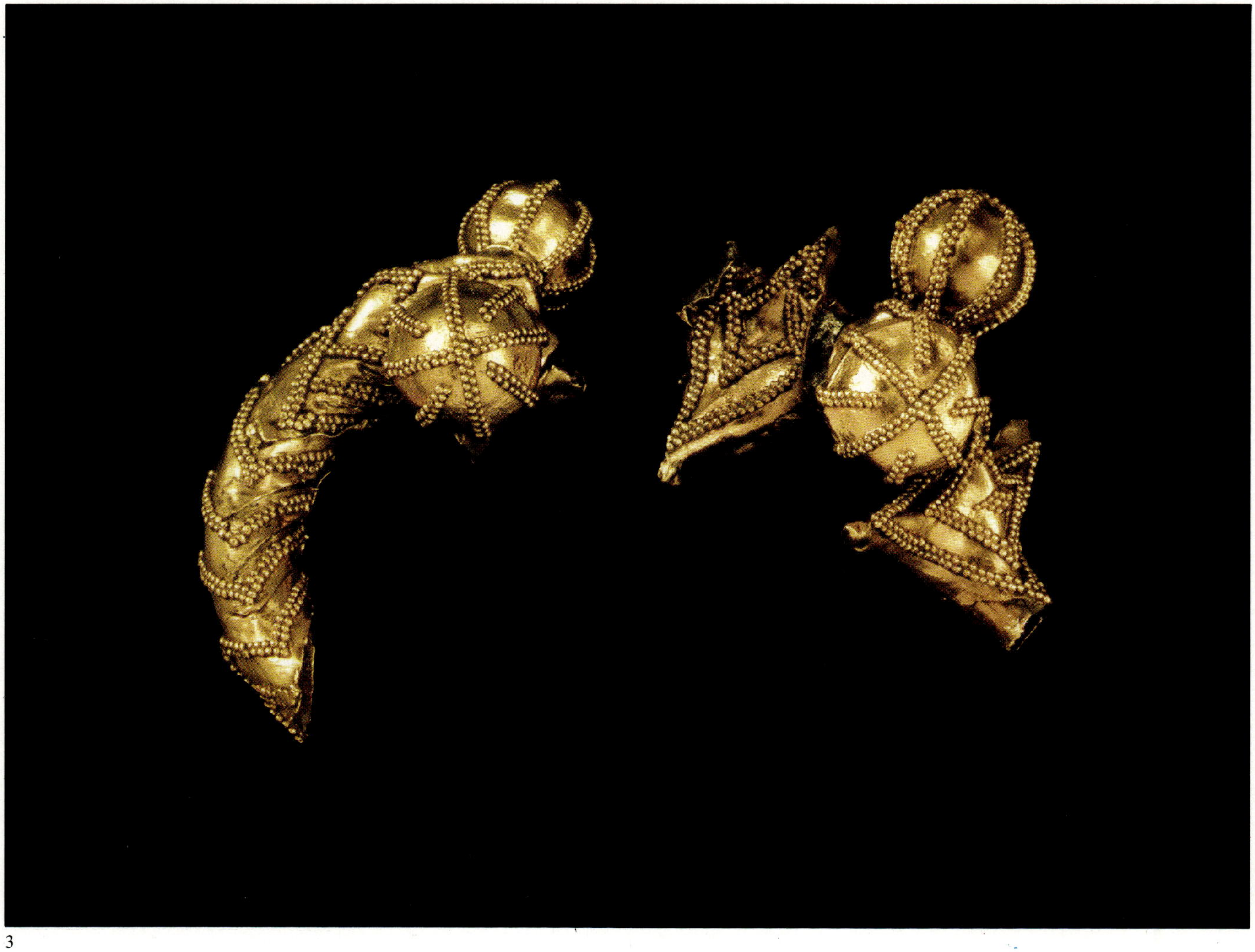

3

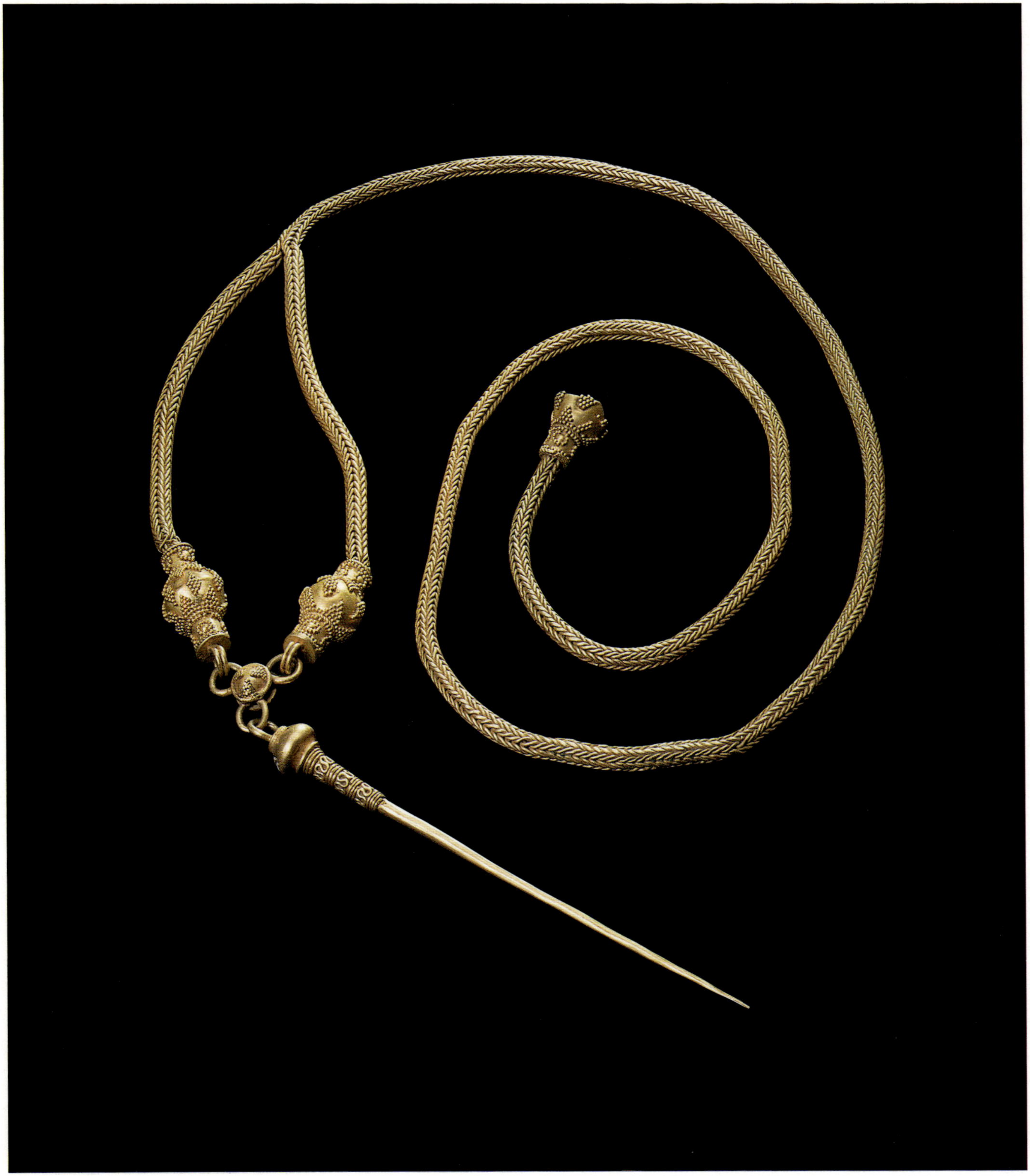

4

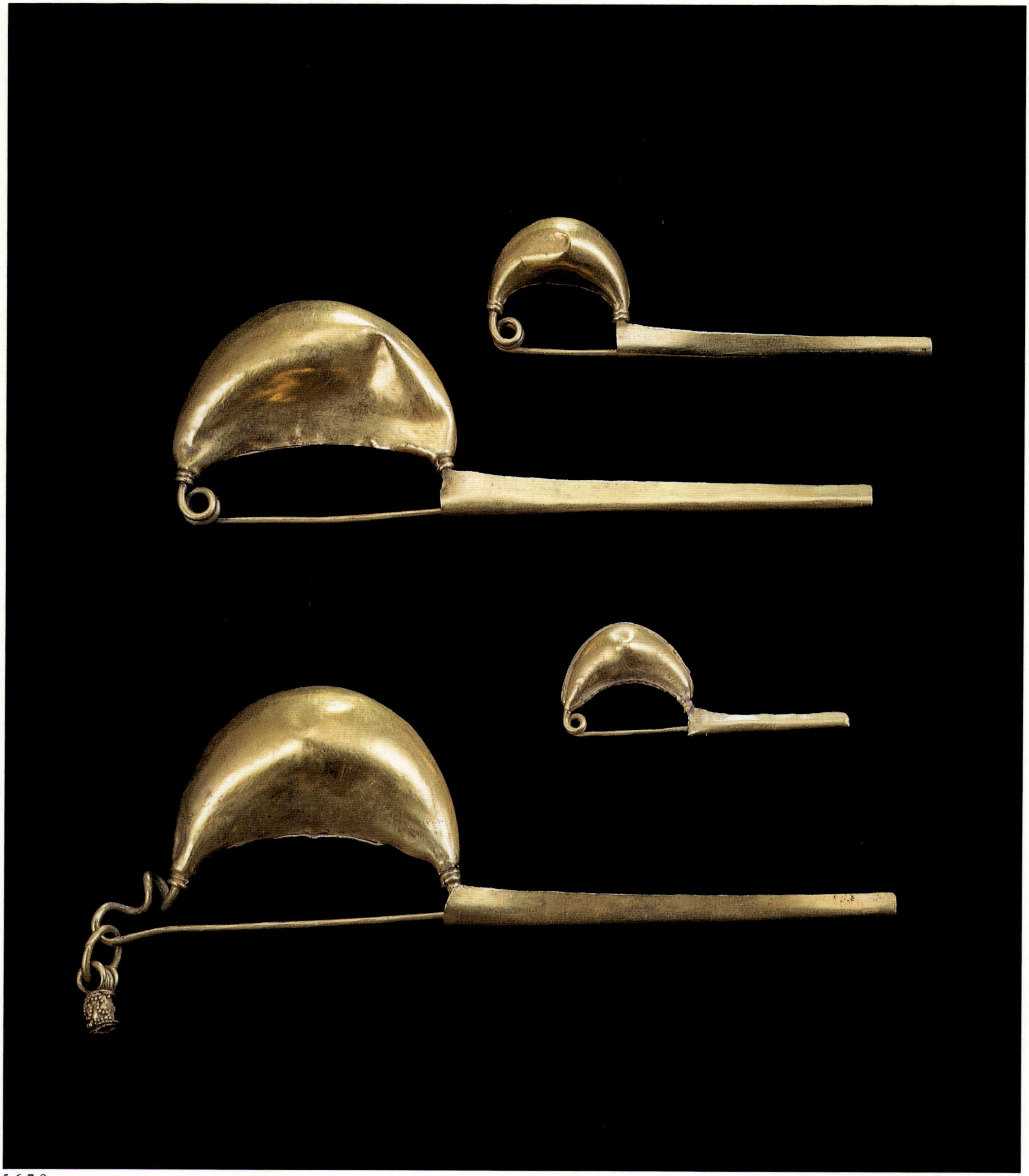

5-6-7-8

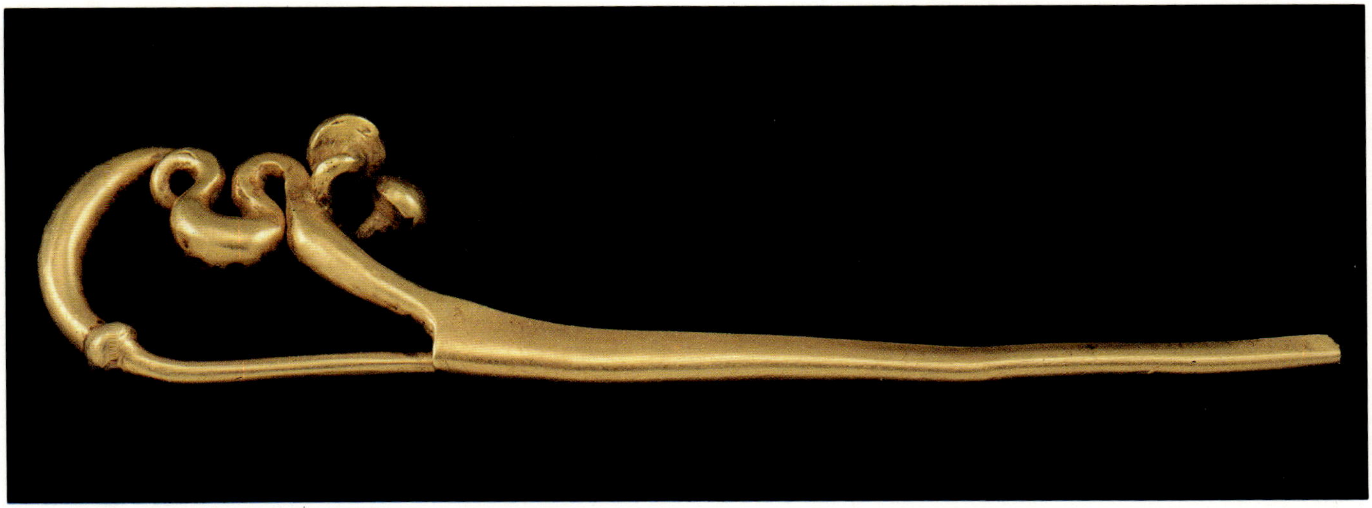
9

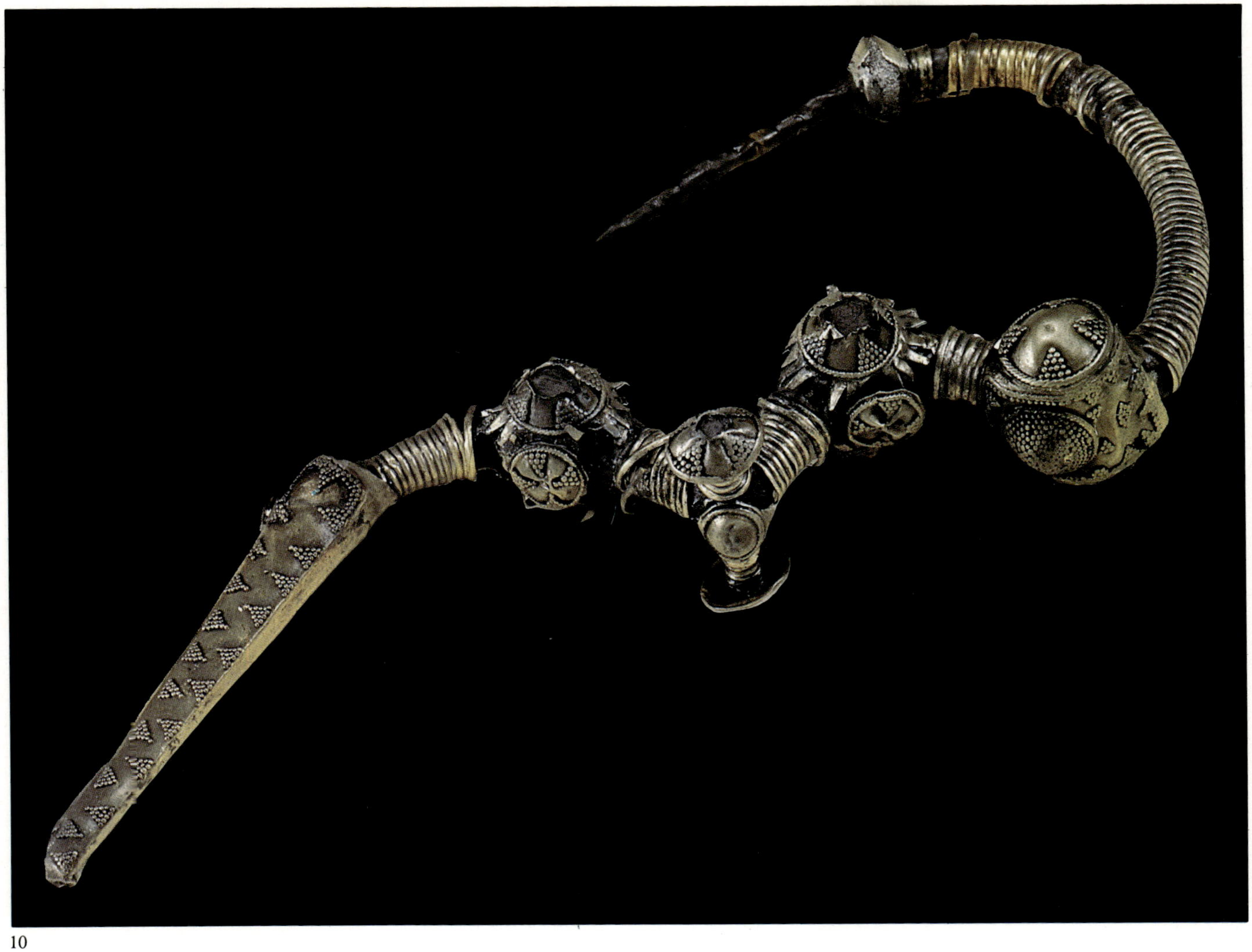
10

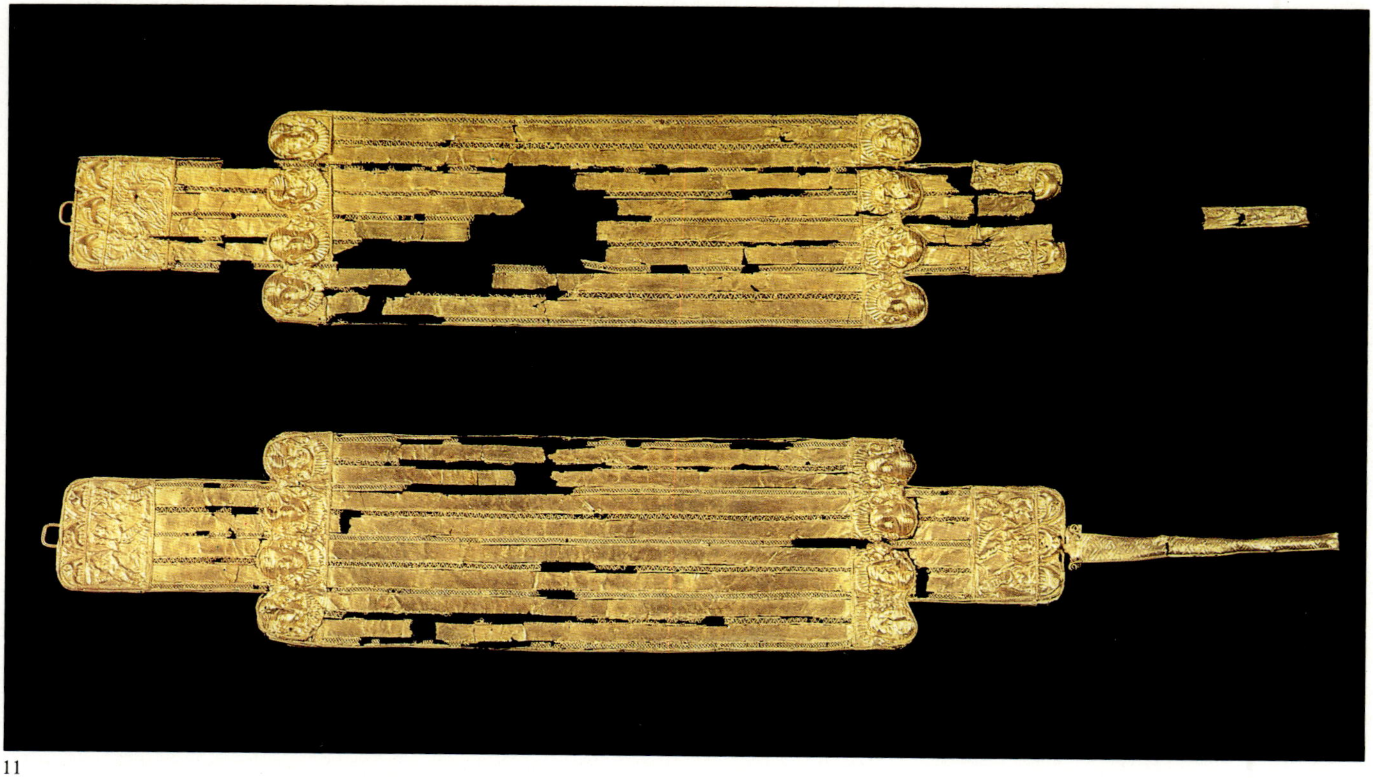

11

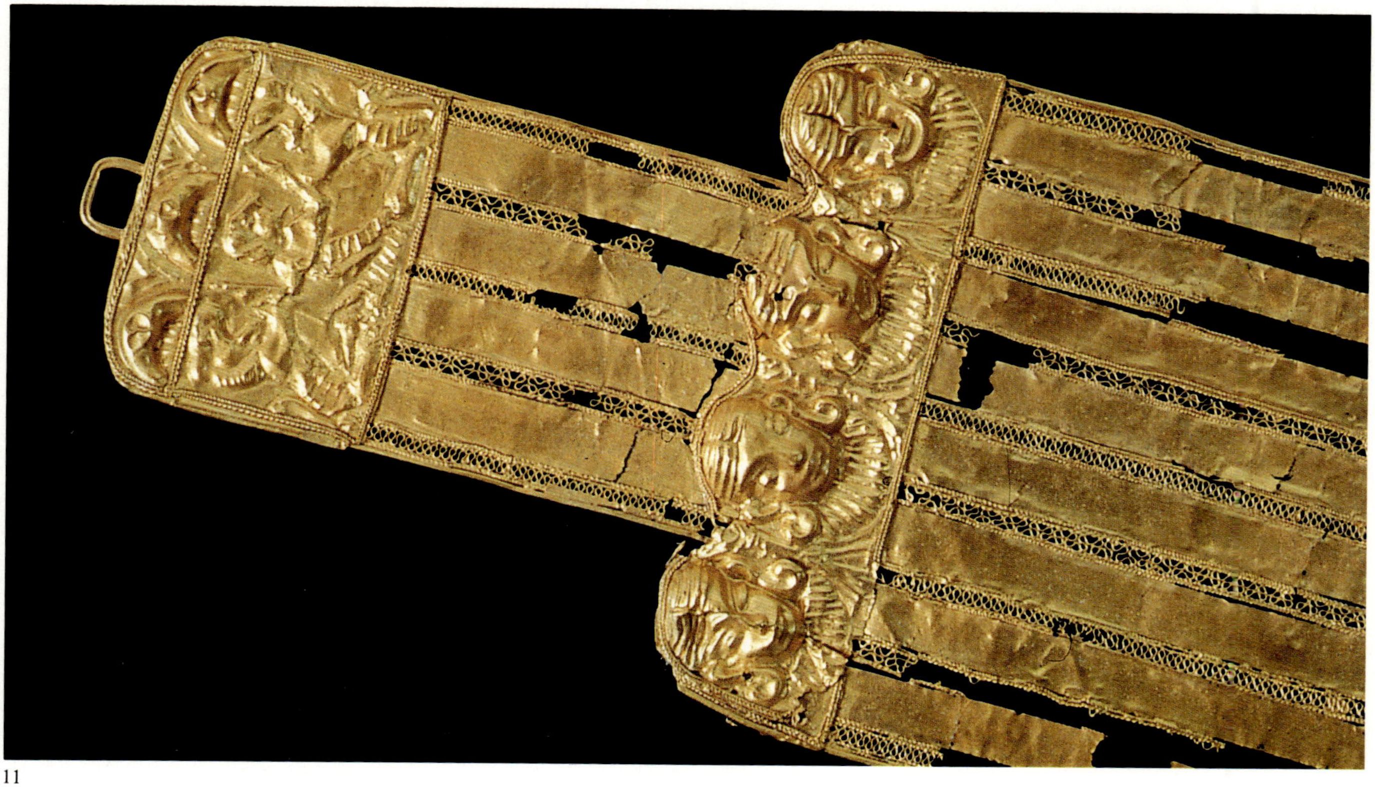

11

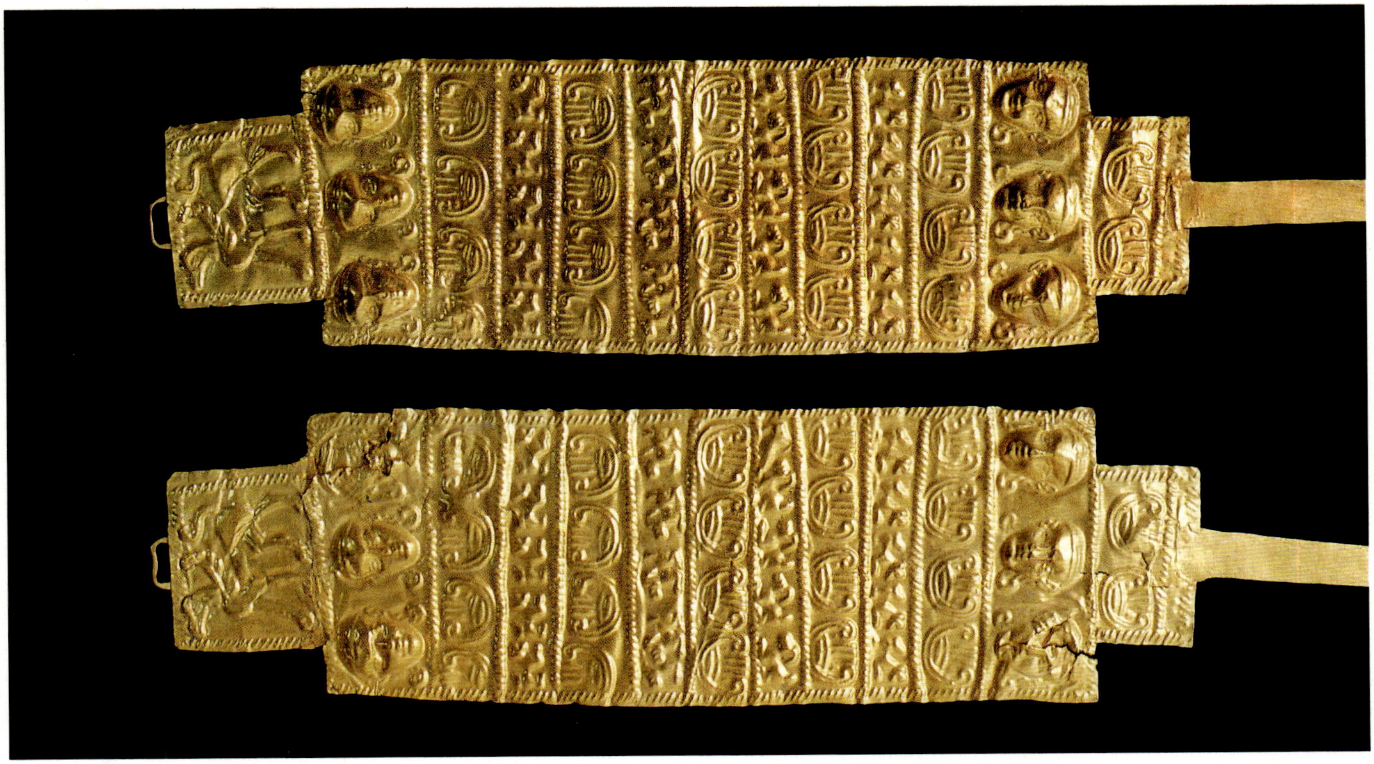

12

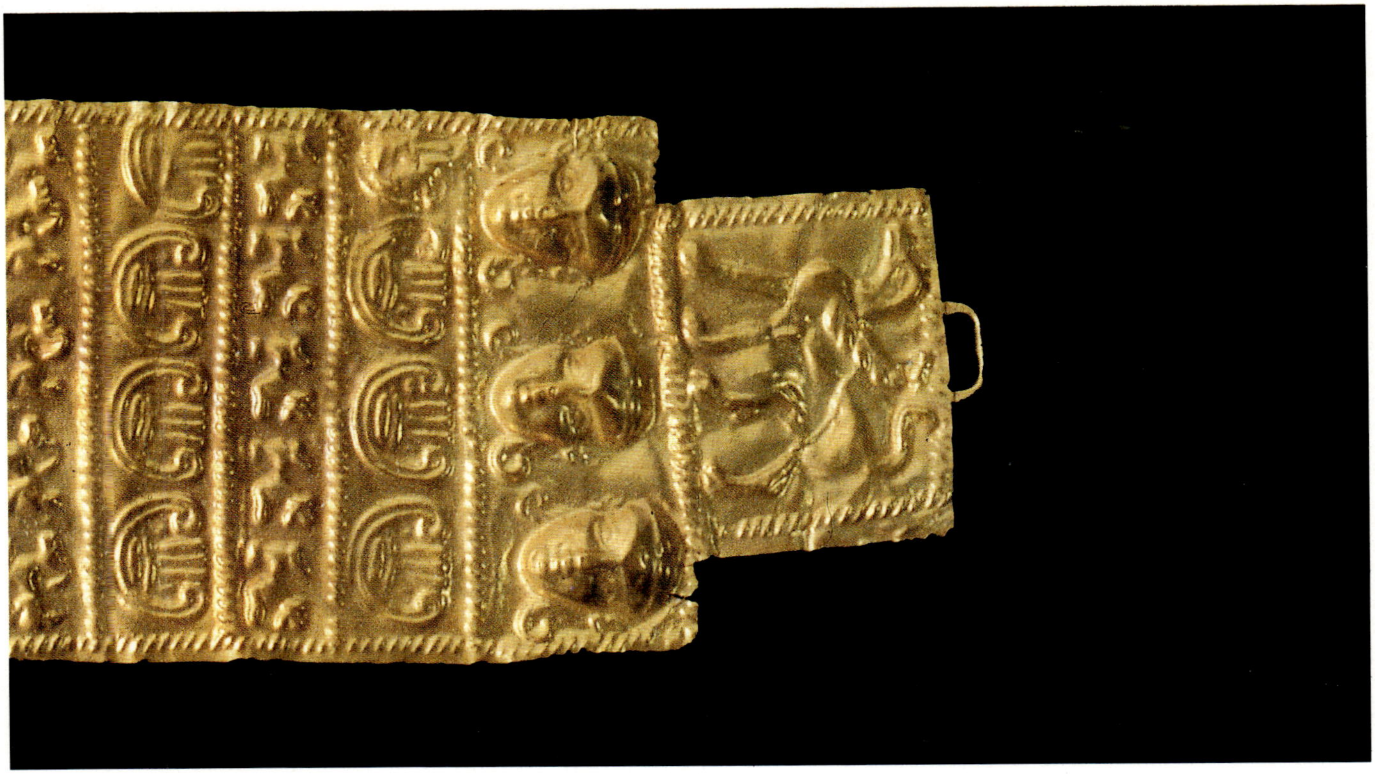

12

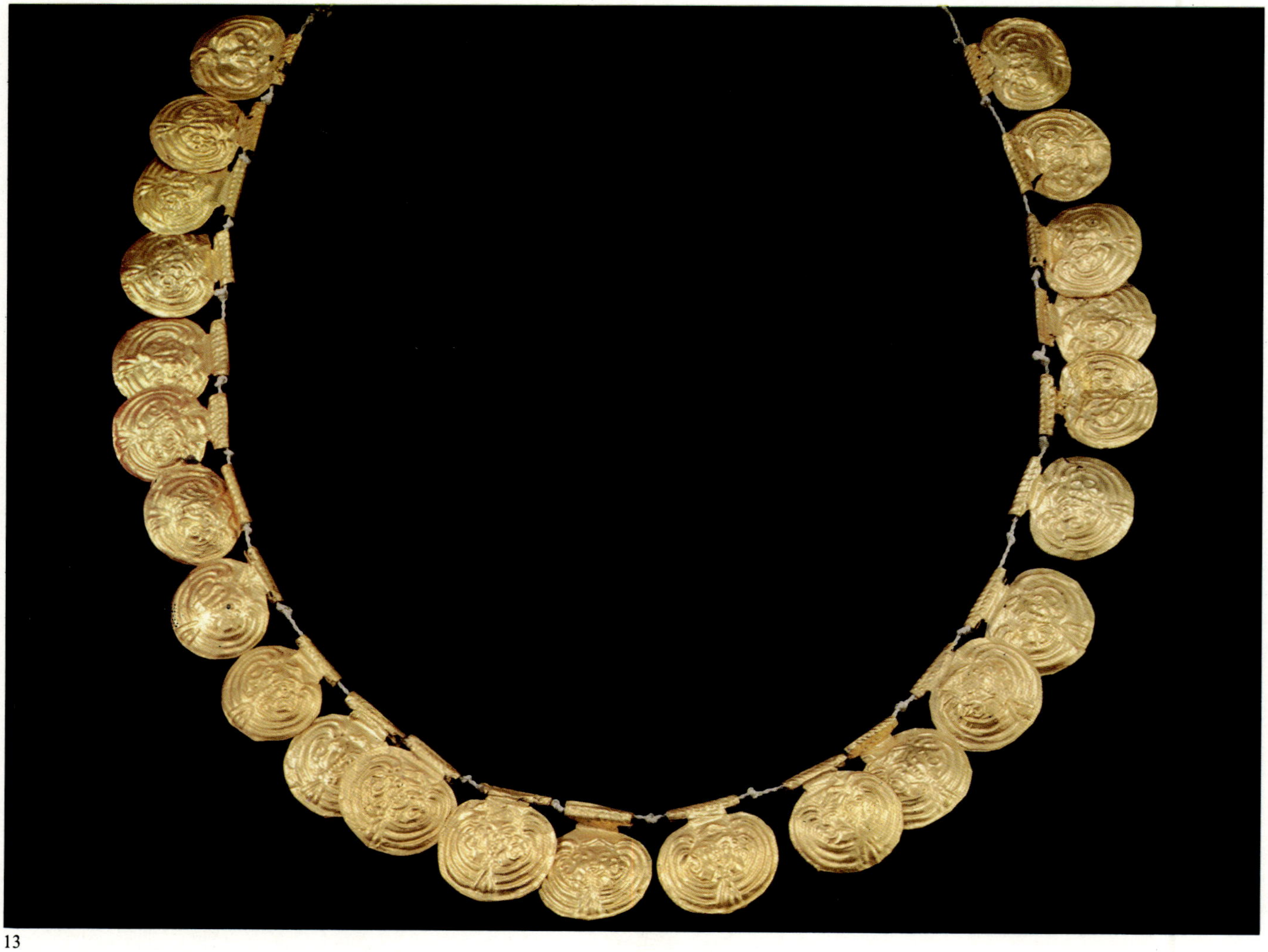
13

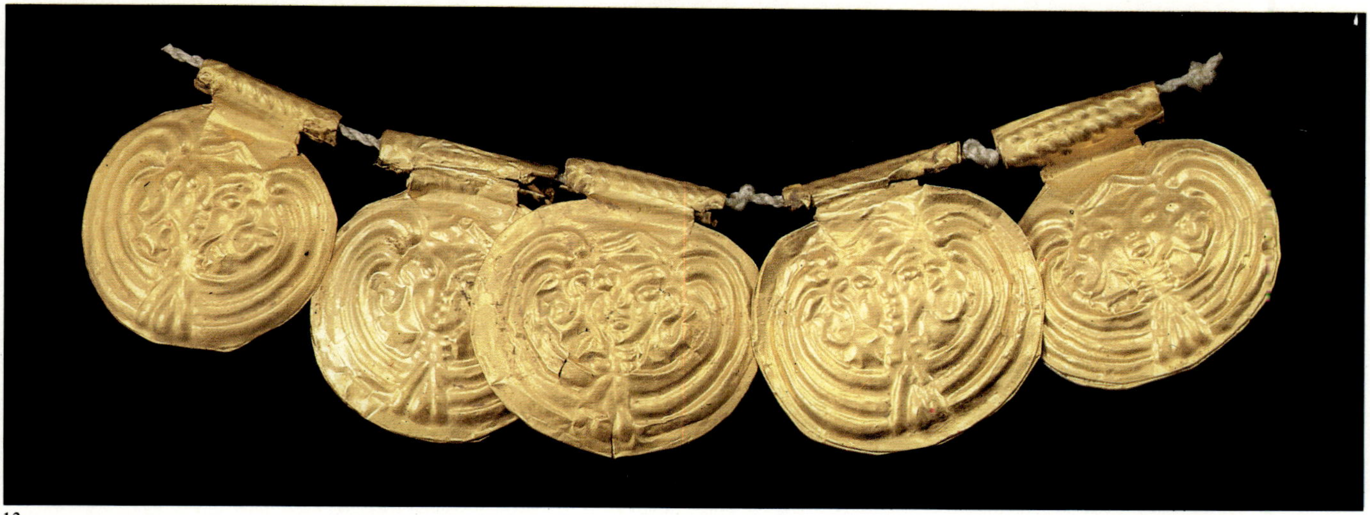
13

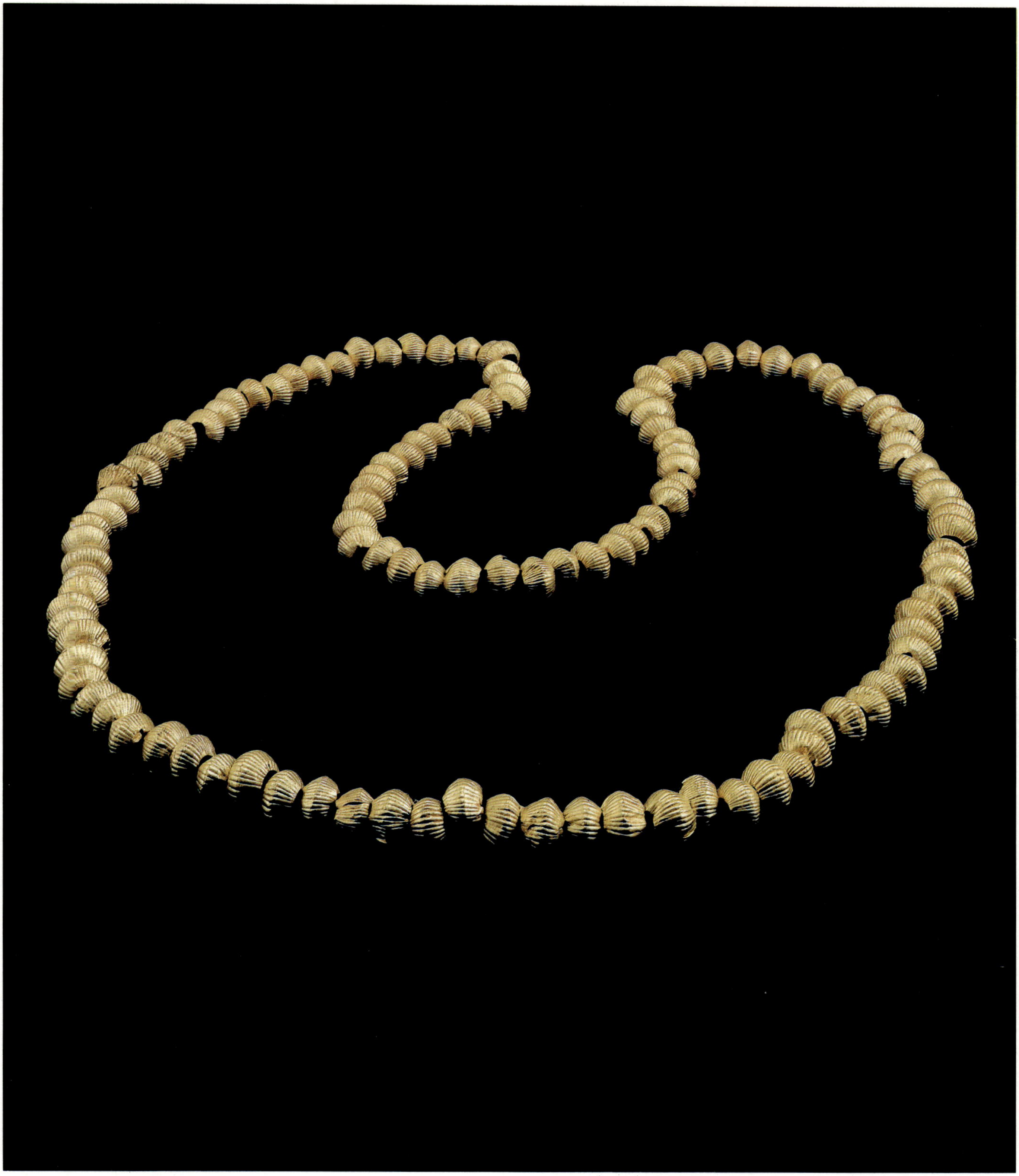

14

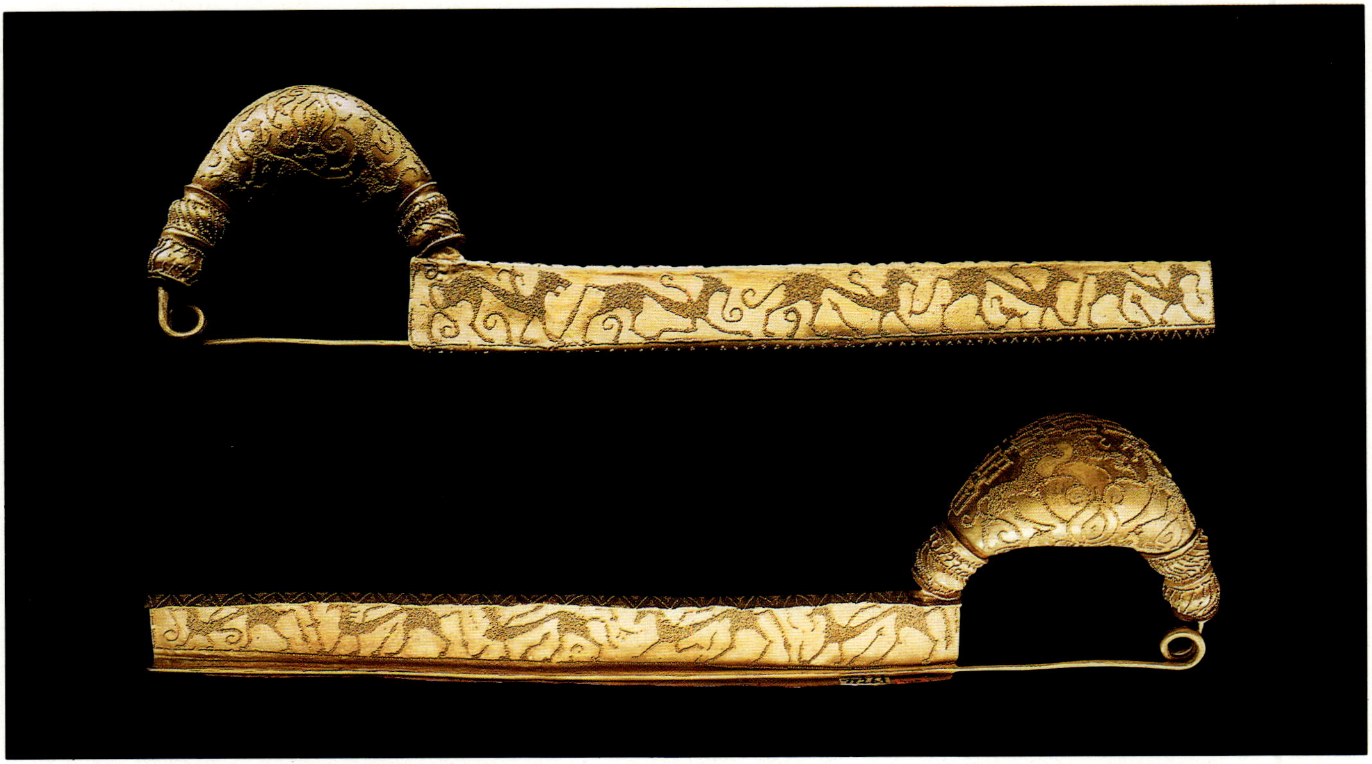

15

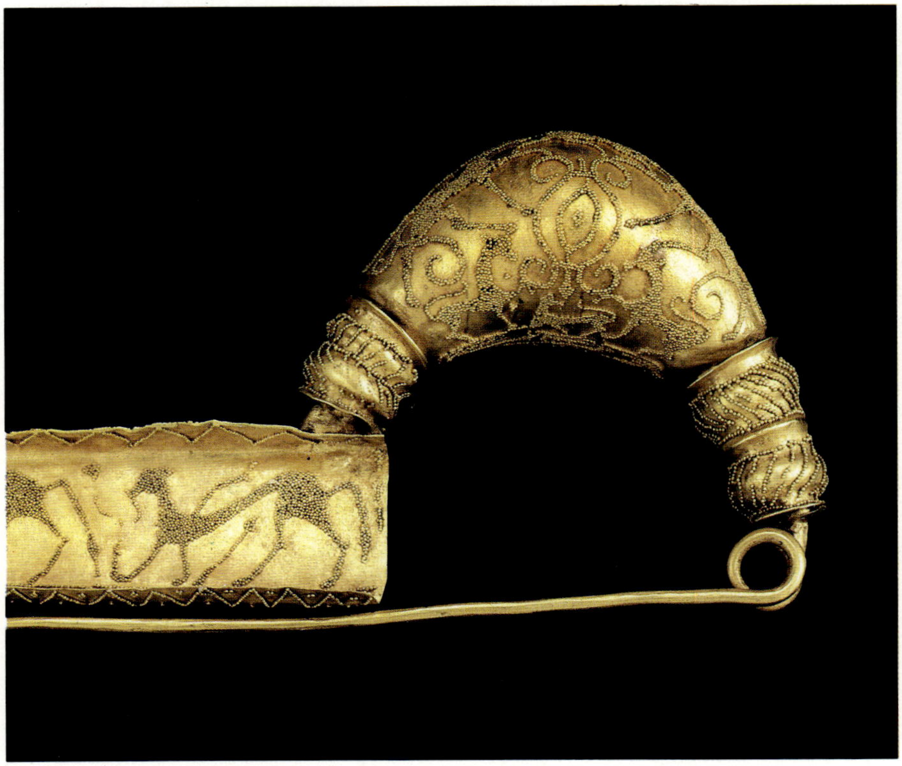

15

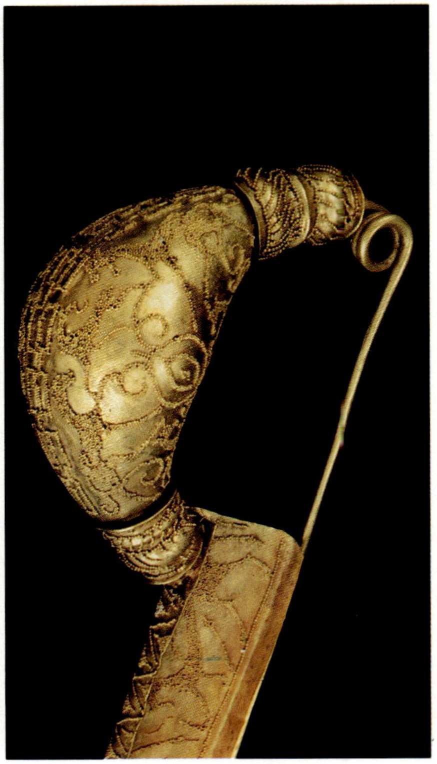

15

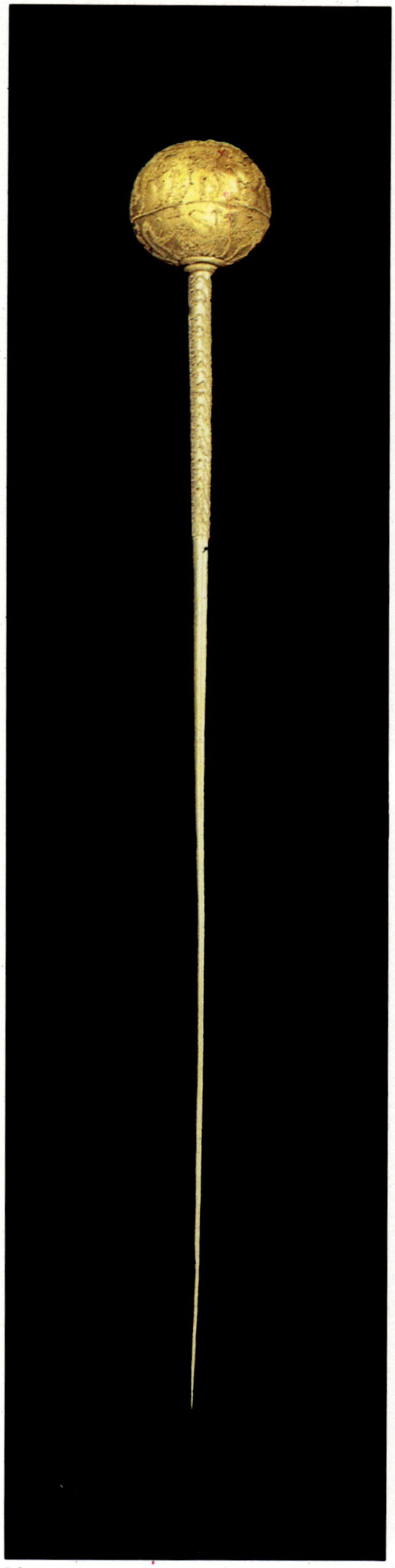

16

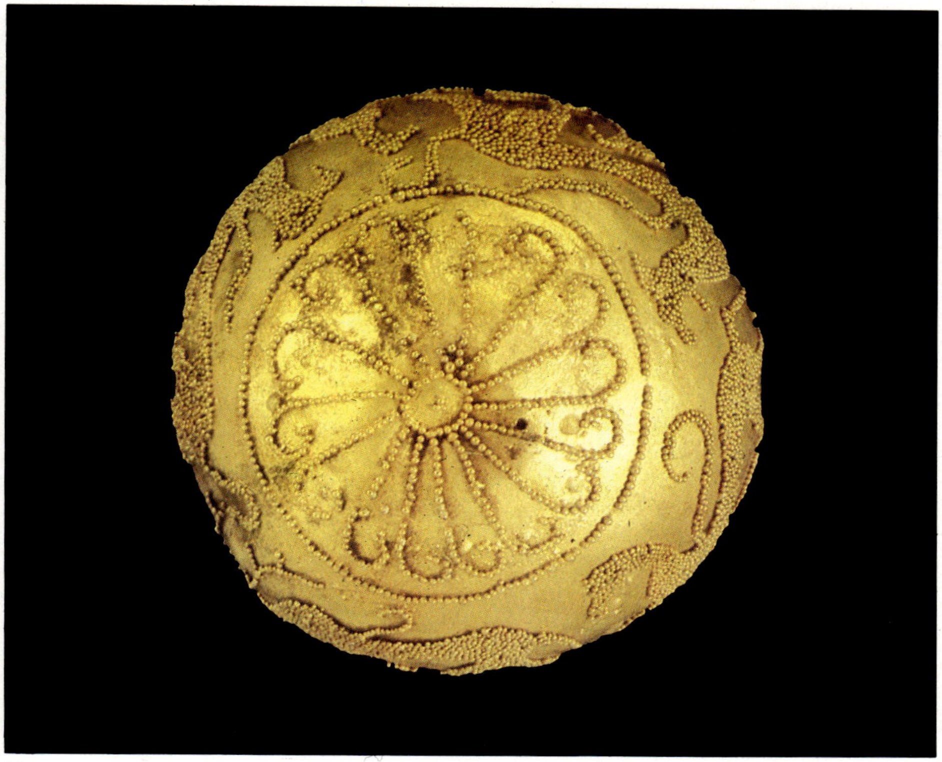

16

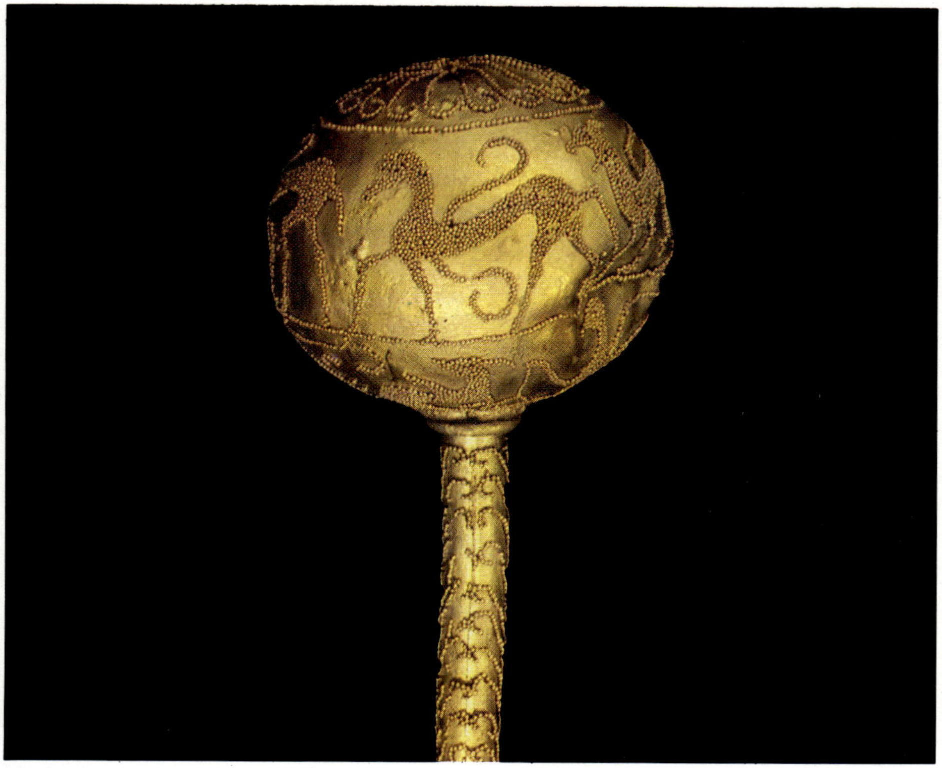

16

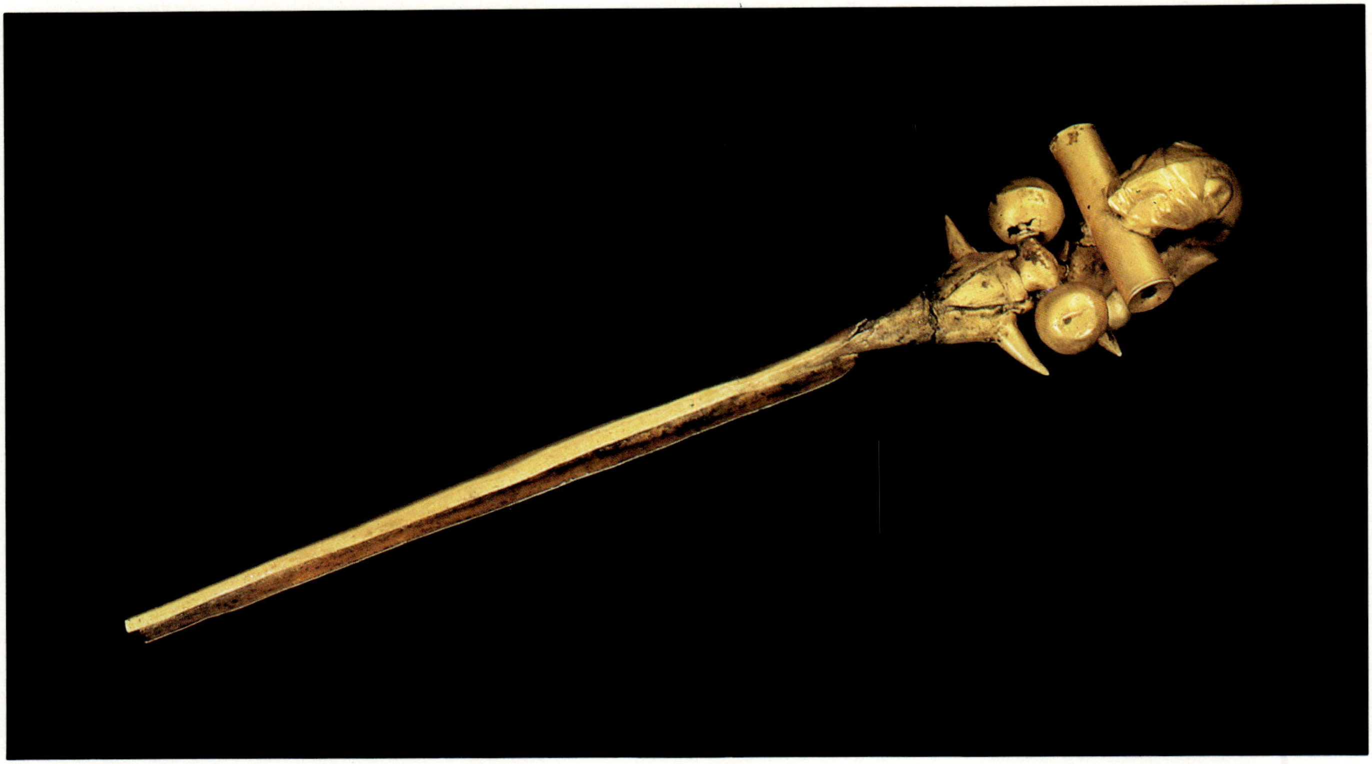

17

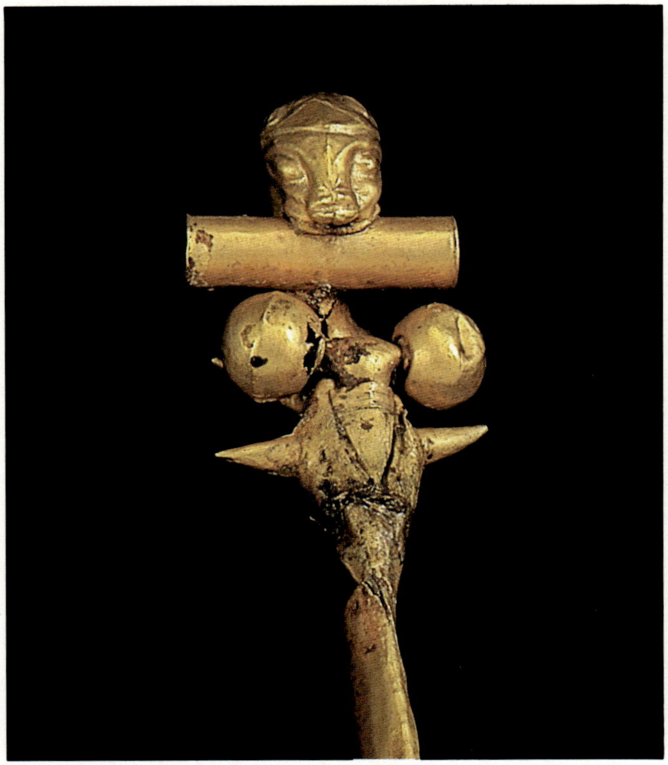

17

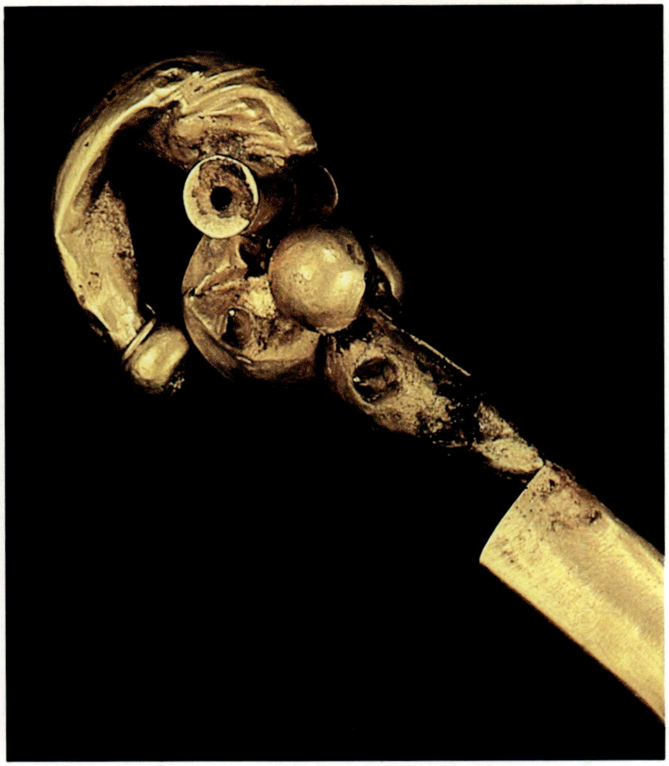

17

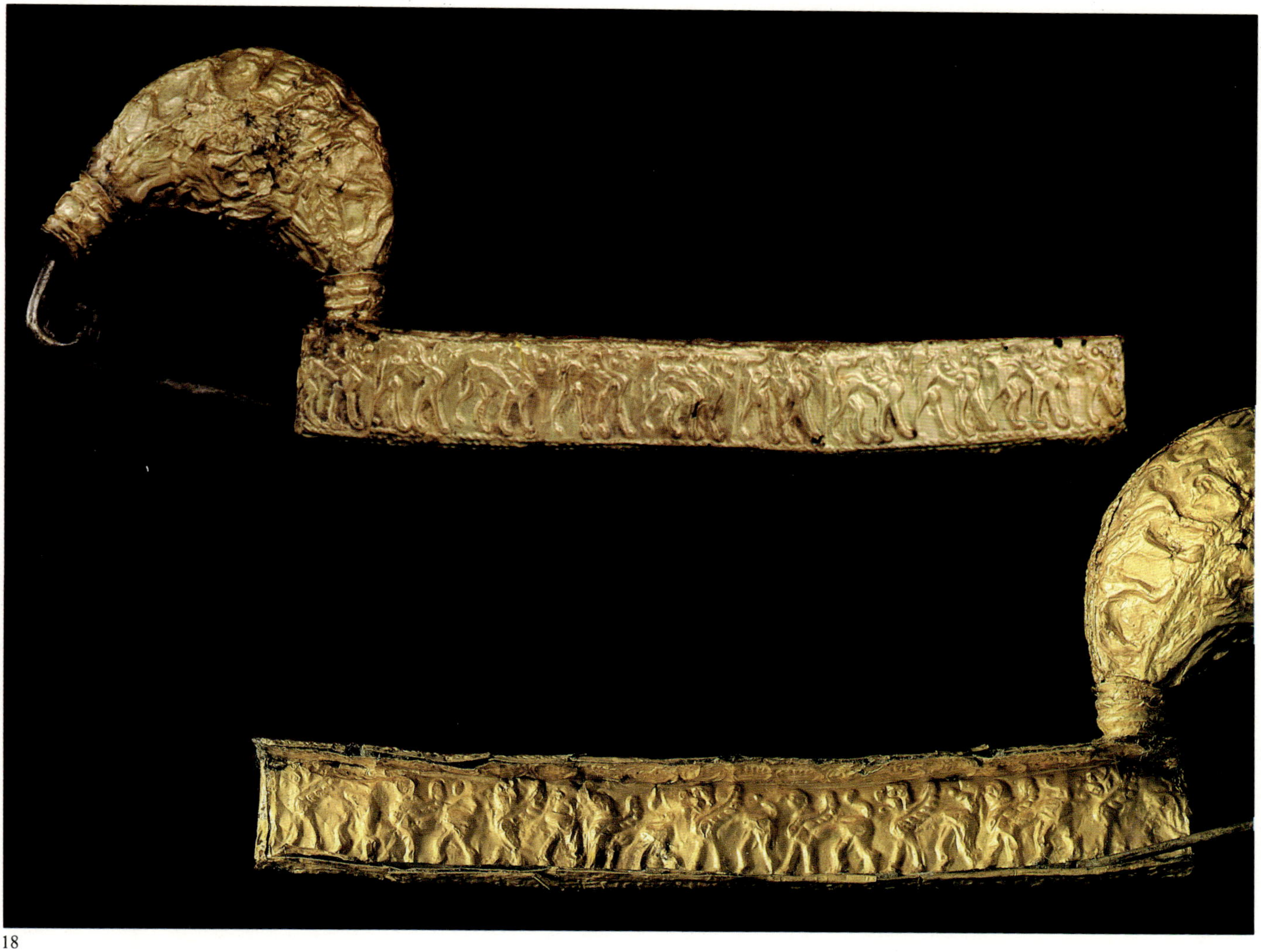

18

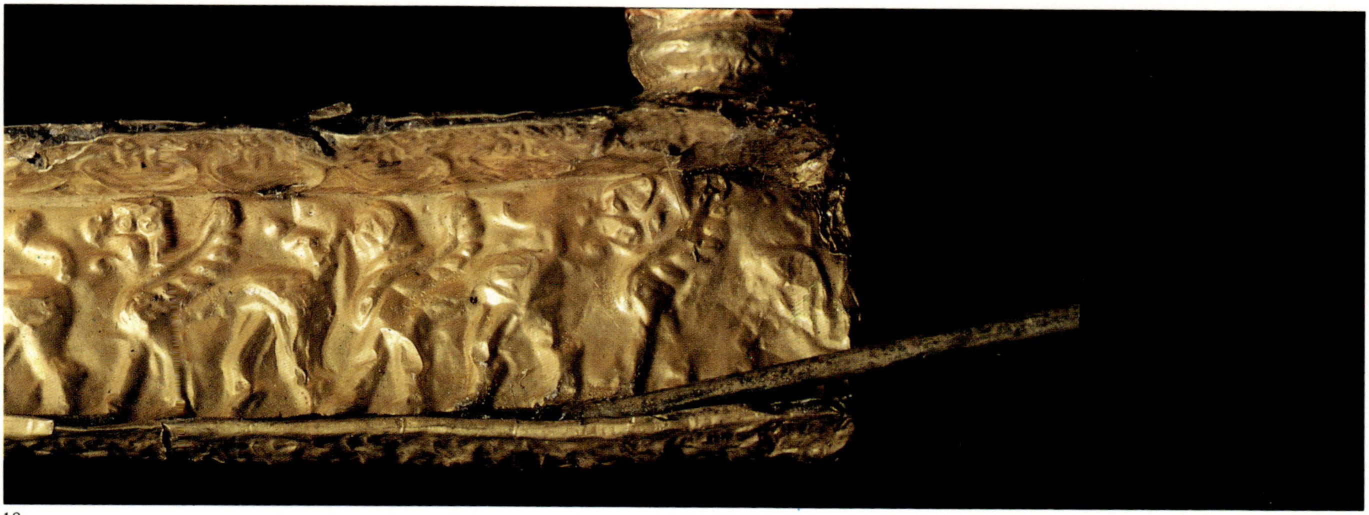

18

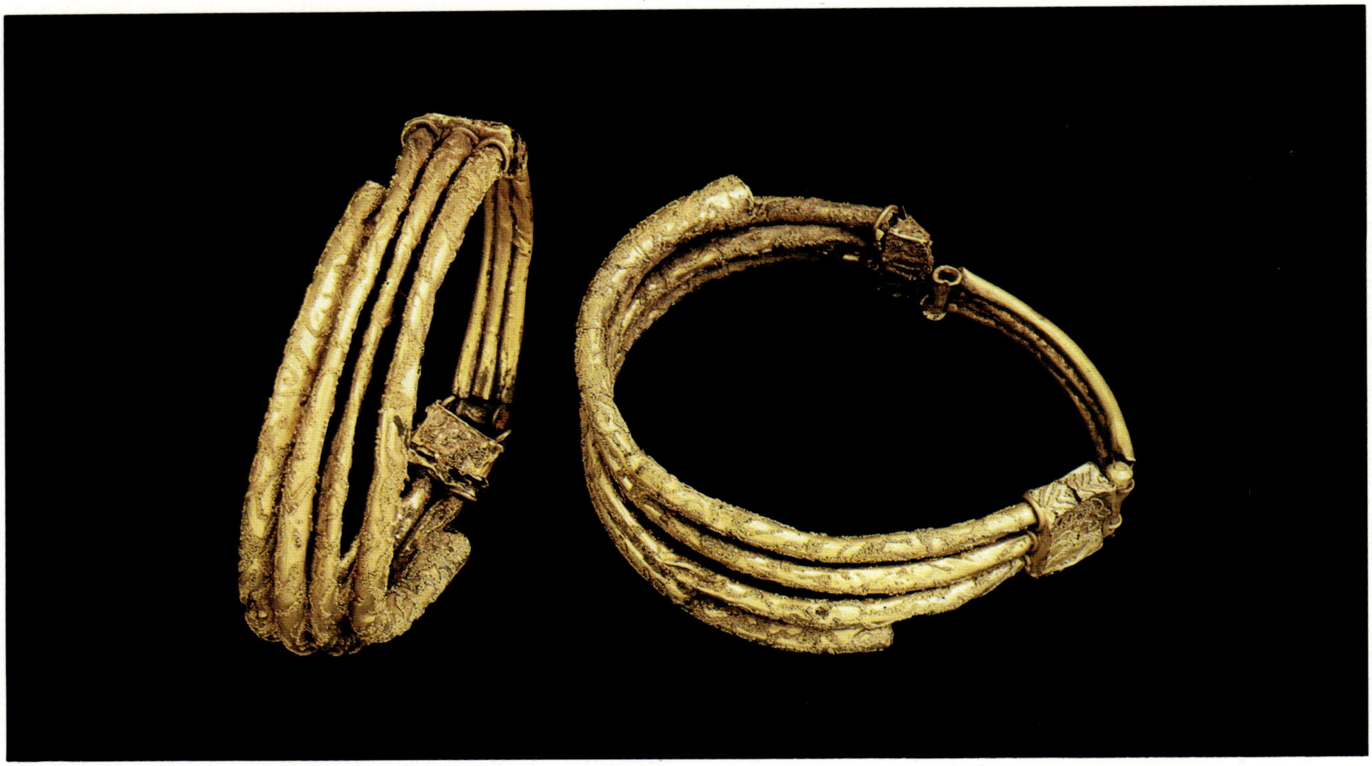

19

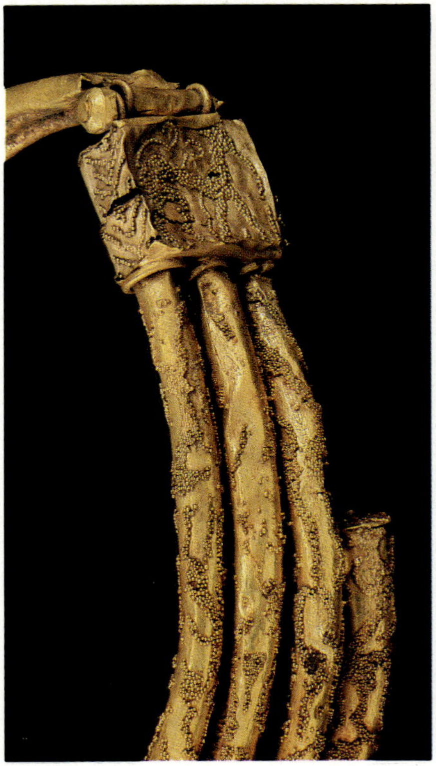

19

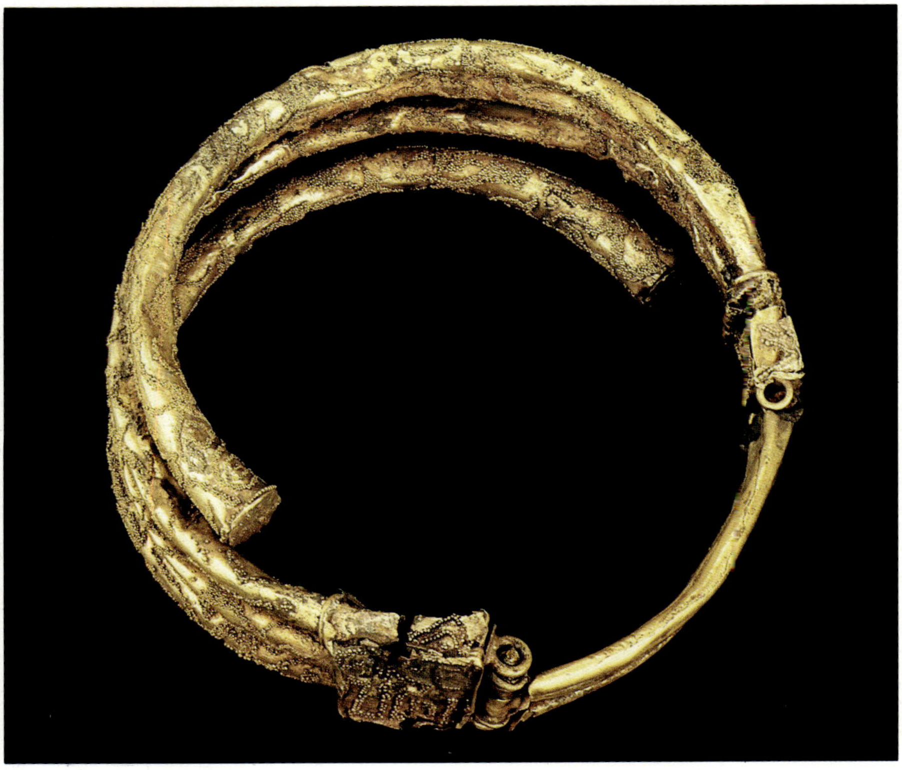

19

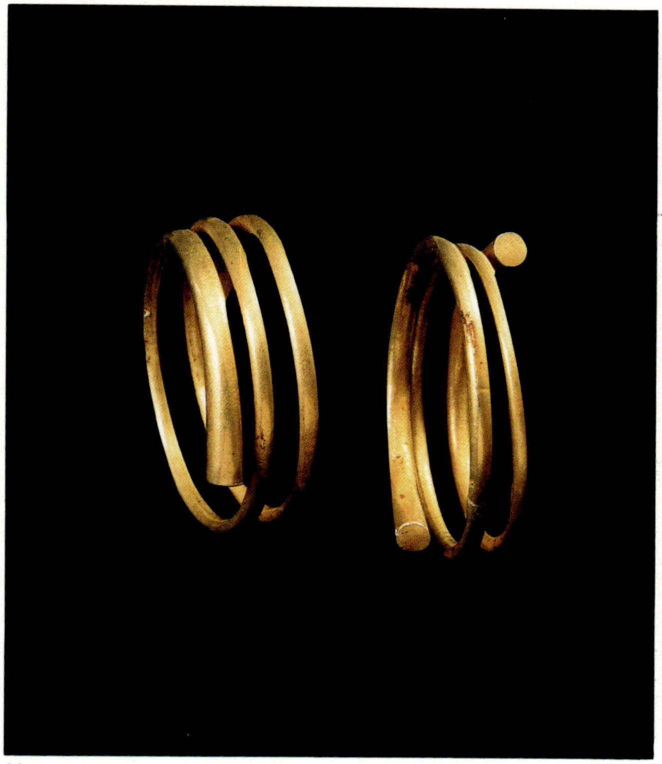

20

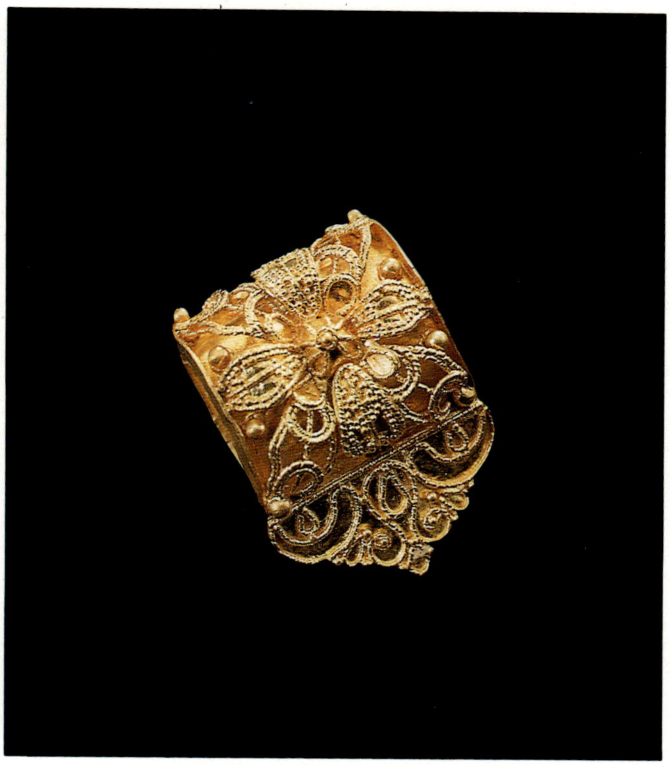

21

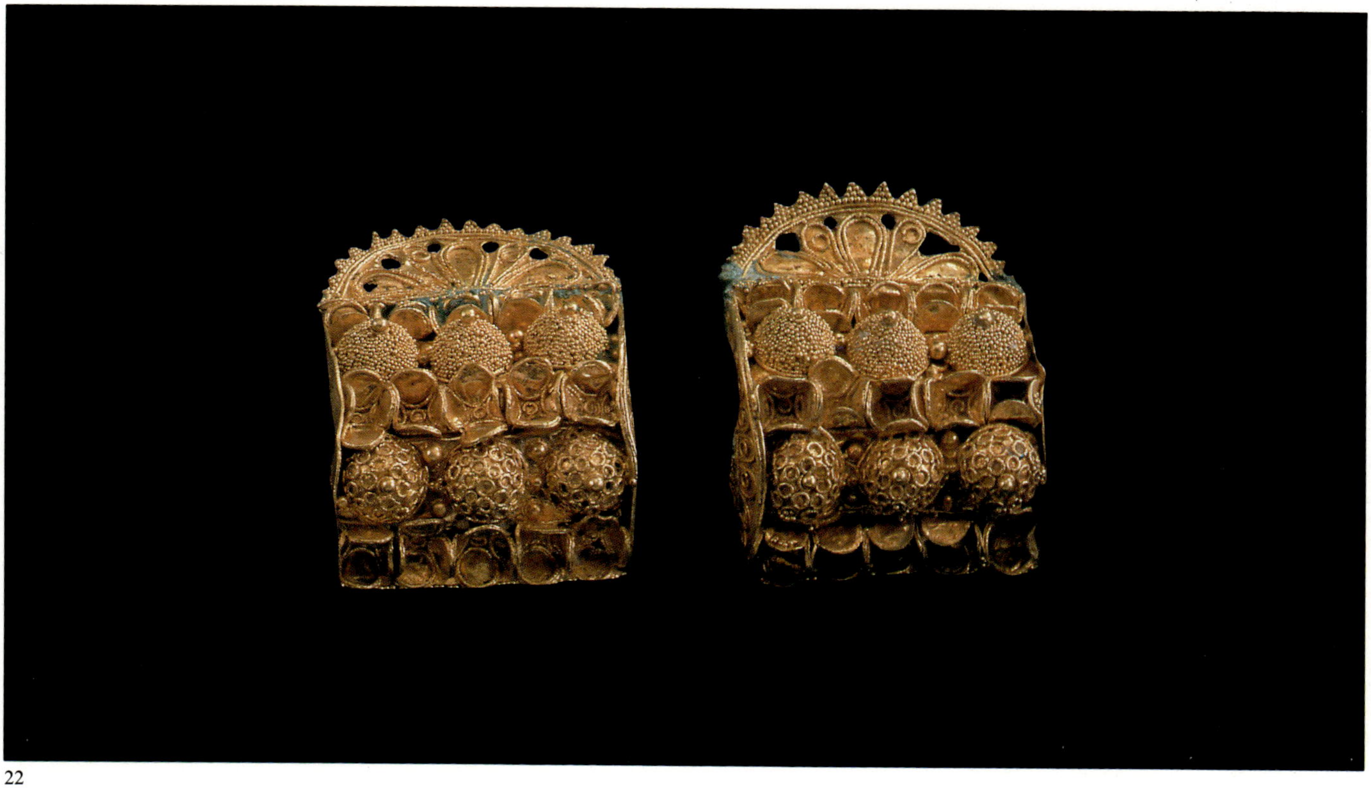

22

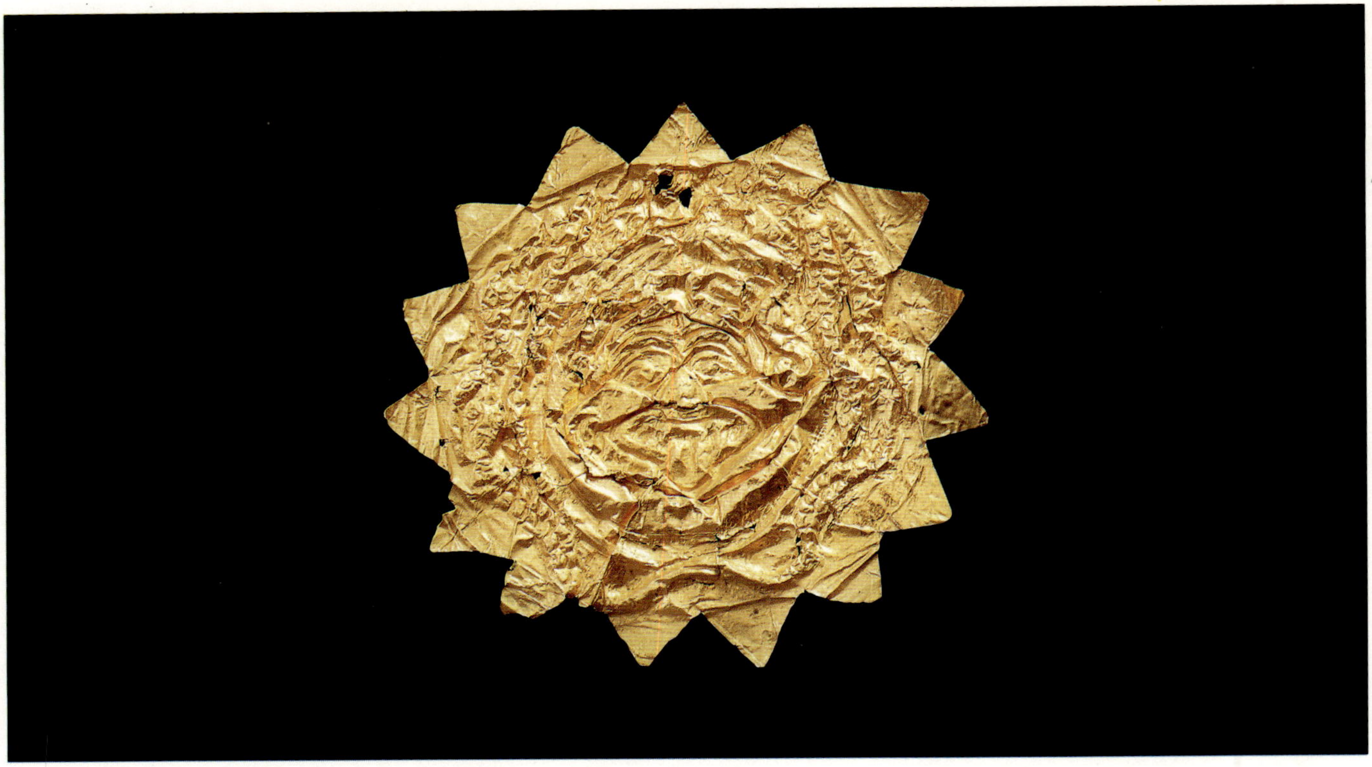

23

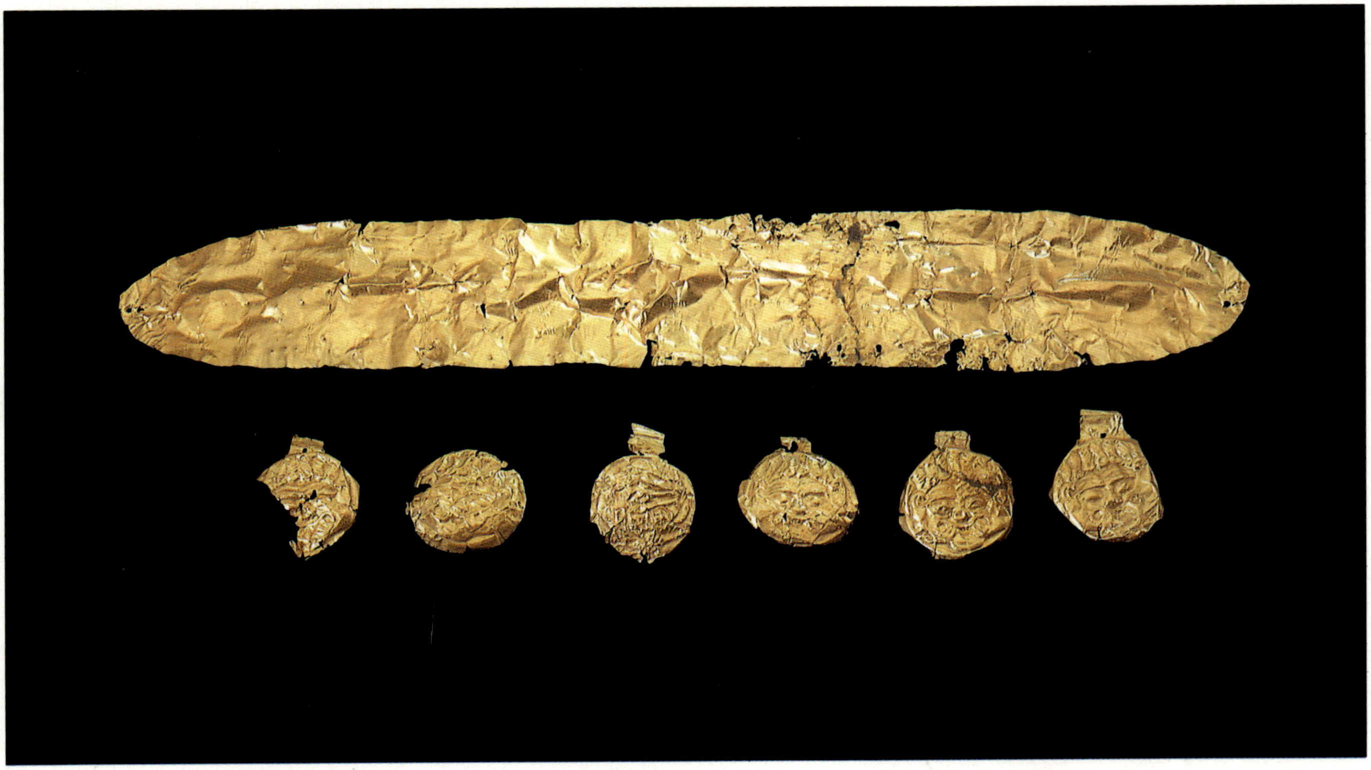

27

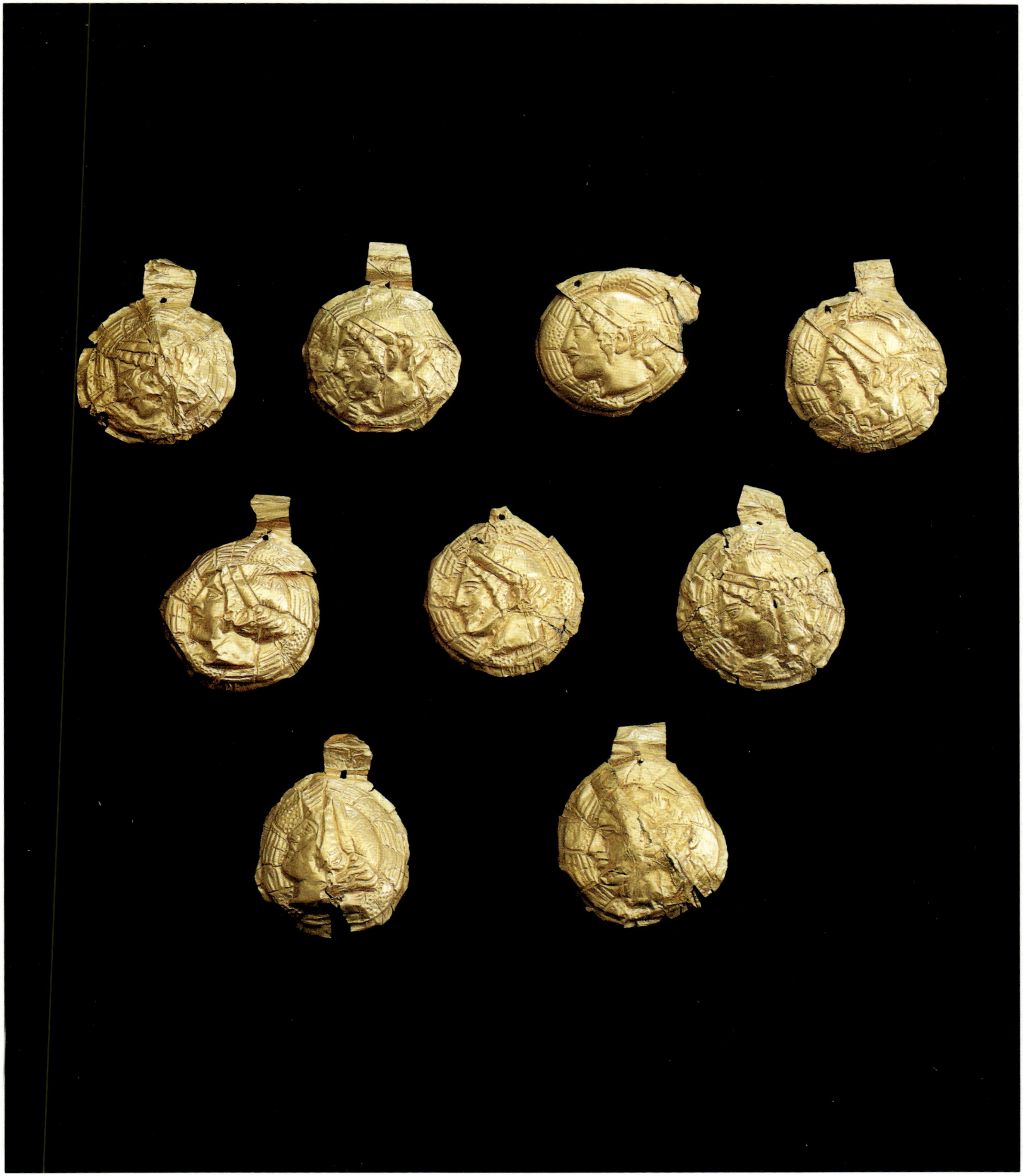

28

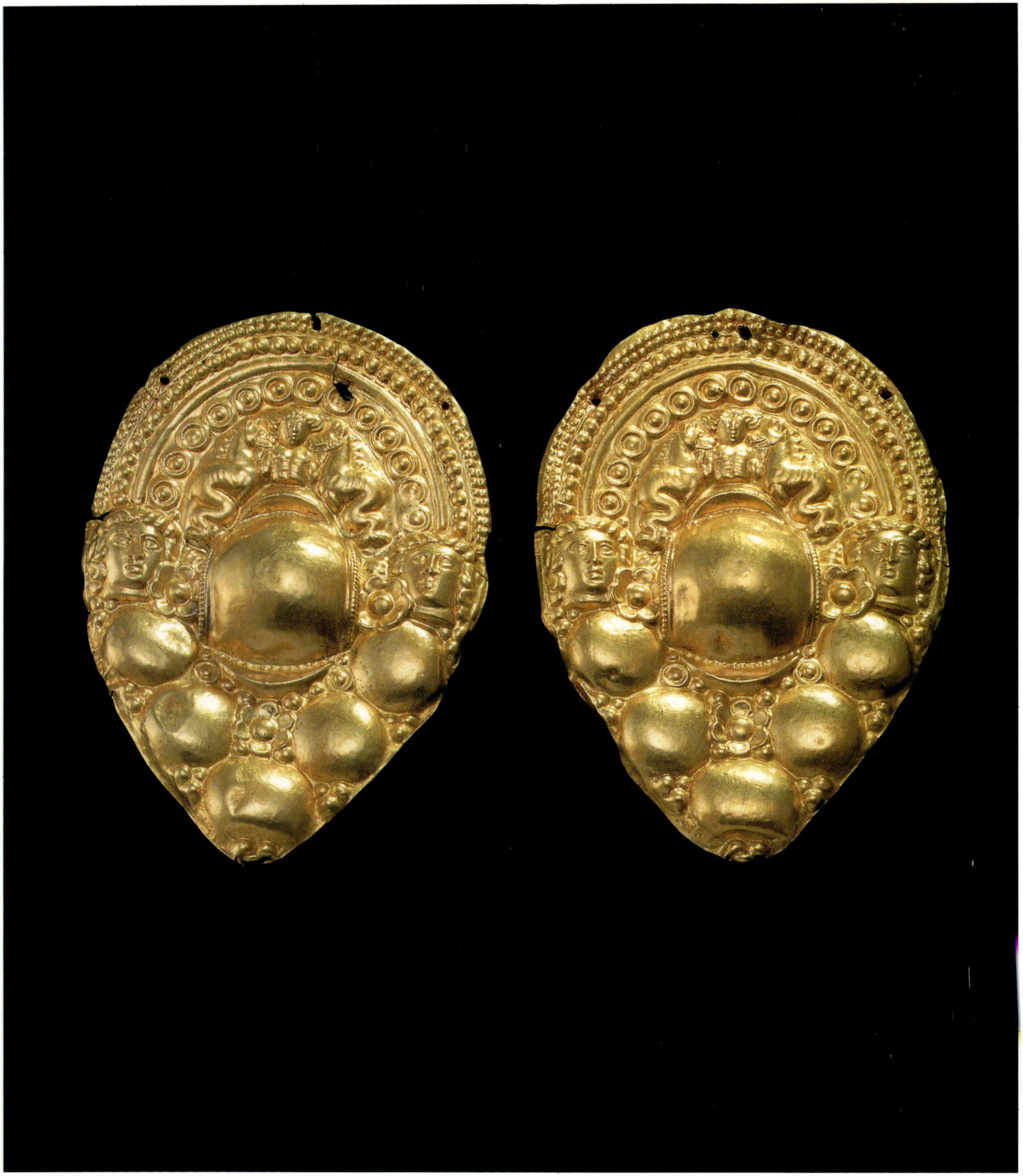

31

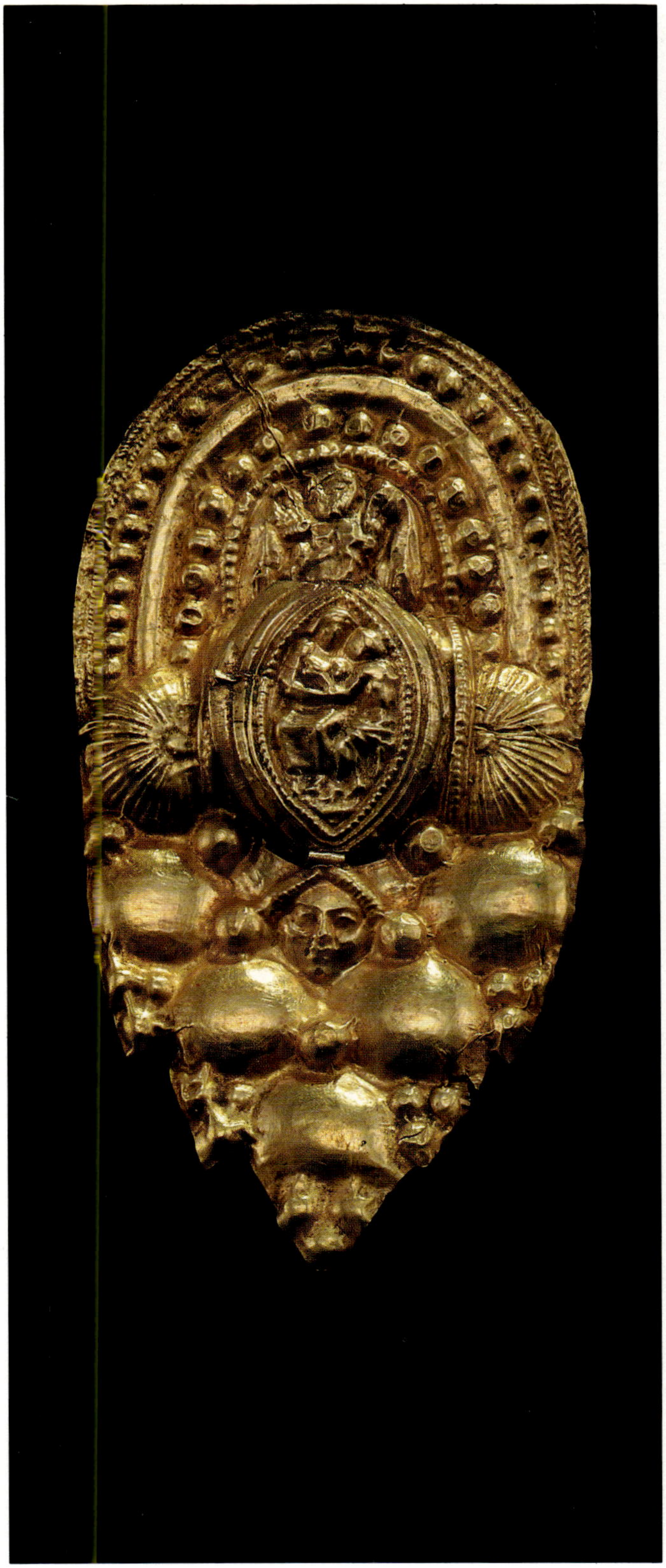

32

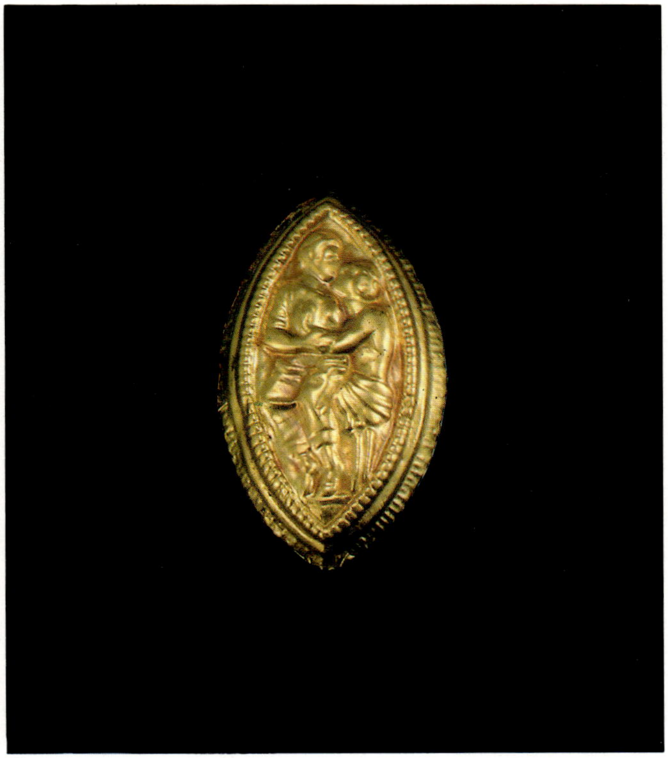

33

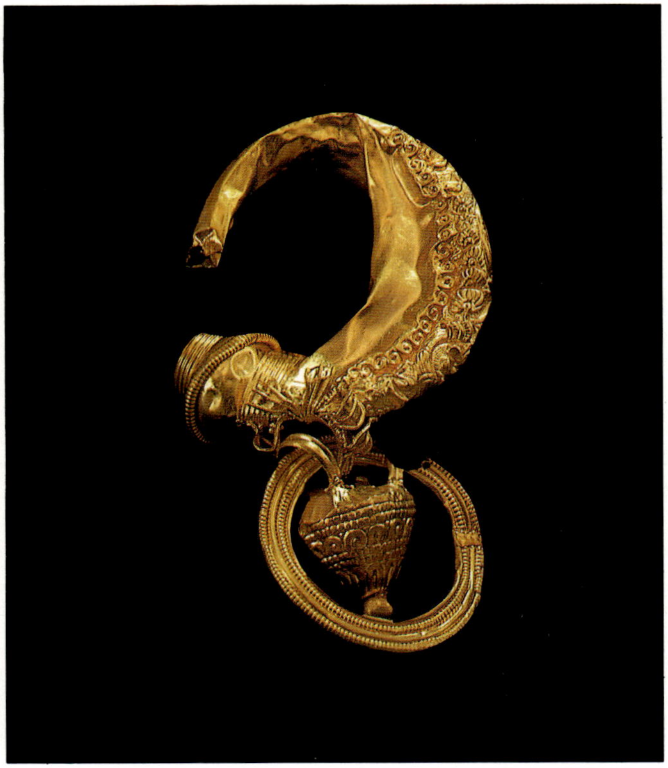

34

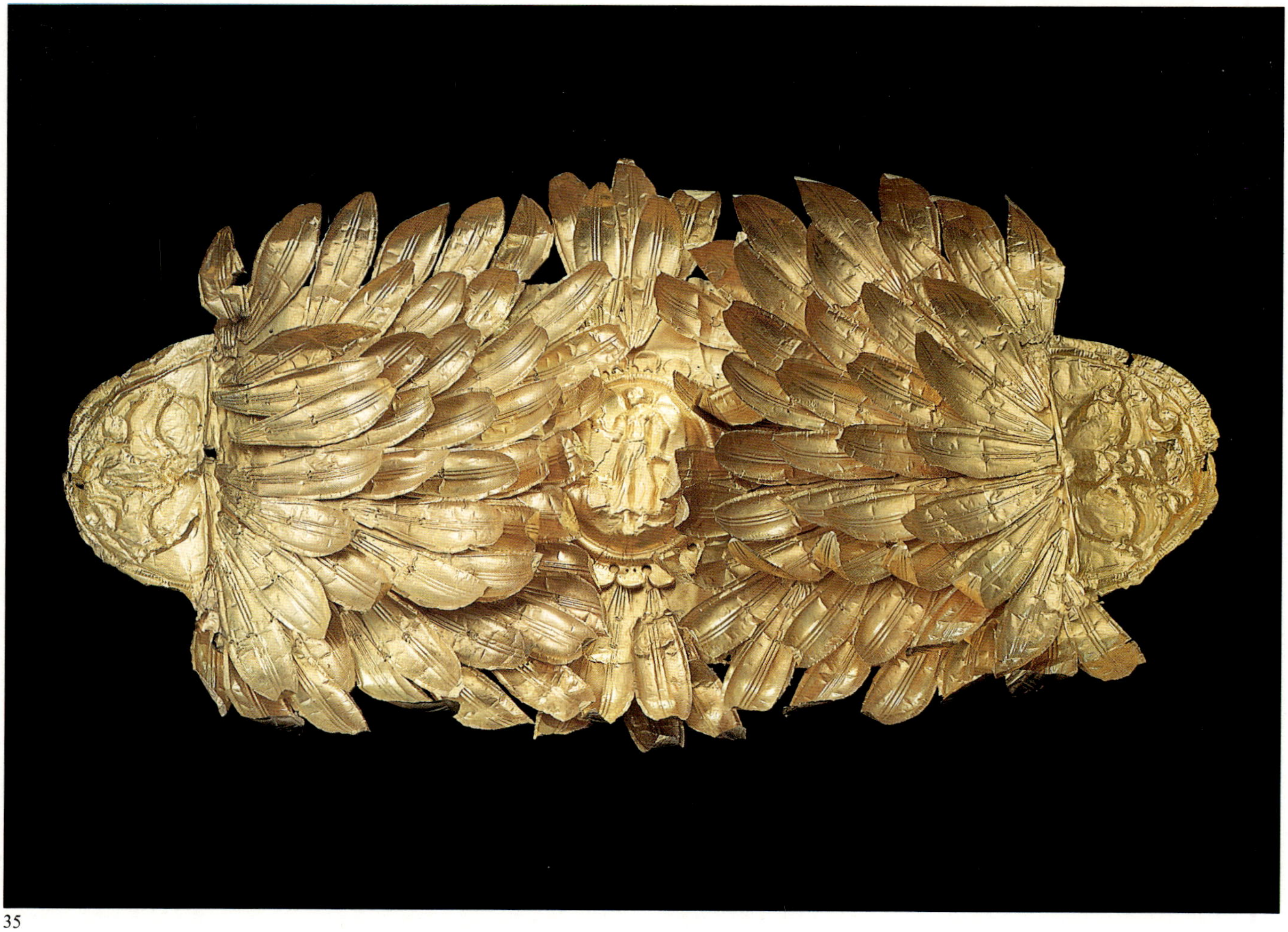

35

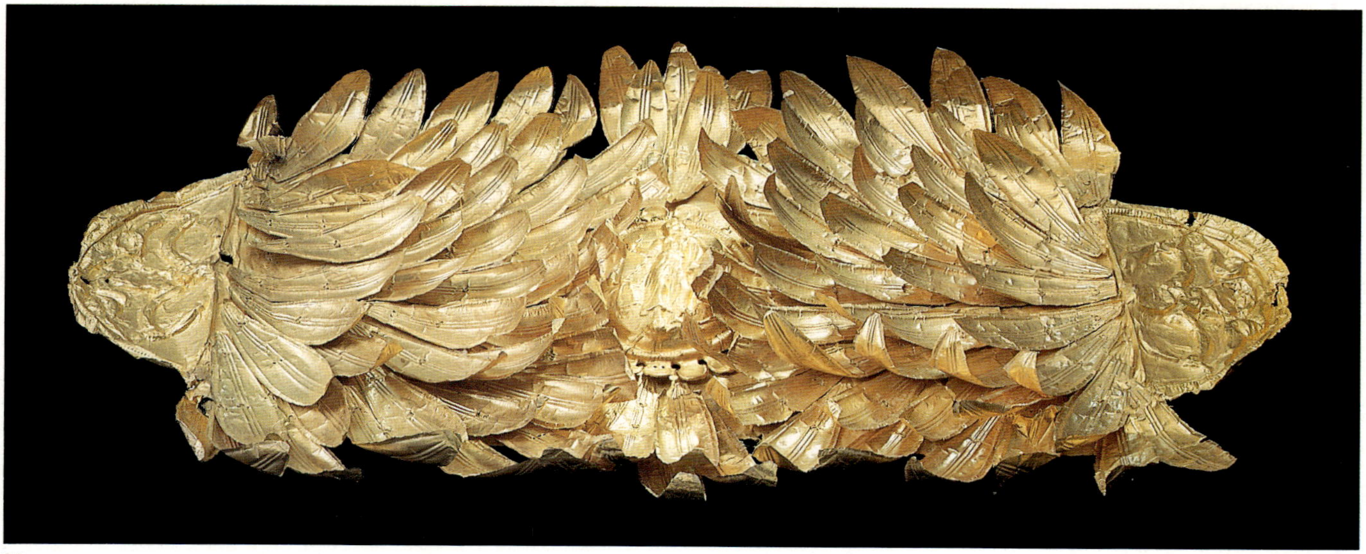

35

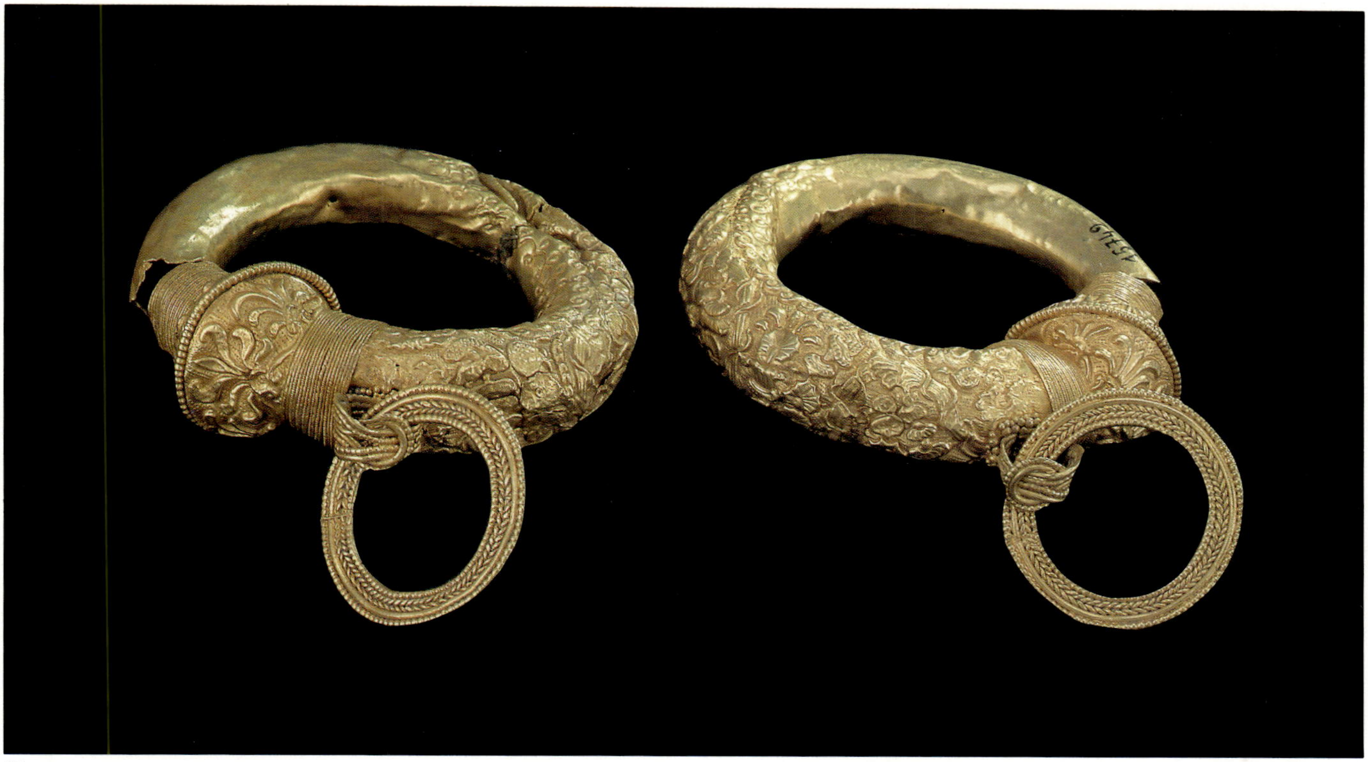

36

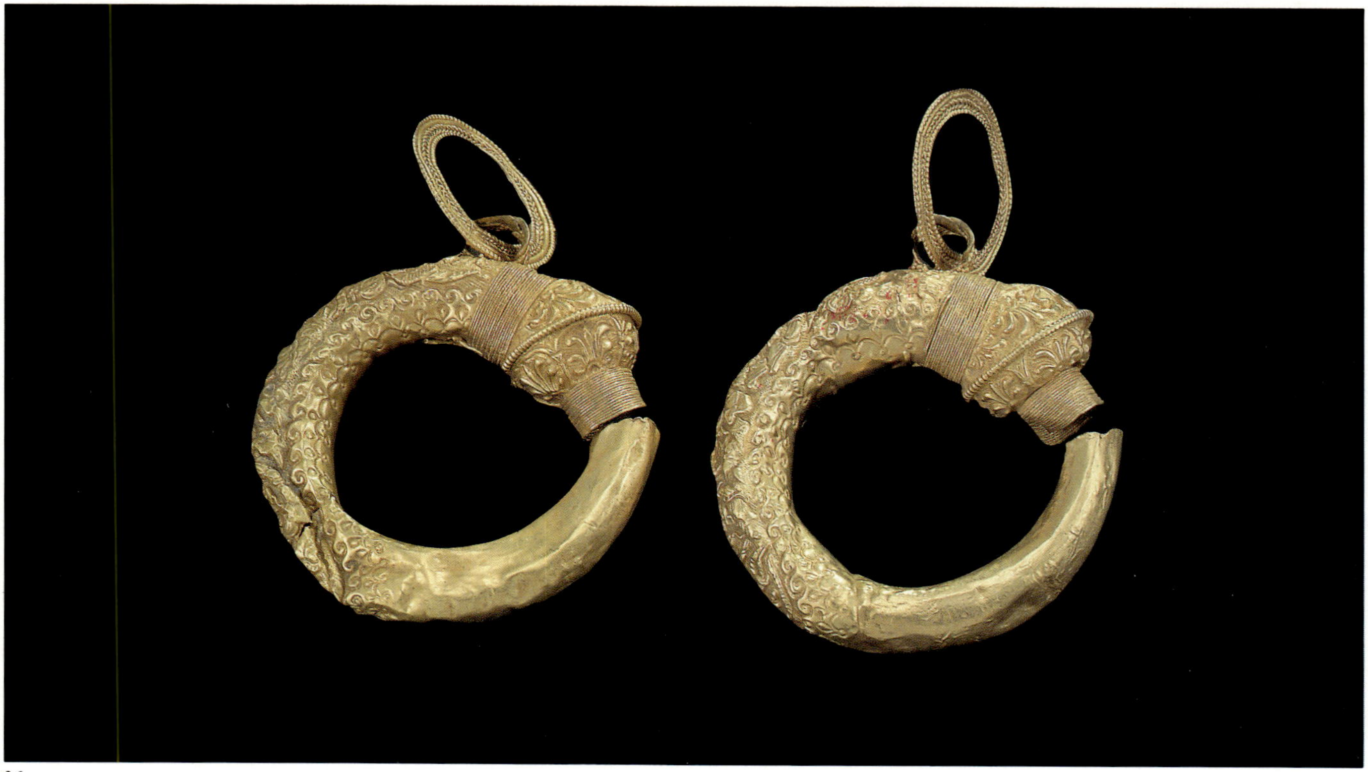

36

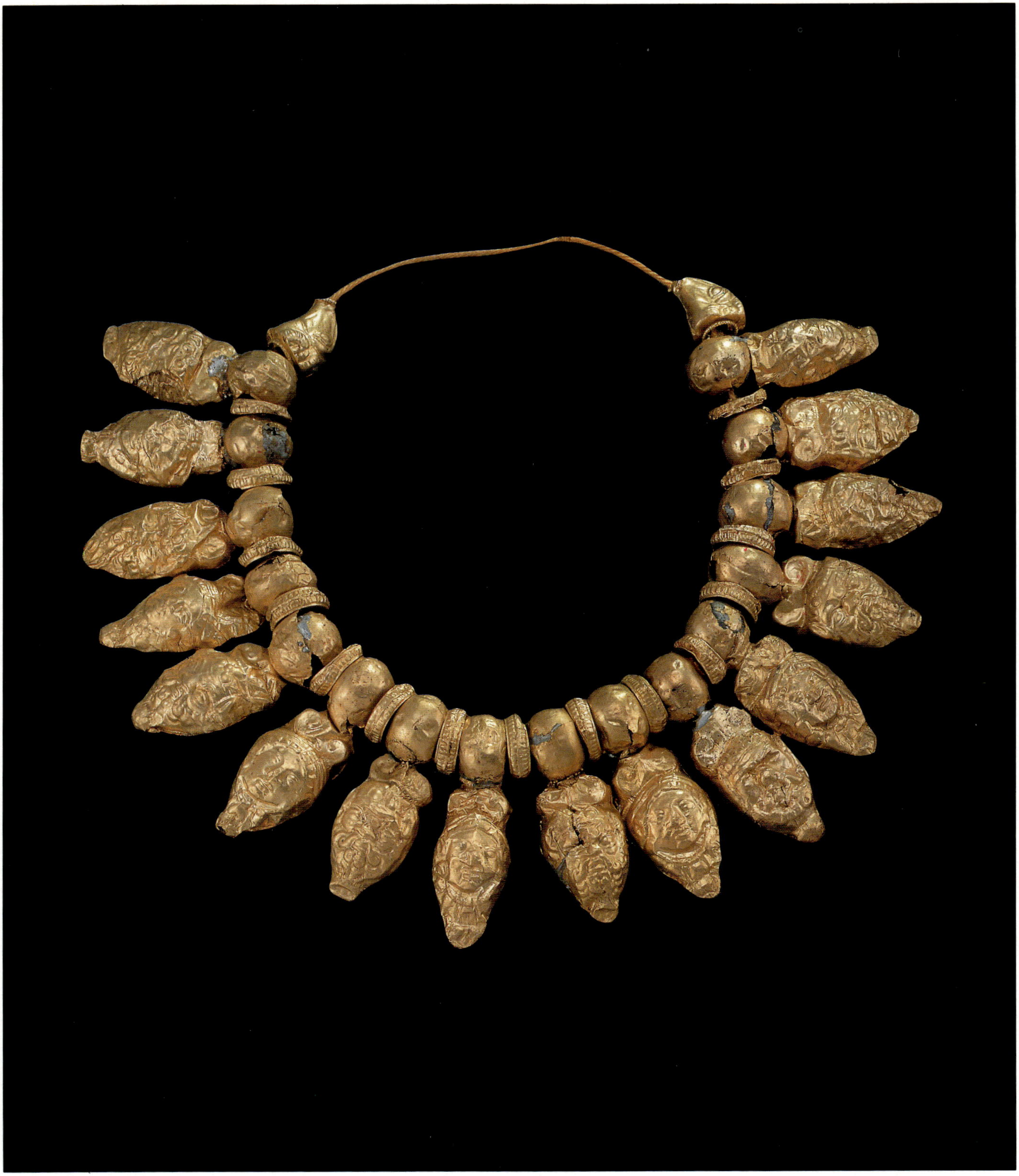

37

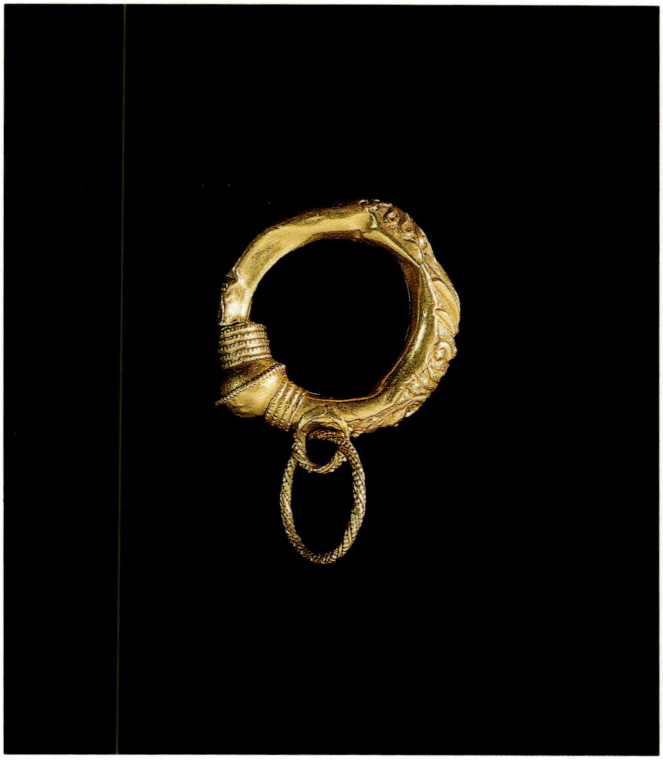

41

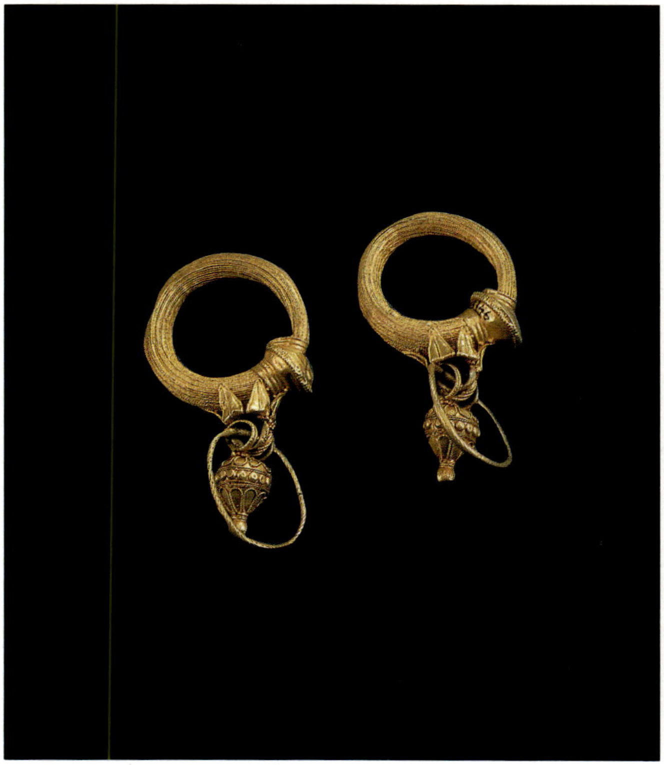

46

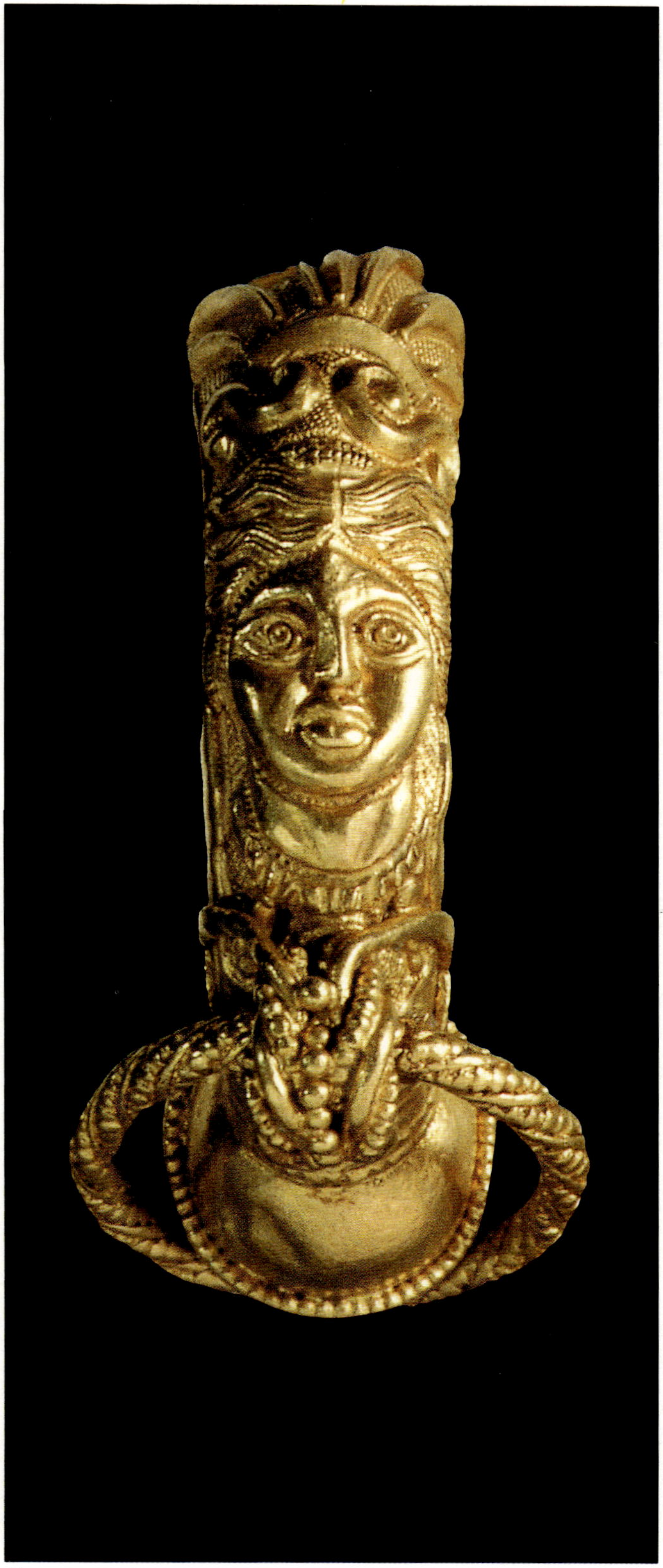

41

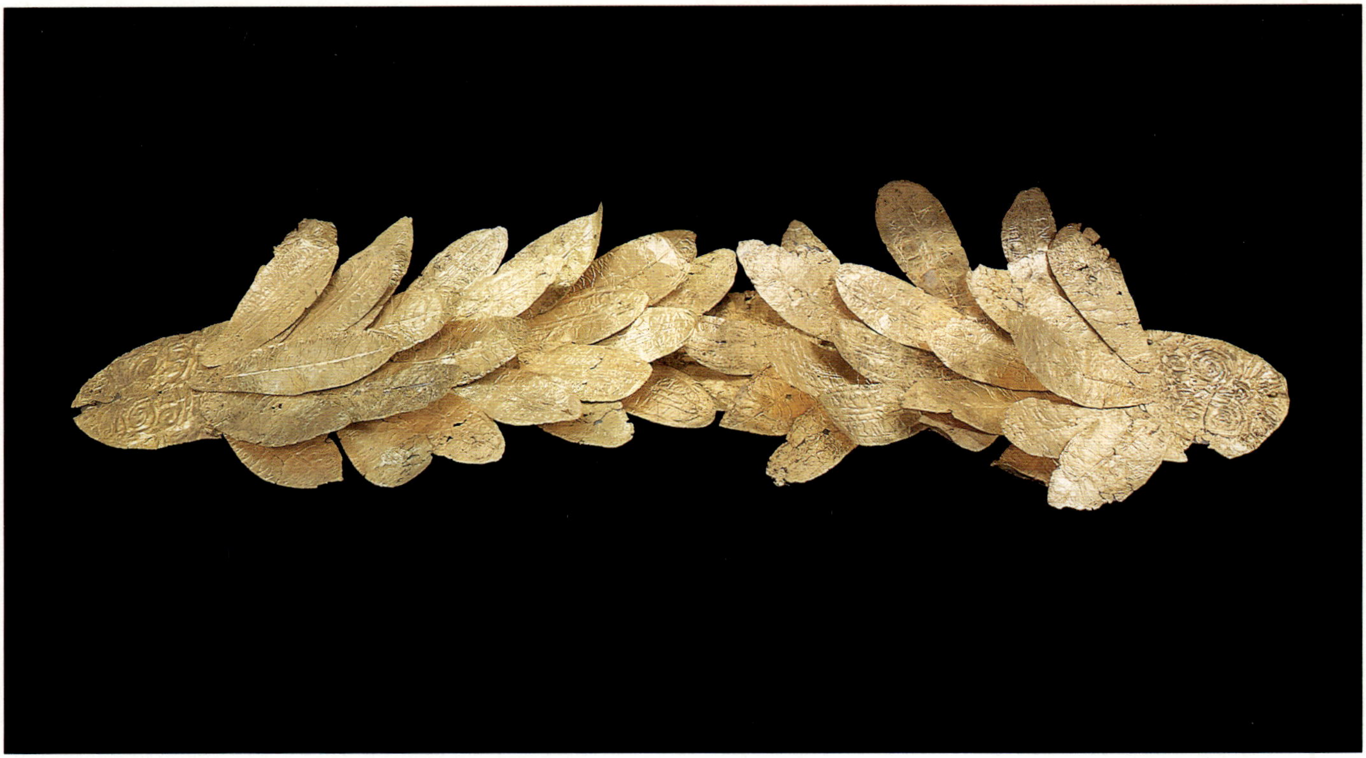

45

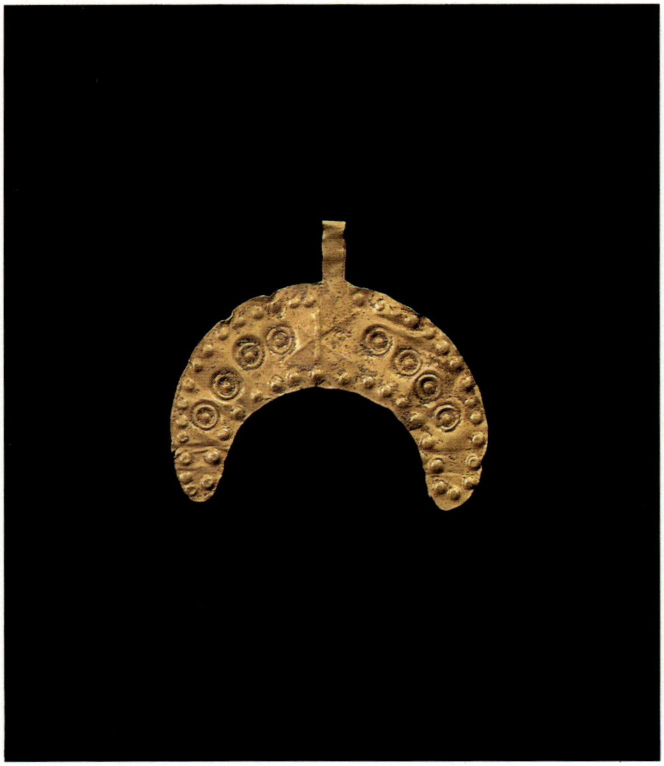

48

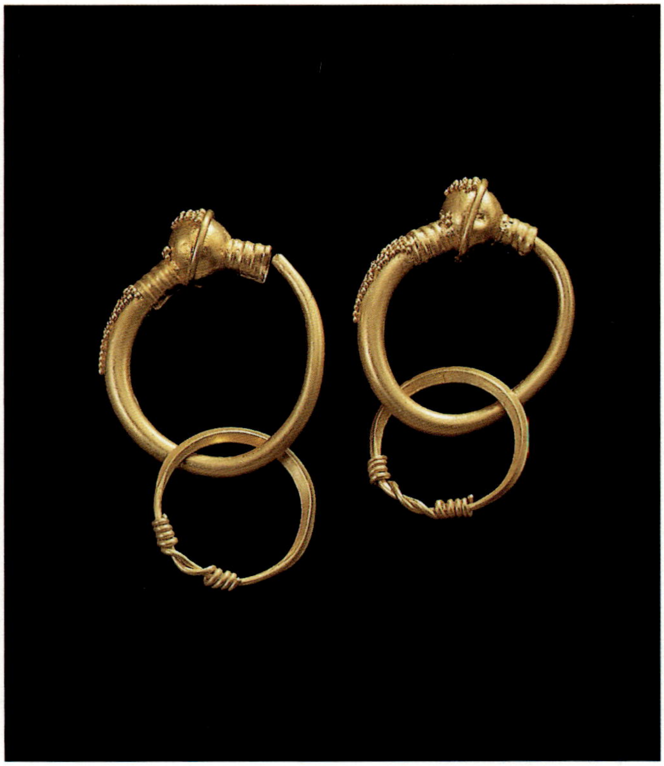

49

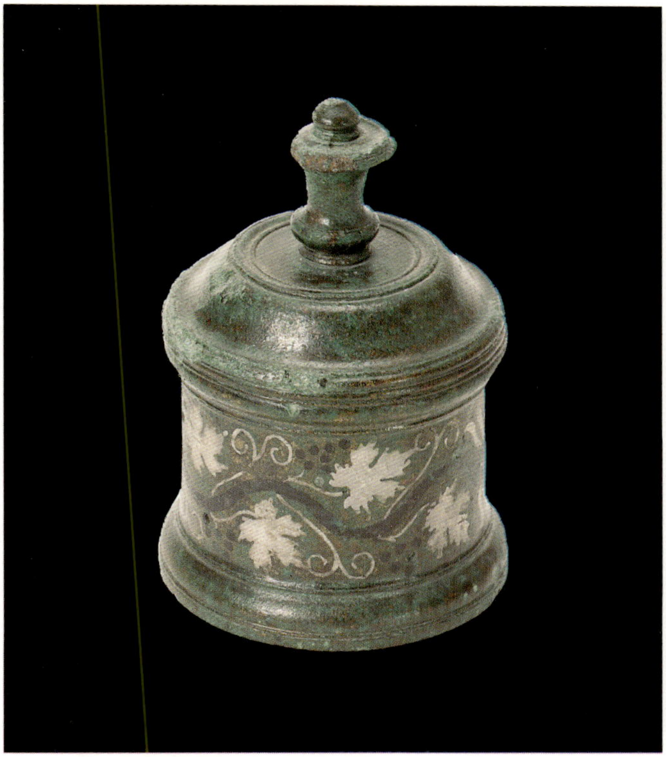
53

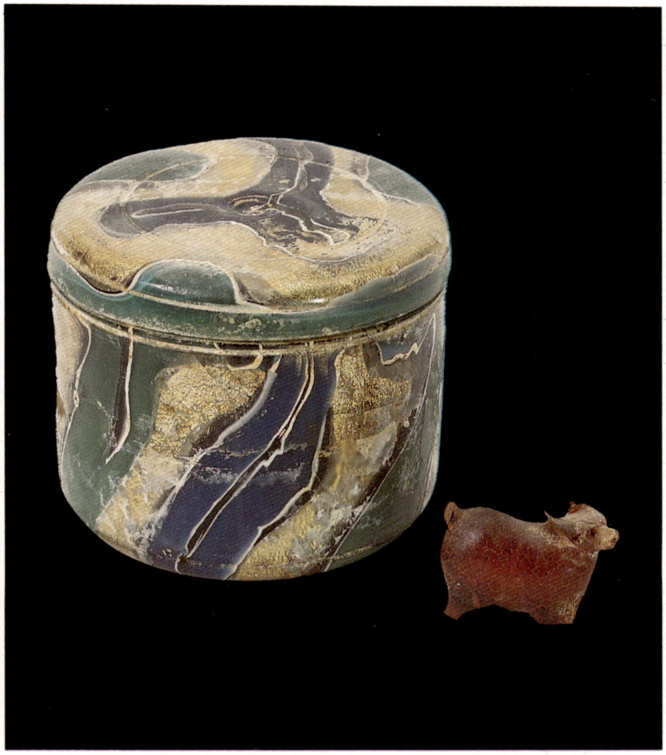
56

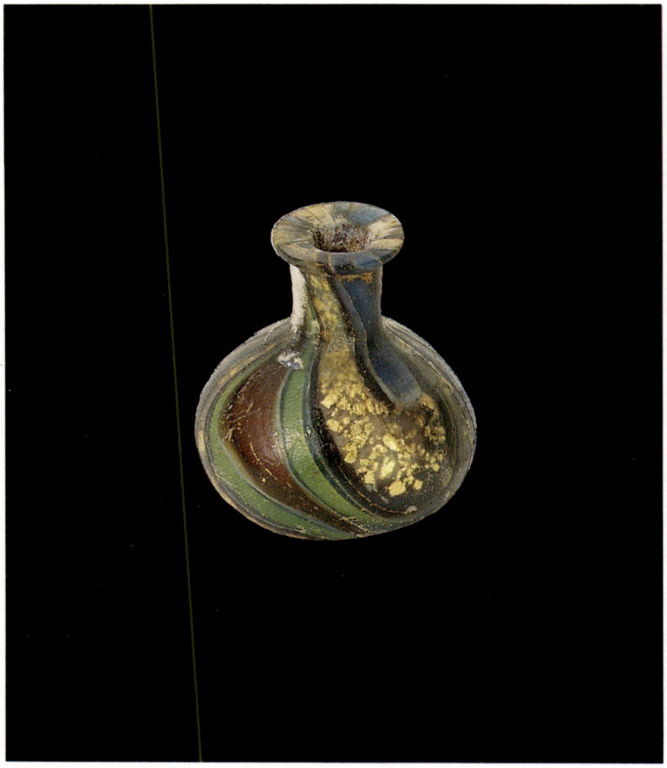
57

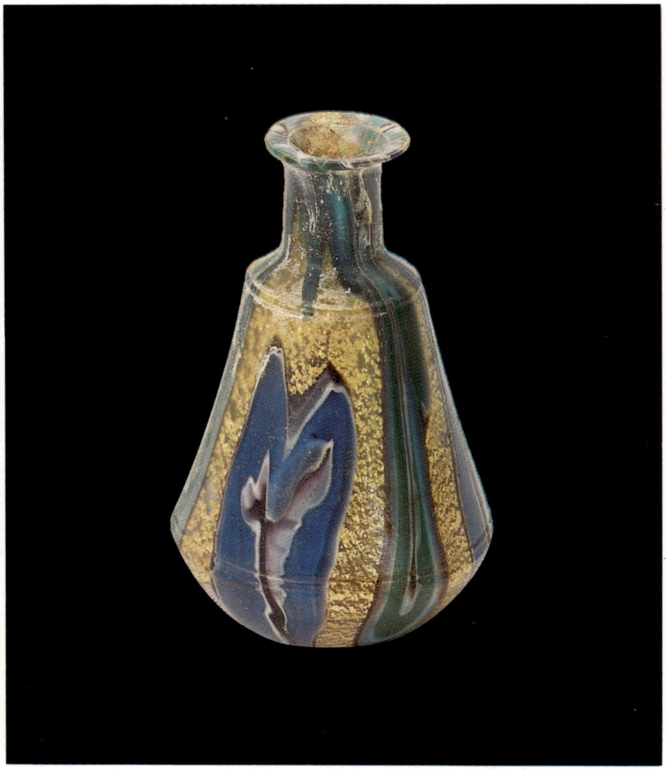
58

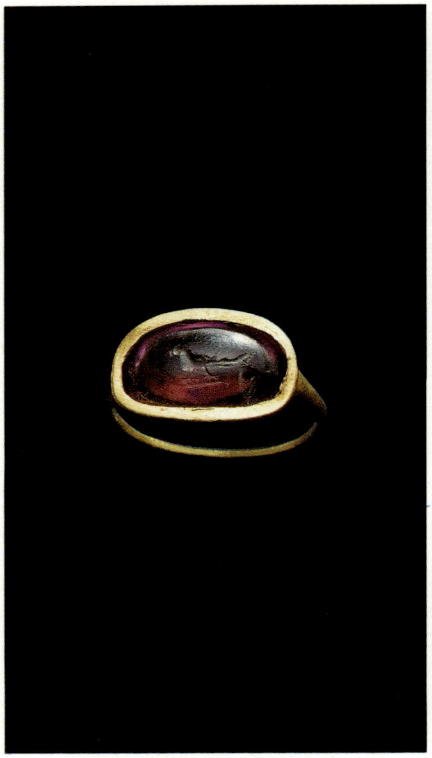
60

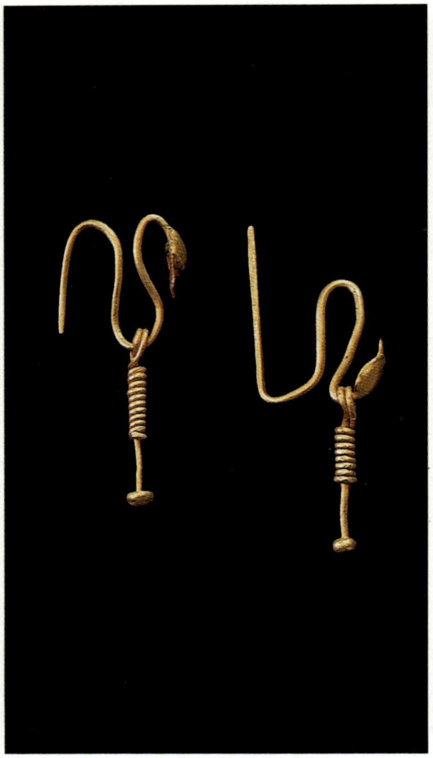
61

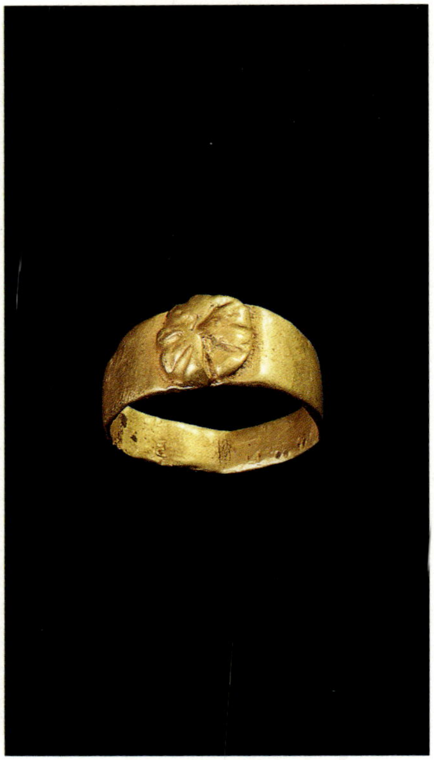
62

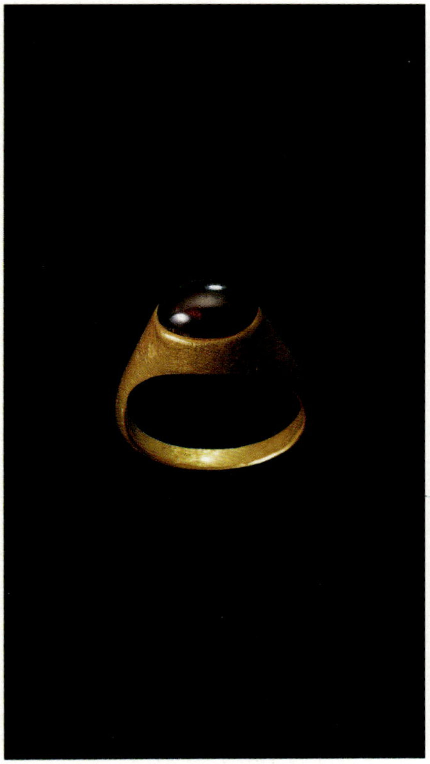
63

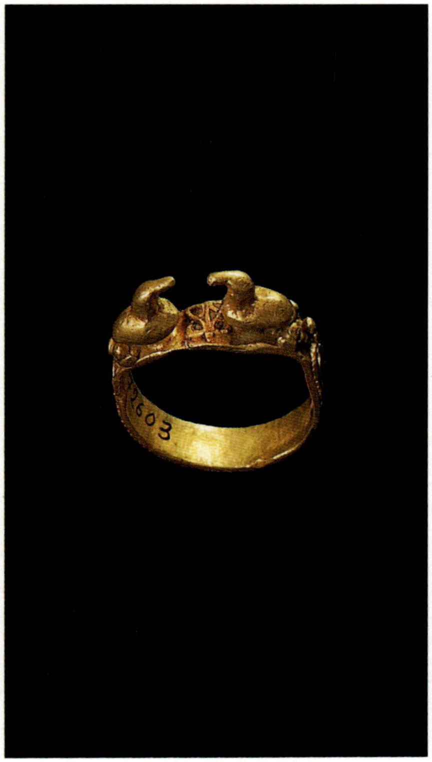
64

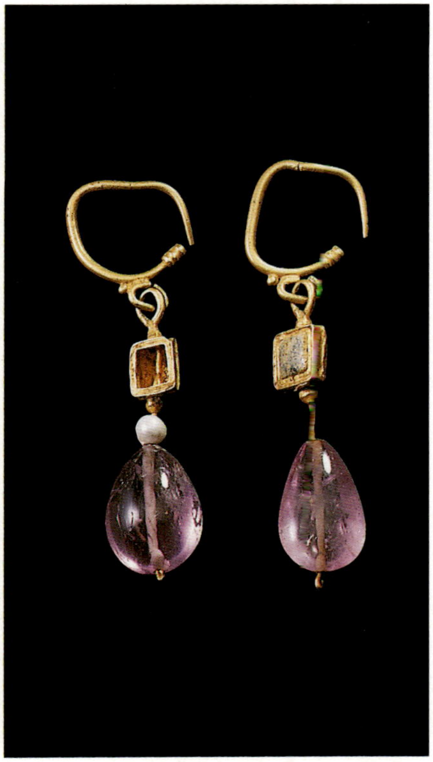
66

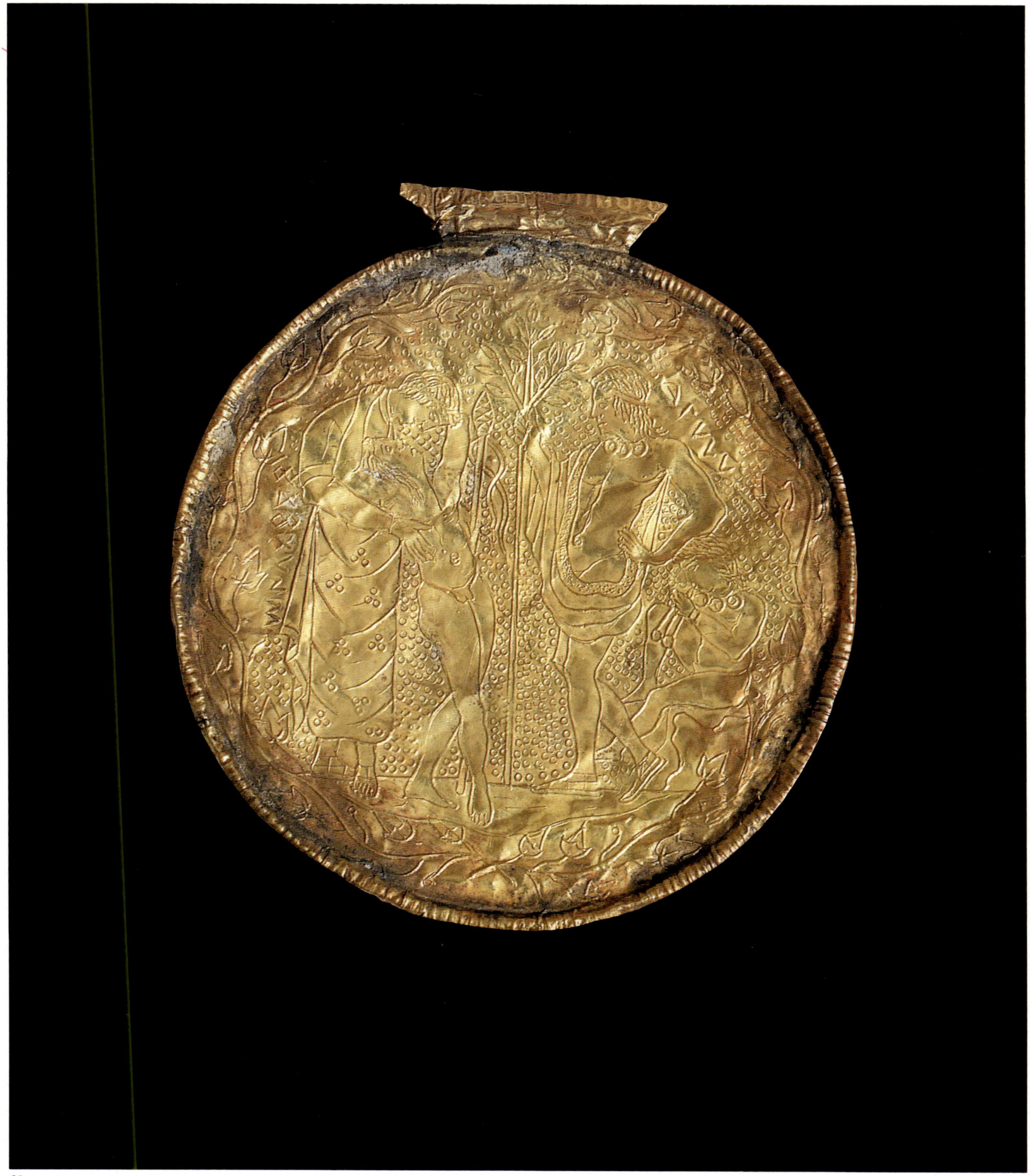

65

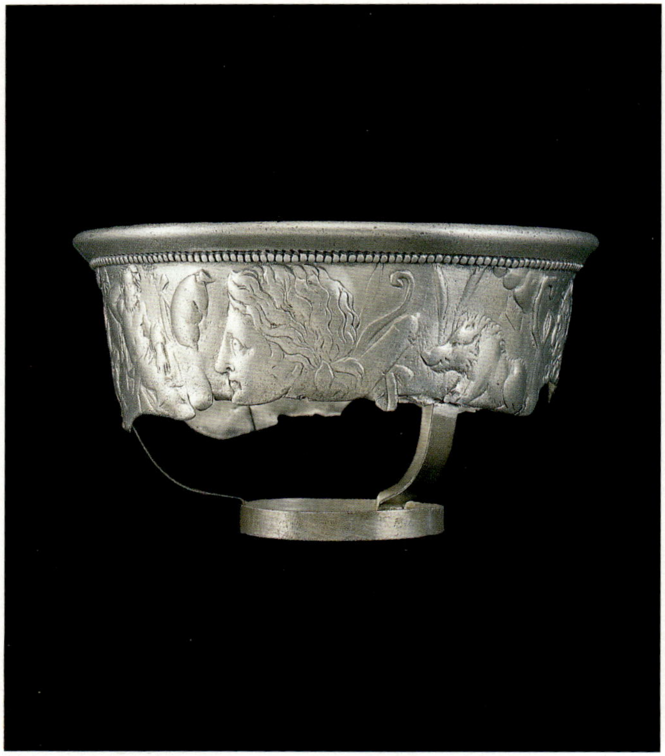
69

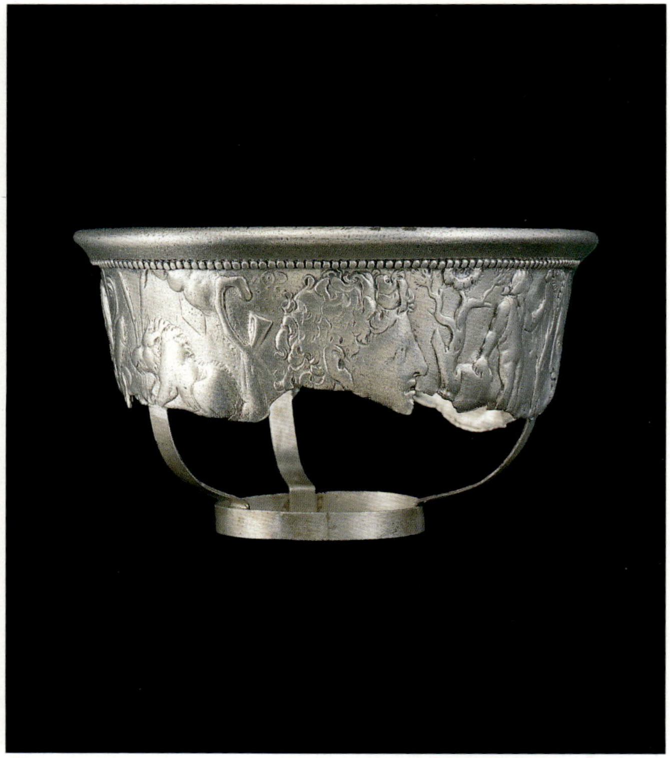
69

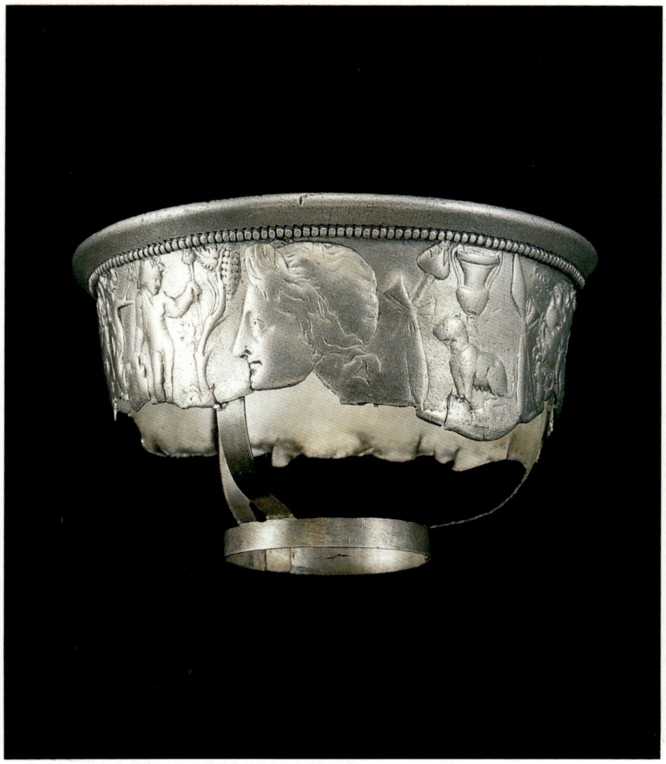
69

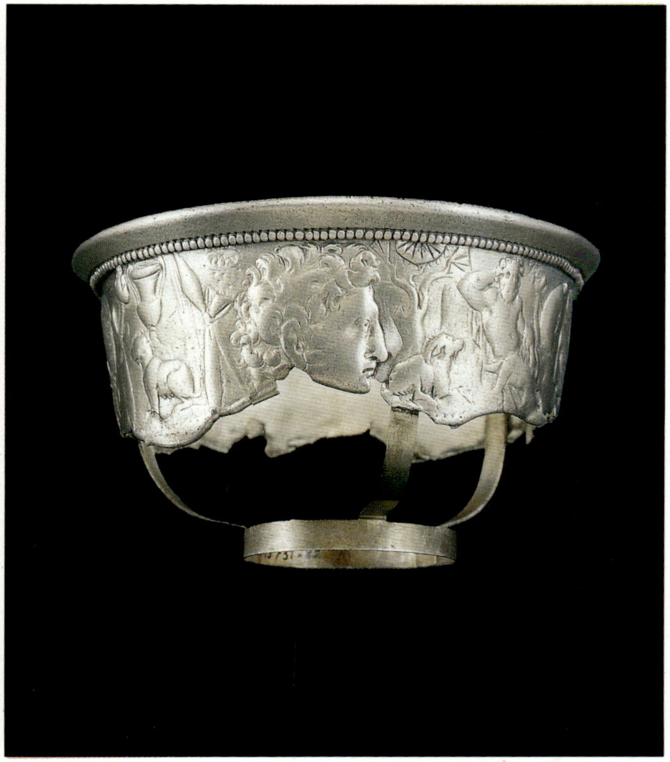
69

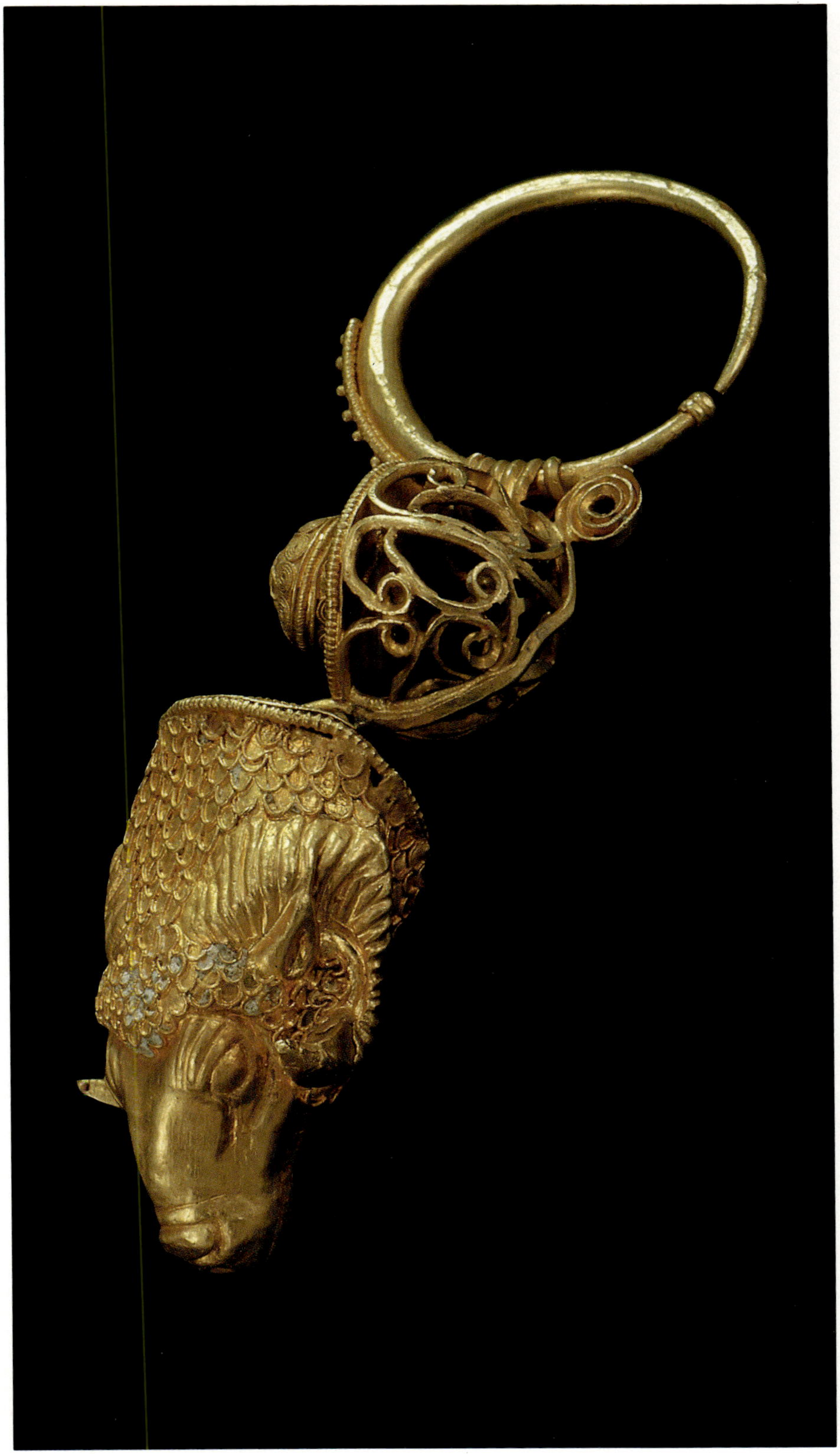

68

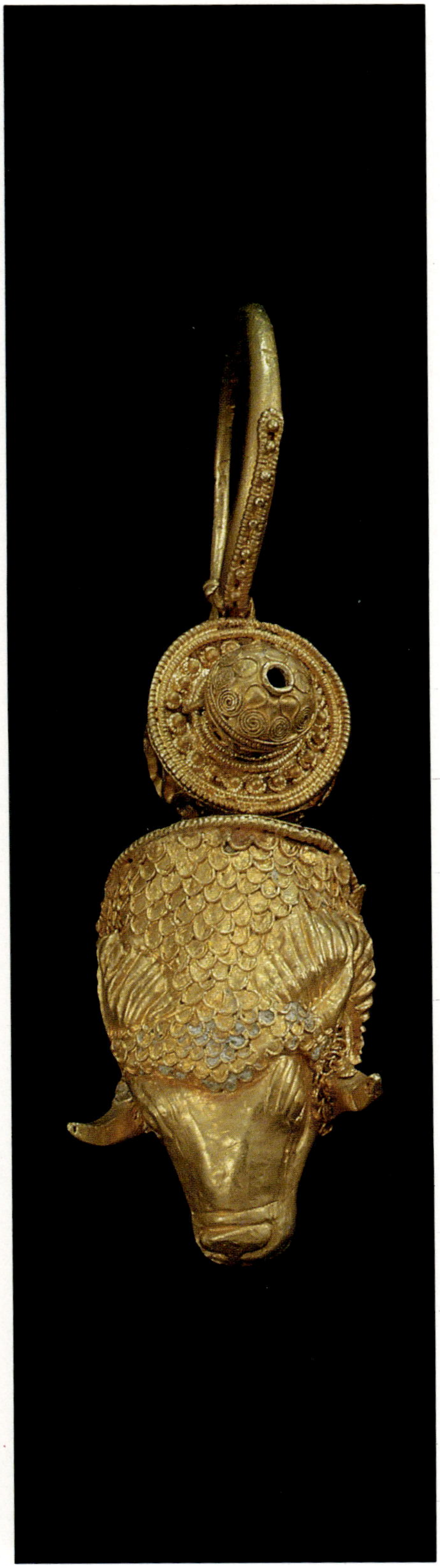

68

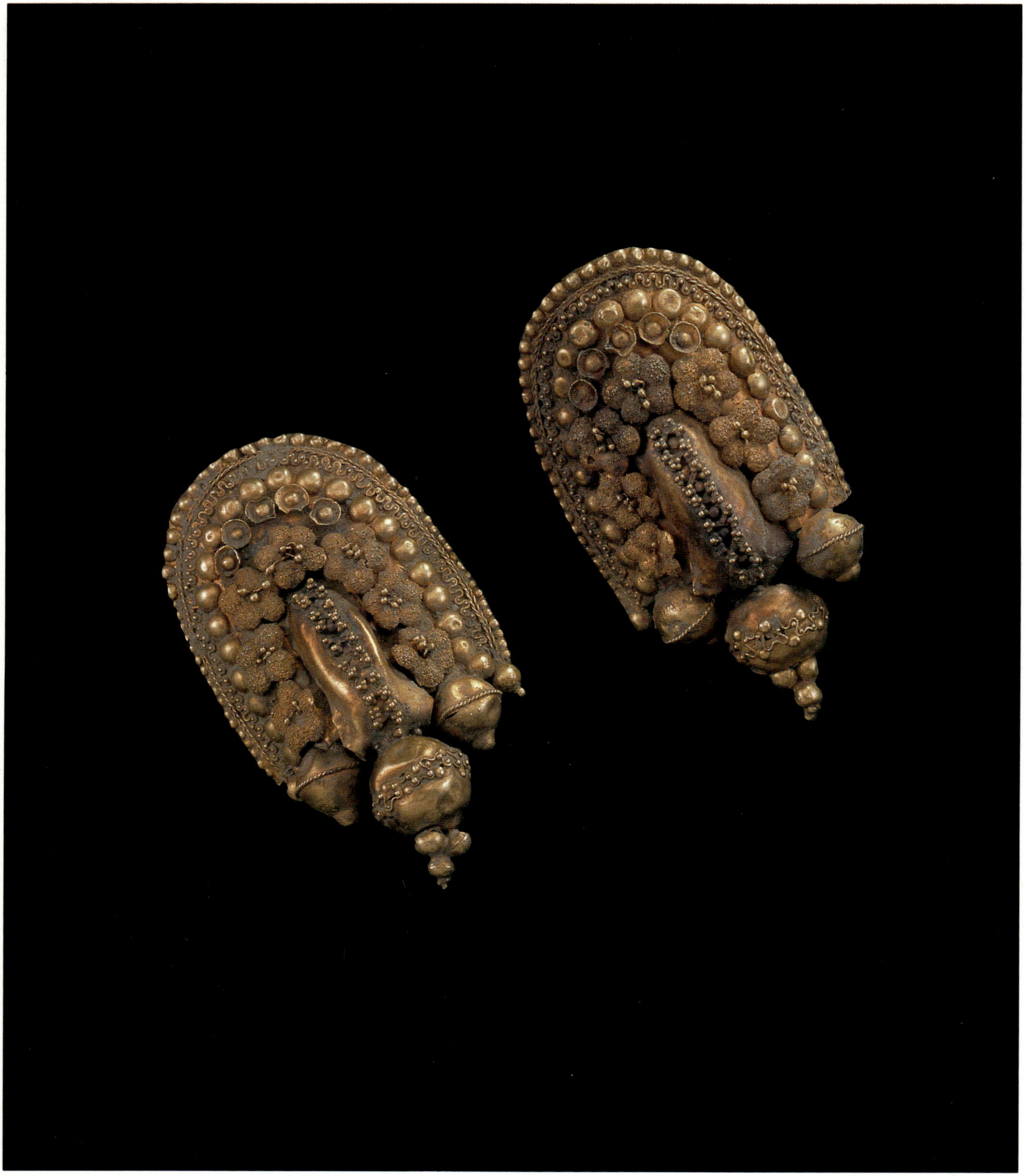

70

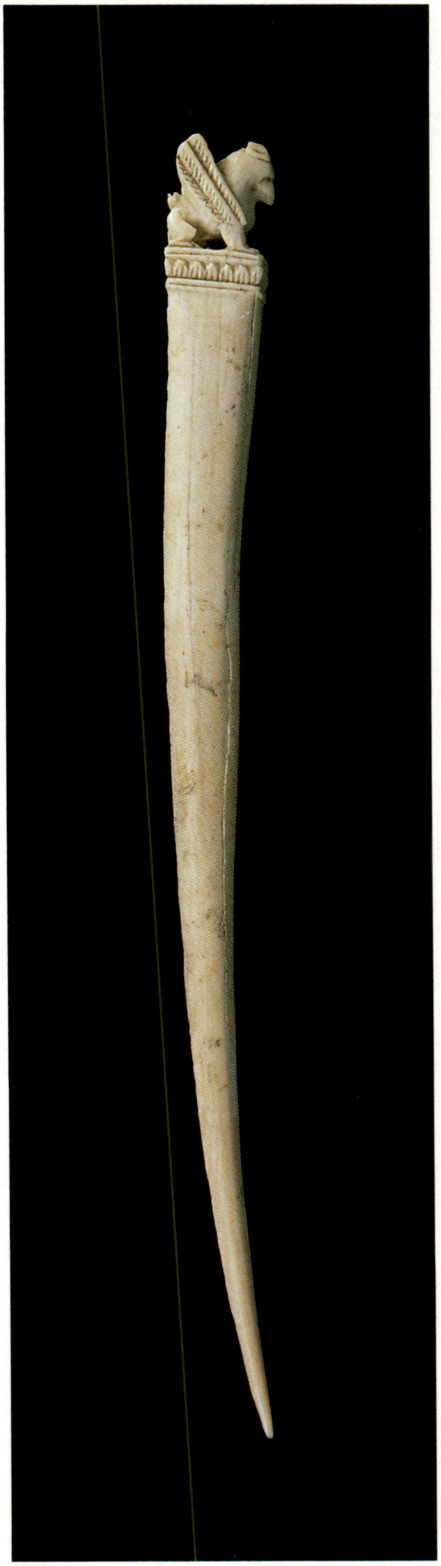

72

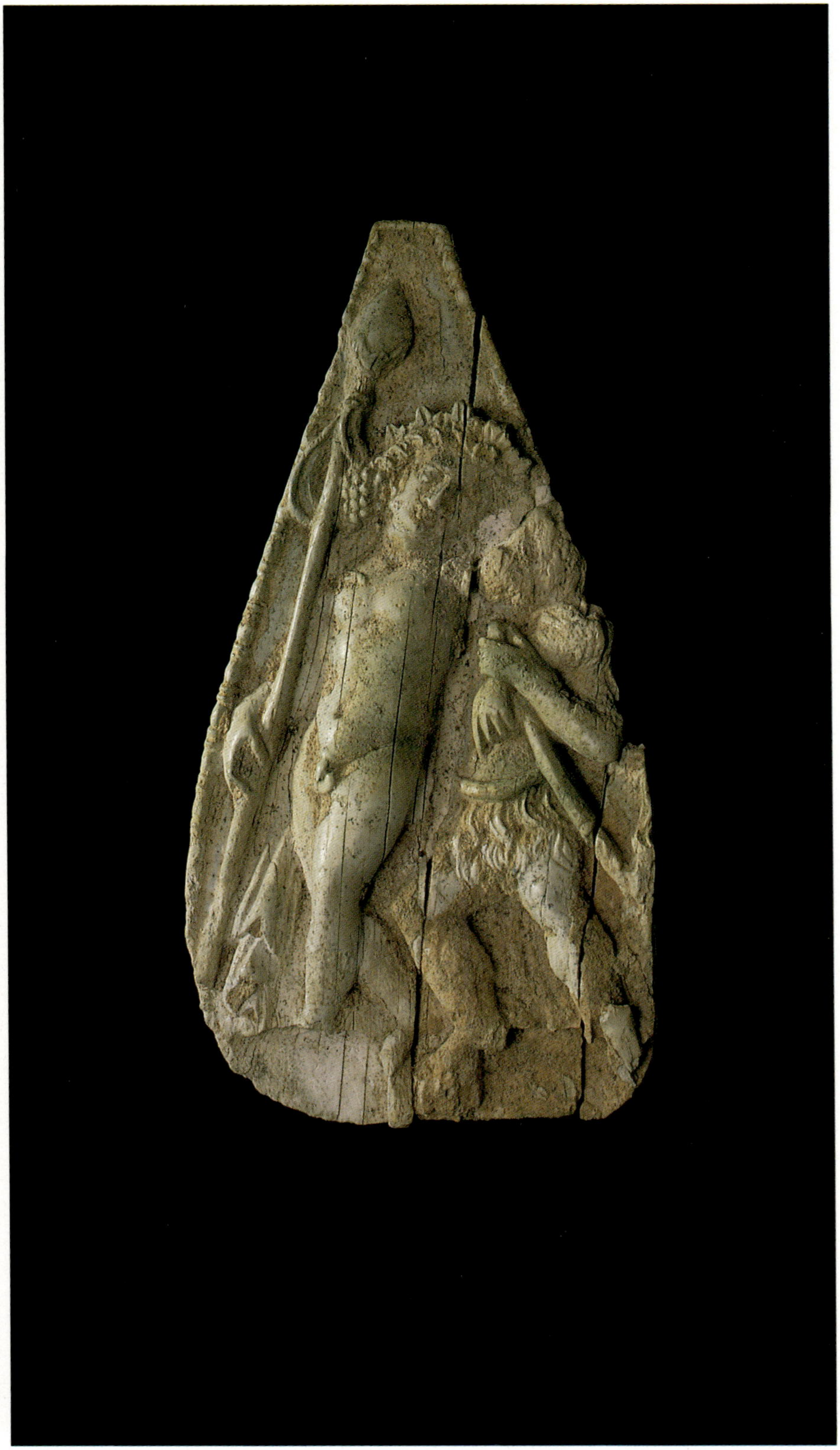

73

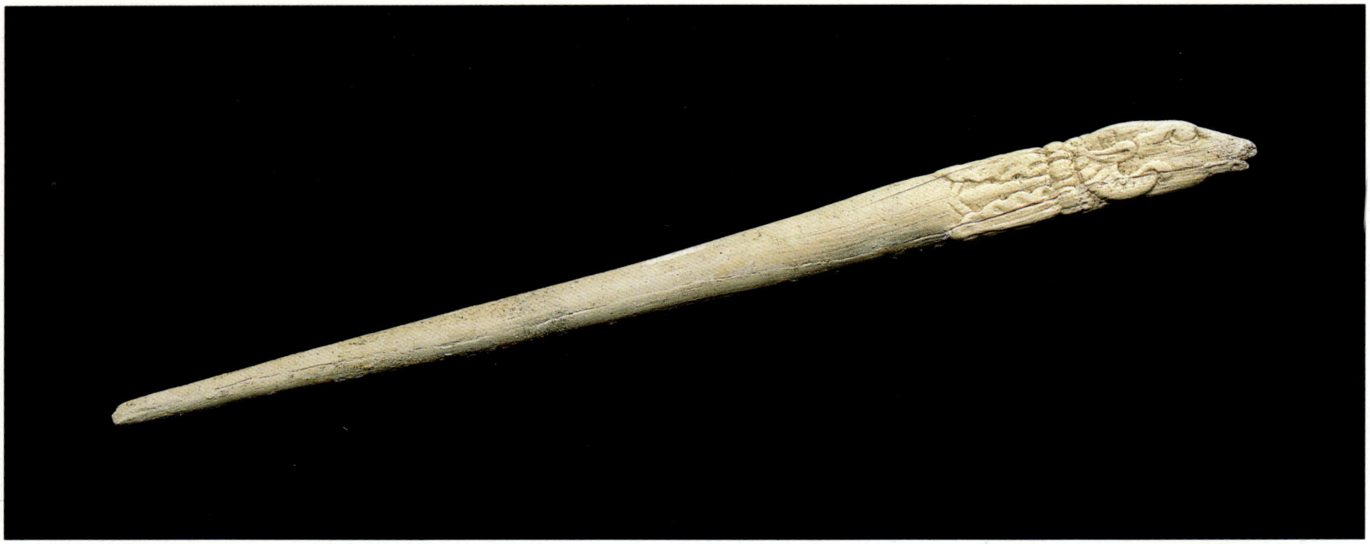

75

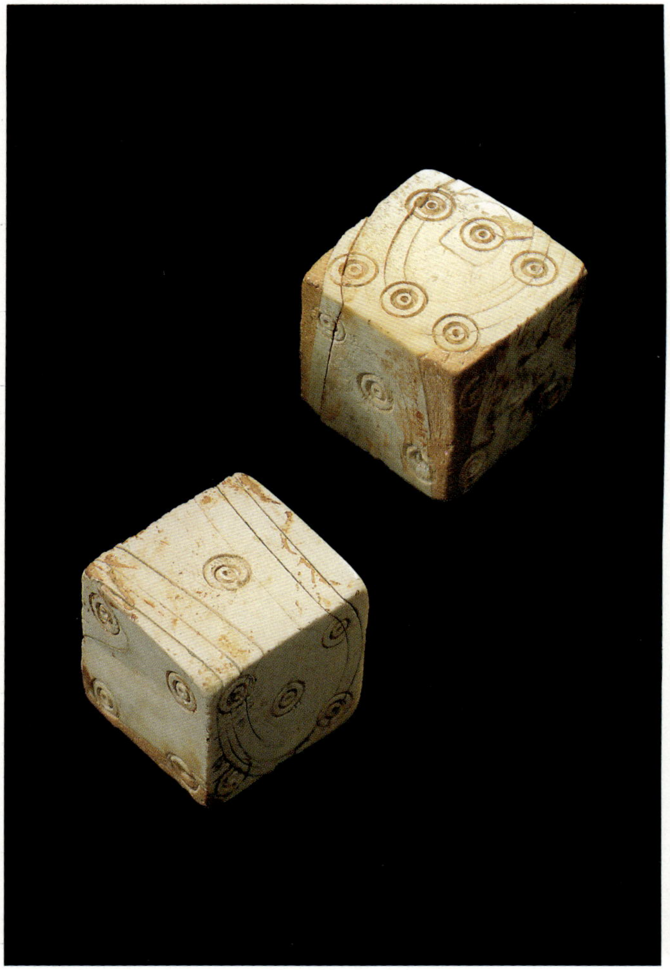

74

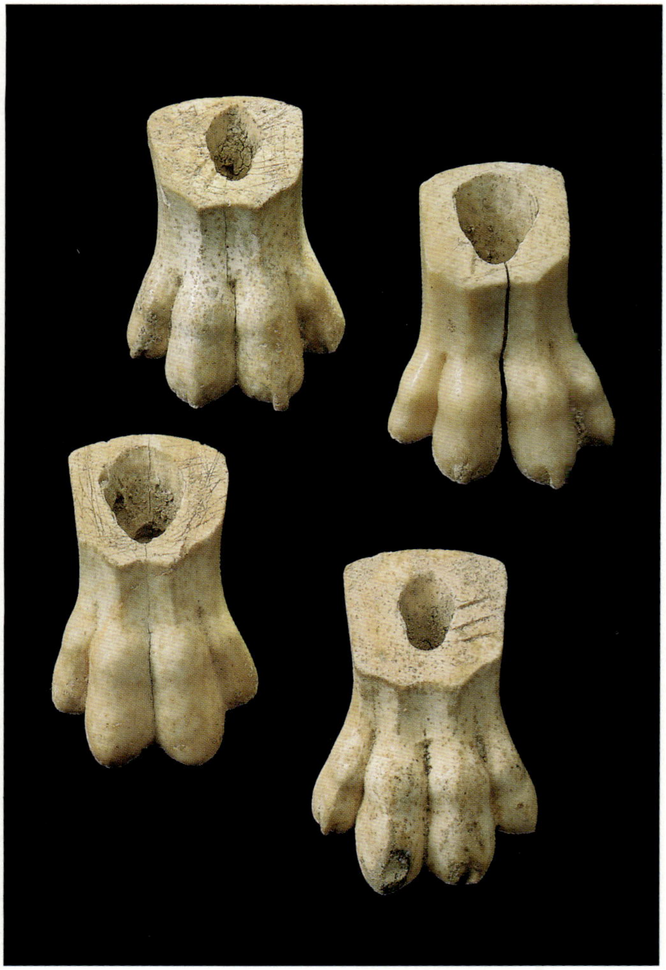

76

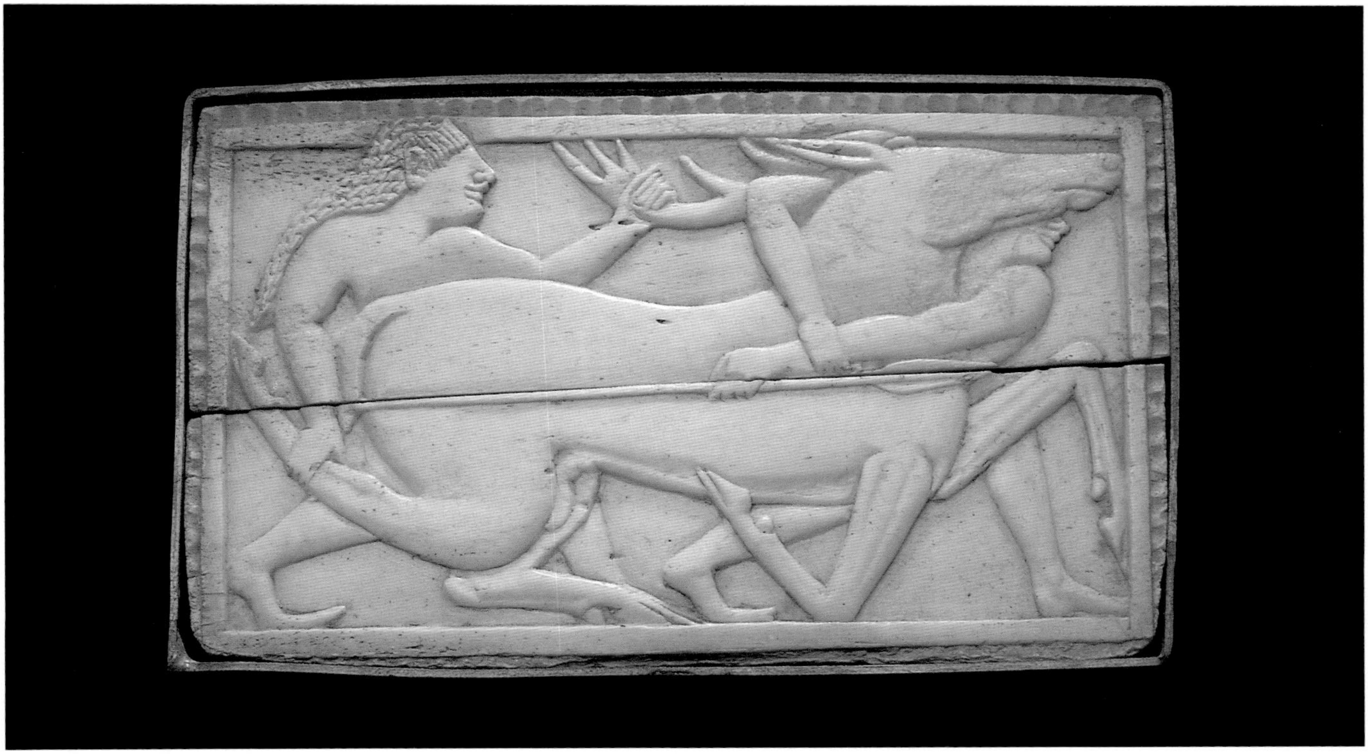
77

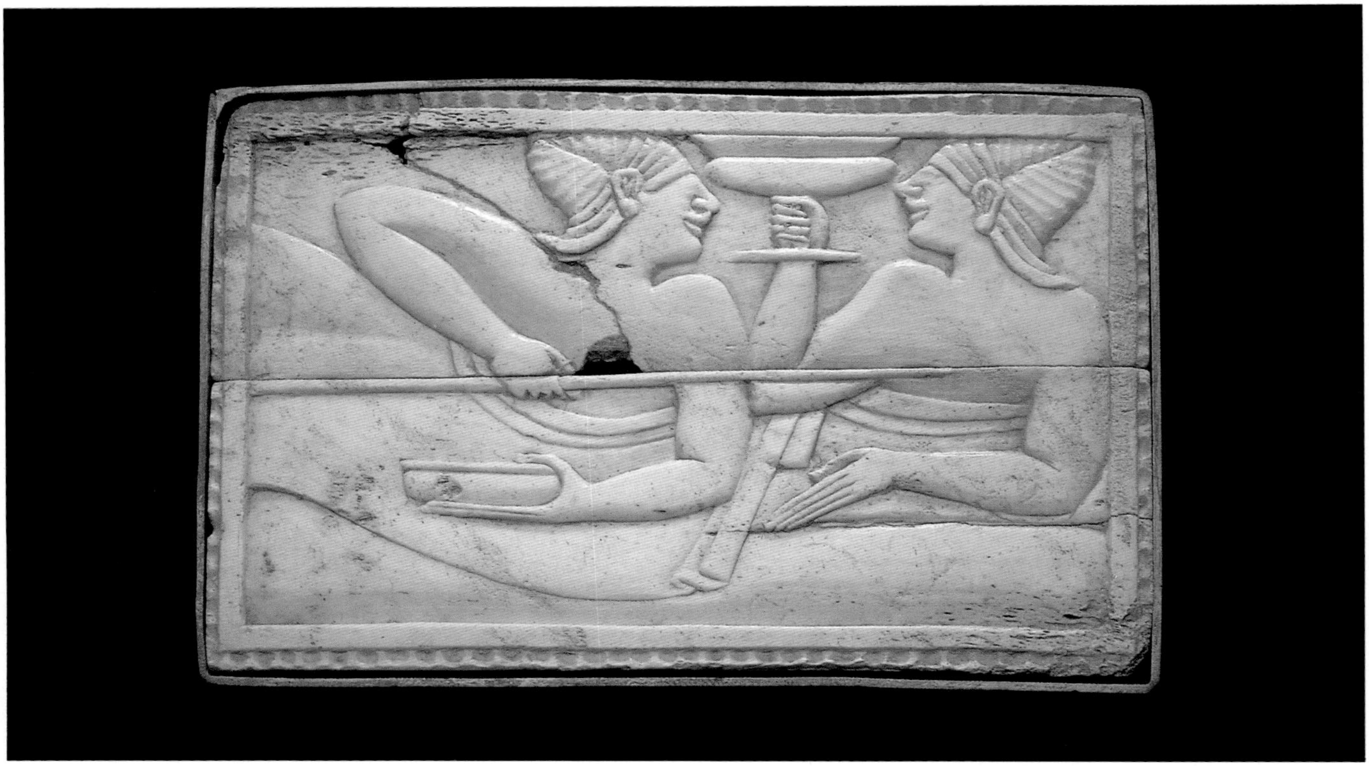
78

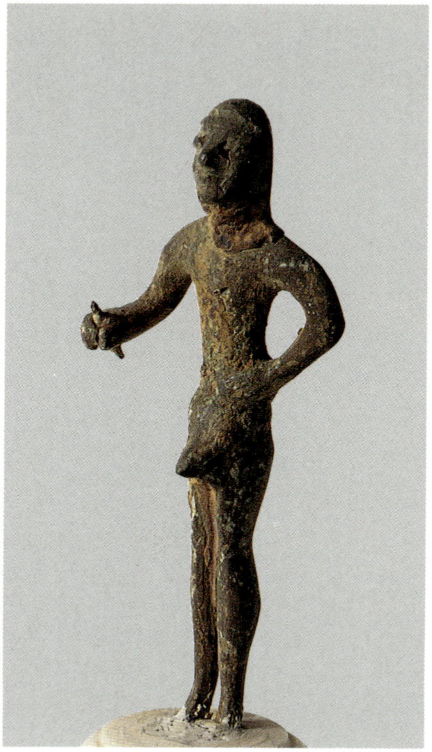

79

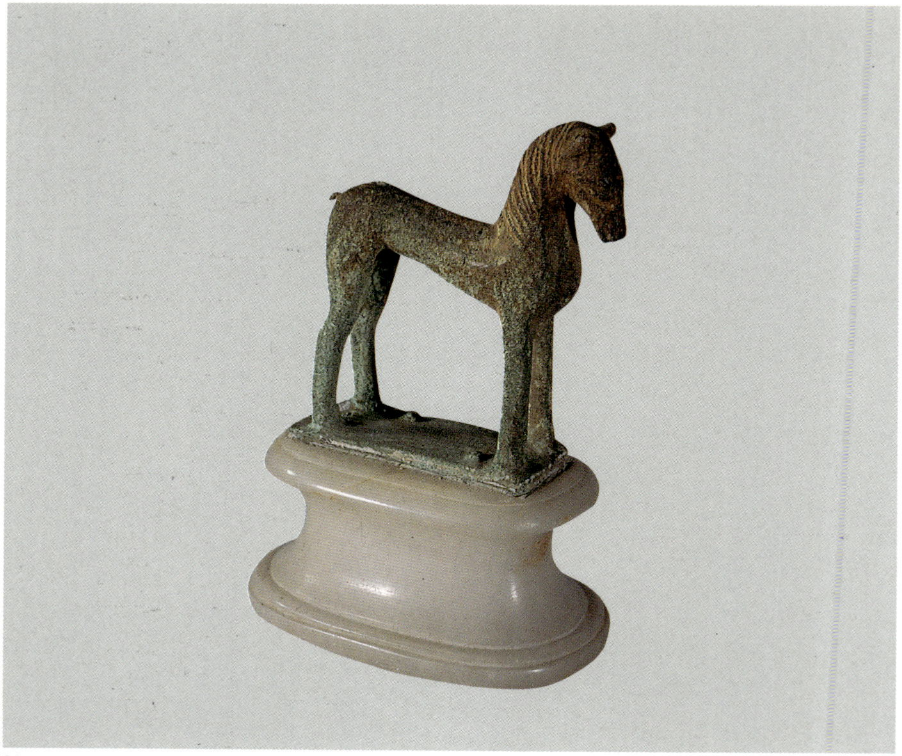

81

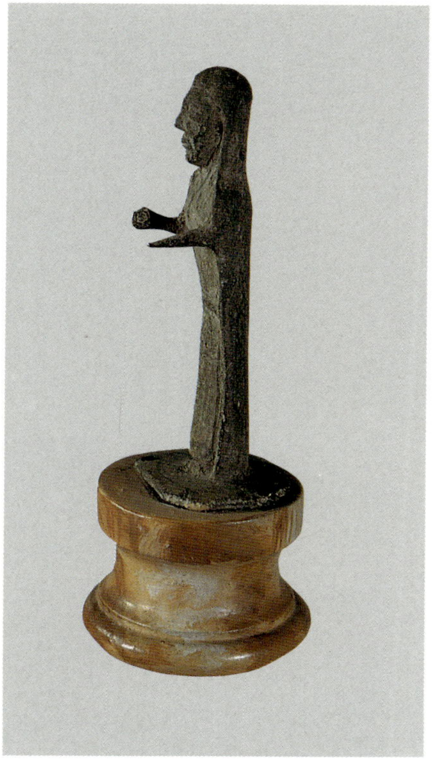

82

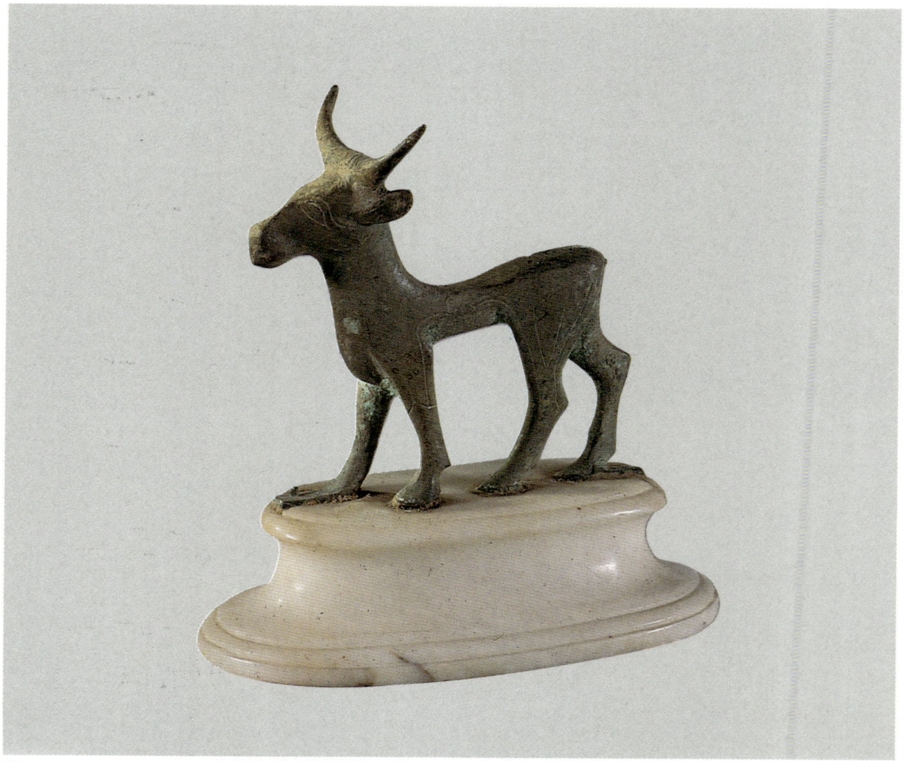

83

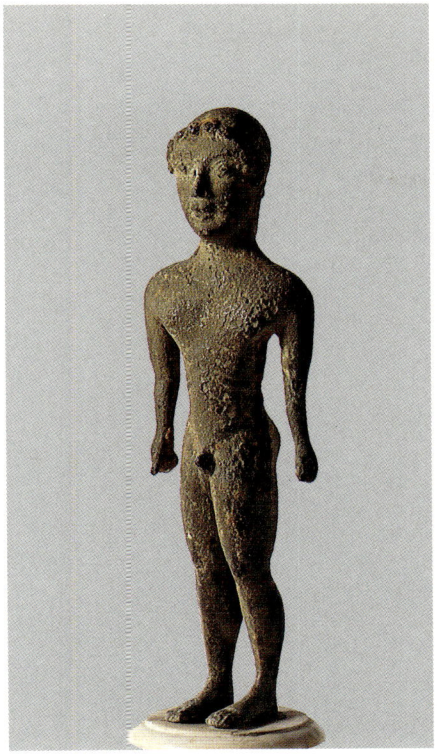
84

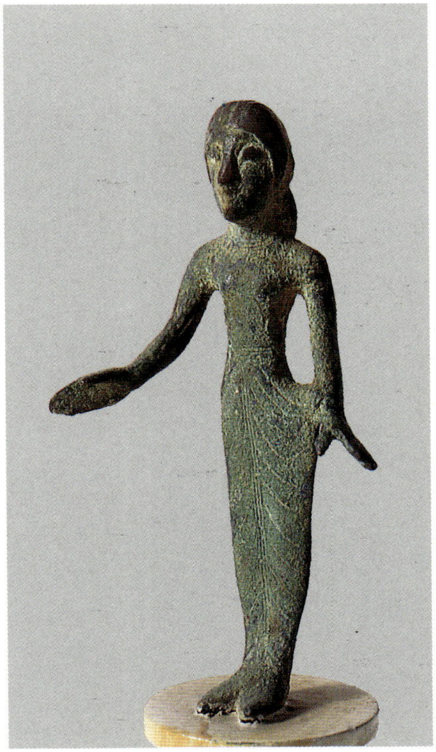
85

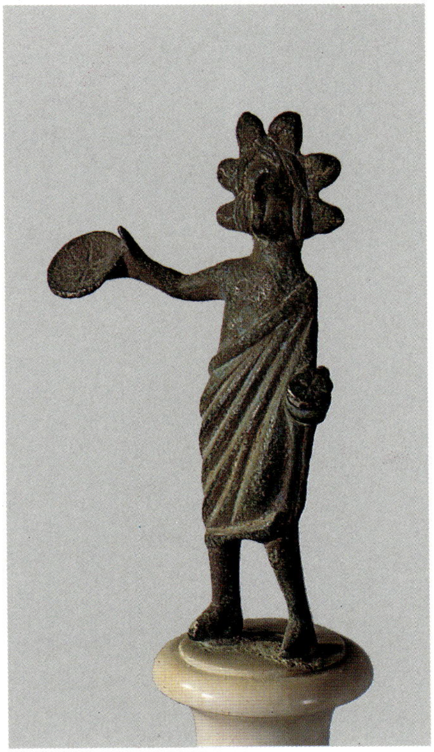
87

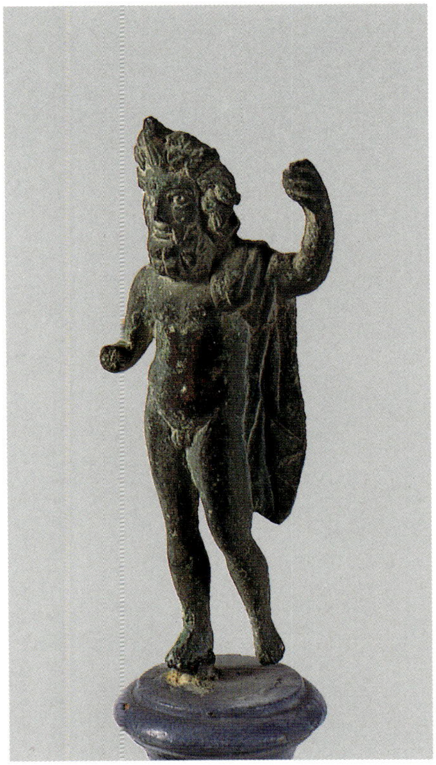
95

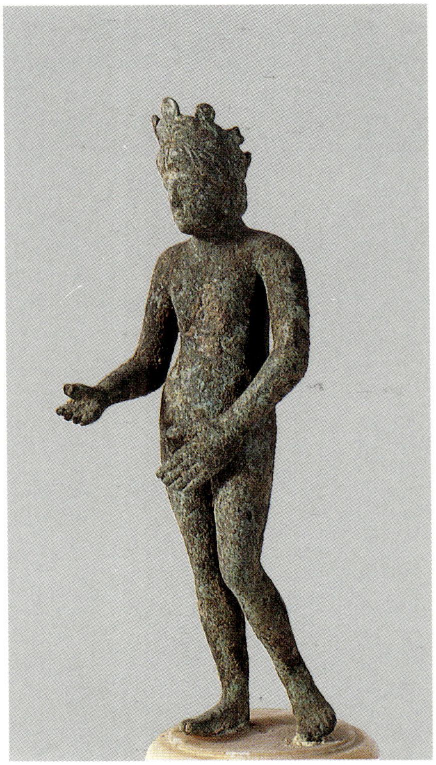
92

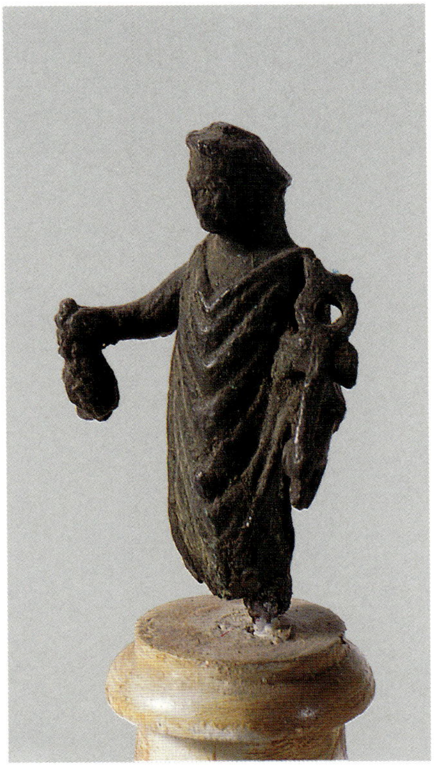
93

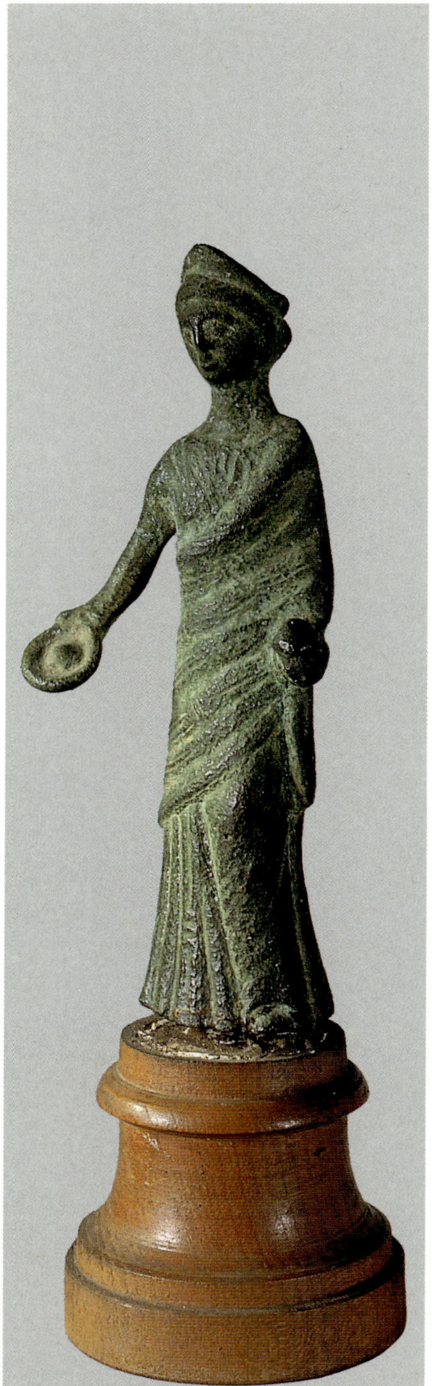

86

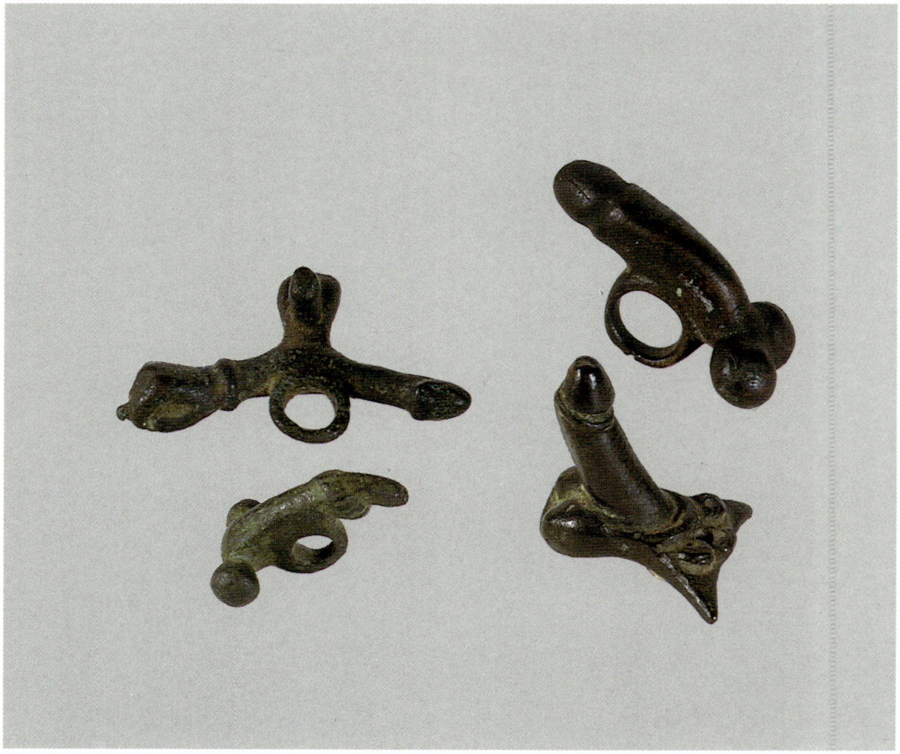

88-89-90-91

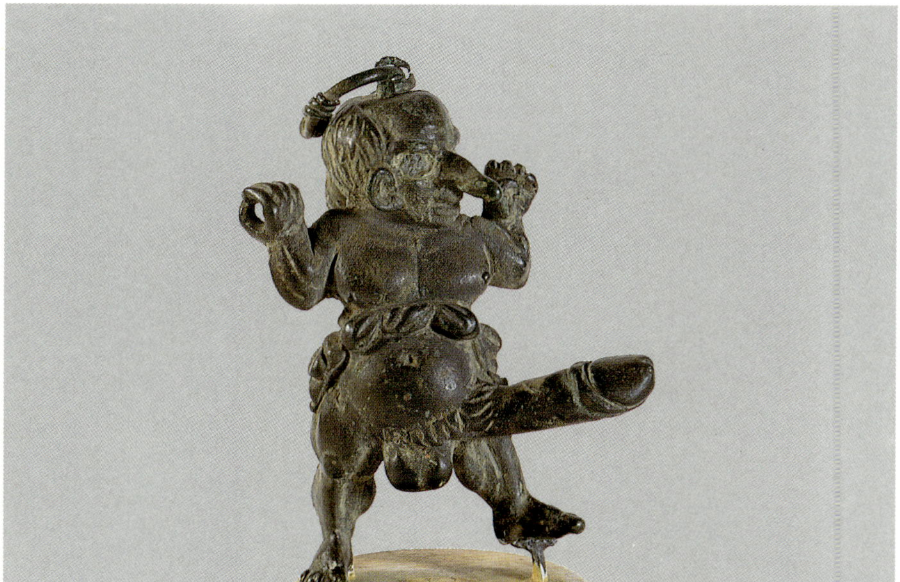

94

THE MIDDLE AGES AND RENNAISSANCE

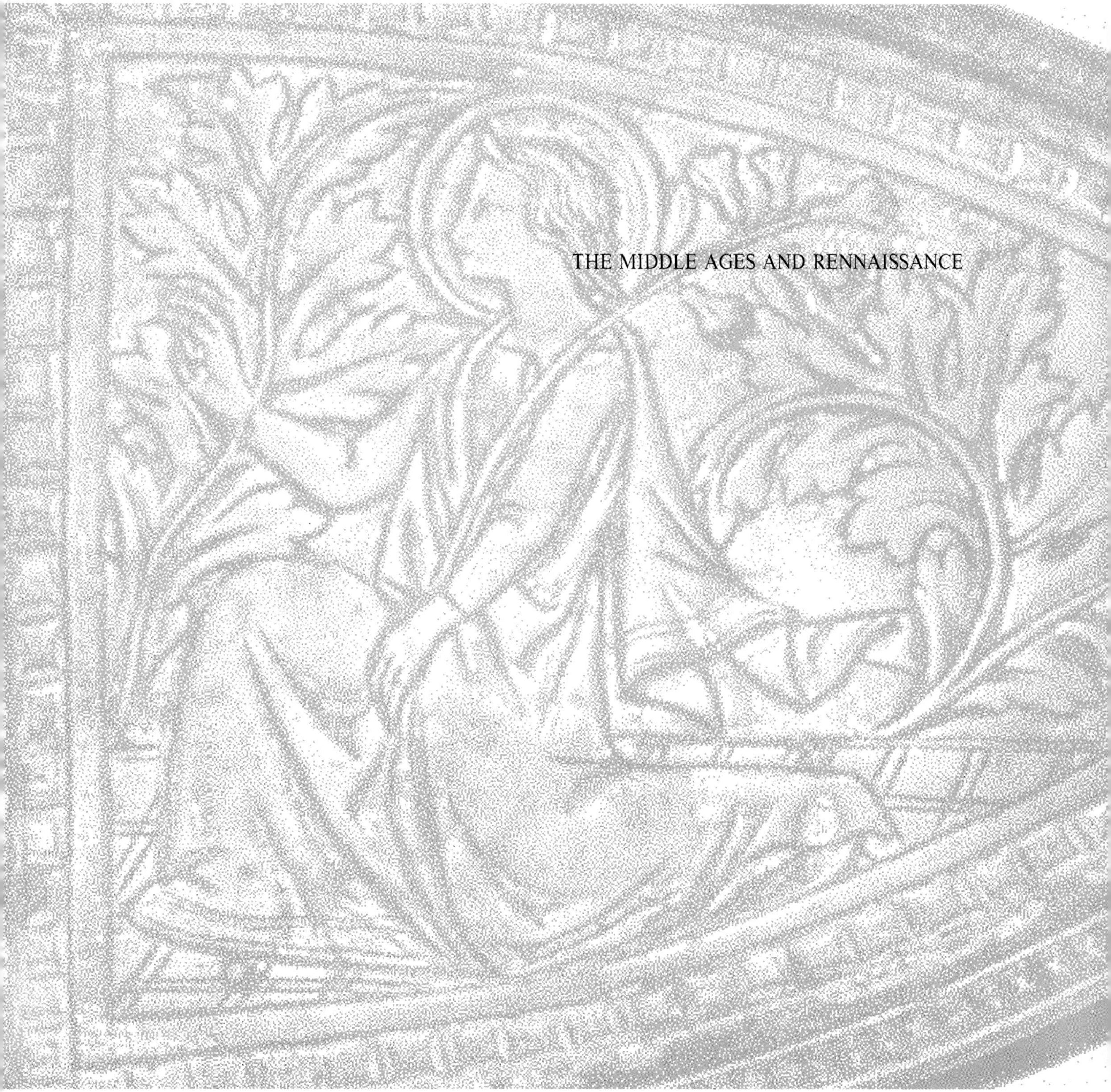

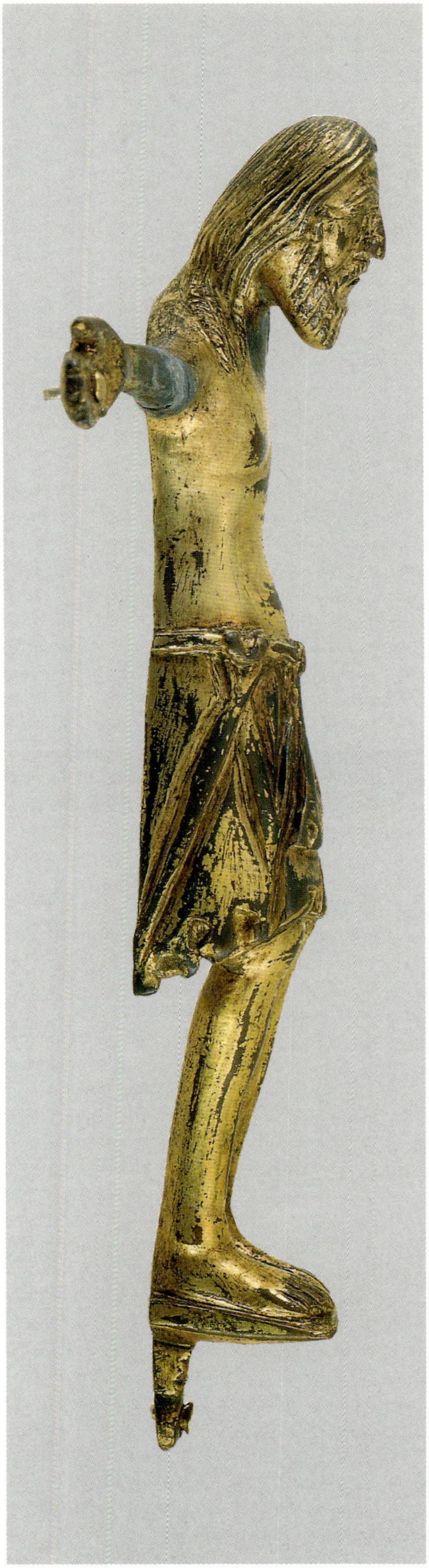

96

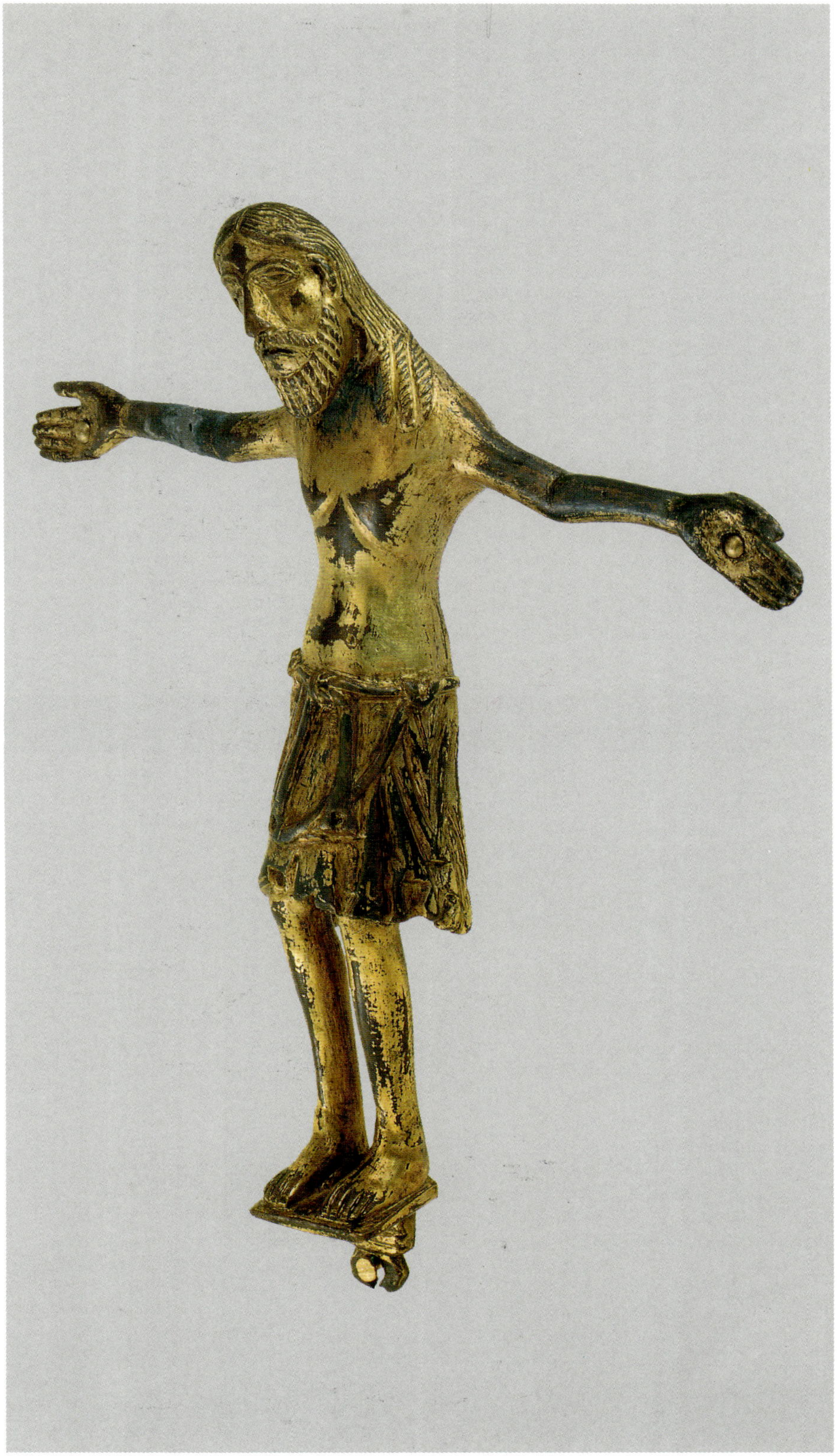

96

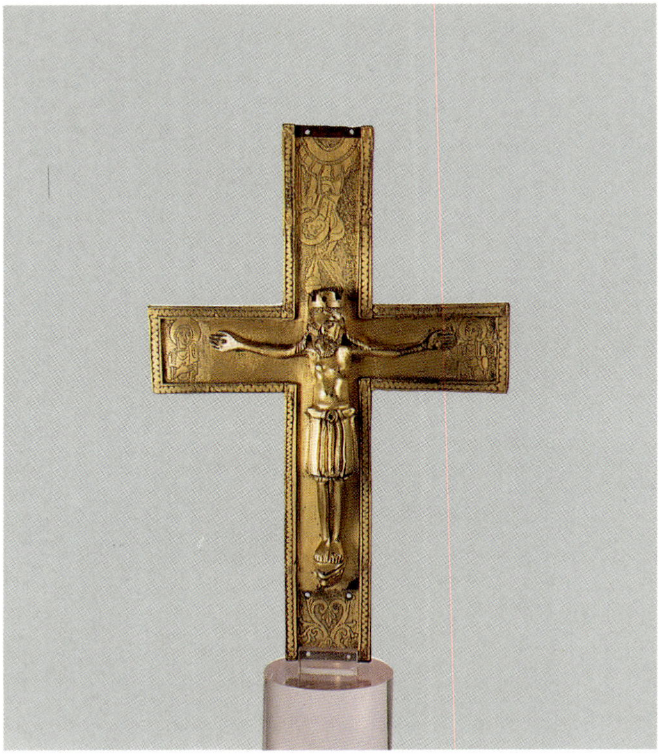
97

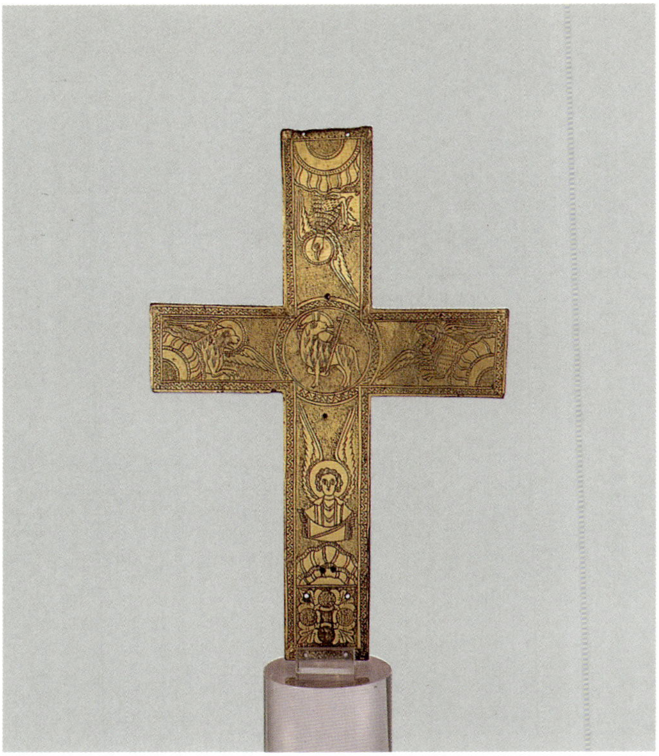
97

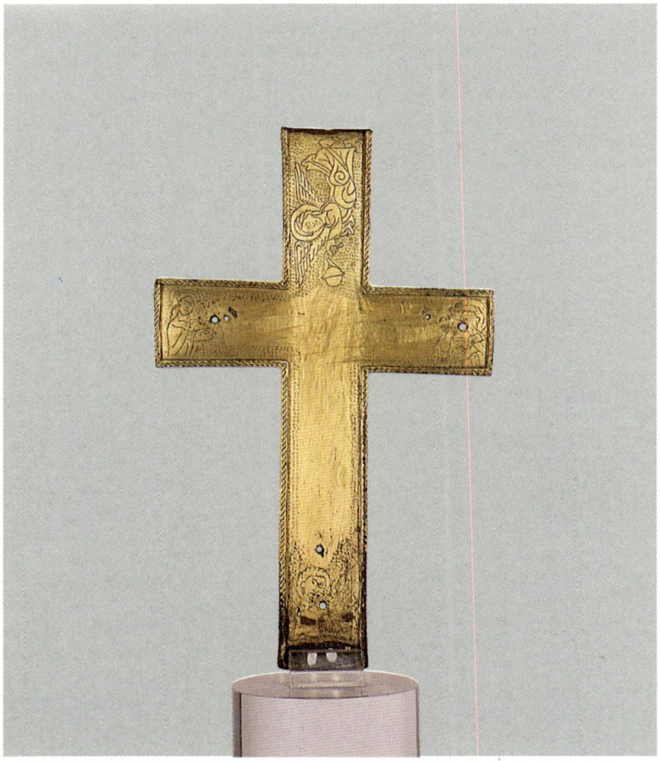
98

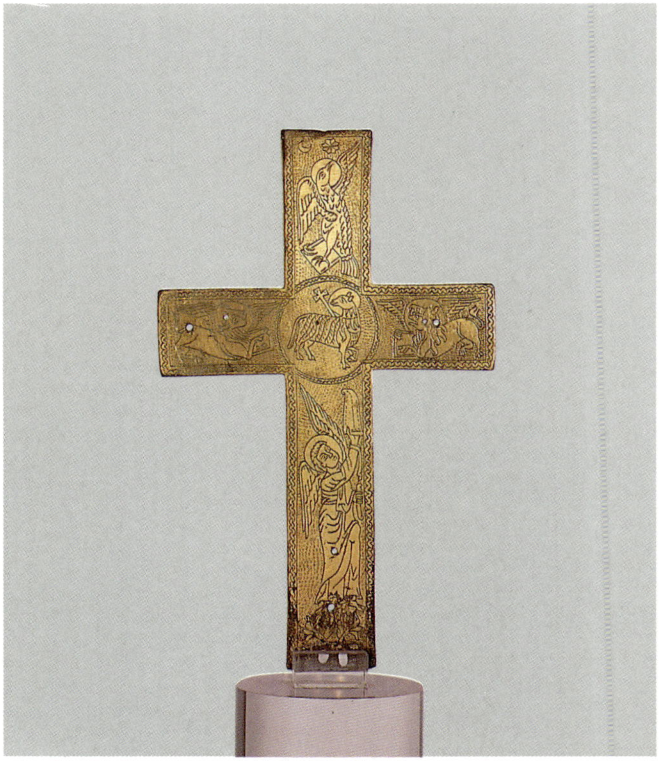
98

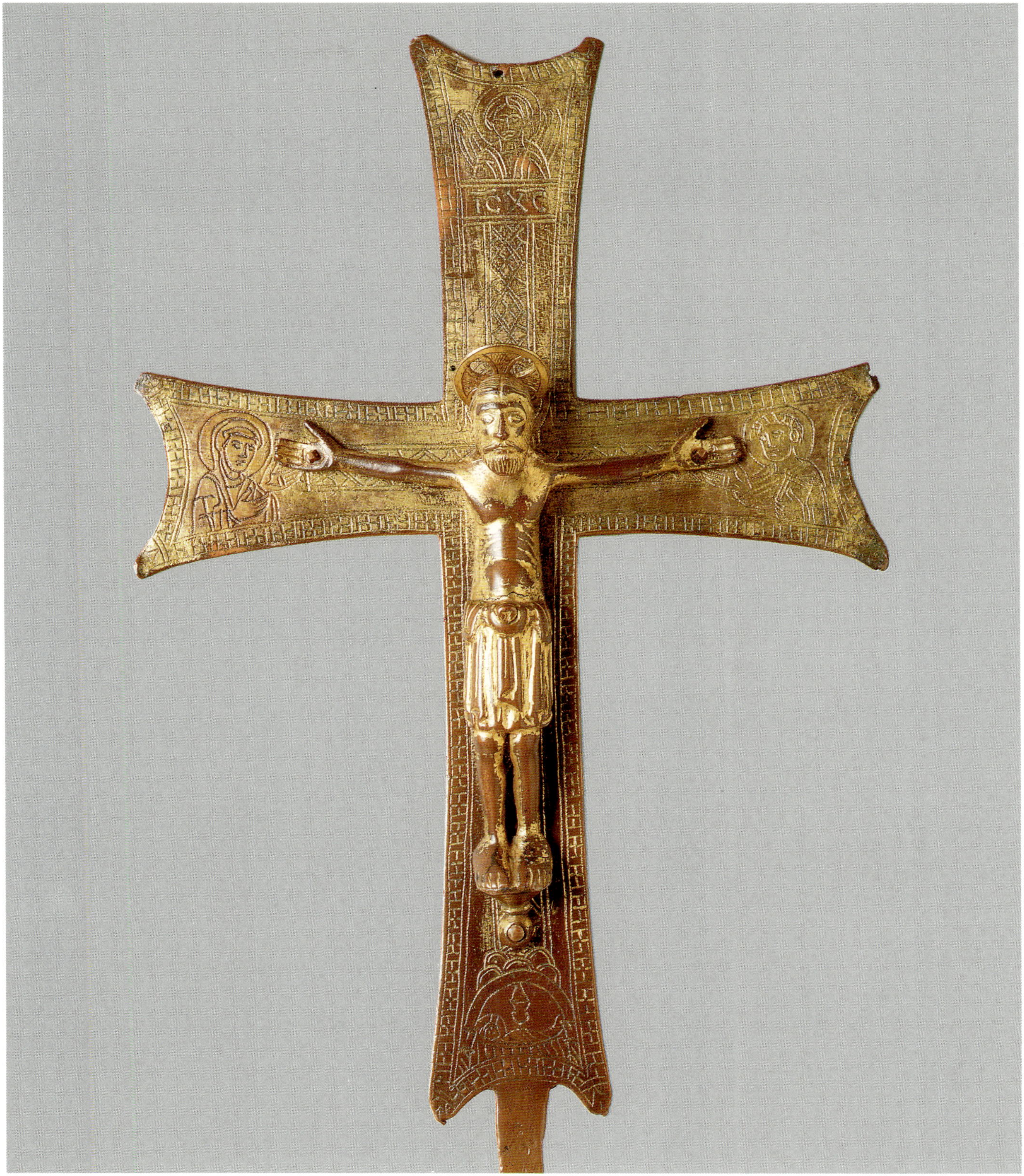

99

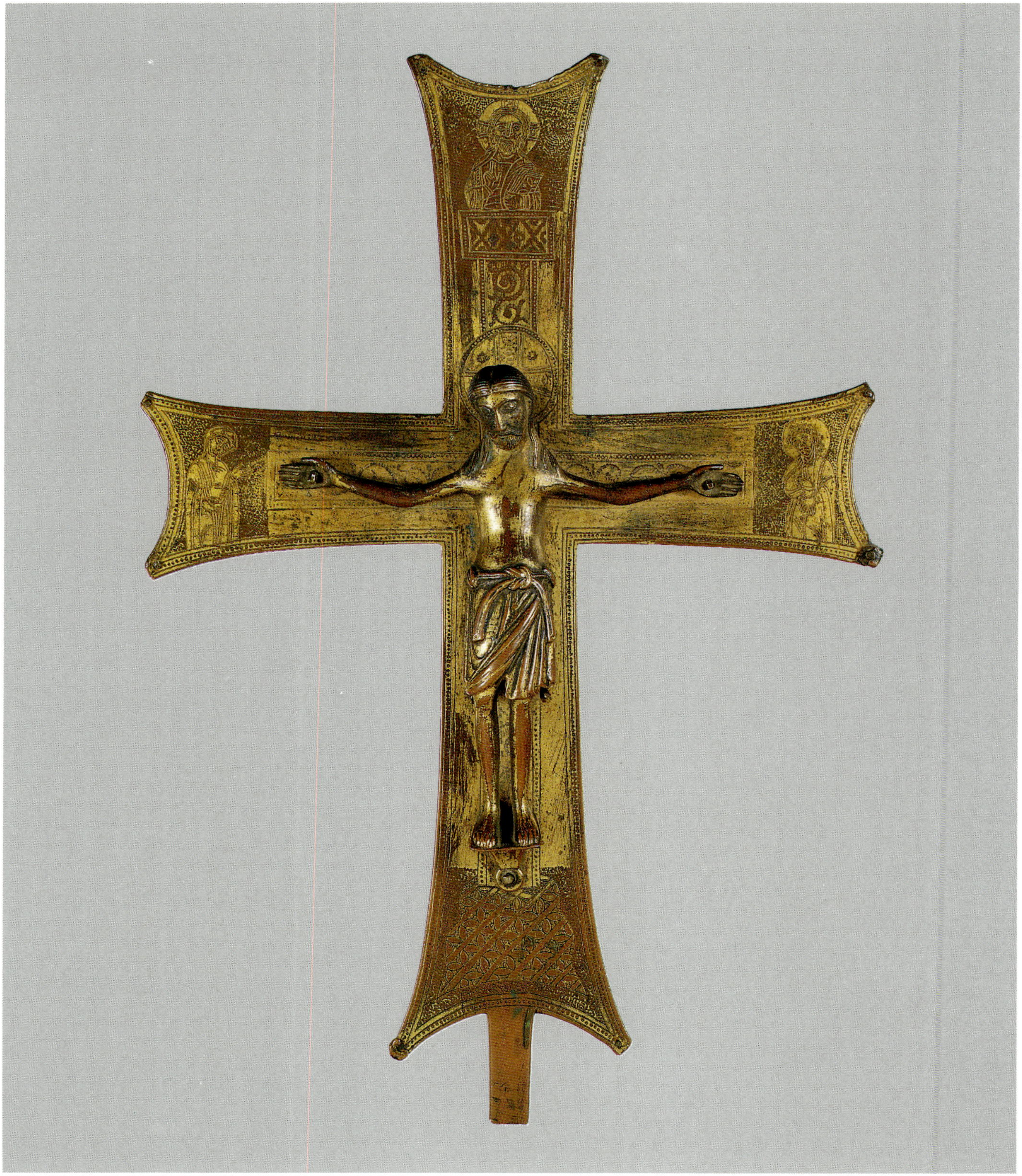

100

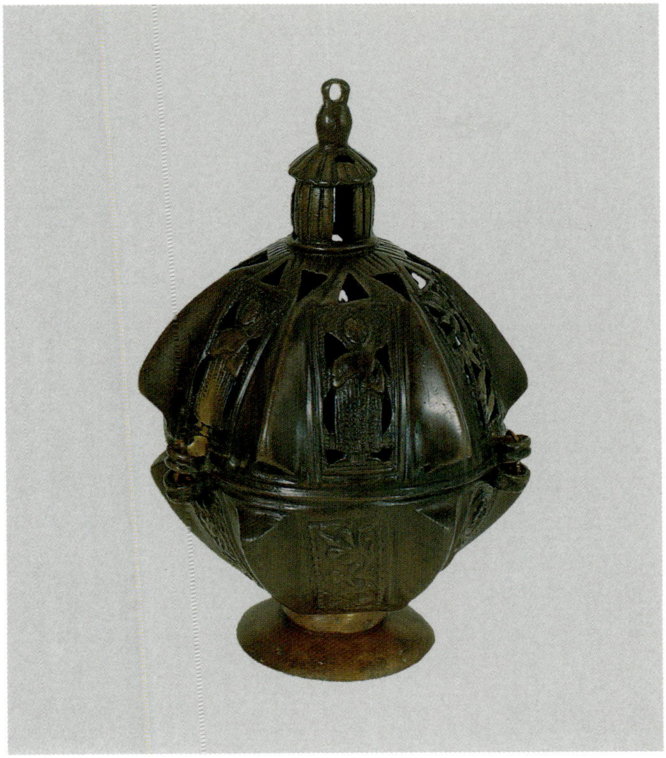
103

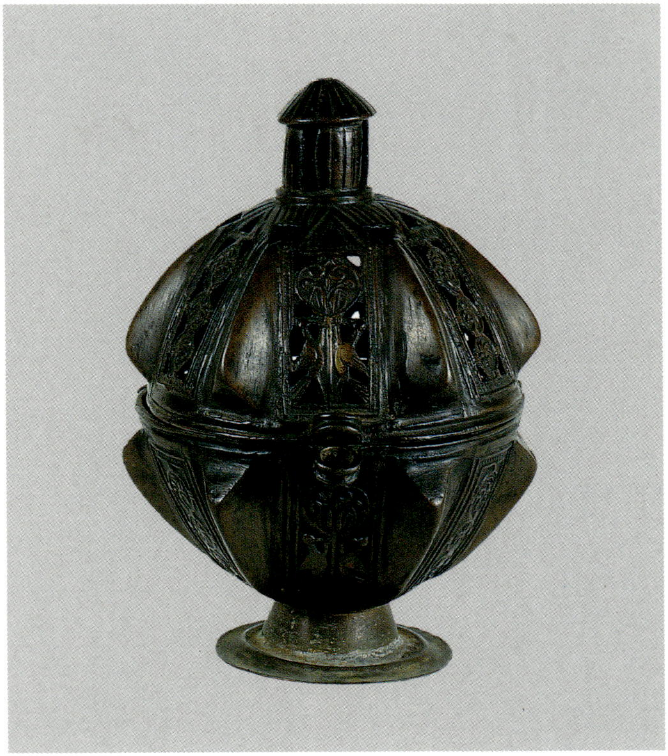
104

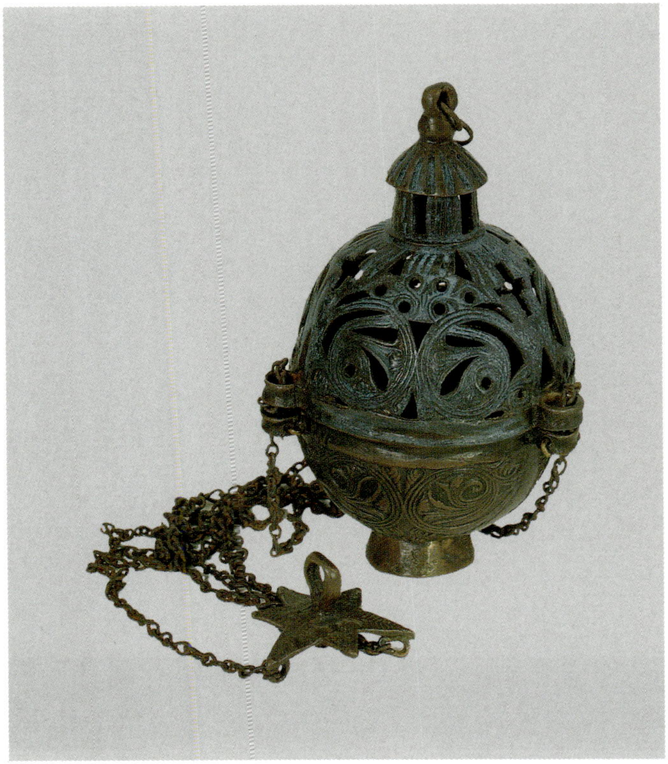
105

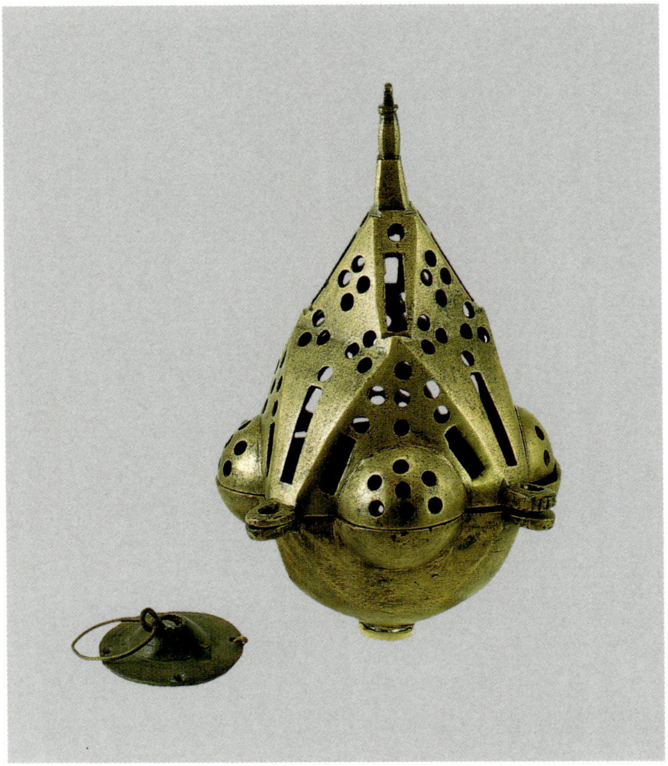
107

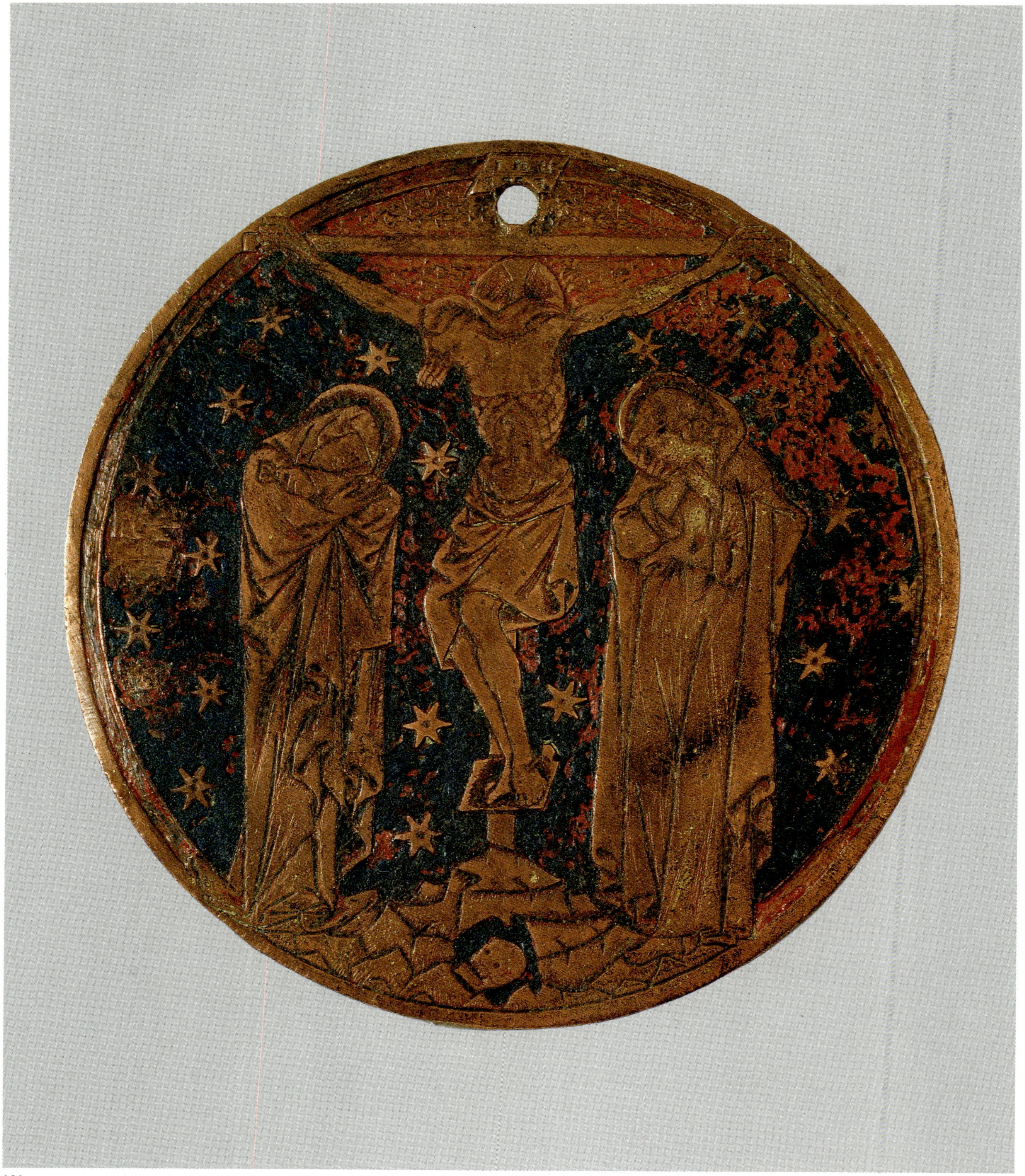

108

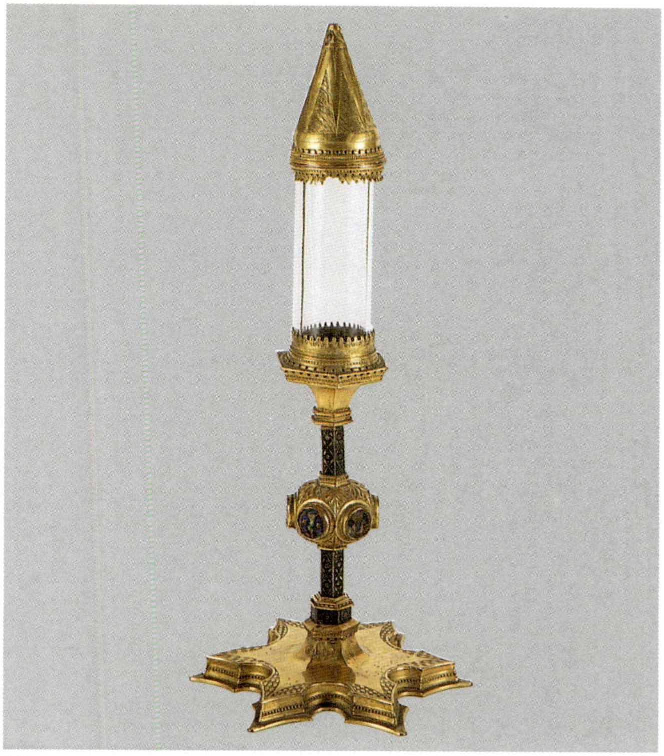
109

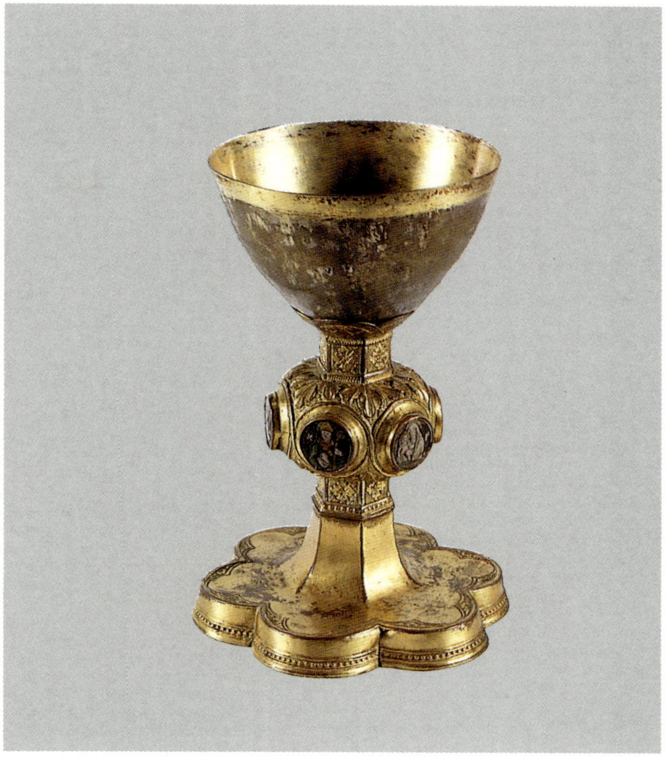
110

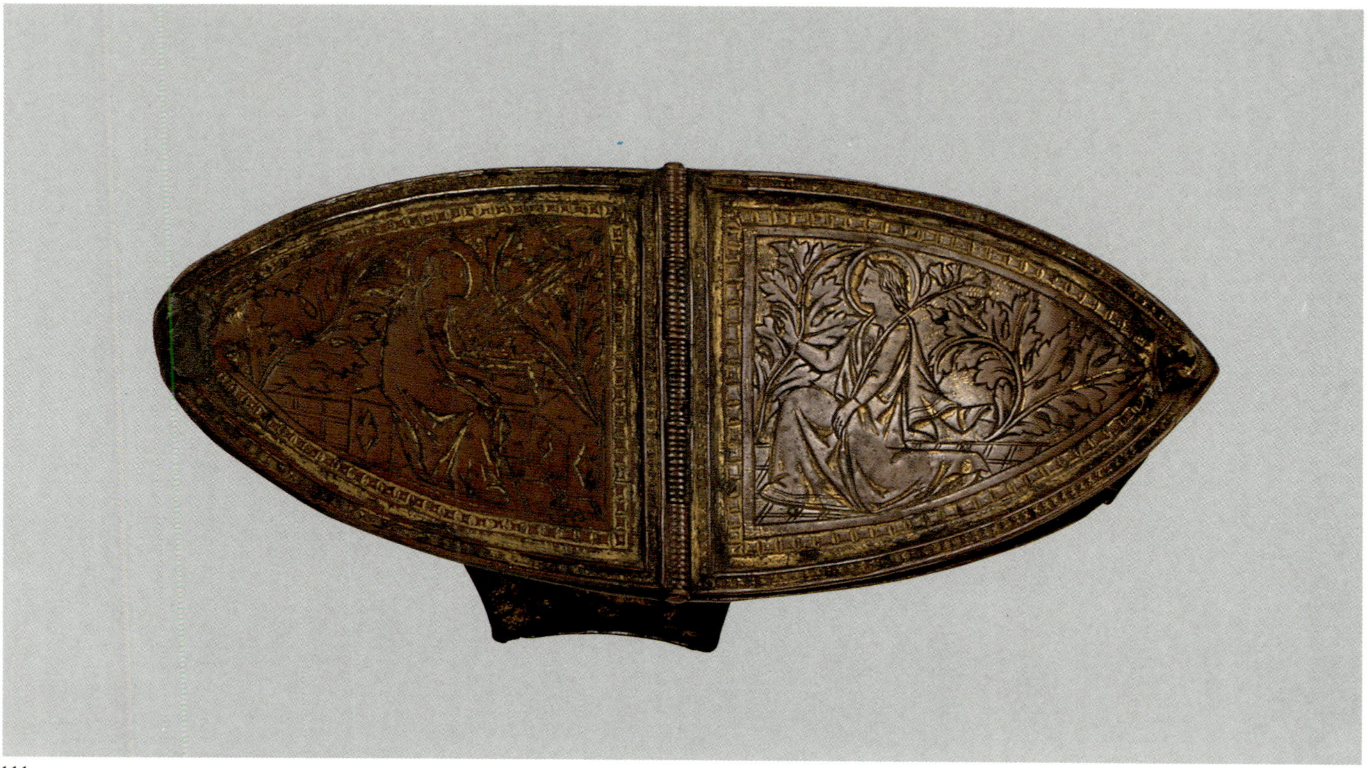
111

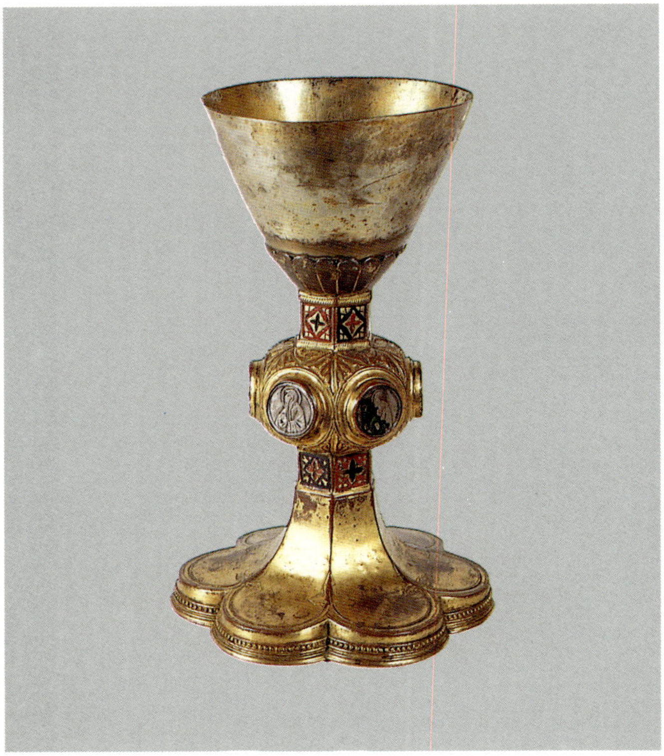

112

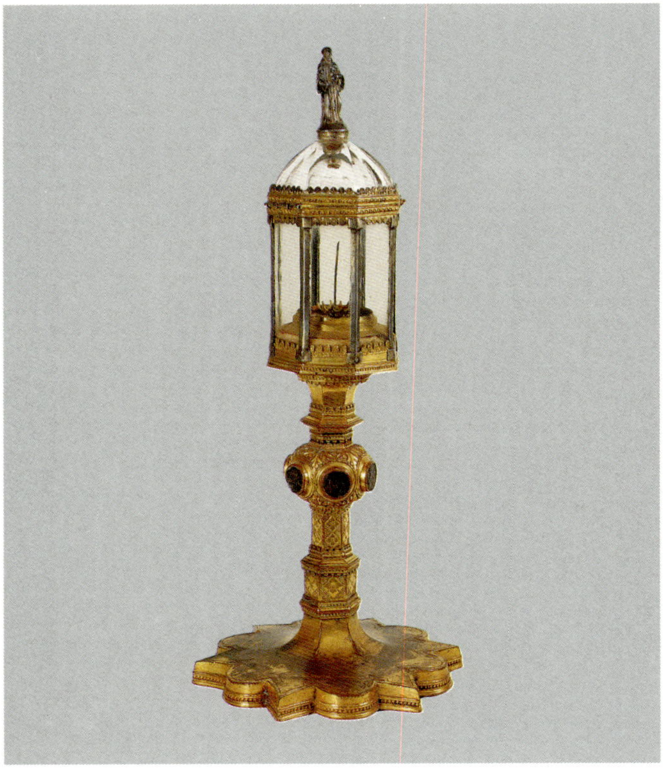

115

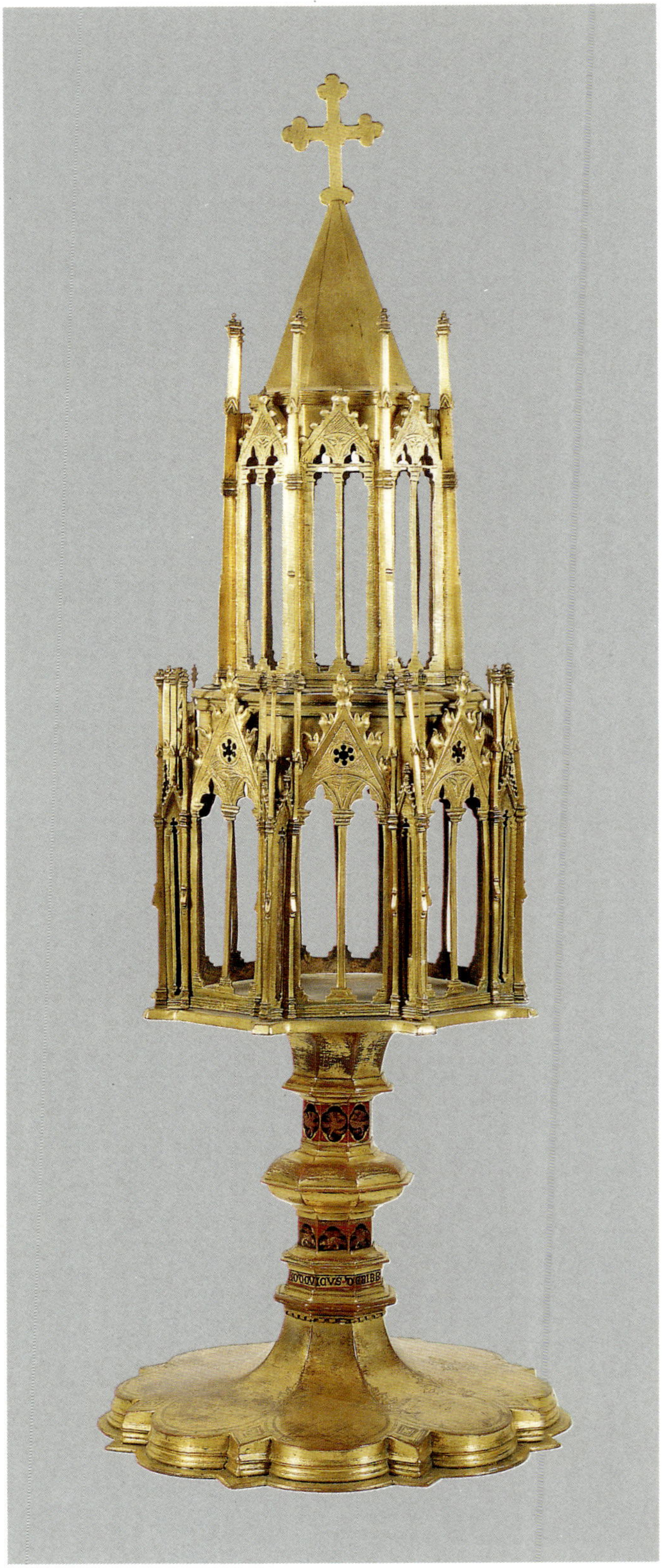

113

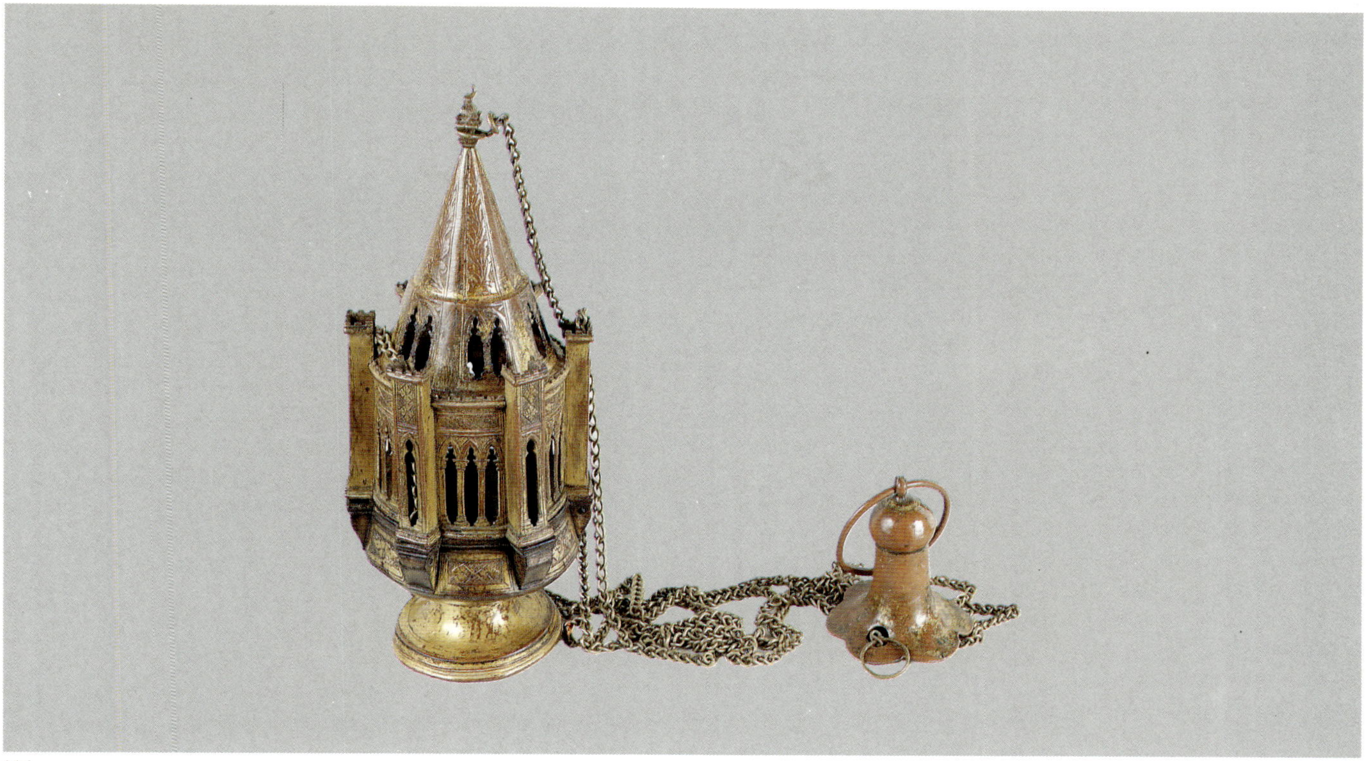

116

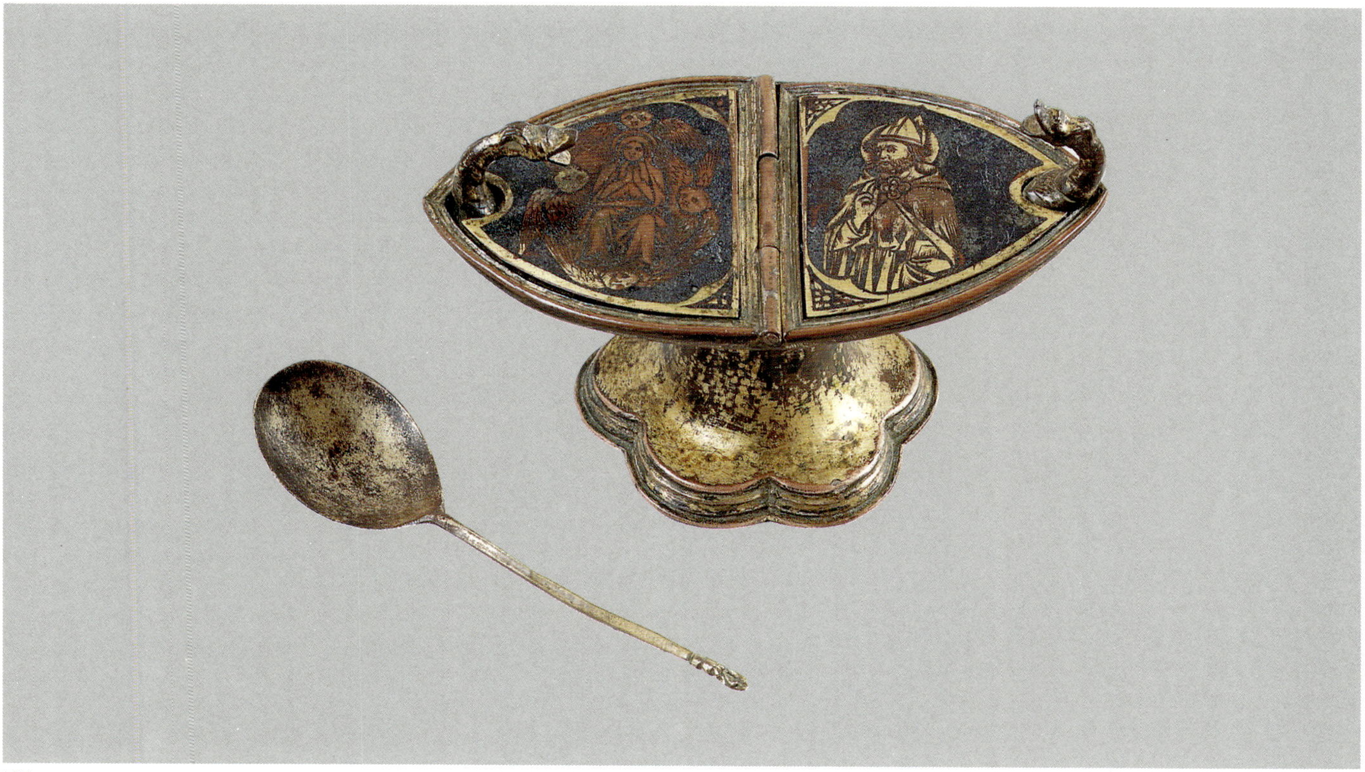

117

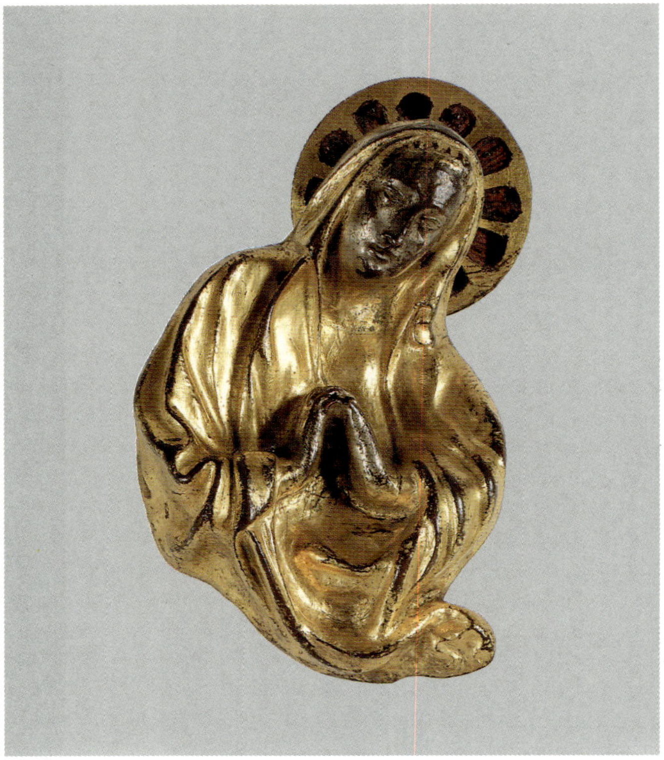
119

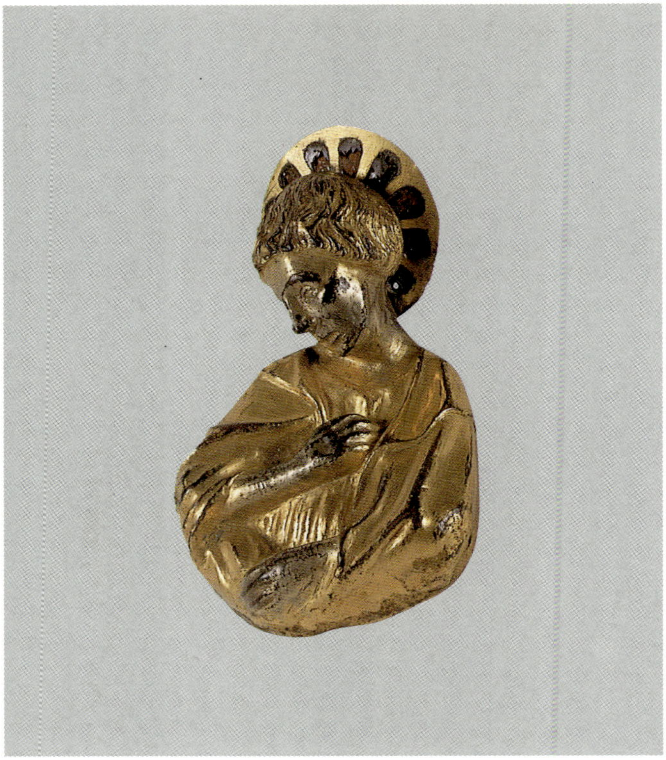
120

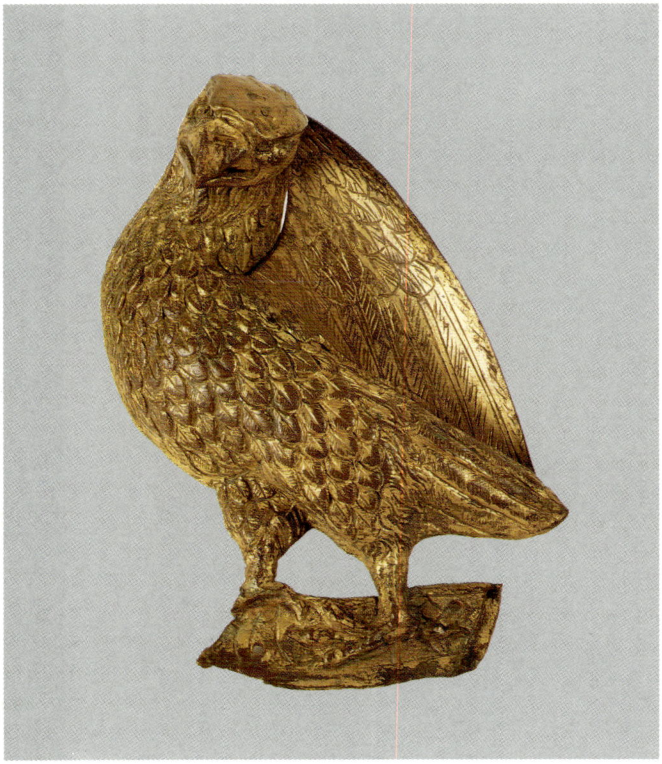
121

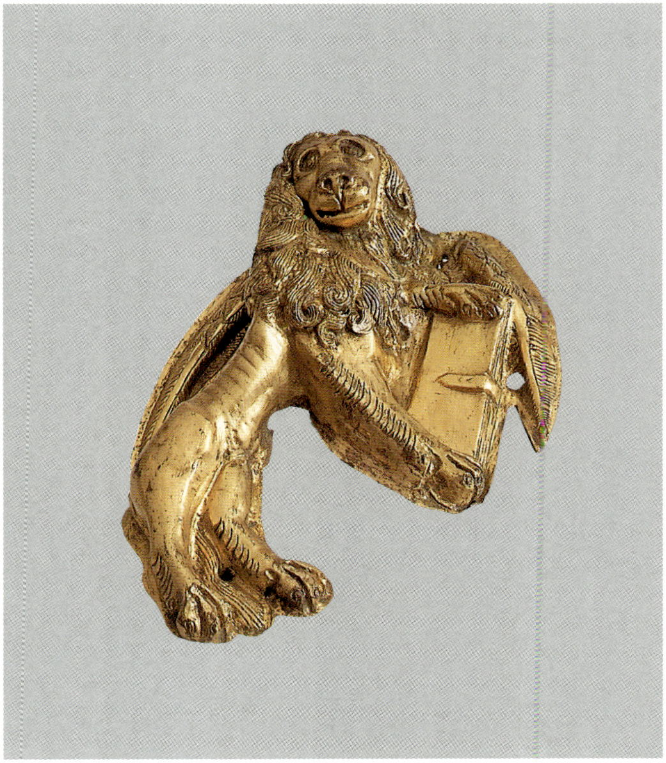
122

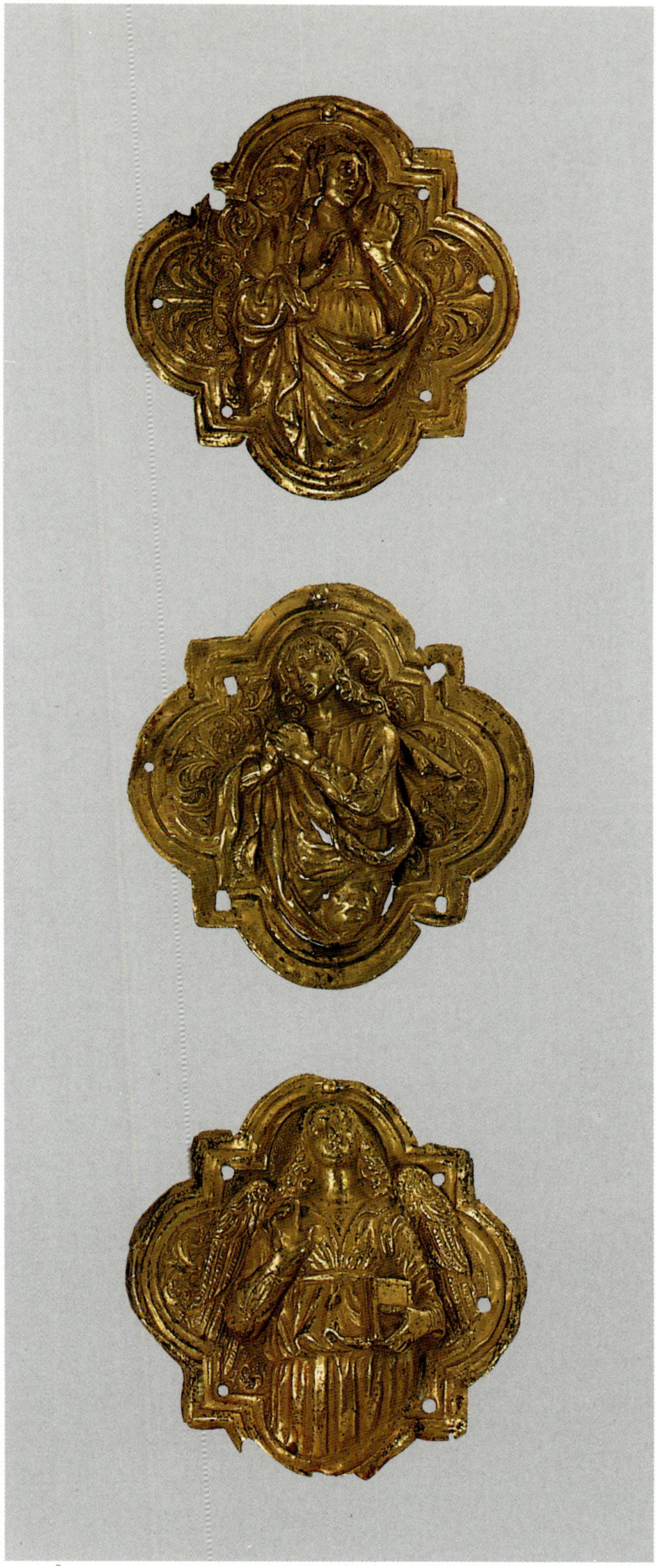

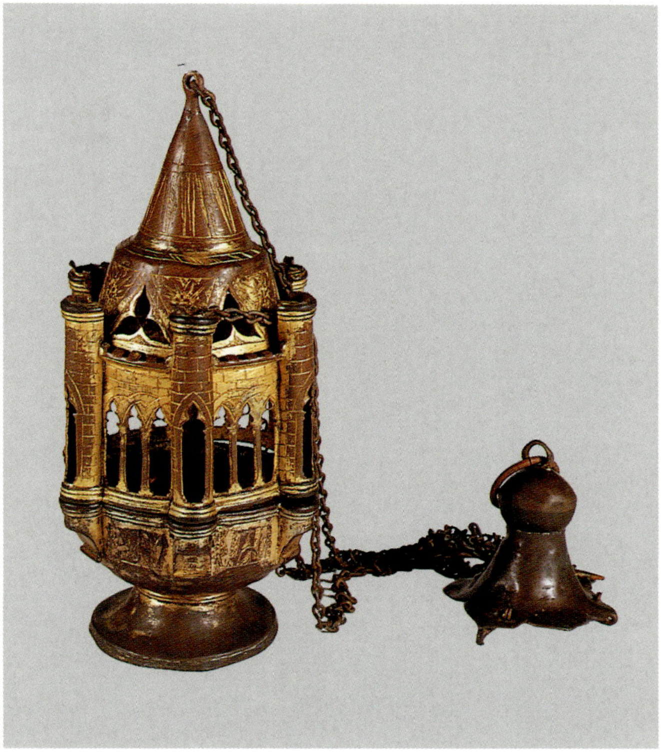

124

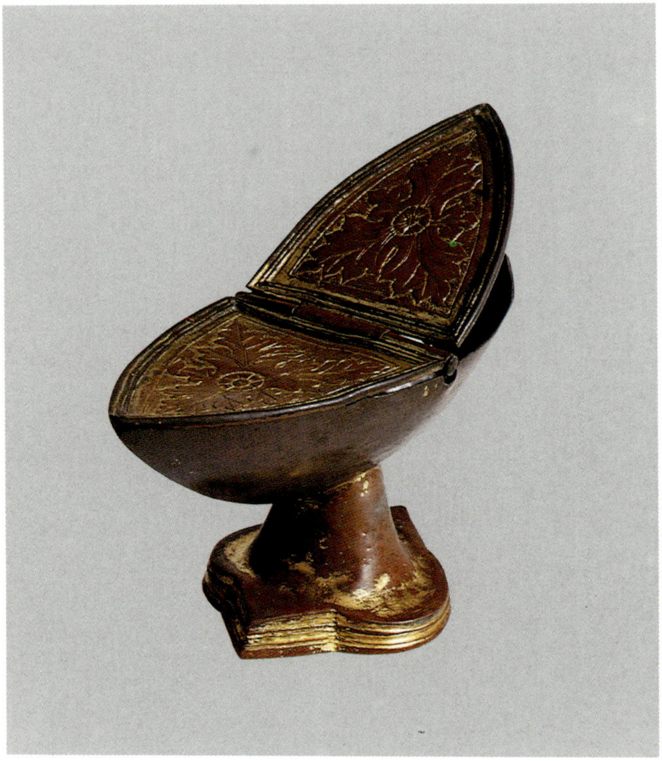

123

124

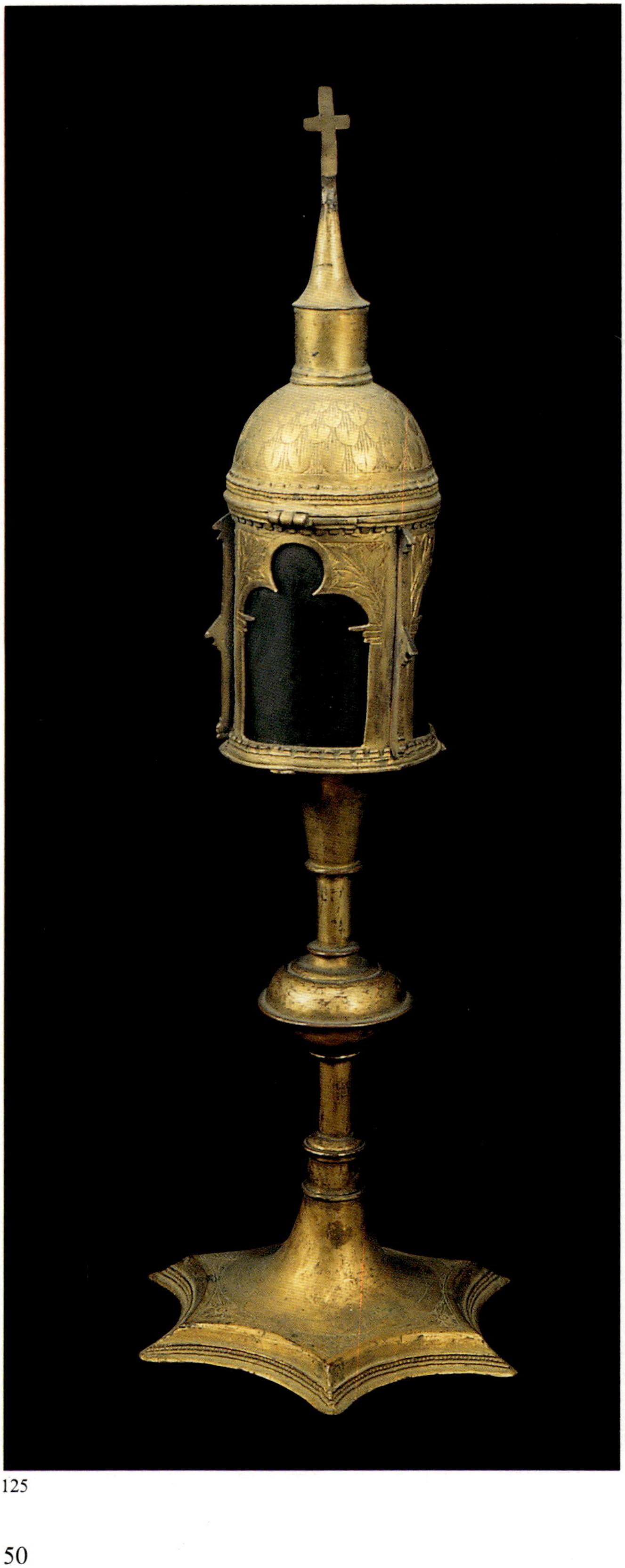

125

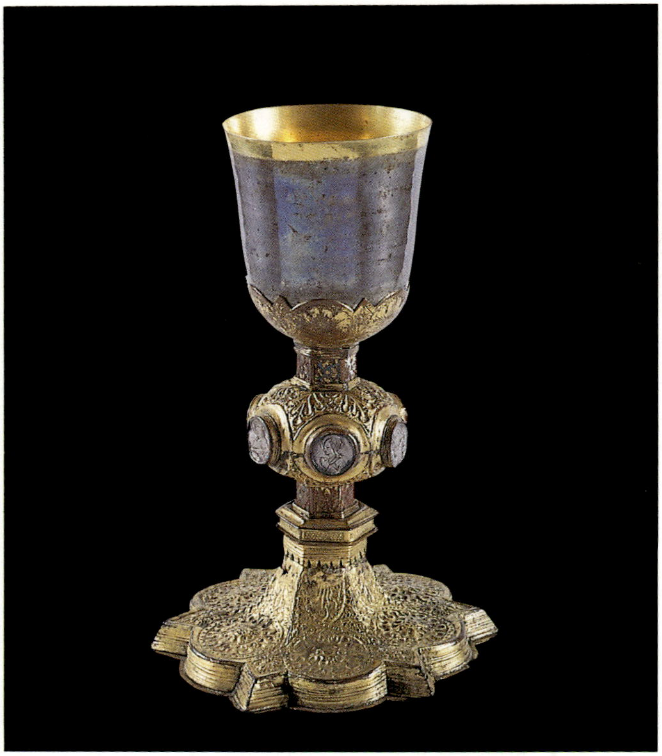

130

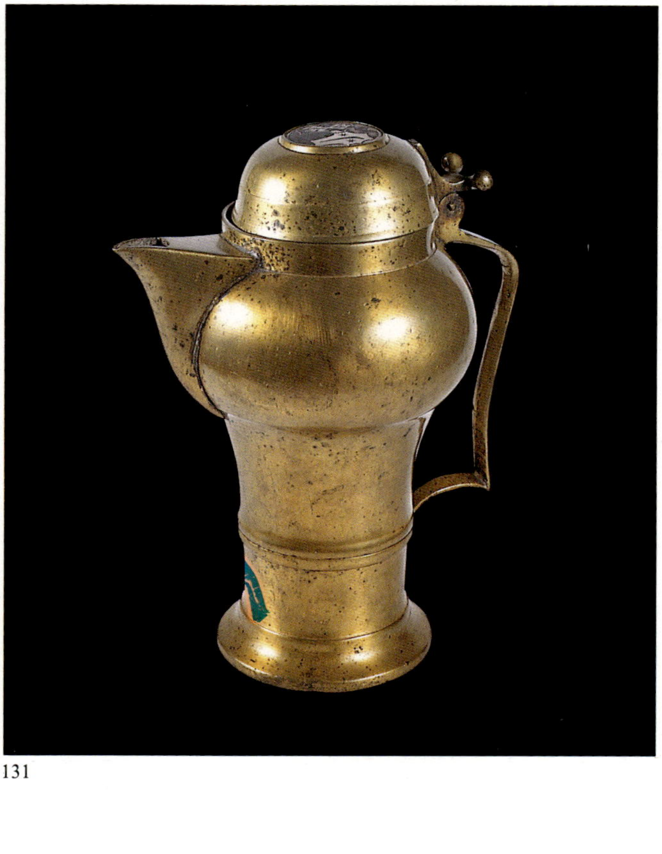

131

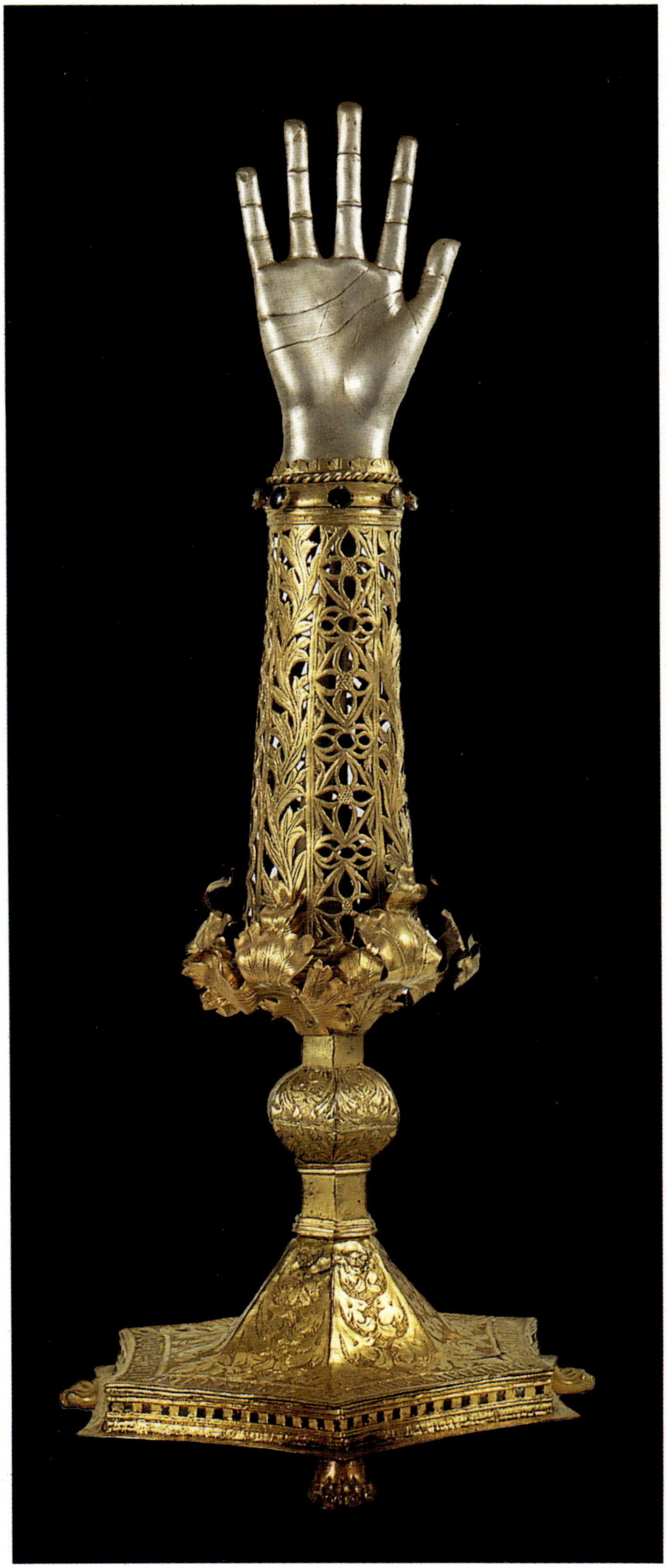

132

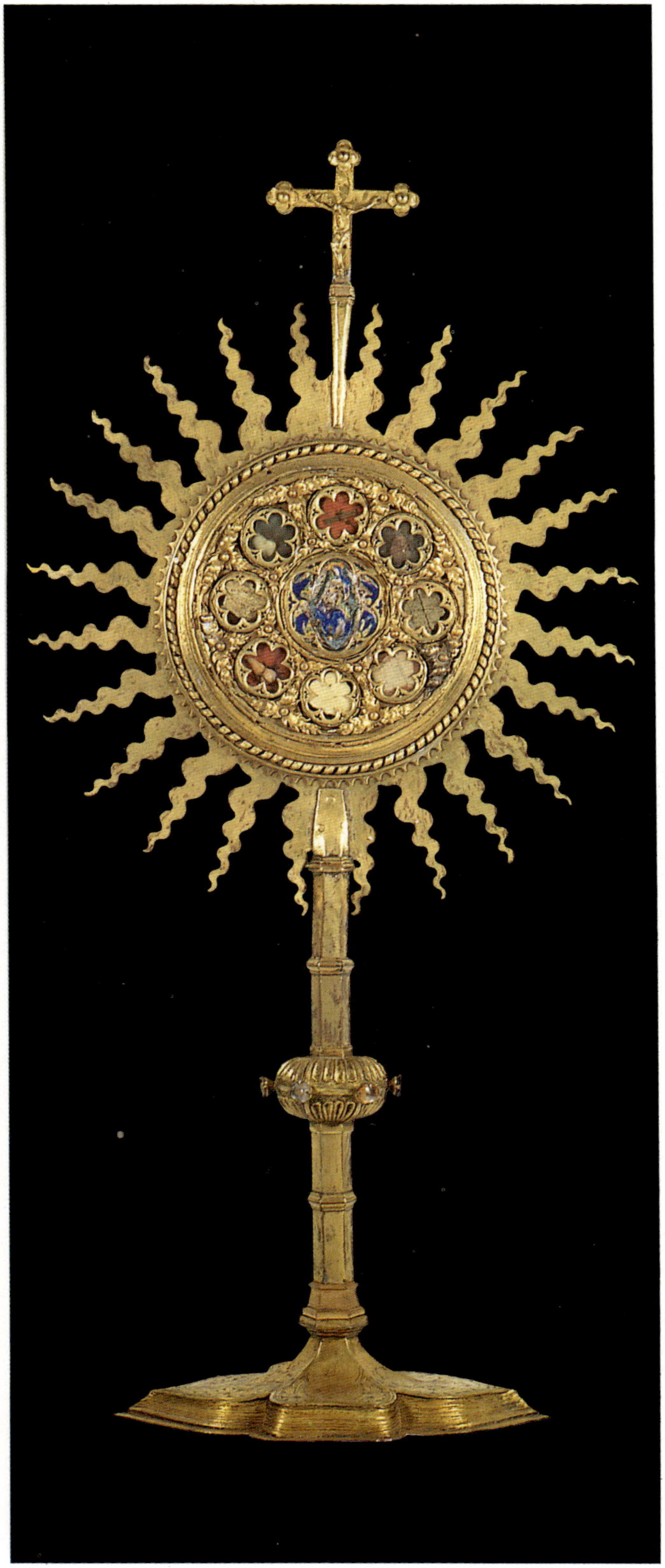

136

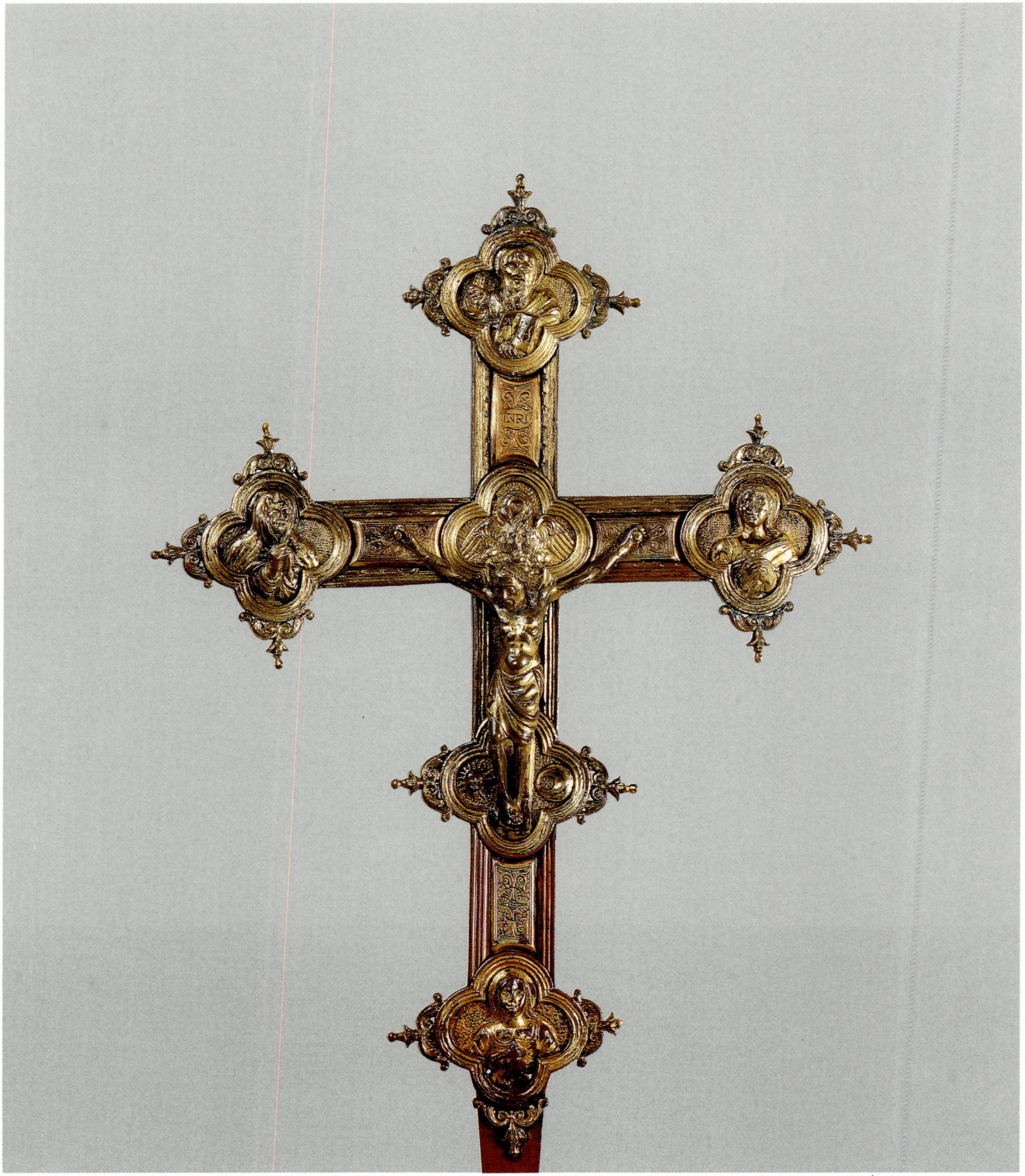

133

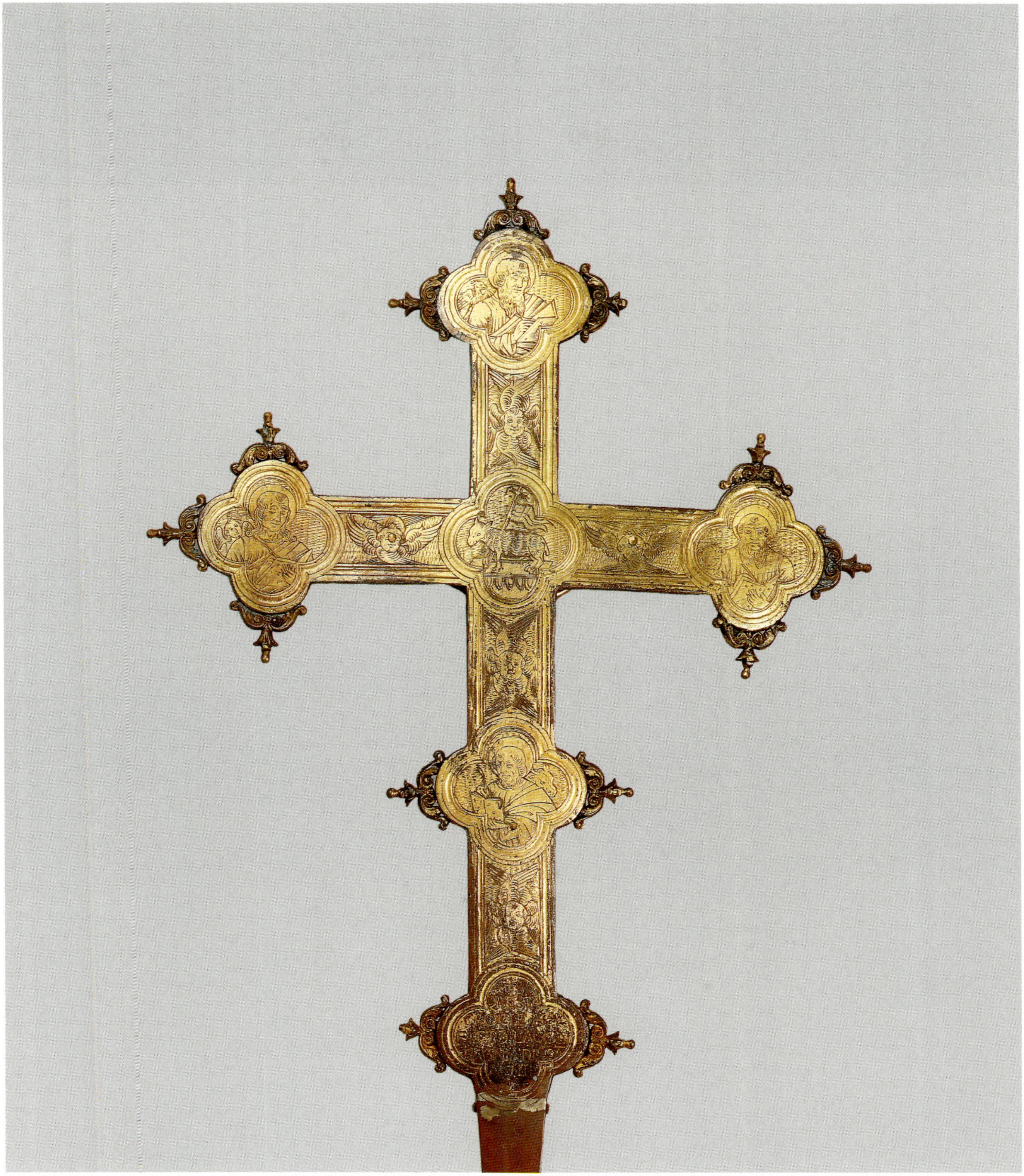

133

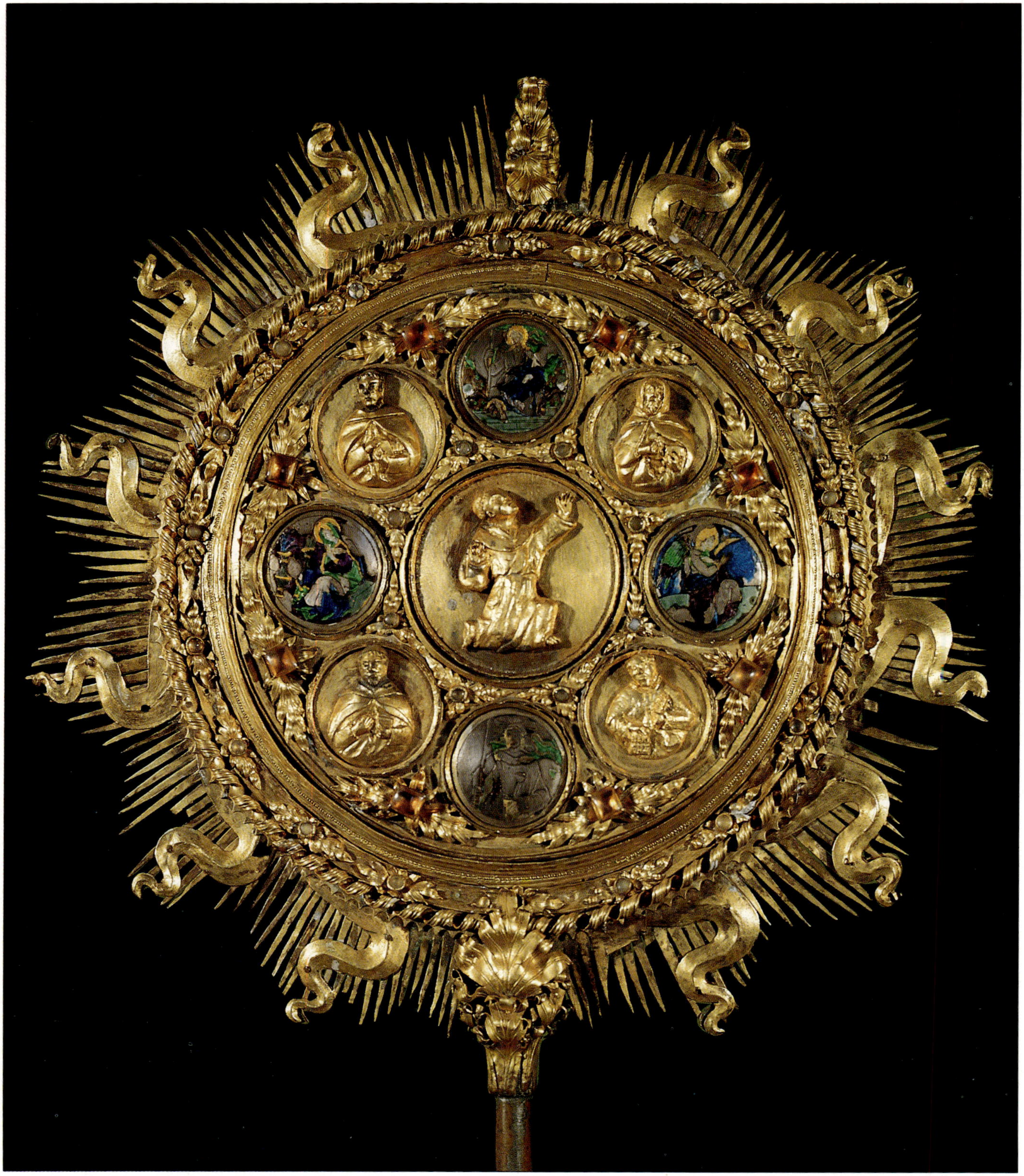

135

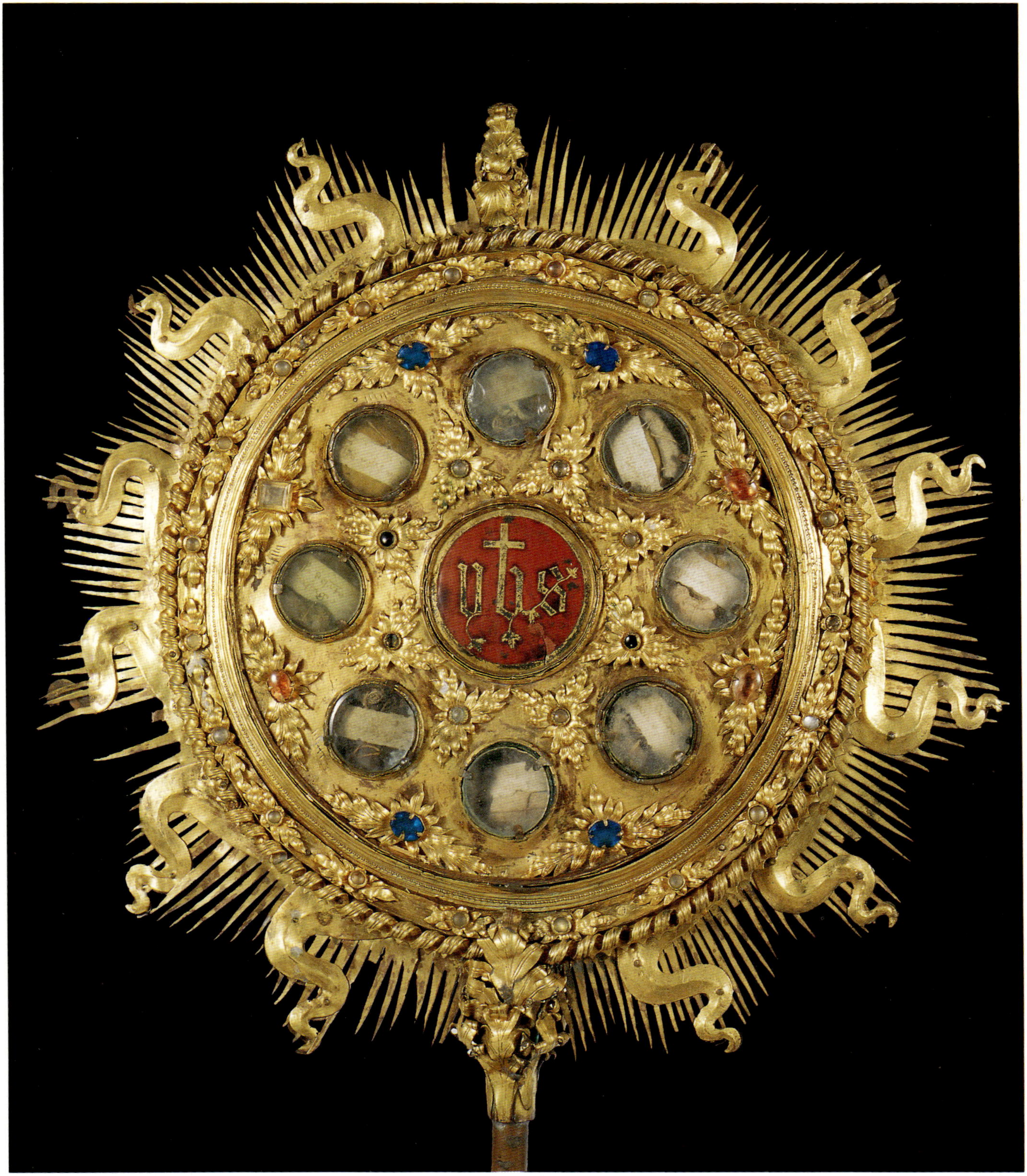

135

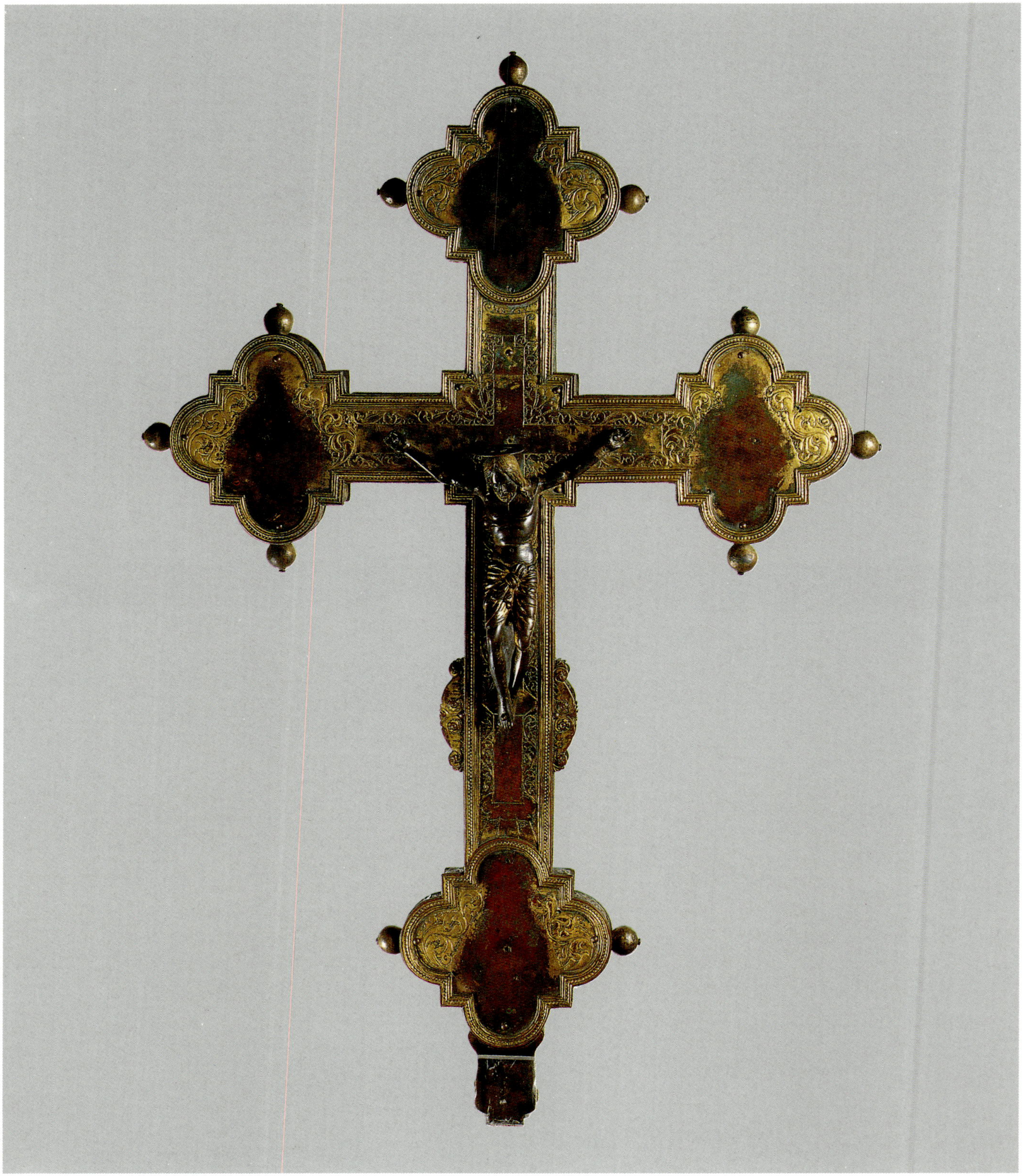

142

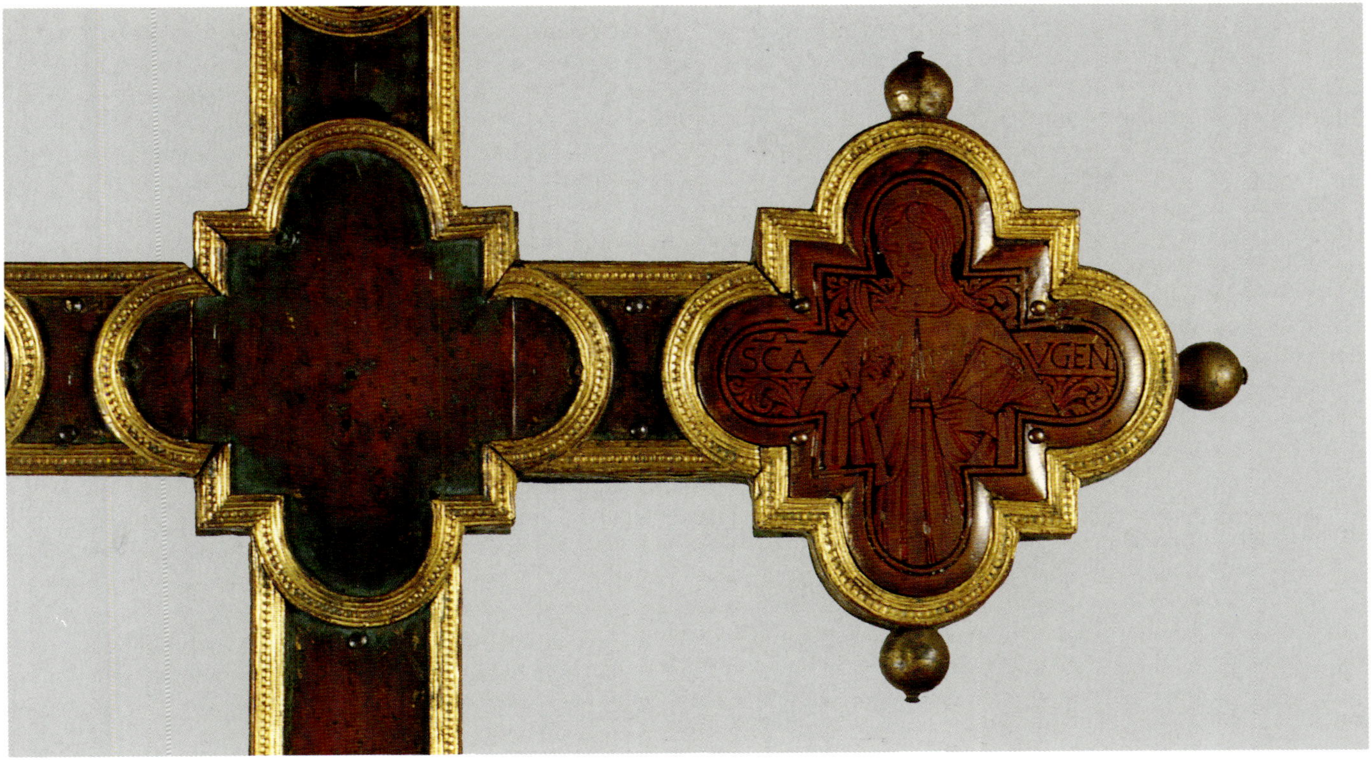

142

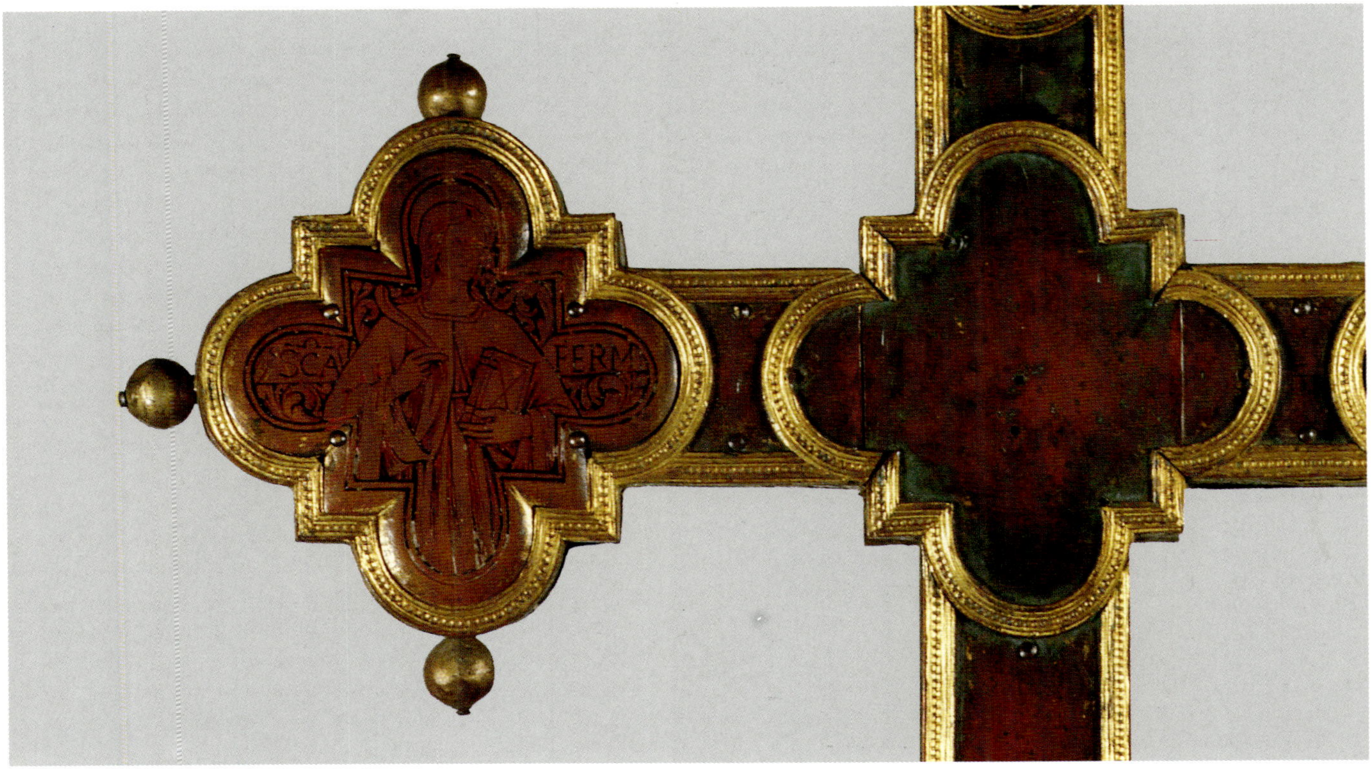

142

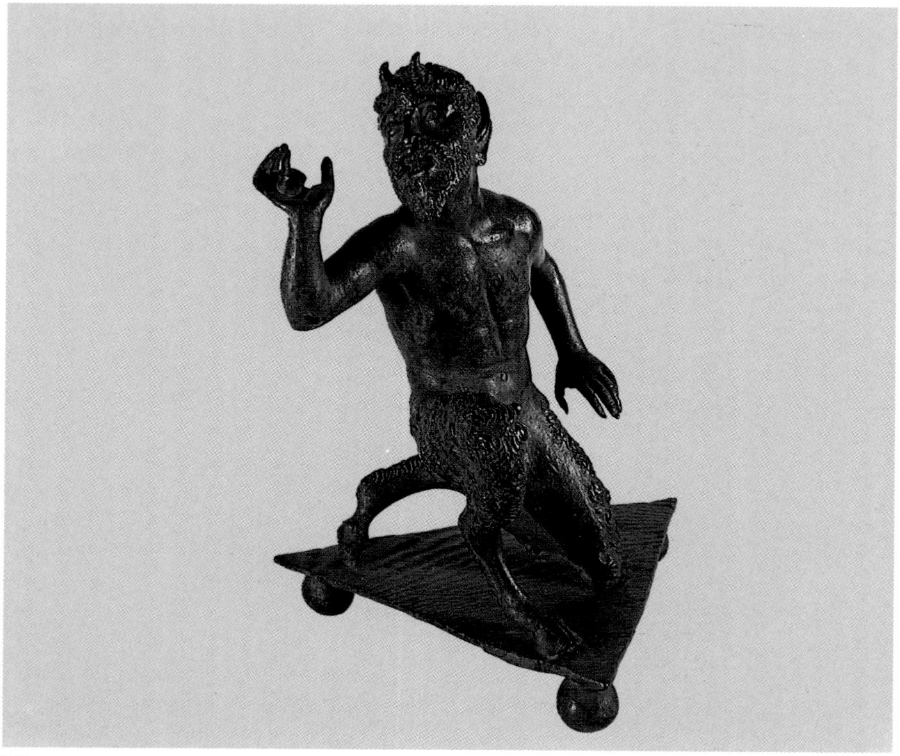
146

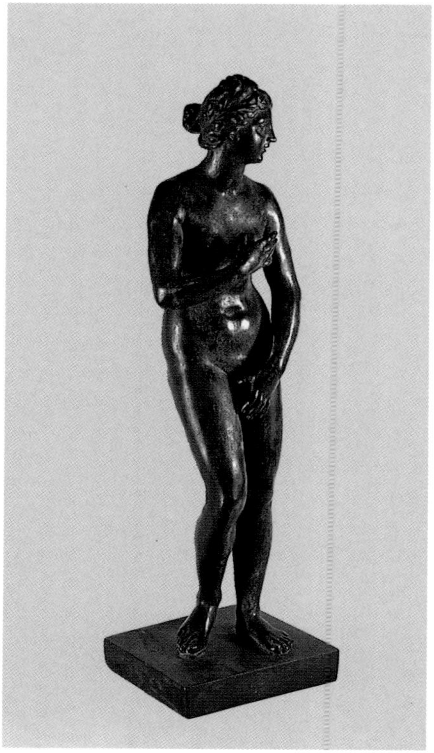
147

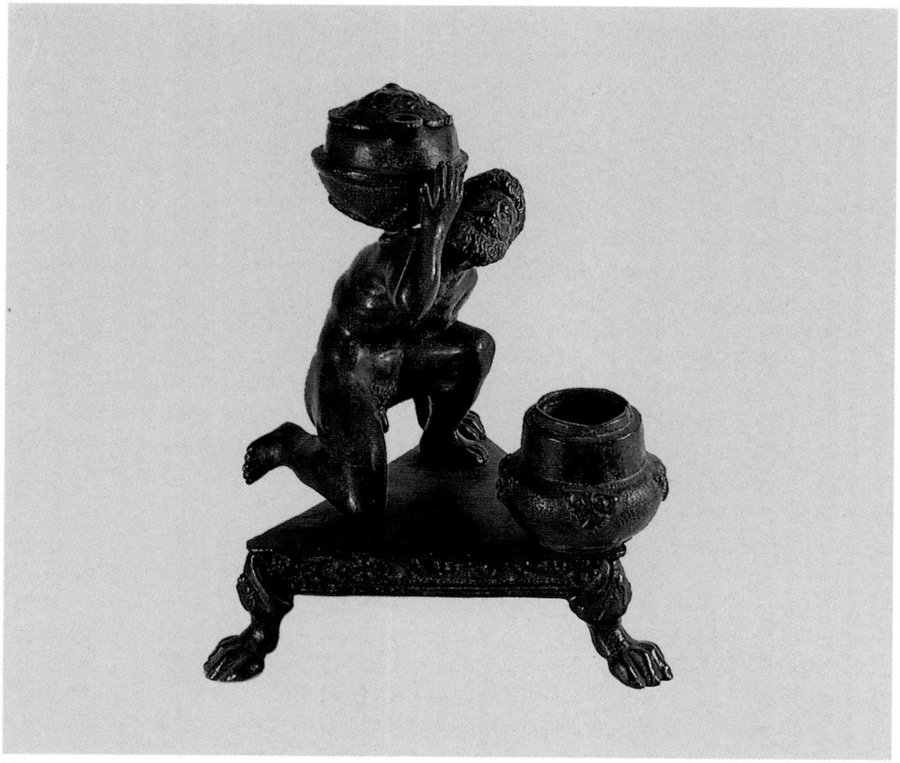
148

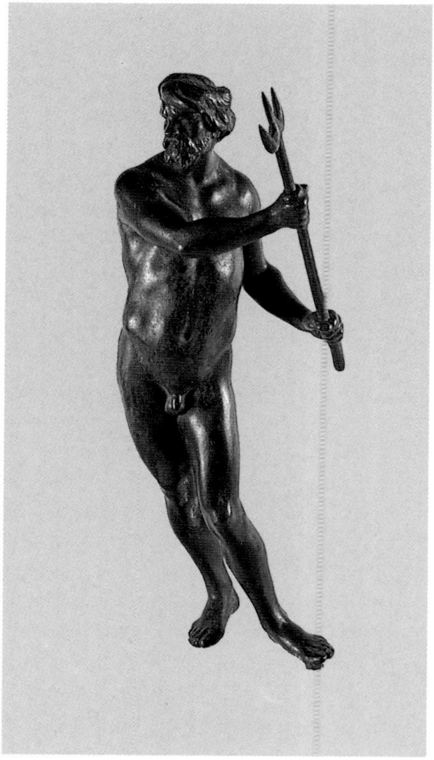
149

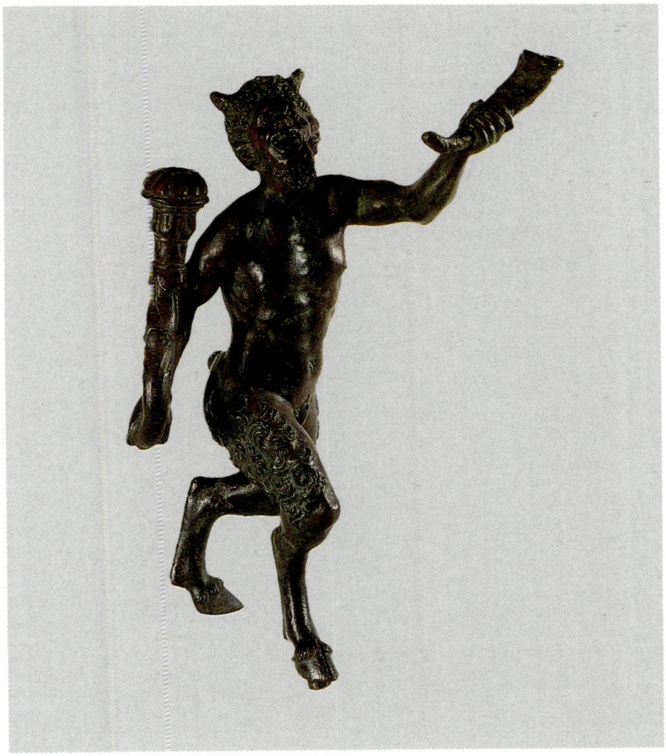

150

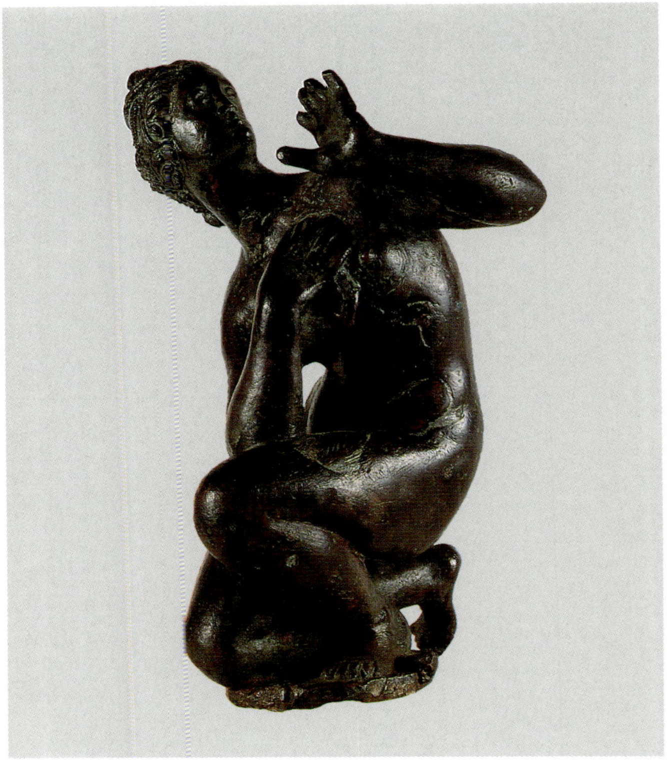

151

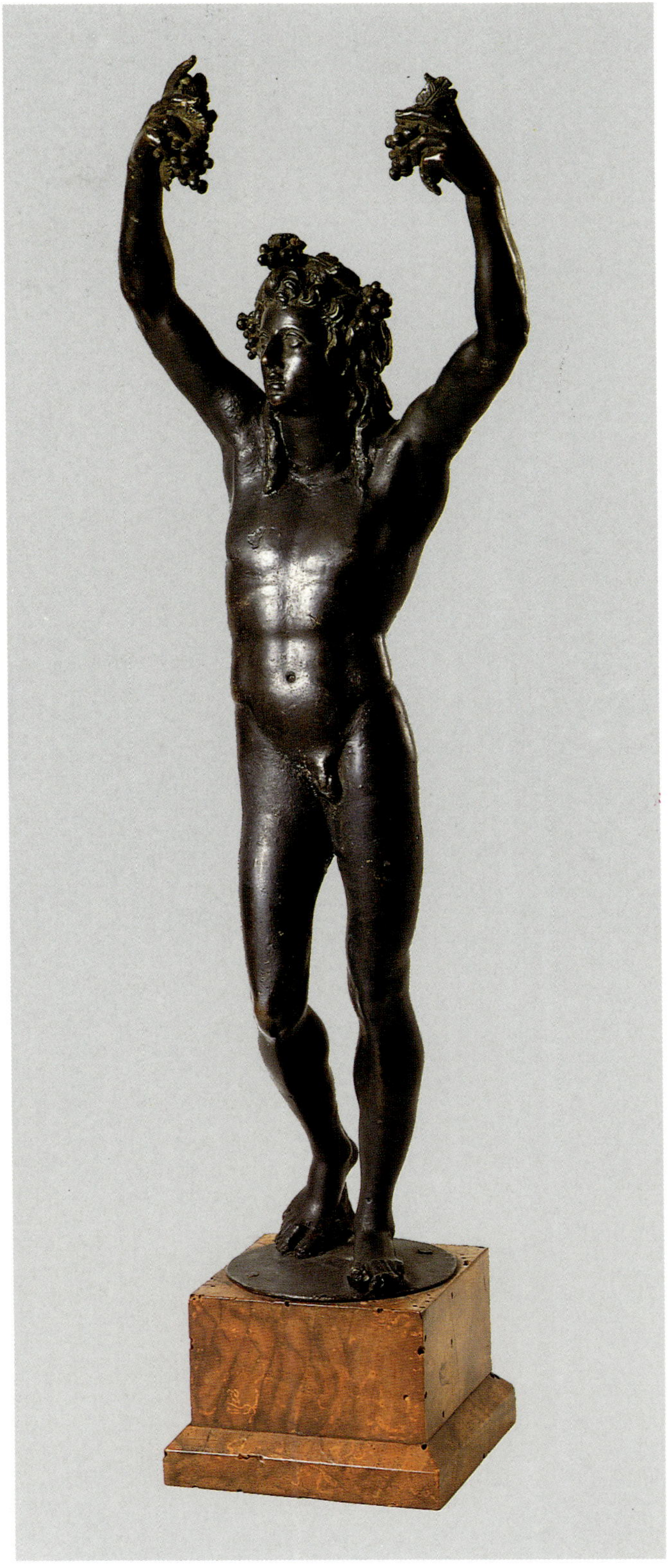

152

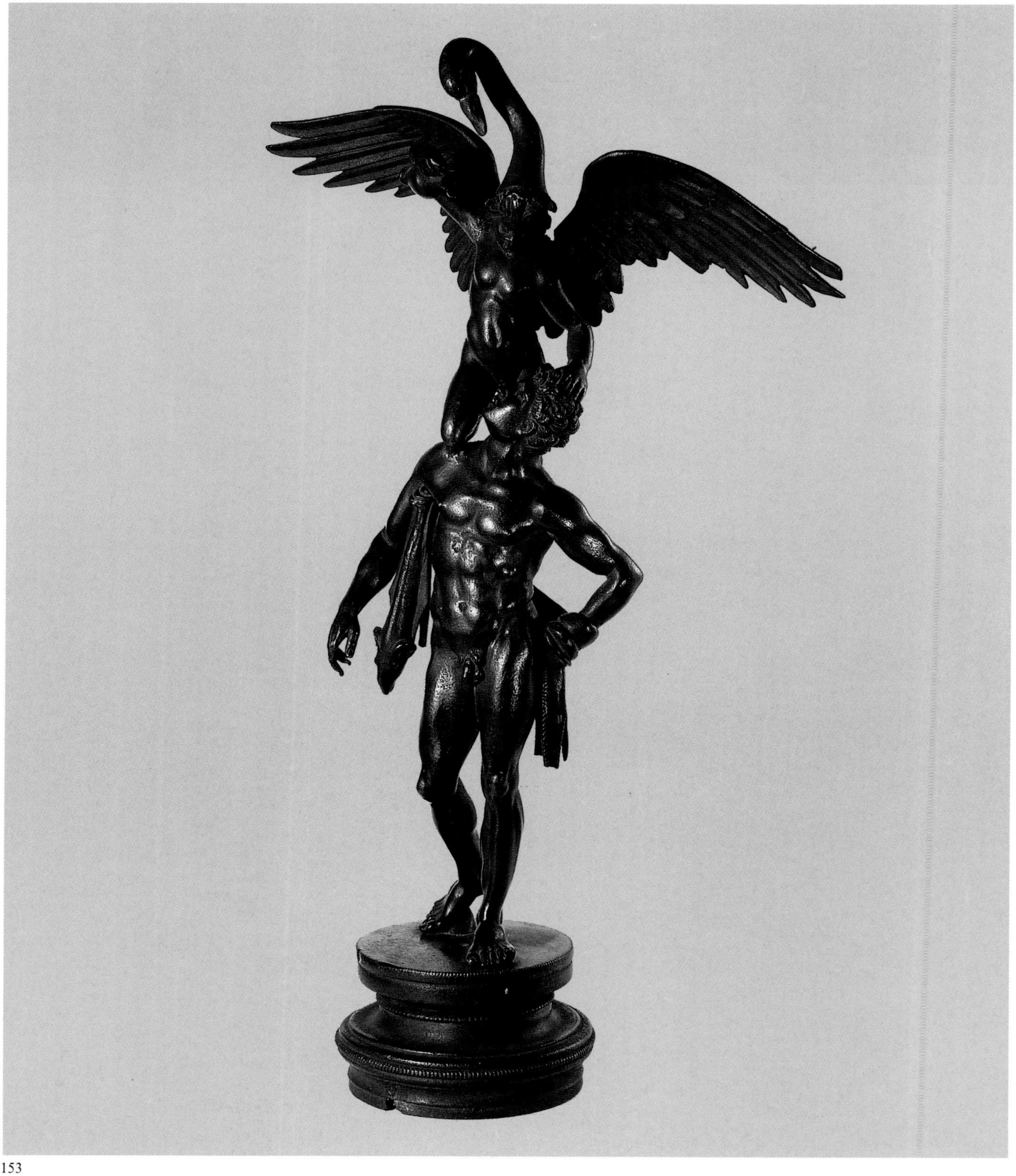

153

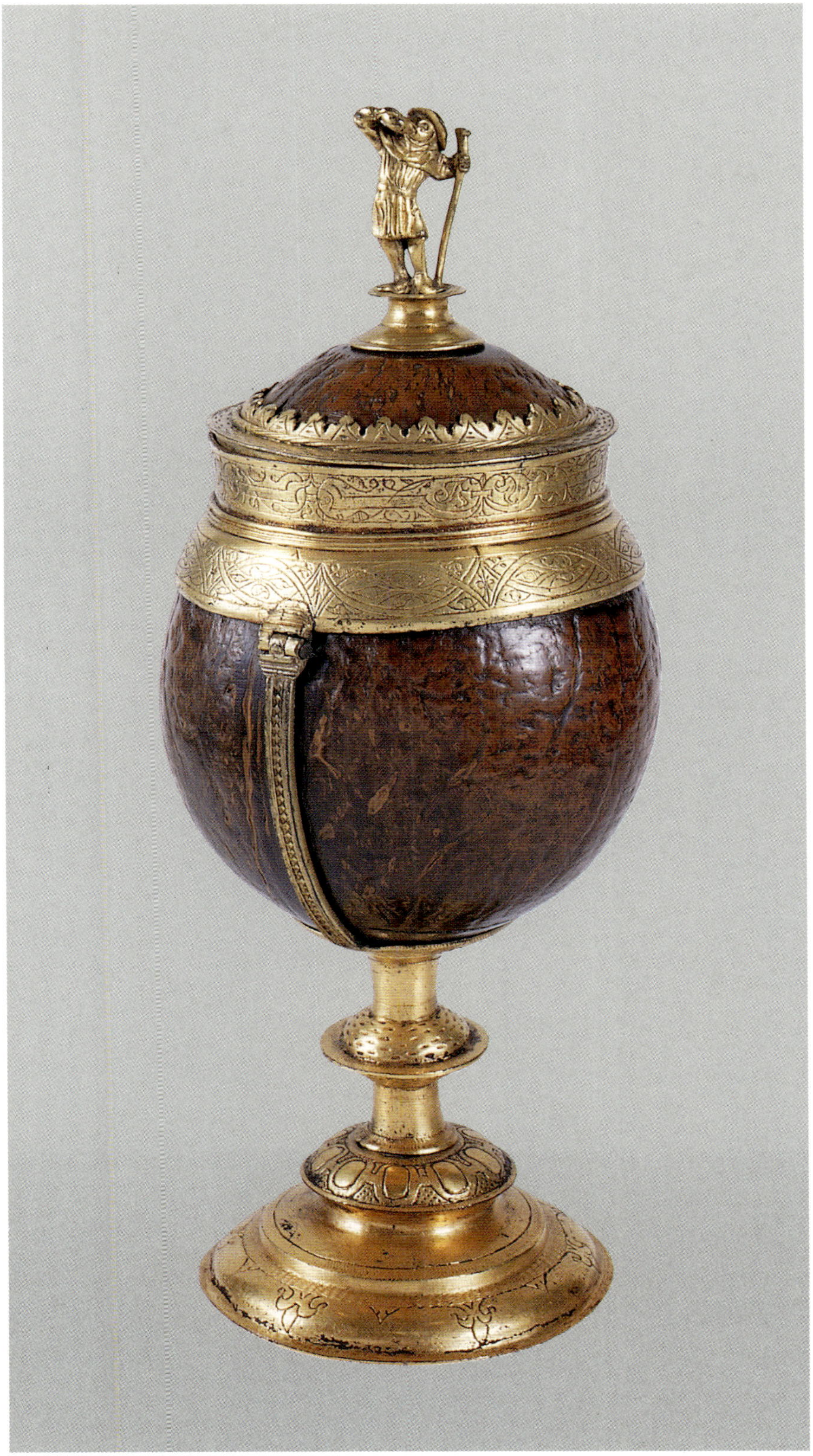

154

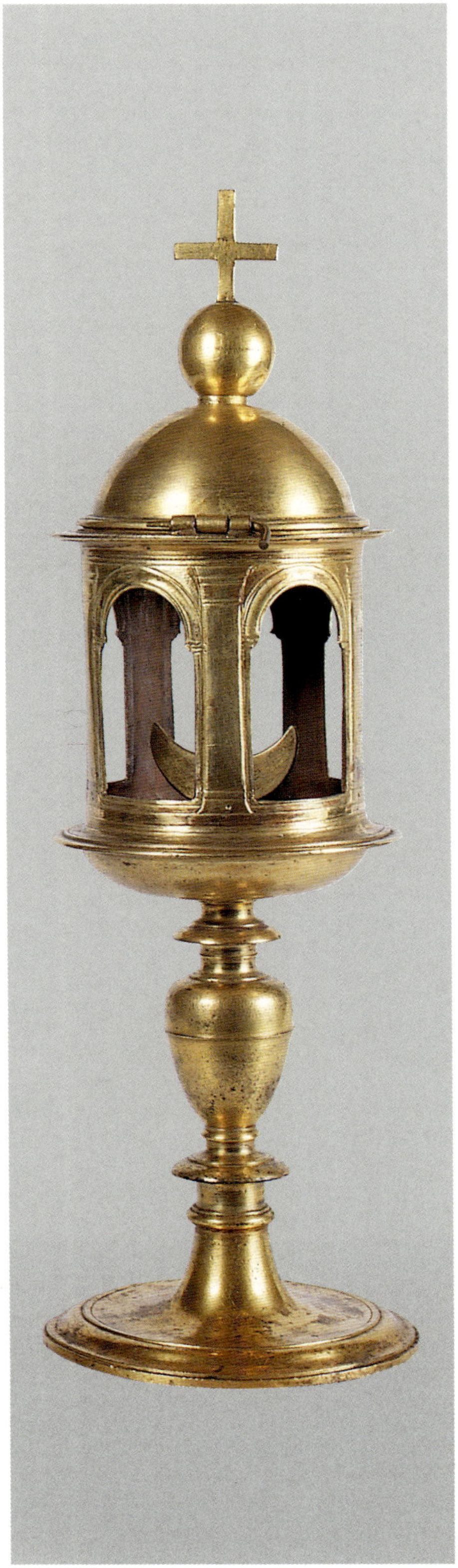

155

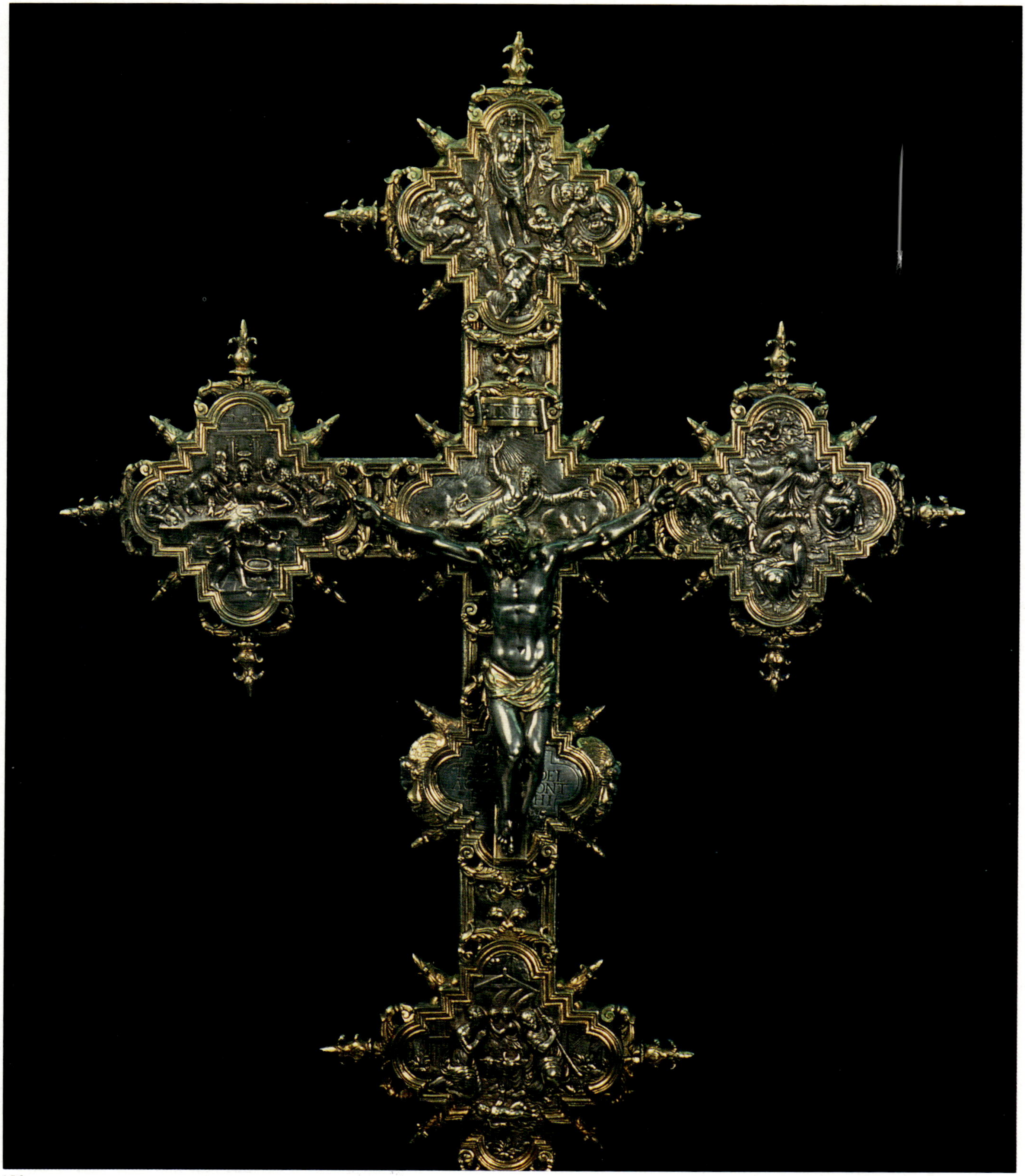

156

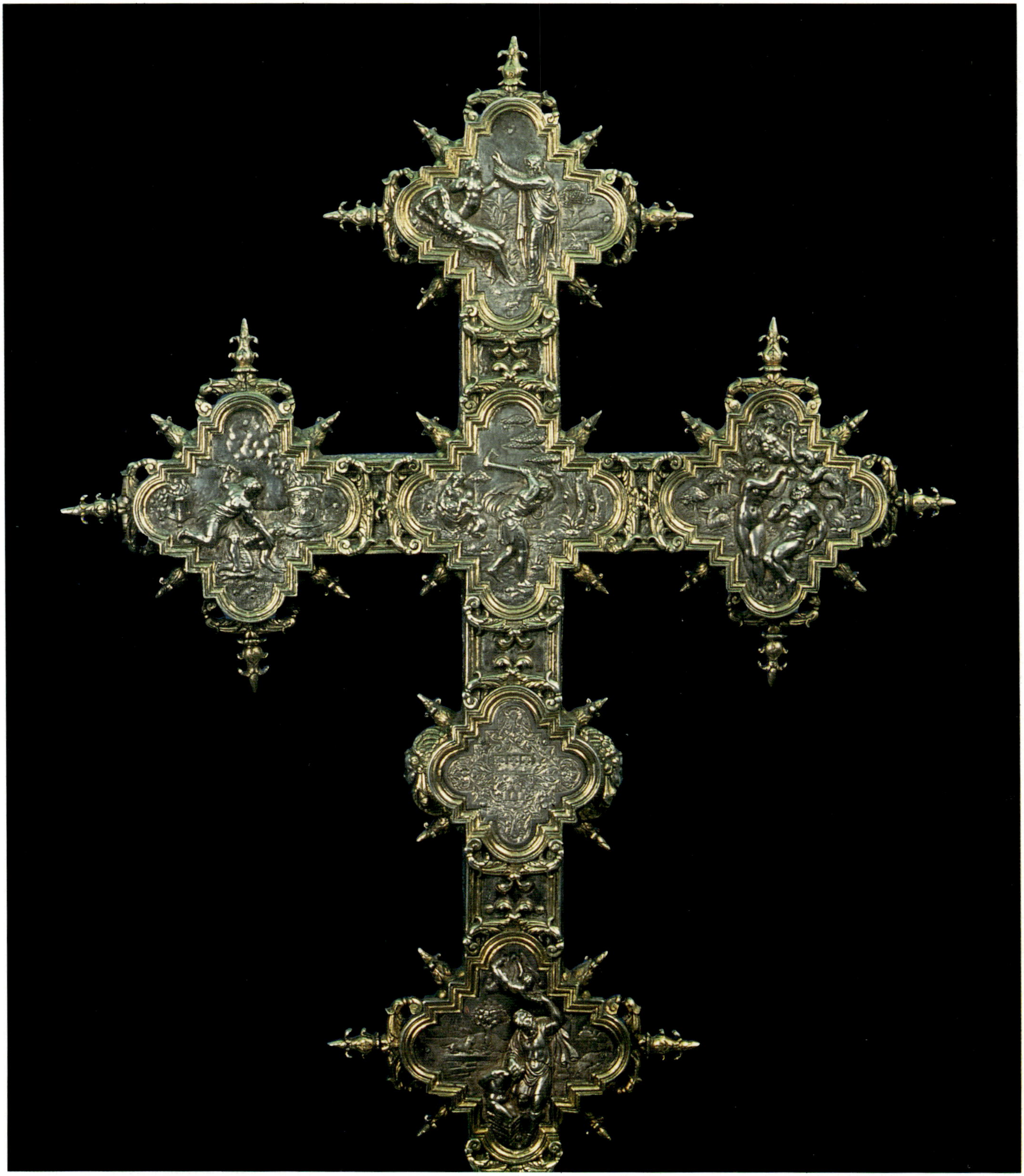

156

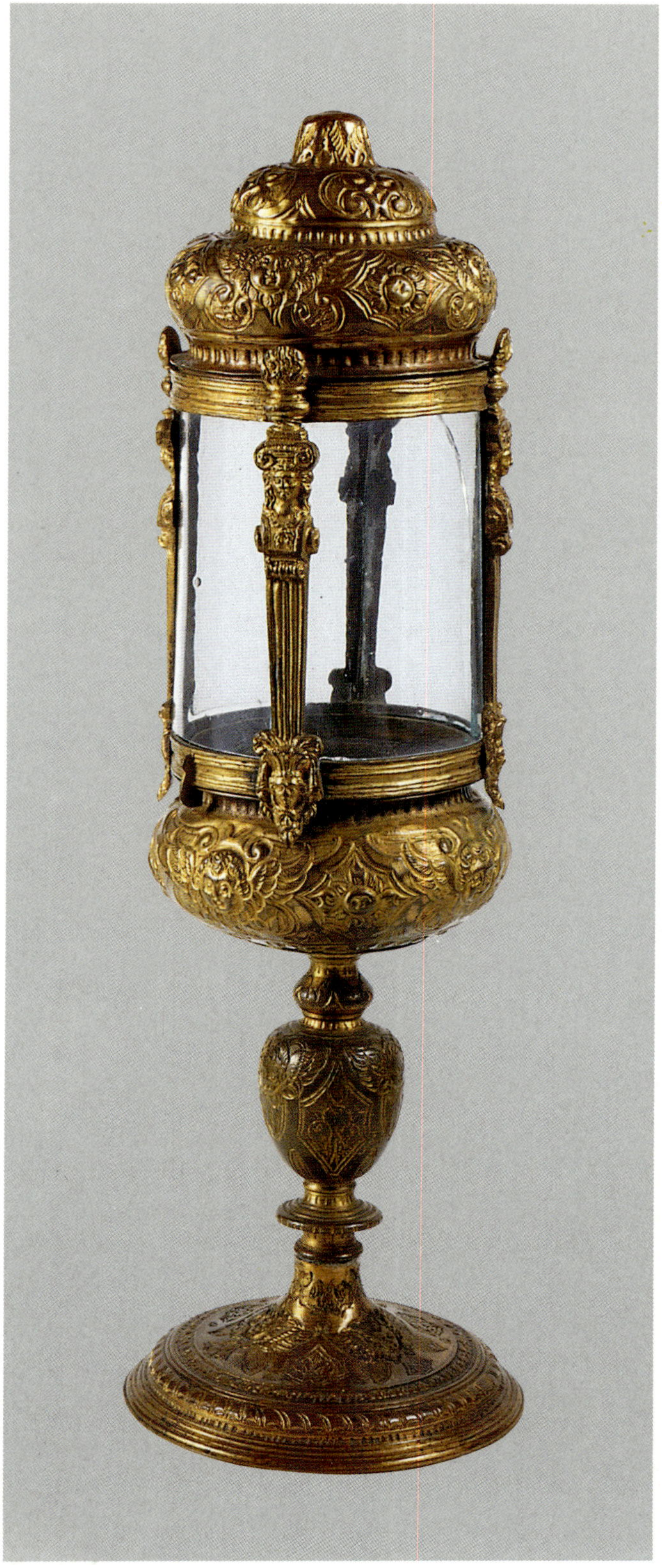

157

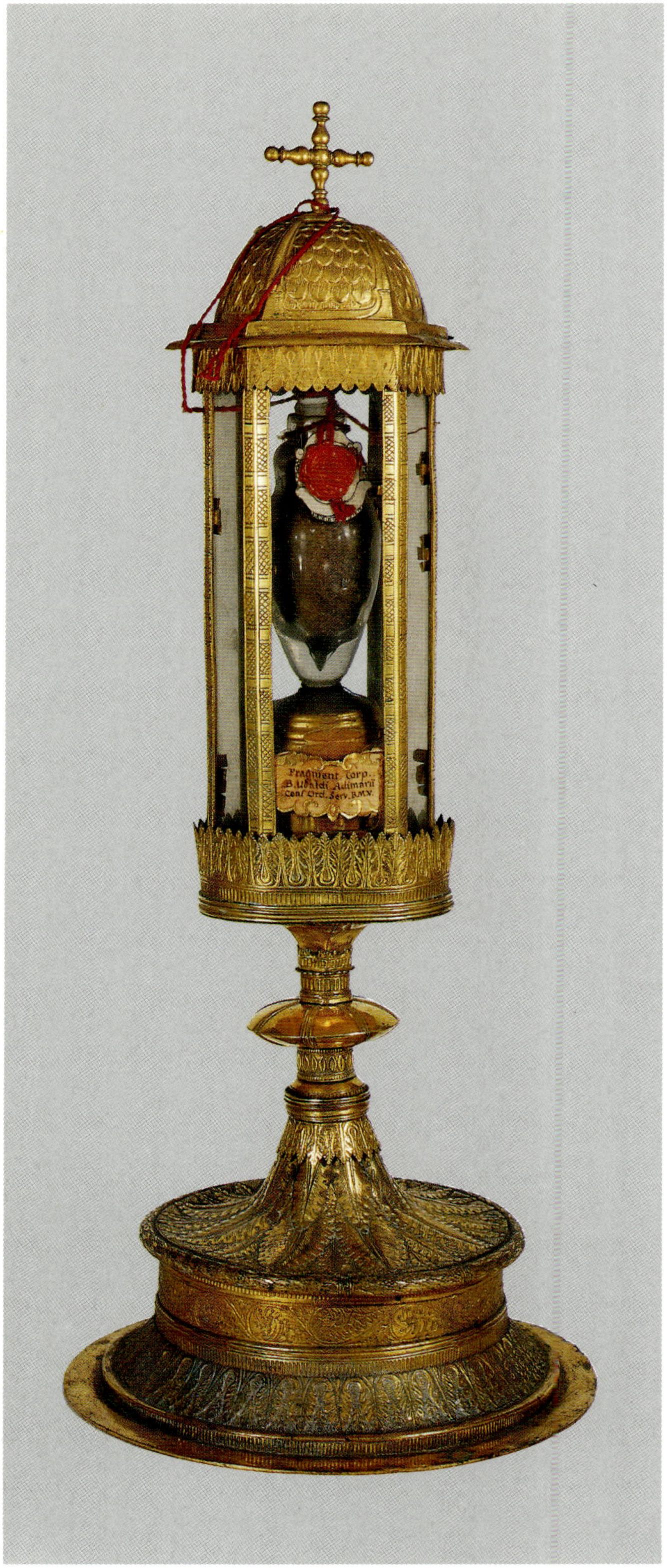

158

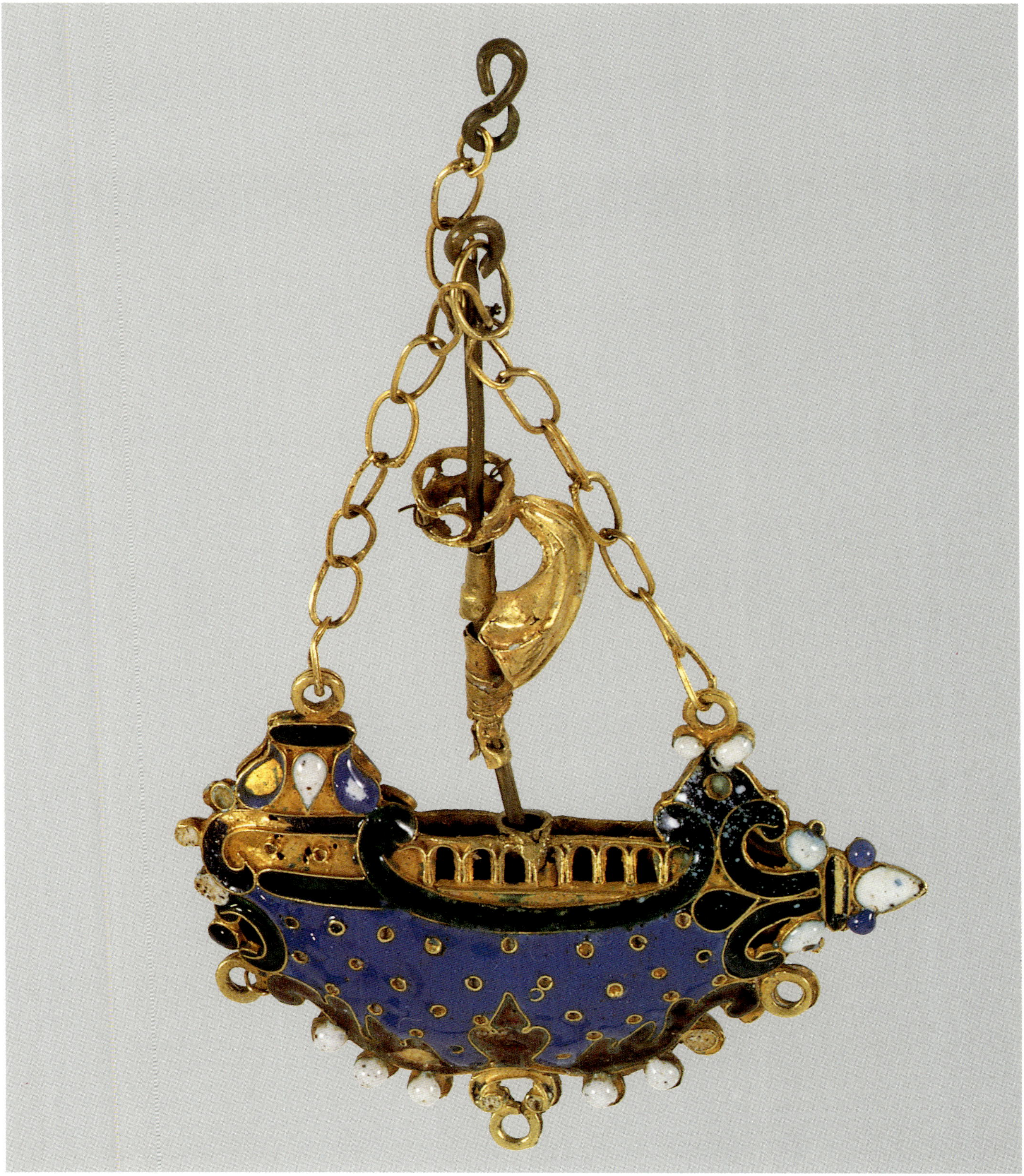

159

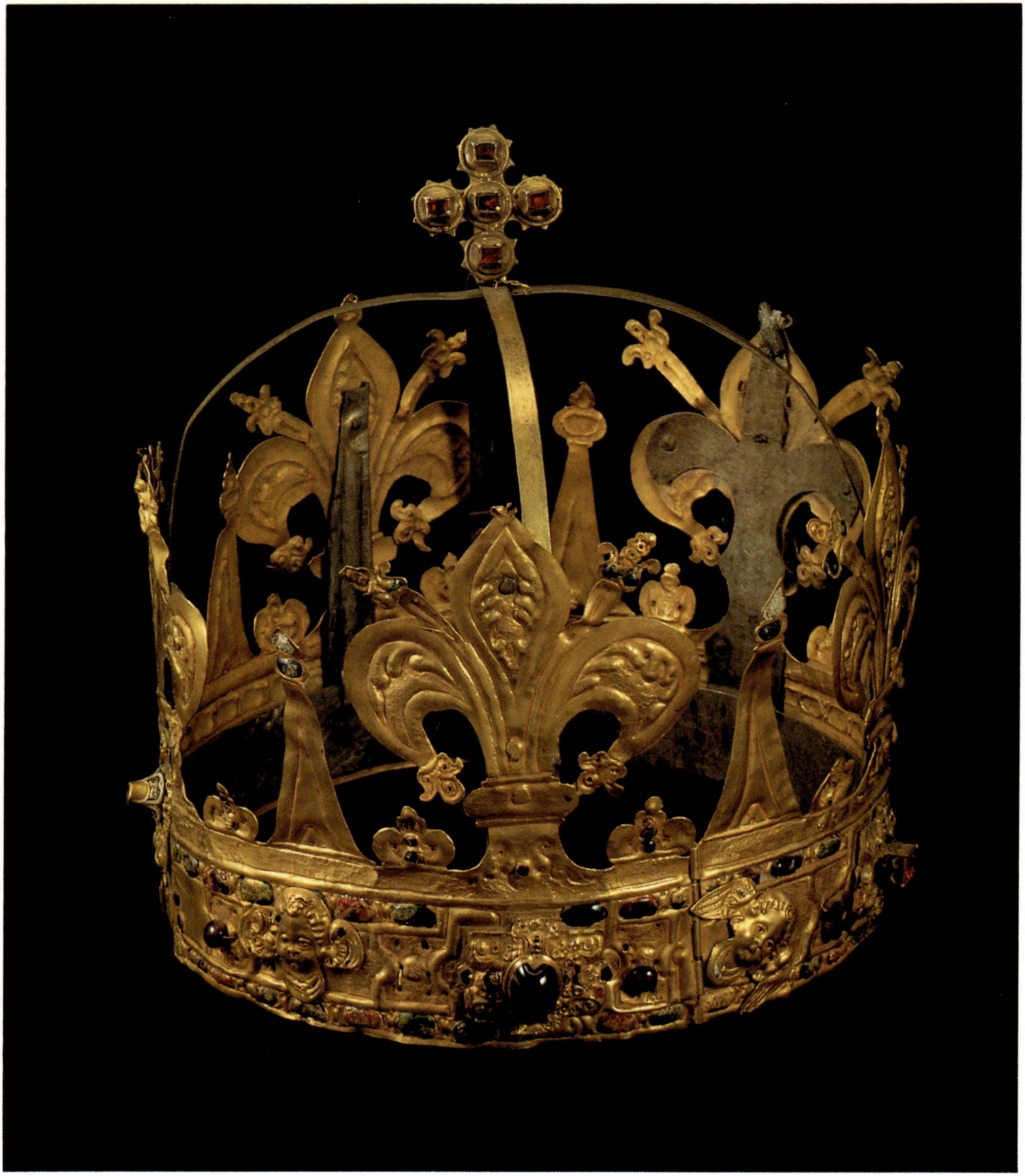

160

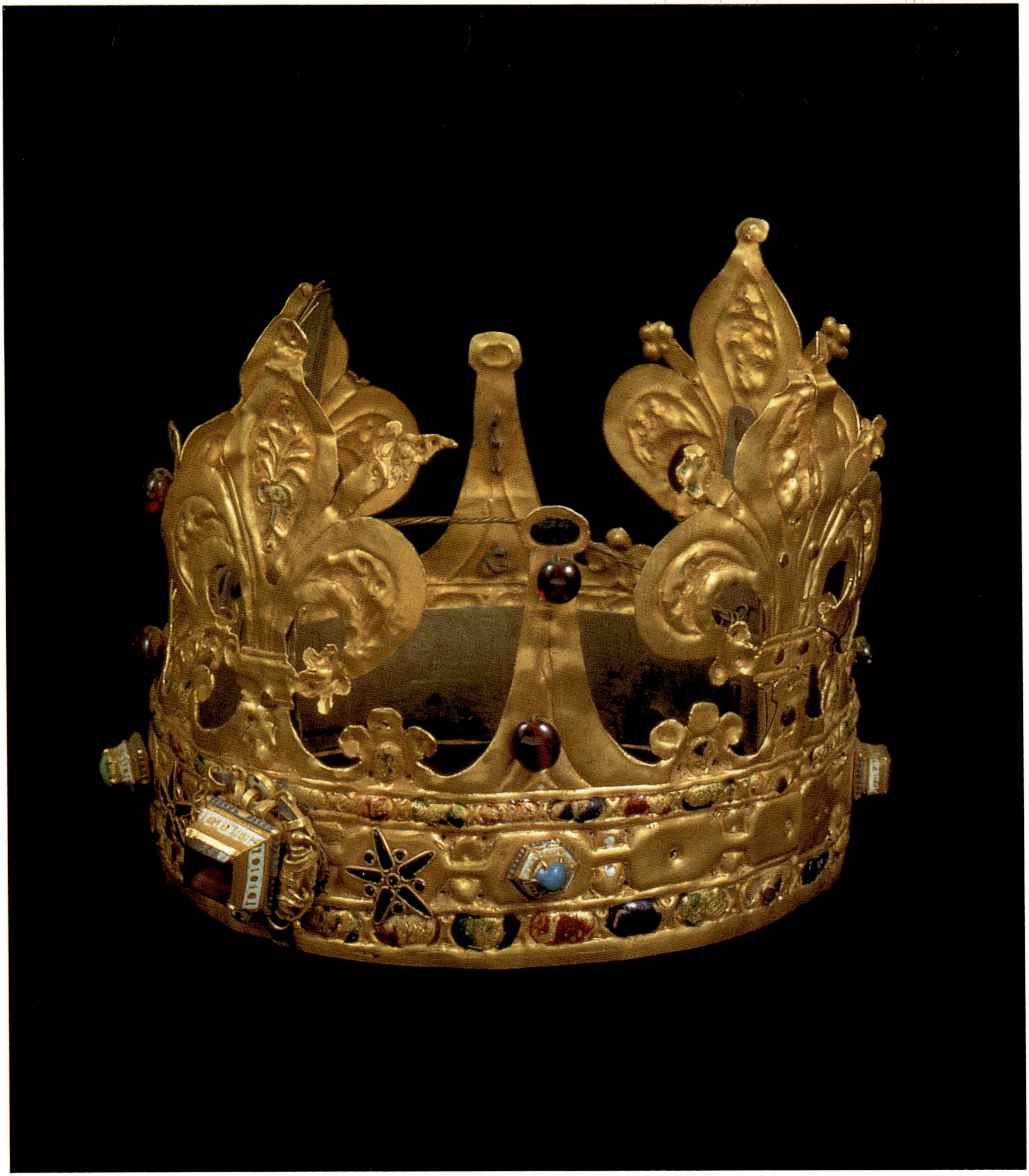

161

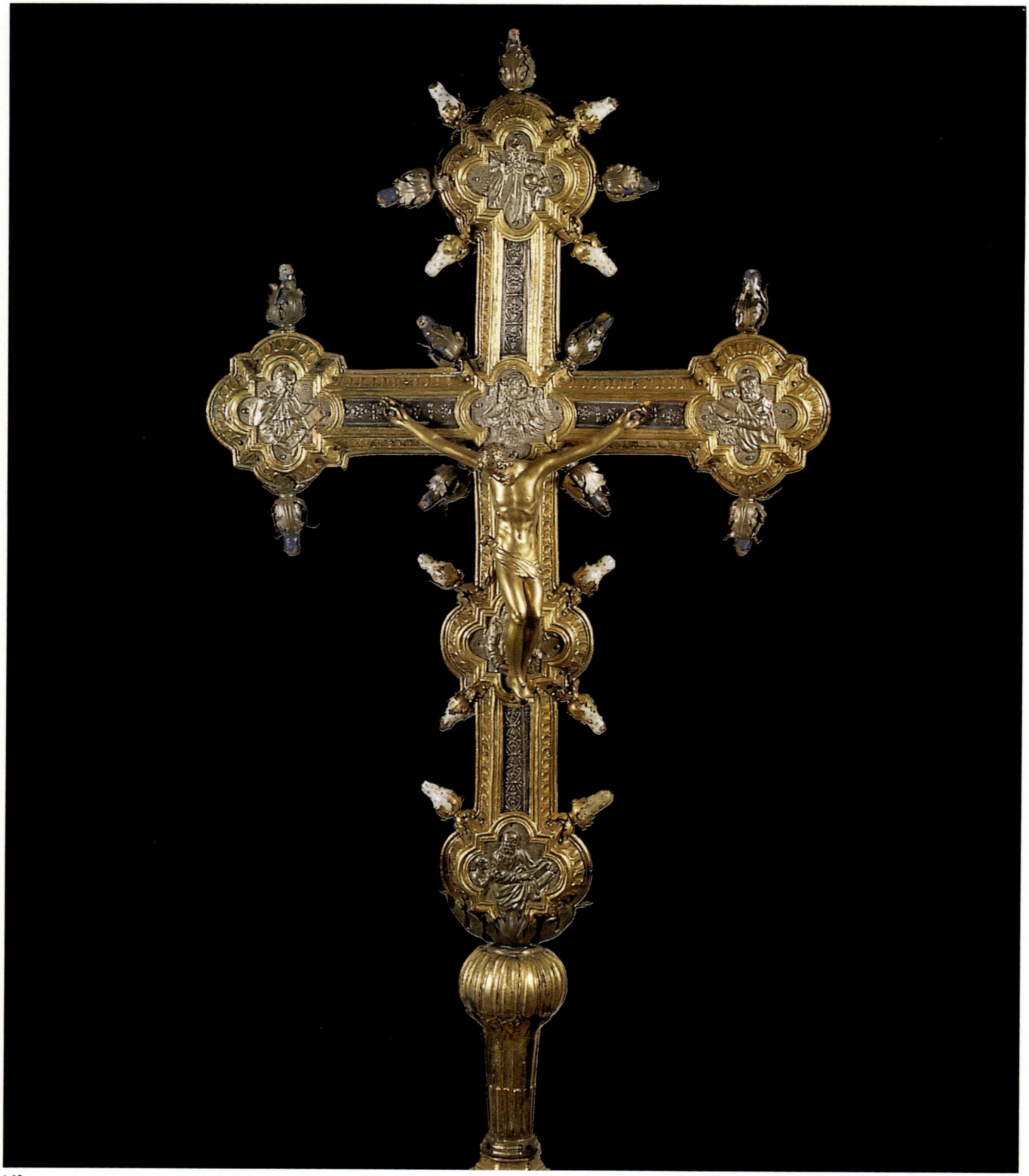

162

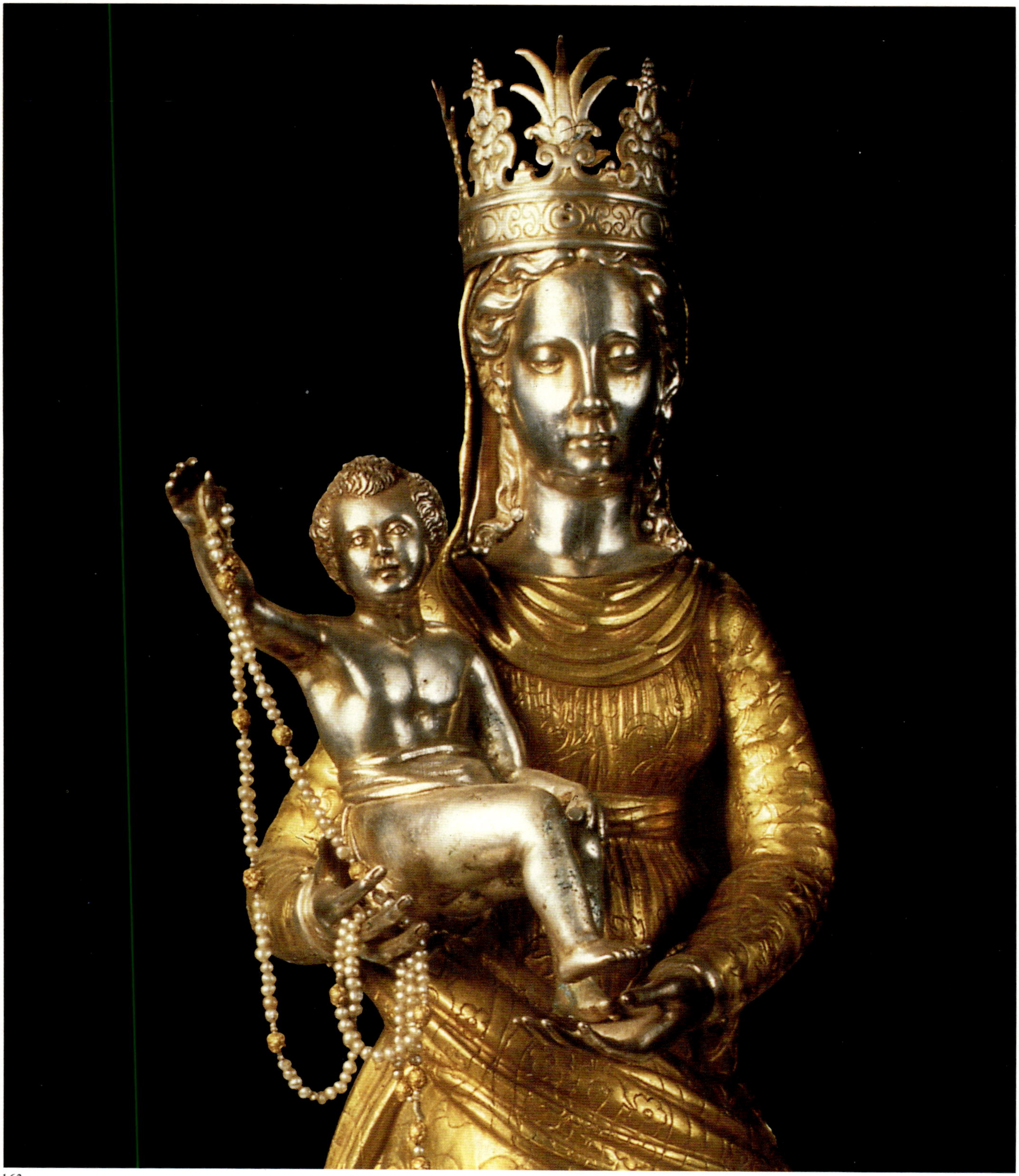

163

MEDALS AND COINS

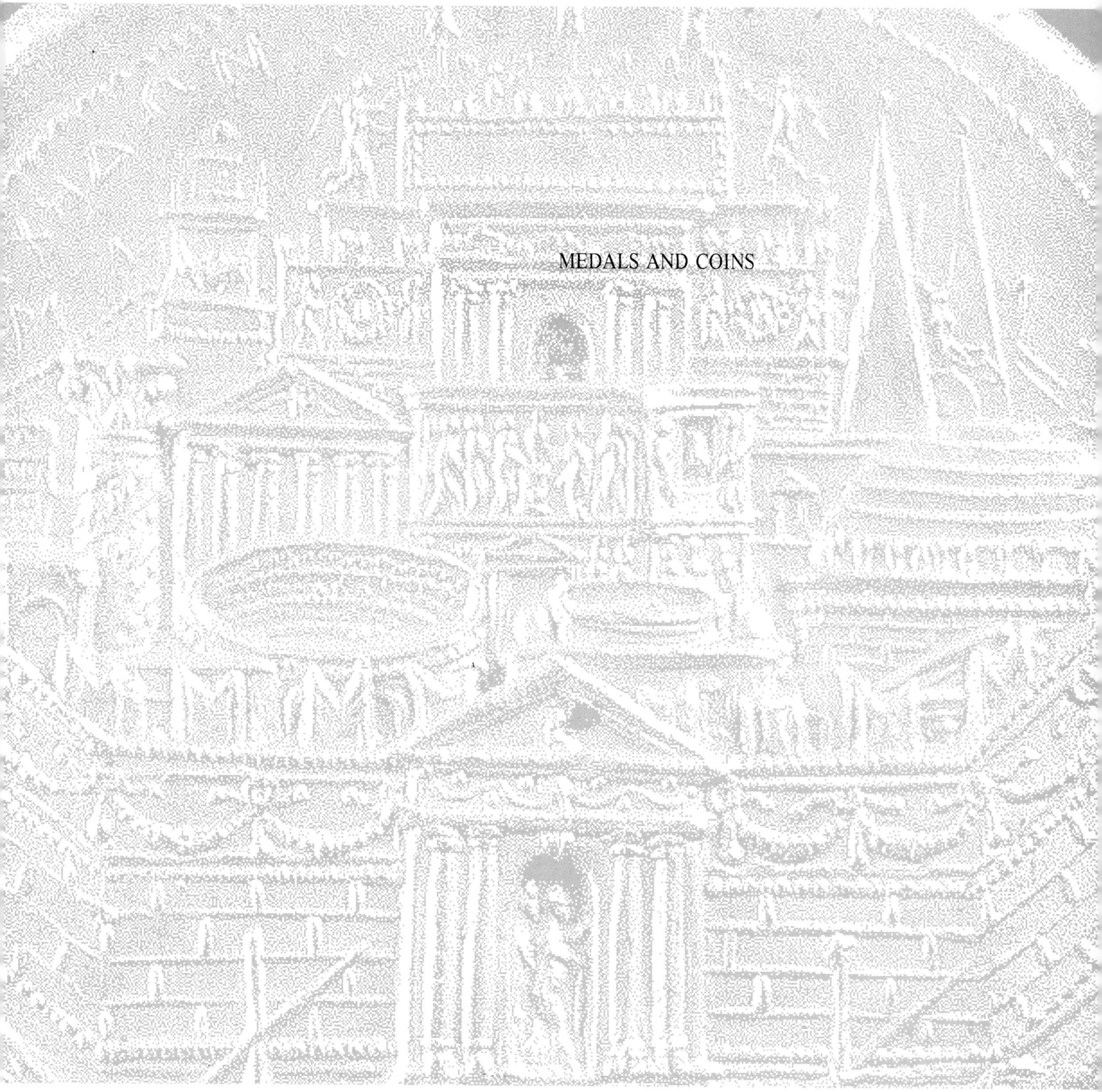

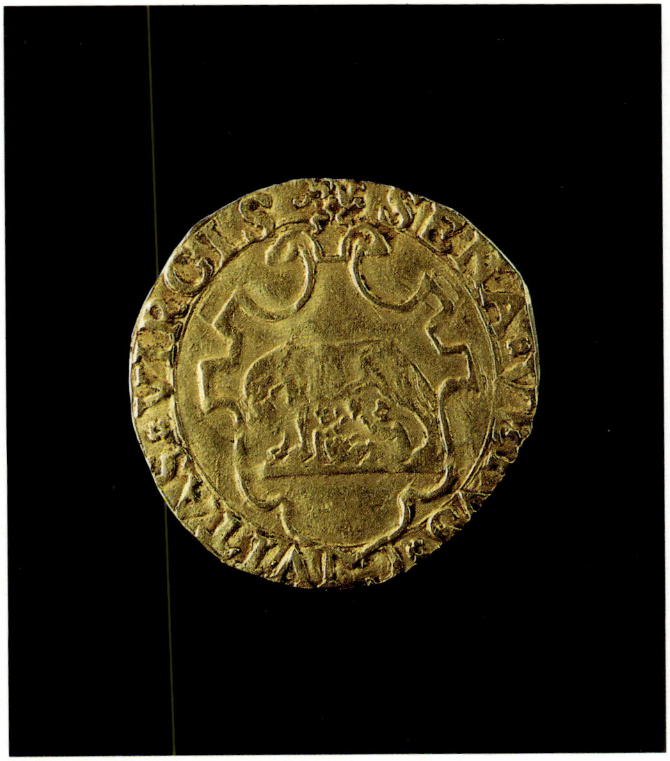

165

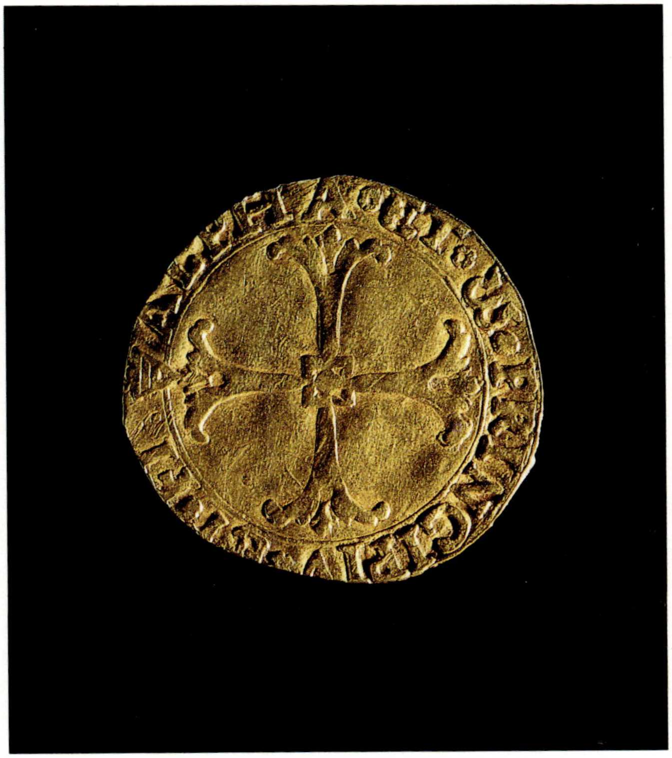

165

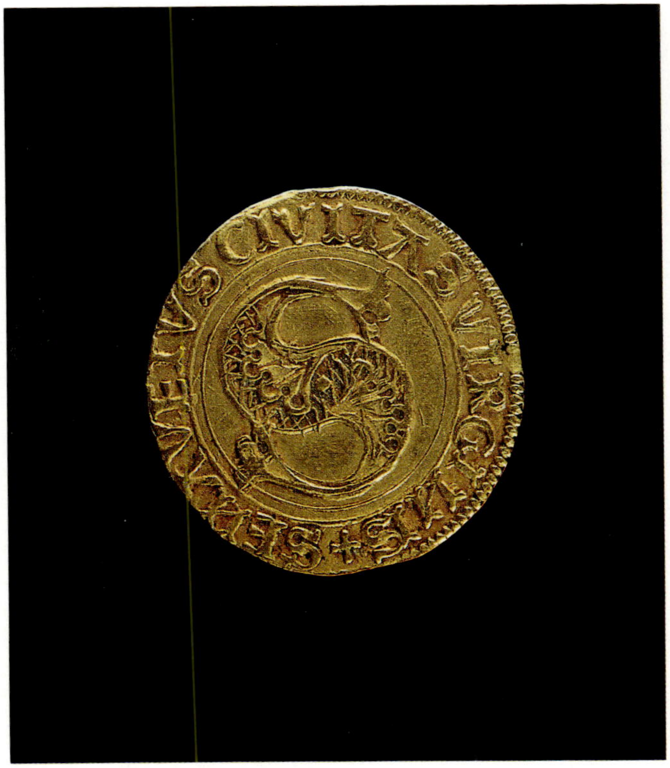

166

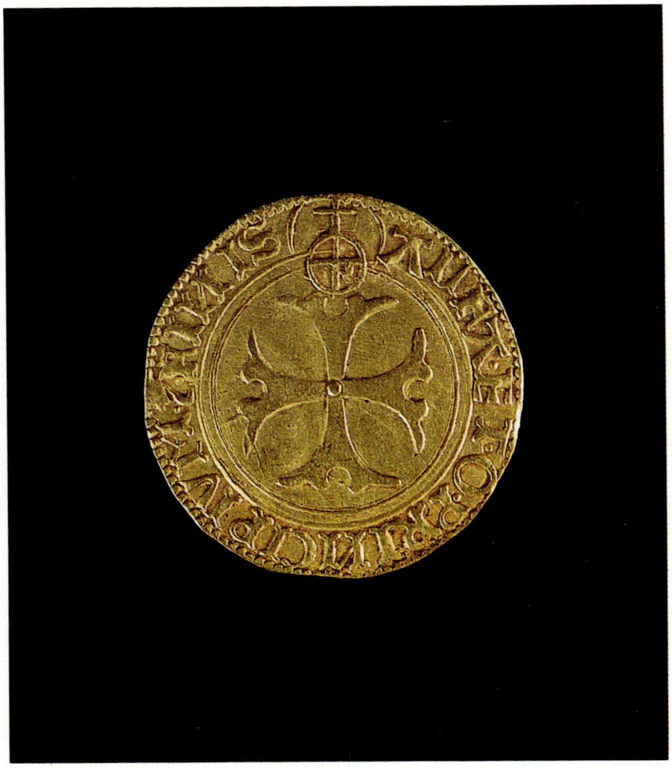

166

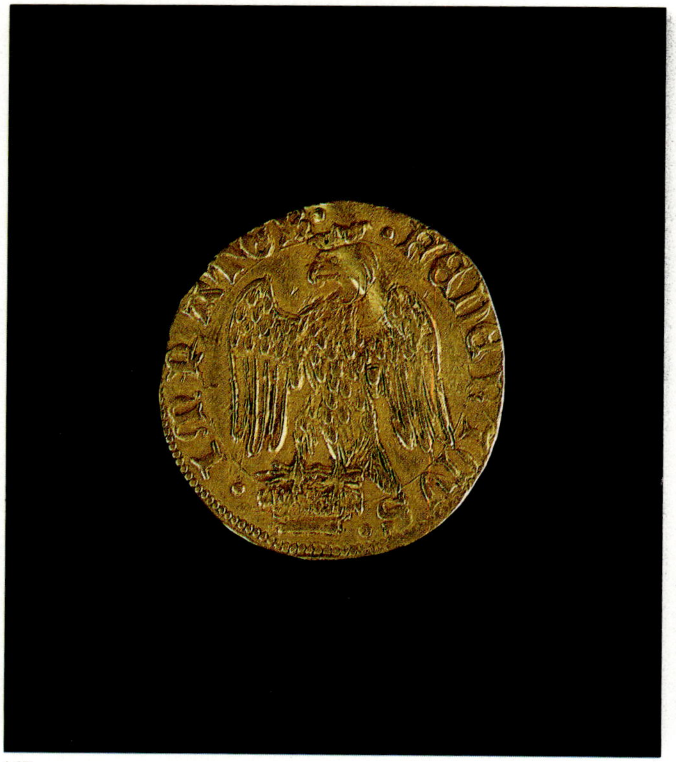

167

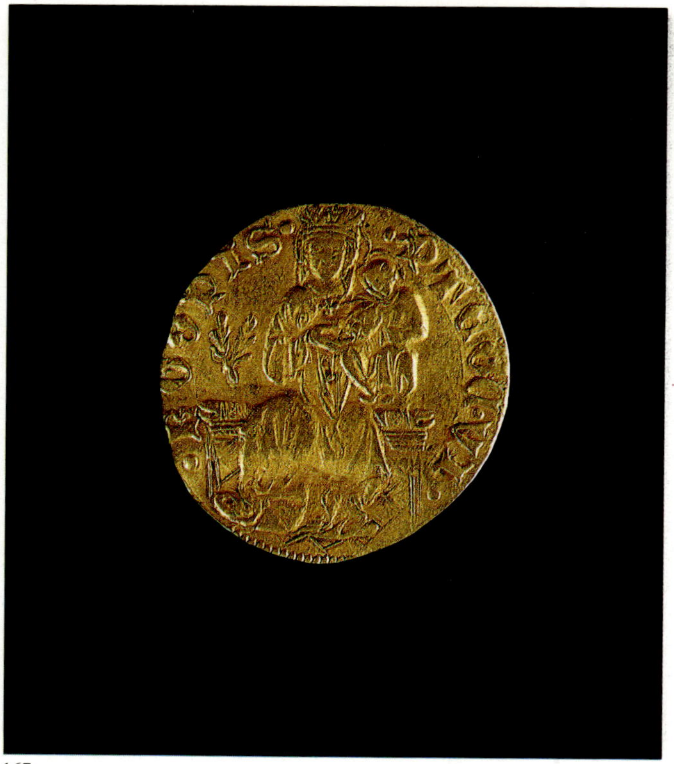

167

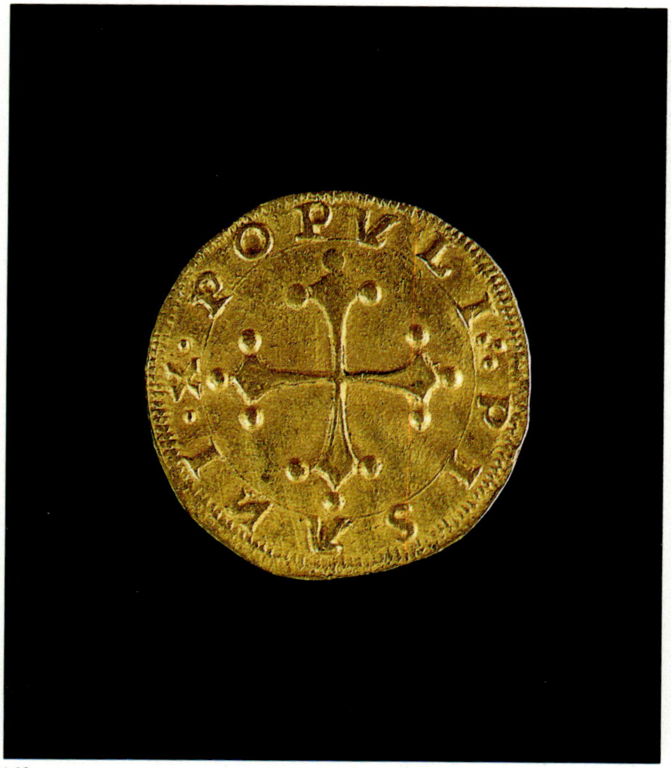

168

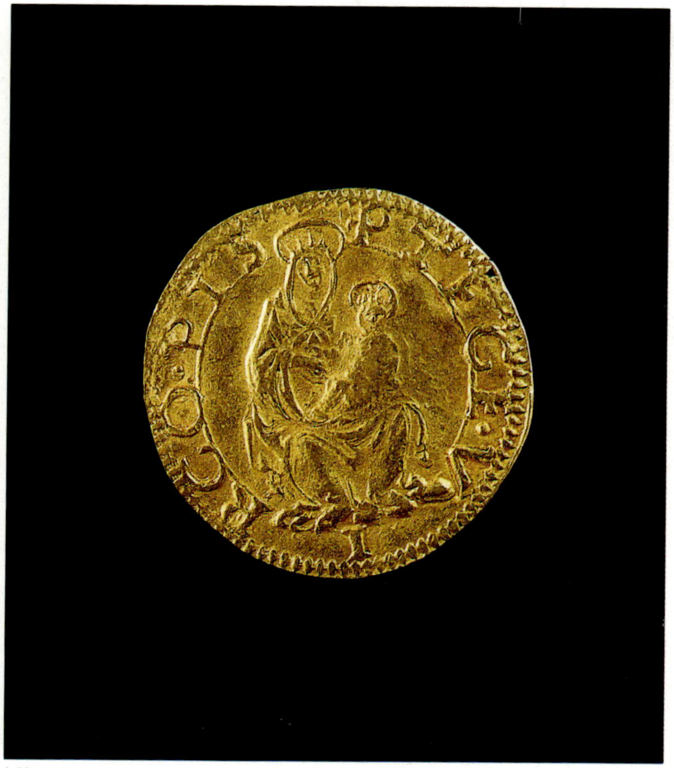

168

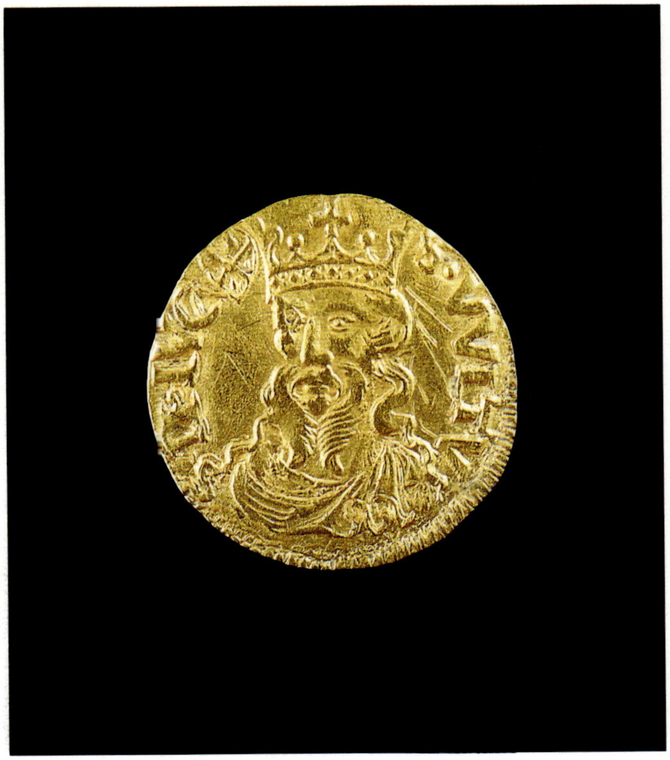

169

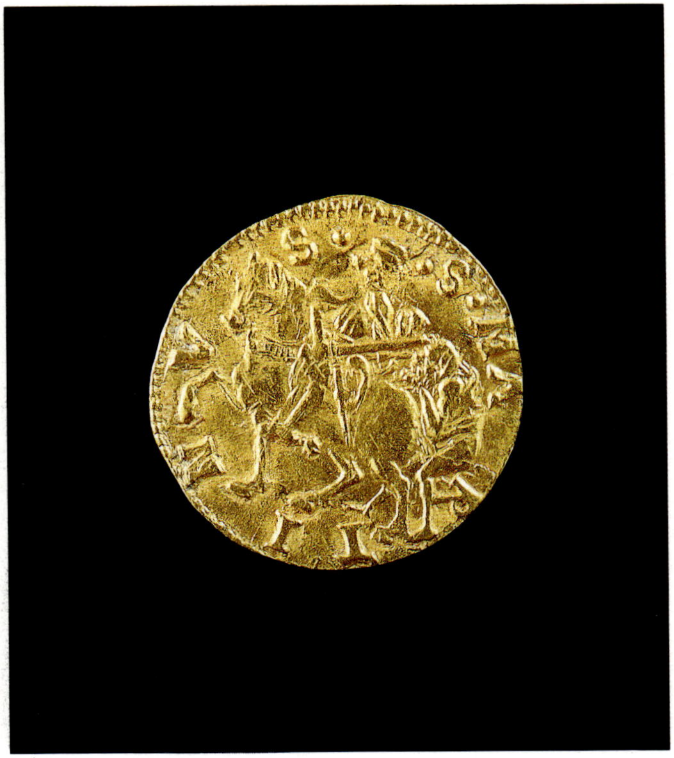

169

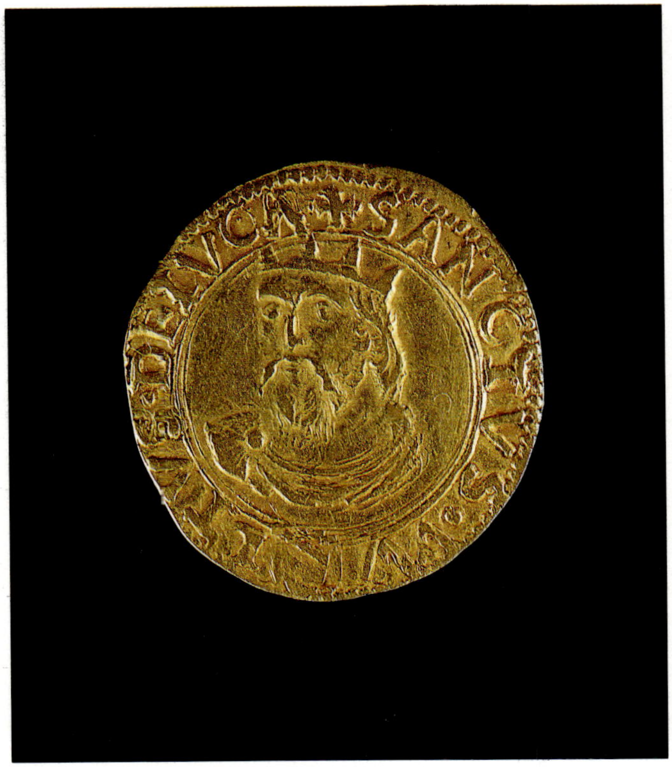

170

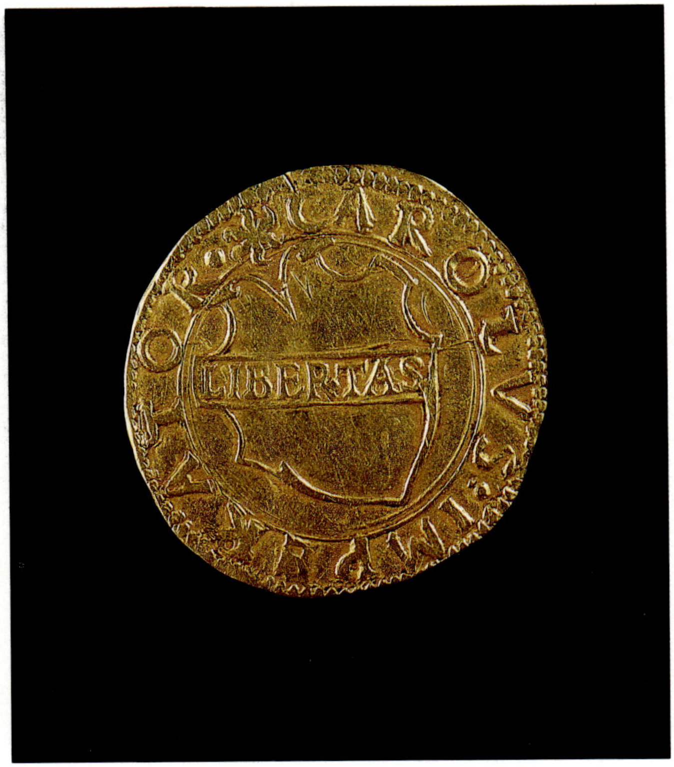

170

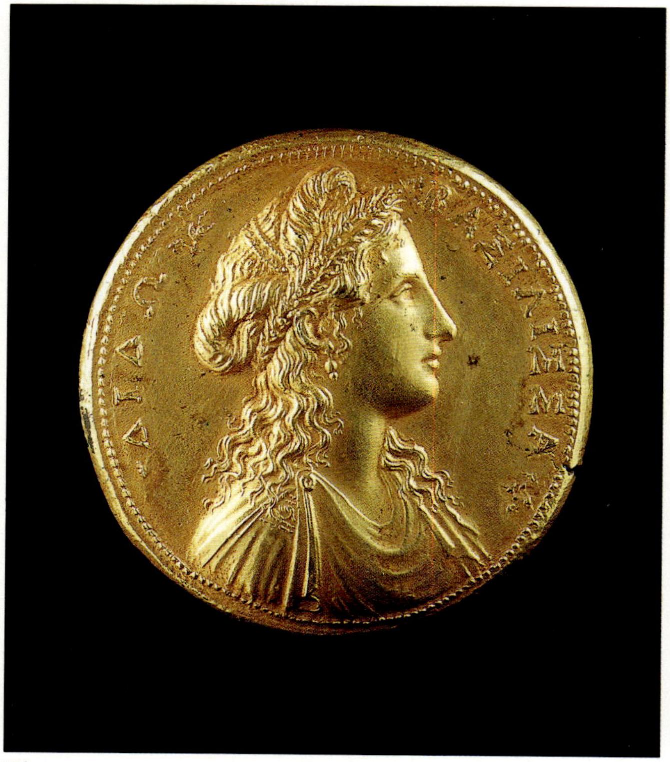

172

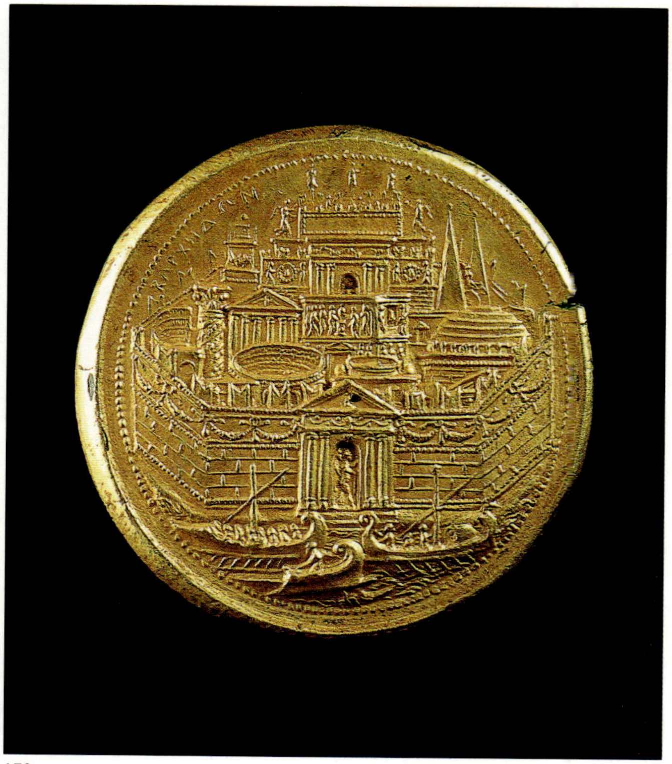

172

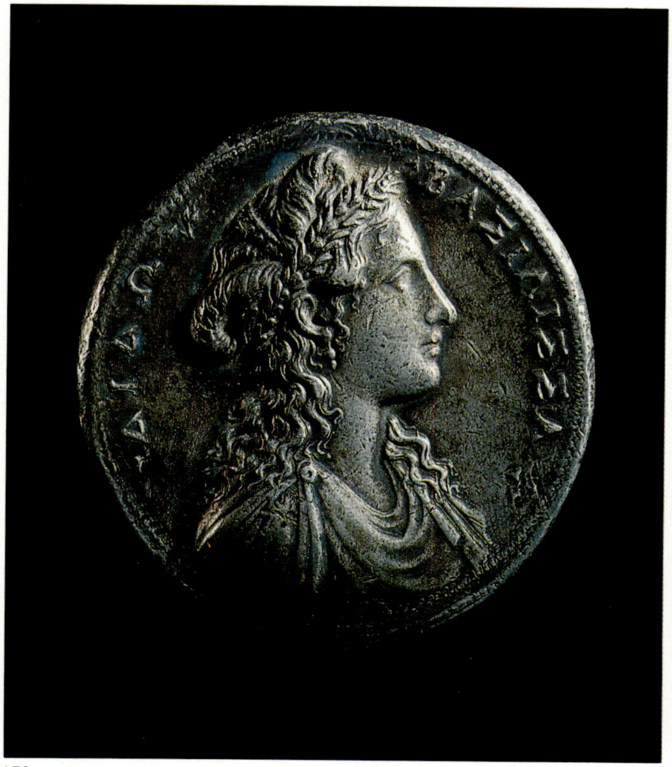

173

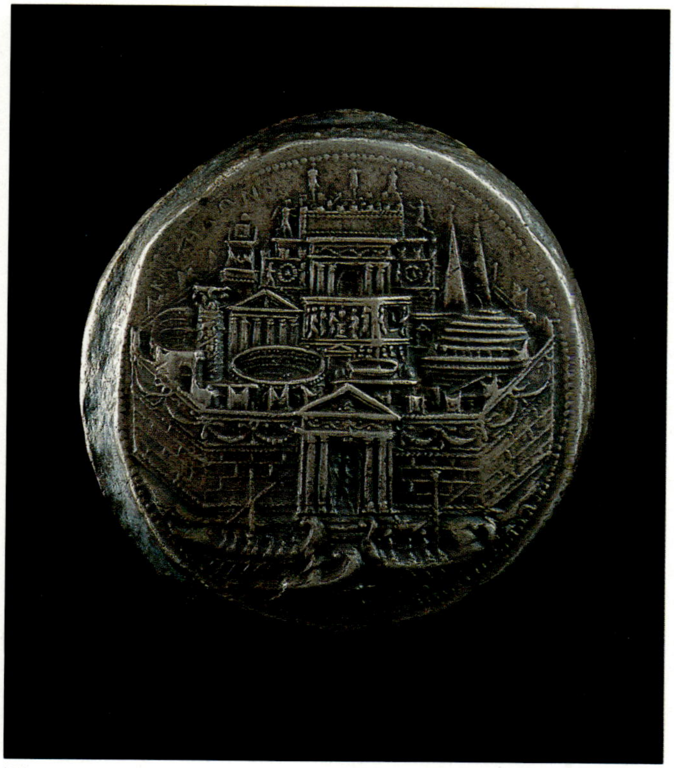

173

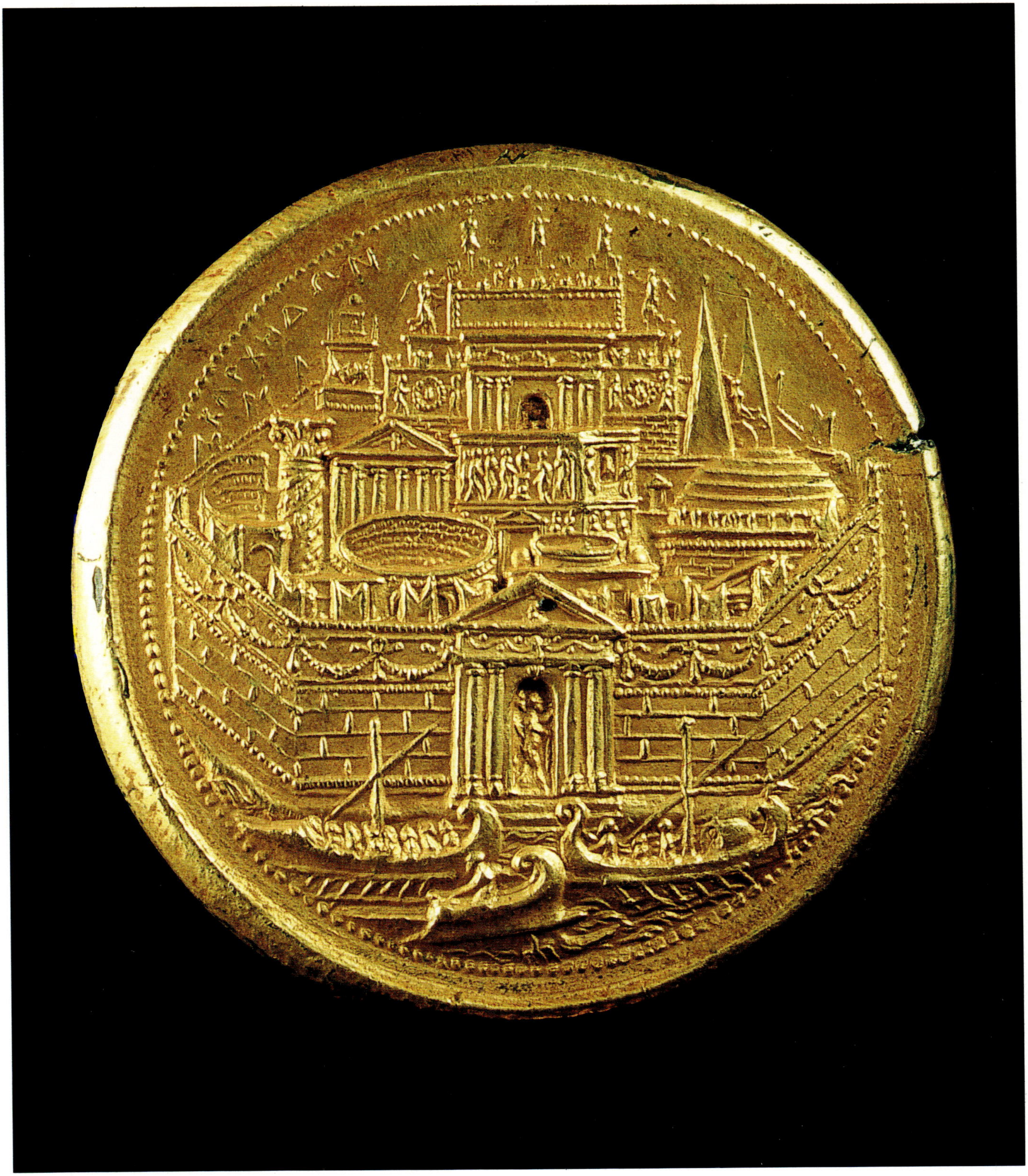

172

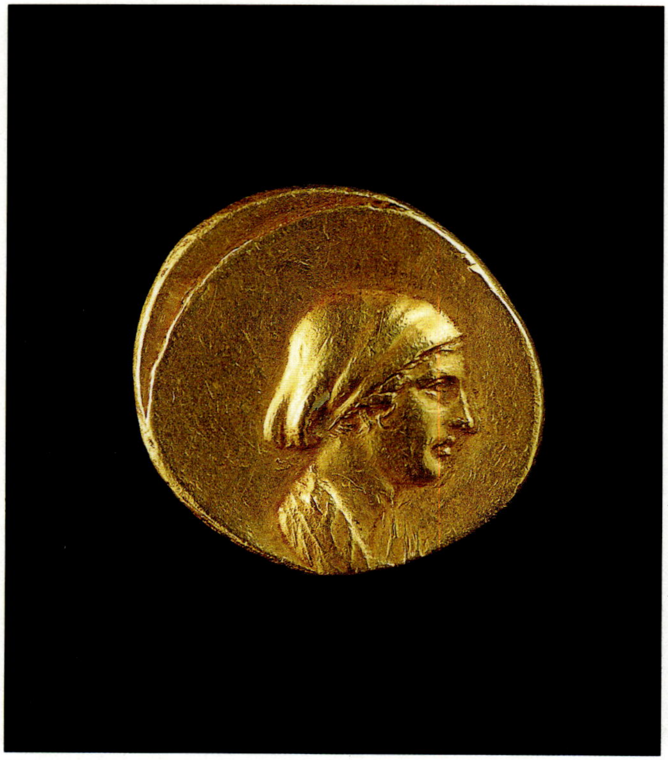

174

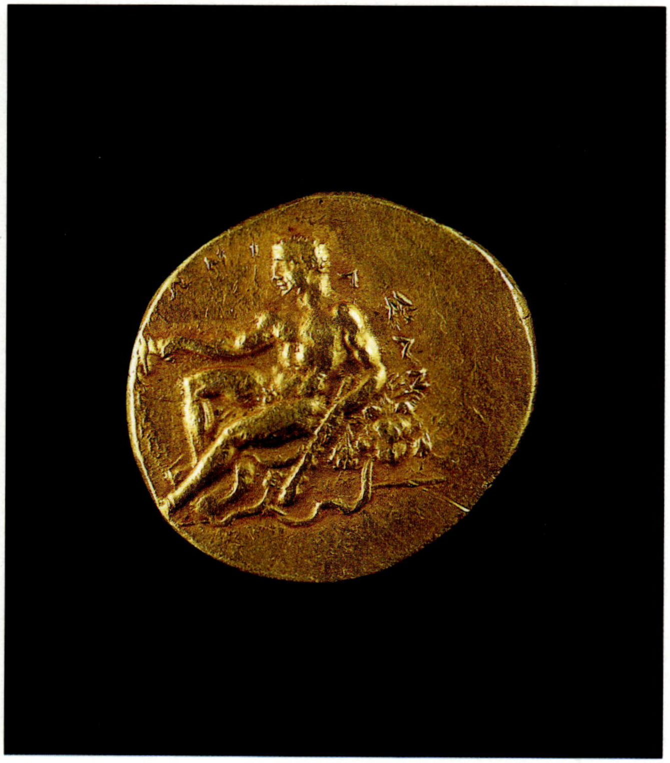

174

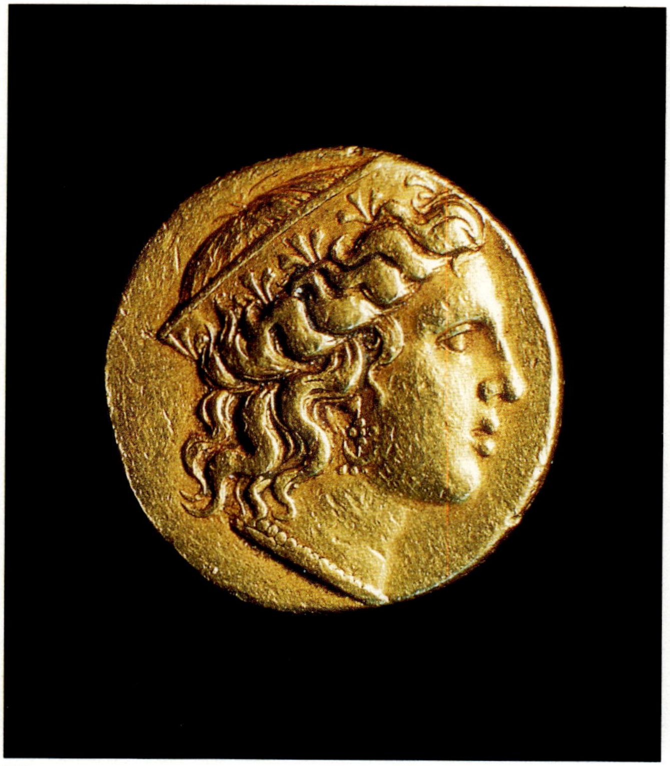

175

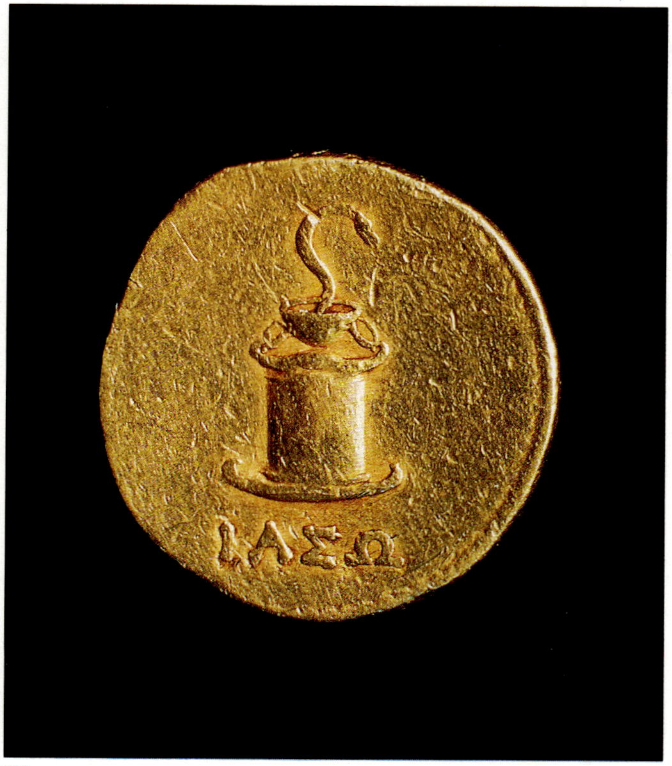

175

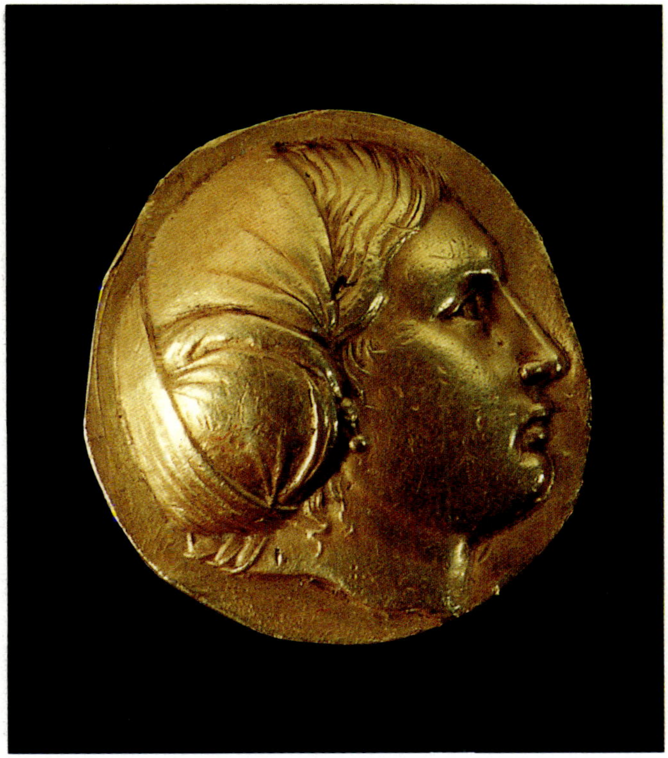

176

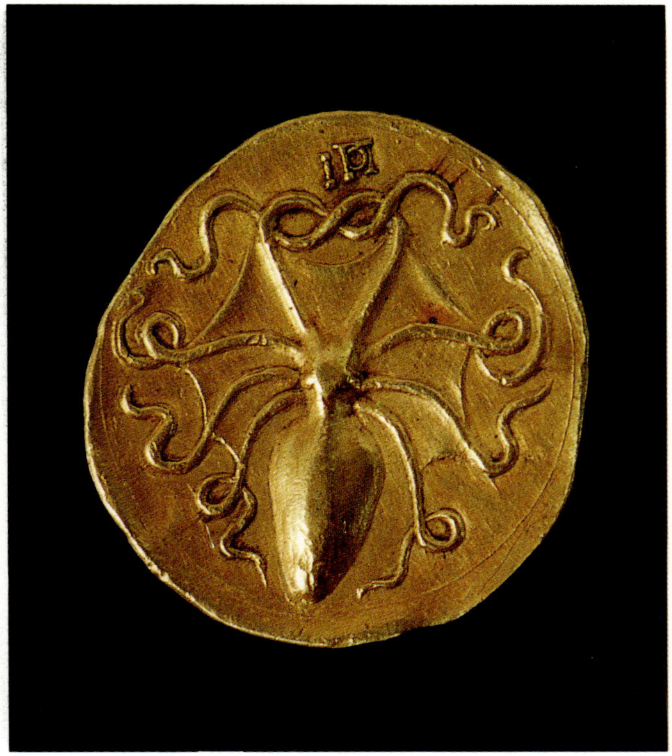

176

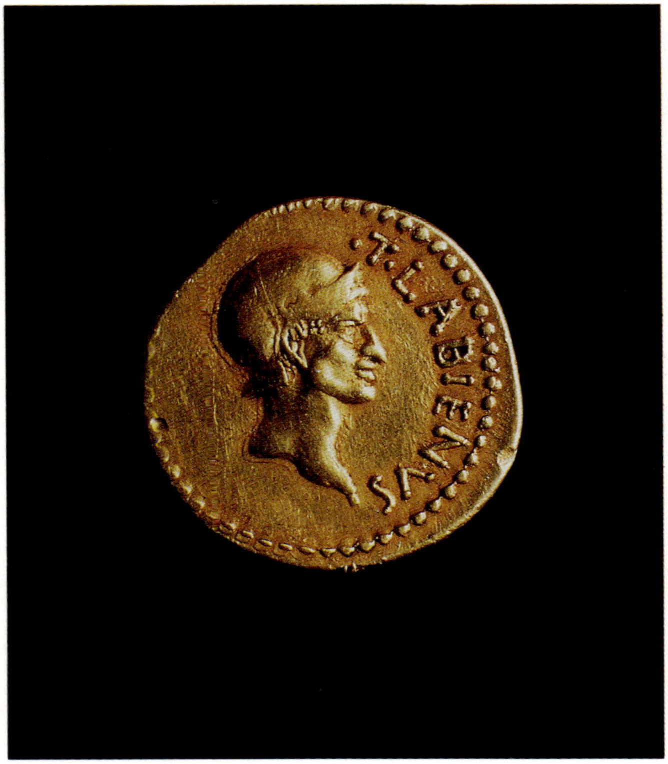

177

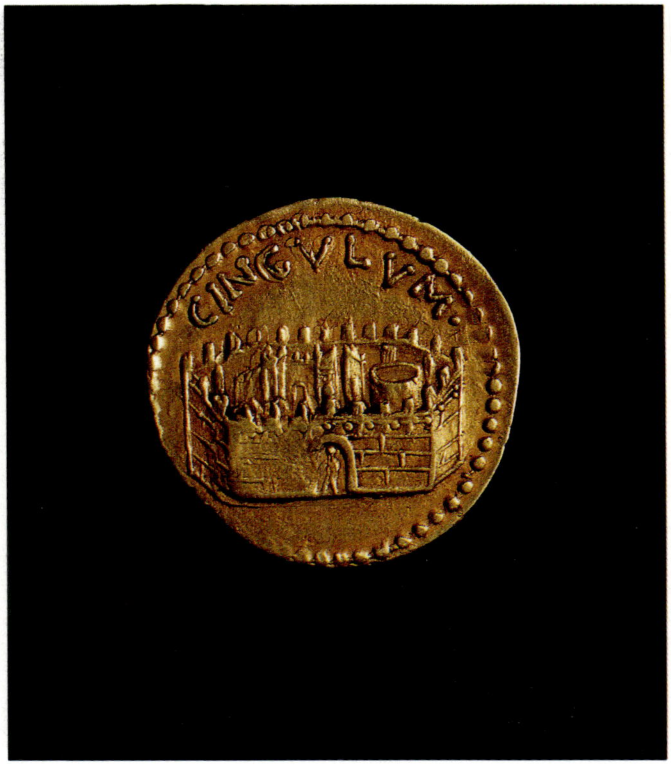

177

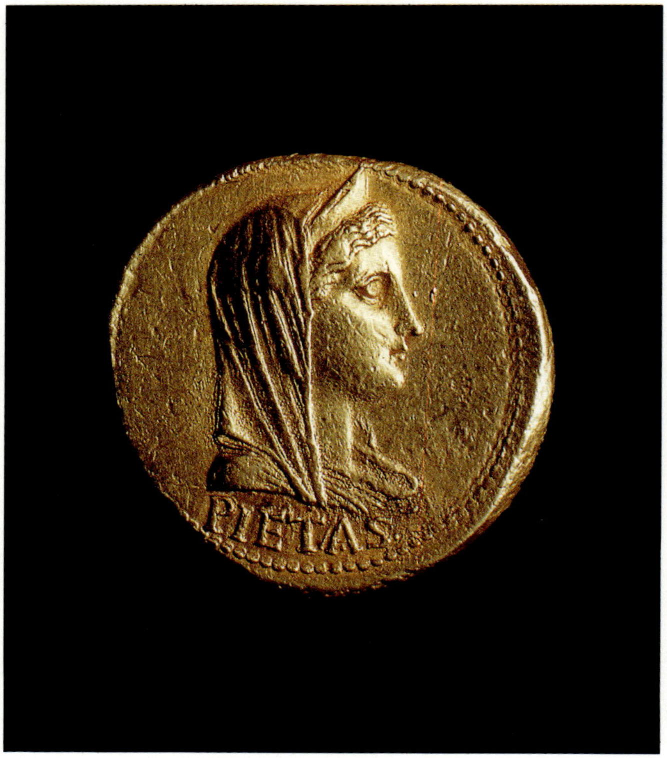

178

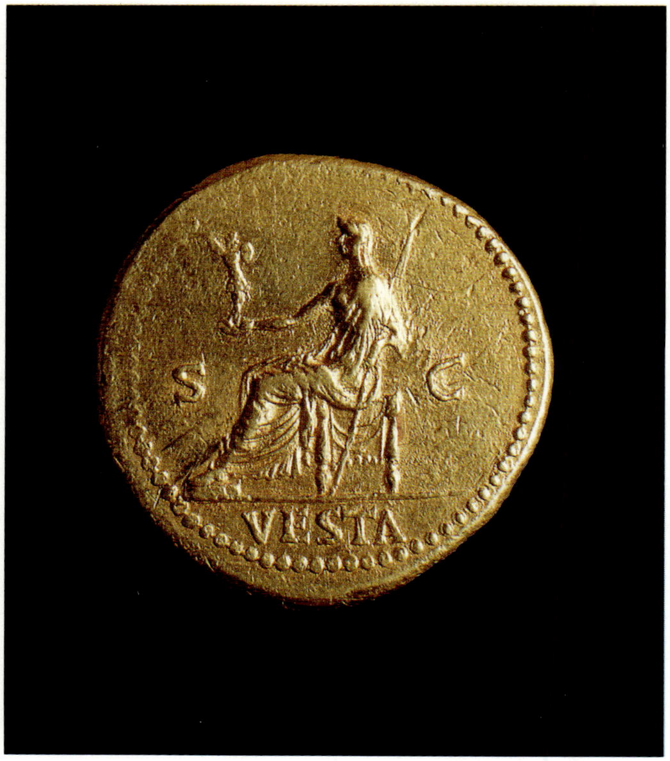

178

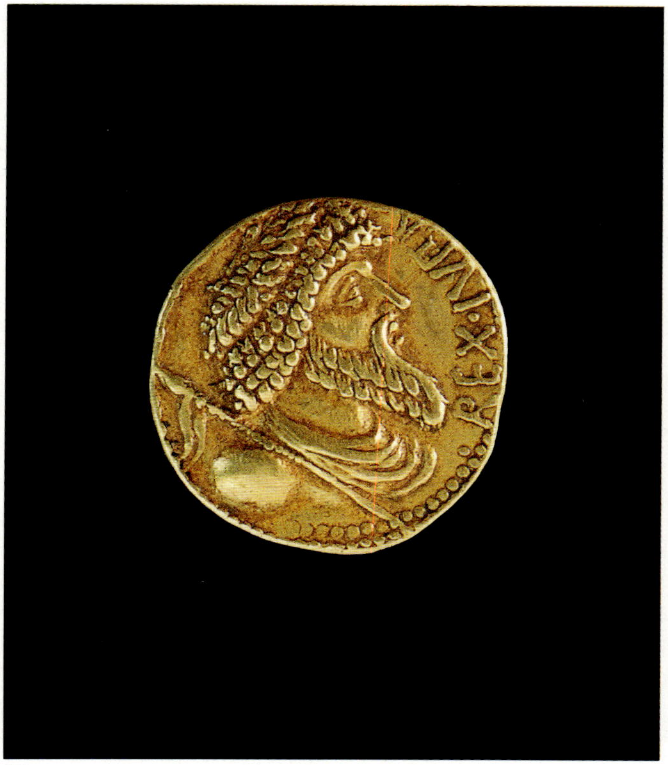
179

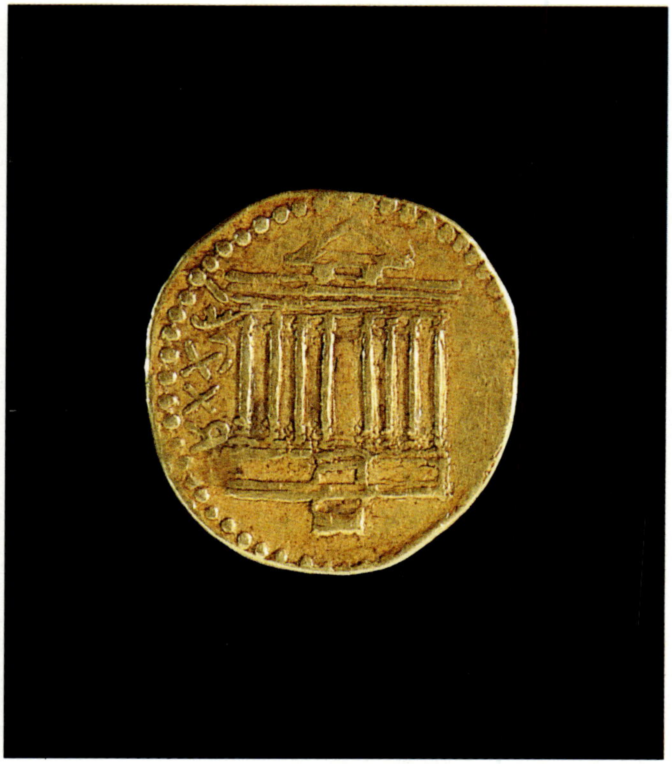
179

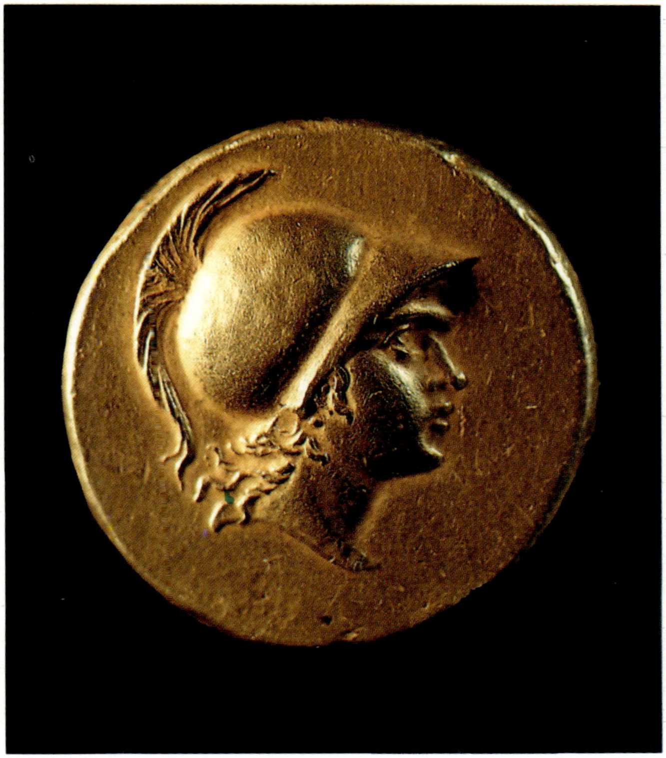

180

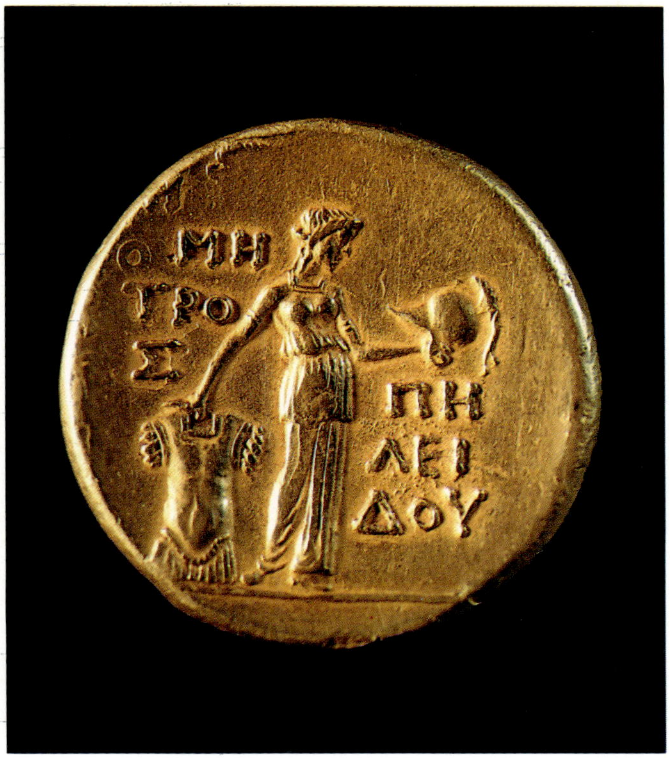

180

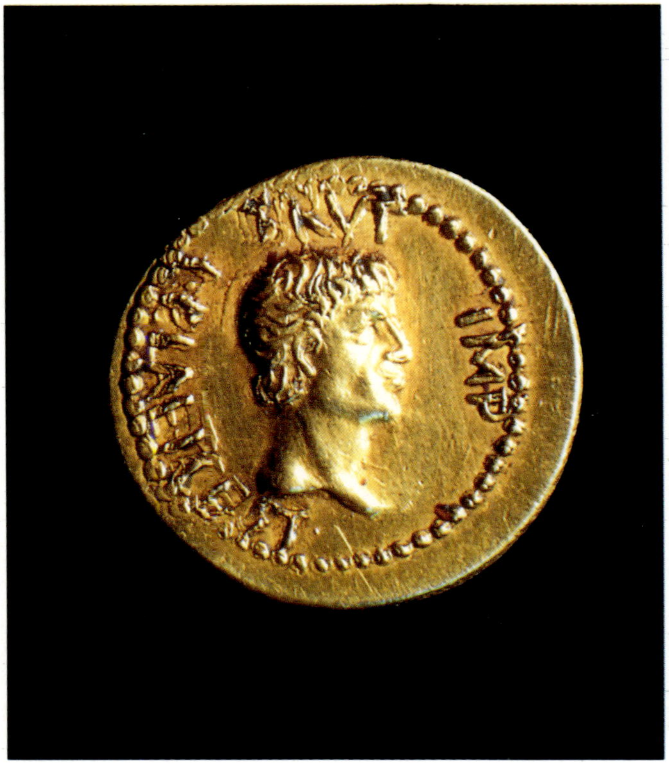

181

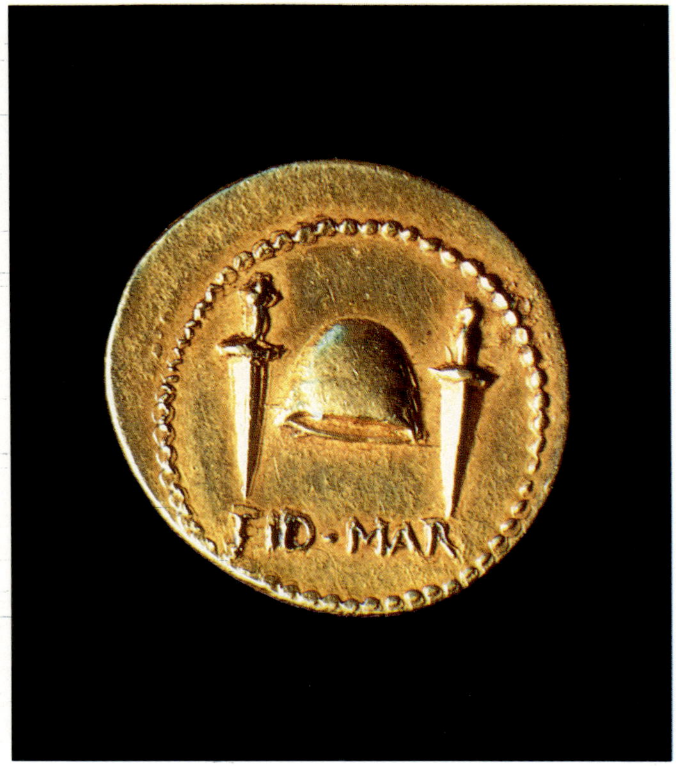

181

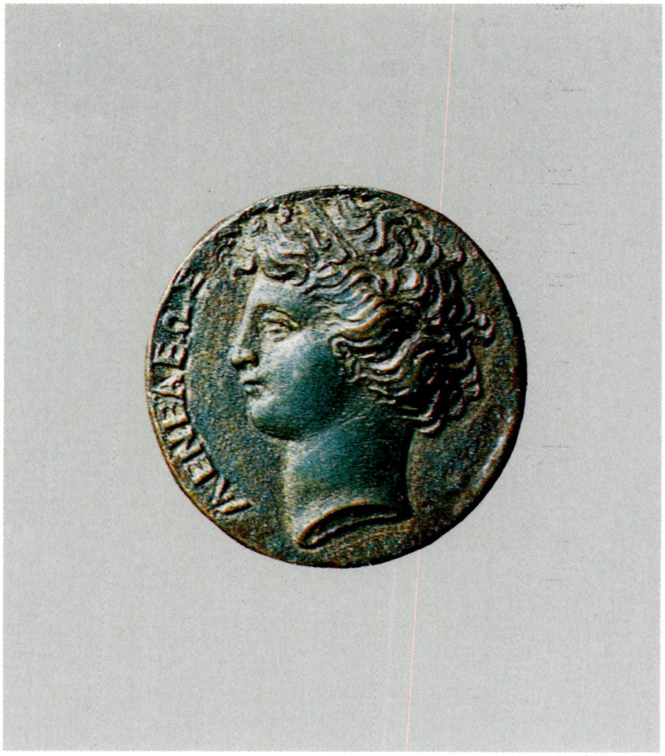

182

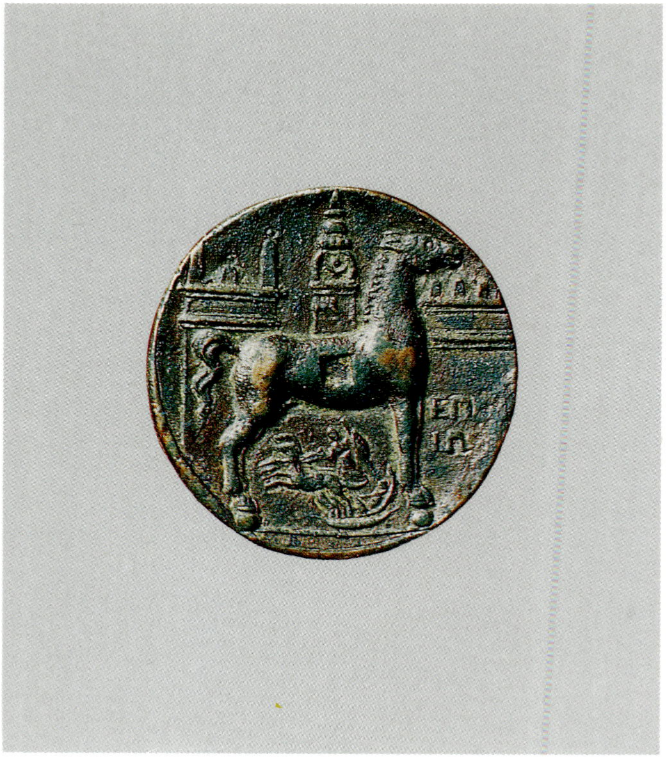

182

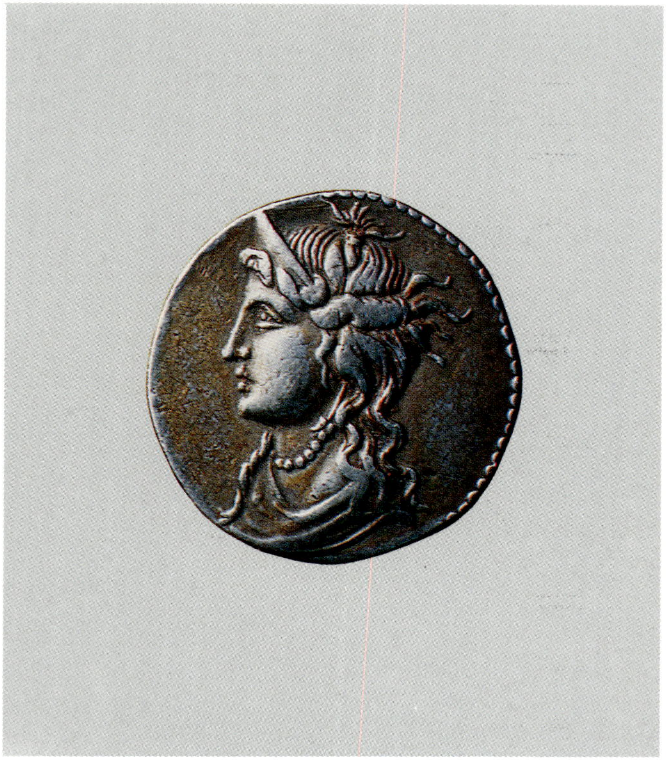

183

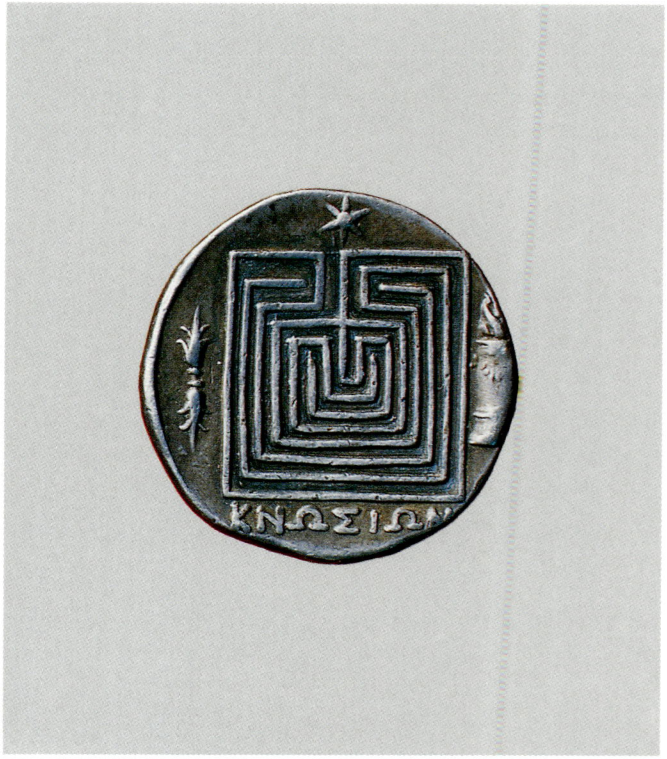

183

GLYPTICS

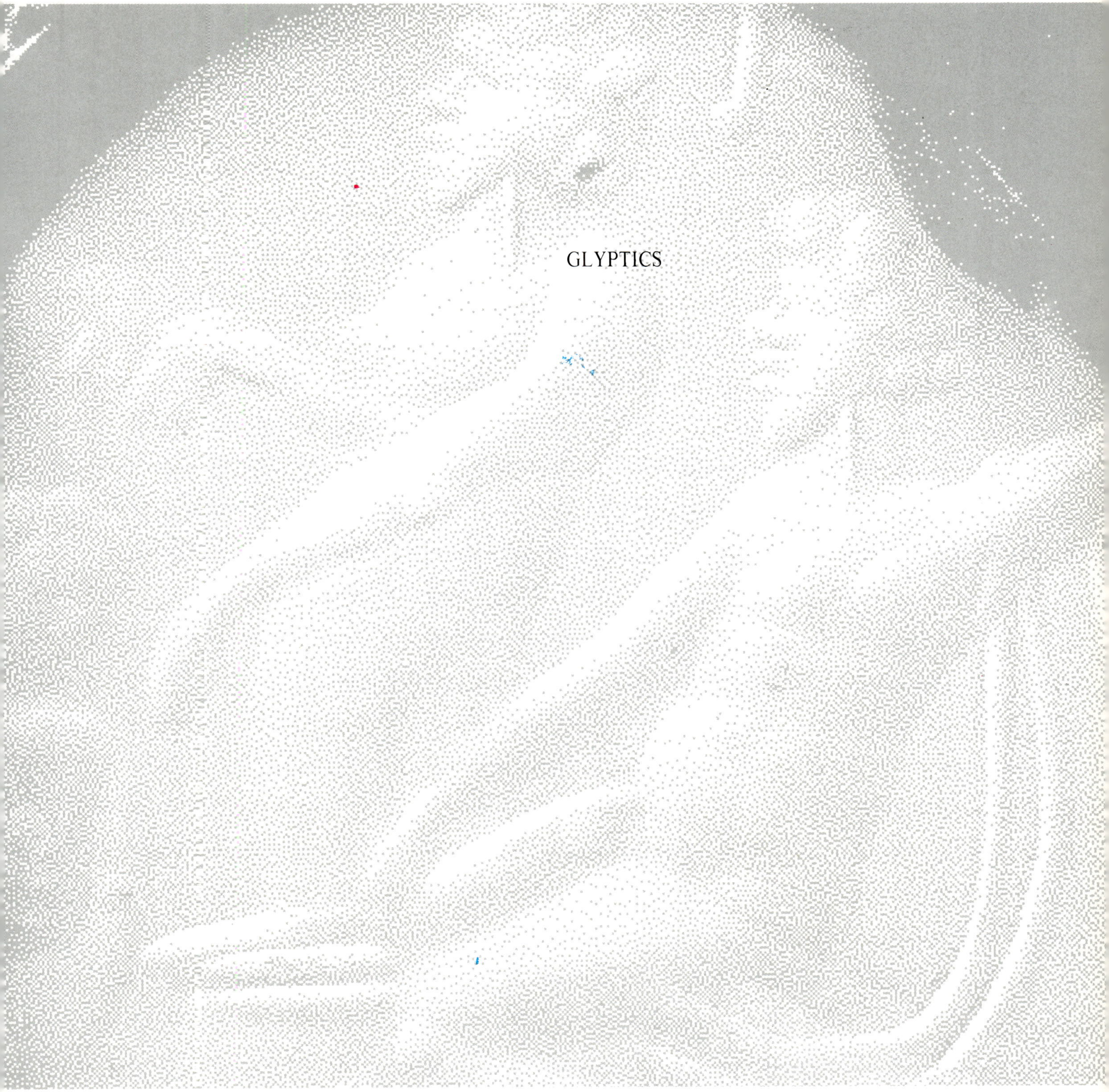

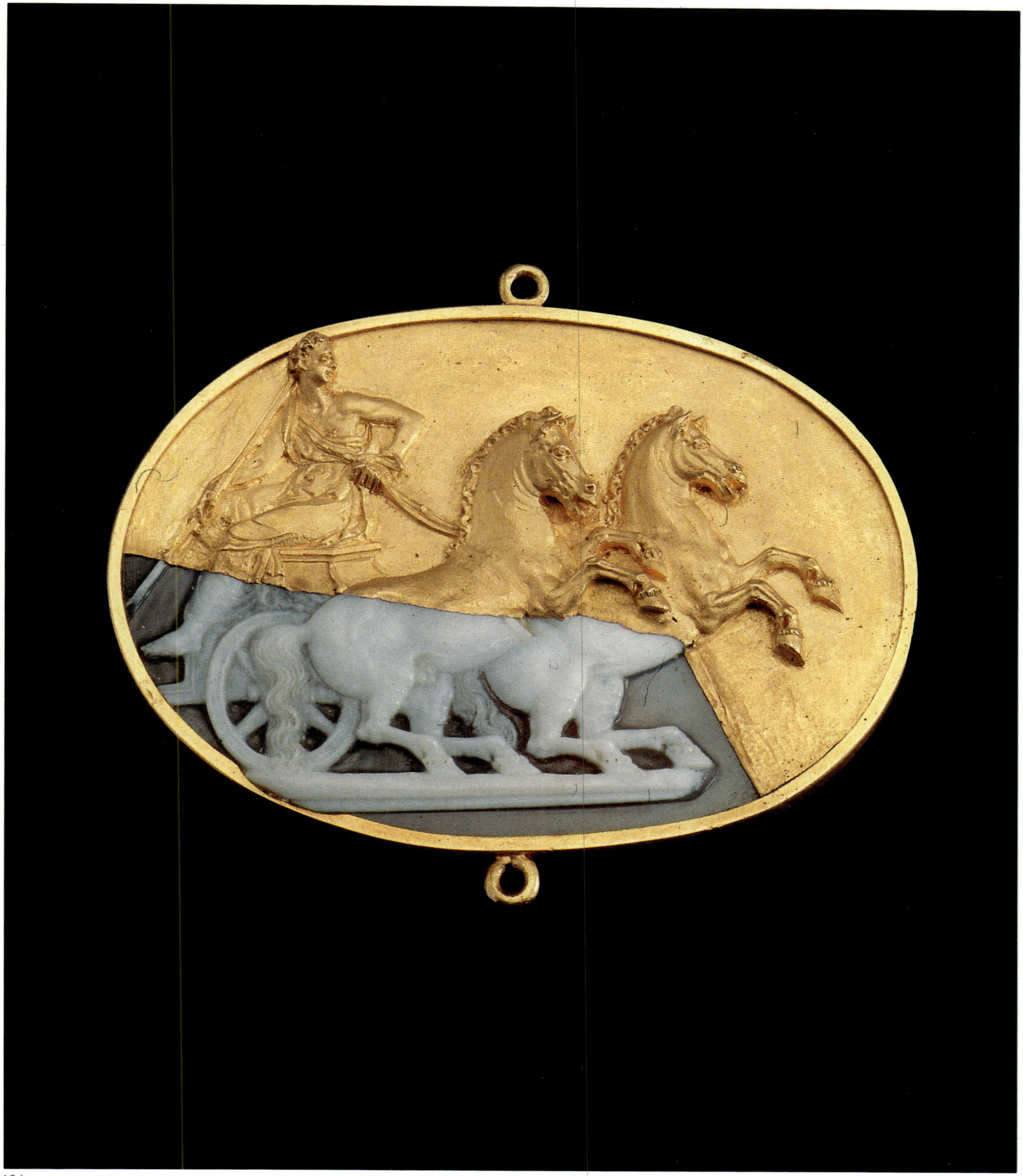

184

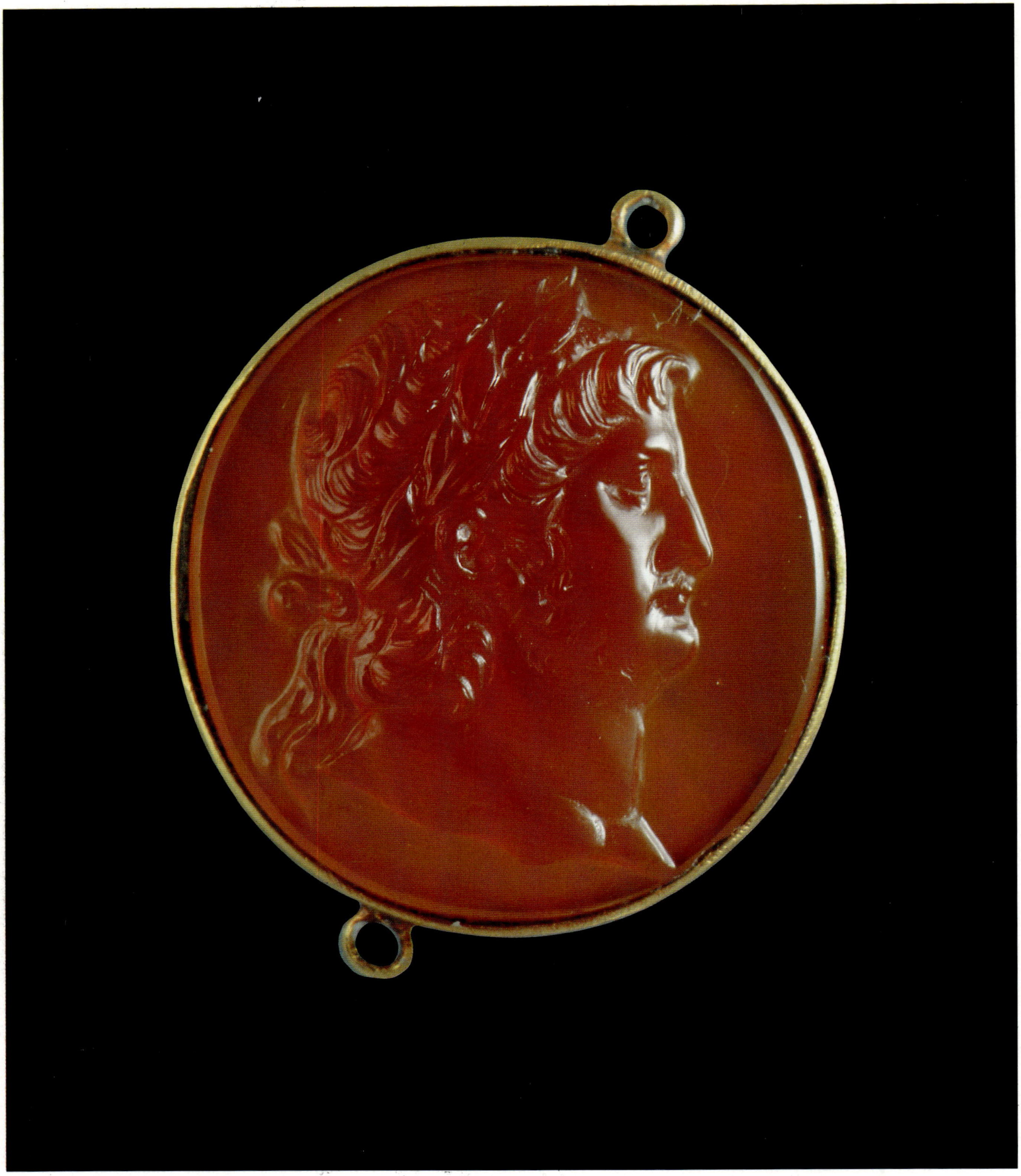

186

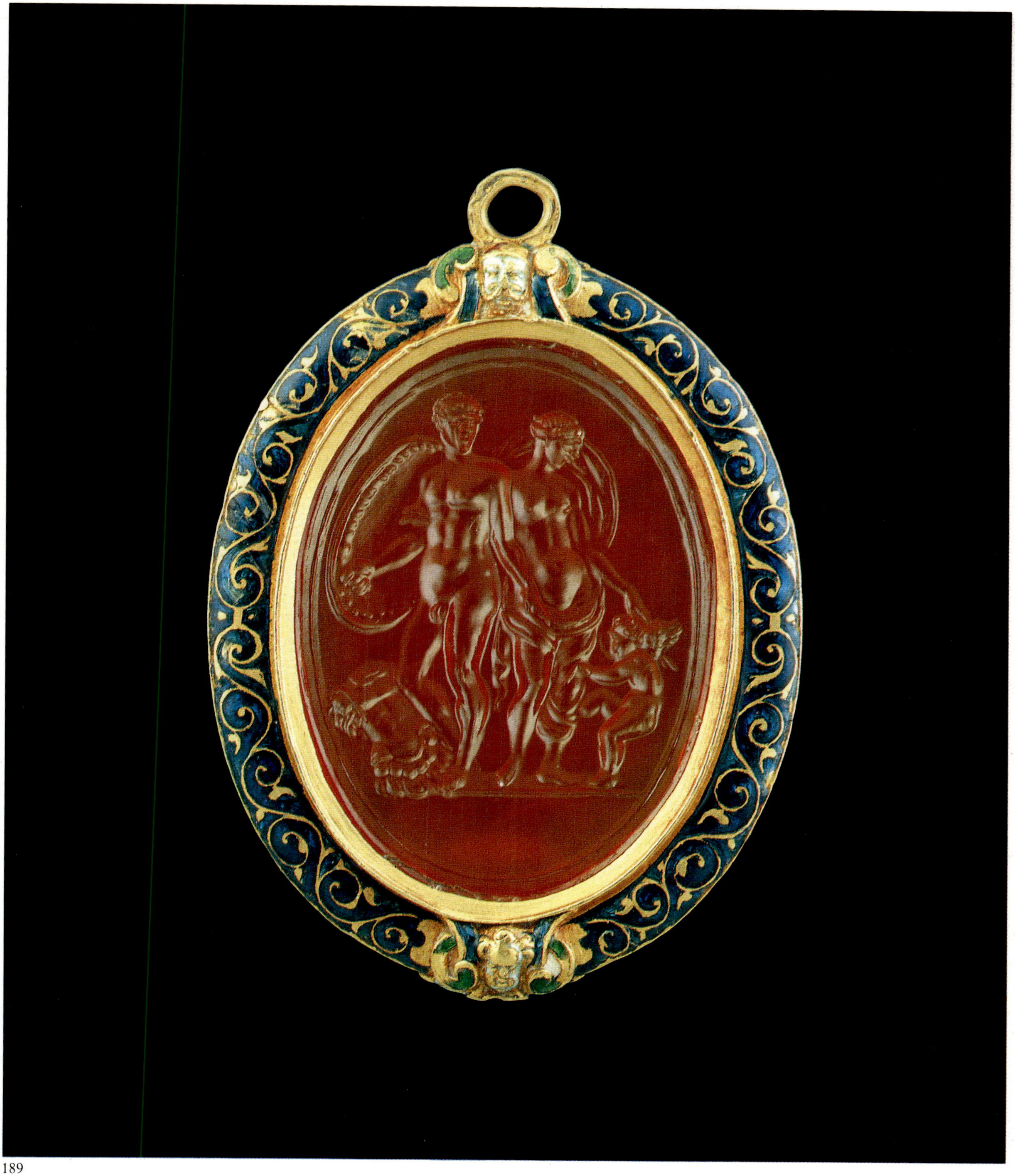

189

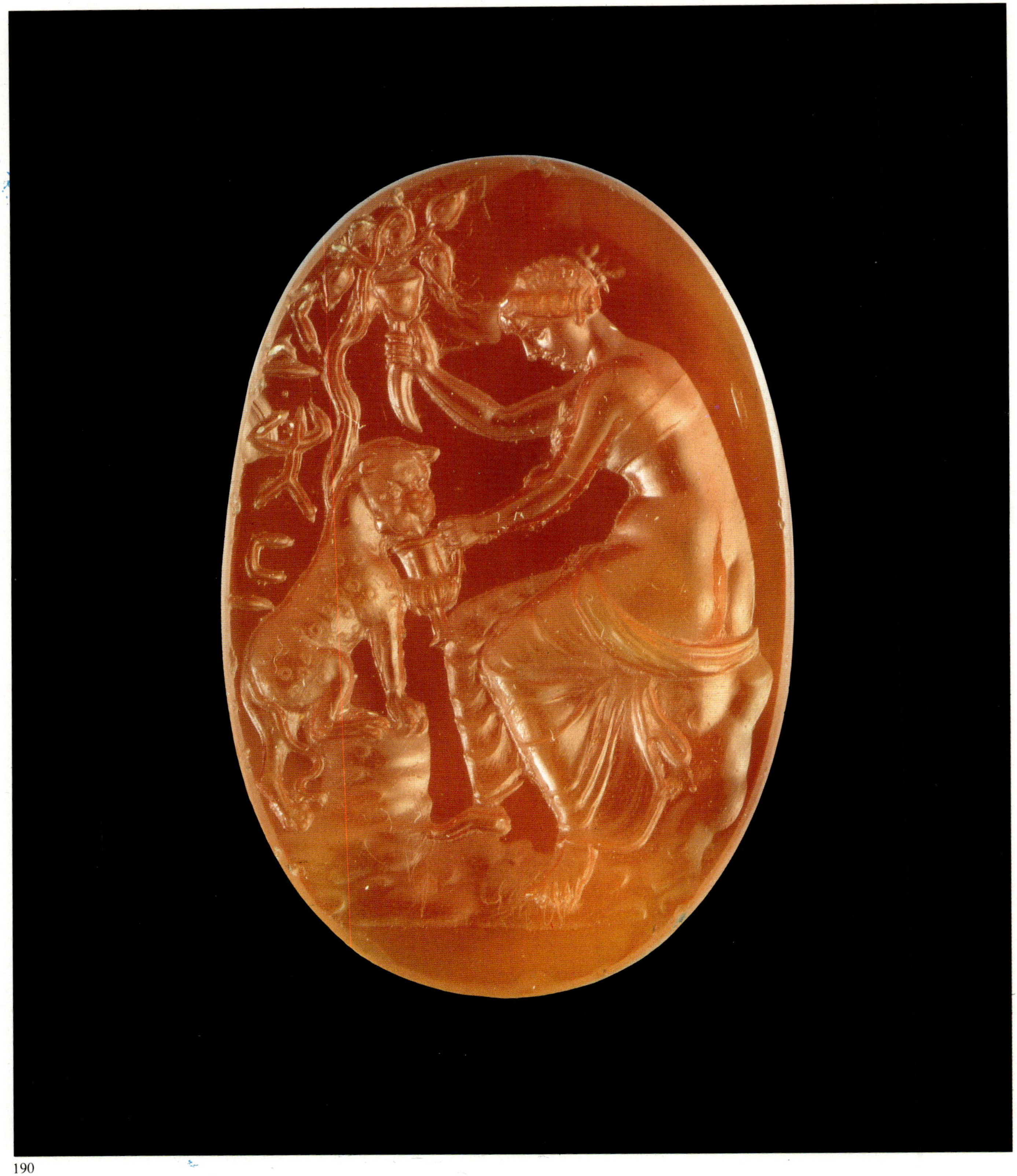

190

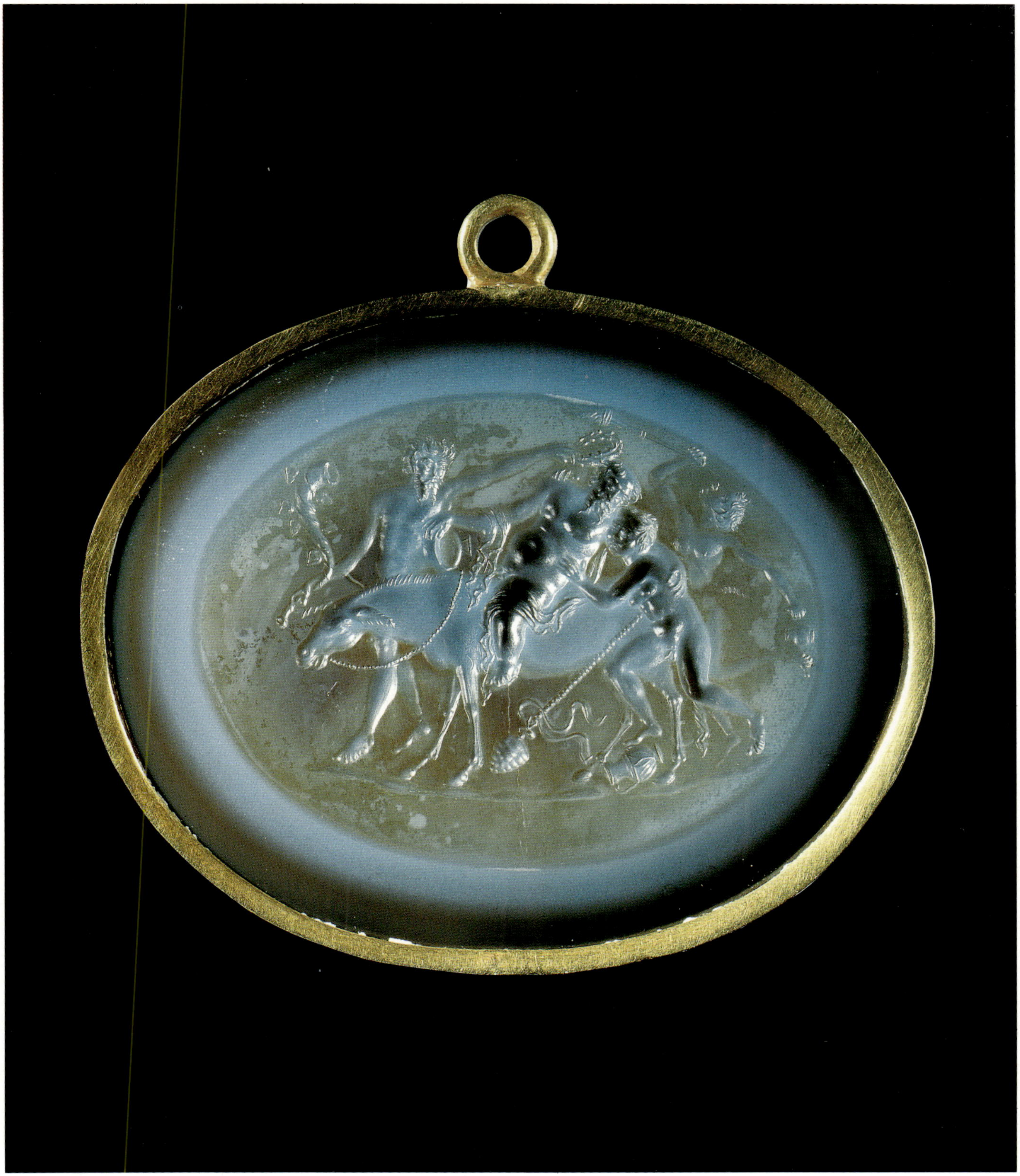

192

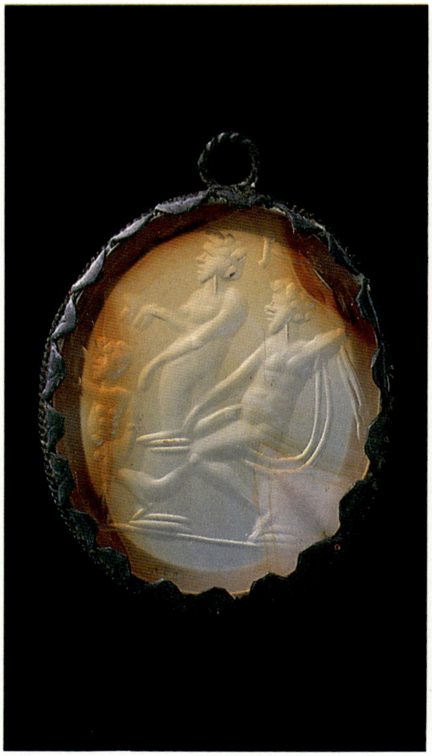
188

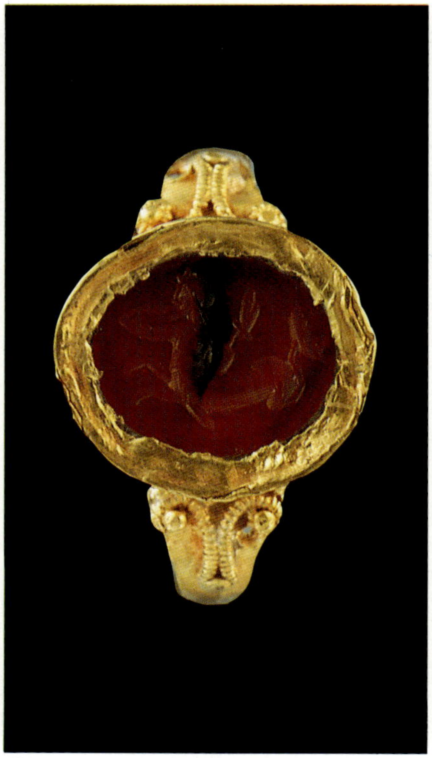
191

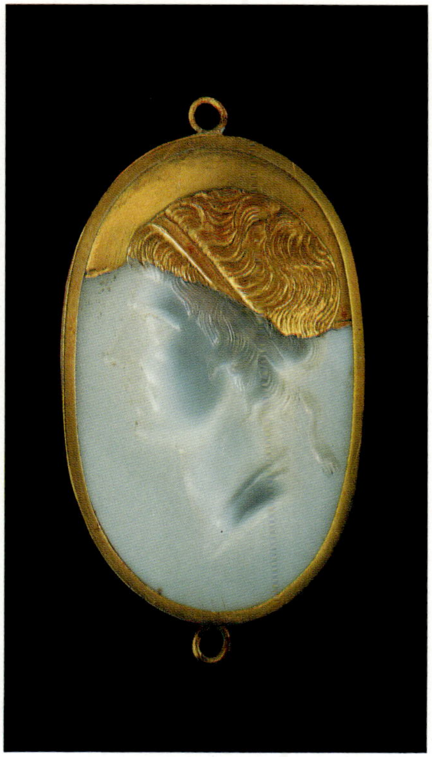
194

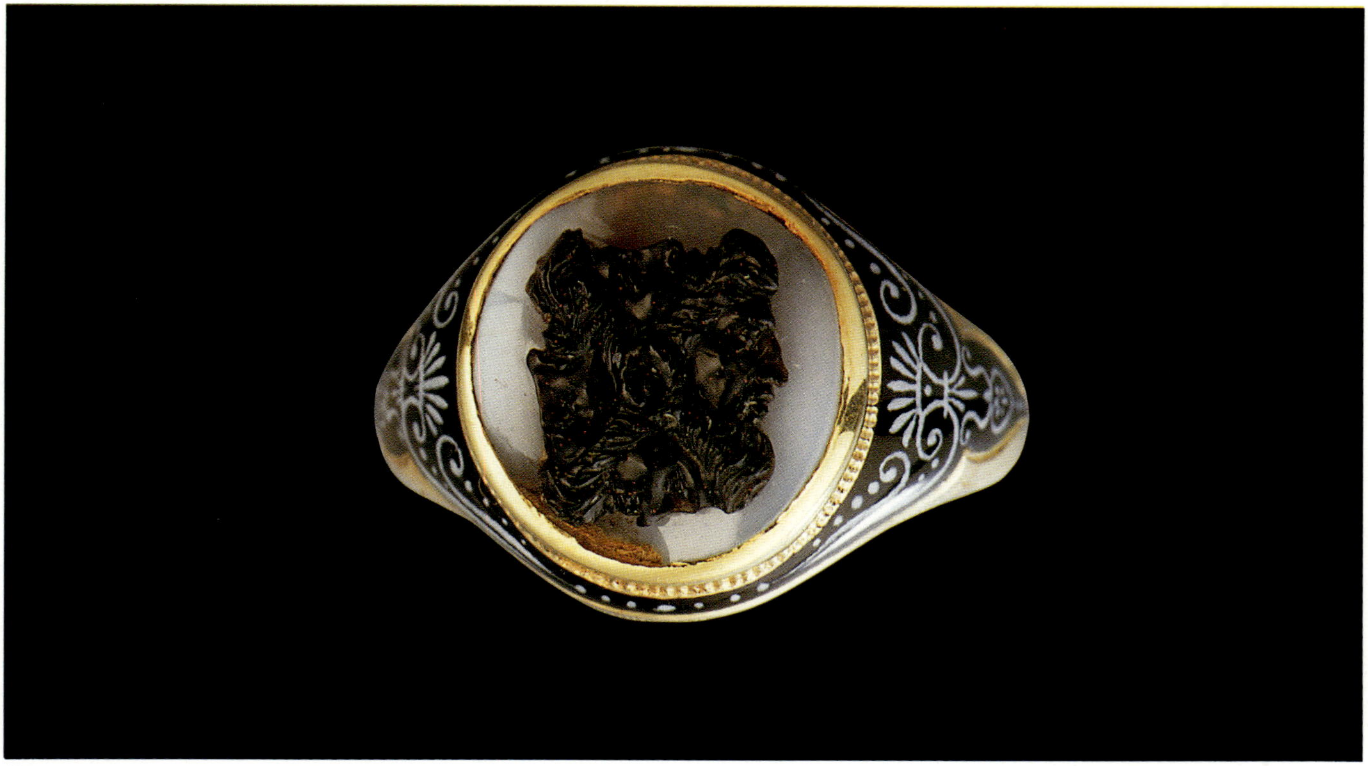
195

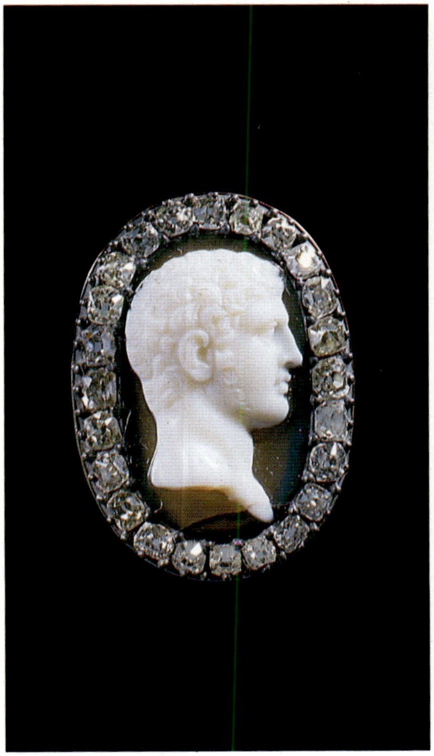
197

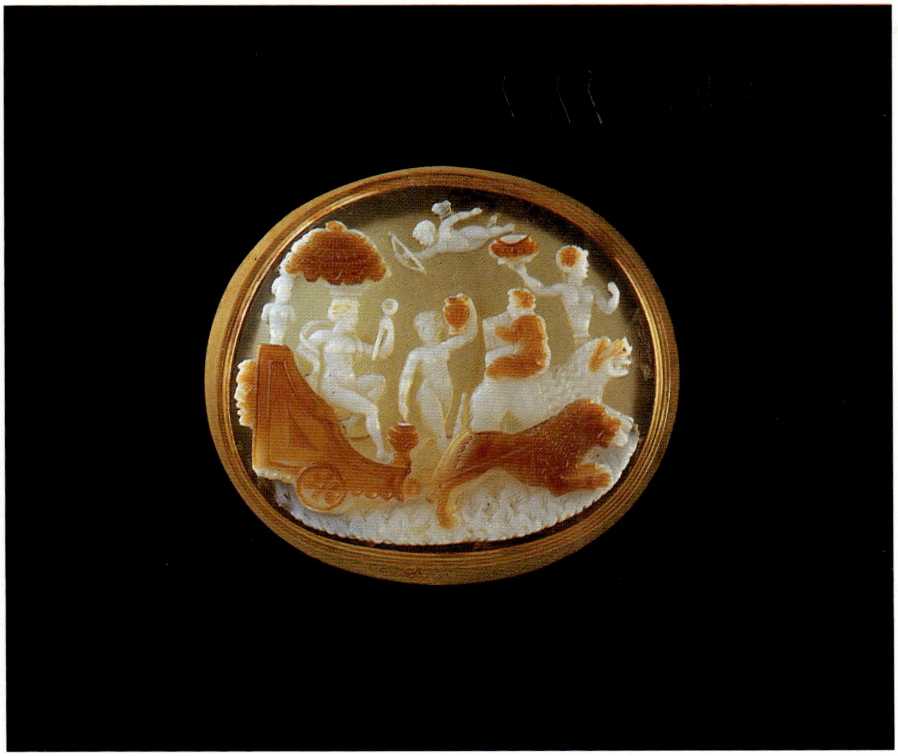
199

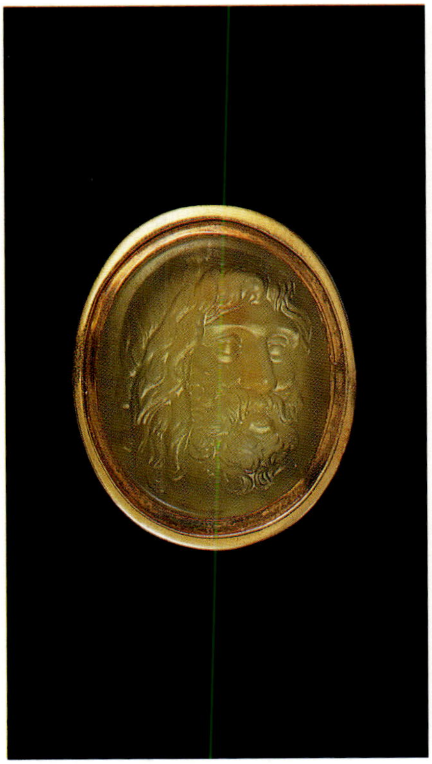
201

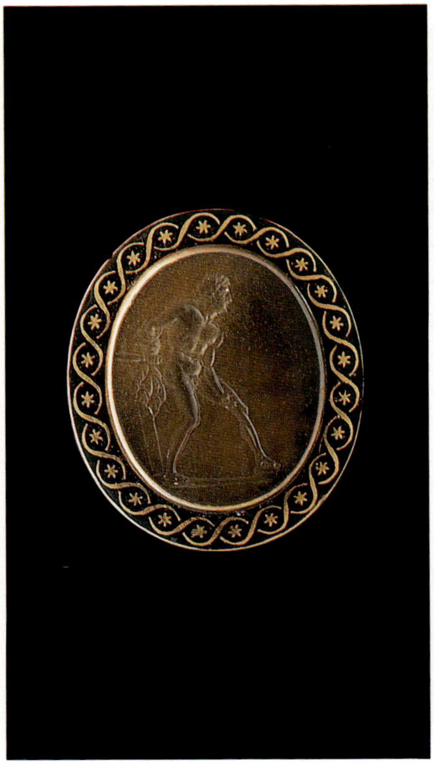
202

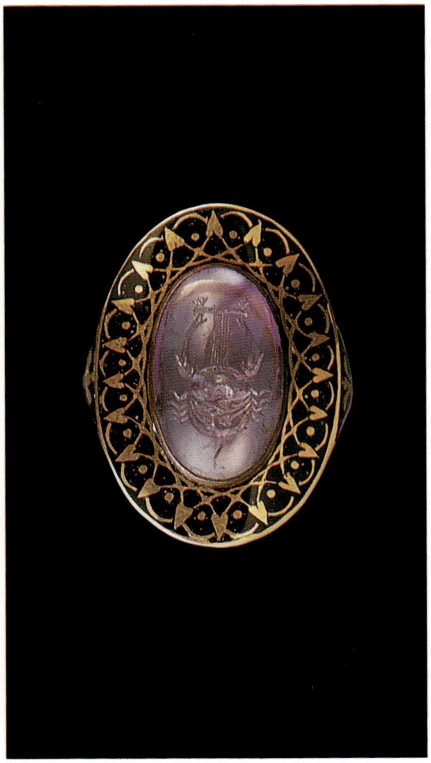
203

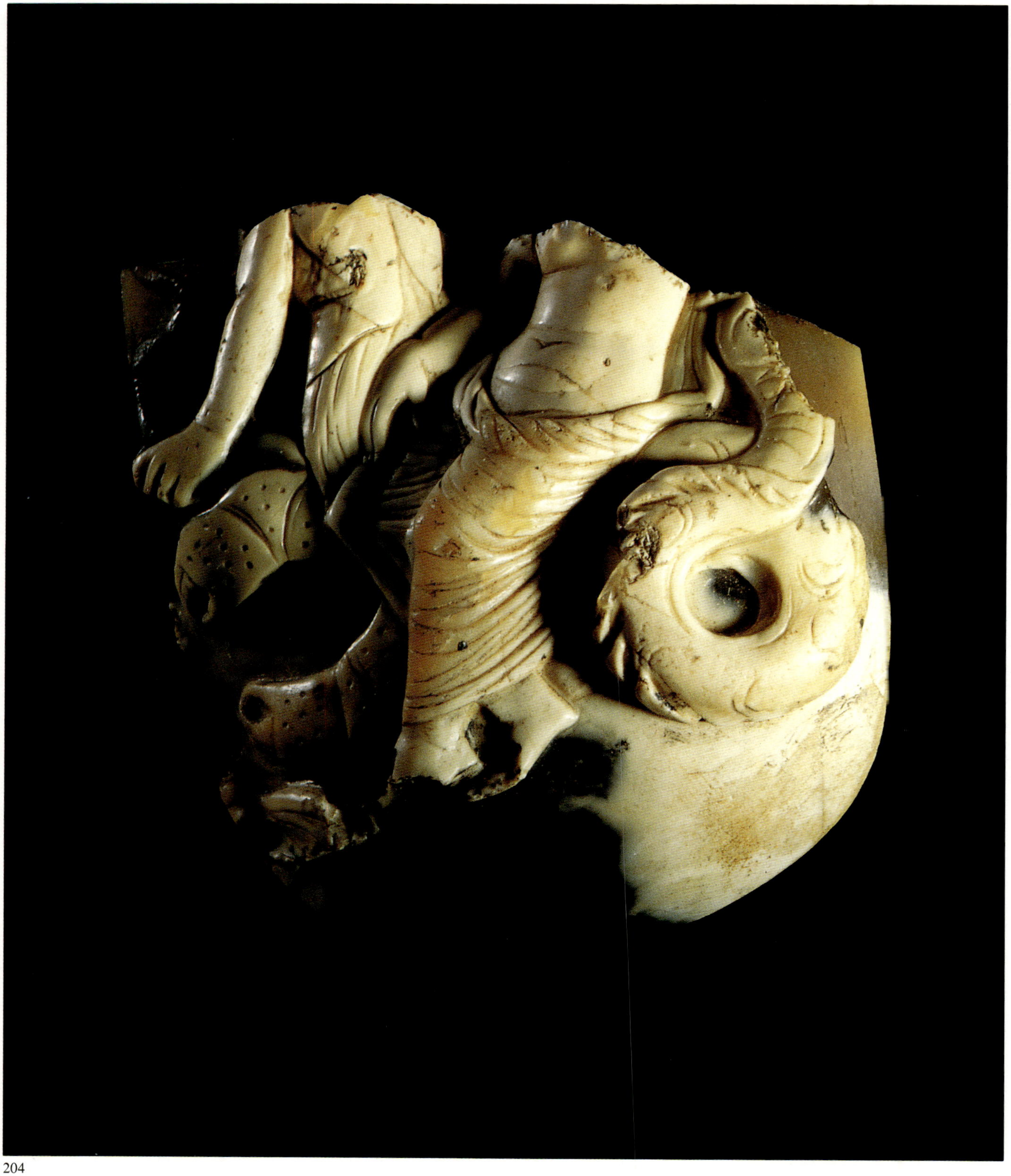

204

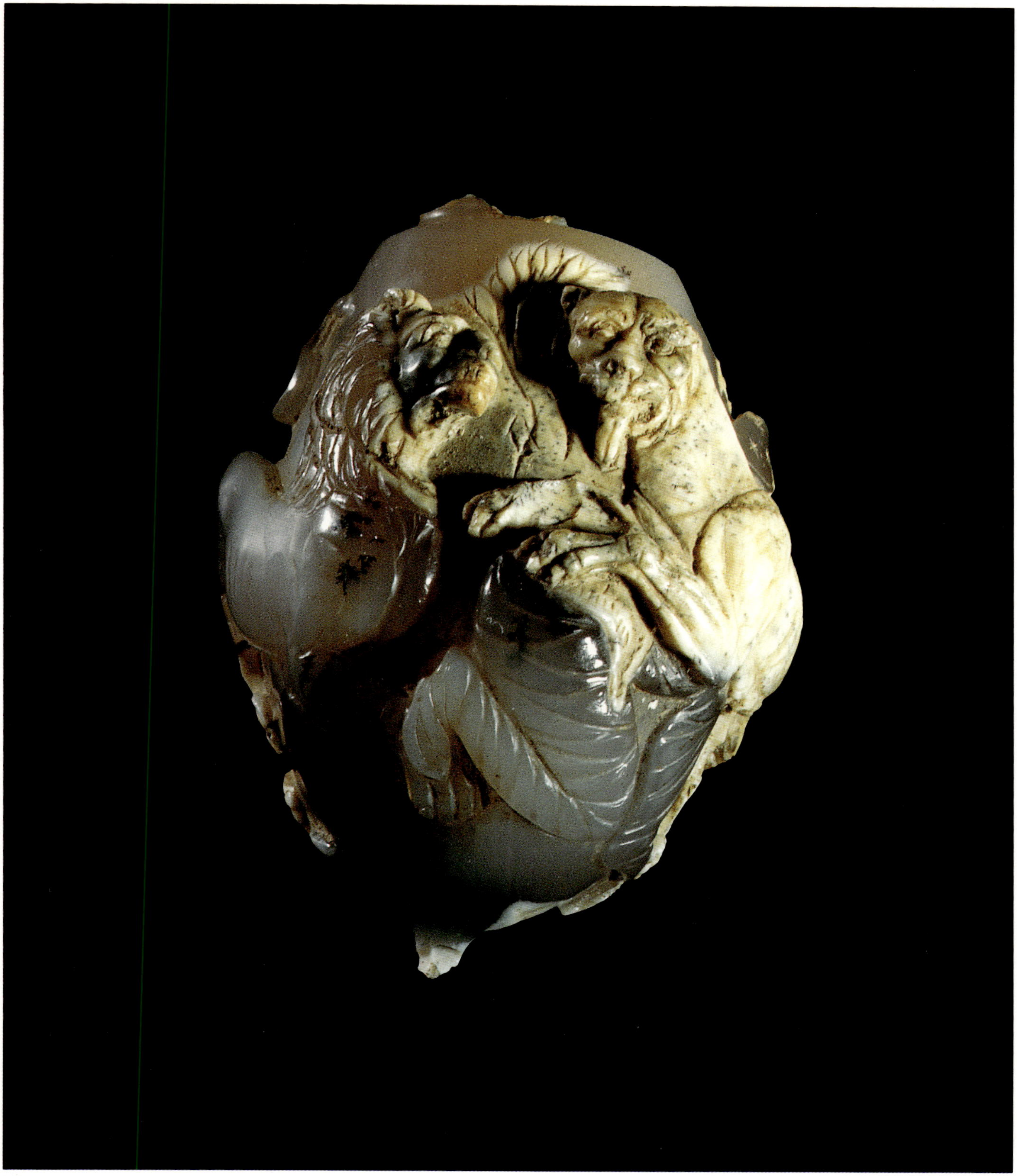

205

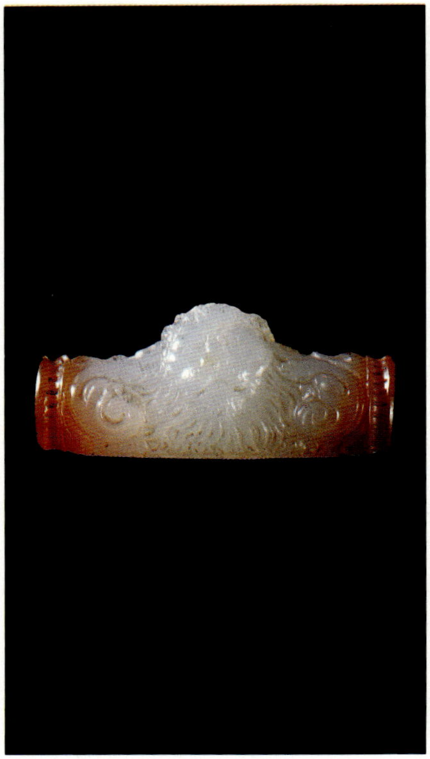
206

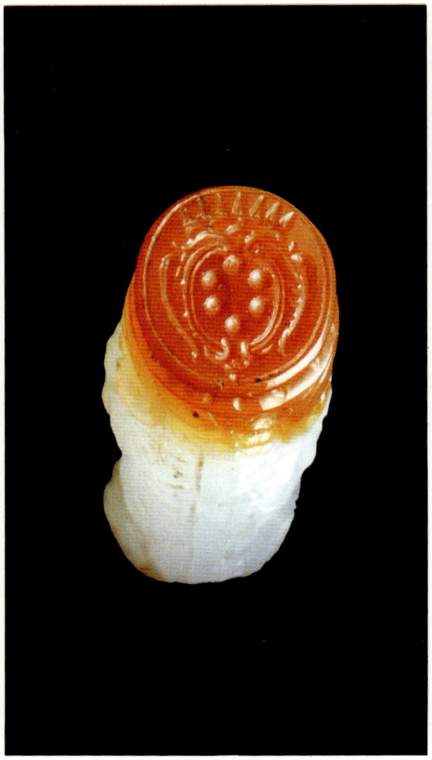
206

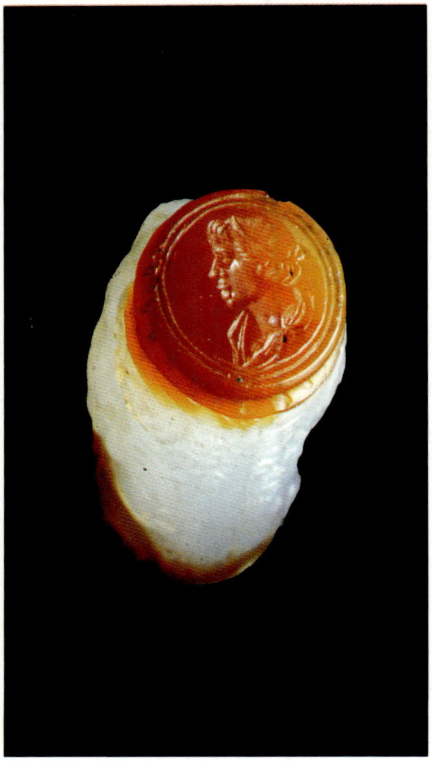
206

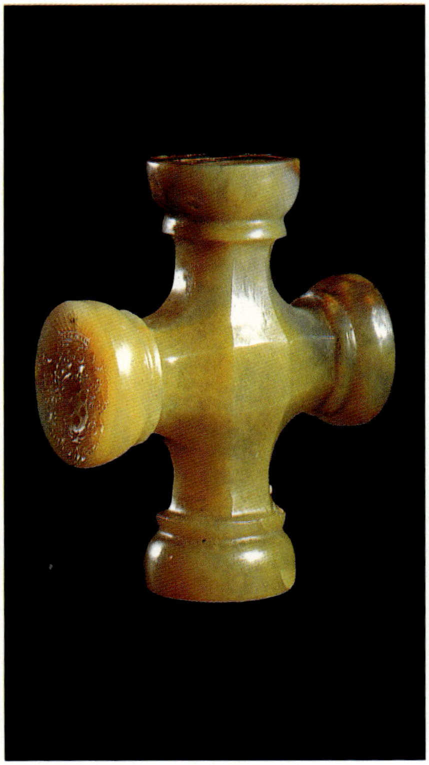
207

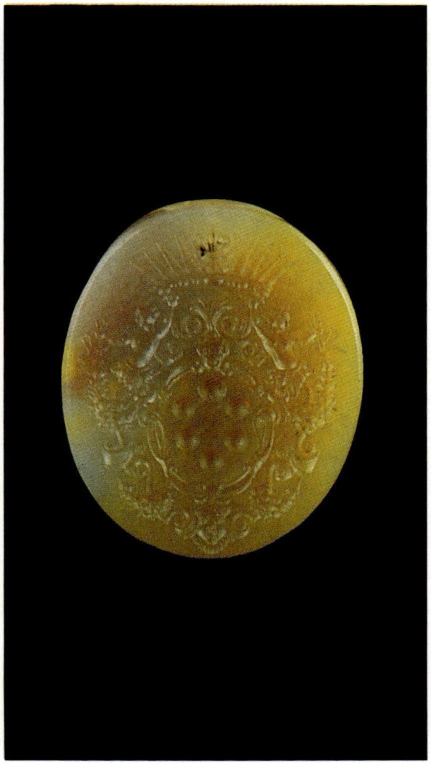
207

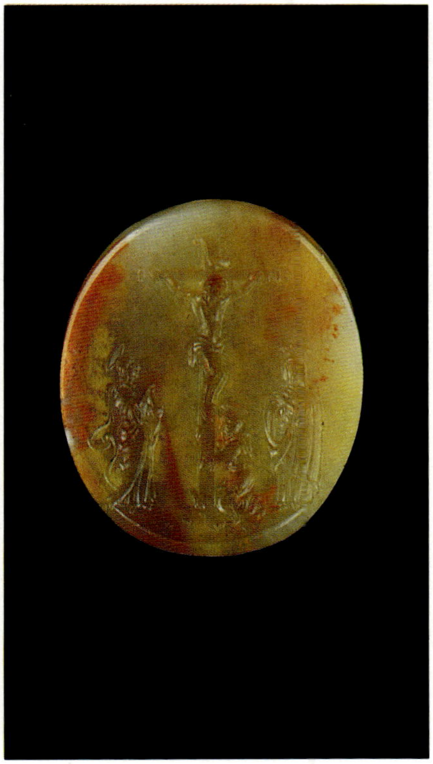
207

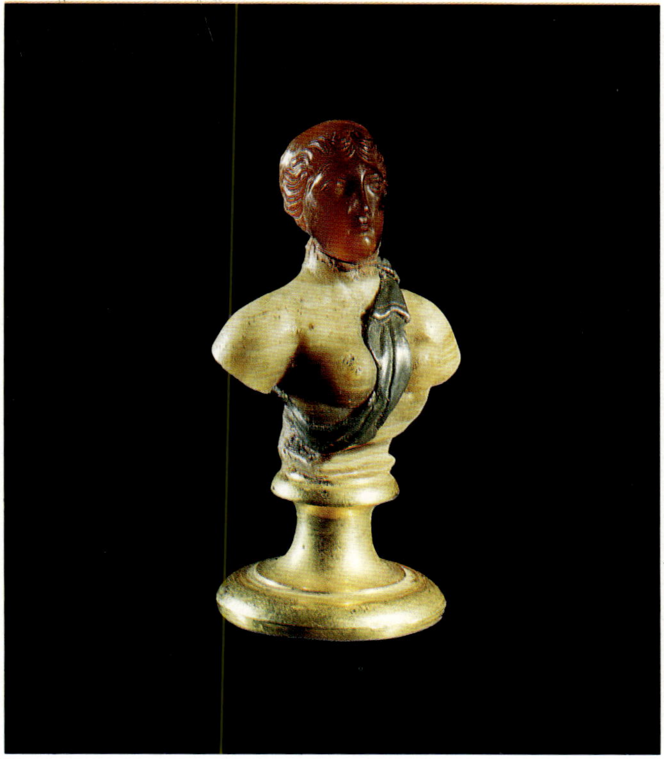
208

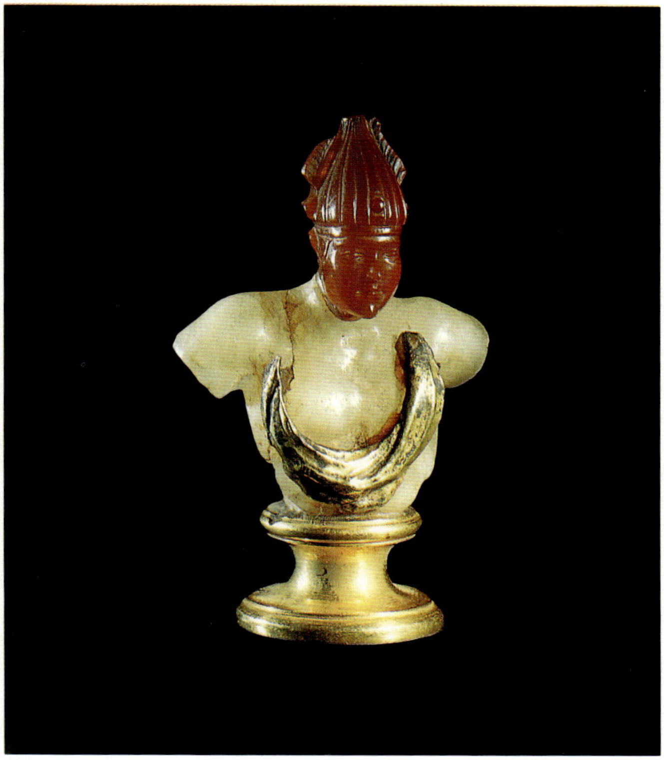
209

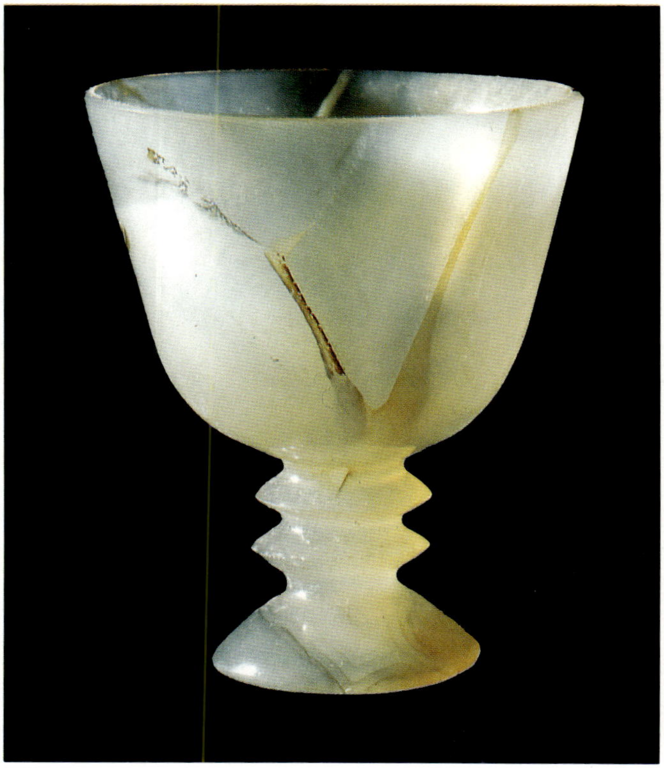
210

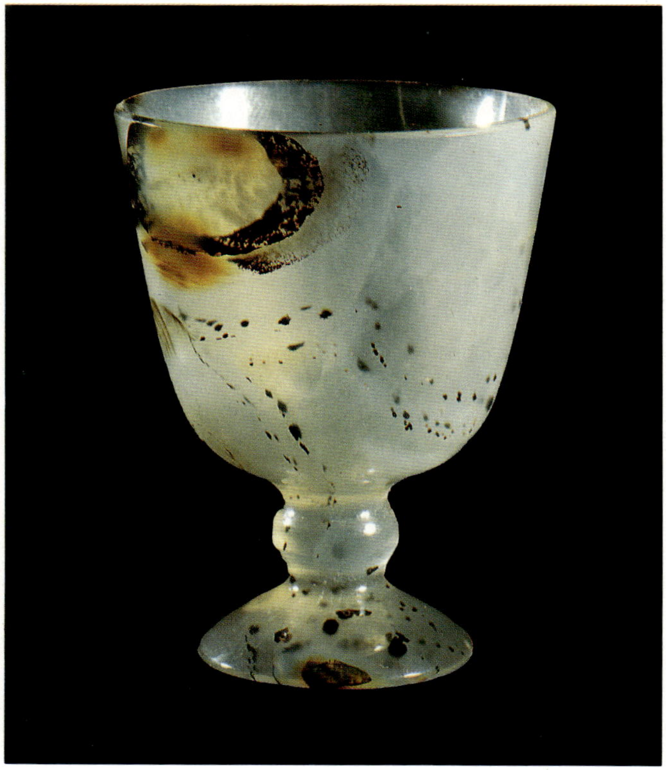
211

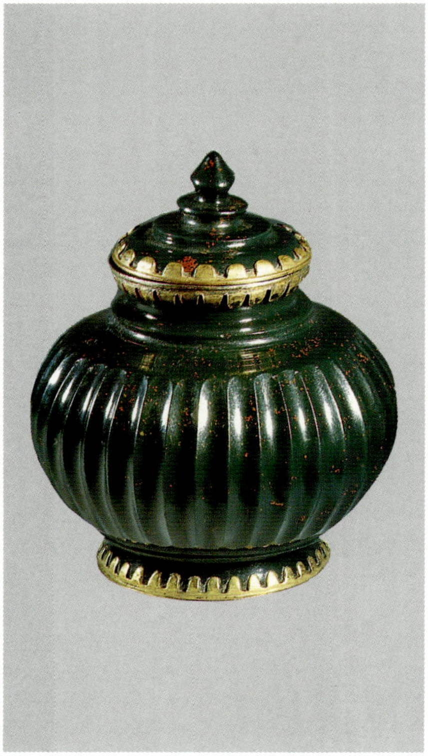
212

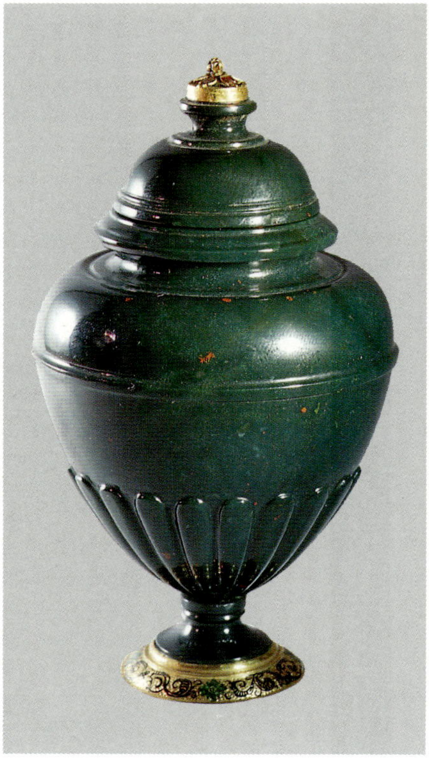
213

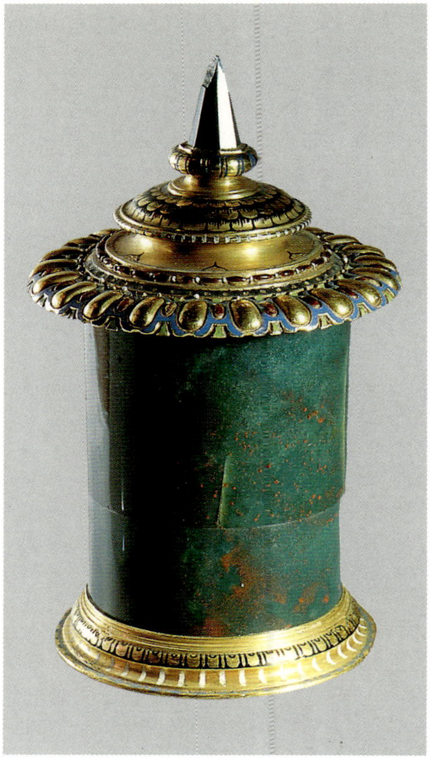
214

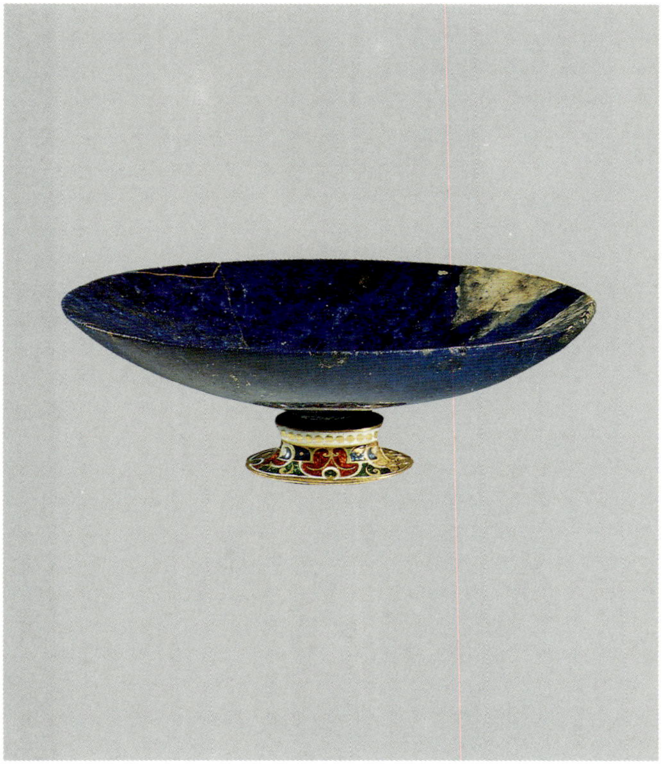
216

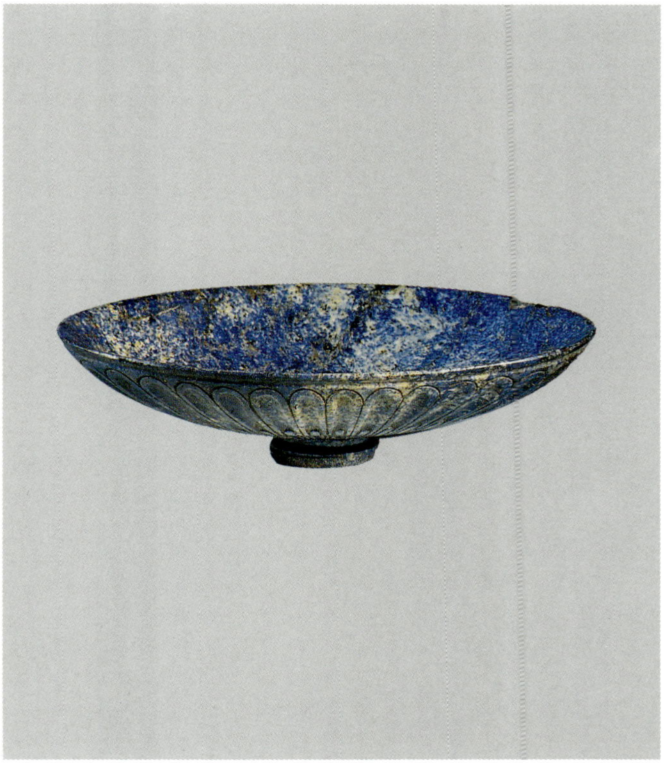
217

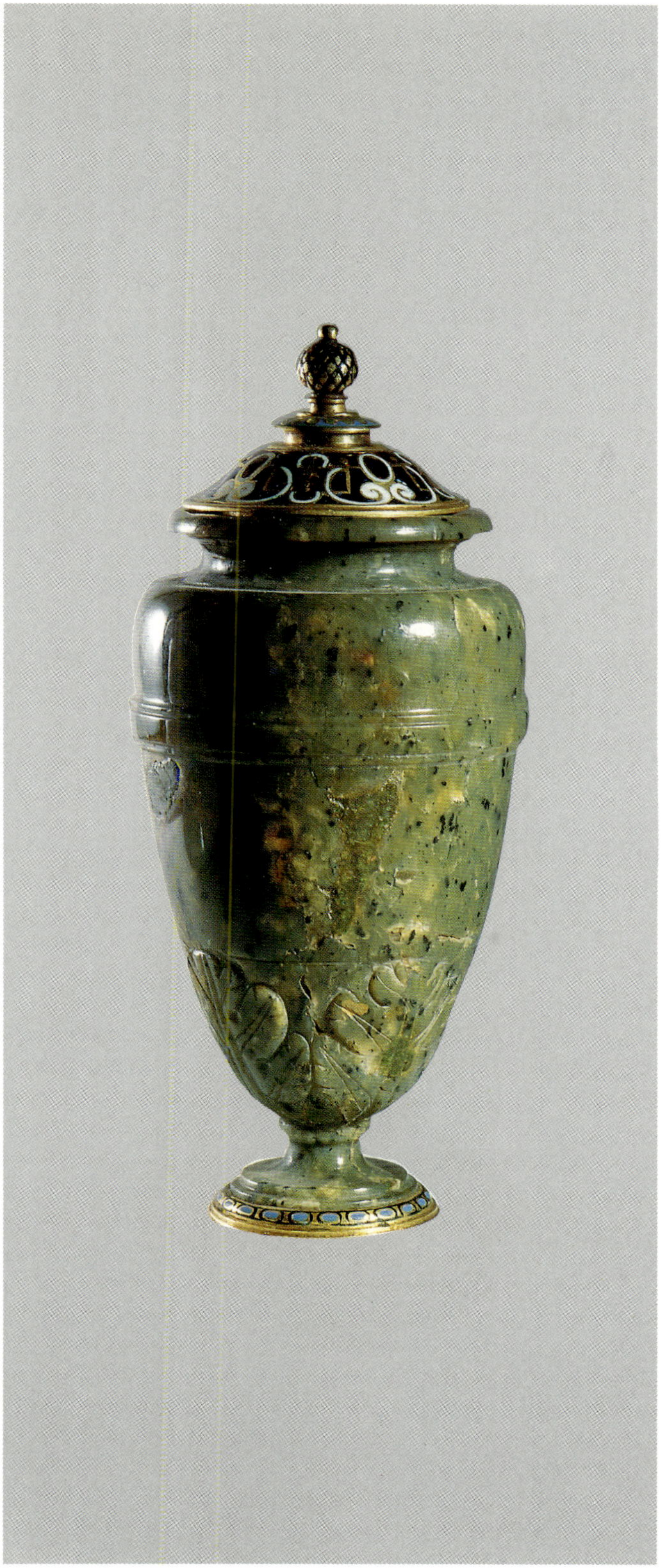
218

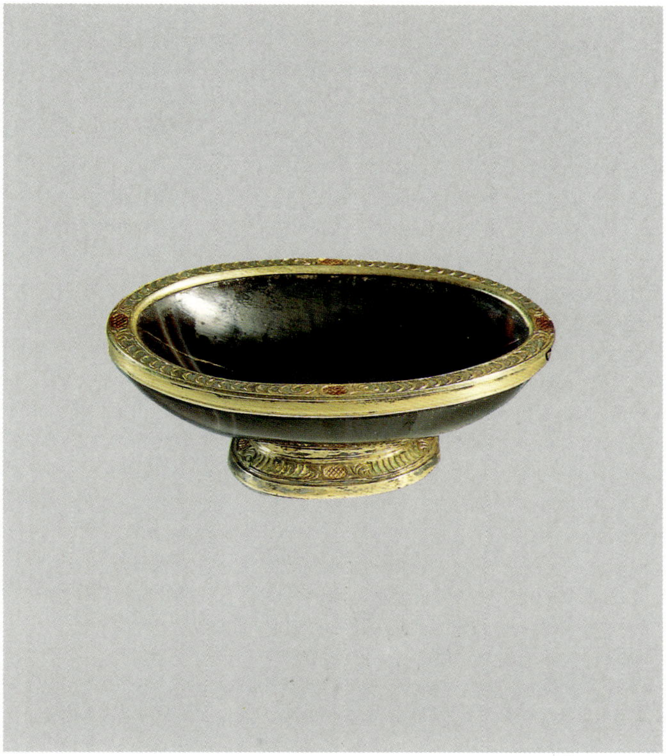
219

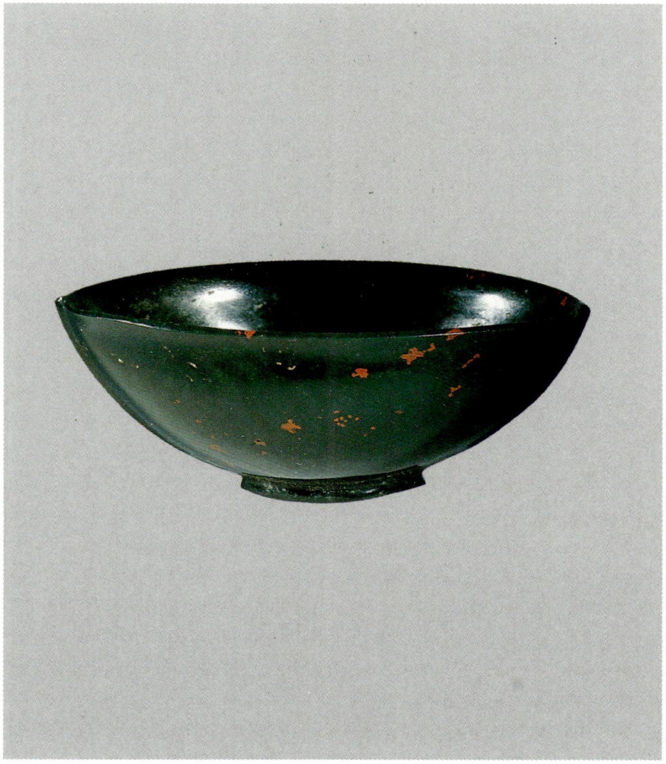
220

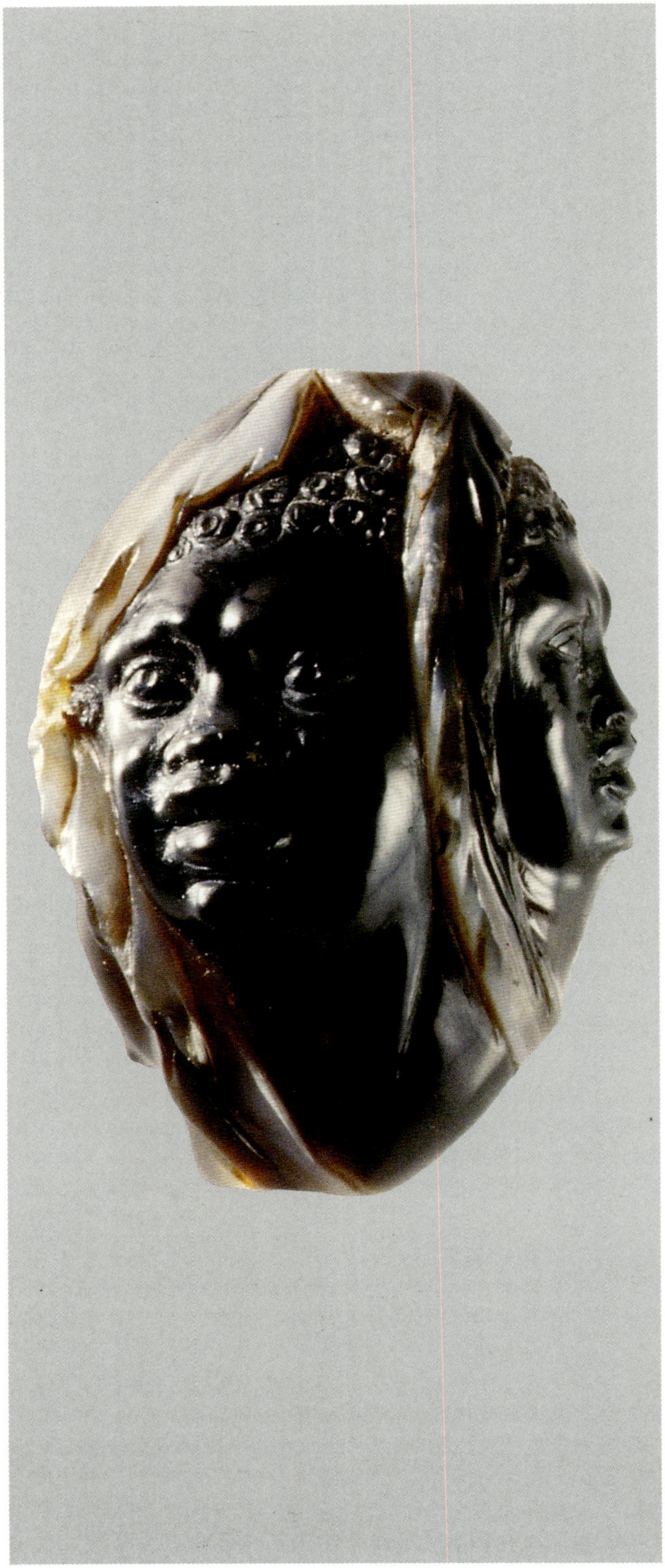

221

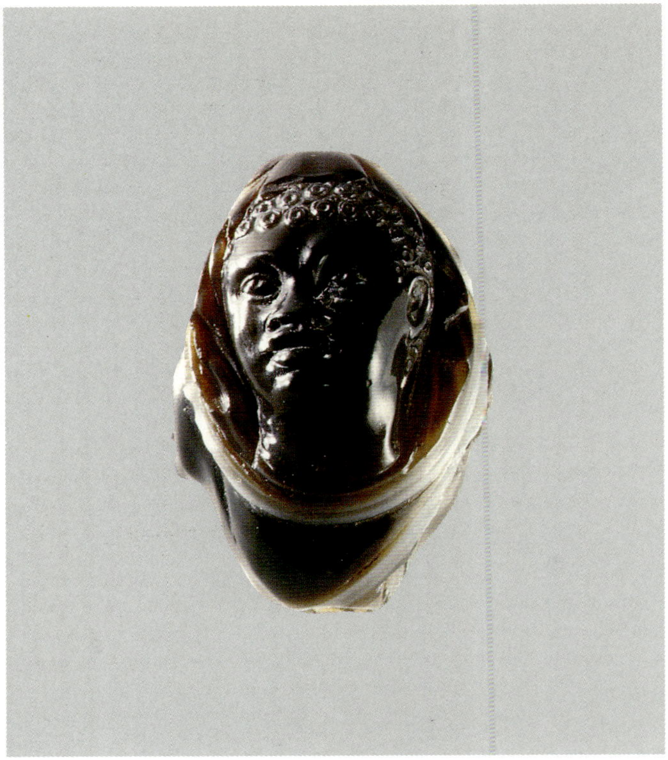

221

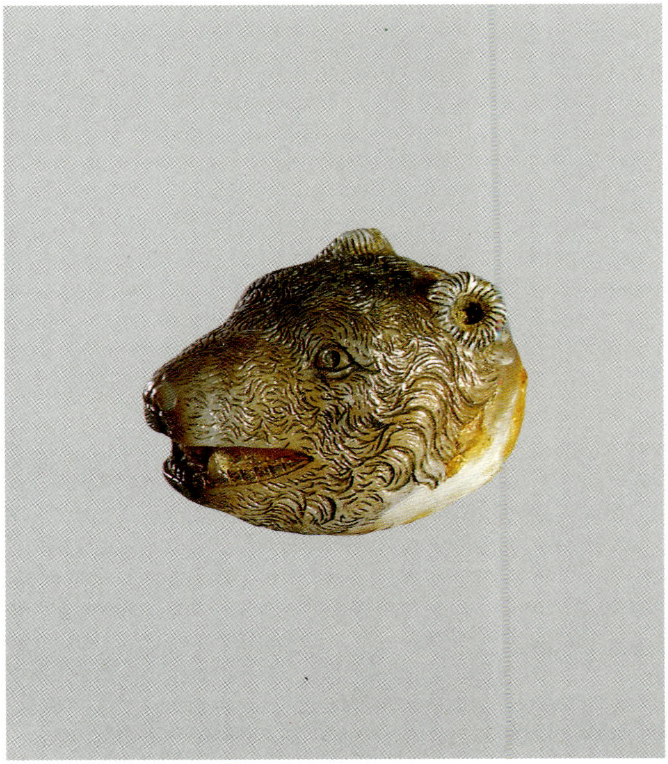

222

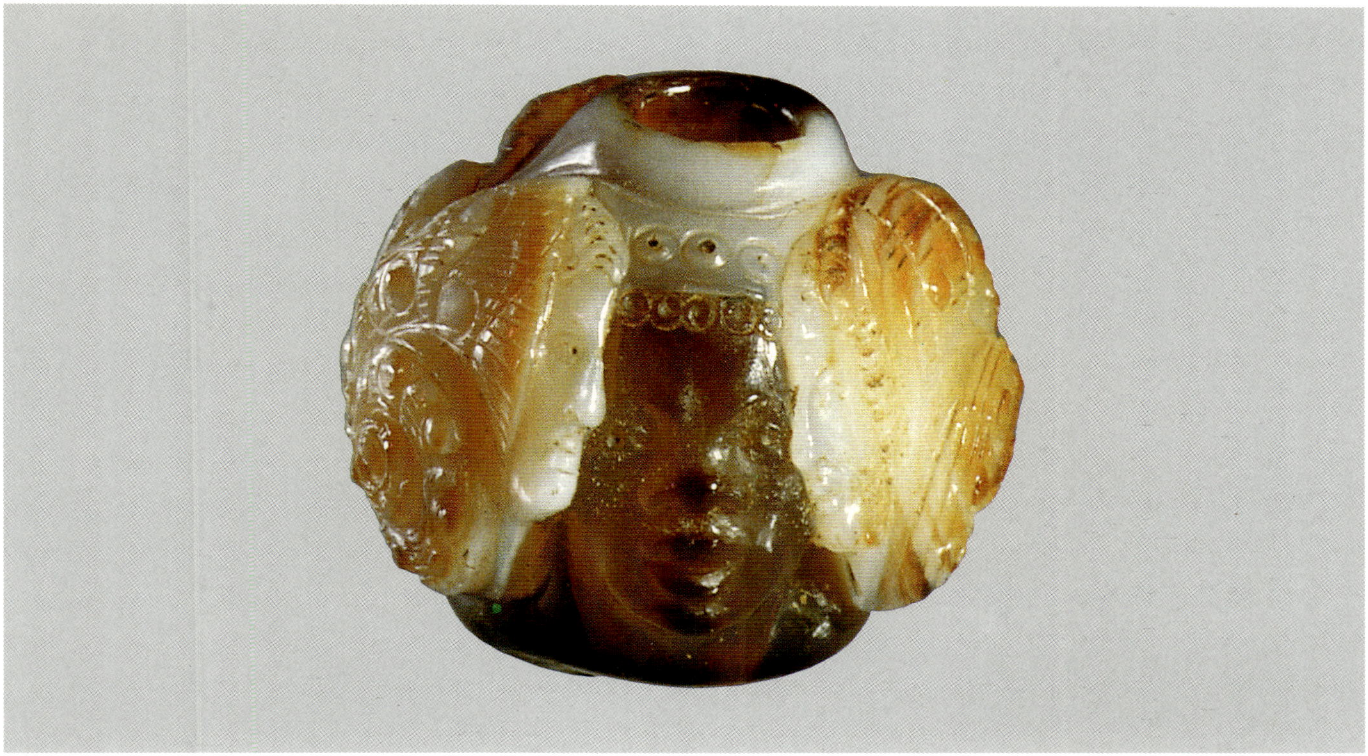
223

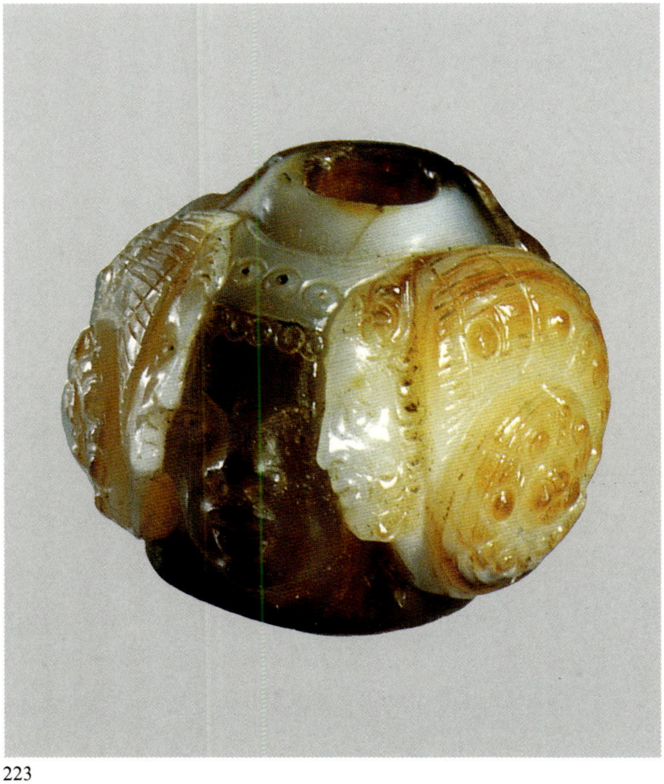
223

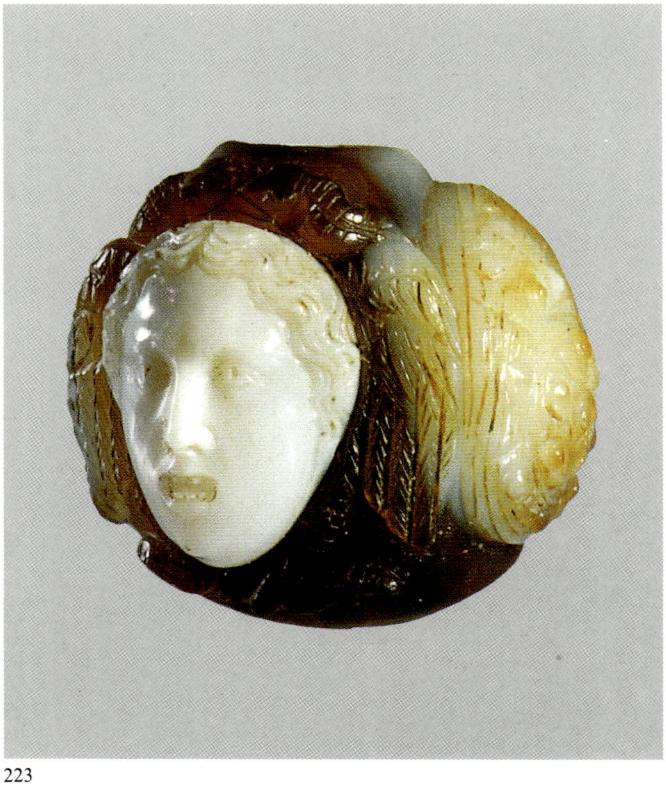
223

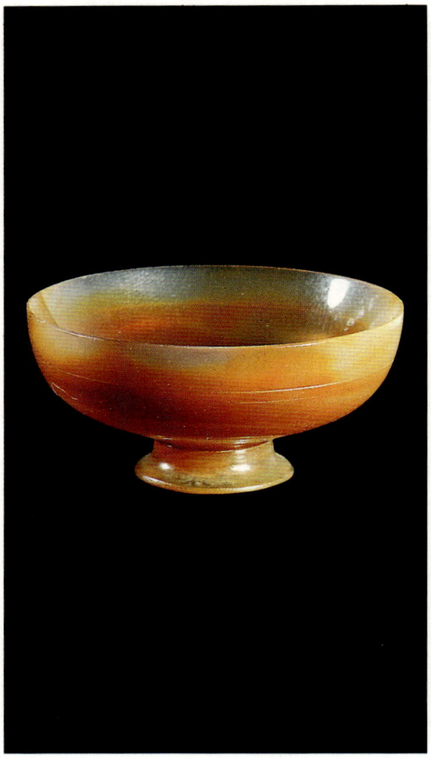
224

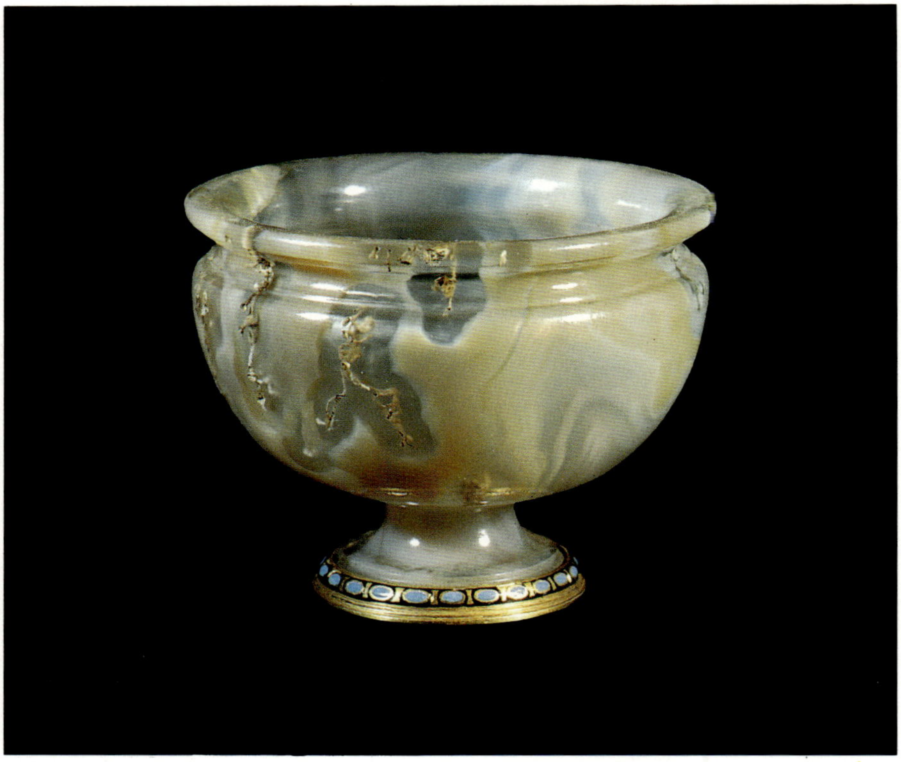
225

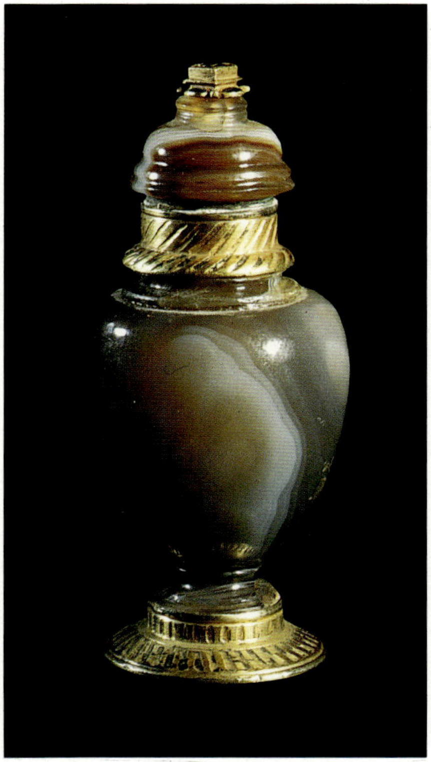
226

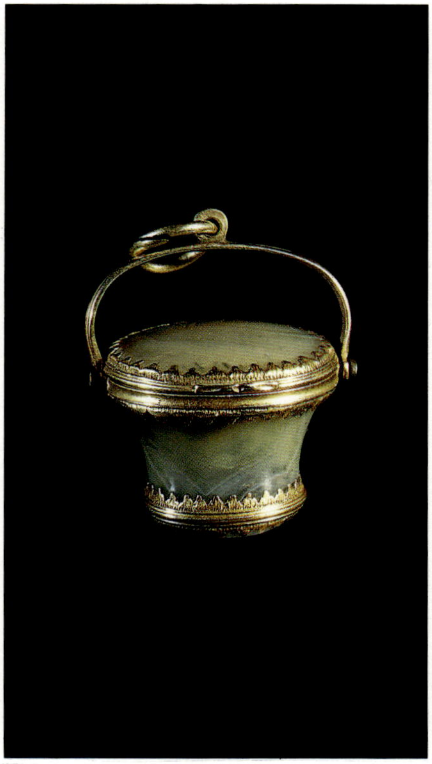
227

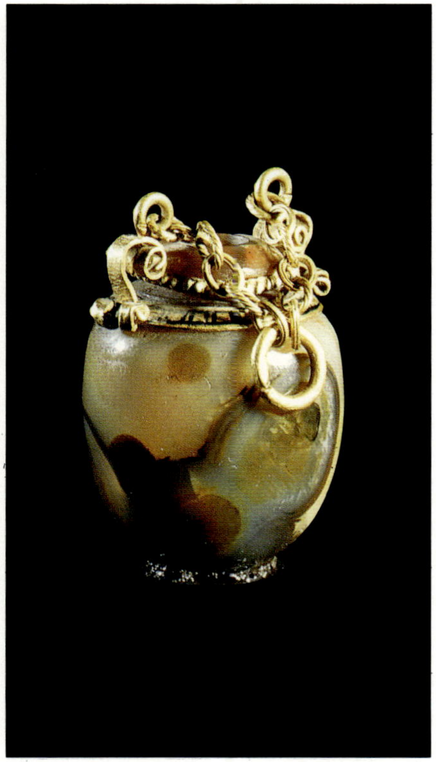
228

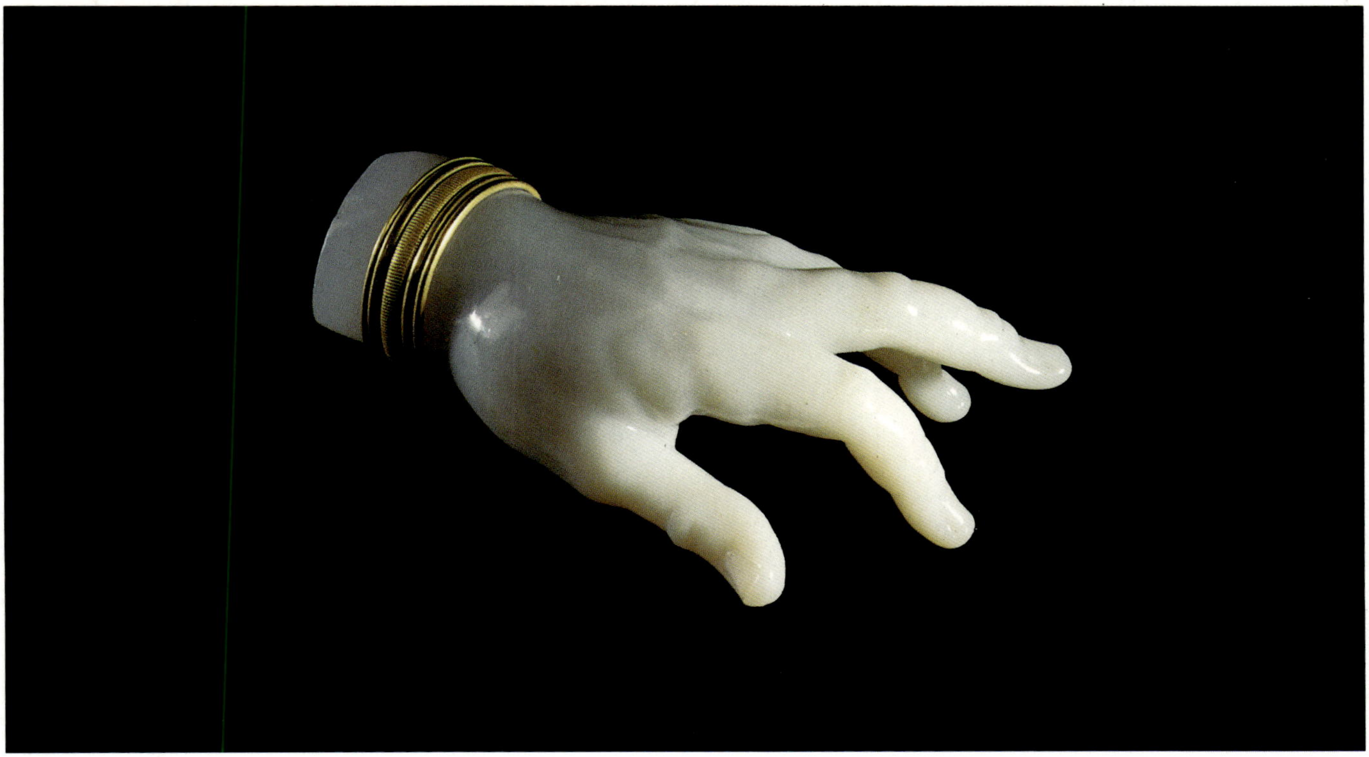

229

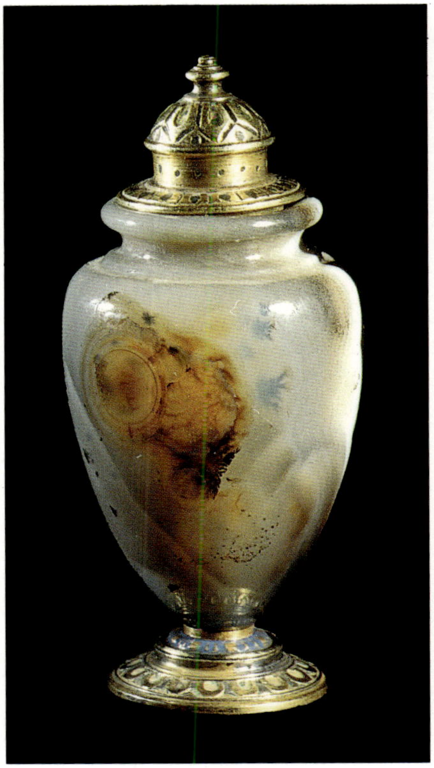

230

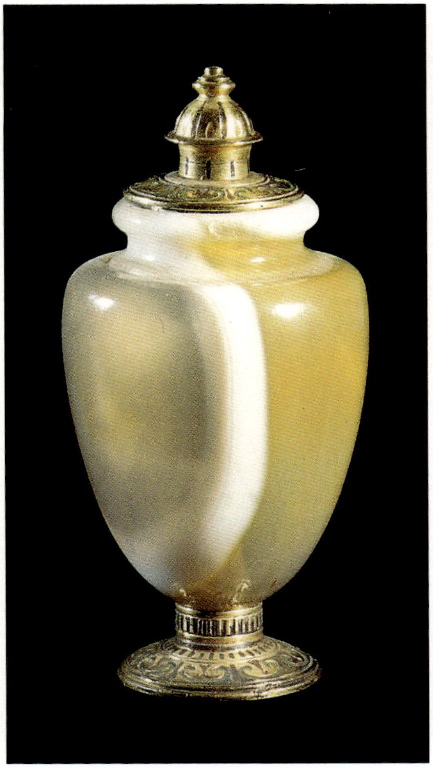

231

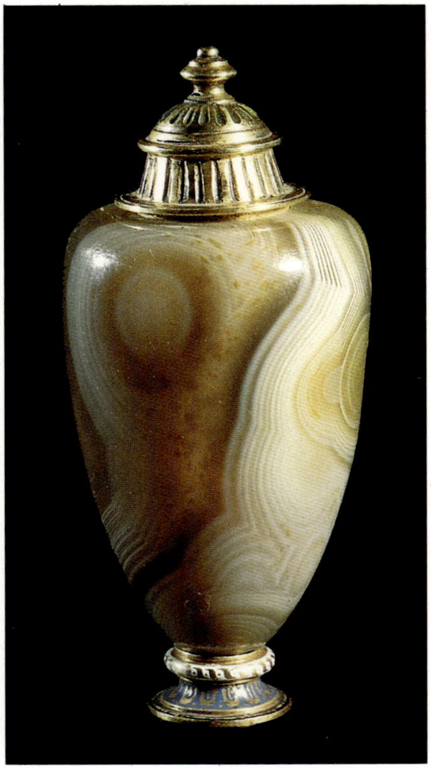

232

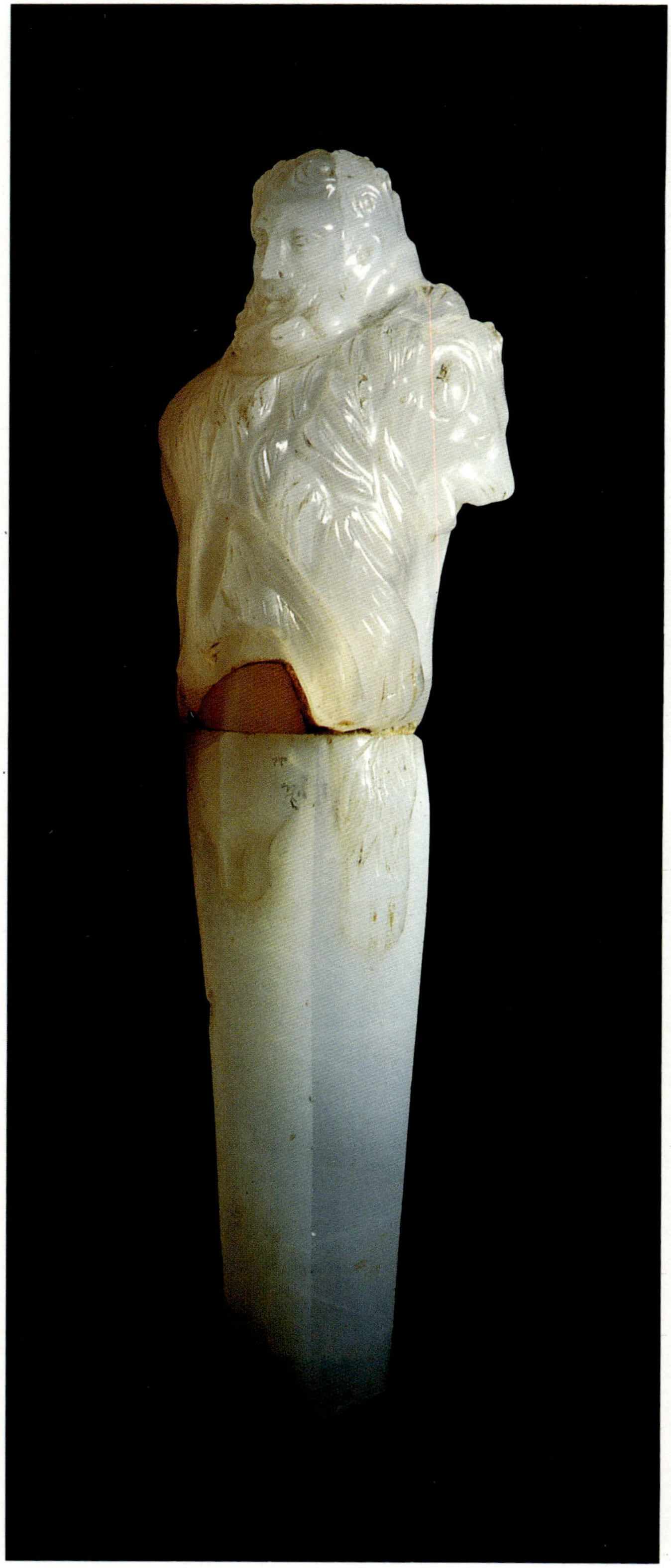
233

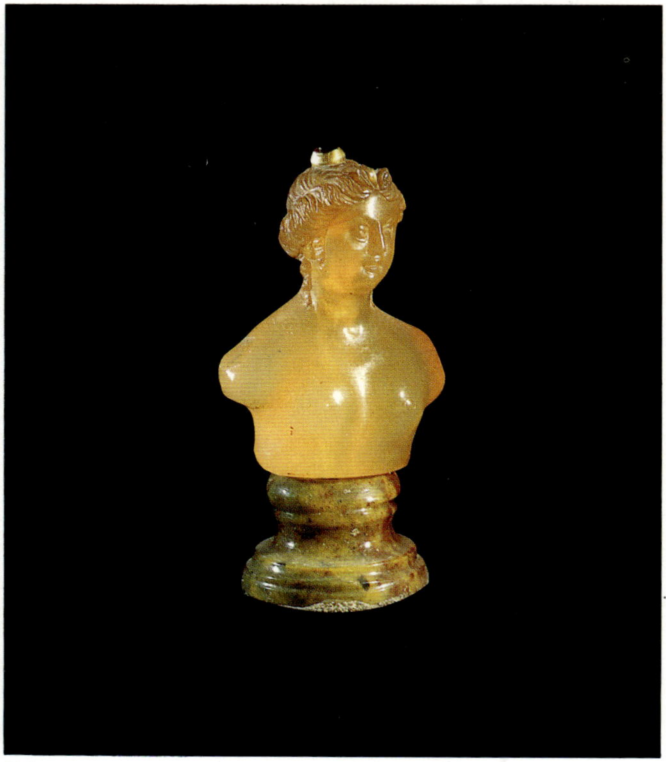
234

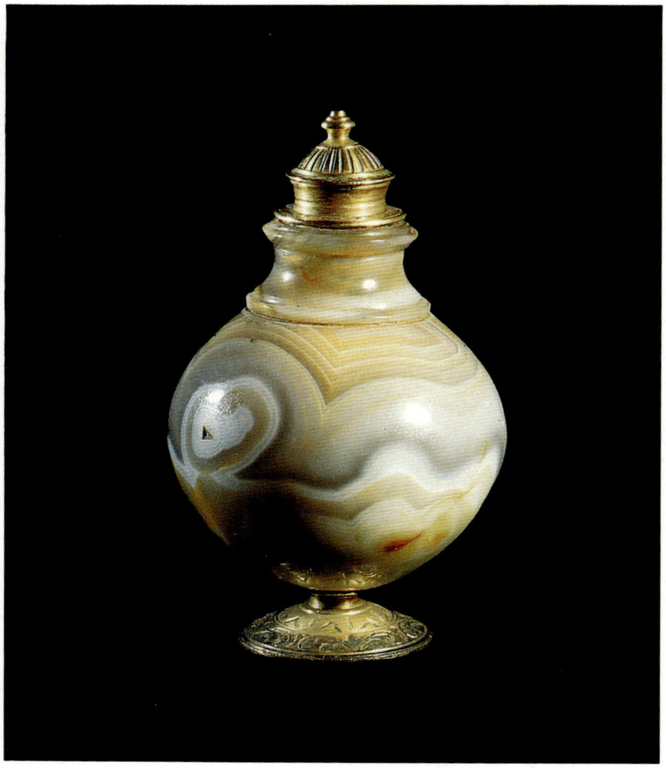
235

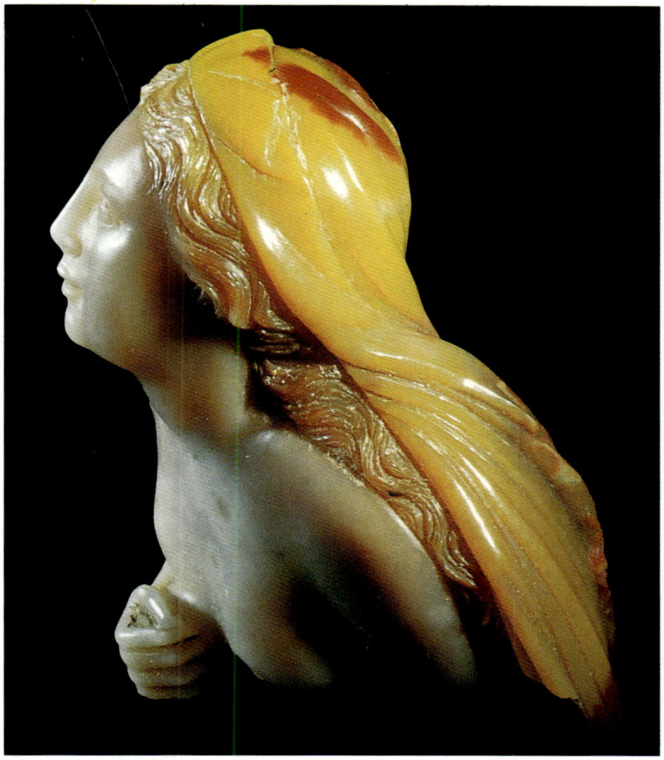
236

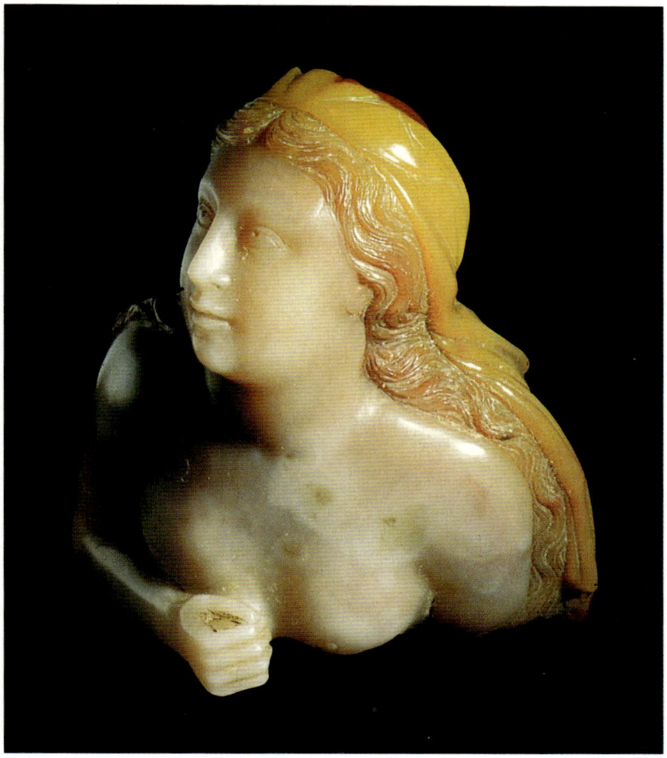
236

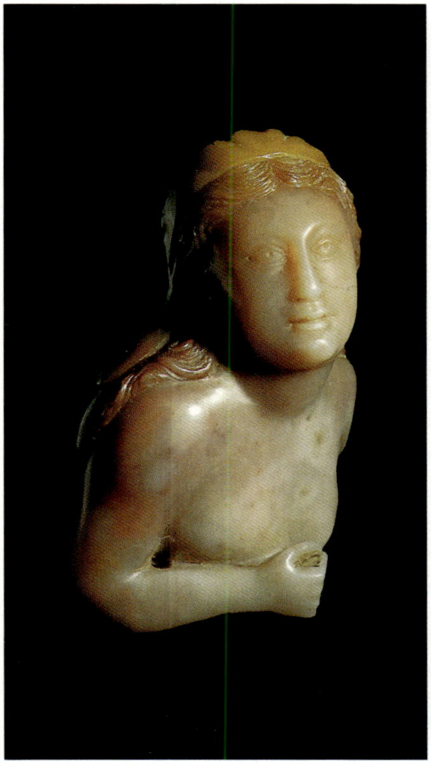
236

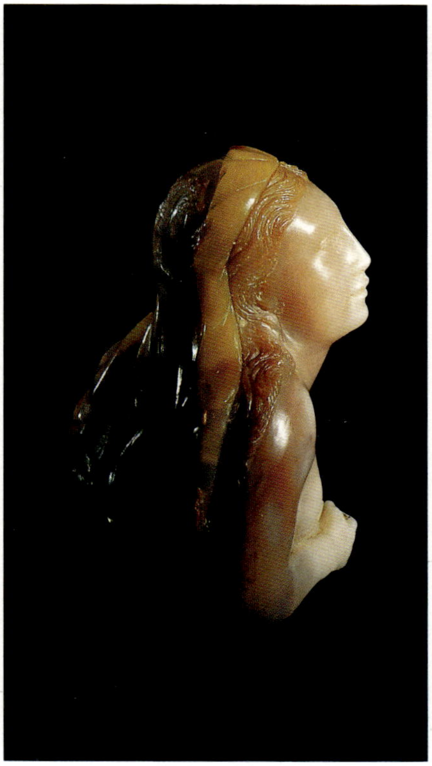
236

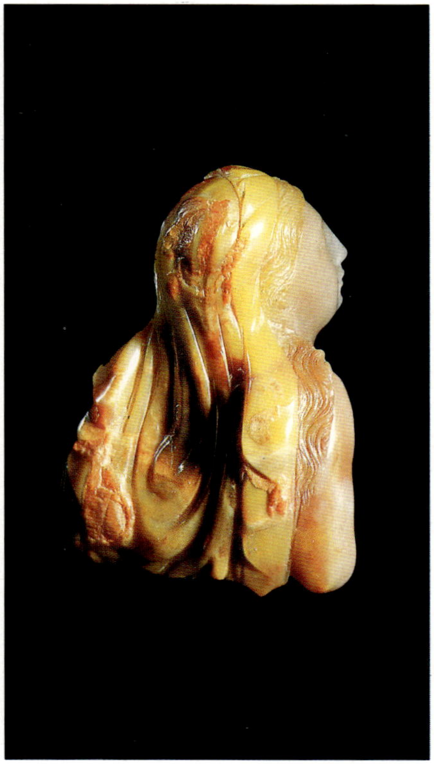
236

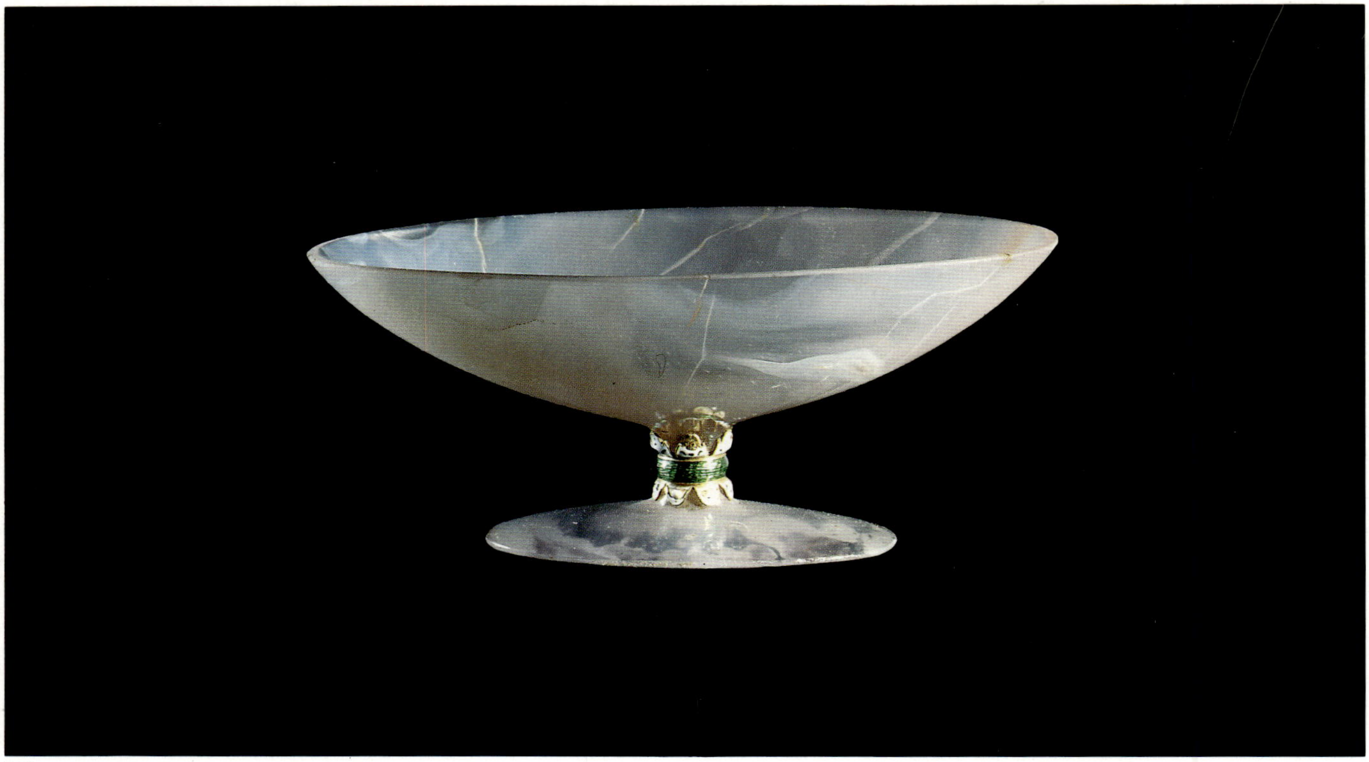
237

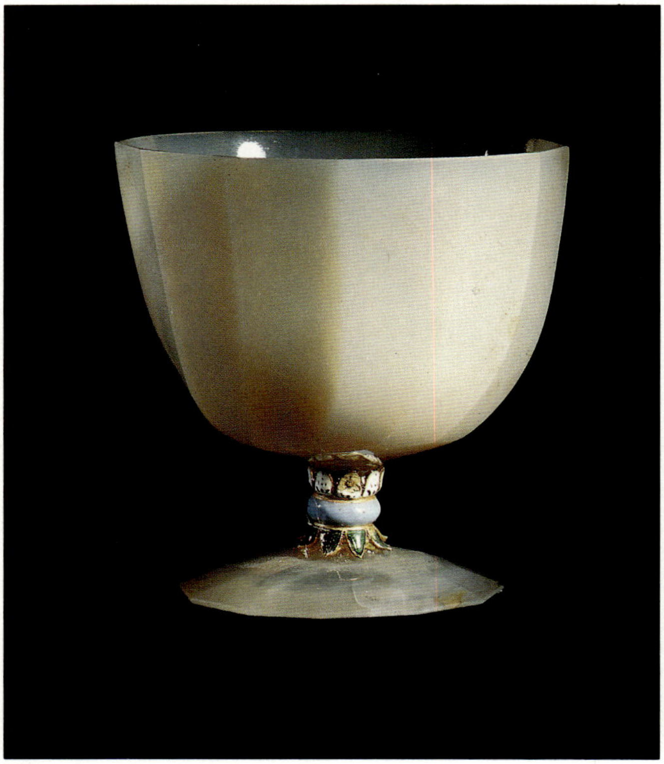
238

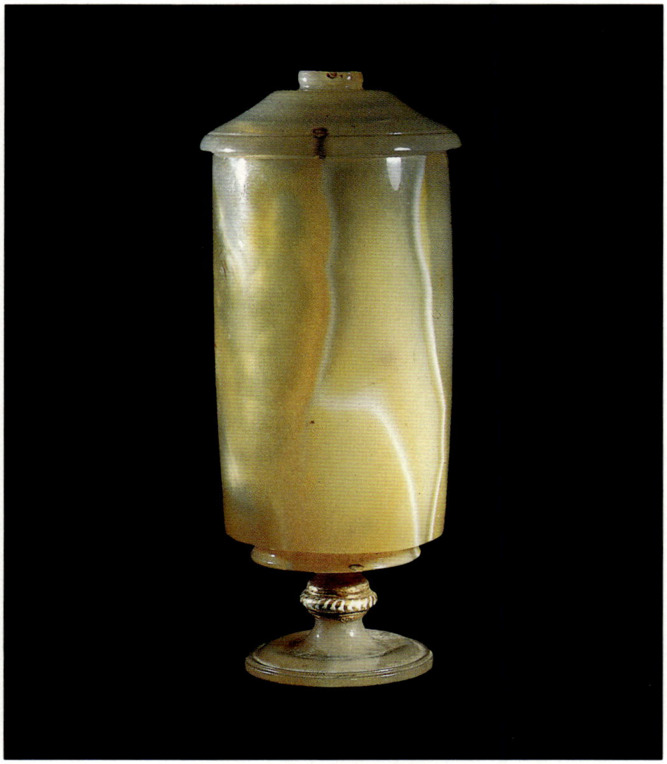
239

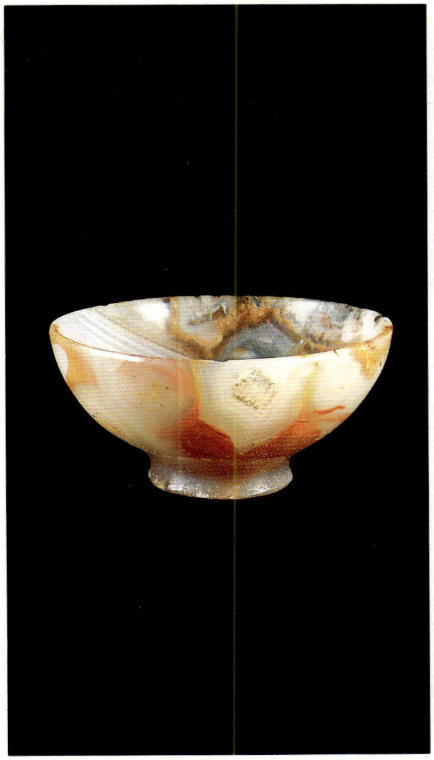
240

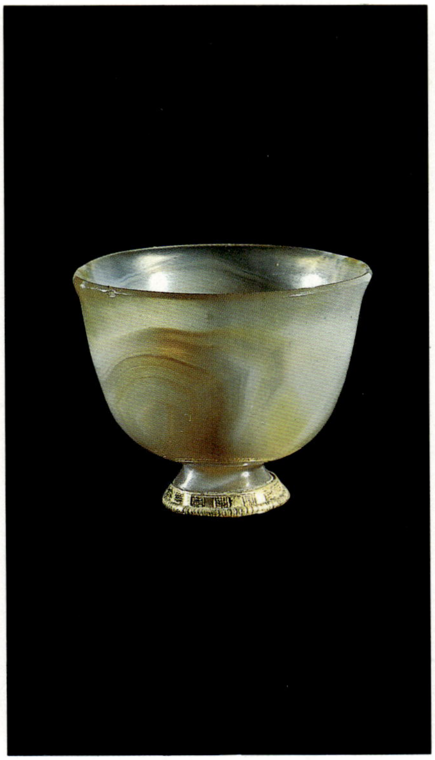
241

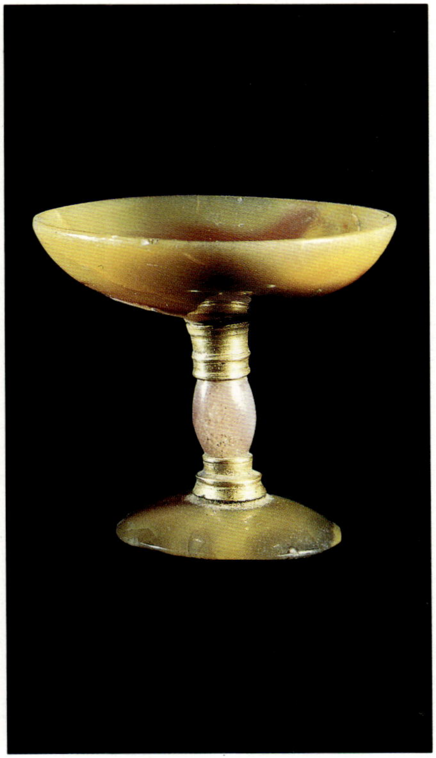
242

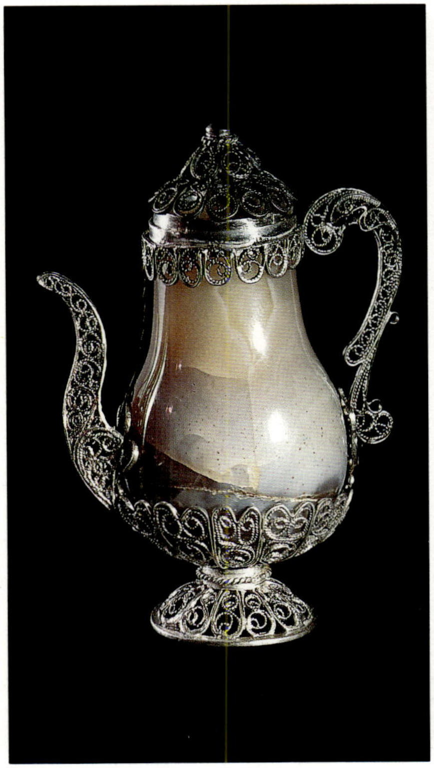
246

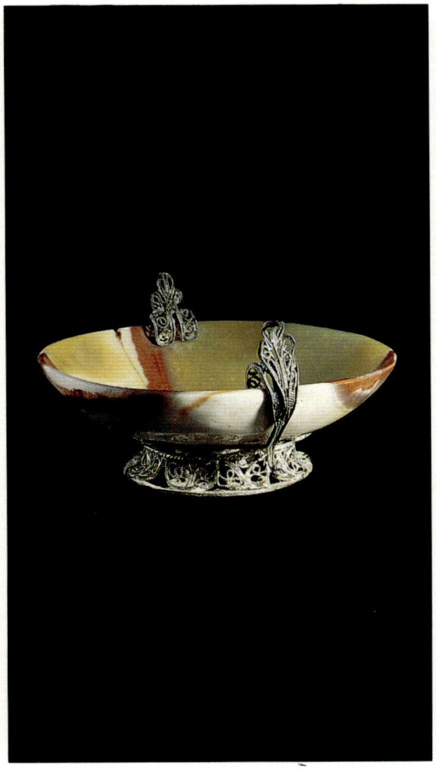
247

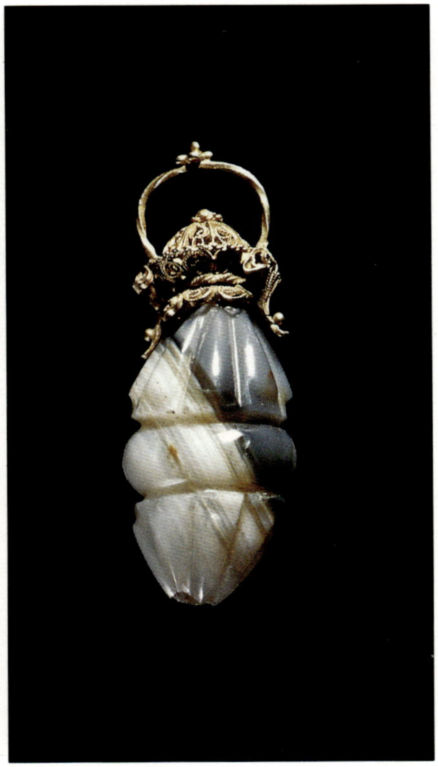
248

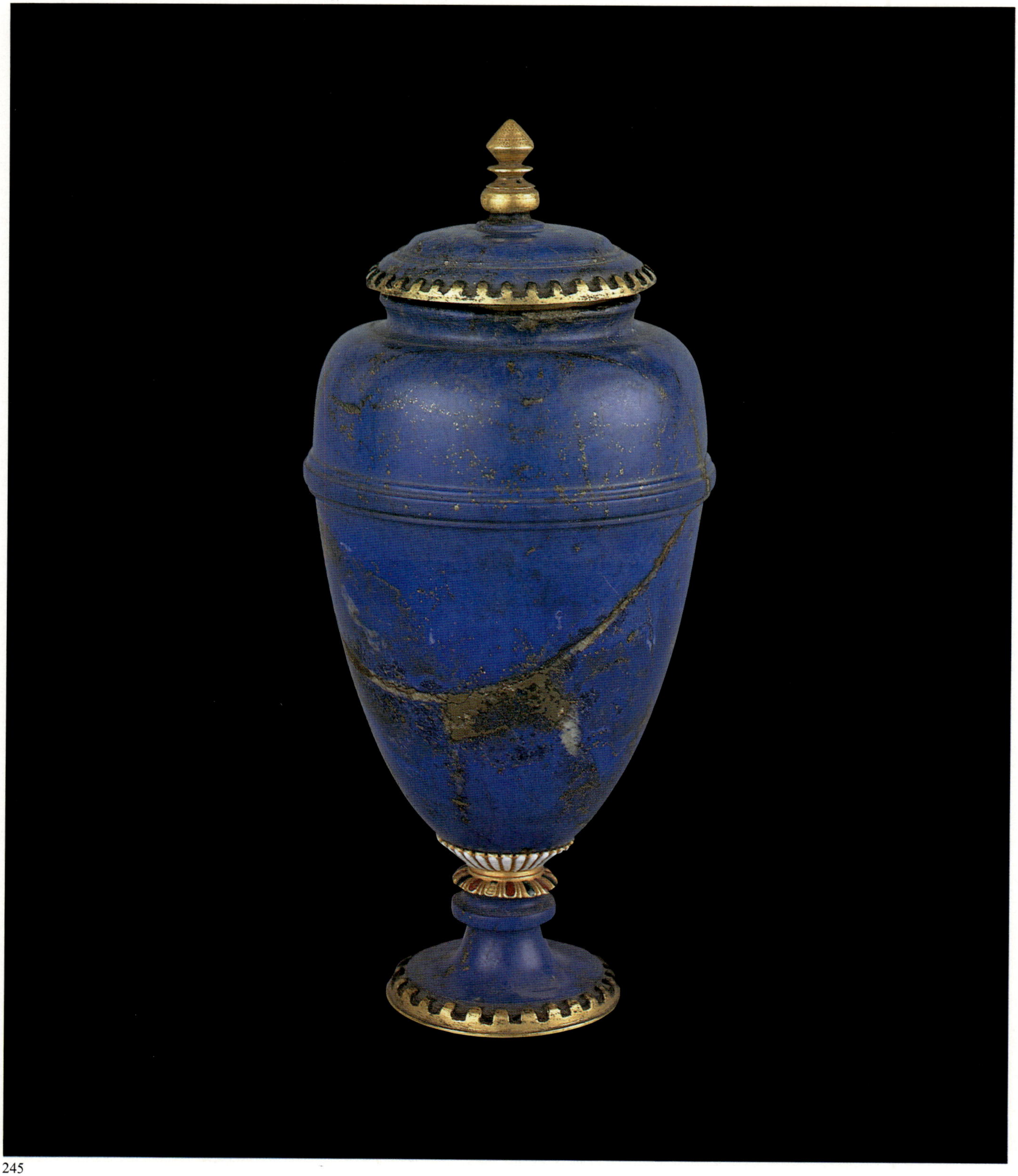

245

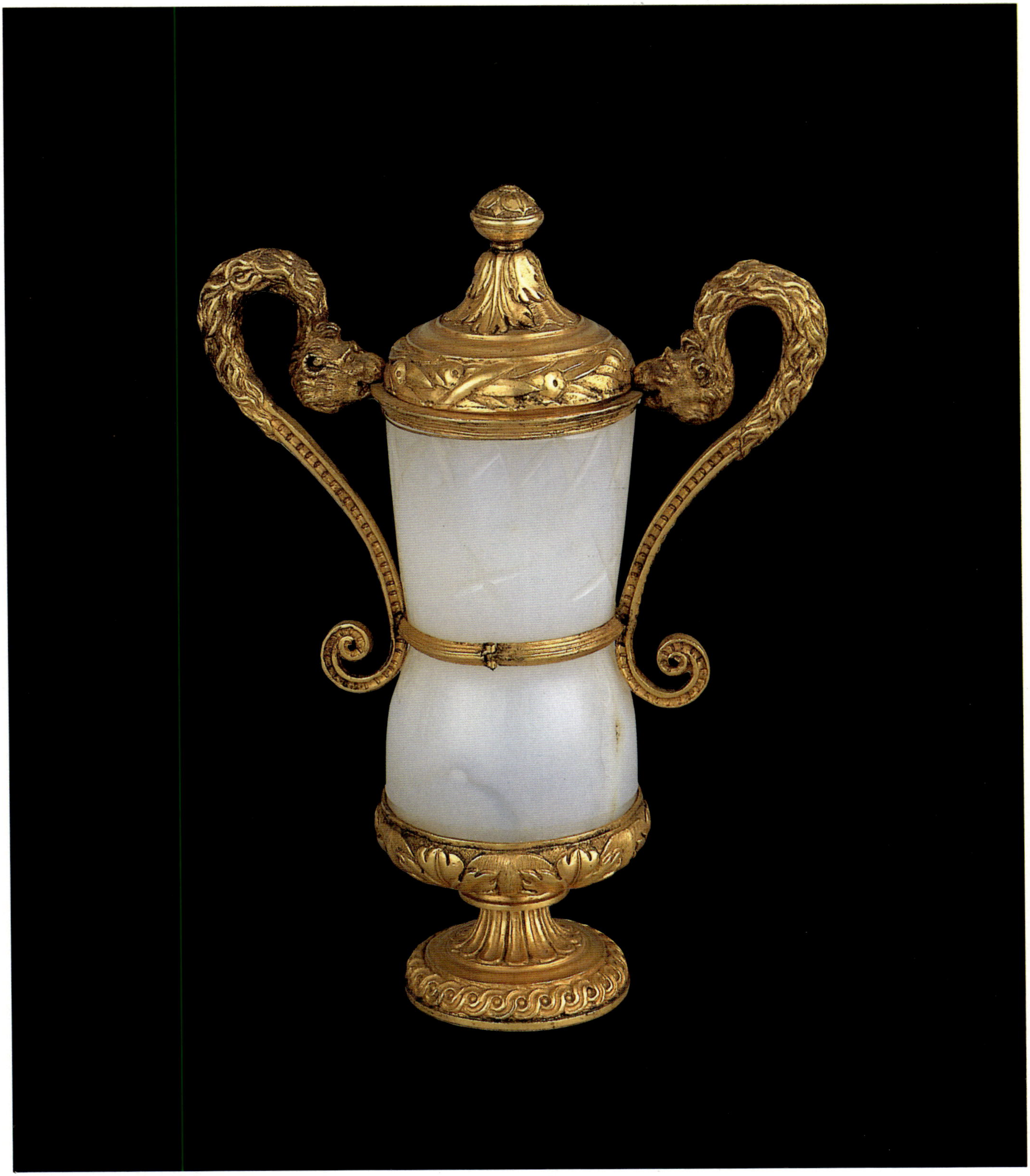

249

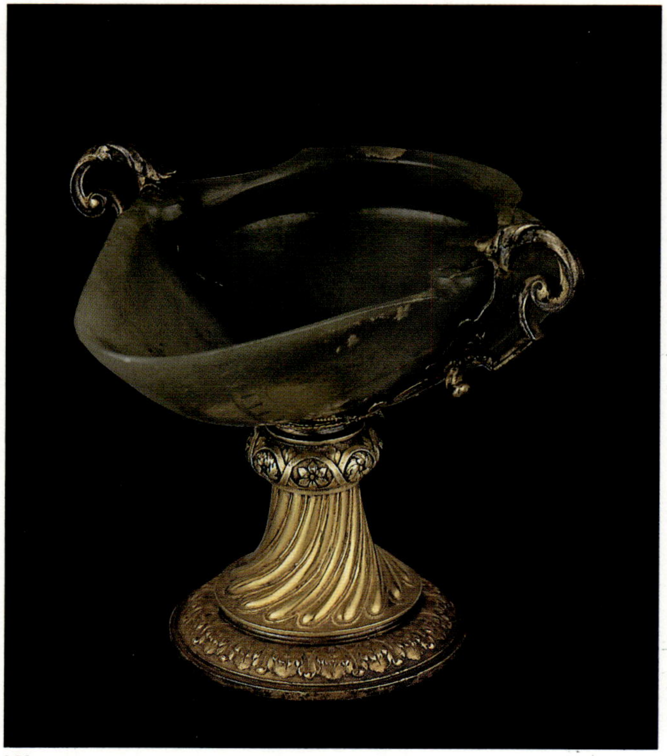
250

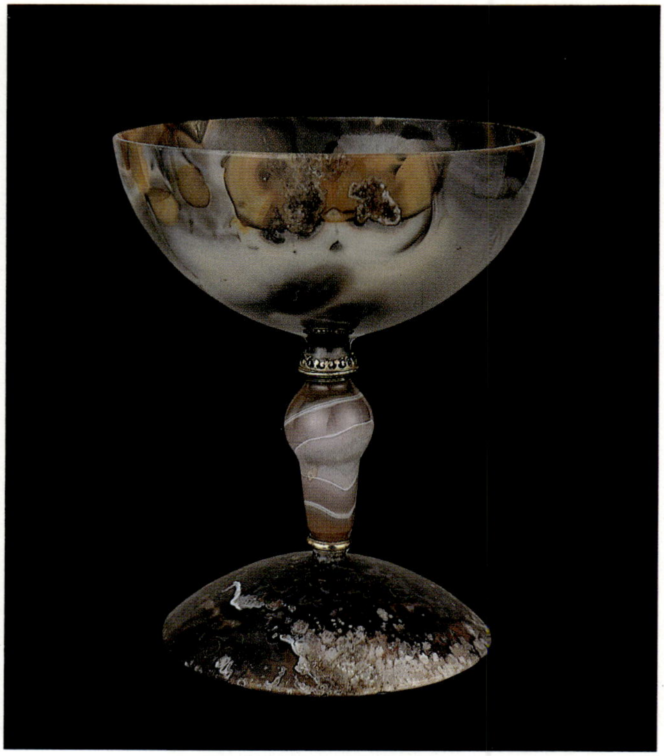
251

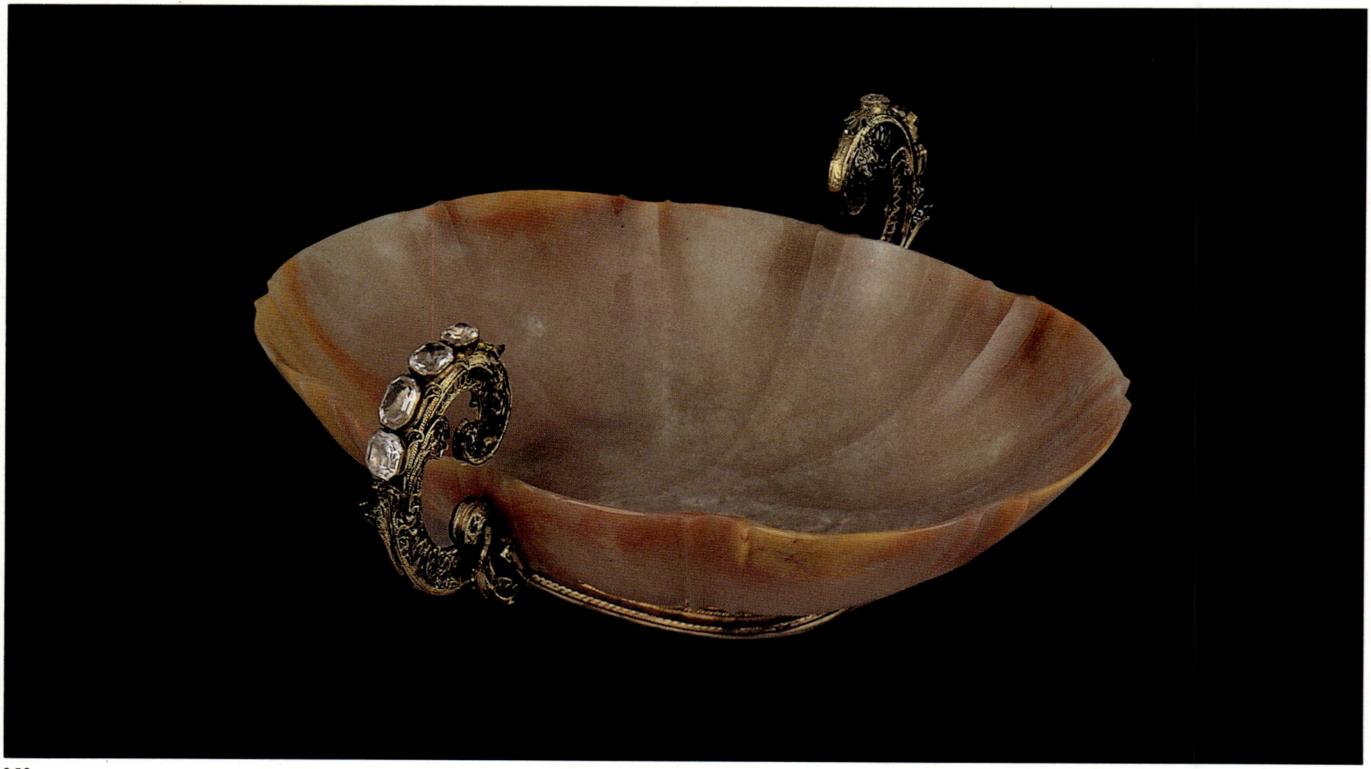
252

CATALOGUE

GOLDWARE
by *Mario Cygelman*

When one is discussing the introduction of new techniques for the working of gold in Tyrrhenian Italy, the contact between the East and the West at the end of the eighth century B.C. can not be left out of the evaluation.

In Etruria, favouring the assimilation process of new techniques for the working of metals, one has to remember the early introduction of personal decorations in gold, silver and other metals by the Villanovans. It is the first sign of class or social differentiation that one finds in the extremely homogeneous cremations practiced in the first period of the Iron Age (ninth century B.C.). Taking an overall look at other cemeteries of the same period, one would find any such type of differentiating fibulas , silver hairpins, pins, medallions, etc. which represent the first evidence of these artifacts.

The fact that cremation was practised widely during the Iron Age does not permit a complete understanding of fashions and shapes of the garments worn by the deceased. Archaeological evidence has however uncovered laying beside the «parures» thin bronze leaves covered with a layer of gold that was probably used to decorate the clothes of the deceased. Already at the end of the tenth century B.C. the local population have reached such highly skillful techniques that a rich metallurgy tradition had evolved. At the end of the seventh century B.C., when new techniques arrived from the eastern Mediterranean, they find a population mature enough for their arrival. From that moment on filigree, knurling and granulation along with techniques from toreutic art and carvings in relief support each other to assume a specific character in the gold working field.

An example of a technique that has its origins in the East is granulation. This technique consists of soldering small sphere to a thin metal sheet. Mesopotania, Syria, Palestine, Asia Minor, Crete and Cyprus represent the most ancient centres from where this technique took its first steps. The tomb of Ur, which dates to the third millenium, has the most ancient examples; the ashes of Troy (2350-2100 B.C.); Knossos in Crete has examples dating from 1700-1600 B.C.; Ebla in Syria has jewellery dating back to 1600 B.C.; and last, the tomb of Tutench-Amun (1352 B.C.) contained buckles and swords also exhibiting this type of technique.

In Greece and on the surrounding islands these techniques especially granulation, which were very well known during the Mycenean period, reappeared at the end of the ninth century B.C., and were reintroduced by Eastern craftsmen. The jewellery recovered at Khaniale Tekke, Knossos (J. Boardman, in *Annual of the British School at Athens*, 62, 1967, p. 571, Pls. 7-12), inside a Minoan Tholos tomb constitutes the most prestigious example of this type of phenomena.

The opening of the Syrian coasts, the markets of Cilicia such as Al-Mina or Tell Sukas and the Phoenician stops at Cyprus, represent the meeting point between the Greek and Eastern communities. It is here that the new techniques are exchanged.

The economic collapse, due to the Assyrian invasion by Sargon II at the end of the eighth century B.C., destroyed the equilibrium of trade. Thus forcing the Phoenicians and the Greeks, at the end of the ninth century B.C., to turn towards the western Mediterranean for their economic interests. They founded new colonies and amplified the ports already in existence (a Phoenician example is the founding of Carthage dating to the end of the ninth century B.C. or Cuma in Campania by the Greeks in the middle of the eighth century B.C.).
The need in finding new mineral sources above all metals, pushed the Greeks and Phoenicians towards Etruria, Sardinia and Spain. The fact that these areas guaranteed a continuous supply for stocks and the pressure of the Assyrian invasion forced the Eastern people to search for a new life in these areas.
The interest in the metal sources in the West brings to Tyrrhenian Italy (Etruria, Latium, Campania) a rapid concentration of wealth which accelerates the process of social-economic differentiation already in action during the Iron Age (middle eighth century B.C.) by the local communities in Etruria and Latium. This phenomena also takes place a little later between the people of the South-Western Mediterranean such Iberian peninsula (El Carambolo, Sines, La Aliseda, Lugo, etc...).
Burial rituals also change. Large tombs like the ones in the East are constructed for entire families or clans. Identical characteristics can be found between the tomb of «Il Duce» di Vetulonia (G. Camporeale, *La tomba del Duce*, Firenze, 1967) or the tombs of Pontecagnano in Campania (B. D'Agostino, *Tombe «Principesche» dell'orientalizzante antico da Pontecagnano*, in Mon. Ant. XLIX, 1977) and the royal tombs of Salamis of Cyprus and Lefkandi in Eretria. There is a need to describe the deceased with a eulogy of wealth and power. Carts, weapons, bronze and silver vases make up the basis of the artifacts. Also found are the religious artifacts such as ostrich eggs decorated with historical scenes, inlaid ivory and rare oriental glassware. Eastern artisans that migrated to the West played a determining role when talking about the preceding artifacts. In addition to transferring new techniques they are also the go between for the new figurative style known conventionally as «Orientalising».
The royal tombs of Etruria and Latium with all their splendid artifacts illustrated this fact to the upmost. Goldware, more than any other type of product was used to show the rapid gain of power and wealth.
Objects that decorated the clothes of the deceased enriches the funerary offerings. Artifacts such as fibulas, buckles, bracelets, hairpins and necklaces with mythical animals (mermaid, sphinx, chimaera, etc...) together with goats, lions, alternated by palmettes or floral patterns and geometric shapes represent a favourite subject. It is on these artifacts that the artisan applies his various techniques.
Along with the splendid artifacts mentioned above, there are also female heads done in relief representing Ishtar, or more genuine Etruscan artifacts.

One has to be aware that the artisans who produced these beautiful jewels also produced vases in the same precious metals. A noticeable stylistic connection can be seen between the decorations of a golden *kotyle* from the tomb Bernardini and the large plaques from the tombs Bernardini and Barberini at Preneste (M. Cristofani - M. Martelli, *L'Oro degli Etruschi*, Novara 1985, Pls. 19-21), the buckles at Preneste, the fibulas at Cerveteri or the Corsini from Marsiliana (idem, Pls. 24; 32; 50). All these artifacts can be connected to a single manufacturer probably close to Cerveteri.
Writing, introduced by the Greek colonies in Southern Italy such as Cuma in Campania also appears at the end of the eighth century B.C. in the Etruscan society. This becomes another way to decorate the surface of a fibula like the one that can be found at the Louvre today originally from Chiusi (cfr. *L'oro degli Etruschi*, Pl. 103).
Other types of personal decorations that can be seen as status symbols and that show the opulence and the lavishness of the Etruscan aristocracy at the end of the eighth century B.C. and the first half of the seventh century B.C., are the golden chest plates decorated in relief. An example of this can be found in the Regolini-Galassi tomb of Cerveteri (see *L'oro degli Etruschi*) with its true collection of Eastern motives. Identical punch marks can be found on the silver sheet at Vetulonia in the tomb of the «Duce» (cfr. Camporeale, Pl. XXV), allowing these artifacts to be attributed to the same Ceretan workshop.
A special importance should be given to the silver pateras decorated in relief and usually gold plated. They are known as Phoenician but even today there still exists some confusion amongst scholars about their origins. Hypothesis about their origins are Cyprus, Northern Syria or a Levantine who immigrated to Italy. None of these can be excluded if one compares these cups with the «situla chiusina» of Plikasna (see *L'oro degli Etruschi*) or the golden cup found today at the Victoria and Albert Museum in London (see J. Wolters, *Die Granulation*, München, 1983, Pl. 139).
However, the silver pitchers found only in royal tombs in Italy and that probably had to do with some type of wine ritual are attributed to Cypriot or Northern Syrian production (see *L'Oro degli Etruschi*, Pl. 42).
If Southern Etruria was the most intense centre around the middle of the seventh century B.C. for the receiving and distribution of new techniques and religious artifacts coming from the East, Vetulonia in Northern Etruria was then without a doubt the centre of a rich and active production of goldware with its own particular characteristics.
Due to the habits and enormous request of buying luxury items like vases and personal decorations made out of precious metals in Southern Etruria made goldware workers from this area come to Vetulonia. Most of the jewellery is destined to women and is usually done in relief, pressed or repoussé and with a «pulviscolo technique».
With these techniques one sees the usual figurative artifacts but excessively decorated which

contrasts with the plain modules of the South etruscan artisans. Above all the «pulviscolo» with the realization of silhouettes allows narrative scenes to be placed in small spaces. The utilization of these figurative patterns that the goldware workers of Vetulonia used and which have their origins in the East become more and more baroque in style. The popularity of these techniques beyond the borders of Vetulonia make one think of a migration of artisans from this centre to Bologna, where several examples showing this kind of decoration come from. If all these techniques had their highest peak during the Orientalising period (end of eighth-seventh century B.C.) they remained an indestructible heritage for the Etruscan artisans during the following periods.

From the sixth century B.C. onward, the concentration of precious metals found in tombs is much less in respect with the luxurious ornaments found dating to the Orientalising period. This probably has much to do with a change in social and political climate bringing a new type of investment instead of personal wealth accumulation like in the preceding period. The luxury objects, influenced by the contact of the Ionic and Lydian world, assume a value connected to fashions: a sign of true pretentiousness.

«Bauletto» shaped earrings, a typical Etruscan creation align themselves with the sphere like shaped earrings of the Eastern Greek tradition. Different techniques are also used on necklaces which are vaguely decorated with granulation or filigree and alternated with hanging configurations like a satyr's head or Acheloo and colourfully alternated by stones. It is difficult to rediscover their real form due to the handling and juxtaposition of the previous century.

All in all goldware working in the Archaic Period reveals new styles and manufacturing thanks to the hellenization that is carried out in a new figurative language. Vulci and Cerveteri undoubtedly represent the two most intense centres even though Orvieto and Chiusi during the same period also must have represented important areas for the working of metals.

If the fifth century B.C. saw a considerable reduction in the production of goldware, the fourth century B.C., due to the Greek and Tarantine influence, brought new life in the field to which the affluent classes willingly took to.

The results were seen more in women's clothes and jewellery such as cluster, tube and pelta earrings or earrings decorated with heads or hanging amphora, plus rings with sardonyx. Granulation, filigree, knurling and relief remain the principal decoration techniques in a collection that will not find any new sources to renew itself with.

During the Roman Period, goldware will be accompanied by semi-precious stones (granite, quartz, amethyst, etc..., glass and enamels), sometimes acquiring new life due to new fashions but acquiring new techniques like in the preceding periods. One can see more stress towards colourist aspects of the decorations which will rule all through the Byzantine and Medieval periods but becoming more overloaded and gaudy.

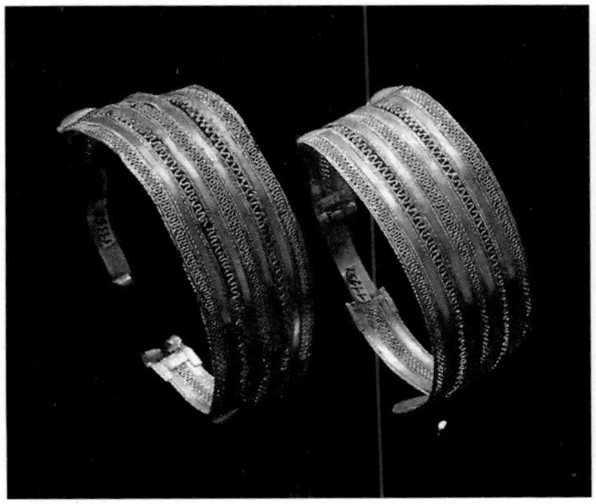

1. PAIR OF ARMLETS
Museo Archeologico, Florence
Inv. 11151-11152
From Marsiliana d'Albegna, necropolis of Banditella, tomb II
Diam. 5.5 cm.
Rolled gold, filigree decoration. Intact
Etruscan production of the 1st quarter of the 7th century B.C.

Armlets consisting of three overlapping bands, formed by fine smooth leaves alternating with bands of corrugated wire, interconnected by means of a pair of ultra-fine corded wires arranged in the shape of a plait. The outer, shorter bands end in a smooth bead with a corded edge; the inner band extends in two tongues featuring cylindrical tube claps interconnected with a small pin.

L'Oro degli Etruschi, p. 266 n° 47, with bibl., *Schätze der Etrusker*, p. 164, nos. 16-17; *Etrusker in der Toskana*, p. 19.

G.C.C.

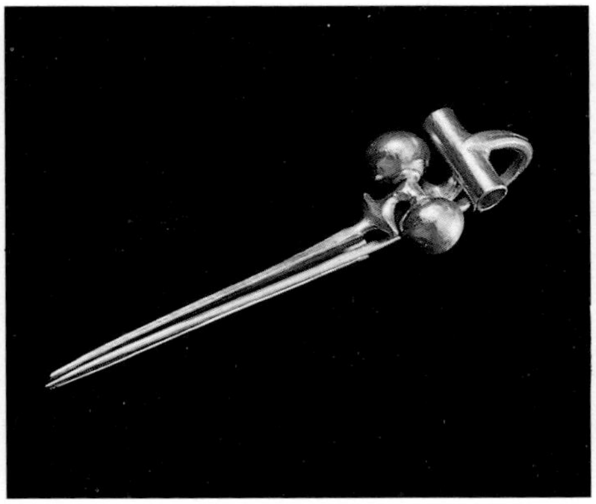

2. DRAGON FIBULA
Museo Archeologico, Florence
Inv. 76344
From Foiano della Chiana - Arezzo, Bought by Pacini in 1895
Length 9 cm.
Cast gold. Intact
Etruscan production of the second quarter of the 7th century B.C.

The bow, consisting of a polygonal-section rod, is twisted and breaks up into two spheres and in two pointed lateral apophyses. A small crosstube crowns the rear curvilinear section, which bears a three-ribbed fastener at the bottom. The strap is long and consists of a bent leaf tapered towards the ends.

F. Lo Schiavo, *«La fibula prenestina»: typological considerations* in BPI LXXXII, 1975 (1980/1981), p. 290 n° 5; *L'Oro degli Etruschi*, p. 267, n° 51 with comparisons and bibl. on the type; *Gioielli e Ornamenti*, p. 23, n° 43.

P.Z.G.

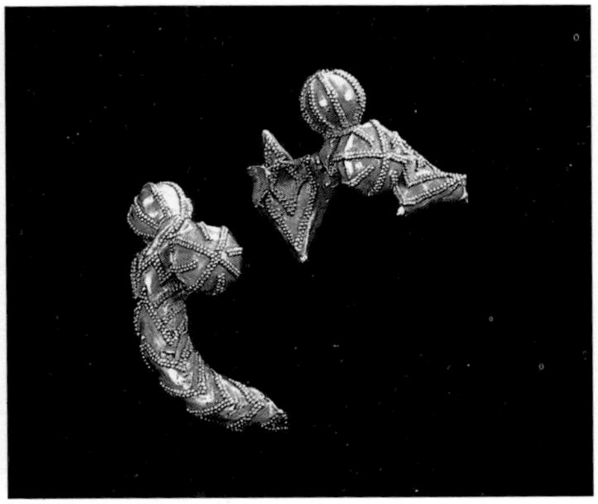

3. FRAGMENT OF FIBULA WITH DRAGON BOW
Guarnacci Museum, Volterra
Inv. 17a, b.
From Gesseri di Berignone - Volterra
L. of fragment a 2.5 cm.; l. of frag. b 3.5 cm.
Extremely oxidated
Etruscan production of the third quarter of 7th cent. B.C.

In all likelihood the two fragments belong in part to the bow and pin of just one fibula.
Very recent restoration work and the analysis of the objects have ascertained that Karo's conjecture, subsequently taken up by Fiumi, that they were of the double-content alloy electrum is wrong. They have a core of a metal alloy clad in thin gold-sheet with granulation-decorated globules and mounds.
L'Oro degli Etruschi, p. 273, n° 70, with bibl.; *Cento Preziosi Etruschi*, p. 119, n° 61; *Gioielli e Ornamenti Preziosi*, n° 121.

Ga.C.

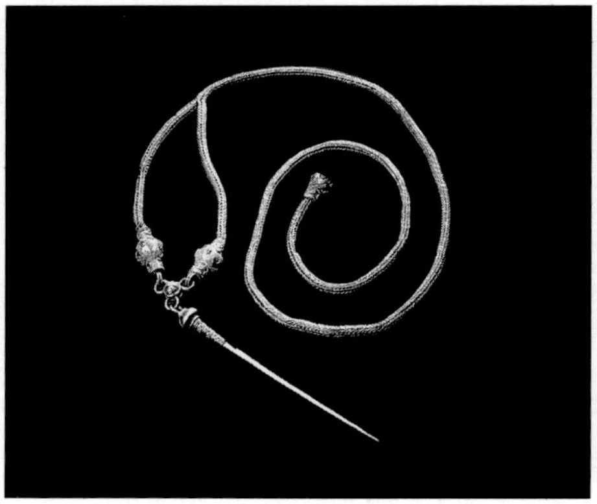

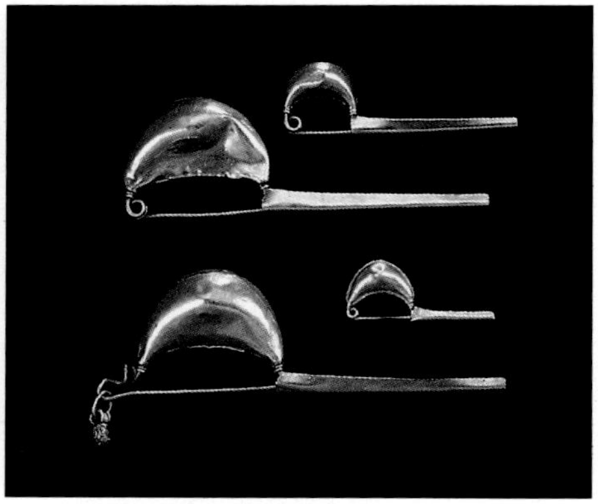

4. CHAIN
Guarnacci Museum, Volterra
Inv. 3.
From Gesseri di Berignone - Volterra
L. 52 cm.
Gold. Gaps at one end. Part of the globule and the pin underneath missing
Etruscan production from the third quarter of 7th cent. B.C.

The chain is the link type consisting of two pairs of very fine gold wires crosslinked so as to form a double herringbone pattern. One end has gaps in the work and conserves only the upper hemisphere of a hollow globule, surmounted by a cylinder welded to the chain. The welding point is concealed under a double row of granulated balls. The shank, on the contrary, exhibits a series of rosettes with a pistil standing out in the centre, bordered with granulated balls. The other intact part of the chain divides into two segments both ending in a globule surmounted by cylinders which are decorated as described above. The lower base of the cylinders displays a double-spiralled hook into which is inserted an assembly of three little loops joined to each other and linked by means of a disc to the false corded flange and the interior, decorated with granulated triangles. The lower hook is tied, by means of another suspension loop, to the round head of a pin, with, on the neck, a filigree decoration of corded motifs in relief, alternating with areas with wavy lines.
The article, similar examples of which are known in the oriental Etruscan period, seems to have fulfilled the function of a «plait clasp», or at any rate to have been connected with hair styles.

L'Oro degli Etruschi, p. 273, n° 68, with bibl.; *Cento Preziosi Etruschi*, p. 120, n° 66; *Gioielli e Ornamenti Preziosi*, n° 119.

Ga.C.

5. FIBULA WITH LEECH BOW
Guarnacci Museum, Volterra
Inv. 20.
From Gesseri di Berignone - Volterra
L. 6.2 cm.; ht. 2 cm.
Sheet gold
Etruscan production from the third quarter of 7th cent. B.C.

In gold-sheet which is hollow inside, it has a long foot with a double-spiralled spring. The bow consists of two welded gold-sheets, terminating at either end in a pair of annular knots. The bow spring and the foot groove are directly welded to the main body of the fibula.

L'Oro degli Etruschi, p. 273, n° 71, with bibl.; *Cento Preziosi Etruschi*, p. 119, n° 62; *Gioielli e Ornamenti Preziosi*, n° 122.

Ga.C.

6. FIBULA WITH LEECH BOW
Guarnacci Museum, Volterra
Inv. 21
From Gesseri di Berignone - Volterra
L. 9.4 cm.; ht. 3 cm.
Etruscan production from the third quarter of 7th cent. B.C.

Of the same type as the one described above. The bow is slightly fuller.

L'Oro degli Etruschi, p. 274, n° 72, with bibl.; *Cento Preziosi Etruschi*, p. 120, n° 63; *Gioielli e Ornamenti Preziosi*, n° 123.

Ga.C.

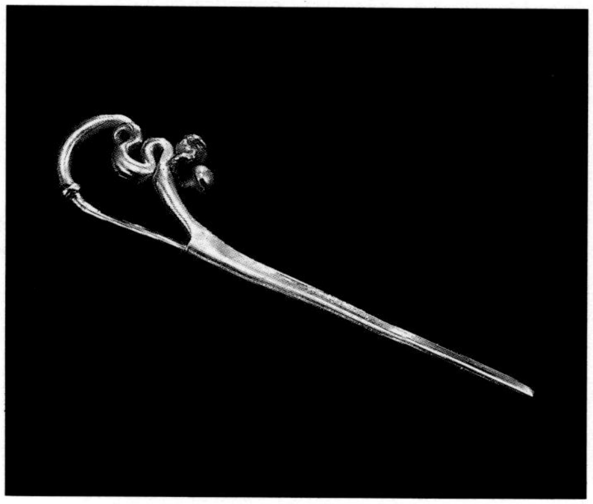

7. FIBULA WITH LEECH BOW
Guarnacci Museum, Volterra
Inv. 23
From Gesseri di Berignone - Volterra
L. 9.6 cm.; ht. 3 cm.
Etruscan production from the third quarter of 7th cent. B.C.

The bow is swollen like in the previous example. The pin spring is deformed and a hook from one of its spirals connects it to a cylinder with granulated decoration, perhaps belonging to an article of toiletry.

L'Oro degli Etruschi, p. 274, n° 73, with bibl.; *Cento Preziosi Etruschi*, p. 120, n° 64; *Gioielli e Ornamenti Preziosi*, n° 124.

Ga.C.

8. FIBULA WITH LEECH BOW
Guarnacci Museum, Volterra
Inv. 24
From Gesseri di Berignone - Volterra
L. 3.3 cm.; ht. 1.5 cm.
The whole foot is missing
Etruscan production from the third quarter of 7th cent. B.C.

Like the previous one. Within a thin, flattened band, a filigree decoration consisting in a continuous wavy line runs along the welding line of the two laminates in the bow.

L'Oro degli Etruschi, p. 274, n° 74, with bibl.; *Cento Preziosi Etruschi*, p. 120, n° 65; *Gioielli e Ornamenti Preziosi*, n° 125.

Ga.C.

9. FIBULA WITH DRAGON
Guarnacci Museum, Volterra
Inv. 6
From Gesseri di Berignone - Volterra
L. 8.1 cm.; ht. 1.7 cm.
Etruscan production from the third quarter of 7th cent. B.C.

Dragon fibula with «antennas»; the rod of the bow with an eyelet; a little knot as a pleat clasp; long, open foot. This is the H IIßb type of Sundwall 1943, well-affirmed in oriental-style series.

L'Oro degli Etruschi, p. 273, n° 69, with bibl.; *Cento Preziosi Etruschi*, p. 119, n° 60; *Gioielli e Ornamenti Preziosi*, n° 120.

Ga.C.

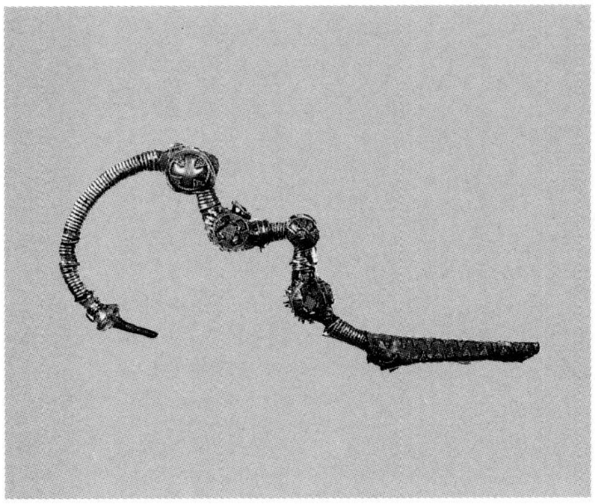

10. FIBULA WITH DRAGON BOW
Museo Archeologico, Florence
Inv. 22419
From Marsiliana D'Albegna, circle of Perazzetta
Length 8.7 cm.
Cast silver, rolled gold; decorated by means of granulation technique. Part of the shank and clasp missing
Etruscan production from the second quarter of the 7th century B.C.

Twisted bow-shaped fibula, in silver rod coated with thin sheet-gold, bearing two couples of lateral apophyses alternating with two lozenge expansions and provided at the base with pleat clasp globule. Long shank. The apophyses and lozenges which decorate the bow culminate at the edges with small hemispheric knobs on expanded flanges; similar knobs, but of smaller dimensions, recur on the upper part of the bow corresponding to the intermediate points of the apophyses and lozenges.

Crf. *L'Oro degli Etruschi*, n° 54, pg. 268, with bibl.; *Etrusker in der Toskana*, n° 73, pg. 119.

G.C.C.

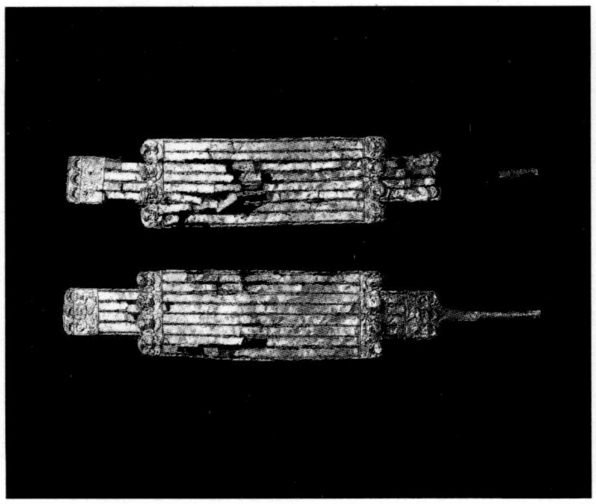

11. PAIR OF ARMLETS
Florence, Museo Archeologico
Inv. 74837-74838
From Vetulonia, tumulus of Pietrera, IV peripheral tomb.
Tot. l.: (74837) 34.7 cm.; (74838) 33.5 cm.; max. w. 6.2 cm.
Sheet-gold. Spaces along the central strip and in one of the plates: the second has no end clasp.
Etruscan production from the second quarter of 7th cent. B.C.

Central band formed of eight thin, smooth strips alternating with filigree work which terminates at both ends in a rectangular laminate with four embossed female heads characterized by a skullcap headdress, divided in two, ending in a hathoric plait and crescent-shaped collar band; the heads alternate with double palmettes. From the ends two bands branch off, of the same type as the central one only narrower, as they consist in only four strips. They are closed at the end by two plates embossed on two registers: in the upper, narrower register, half moons and stylized palmettes; in the lower register an armlet (74837) exhibits a bare-chested male figure kneeling dexter, with short, plaited hair and wearing a long, striped robe, with arms reaching out towards two winged lions rampant arranged heraldically at his sides; the other (74838) has a female, bare-chested figure kneeling sinister, with long plaits and wearing long clothes engraved with rhombi and dots, her arms raised towards two winged felines, also in heraldic composition. At the edges a wire eyelet and a strap with a series of counterposed zig-zags have been used; a scroll motif unites the straps and the band.

Schätze der Etrusker, p. 184, n°s. 1-2; *Etrusker in der Toskana*, p. 213, n°s. 133-134.

M.C.

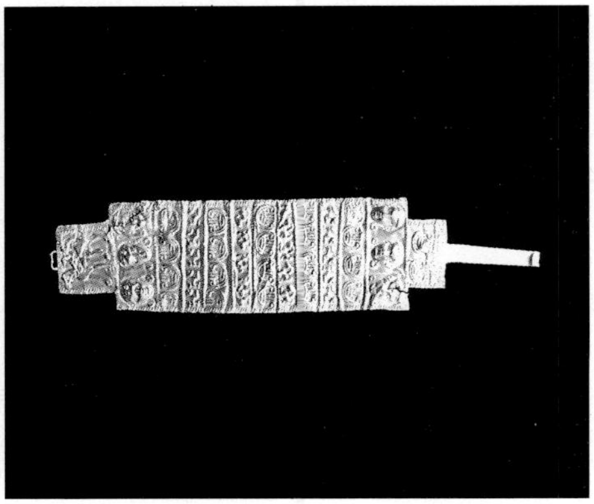

12. PAIR OF ARMLETS.
Florence, Museo Archeologico
Inv. 92600-92601
From Vetulonia, Circle of the Silver Lions, III deposition.
Total l.: 16.5 cm.; max. w. 3.8 cm.
Sheet-gold with probable traces of bronze supports. Intact.
Etruscan production from the third quarter of 7th cent. B.C.

Unlike the previous ones, these armlets were made entirely in sheet-gold, cut into rectangular strips and finished at the ends in smaller rectangles. The close-knit, chisel-embossed decoration consists in eleven separate horizontal registers, limited by the ribbed borders. The arrangement of the registers is approximately symmetrical: the two external ones each exhibit three female heads in profile with hathoric plaits; the others alternate respectively with four Phoenician palmettes, five winged lions couchant facing right and four ibices with the fore quarters of a fifth. The four end plates exhibit respectively a griffon passant sinister and two Phoenician palmettes. At the ends, a bent-up catch-plate and a wire eyelet.

L'Oro degli Etruschi, p 280, n° 96, with bibl. *Schätze der Etrusker*, p. 185, n°s. 6-7; *Etrusker in der Toskana*, p. 215, n°s. 136-137.

M.C.

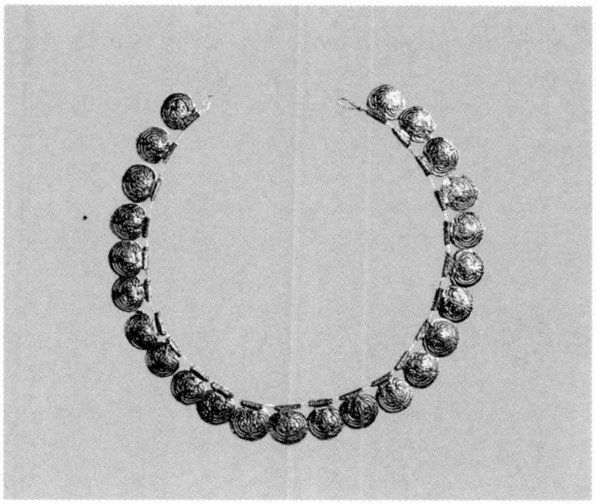

13. PENDANT NECKLACE
Museo Archeologico, Florence
Inv. 92602
From Vetulonia, Circle of the Silver Lions, III deposition.
Average ht. of pendants 1.8 cm.; w. 1.9 cm.
Sheet-gold. Intact.
Etruscan production from the third quarter of 7th cent. B.C.

Consisting in 24 discoid pendants; each embossed with a female head with hathoric plaits, compressed into a scroll motif springing from a lotus bud. On the top edge of the disk, the laminate extends into a fine tube for the insertion of a wire.

L'Oro degli Etruschi, p. 280, with bibl.; *Schätze der Etrusker*, p. 185, n° 8; *Etrusker in der Toskana*, p. 215, n° 138.

M.C.

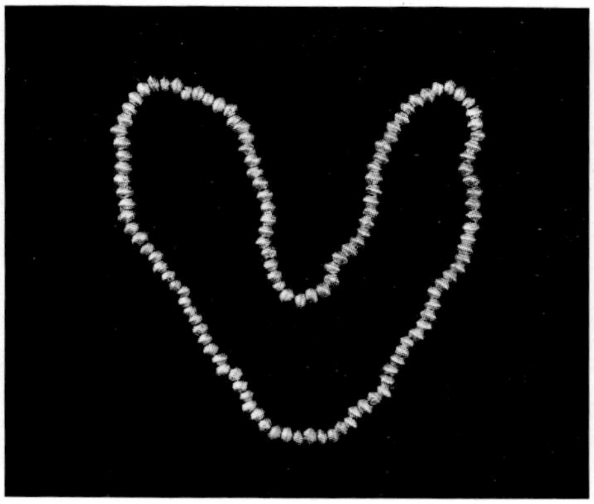

14. NECKLACE
Museo Archeologico, Florence
Inv. 77265
From Vetulonia, the Lictor's tomb
Average diam. of beads 0.71 cm.
Sheet-gold. Intact
Etruscan production from the third quarter of 7th cent. B.C.

Necklace formed with 126 streaked, bean-shaped beads of sheet metal.

L'Oro degli Etruschi, p. 271, n° 60; *Schätze der Etrusker*, p. 186, n° 15; *Gioielli e Ornamenti*, p. 137, n° 39.

M.C.

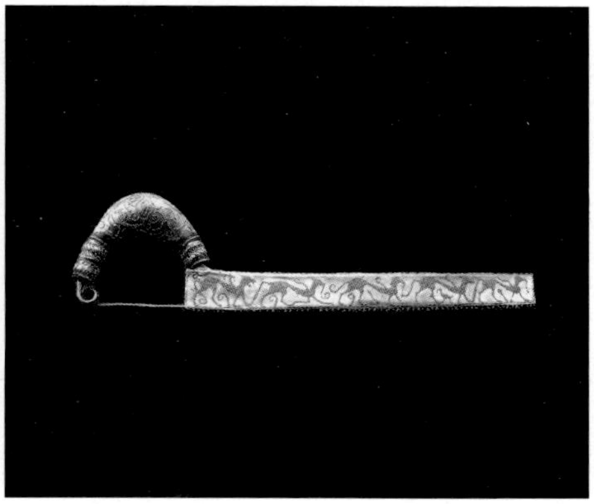

15. LEECH-SHAPE FIBULA
Museo Archeologico, Florence
Inv. 77261
From Vetulonia, the Lictor's tomb
L. 15.6 cm.
Sheet-gold. Intact
Etruscan production from the third quarter of 7th cent. B.C.

The bow is formed by two welded sheets, joined at the tongue and the foot by a reel diagonally crossed with granulated, curved lines.
The bow and the foot constitute a conspicuous example of the colouring potential of the «dust» decoration. Along the welding line on the bow, there runs a meander motif; on both faces of the leech, groups of quadrupeds rotate around a plant arabesque. Along the external side, the foot exhibits five fantastic quadrupeds passant dexter, some with sinuous tails, some with curved elements hanging from their mouths, with, among them, cirri arising from the ground and a small fowl serving as fillers. Recognizable in the last animal is one of the most ancient Etruscan renderings of the chimera. On the inside the zoomorphic frieze is repeated passant sinister. On the sides, there are a series of triangles and zig-zags.

Schätze der Etrusker, p. 188, n° 21 with bibl.; *Gioielli e Ornamenti*, p. 22, n° 40.

M.C.

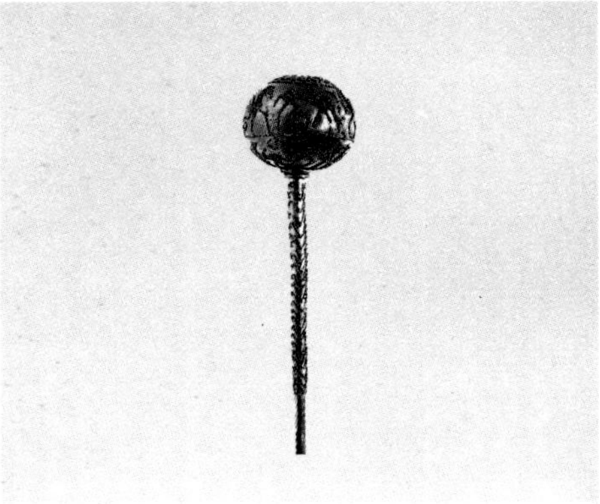

16. PIN
Museo Archeologico, Florence
Inv. 77260
From Vetulonia, the Lictor's tomb
L. 20.7 cm.; diam. of head 2.2 cm.
Sheet-gold. Intact
Etruscan production from the third quarter of 7th cent. B.C.

Spherical head, joined to a double collar band concealing the welding to the pin. The latter, considerably long, exhibits a decoration in «gold dust» with geometrical motifs (the corners ending in scrolls) limited to the upper part. The head is divided into three zones, decorated in the «dust» technique: the top crown displays a circle, which gives off rays of cirri, the median area displays a procession of fantastic animals (winged deer and horses passant sinister), among which are inserted birds and plant motifs as fillers. An analogous procession is repeated, but with a quadruped passant reguardant, in the part underneath.

L'Oro degli Etruschi, p. 270, n° 58, with bibl.; *Schätze der Etrusker*, p. 186, n° 12.

M.C.

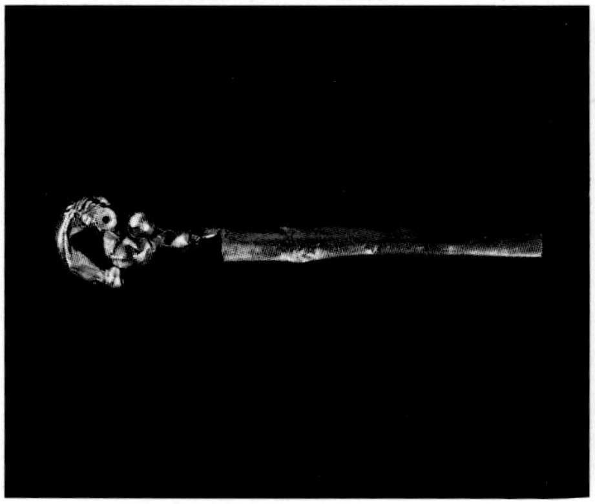

17. FIBULA WITH DRAGON BOW
Museo Archeologico, Florence
Inv. 77263
From Vetulonia, the Lictor's tomb
L. 11.7 cm.
Silver mandrel, gold laminated. By and large intact, with the exception of a part of the tongue missing.
Etruscan production from the third quarter of 7th cent. B.C.

The scroll of the bow stems from part of a pleat clasp globule, distinguished by a minute hole and terminating in a feline protome, holding a tube crosswise in gaping jaws. The upper part of the bow continues from this, articulated in three pairs of pointed lateral apophyses: the median pair corresponding to the elbow carries two applied globules. The long shank consists in a bent-over sheet tapered towards the end.

L'Oro degli Etruschi, p. 271, n° 61, with bibl.; *Schätze der Etrusker*, p. 186, n° 16.

M.C.

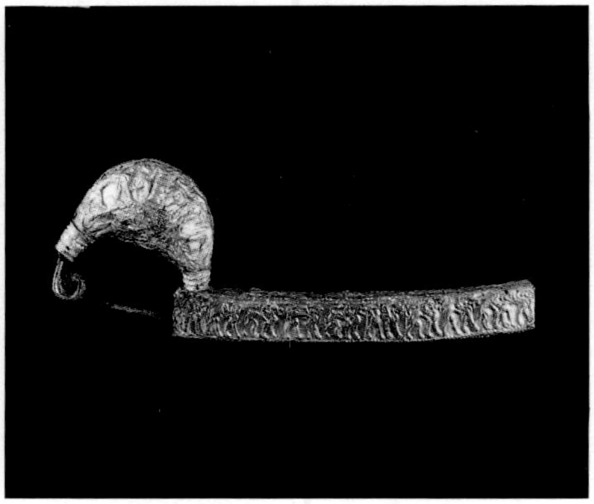

18. FIBULA WITH LEECH BOW
Museo Archeologico, Florence
Inv. 77258
From Vetulonia, the Lictor's tomb
L. 20.8 cm.
Bow-shaped tongue in silver, gold laminated; foot in gold laminate. Intact
Etruscan production from the third quarter of 7th cent. B.C.

Leech bow clad in two gold laminates on the front and back: the welding flanges are clad in a thin laminate with an embossed decoration of circles between wire cord. On the leech there runs an embossed decoration in double register: the upper one with two bearded shinxes arranged heraldically with a plant-scrolled helmet at the centre, the lower one with two griffons counter reguardant divided by a palmette-scroll pendant hanging from above. The bow is joined to the foot by a profiled spool. The foot, slightly tapered, is embossed; it exhibits a procession of nine winged sphinxes and the hindquarters of a tenth passant dexter on the external face; on the upper side, series of upside-down, Phoenician palmettes between two wire cords. Internally, six sphinxes and two griffons and the forequaters of a sphinx are alternated with scrolls; the upper side exhibits 18 Phoenician palmettes. The lower side is smooth both externally and internally.

L'Oro degli Etruschi, p. 271, n°s. 62-64, with bibl.; *Schätze der Etrusker*, p. 187, n° 17.

M.C.

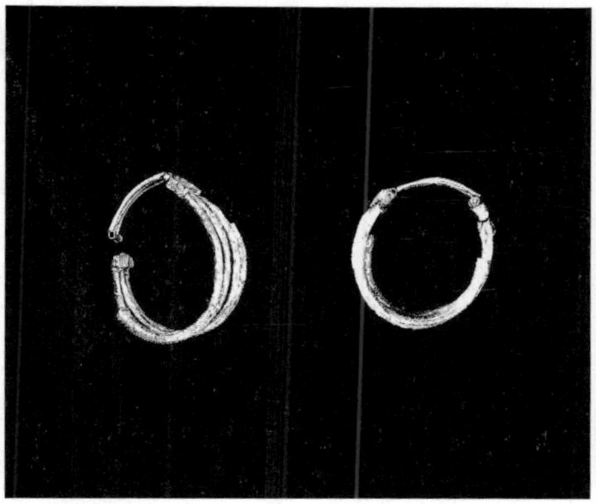

19. PAIR OF ARMLETS
Museo Archeologico, Florence
Inv. 77266-77267
From Vetulonia, the Lictor's tomb
Diam. *ca.* 6.5 cm.
Sheet-gold. The first is intact, fragmentary the second
Etruscan production from the third quarter of 7th cent. B.C.

Each armlet is formed by four hollow, curved tubes, the central ones having the ends welded to a parallelepiped capsule, while the two shorter lateral ones are joined at only one end, the other being free and sealed by a discoid plate. The fastening is effected by three arcuate sticks, joined by hinges to the clasps. Gold dust decoration with a zoomorphic frieze (lions and sphinxes) and geometrical and plant fillings. On the bigger sides of the clasp, a winged lion facing right: on the smaller sides zig-zags and multiple corners.

L'Oro degli Etruschi, p. 272, n° 67, with bibl.; *Schätze der Etrusker*, p. 188, n°s. 22-23.

M.C.

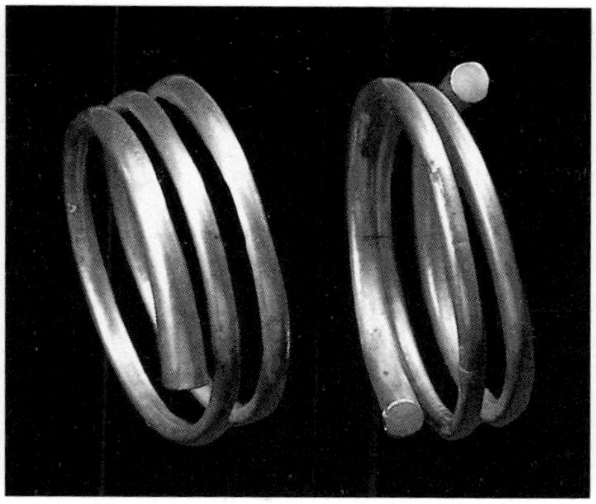

20. PAIR OF PLAIT-CLIPS
Florence, Museo Archeologico
Inv. 74013-74014
From Vetulonia, Bought by Guidi in 1890
Diam. 4.5 cm.
Rolled gold. Intact
Etruscan production of the 7th century B.C.

Tabular leaf twisted in three coils.

Gioielli e Ornamenti Preziosi, n° 4.

M.C.

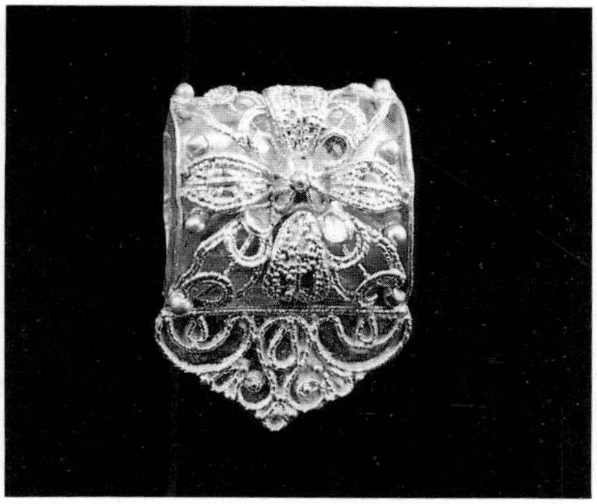

21. *BAULE* (BASKET) EARRING
Museo Archeologico, Florence
Inv. 132292
From Vetulonia. Lancetti Purchase 1903
Ht. 2 cm.; w. 1.5 cm.
Sheet-gold; stamped decoration, granulation and filagree. Intact
Etruscan production from the second half of 6th cent. B.C.

Rectangular, curved band, divided into two sections. In the front one, a large rosette of eight plastic petals has granulated motifs running through it which join up at the corners with globules and filagree knots. All this is surmounted by a granulated crowning of palmettes and half-moons. The back is formed with a thin metal sheet crossed by little ribs in relief. At one end there is a hinge consisting of two welded cylindrical tubes.

Gioielli e Ornamenti Preziosi, n° 5.

M.C.

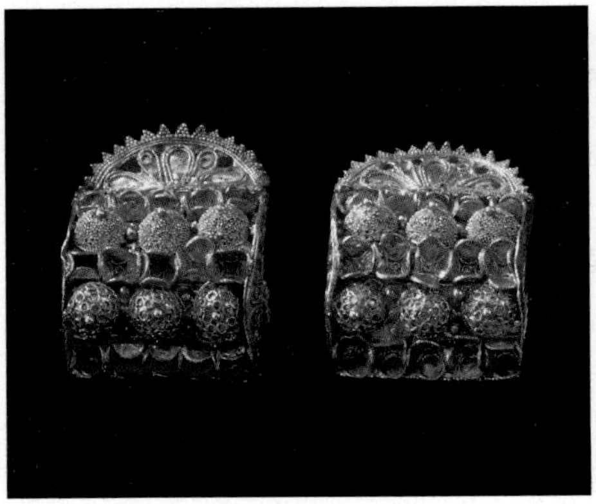

22. PAIR OF *BAULE* EARRINGS
Museo Archeologico, Florence
Inv. 15748-15749
Ht. 2 cm., w. 1.5 cm.
Sheet-gold; filigree and granulation decoration. Intact
From Volterra, Portone necropolis
Etruscan production from the second half of 6th cent. B.C.

Curved, rectangular band ending in a semi-circular tongue. The decorative motif of the body consists in two series of three globules, decorated in filagree and granulation, alternating with three strips of four-petalled rosettes. Palmettes on the tongue.

Ori e argenti, p. 9, n° 101.

M.C.

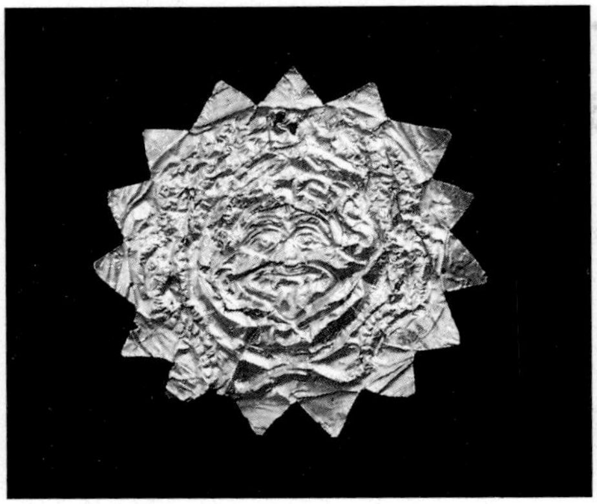

23. STUD
Museo Archeologico, Florence
Inv. 81095
From Vetulonia. Lancetti Purchase 1903
Diam. 4.5 cm.
Sheet-gold, stamped decoration. Intact
Etruscan production from the 6th-5th cent. B.C.

At the centre of the circular, convex stud with fringed, triangular flanges, there is a Gorgon head around which a double plant motif extends sinuously.

Gioielli e Ornamenti Preziosi, n° 7.

M.C.

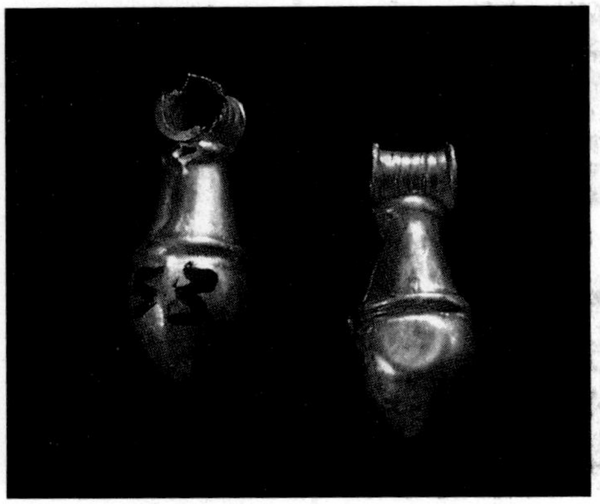

24. PAIR OF NECKLACE PENDANTS
Museo Archeologico, Florence
Inv. 138453-138454
From Vetulonia, Lancetti Purchase 1903
L. 1.2 cm.
Sheet-gold. Intact
Etruscan production from 6th-5th cent. B.C.

Pendants shaped as acorns, surmounted with tubular loops.

Gioielli e Ornamenti Preziosi, n° 10.

M.C.

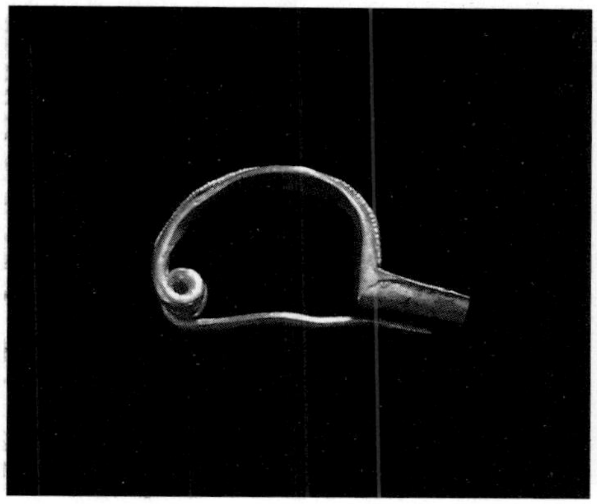

25. FIBULA
Museo Archeologico, Florence
Inv. 81111
From Vetulonia. Lancetti Purchase 1903
L. 2 cm.
Sheet-gold; knurled decoration. Intact
Etruscan production from the end of 6th-5th cent. B.C.

Slightly expanded bow, crossed lengthwise by a knurled wire. The foot consists of a bent-over laminate.

Gioielli e Ornamenti Preziosi, n° 6.

M.C.

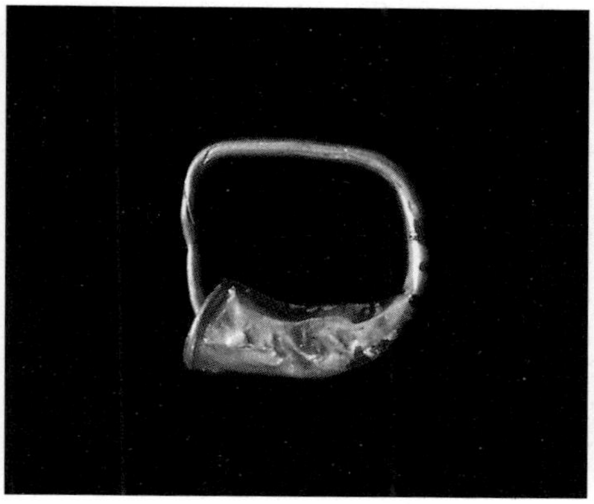

26. BUGLE EARRING
Museo Archeologico, Florence
Inv. 138449
From Vetulonia. Lancetti Purchase 1903
Diam. 1.5 cm.
Sheet-gold. Deformed
Etruscan production from the 6th-5th cent. B.C.

Consists in a bent-up laminate, splayed at one end.

Gioielli e Ornamenti Preziosi, n° 9.

M.C.

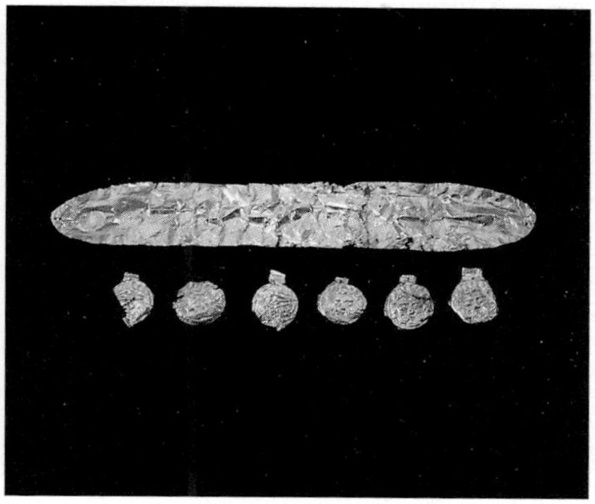

27. BAND WITH FIVE STUDS
Museo Archeologico, Florence
Inv. 81094
Lancetti Purchase 1903
L. 18.2 cm.; diam. of studs 1.8 cm.; l. of band 0.9 cm.
Sheet-gold; stamped decoration. Intact
Etruscan production from the 6th-5th cent. B.C.

Smooth, rectangular band, rounded along the short sides, accompanied by five circular, convex studs, which exhibit a stamped Gorgoneion at the centre; at one end a rectangular bent-up catch-plate for suspension.

Gioielli e Ornamenti Preziosi, n° 8.

M.C.

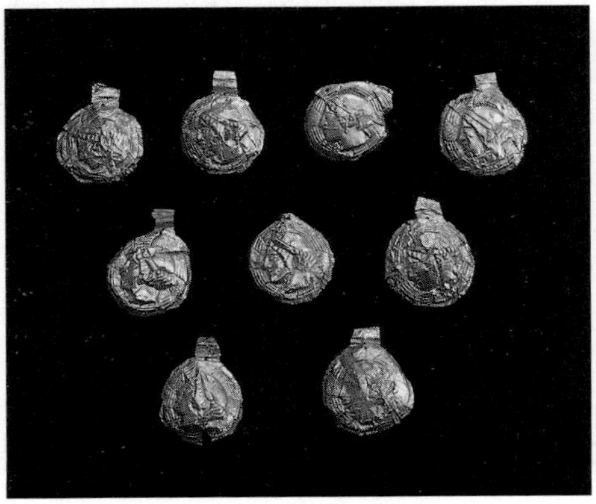

28. STUDS
Museo Archeologico, Florence
Inv. 81100-81108
From Vetulonia. Lancetti Purchase 1903
Diam. 2.4 cm.; l. of strap 0.6 cm.
Sheet-gold; stamped decoration. Intact with superficial dents
Etruscan production from the first half of 5th cent. B.C.

At the centre of the circular convex sheet, a stamped female head in the left profile is realized, with a ribbon diadem and hair tied at the back of the neck. A knot and fascia motif surrounds the head.

G. Becatti. *Oreficerie antiche*, Rome 1955, tav. 78, n° 315. *Gioielli e Ornamenti Preziosi*, n° 11, with bibl.

M.C.

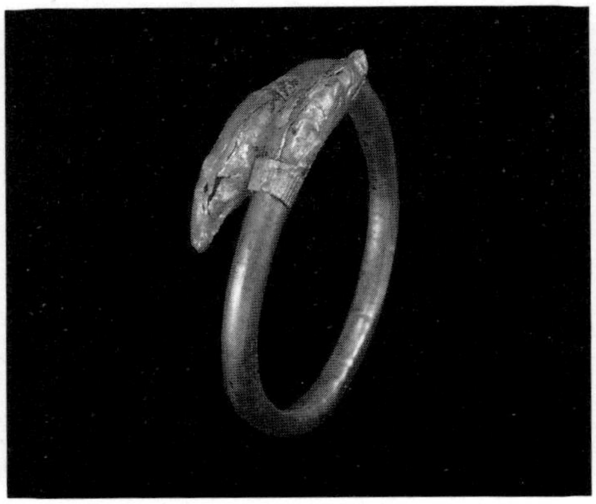

29. ARMLET
Museo Archeologico, Florence
Inv. 15741
Presumably from Volterra, previously Cinci Coll. (erroneously indicated from Pescia Romana)
Diam. 5.8 cm.; diam. of shaft 0.5 cm.
Gold. Intact
Etruscan production from the mid 5th cent. B.C.

Barred armlet in circular sections with overlapping heads; at the ends two whale protomes in embossed and chiselled sheets on a bronze mandrel are inserted. At the base of the protomes there is a collar band decorated with rhomboid motifs, applied with the aid of a burin.

E. Fiumi, «Materiali volterrani del Museo Archeologico di Firenze. La Collezione Cinci» in *StEtrXXV*, 1957, p. 474; *Gioielli e Ornamenti Preziosi*, p. 143, n° 63; *Ori e Argenti*, p. 9, n° 119.

S.B.

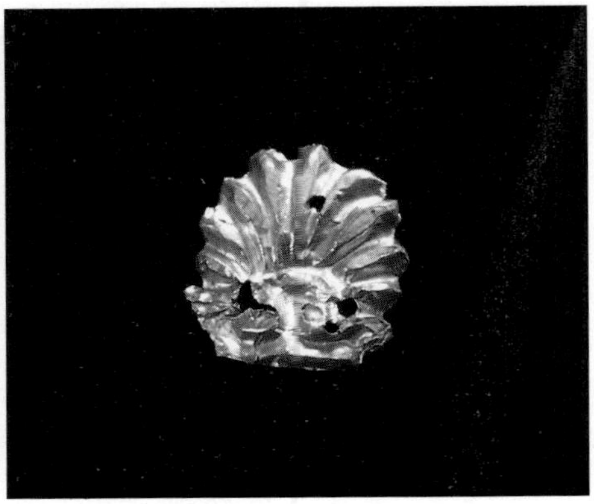

30. PALMETTE STUD
Museo Archeologico, Florence
Inv. 138455
L. 1.3 cm.
Sheet-gold; stamped decoration. Intact
Etruscan production from 5th-3rd cent. B.C.

The sheet, concave on the surface, is shaped as a palmette.

Gioielli e Ornamenti Preziosi, n° 12.

M.C.

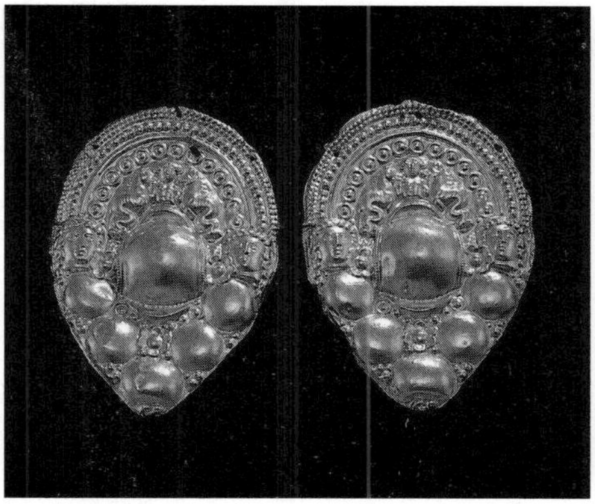

31. CLUSTER EARRINGS.
Museo Archeologico, Florence
Inv. 15803-15804.
Currie Coll.
Ht. 8.65 cm.; max. w. 6 cm.
Sheet-gold with embossed decoration. Intact
Etruscan production of the second half of 4th cent. B.C.

Upper circular shield, with strips decorated respectively with a double series of little knobs, a series of knobs of greater dimensions, and umbilicate circles preceded by a fillet. In the central lunette, a nude male half-figure holds two sea-horses respectant.

At the centre, a sphere segment bordered above and below by a half-moon surrounded by wires; at the sides, two female heads. In the lower part, five spheres, each with three globules at the base; the decoration is enriched by three six-petalled rosettes and two encircled bosses.

L'Oro degli Etruschi, p. 63, p. 68 note 6; *Gioielli e Ornamenti*, p. 145, n° 70, with bibl.; *Ori e Argenti*, p. 7. n° 71.

M.C.

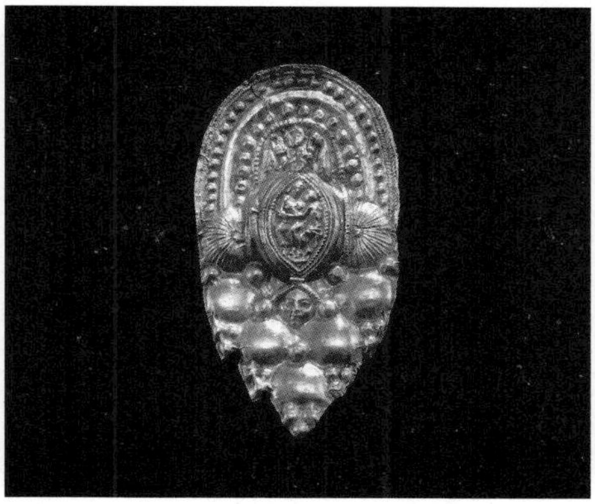

32. CLUSTER EARRING.
Museo Archeologico, Florence
Inv. 15802
Currie Collection
Ht. 9.05 cm.; max. w. 4.75 cm.
Sheet-gold; stamped decoration. Intact
Etruscan production of 4th cent. B.C.

Oval upper shield, decorated by means of a series of knobs, included respectively between two strips of knurled wire, a smooth ribbing and a filletted ribbing. In the central lunette, a nude, male half-figure holds two sea-horses respectant. At the centre, an elliptical helmet, consisting in an isolated metal sheet, on which a male and a female embracing are represented; at the sides, two palmettes. In the lower part, five spheres, each with three globules at the base; at the centre, a Medusa head between globules.

Gioielli e Ornamenti, p. 145, n° 71; *Ori e Argenti*, p. 7, n° 72.

G.P.

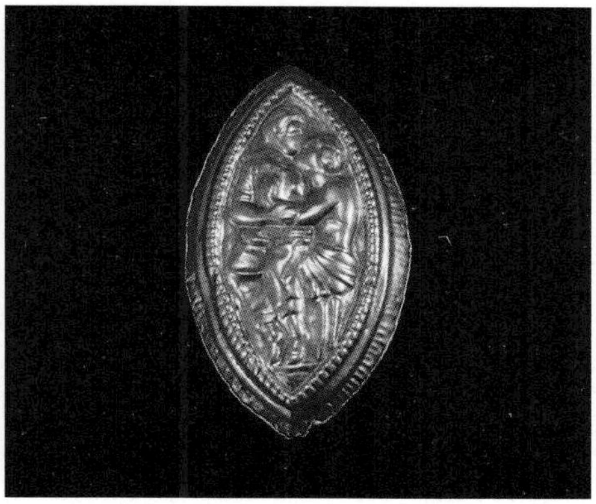

33. FINGER-RING
Museo Archeologico, Florence
Inv. 15733
From Orbetello, purchased in 1820
Diam. 2.5 cm.; diam. of bezel 2.5 x 1.5 cm.
Sheet-gold; stamped decoration. Intact
Etruscan production from the first half of 4th cent. B.C, which can be included in the so-named Fortnum Group.

Banded ring with almond bezel. In the bezel, bordered by a series of tongues, a seated youth in the act of embracing a woman seated on his knee is portrayed in a pearly frame.

J.D. Boardman, *Etruscan and South Italian Finger Rings, cit.* p. 11, n° X, tav. IV; *Gioielli e Ornamenti*, p. 145, n° 74. *Ori e Argenti*, p. 7, n° 74.

G.C.C.

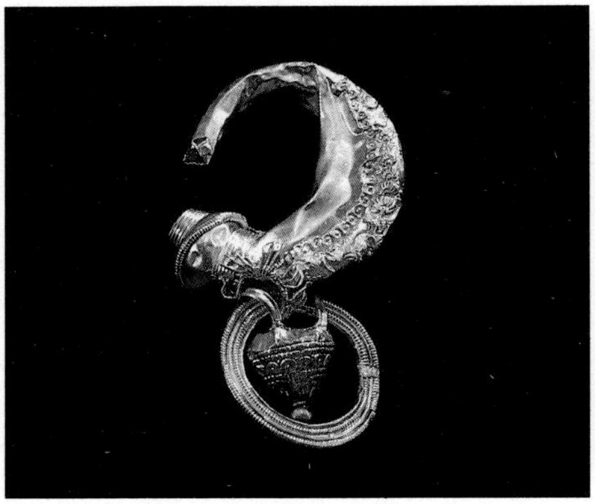

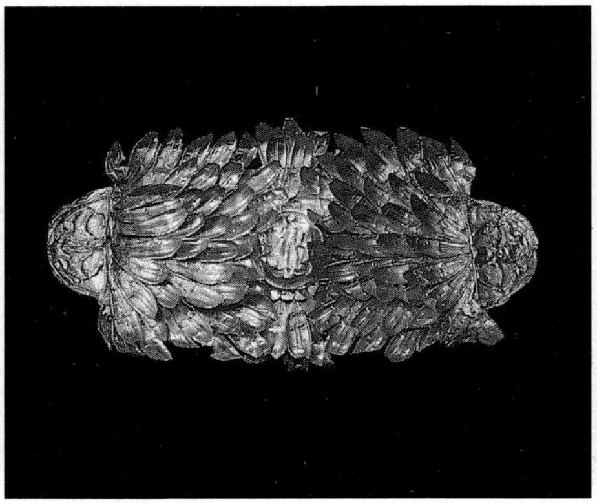

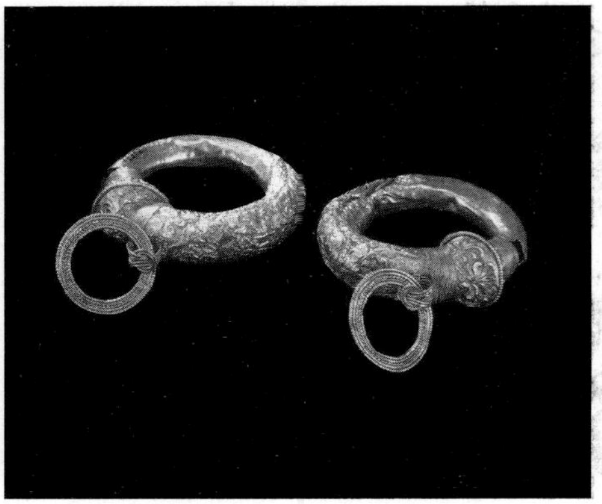

34. TUBULAR EARRING WITH PENDANT
Museo Archeologico, Florence
Inv. 81092
Ht. 7 cm; max. w. 4 cm.
Sheet-gold; embossed and knurled decoration. Intact with dented surface
Etruscan production from the end of 4th cent. B.C.

Hollow ring consisting in a fine sheet bent into a tube, broadened at the ends and terminating in a little double-cylindrical globule decorated with a knurled collar band at the fullest spot. The front of the ring is decorated with an embossed motif with plaits, plant elements and cirri. A knurled knot supporting a hoop pendant is welded near the globule. This consists of intertwined wires having at the centre an amphora crossed with embossed motifs.

Gioielli e Ornamenti Preziosi, n° 14.

M.C.

35. DIADEM
Museo Archeologico, Florence
Inv. 84339
From chamber Tomb with coffin at Sperandio (Perugia)
Ht. 19.1 cm., w. 33 cm.
Gold; applied and stamped, embossed decoration. Small gaps, worn at the edges
Etruscan production datable from about 300 B.C.

It consists in a rectangular metal sheet, with semicircular, embossed tongues at the ends, on which cut-out olive or laurel leaves have been applied using gold wires. The leaves have stamped decorations of three central, longitudinal veins and prominent flanges and are placed on each side in five rows radiating towards the centre and also in two smaller groups which all divide the diadem axially into two parts. They are fixed at the base and at the top of an eliptic boss, placed at the centre, with a cornice of pelta-shaped petals.
On the boss a winged, female figure, stamped in relief, is portrayed. She stands to the left, dressed in a girdled chiton, with a mirror in the right hand and an unguentarium in the left. A cist surmounted with drapery is on her right. An oenochoe with keel-shaped shoulder lies near her left foot. Using the same technique on the lateral plates, a figure of Typhon, full-face, is portrayed. He is arranged heraldically, with his lower, serpentine limbs curled in a spiral and with a delphin held aloft in each hand.

Gioielli e Ornamenti, p. 148, n° 84. *Gioielli e Ornamenti Preziosi*, n° 42.

M.M.

36. PAIR OF TUBULAR EARRINGS
Museo Archeologico, Florence
Inv. 15742-15824
Targioni Tozzetti Purchase 1823
Etruscan production from the second half of 4th cent. B.C.
Ht. 7.3 cm.
Sheet-gold. Intact

They consist in a tubular, expanded, circular sheet. One end terminates in a double-cylindrical globule, between two bands covered with twisted wire, crossed horizontally with a series of little spheres and decorated with a chain of palmettes and cirri. The loop pendant, consisting of knurled, plaited wires, is joined to the laminate by a knot of knurled wires.

Gioielli e Ornamenti, p. 150, n° 90. *Ori e Argenti*, p. 8, n° 99.

M.C.

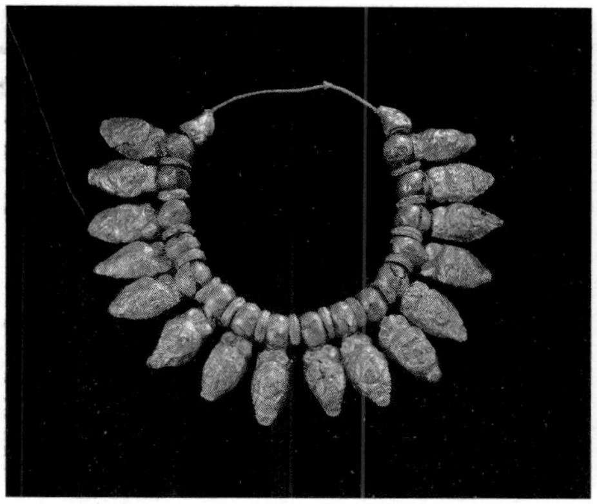

37. NECKLACE
Museo Archeologico, Florence
Inv. 15951
From Volterra, necropolis of Portone, previously Cinci Coll.
Total l. 2 cm.; pendants ht. 4 cm.; spacer diam. 1 cm.
Sheet-gold. Intact
Etruscan production of 4th cent. B.C.

Consisting in 16 pendants of metal sheet, separated by spacers decorated with streaks, it has two ram's heads at the ends in laminate. The pendants are soldered to a spheric globule by means of a double volute joint and represent an embossed Silenus head alternating with a maenadic head.

E. Fiumi, «Materiali volterrani nel Museo Archeologico di Firenze», in *StEtr.* XXV, 1957, p. 481, fig. 6; *L'Oro degli Etruschi*, p. 316, n° 265, with bibl. (of erroneous provenance); *Gioielli e Ornamenti*, p. 146, n° 78; *Ori e Argenti*, p. 9, n° 104.

M.C.

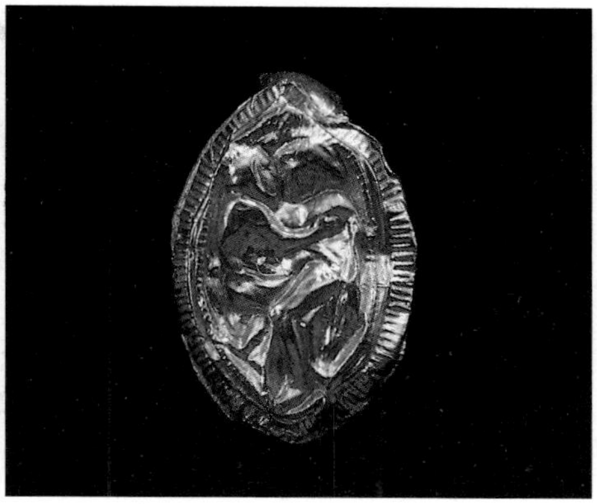

38. FINGER-RING
Museo Archeologico, Florence
Inv. 81113
W. 3.2 cm.; ht. 2.3 cm.
Sheet-gold; stamped decoration. Intact with superficial dentation
Etruscan production belonging to the «Fortnum» Group; first half of 4th cent. B.C.

Banded ring with an almond bezel. Embossed on the latter is a seated male figure embracing another cloaked figure seated on his knee.

Gioielli e Ornamenti Preziosi, n° 13.

M.C.

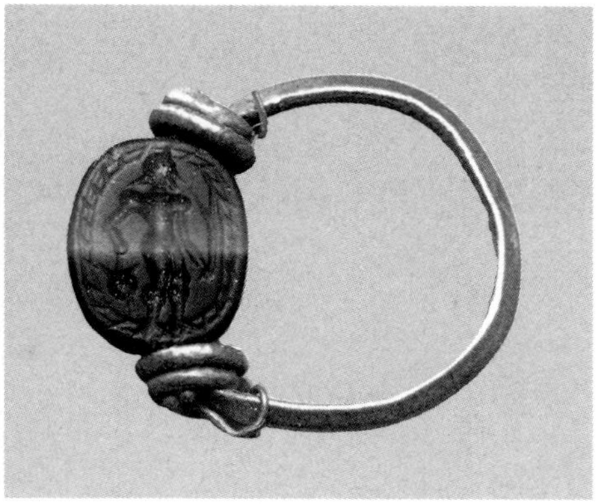

39. RING WITH SCARAB
Guarnacci Museum, Volterra
Inv. 99
Ancient deposits of the Guarnacci Museum going back to 18th cent.
Diam. 1.1 cm.
Gold. Agate
Etruscan production from the 4th cent. B.C.

Gold bar ring with a banded agate scarab fixed to the bar by a gold wire twisted around it. On the flat base, within a frame of a series of hyphening, a male figure in profile dexter is engraved in the globule style. He holds a long, crooked stick in his left hand and in the right an unidentifiable spheroid object.

Gioielli e Ornamenti Preziosi, n° 128.

Ga.C.

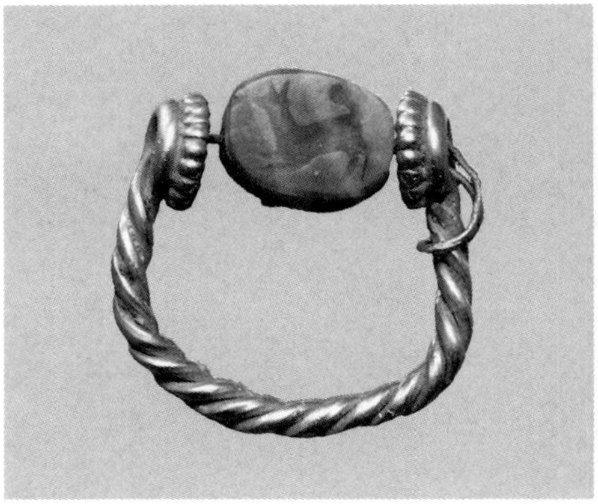

40. RING WITH SCARAB
Guarnacci Museum, Volterra
Inv. 102
Ancient deposits of the Guarnacci Museum going back to 18th cent.
Diam. 0.8 cm.
Gold. Agate
Etruscan production from the 4th cent. B.C.

Spiral bar ring with banded agate scarab, fixed to the bar with a gold wire twisted around it. The figure of a fox on the run is engraved on the whole of the flat part.

Gioielli e Ornamenti Preziosi, n° 129.

Ga.C.

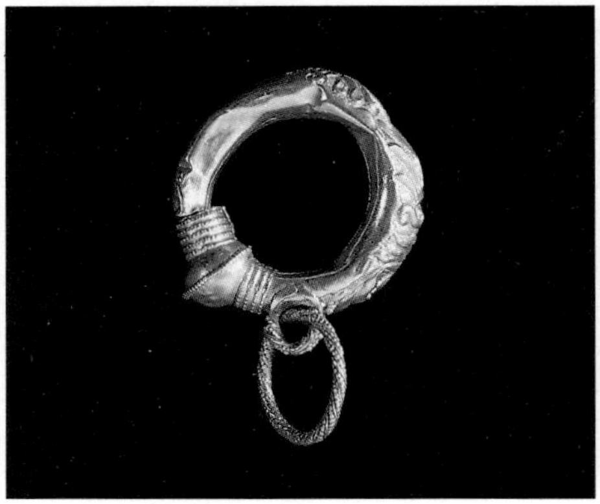

41. TUBULAR EARRING
Museo Archeologico, Florence
Inv. 15765
Unknown provenance, previously Currie Coll.
Diam. of ring 3 cm.; diam. of pendant 1 cm.
Sheet-gold; granulated and embossed decoration. Intact
Etruscan production from the second half of 4th cent. B.C.

Hollow ring, consisting of a thin metal sheet bent into a tube, broadened at the ends and terminating in a biconic globule compressed between two series of granulated collars. In the front the ring is embossed with a full-face female head, locks of hair parted on the forehead, surmounted by a counter scroll-and-palmette motif. Welded near the globule is a smooth knot which holds a hoop pendant consisting of gold knurled and plaited wires.

Gioielli e Ornamenti, p. 149, n° 88; *Ori e Argenti*, p. 11, n° 150.

G.C.C.

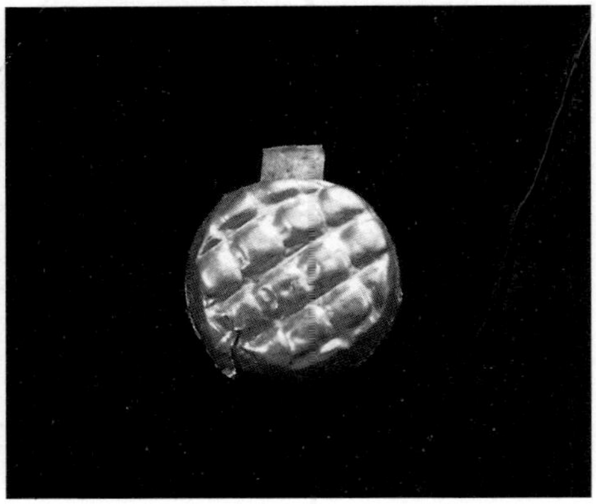

42. STUD
Museo Archeologico, Florence
Inv. 81099
Diam. 1.5 cm; max l. 1.6 cm.
Sheet-gold; stamped decoration. Intact
Etruscan production from 4th - 3rd cent. B.C.

Concave-convex circular surface, the latter being crossed by rhomboid motifs and surmounted at one end by a square clip to hang them by.

Gioielli e Ornamenti Preziosi, n° 15.

M.C.

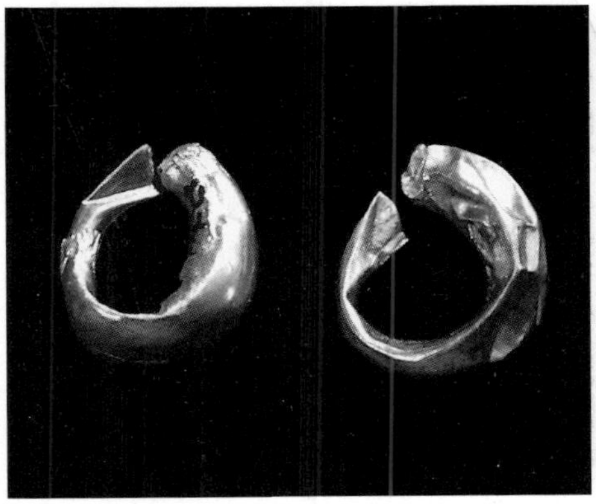

43. PAIR OF EARRINGS
Museo Archeologico, Florence
Inv. 138447-138448
Diam. 1.2 cm.
Sheet-gold. Deformed with gaps at one end
Etruscan production from 4th - 3rd cent. B.C.

Sheet bent into a tube, thickened at one end.

Gioielli e Ornamenti Preziosi, n° 19.

M.C.

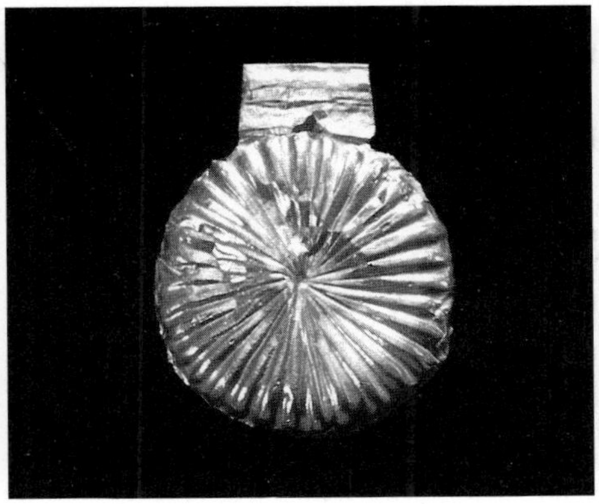

44. PAIR OF PENDANTS
Museo Archeologico, Florence
Inv. 81097-81098
Diam. 1.7 cm.; clasp l. 1.2 cm.; 0.4 cm.
Sheet-gold; stamped decoration. Intact
Etruscan production from 4th - 3rd cent. B.C.

Concave-convex circular sheet with stamped ray motifs. At one end a rectangular clip to hang them by.

Gioielli e Ornamenti Preziosi, n° 16.

M.C.

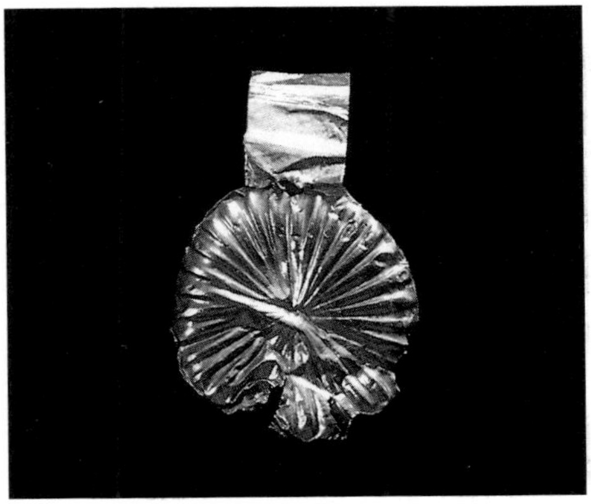

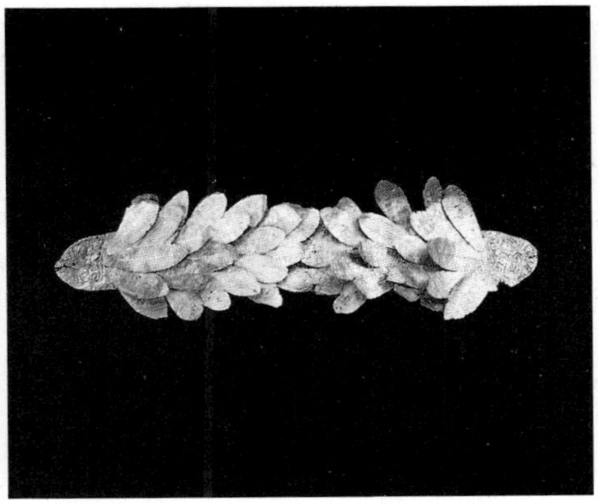

45. FUNERARY BAND
Guarnacci Museum, Volterra
Inv. 4
Portone necropolis. Purchase 1861
L. 28.5 cm.
Gold
Etruscan production from the late 4th - 3rd cent. B.C.

Onto a narrow gold sheet band, with semi-circular tongues at the ends, are applied thin leaves, veined like those of the olive tree and superimposed in a closely-packed symmetrical mass. The lateral tongues, which have a loop hole, are decorated with stamped palmettes on volutes bordered with tiny olive leaves.

L'Oro degli Etruschi, p. 310, n° 236; *Gioielli e Ornamenti Preziosi*, n° 132.

Ga.C.

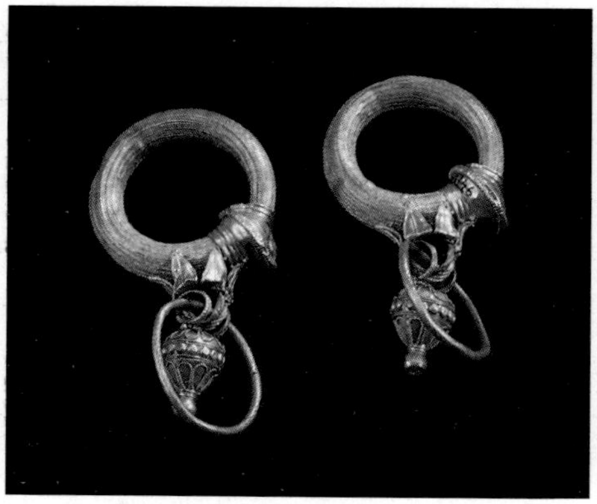

46. PAIR OF TUBULAR EARRINGS, with pendant
Museo Archeologico, Florence
Inv. 15745-15746
Diam. of ring 2.8 cm.; overall ht. 5.2 cm.
Sheet-gold with embossed and filigree decoration. Intact
Etruscan production from the end of 4th cent. - beginning of 3rd cent. B.C.
From Orbetello, Purchase 1820.

Hollow ring consisting in a thin sheet bent into a tube, thickened at one end and terminating in a double-cylindrical globule. The ring has a series of closely packed knurled wires. Near the globule, a lotus flower holding a hoop pendant with an amphora at the centre is welded.

Ori e Argenti, p. 7, n° 73.

M.C.

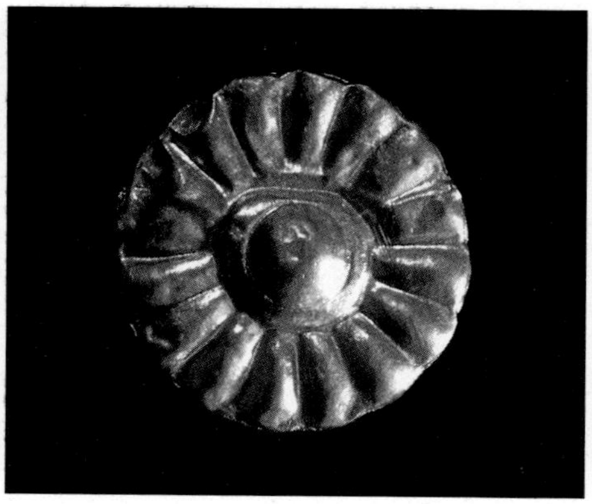

47. STUD
Museo Archeologico, Florence
Inv. 81096
Diam. 2 cm.
Sheet-gold; stamped decoration. Intact
Etruscan production from 4th - 2nd cent. B.C.

Formed of two sheets welded together and traversed by a stamped rosette motif, with a central boss in relief. At the back there is a clip, bent over and welded, to hang it by.

Gioielli e Ornamenti Preziosi, n° 18.

M.C.

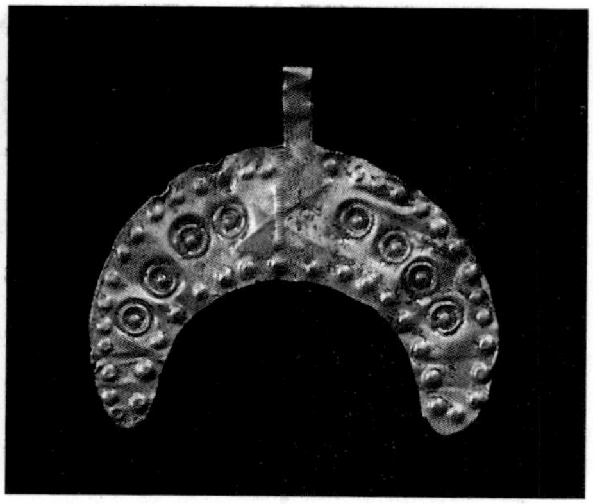

48. NECKLACE PENDANT
Museo Archeologico, Florence
Inv. 72614
From Luni, previously Remedi Coll.
Ht. 2.4 cm; w. 2.7 cm.
Sheet-gold; embossed and stamped decoration. Intact
Etruscan production from 3rd cent. B.C.

Formed from a flat sheet fashioned as a half-moon, stamped with series of cuppels along the external strip. On both sides, quadruple embossed, concentric circles, divided by a thin, engraved St Andrew's cross. At the upper end of the convex side, a flat suspension clip.

Gioielli e Ornamenti Preziosi, n° 26.

M.C.

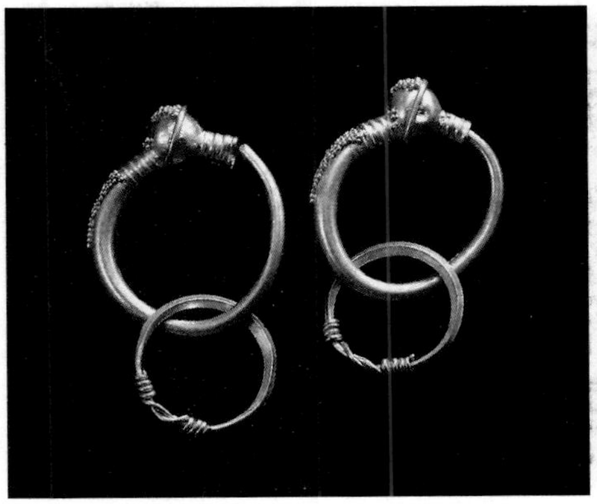

49. PAIR OF TUBULAR EARRINGS with pendant
Museo Archeologico, Florence
Inv. 81114-81115.
Tot. ht. 2.5 cm.; diam. 1.5 cm; diam. of pendant 1 cm.
Sheet-gold; granulated decoration. Intact
Etruscan production from 3rd - 2nd cent. B.C.

Hollow ring consisting in a thin sheet, bent into a tube, thickened at one end and terminating in a double-cylindrical globule. On this and on the frontal end of the ring, there is a triangular, granulated motif. Hooked to one end is a hoop pendant with two sections traversed with wire twisted around.

Gioielli e Ornamenti Preziosi, n° 17.

M.C.

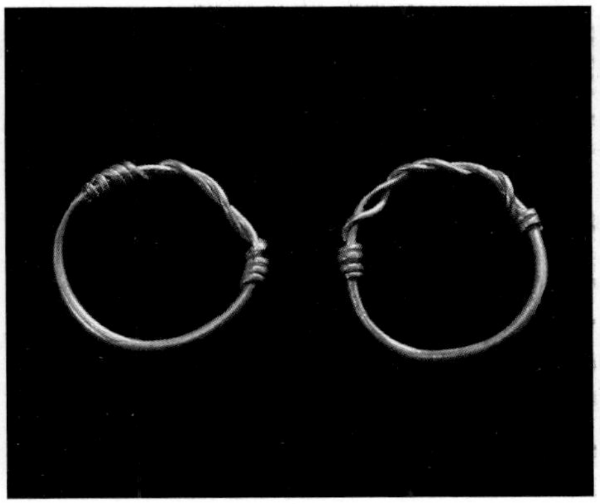

50. PAIR OF EARRING PENDANTS
Museo Archeologico, Florence
Inv. 81116-81117
Diam. 0.6 cm.
Sheet-gold. Intact
Etruscan production from 3rd - 2nd cent. B.C.

Hoop pendants with two sections traversed by wire twisted around.

Gioielli e Ornamenti Preziosi, n° 20.

M.C.

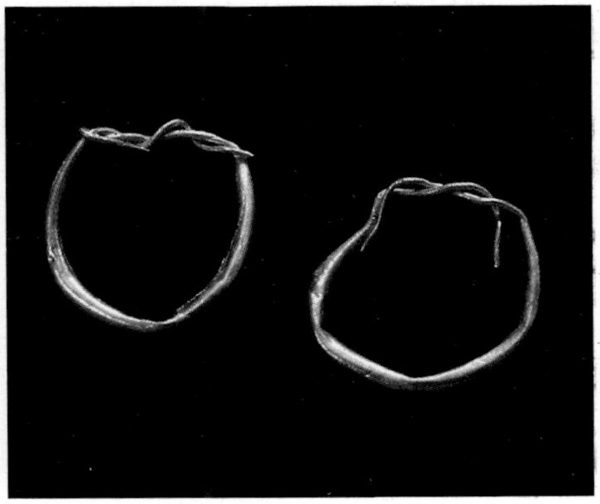

51. PAIR OF EARRING PENDANTS
Museo Archeologico, Florence
Inv. 81118-81119
Diam 0.7 cm.
Sheet-gold. Intact
Etruscan production from 3rd - 2nd cent. B.C.

Hoop pendants with two sections traversed by wire twisted around.

Gioielli e Ornamenti Preziosi, n° 21.

M.C.

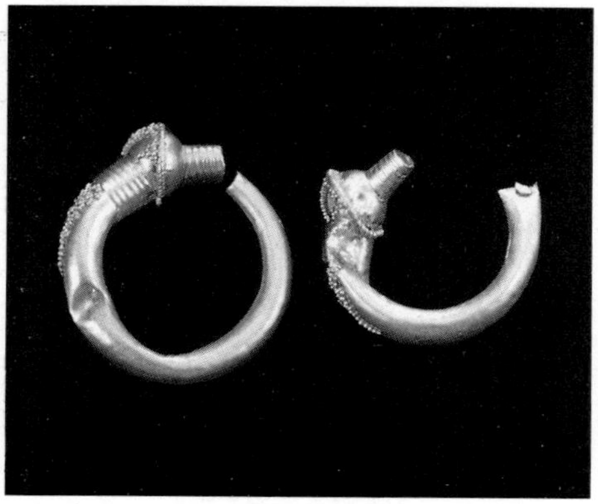

52. PAIR OF TUBULAR EARRINGS
Museo Archeologico, Florence
Inv. 81109-81110
Diam. 2 cm.
Sheet-gold; granulated decoration. Intact
Etruscan production from 3rd cent. B.C.

Hollow ring consisting of a thin sheet bent into a tube, broadened at one end and terminating in a biconic globule. On this and on the front end of the ring, triangular, granulated motifs.

Gioielli e Ornamenti Preziosi, n° 22.

M.C.

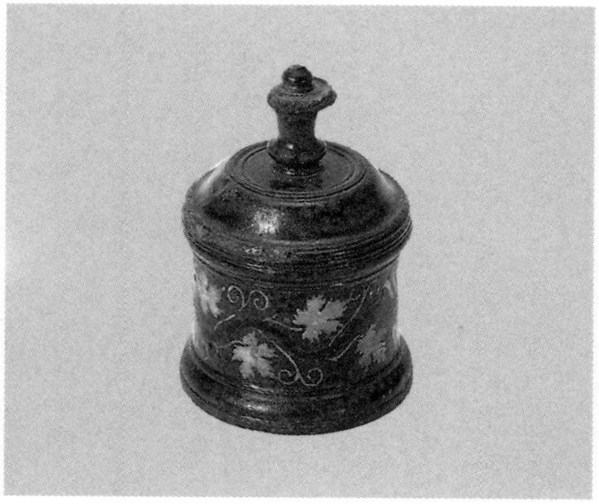

53. PYX
Guarnacci Museum, Volterra
Inv. 5012
Ancient deposits of the Guarnacci Museum going back to 18th cent.
Ht. 7.5 cm.; diam. 4.5 cm.
Bronze with damascene silver decorations
Etruscan production from the 3rd - 2nd cent. B.C.

Cylindrical in shape, it has a conical lid with a moulded knob. The central band exhibits a decoration of a rich garland of vine leaves alternating with flower clusters in silver damascene.

Gioielli e Ornamenti Preziosi, n° 134.

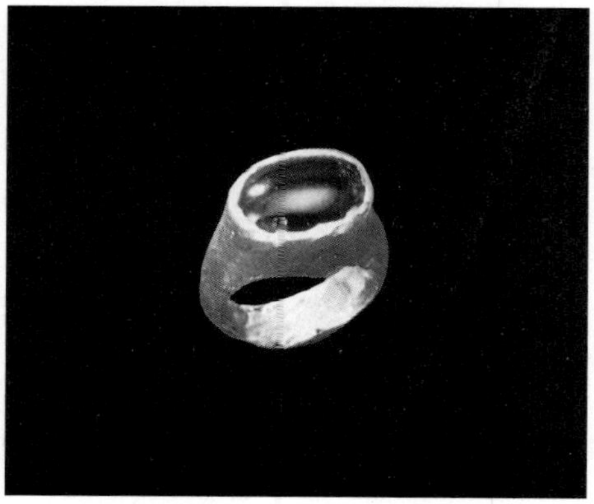

54. FINGER RING
Guarnacci Museum, Volterra
Inv. 115
Ancient deposits of the Guarnacci Museum going back to 18th cent.
Diam. 1.6 cm.
Gold. Ruby
Etruscan production from the Hellenistic Age.

Hollow band with a hoop complete with an oval bezel in which a ruby is set.

Gioielli e Ornamenti Preziosi, n° 131.

Ga.C.

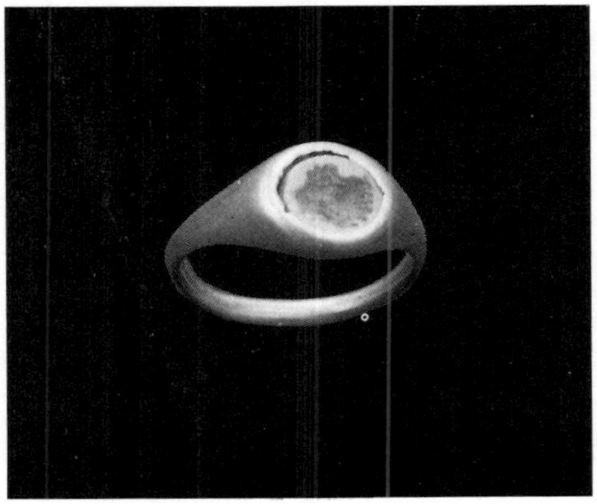

55. FINGER RING
Guarnacci Museum, Volterra
Inv. 116
Ancient deposits of the Guarnacci Museum going back to 18th cent.
Diam. 2.8 cm.
Gold. Vitreous paste
Etruscan production from the Hellenistic Age.

Hoop provided with an oval bezel where a vitrous paste or blue gem is set, engraved with a Moor's head.

Gioielli e Ornamenti Preziosi, n° 130.

Ga.C.

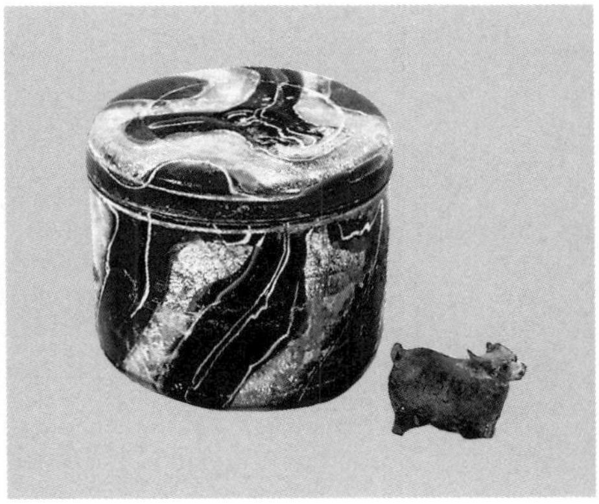

56.-57.-58. PYXIS AND TWO UNGUENTARIA
Guarnacci Museum, Volterra
Inv. 4, 6,7
Necropolis of Portone (1860-1873 excavations)
Ancient deposits of the Guarnacci Museum going back to 18th cent.
Pyxis: ht. 5.3 cm., diam. 5 cm. Pyriform aryballos: ht. 8 cm. Globular aryballos: ht. 3 cm., max. diam. 2.8 cm.
Vitreous paste and gold bands
Italic production of Augustan age.

Cylindrical pyxis with a lid; pyriform aryballos with double careen; compressed globular aryballos. The polychrome ointment jars and pyxis, with serpentine filaments (some in gold dust), were produced using a system like the one used for the so-called «barbotine» pottery.

Gioielli e Ornamenti Preziosi, n° 127, with bibl.

Ga.C.

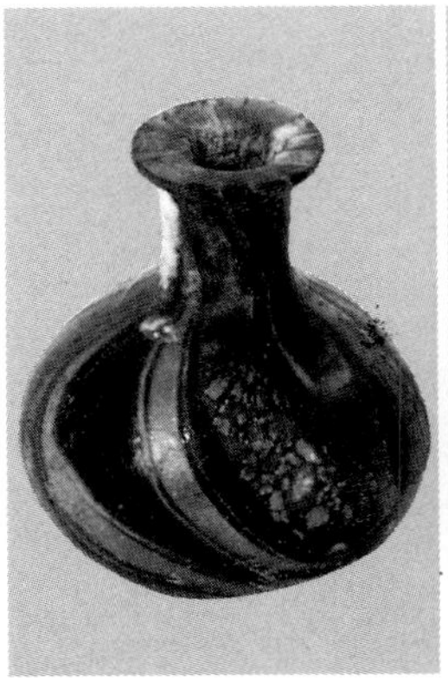

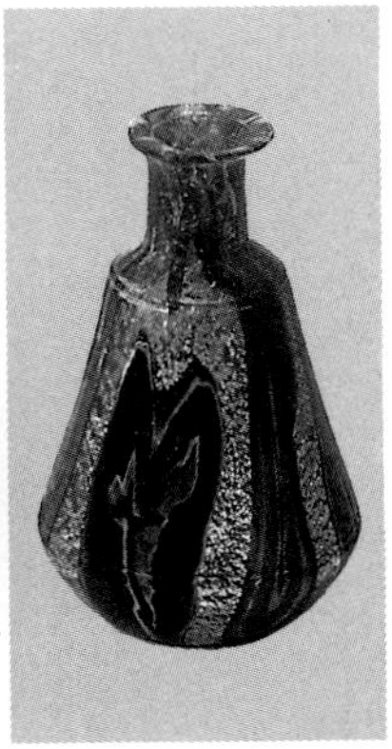

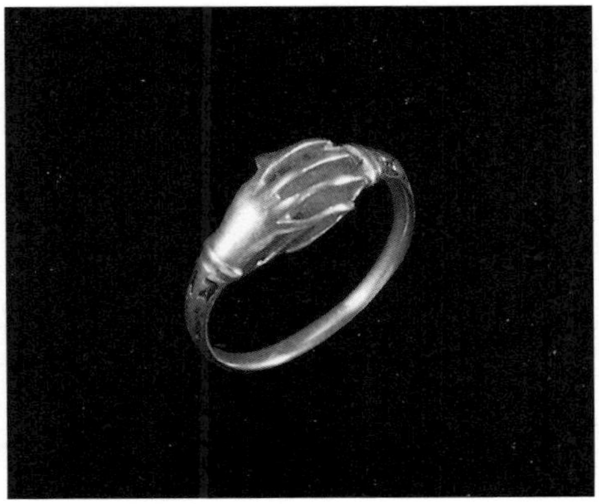

59. FINGER RING
Guarnacci Museum, Volterra
Inv. 133
Ancient deposits of the Guarnacci Museum going back to 18th cent.
Diam. 2.2 cm.
Cast and chiselled gold. Intact
Roman production from 1st cent. B.C. - 1st cent. A.D.

The object is formed by a circular, flattened bar, modelled at the top in the shape of two intertwined hands.
This little finger ring from Volterra is difficult to collocate chronologically. The motif repeated on it, that of the intertwined hands in the *dextrarum iunctio*, is noted not only in the farewell scenes on the funerary urns, but also on a gem belonging to the Guarnacci Collection.

Gioielli e Ornamenti, p. 159, *Gioielli e Ornamenti Preziosi*, n° 126.

Ga.C.

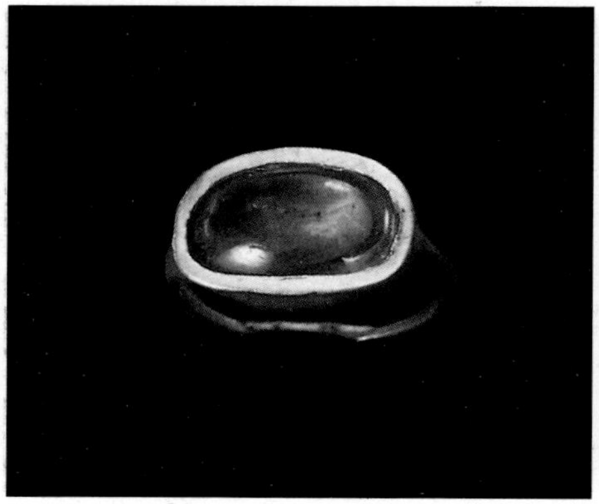

60. FINGER RING
Museo Archeologico, Florence
Inv. 72588
From Luni, previously Remedi Coll.
Diam. 2 cm.
Sheet-gold and amethyst. Intact

Consisting in a thin sheet which is expanded at the top with an oval bezel in which an amethyst bearing the engraving of a bird is set.

Gioielli e Ornamenti Preziosi, n° 29.

M.C.

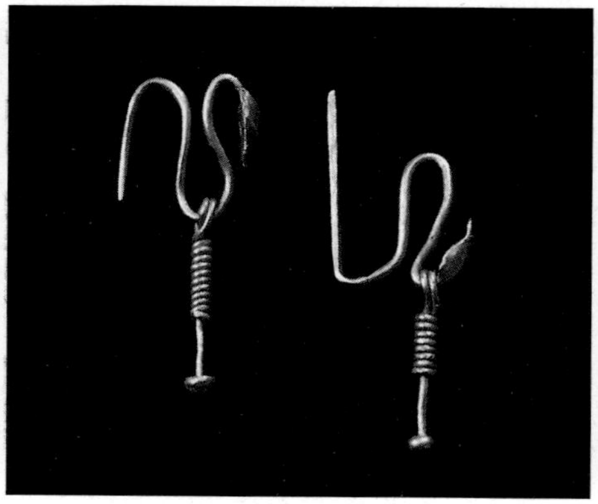

61. PAIR OF EARRINGS
Museo Archeologico, Florence
Inv. 72607
From Luni, previously Remedi Coll.
Ht. 2.5 cm; w. 1 cm.
Sheet-gold. Intact
Roman production from 1st - 2nd cent. A.D.

Serpentine pin surmounted at one end by a thin convex ovoid metal sheet, terminating in a short rectangular tongue.In a bend of the serpentine, a pendant is hooked on by means of an eyelet. This wire pendant has another wire twisted several times round the upper half and terminates in a button.

Gioielli e Ornamenti Preziosi, n° 33.

M.C.

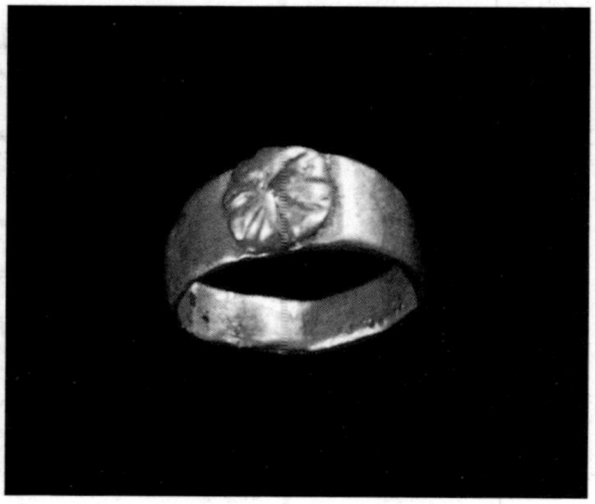

62. FINGER RING
Museo Archeologico, Florence
Inv. 72600
From Luni, previously Remedi Coll.
Diam. 1.4 cm.
Sheet-gold; relief decoration. Intact
Roman production from 1st - 2nd cent. A.D.

Consisting in a flat sheet, expanded at the top, it exhibits a flower with petals in relief on the upper exterior band.

Gioielli e Ornamenti Preziosi, n° 34.

M.C.

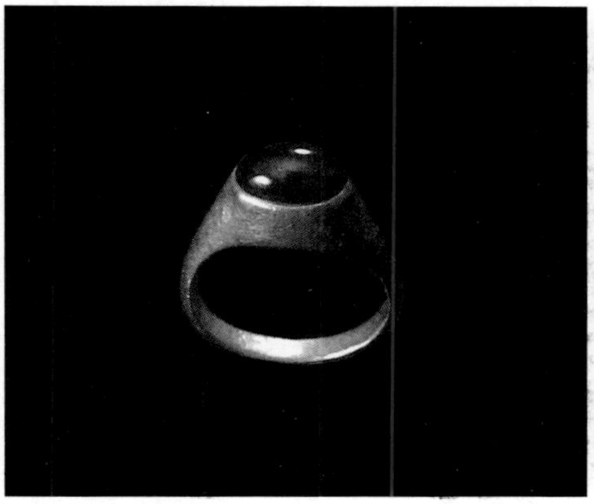

63. FINGER RING
Museo Archeologico, Florence
Inv. 72599
From Luni, previously Remedi Coll.
Ht. 1.7 cm; w. 1.5 cm.
Sheet-gold, granite almandine. Intact
Roman production from 1st - 2nd cent. A.D.

The circle is formed by a smooth metal sheet which broadens into the upper area where an oval granite almandine is set.

Gioielli e Ornamenti Preziosi, n° 36.

M.C.

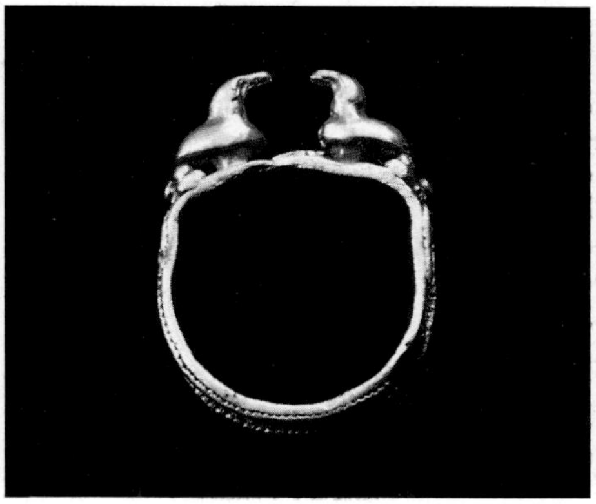

64. FINGER RING
Museo Archeologico, Florence
Inv. 72603
From Luni, previously Remedi Coll.
Ht. 2.5 cm.; w. 2 cm.
Sheet-gold; knurled and relief decoration. Intact
Roman (?) production from 3rd - 5th cent. A.D.

The circle consists of a flat metal sheet, bordered along the outside by a knurled wire that joins up in a double volute, and carries on the sheet the inscription AGNES preceded by a cross. It is surmounted by two birds facing each other in full relief, made in two welded metal sheets. Behind them are three litle balls, arranged in a triangle and surrounded by a wire. At the centre there is a double 8 motif in relief with residues of brown glass on the bezels.

Gioielli e Ornamenti Preziosi, n° 37.

M.C.

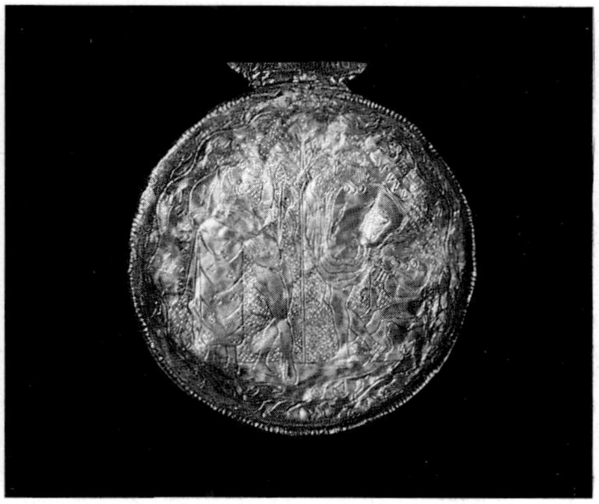

65. BULLA
Museo Archeologico, Arezzo
Inv. 1954 B
Funghini Collection
Diam. 6.5 cm.
Sheet-gold, burin-engraved. Intact
Etruscan production from mid 4th cent. B.C.

The disc with a knurled rim has a grip. At the centre, a scene with four personages is portrayed: on the right, a standing female figure (*Semla?*) bends over a nude, adolescent (*Fufluns*) who leans back, holding a thyrsus in his hand; opposite, an upright youth (*Aplu*) with long hair held back by a taenia is placing a laurel branch on the ground; below left, a seated Silenus is playing the double flute. The figures stand out from the granulated background; the scene is bordered by an ivy frame. Captions in Etruscan letters distinguish the two male figures as *Fufluns* and *Aplu*.

Il Museo Archeologico Nazionale G.C. Mecenate in Arezzo, Florence 1987, p. 183, with bibl.; *Gioielli e Ornamenti*, p. 148, n° 82.

D.B.

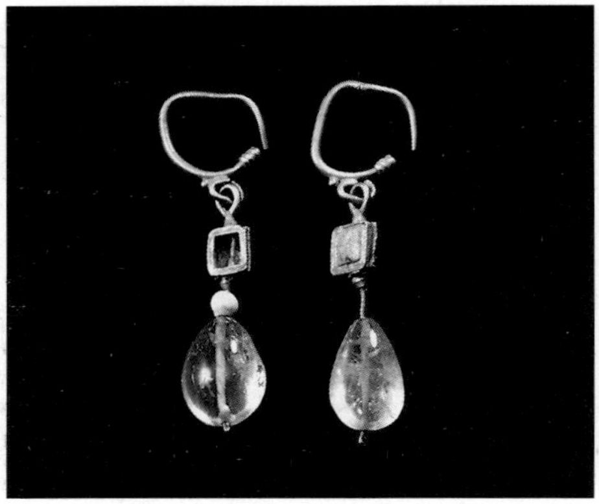

66. PAIR OF EARRINGS
Museo Archeologico, Florence
Inv. 72605
From Luni, previously Remedi Collection
L. 6.7 cm.
Sheet-gold; enamel and amethyst. Intact
Roman production from 4th - 6th cent. A.D.

A thick, curved wire hoop terminating at one end with a stamped, cylindrical swelling is welded onto an eyelet hooked onto a ring where a pendant hangs. The latter is articulated in a rectangular bezel, convex behind and hollow at the front to accommodate a grey enamel. Joined to this are a globule and a pin, curved at the bottom, onto which a white pearl and a drop-shaped amethyst are threaded.

G. Ciampoltrini, «Due orecchini "bizantini" da Luni», in *Archeologia Medievale XVI*, 1989, pp. 737 ff; *Gioielli e Ornamenti Preziosi*, n° 38.

M.C.

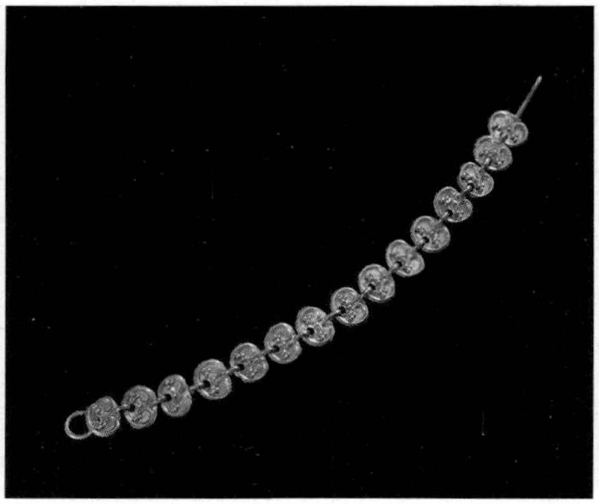

67. BRACELET
Museo Archeologico, Arezzo
Inv. 124971
L. 14.8 cm.
Gold. Intact
Longobard production from 7th cent. A.D.

The bracelet is formed by fifteen heart-shaped plate elements, outlined with a wire ending in volutes which terminate in three closely-spaced granules. The flexible plates are joined by links. The bracelet fastening consists in an eyelet at one end and a hook on the other.

Gioielli e Ornamenti, p. 165, n° 161a.

P.Z.G.

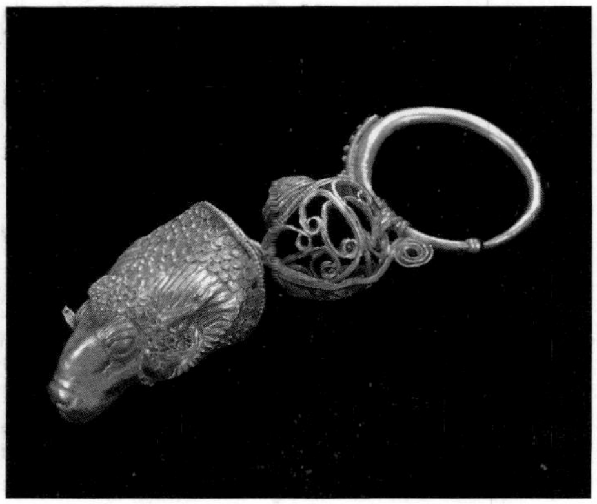

68. EARRING
Museo Archeologico, Florence
Inv. 15698
Currie Coll.
Suspension hoop - diam. 2.5 cm; basket
W. 1.7 cm., ht. 1.8 cm.; pendant - l. 3 cm.
Ht. 1.6 cm., w. 1.95 cm.

Suspension hoop partially decorated by eight globules within a double row of beaded wire. Open basket, formed by four double volutes, closed in a heart shape; the front disc decorated with globules within a double series of beaded wire; in the central bezel, a gold ball. Pendant shaped as an embossed, scaly-skinned, taurine protome.
Authentic antiquarian collector's *pastiche*, the earring is the result of the union of elements referring to different ages. The principle nucleus consists of a basket with relative suspension hoop, which can be attributed to a type amply exemplified in the circles of the Italian Lombards of the first half of the 7th century A.D.
On the contrary, believed to be the work of Etruscan goldsmith's art are both the gold ball in substitution of the stone normally set at the centre of the disc and the pendant shaped as a taurine protome, which may be dated to the classical age.

O. von Hessen, in *Studi Colombaria XLI*, 1975, p. 85, n° 3, fig. 9.4; *Gioielli e Ornamenti*, p. 171, n° 181; *Ori e Argenti*, p. 13, n° 186.

M.C.

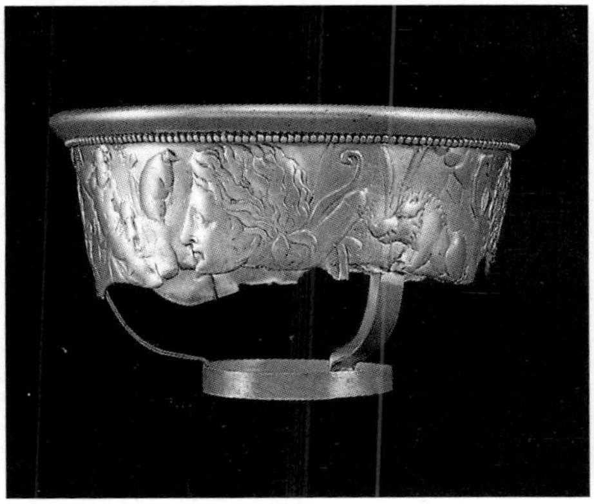

69. CUP
Museo Archeologico, Florence
Inv. 15731
Purchase 1863, previously Currie Coll.
Ht. 3.9 cm; diam. 10.2 cm.
Cast silver, stamped decoration. Lower half lost. Unlikely to be antique.

Hemispheric cup with expanded rim, emphasized at the joining by a collar band of beads. Four large male heads in profile on the basin, inserted into a Dionysian frieze.

Ori e Argenti, p. 13, n° 189.

M.C.

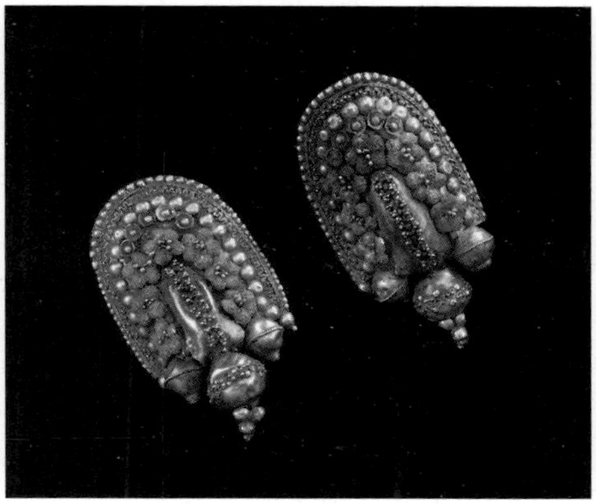

70. PAIR OF CLUSTER EARRINGS
Museo Archeologico, Florence
Inv. 85036
Supposedly from Populonia, Maruzzi purchase 1911
Ht. 6 cm; w. 3.5 cm., wt. 27.70 gr.
Gold; stamped granulated decoration, with applied wires. Intact
Modern production.

They consist in the top horseshoe-shaped part, from the ends of which hang two globules decorated at the centre with a knurled wire, and in the central elongated body from which hangs a sphere terminating in three globules. At the back the fastening consists in a wide oval clasp. The higher part is decorated with a band of small globules, a plaited wire, a row of small dots around which a wavy wire is wound, a band of globules, a strip formed by seven flowers with four or five petals ornate with gold dust and surmounted with five rosettes with a central globule. The central body is decorated by a longitudinal strip with groups of small globules. The central sphere exhibits an applied ribbon with two rows of globules around which a wavy wire is wound.

L'Oro degli Etruschi, p. 311, n° 238, with bibl.; *Gioielli e Ornamenti*, p. 174, n° 89; *Ori e Argenti*, p. 16, n° 231.

G.P.

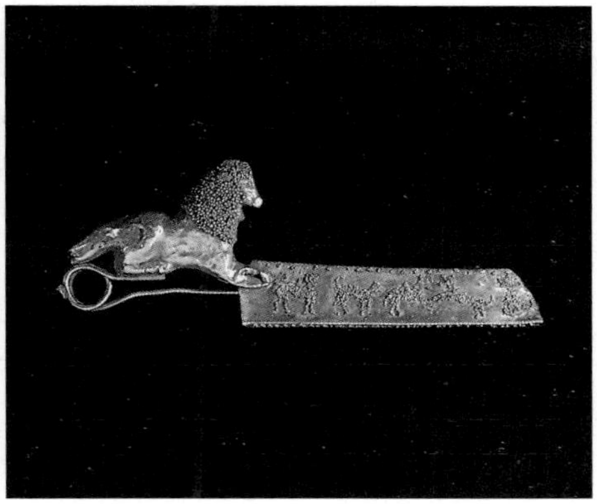

71. FIBULA
Museo Archeologico, Florence
Inv. 85037
Supposedly from Populonia, Lunghi Purchase
L. 9.4 cm.; wt. 14.05 gr.
Sheet gold; embossed, granulated and gold dust decoration. Missing in part
Modern production.

Bow-shaped fibula in the form of a lion, obtained from joining two embossed metal sheets. He has little, slightly outlined ears and a short, slender muzzle: the fore paws are lengthened and join on to the shank immediately underneath the upper part, the tail is shortened with a hole drilled in it, and the thick mane has been made by granulation. The spring, wound round one and-a-half times, is welded under the lion. The elongated shank terminates obliquely cut at the rounded end and is decorated with a procession of 5 animals in gold dust (after two probably winged lions passant dexter, there are two unidentifiable animals rampant and another lion passant traversed) bordered by two rows of granulated dots.

L'Oro degli Etruschi, note 87, p. 51, with prior bibl.; *Gioielli e Ornamenti*, p. 174, n° 188, with bibl.; *Ori e Argenti*, p. 16, n° 230.

A.R.

IVORY AND BONE CARVING IN THE ANCIENT WORLD

by *Anna Maria Esposito*

Because of their ductility and durability, bone and ivory have been used since earliest times, both for the artefacts on everyday use and for small carvings.

Already by the end of the Neolithic Age small human and animal figures were being carved from the ductile material of mammoth tusks.

In the second millenium B.C. this valuable material, obtained from the hippopotamus or, more commonly, from the elephant, attained enormous popularity throughout the Mediterranean region.

The Old Testament and Egyptian, Assyrian and Greek texts provide much information about the preciousness of this material. Ivory appears among the spoils of war along with gold and silver. Oriental tomb paintings and sculpture depict figures who in making offerings carry horns of ivory or lead elephants. In the Old Testament ivory is the symbol of luxury par excellence and Psalms speak of «houses of ivory». Dionysius of Halicarnassus says that in Etruria ivory was a royal attribute; Homer, Horace and Virgil mention «rooms resplendent with gold, electrum and ivory» and furniture covered with plaquettes of bronze and ivory. The Book of Kings refers to Solomon's throne as «made from ivory and covered with pure gold».

Already in Pre-Dynastic tombs in Egypt there appear objects and statuettes in ivory, carved with great care and subtlety.

In the early Dynasties ivory is commonly used as a decorative element or luxurious furnishings (e.g. the legs of funeral beds, decorative plaquettes or furniture, etc...) but it has also produced small masterpieces, like the statuette of a king with a crown and fringed gown (vid. I. Woldering, *Götter und Pharaonen*, 1967, pp. 32-33, figg. 10-11; Ist Dynasty, from the temple of Abydos, now in the British Museum) or the portrait of the pharaoh Cheops from the fourth Dynasty.

Ivory-working in the ancient Near East, which attained a very high standard, is seen in the carved ivories discovered at Megiddo (thirteenth century B.C.), one of the most important and remarkable centres for the richness and diversity of artefacts and subjects (banquets, chariot battles, etc...); predominantly their style is indigenous, that is, Syrian (that they were made in loco is proved, moreover, by the discovery of elephant tusks, remnants of work, etc...) [cfr. C. Decamps de Mertzenfeld, *Inventaire commenté des Ivoires Phéniciens et apparentés decouverts dans le Proche-Orient*, Paris, 1954).

A more marked Egyptian influence may be seen in ivories from the first millenium B.C., and above all in the subjects, which often represent sphinxes in a frontal position and variations on the floral motif of the palmette. The powerful Assyrian empire, and particularly the Assyrian court, became the principal client of the Phoenician craftsmen who were highly skilled in the art of ivory-working. The Assyrian cities, and Nimrud in particular, have provided us with genuine masterpieces of great artistic value (R.D. Barnett, *A Catalogue of*

the Nimrud Ivories, London, 1975).
From the Near East ivory-working spread throughout the Mediterranean world. From Crete, for example, comes a small sculpture of particular interest for its style and also its subject, an acrobat who is probably leaping over a bull, as depicted in the frescos in the palace of Knossos (C. Davaras, *Guide to Cretan Antiquities*, 1976, p. 155, fig. 89). Particularly worthy of note are the statuettes of youths in loin-cloths of gold from Paleokastro in which appears the combination of ivory and gold, celebrated by ancient authorities and anticipating the precious technique that will be used in Classical Greece for the images of the most venerated deities.
By the second millenium B.C. ivory-working also reaches a high level on mainland Greece from the Acropolis and the royal tombs at Mycenae come small carvings in high-relief which are among the most precious in antiquity. There are, for example, the group with two female deities and a child (R. Hampe - E. Simon, *Tausend Jahre Frügriechische Kunst*, fig. 328) and the carving of a seated female deity (Hampe - Simon, fig. 334), both of them again datable to between the fifteenth and the fourteenth centuries B.C..
The oriental characteristics identified in some examples has led to the assumption that they are Syrian, but there are also numerous similarities with ivories found in Cyprus, at Enkomi. Evidence of Aegean, and in some cases Cypriot influence are, moreover, identifiable in ivories from Nimrud, a testimony to the dense network of trade and other contacts which link these diverse cultures.
The tradition of elegance and luxury in the employment of ivory and evident in the Mediterranean world, is carried on in Greece in the eighth and seventh centuries B.C.. Apart from the Acropolis at Athens, precious and elegant artefacts have been found at the major sanctuaries on the Greek mainland and the islands. Particularly valuable and important are the votive offerings from the sanctuary of Artemis Orthia at Sparta (R.M. Dawkins, *The Sanctuary of Artemis Orthia at Sparta*, London, 1929, Pls. CXI-CLXXVIII), the Heraion at Samos (Hampe-Simon, n. 348) and the sanctuary of Apollo at Delphi, from where, for example, comes the famous group «A deity with a lion» (Hampe-Simon, n. 353).
Later still in Greece, ivory is also used for monumental sculptures: according to the sources, the horses of the Dioscuri at Argos would have been made of ivory and ebony, the work of Dipoinos and Skyllis in the first half of the sixth century B.C., while for the images of the more important deities, from Phidias, the most celebrated artist from Periclean Athens, were commissioned monumental sculptures in precious chryselephantine (ivory and gold): the Athena Parthenos for the Athenian Acropolis and the enthroned Zeus for the Temple of Zeus at Olympia.
The Macedonian court undoubtedly made great use of ivory, but no examples of particular note have come down to us.

On the other hand, a great wealth of material is provided by the ivories of the Orientalizing and Archaic periods found in Etruscan Italy, one of the destinations for Phoenician traders. The Etruscan aristocracy imported from the East articles of high value and exquisite beauty and very early on a local industry developed which often attained such a high level of artistry as to make the attribution of these artefacts difficult.

The royal tombs in southern Etruria, as, for example,those of Regolini-Galassi at Cerveteri, Bernardini and Barberini at Praeneste, have provided ivories remarkable in their typological variety, richness of ornament and artistic value (cfr. for example, the ivory handles in the shape of an arm or the calixes with caryatids from the Barberini tomb). They are modelled on examples from the oriental world but they are the products of workshops in southern Etruria (cfr. Y. Huls, *Ivoires d'Etrurie*, Bruxelles - Roma 1957, Pls. I-III Regolini- Galassi tomb; Pls. IV-VI, Bernardini tomb; Pls. XIII-XVIII, Barberini tomb).

From the second half of the seventh century to the beginning of the sixth century B.C., the use of carved ivory also achieved great success in central and northern Etruria. We need not look further than the important finds among the «Circles» at Marsiliana (Huls, Pls. VII-IX) and Chiusi, from which comes one of the most precious examples of ivory-working in the late-Orientalising period: the situla of Pania, with scenes taken from the Homeric poems (Huls, Pls. XXVII-XXX).

Also of great interest is the discovery, during the excavation of the Orientalising and Archaic structure at Murlo — besides objects in bone and ivory for personal use — of rejects from the manufacturing process, which proves without a doubt that an indigenous industry existed (cfr. *Case e palazzi d'Etruria*, Siena, 1985, p. 94).

Also attributable to the workshops of southern Etruria are the numerous late-Archaic plaquettes ornamented in relief and used to decorate caskets. They are found in various Etruscan centres (Tarquinia, Orvieto, etc..) and they, too, like all of the Etruscan artefacts of this period, reveal a clear Greek and Eastern influence (M. Cristofani Martelli, «Gli avori tardo-arcaici: botteghe e aree di diffusione», from: «*Il commercio etrusco-arcaico*», Rome 1985, pp. 207 et seq.)

More rare, however, or at least not as well documented, is work of a later period, when we find above all objects for personal and everyday use (small ciboria, combs, hairpins, dice, mirror handles) and often made from bone.Ivory attained great popularity in the Roman world, especially with the spread of the «luxus», the lifestyle of the aristocracy, modelled on the Hellenistic monarchy. Furniture inlaid with ivory was widely found while more commonly-used objects, such as combs, styli for writing and small jointed dolls, were made from a less expensive material, ox-horn.

Not surprisingly, during the Imperial Age ivory predominated in the court of the Caesars. The sources (Propertius II 3.1) tell us that the sculptures on the doors of the temple of Apollo

Palatine, with depictions of the Flight of the Celts from Delphi and the Slaying of the Niobids, were made from ivory.
Extant sources provide evidence of the gradual decline in the use of this material during the second and third centuries A.D., while there is evidence of a great revival in ivory-working from the middle of the fourth century A.D. onwards.
This precious material is by this time exclusively reserved for the Emperor and his most high-ranking officials. Work of great finesse and artistry by highly-skilled craftsmen is destined in particular for objects for personal use and diptychs, the pairs of hinged tablets, carved on the outside and on the inside coated with wax, for writing on. These diptychs were used as wedding gifts for those of high rank or given to consular appointees, and very soon they became the prerogative of the consuls themselves (cfr. Milano, *Capitale dell'Impero Romano*, 1990, pp. 338 et seq.). With the establishment of Christianity ivory was also used for sacred artefacts, almost as an assertion of the sovereignty of Christ, which was set against the worldly power of the Emperors.
From the great number of examples that have come down to us and the elaborate refinement of their ornamentation, it can be confidently stated that during the late period of the Ancient world this art attained the same high standards found in work from Greece and the great pre-Classical civilisations of the Mediterranean world.

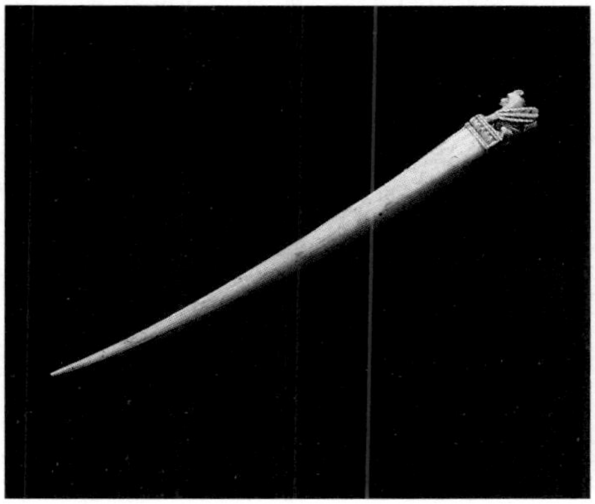

72. PIN OR STYLUS
Museo Archeologico, Florence
Inv. 82311
L. 19.6 cm.
Carved ivory. Homogeneous, yellow finish, surface traversed with multiple cracks
Oriental production from 7th cent. B.C.

Pin of conical shape with a thin, pointed tip. The upper part is squared off progressively towards a small rectangular base at the end with a frame of ovules (double fillet top and bottom) which supports a griffon figurine, crouching on the hind quarters, worked in full relief. The forepaws are straight. The design of the claws and the plummage on the wings is particularly minute. On the muzzle there is the beak, two little holes for the eyes and the ears with a hollow in the centre. On the back, between the wings, there is a small transversal projection (perhaps the tail that curls over the back?).

Gioielli e Ornamenti Preziosi, n° 43.

P.G.

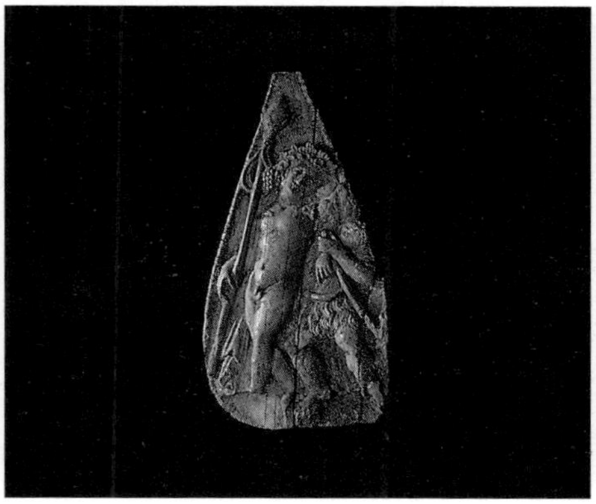

73. COVER PLAQUE
Museo Archeologico, Florence
Inv. 01522
Ht. 11.2 cm.; w. 6.4 cm.
Carved ivory. Homogeneous greeny-blue finish. Encrusted surface with long parallel splinters. Gaps in the area of Dionysius' foot (both are lost) and in the right one of Pan. The whole right margin of the plaque exhibits a gap (obviously because the ovolo frame is missing on this side). Pan's head and face are very worn.
Roman production from the Oriental provinces of the Hadrian - early Antonian Ages.

Between a fillet-and-ovolo decoration, alternating with a double tongue, the god on the left, full-faced, leaning slightly to the right, holds a long thyrsus in his right arm, while in the left he leans against Pan, who supports him by the wrist. The god is surrounded by a rich crown of vine-leaves; the bust is almost full on, slightly turned to the left. The right leg supports the weight of the body, the left being bent backwards, in the position of leaning against someone. His right arm is around Pan's shoulders with the hand falling onto his chest. The god is naked, except for a cloak, the edges of which are visible between the thyrsus and his legs and around his elbow. The facial features are briefly outlined; the hair is just a few locks on the forehead under the crown. Pan's figure is quite worn and corroded facially, seemingly turned upwards to the god. Recognizable is the goat's hair on his legs. He also holds a thyrsus of which there are the remains of the stick on the left side.

Gioielli e Ornamenti Preziosi, n° 44.

P.G.

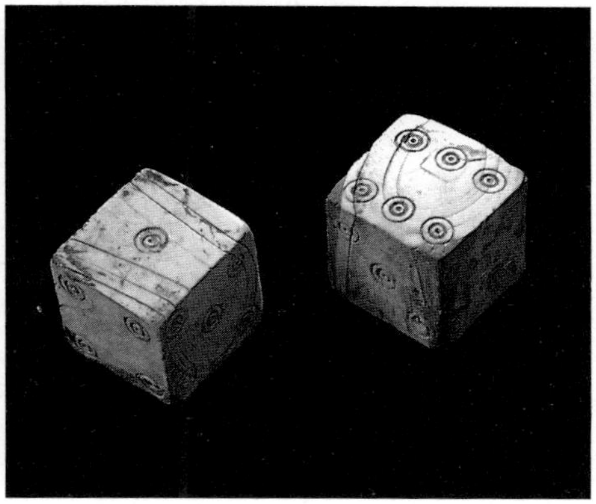

74. PAIR OF DICE
Museo Archeologico, Florence
Inv. 01565A-B
Side 2.7 cm.
Carved ivory. Non-homogeneous dark yellow finish. Corroded and splintered surface. Small gaps all over the surface and integrated by restoration.
Etruscan production from mid 7th cent. B.C.

The dice are numbered from one to six by means of double circles with a little hole in the centre.

Gioielli e Ornamenti Preziosi, n° 46.

P.G.

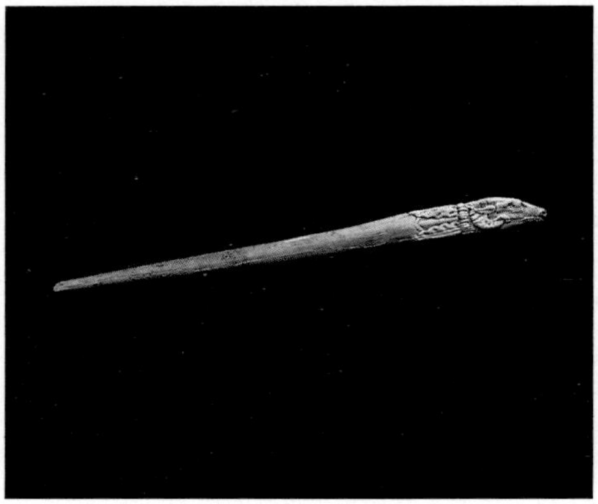

75. PIN OR STYLUS with ram's head
Museo Archeologico, Florence
Inv. 01601
L. 27 cm.
Grey-brown finish. Pointed end broken off. Corroded and splintered surface. Ram's muzzle worn down
Possible Etruscan production from 6th cent. B.C.

Conical pin, ending at the top in a plastic ram's head, quadrangular outline. In the elongated muzzle the carved eyes, mouth and nose are recognizable. The two curled horns are, however, rendered plastically (with a pattern of thin parallel incisions) between which there are the lance-shaped ears, laid backwards. At the end of each horn, a projecting gland typical of the animal's anatomy is revealed. On the upper part of the head, between the two horns, there is a triangle of fleece represented by thin plastic circles. The modelling of the animal's head is interrupted by an ovolo and fillet frame, after which there are four acanthus leaves interspersed with a geometrical, lance-shaped motif.

Gioielli e Ornamenti Preziosi, n° 47.

P.G.

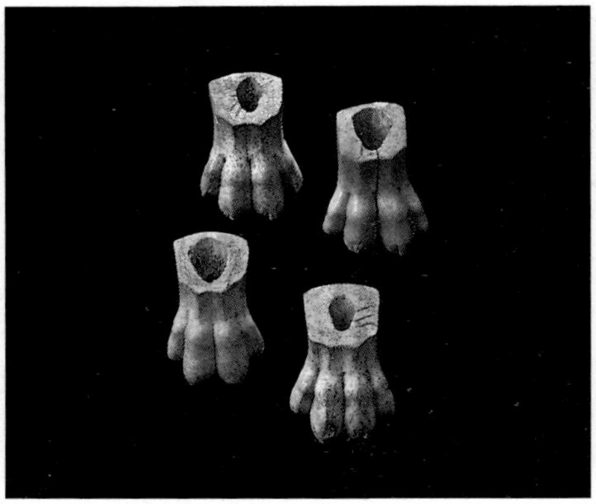

76. FOUR FERINE PAWS.
Museo Archeologico, Florence
Inv. 01492
From Orvieto, Crocifisso del Tufo, Le Conce, Tomb of Panatenaica
Av. ht. 3 cm.; av. w. 4 cm.
Carved ivory. Non-homogeneous yellow finish. Corroded, splintered surface
Etruscan production from 560-520 B.C.

The paw has four elongated digits, modelled in an extremely plastic way. The claws are sharp, extended slightly, on the end of each digit (except on one of the paws which is completely smooth).
The four paws have a circular cavity running right through them. The cut surface at the top is net, like the surfaces on which they rest. The back is completely smooth, except for a slight central depression.
In all probability they were the feet for a casket or a small cist.

Gioielli e Ornamenti Preziosi, n° 48.

P.G.

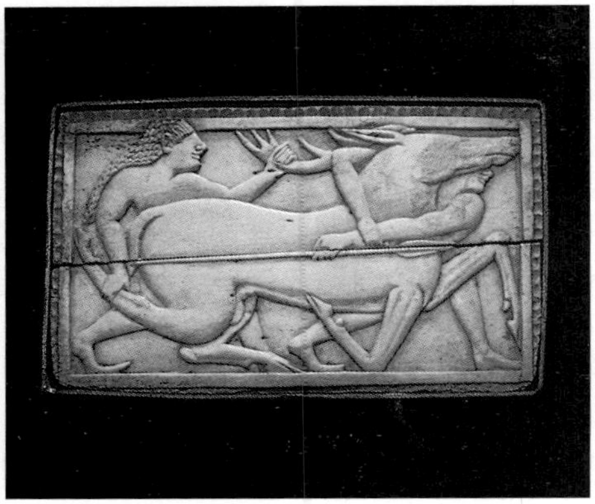

77. CASKET COVER PLAQUE
Museo Archeologico, Florence
Inv. 01507
From Orvieto, Crocifisso del Tufo, Le Conce, Tomb of Panatenaica
Ht. 6.6 cm.; w. 11.2 cm.
Carved ivory. Non-homogeneous brown finish. Corroded, splintered surface. Recomposed from two parts originally joined along the horizontal median line. Generalized cracks. The back is smooth
Etruscan production from 540-520 B.C.

In a double frame (the internal fillet is smooth, the external one notched), two figures of hunters, apparently naked, who grasp a large deer running towards the right. The hunter on the right, with both legs bent at the knee, clutches the animal around the neck with both his arms, and clasps in his right fist a long javelin which runs practically the whole length of the scene. Only the lower part of the hunter's profile can be seen. The hunter on the left, also with his legs bent at the knee, holds the animal firmly by the long visible horn, while with the left hand he clutches the hind hoof of the deer to force it to the ground. The profile of the second hunter, similar to the incomplete one of his companion, exhibits a complicated hair style of parallel plaits flowing down his back, well below the shoulders. The large deer, almost the main protagonist of the scene, extends his muscular body forward, the head slightly forced back by the hunters' grip. The left fore leg is held up and bent at the knee, while the right, also bent, scrapes on the ground. Of the two hind legs, one is held by the hunter and the other is bent under the body. The design of the four hooves is particularly fine and precise. On the muzzle, the lines of the mouth and nostrils as well as the hollow of the long ear are carved.

Gioielli e Ornamenti Preziosi, n° 49.

P.G.

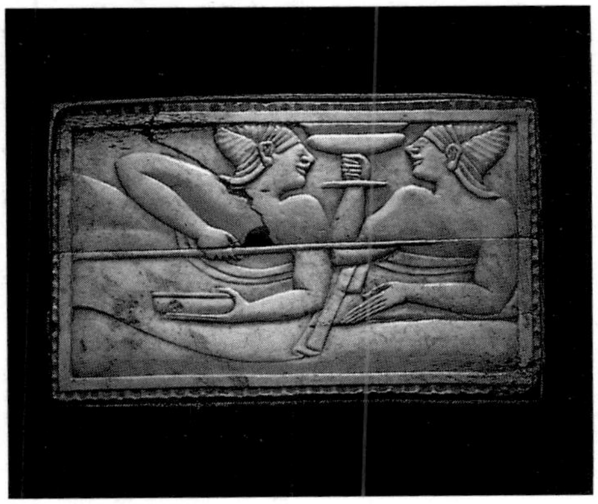

78. CASKET COVER PLAQUE
Museo Archeologico, Florence
Inv. 01506
From Orvieto, Crocifisso del Tufo, Le Conce, Tomb of Panatenaica
Ht. 6.5 cm.; w. 10.6 cm.
Carved ivory. Non-homogeneous brown finish. Along the joining line of the two pieces which make up the plaque itself, there is a median horizontal fracture across the whole width. Corroded, splintered surface. Small gaps on the left-hand figurine's breast and another minor one along the upper margin to the left; generalized cracks. The back is smooth.
Etruscan production from 540-520 BC.

In a double frame (the internal fillet is smooth, the external one notched), two male figures facing each other with their heads in profile and busts facing front are reclining. The one on the left holds a phial, the one on the right holds up a cup. Both wear a conic head covering with thick parallel pleats, terminating on the forehead and the nape of the neck in three wider bands. The figures are naked to just above the waist, while a cloak with a double turn-over at the top hem is wrapped around the rest of the body which is visible.
The figure on the left raises his left arm and seems to clasp a sceptre or rod in his fist. The point of the rod terminates at chest height of the other personage, who leans on his right arm bent at the elbow.
The figure to the right holds up a cup in his left hand, and with his right arm he repeats the same position of his companion. His open right hand has very long fingers. In the profiles of the heads the noses are prominent, the lips fleshy and the ears big and carefully designed. The eyes are just sketched. The arms and shoulders appear robust and muscular. The lower part of the plaque, smooth and slightly bulging, seems to indicate the cushion of the couch.
Gioielli e Ornamenti Preziosi, n° 50.

P.G.

PLASTIC VOTIVE ART
by *Paola Zamarchi Grassi*

Etruscan Period

In Etruria, as in Greece, the forms of worship took the form of offering votive objects to the gods. In fact, the devotees would deprive themselves of personal property and offer them to the deity in order to solicit his benevolence and protection or to thank him for a favour received.

At first the offerings were represented by material property: food, animals offered for sacrifice or precious objects: coins, metal objects, vessels. These gifts later acquired a symbolic value. In fact, at a later period the presence of miniature vessels and bronze or terracotta representions of human bodies or parts of the human body were predominant — either life-size or in reduction —. These representations usually depicted either the doner or the doner's request. For instance, if the request concerned fertility, the devotees would offer figurines representing new-born babies or representing animals if the request concerned animal fertility (birds, cattle, equines, sheep, goats etc.); for a recovery from an illness one would offer reproductions of the anatomical parts concerned (legs, arms, breasts, male or female genitals etc.)

Evidence that there were votive gifts in Etruria goes back to the end of the eighth Century B.C.; the formulas inscribed on these archeological finds, dating back to the seventh and sixth Century B.C., reveal the existence of sanctuaries where these sacred gifts were offered to the gods.

It was probably in this period that monumental structures were built for the purpose of worshipping the gods. Previously these cerimonies usually took place outdoors or under temporary structures.

In fact, during this period artisanship was dedicated to the creation of gifts intended as offerings, which were placed within the sanctuaries. The more precious gifts (tripods, gold and silver vessels, parade arms etc.) were placed in the so called «Thesauroi» (Treasuries) of the Temple, whilst the more modest gifts were placed inside the sanctuary.

The offerings being sacred objects, could not be thrown away. So when they became too numerous to be arranged in the sanctuary or when restoration of the temple was necessary, they were removed and crammed into the sanctuary's «temenos» (sacred enclosure) or in a protected pit, purposely excavated nearby the temple, called «bothros» in Greek and «favissa» in Latin. These sacred objects were then buried in order to protect them from desecration.

Votive deposits are often the only evidence of the existence of a destroyed temple which helps archaeologists to determine the duration of the cult, and by means of the dedications, the deity to whom the temple was dedicated.

«Jactatae» coffers go back to prehistoric and proto-historic cultures (i.e. Etruscan culture and the Palaeo-culture of Veneto region). These coffers were thrown into lakes (for instance

the jactatae coffer of Falterona - Arezzo), pools and hot springs to which therapeutic virtues were attributed and might be associated with a sacellum.
In Etruria and especially in Arezzo (where at least two famous coffers existed, the Fonte Veneziana coffer and St. Bartholomew's coffer) small votive objects represented characteristic outputs. The presence of many metalliferous deposits (Colline Metallifere, Campiglia, Massa Marittima, Lago dell'Accesa, the Isle of Elba and in the Arezzo area the mines of Monti Rognosi) encouraged this craft, which was probably introduced by itinerant merchant-artists who at the beginning of the sixth Century settled permanently in various centres, including Arezzo.
At first this type of artisanship was practiced by means of full casting using stone moulds. Later, hollow-casting methods were used with direct or indirect lost-wax casting techniques. The finishing touches were executed by punching the hot metal or by filing the cold metal.
In visiting the Museum of Arezzo one can find three different types of Etruscan bronze statuettes which probably belonged to lost coffers. These statuettes illustrate the development in technique from the Archaic and Late Archaic period (seventh - fifth Century B.C.) to the Hellenistic period (fourth - second Century B.C.) revealing the constant influence of Greek art which played an important role in the evolution of Etruscan art.
The first type (Nos. 79 - 80) represents two warriors (one is a carrying a lance, the other one is wearing a loin-cloth, mistakenly called a «gladiator»), a veiled female figure and two animals: an ox and a horse (Nos. 82, 81, 83).
These characters are central to the Archaic social structure (from the seventh Century to the first half of the sixth Century B.C.) and represent the main activities during this period: war, agriculture and activities relative to the home and family.
The second type (second half of the sixth-fifth Century B.C.) (Nos. 84 - 85), which was spread throughout Etruria and all the Etruscan areas, was inspired by the kouroi (young naked heroes offered to the god as a supreme gift) and the korai (virgins) originating from Greek stone statuary art. This type not only represents the male and female components of society but also represents the strong influence of Greek art in Etruria during the period in which well-defined urban centres were established.
The third type (third-second Century B.C.) (Nos. 86 - 87), which is present in many Italian and foreign museums, was widely spread in the Italic territory from the end of the Republic to the early Imperial Age. This type includes devotees (without attributes) and doners — often with patera and acerra (incense containers) — and is composed of several groups with numerous variations that can be determined from observing the pose and clothing.
The male figure completely covered up, at times *capite velato* (with veil over the head), is less common than the models with toga with one shoulder uncovered, with a mantle wrapping the lower part of the body. In the female version only the hips are covered, with tunic

and toga and with chiton and himation.
Parallel to the above-mentioned types is the analogous one introduced in this catalogue, divided into just as many variations, which seems to be the most widely spread and the most typical. This type is made up of crowned bronze statuettes, usually called «priests» and «priestesses» and generally referable, for the crown, to the Dionysiac cult.

Roman Period
During the Roman period, parallel to the official religion, and to the ceremonies which governed the official life of the town and of the empire, there is evidence of a private cult which was usually practiced within the home and the priest was the pater familias. The home was protected by the «Genius Familiaris», the Penates and the Lares. The Penates protected the provisions (penus) and were thanked at every meal, whilst the Lares influenced the fortunes of the house, the family, including the servants, and on the fields particularly on the boundaries where an aedicula dedicated to the Lares was usually placed. Their cult revived a new impulse during the religious restoration under the Emperor Augustus and was combined with the Genius Augusti cult, later assimilated into the Genius Familiaris.
Every home guarded a lararium: a household sacellum where the divine protectors of the home and family were kept. It was usually situated in the atrium but could also be found in the kitchen and in the peristyle. The most complete typology of lararii is preserved in Pompei where one can find two different models: some are found in hollow niches on walls, others are in the shape of an aedicula with its façade in a form of a temple; in some cases the lararium was substituted by a painting depicting the lararium.
Very often thaumaturgical deities or those which protected the prosperity of the home — for instance Mercury and Jupiter — or bronze statuettes, charms and other objects with apotropous functions, (i.e. which chased away the evil from the home) for example phallus (male sexual organs) or ludicrous figures were part of the lararium.
Phallic amulets, which were worn round the neck, had the function of bringing fertility. These amulets were occasionally complex in shape (Nos. 88 - 91) assuming different forms with a closed fist which also represented the warding off of misfortune.
The bronze statuettes illustrated below, property of the Archaeological Museum of Arezzo, are related to the household cult.

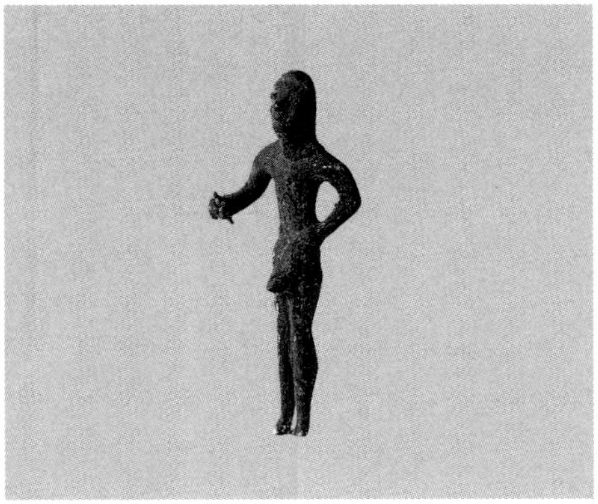

79. STATUETTE of warrior
Museo Archeologico, Arezzo
Inv. 11483
Lay Fraternity Coll.
Ht. 5.6 cm.; w. 3.7 cm.
Bronze. Feet missing
Etruscan production from the third quarter of 7th cent. B.C.

The head is ovoid with hair flowing down the nape of the neck, with an elongated face, a receding forehead, big, oblique, slightly elongated eyes, a prominent nose, a barely oulined mouth, a short, stocky neck, rounded shoulders, and stocky arms. His left arm is bent at the elbow with his hand resting on his side, the fingers engraved; the right arm is extended forwards, holding a fragment of an iron lance (1 cm. high) in his hand. The torso is outlined with a narrow waist and his legs together as far as the knees, with well-formed calves. He wears a belt round the waist which also covers the genitals, forming a loincloth.

Gioielli e Ornamenti Preziosi, n° 135.

P.Z.G.

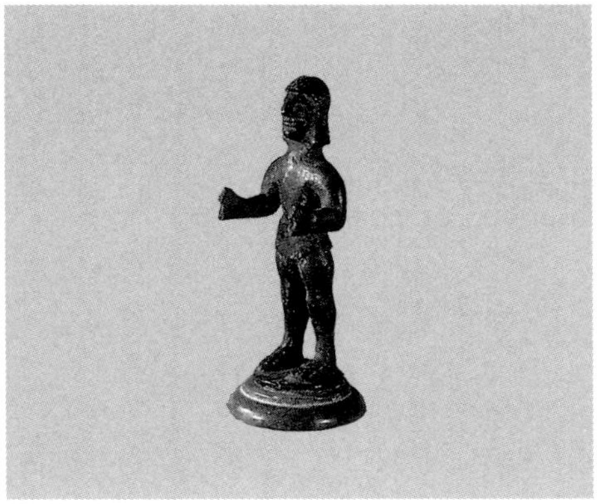

80. STATUETTE of warrior, the so-called «gladiator»
Museo Archeologico, Arezzo
Inv. 11495
Lay Fraternity Coll.
Ht. 7.7 cm.; w. 2.7 cm.
Bronze. Part of the hands missing
Etruscan production from the second half of 7th cent. B.C.

The face is round with hair flowing onto the shoulders in a strip outlined by thin, vertical, parallel lines. Prominent in the lower part are two horizontal, parallel incisions. The anatomical features are well marked; the enormous eyes, prominent nose, wide mouth with thin lips, a pronounced chin. The arms are robust, bent at the elbows and stretched forwards, the open hands have external engraved lines which summarily indicate the fingers. His legs are straight, stiff and slightly apart, with his knees and calves well-oulined, and the small feet with toes indicated by thin, engraved lines. He wears a tight loincloth round his hips. He stands on a discoid base without holes.

Arte Aurea Aretina, p. 54.; *Gioielli e Ornamenti Preziosi*, n° 136.

P.Z.G.

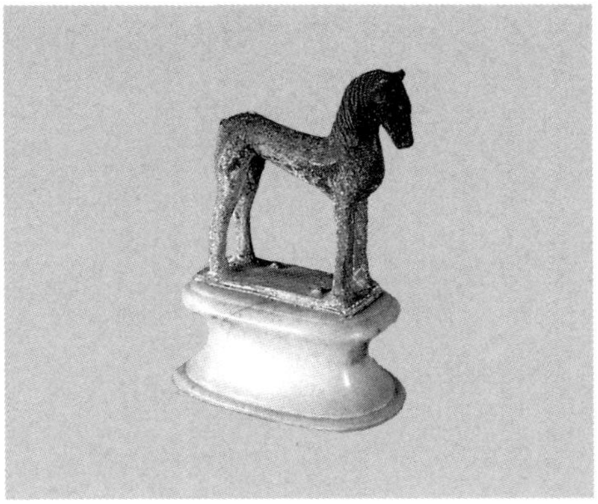

81. STATUETTE of equid
Museo Archeologico, Arezzo
Inv. 11541
Lay Fraternity Coll.
Ht. 6 cm.; w. 5.3 cm.
Bronze. Tail missing
Etruscan production from the 6th cent. B.C.

Figurine of a standing horse of a stylized type. It has an elongated muzzle; wide, ovoid, protruding eyes emphasized by an engraved line; the open mouth is formed by a transversal line; the ears are small and roundish; the mane is outlined with the use of deep, carefully-cut lines; the body is slender and flat, slightly elongated and rendered almost plastically; the legs are very long, separated and placed two by two along the same line; the posterior ones have fine transversal lines cut to indicate the fetlocks. It stands on a rectangular, bronze base with a nail near the hind leg.

Arte Aurea Aretina, p. 54; *Gioielli e Ornamenti Preziosi*, n° 138.

P.Z.G.

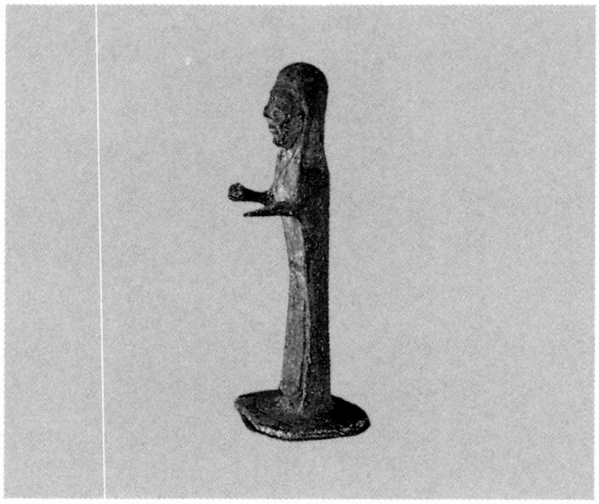

82. STATUETTE of female offerer
Museo Archeologico, Arezzo
Inv. 11502
Lay Fraternity Coll.
Ht. 7.9 cm.; w. 2.8 cm.
Bronze. Intact
Etruscan production from the first half of 6th cent. B.C.

She has a regular-shaped face with well-marked features: wide eyebrows, elongated and slightly oblique eyes which are open, a straight, regular nose, a narrow mouth and a round chin. The arms are perpendicular to the body and grow out of the body directly from the mantle brought forward with outstretched hands: the right one is in a vertical position and must have held an object as demonstrated by the remains of a nail in the centre on the back; the left has the palms raised upwards. She wears a long tunic which reaches the base, with a belt at the waist and a large veil which covers the head and also hides her hair.

Arte Aurea Aretina, p. 52; *Gioielli e Ornamenti Preziosi*, n° 137.

P.Z.G.

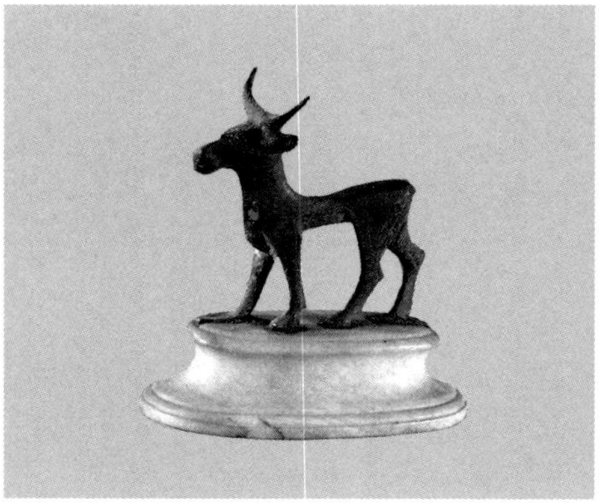

83. STATUETTE of bovid.
Museo Archeologico, Arezzo
Inv. 11524
Lay Fraternity Coll.
Ht. 8.8 cm.; w. 8.5 cm.
Bronze. Tail and base missing
Etruscan production from 6th cent. B.C.

Figurine of an ox in movement of a stylized type. The muzzle is short and outlined, with eyes marked by thin, ovoid, engraved double lines; the large, moon-shaped horns and the ears are proportionate, the eyelashes are formed by thin, parallel, engraved lines, the nostrils are also marked and the mouth is formed by a wide transversal line. It has a wide, mighty neck, a flat body narrowed in the centre, and robust but proportionate hind legs. The right fore leg and the left hind leg are advanced. It stands on a rectangular bronze base with nails at the height of the right fore and hind hooves. Both body and legs of the figurine are decorated with incised lines, in all probability to indicate the muscles.

Arte Aurea Aretina, p. 54; *Gioielli e Ornamenti Preziosi*, n° 139.

P.Z.G.

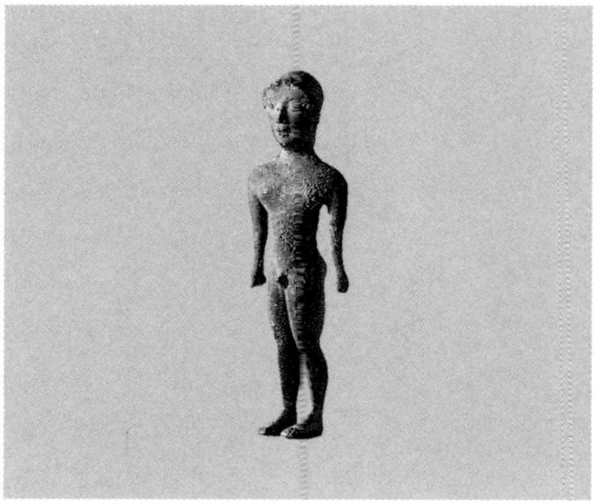

84. MALE VOTIVE STATUETTE
Museo Archeologico, Arezzo
Inv. 11564
Lay Fraternity Coll.
Ht. 16.5 cm.; w. 5.2 cm.
Bronze. Intact
Etruscan production from the second half of 6th cent. B.C.

The upright figurine, with a wide face and slightly marked anatomical features, has large, protruding eyes with a hole for pupils, a straight nose, a narrow mouth with a thick upper lip and a powerful, rounded chin. He has a shock of hair which from the centre of the nape of the neck flows onto the forehead where it ends in a round line and curly locks. The hair is marked by means of thin, incised, wavy lines which are arranged irregularly. His neck is stocky and short, the shoulders wide and square, the chest robust and slightly out of proportion with the rest of the body. The thick legs are separated from the body, and the arms hang with the hands closed in fists with only the thumbs upraised.

Gioielli e Ornamenti Preziosi, n° 140.

P.Z.G.

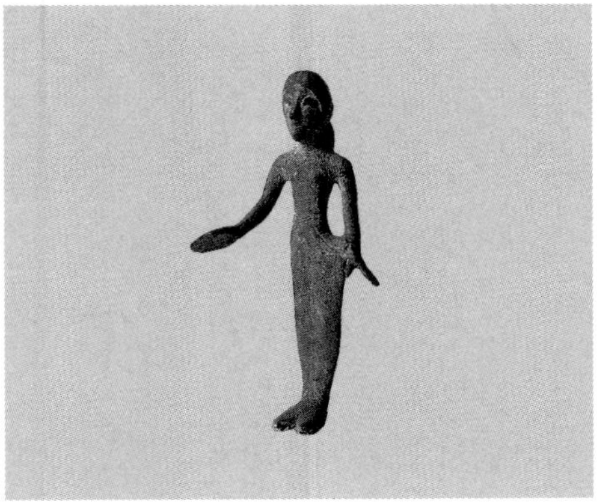

85. FEMALE VOTIVE STATUETTE
Museo Archeologico, Arezzo
Inv. 11618
Lay Fraternity Coll.
Ht. 9.5 cm.; w. 5.1 cm.
Bronze. Intact
Etruscan production from the second half of 6th cent. B.C.

Upright figurine, dressed in a long chiton to the feet, with a round, fleshy face with well-marked anatomical features. She has a receding forehead, oblique, slightly elongated eyes, a big, prominent nose, a small mouth with thick lips and a rounded chin. Her ample hair, flowing to a point on the shoulders, is marked by thin, vertical, incised, wavy lines. Her right arm is held aloof from the body, slightly bent at the elbow and outstretched with open hand. The left, contrariwise, is close to the body with the open palm facing downwards and the thumb separated so as to lift up the dress which is tied to the wrist.

Gioielli e Ornamenti Preziosi, n° 141.

P.Z.G.

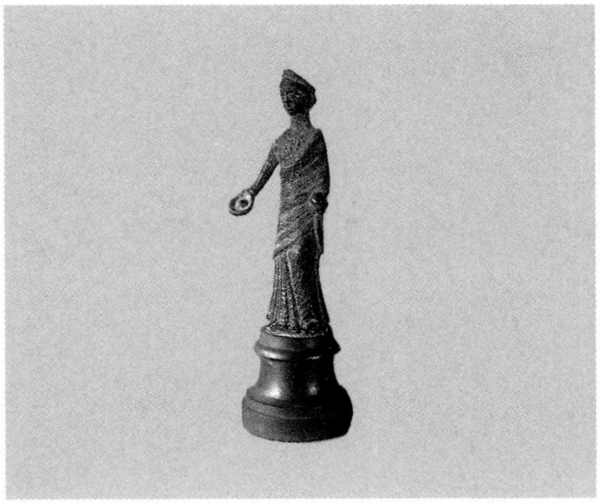

86. STATUETTE of female offerer
Museo Archeologico, Arezzo
Inv. 12033
Lay Fraternity Coll.
Ht. 12.7 cm.; w. 5.4 cm.
Bronze. Intact
Etruscan production from 3rd - 2nd cent. B.C.

The standing female figurine with a diadem has marked facial anatomical features, though they are roughly expressed. The low forehead; has wide, arched eyebrows from which the long, straight nose stems. The pupils are large but the mouth small, with thick lips. Her hair frames her forehead and is gathered in a bun on the neck. She wears a chiton and is wrapped in a himation which uncovers the upper part and continues down below the waist with well-modelled drapings which are further engraved in front though only slightly marked behind. Her right arm is outstretched in front and she holds in her hand an umbilicate patera. The left arm, close to the body and covered by the mantle, holds an unidentifiable object (casket?).

Arte Aurea Aretina, p. 59; *Gioielli e Ornamenti Preziosi*, n° 143.

P.Z.G.

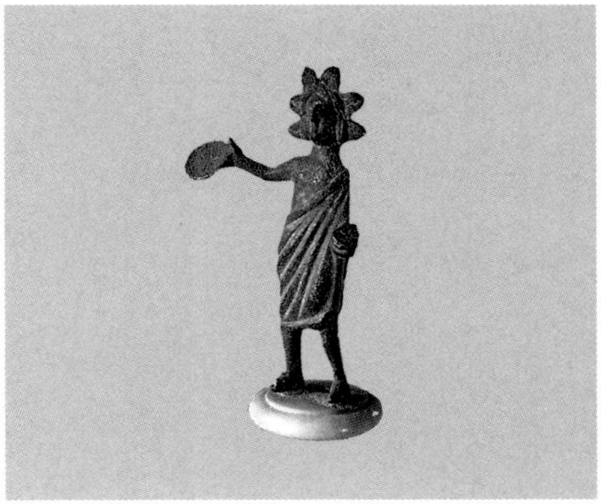

87. STATUETTE of male offerer.
Museo Archeologico, Arezzo
Inv. 12019
Lay Fraternity Coll.
Ht. 10.6 cm.; w. 7.2 cm.
Bronze. Intact
Etruscan production from 3rd - 2nd cent. B.C.

An upright male figurine with a radiating crown consisting of six rectangular triangles.
The anatomical facial features are well-marked: the arched eyebrows, the large eyes, the straight, tapering nose, the little mouth with thin lips and the rounded chin can all be noted. A shock of hair frames the face and reaches almost to the shoulders. His neck is stocky and is grafted directly onto the small, narrow shoulders. The figurine wears a himation which leaves the top right side of the body uncovered and which exhibits numerous oblique pleats. The left arm is covered by a mantle from which his hand stretches out, grasping an unidentifiable object (pyxis?).

Arte Aurea Aretina, p. 59; *Gioielli e Ornamenti Preziosi*, n° 142.

P.Z.G.

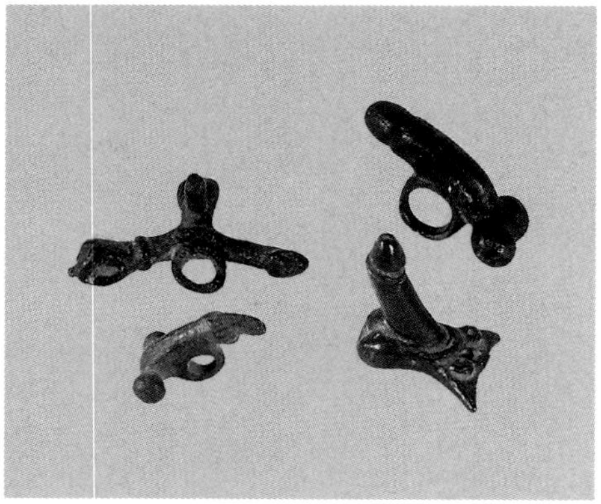

88. PENDANT
Museo Archeologico, Arezzo
Inv. 11303
Lay Fraternity Coll.
L. 4.5 cm.; w. 3.1 cm.
Bronze. Intact
Roman production from the Imperial Age.

It has the shape of an erect phallus with a little hole to hang it by situated among the pubic hairs.

Arte Aurea Aretina II, p. 57; *Gioielli e Ornamenti Preziosi*, n° 147.

P.Z.G.

89. PENDANT
Museo Archeologico, Arezzo
Inv. 11311
Lay Fraternity Coll.
Ht. 3.4 cm.
Bronze. Corroded
Roman production from the Imperial Age.

It has the shape of an erect phallus. Similar to the previous one, only it exhibits more schematized anatomical details.

Arte Aurea Aretina II, p. 57; *Gioielli e Ornamenti Preziosi*, n° 148.

P.Z.G.

90. PENDANT
Museo Archeologico, Arezzo
Inv. 11306
Lay Fraternity Coll.
Ht. 5.5 cm.; w. 2.7 cm.
Bronze. Intact
Roman production from the Imperial Age.

It has the shape of an erect phallus which is surmounted by a small hoop in the lower median part.

Arte Aurea Aretina II, p. 57; *Gioielli e Ornamenti Preziosi*, n° 149.

P.Z.G.

91. PENDANT
Museo Archeologico, Arezzo
Inv. 11305
Lay Fraternity Coll.
Ht. 6.1 cm.; w. 3.1 cm.
Bronze. Intact
Roman production from the Imperial Age.

It has the shape of an erect phallus, surmounted transversally by another erect phallus which has a hoop above it and terminates at the other end in a closed fist, but with an outstretched thumb inserted between the index and middle fingers.

Arezzo, 1987, p. 201; *Gioielli e Ornamenti Preziosi*, n° 150.

P.Z.G.

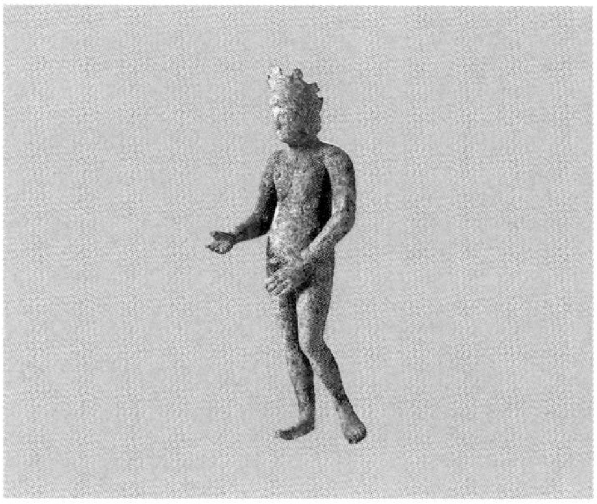

92. STATUETTE of Venus
Museo Archeologico, Arezzo
Inv. 11697
Lay Fraternity Coll.
Ht. 13.2 cm.; w. 4.3 cm.
Bronze. Intact
Roman production from 1st - 2nd cent. A.D.

The goddess is portrayed nude, upright and adorned with a diadem. The anatomical features of her face are highlighted: noticeable is the low forehead, bordered by her hair which follows the line of the diadem, her large eyes with engraved pupils, her regular nose and her small mouth.
The modelling of the figurine is careless and without plastic notation. The arms, especially the hands, are rendered in a disproportionate way with regard to the rest of the figurine. Her right arm is stretched forward with an upturned, open hand; the left arm is flexed and the hand held in front in the gesture of covering the pubic area. The weight of the figurine is borne on the right leg, while the left is flexed and shifted to one side.
The goddess of love is here represented according to the combination between two models derived from the Greek protoypes, that of the modest Venus and that of the Venus of Melos.

Arezzo, 1987, p. 199; *Gioielli e Ornamenti Preziosi*, n° 145.

P.Z.G.

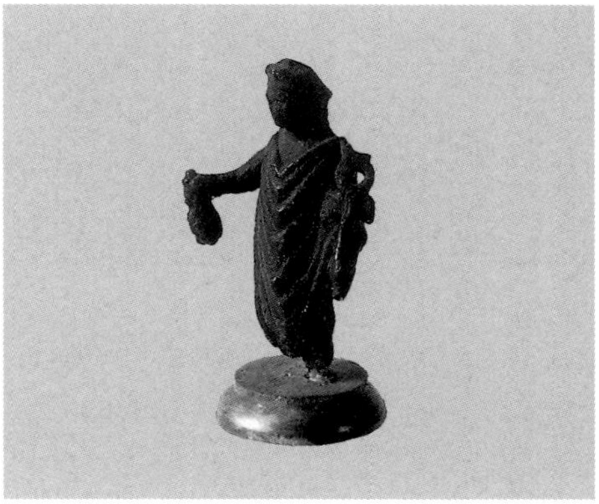

93. STATUETTE of Mercury
Museo Archeologico, Arezzo
Inv. 11659
Lay Fraternity Coll.
Ht. 5.6 cm.; w. 3.9 cm.
Bronze. Lower part of the legs missing
Roman production from 1st - 2nd cent. A.D.

The god, complete with petaso (winged hat), wears a paenula which, attached on the right shoulder, covers the whole body and falls in deep folds placed horizontally. His face, bent towards the right, exhibits features which are difficult to read as the object is so worn. The right arm is extended forwards and he holds a bag in his hand; in the left one he holds the caduceus. It is probably a Roman re-elaboration of a Greek typology.

Gioielli e Ornamenti Preziosi, n° 146.

P.Z.G.

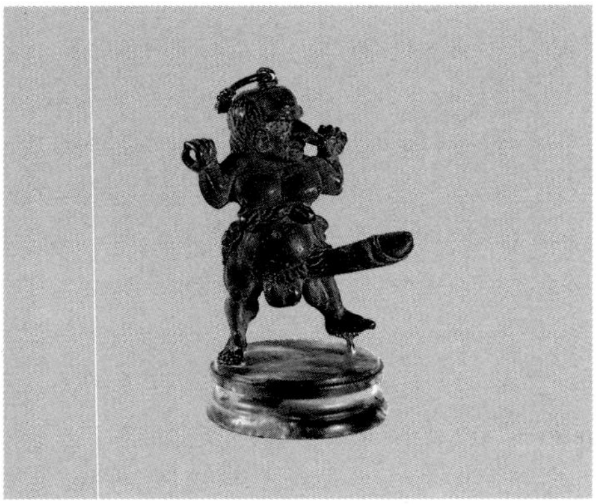

94. PENDANT in the shape of a dwarf or pygmy
Museo Archeologico, Arezzo
Inv. 11700
Lay Fraternity Coll.
Ht. 10.1 cm.; w. 7.3 cm.
Bronze. Intact
Roman production from 1st - 2nd cent. A.D.

The figurine is nude, covered only by a kind of loincloth, twisted round the waist and knotted, the corners of which cling to the thighs. He stands on parted legs with the left one slightly forward, and he raises his arms with closed fists to indicate the presence originally of an attribute, no longer conserved. The muscles in the limbs are well-marked. The short, fat body is portrayed in caricature, chest and paunch prominent and with an enormous sexual organ. His head, grafted directly onto the shoulders, has very strong features. The forehead is high and hairless, the nose long, the mouth fleshy. There are short locks on the temples, represented by incisions. The hair at the back is gathered into a kind of phallus-shaped knot.

Two hooks are present on the head into which some rings are inserted and which indicate that the object was meant to be suspended, probably with a magic, apotropaic function, as the exaggerated priapic characteristics also indicate (Priapus was the god of masculine sexuality). The statuette is a work of considerable quality which is inspired by Hellenistic caricatural personages.

Arezzo, 1987, p. 203; *Gioielli e Ornamenti Preziosi*, n° 151.

P.Z.G.

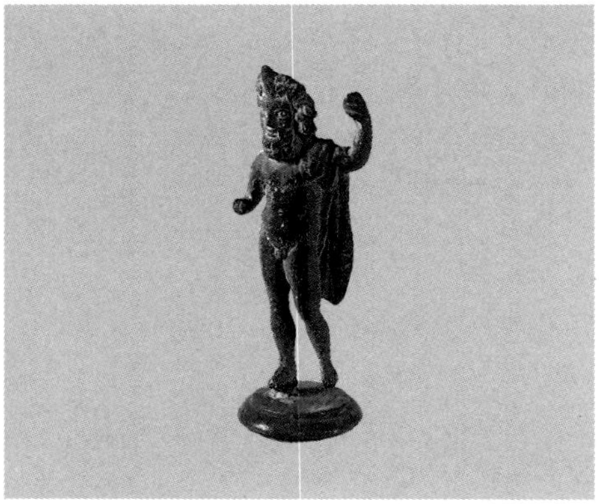

95. STATUETTE of Jove/Jupiter
Museo Archeologico, Arezzo
Inv. 11643
Lay Fraternity Coll.
Ht. 6.1 cm.; w. 2.7 cm.
Bronze. The left forearm and the left hand are missing
Roman production from 2nd cent. A.D.

The god is completely nude. His head has rough features and a mane of hair, with a voluminous beard. The eyebrows are bushy, the big eyes have hollow pupils, the elongated nose is regular and the mouth fleshy. On the left shoulder he has a chlamys which forms a pleat and which falls the length of the left side of the body with stiff folds marked by incised lines. His right arm is raised, perhaps in the act of leaning on the sceptre and the right one is bent and held in front. The weight of the body falls on the right leg, while the left is raised and moved slightly back.

The god, called Zeus in Greek and Tinia in Etruscan, is the father of all the gods and the lord of lightening. This representation is inspired by the statue of Juppiter Conservator which was found in Rome on the Capitol and follows the prototype of a Greek statue of the 5th cent. B.C.

Arezzo, 1987, p. 198; *Gioielli e Ornamenti Preziosi*, n° 144.

P.Z.G.

THE ART OF METALWORKING IN TUSCANY FROM THE MIDDLE AGE TO THE RENAISSANCE AND THE BAROQUE ERA

by *Anna Maria Maetzke*

The working of precious metals, principally gold and silver but including also a wide range of other metals from copper to platinum, is common to all ages and every society with a developed culture. The brilliance and colour of these materials, as well as the characteristic ductility and malleability that allows delicate and refined workmanship, confers on them a particular fascination and value.
The high cost of precious metals and the considerable technical ability and artistic skill required to work them has meant that, generally speaking, the products of this art were confined to a social elite, for necklaces and other jewellery and to monarchs for their regalia, and above all to those objects intended for use in religious ceremonies; the inherent beauty of the objects used for divine worship emphasizes the sacredness of the ceremony.
In the Middle Age, in the West as well as in the Christian East, centred on Byzantium, the courtly and symbolic significance of objects worked in metal particularly lent itself to the creation of objects used in religious ceremonies. The liturgy requires solemnity and reveals its transcendent significance through the use of precious objects. These are often of very high quality and the product of the great skill of artists who knew how to combine elegance of workmanship with the decorativeness achieved by applying precious stones, enamel, cameos and pearls.
Most of these liturgical objects are intended for the fundamental, central rite of the Christian religion, the celebration of Mass, which is centred around the constant renewal of the miracle of the Eucharist, that is to say, the body of Christ materialised in the consecrated bread and wine. The most common of the objects required for this rite are therefore the chalice, the pyx (the cup for the Eucharist), the ampulla for the wine and water, and also the thurible (in which grains of incense are burnt to fill the church with a fragrance during the adoration), the navicula, or incense-boat, in which the incense is kept, and the mostrance, the precious container used to display the Host, or the body of Christ, for the adoration of the faithful.
To these objects fundamental to the Mass can be added innumerable reliquaries intended to contain the relics of saints, that is to say, fragments of their bones and even of their clothing, and to display them for the adoration of the people. Candelabra, also, are to be found in all churches for the illumination of the altars and votive lamps, and altar-cards, which display in precious frames on the altar the text of various prayers.
Essentially present in Christian churches in the West, and bound up with the veneration of images, is the image of Christ Incarnate, the Son of God represented at the culminating moment of His earthly mission, the Crucifixion. The presence of the Crucifix in churches has been recorded since earliest times. In the Middle Age the Crucifix dominated the centre of the church and drew the attention of the faithful to the presence of the Divinity upon the Cross. In early times this presence was underlined by the splendour of precious metals,

the figure of Christ being wrapped with a lamina of gold and silver. These monumental images were then reproduced in the smaller processional crosses (called «croci astili» because they were placed upon poles, or «aste» and carried in procession). In order to create objects such as these, from the eleventh and twelfth centuries onwards the great goldsmith's Guilds were founded throughout Europe, from Northern Germany to Lower Germany, France, Spain and Italy. These Guilds remained active throughout the Renaissance and Baroque periods and up until the present day.

In the province of Arezzo, densely settled and with a diversity of cultures, the art of metalworking, much of it of very high quality and sophistication, represents an aspect of by no means secondary importance over the centuries in the rich artistic heritage of Tuscany and its major centres of activity.

In the present day, such work, predominantly of a religious nature, forms an integral part of an artistic output at the highest level. The metalworking heritage of the Arezzo region is only in part of local manufacture for we should recognize the presence of works of very high quality and, indeed, great masterpieces, originating from different parts of Italy and Northern Europe as a result of various historical events.

For the entire period of the Middle Age, from as early as the Carolingian era, there must have been a wide diffusion of small crucifixes and processional crosses in copper and gilded bronze. They reproduced the typology and iconography of «The Living Christ» or «Christ Triumphant», that is to say, the image of Christ represented frontally, with eyes open, in as much as He is victorious in death, and which is analogous to, and perhaps even imitating, contemporary monumental sculpture. Three exceptional examples of this work are in the Museo del Duomo in Arezzo, where they have been put on display after painstaking restoration. Broadly speaking, these small crucifixes and processional crosses, in copper and gilded bronze, were created by local smiths, influenced by examples from the Rhineland and by late Ottonian art.

Crucifixes of this type, most of them very well preserved, would have been found in every parish church in the province of Arezzo and its vast Diocese. In this exhibition there are examples from the Museo del Duomo and the Museo Statale d'Arte Medioevale e Moderna in Arezzo, as well as a splendid example from the parish church of Cavriglia and another from the Chianti region of Siena, all of them from around the twelfth and thirteenth centuries. The rounded figure of Christ often turns out to be older than the cross it is attached to, and therefore unrelated to it, but often reproducing an earlier configuration. In the Arezzo Museo Statale this phenomenon is seen in other precious crucifixes of the same type and embellished with enamel. This museum, together with the Museo del Duomo, also contains some rare thuribles and naviculae of the Romanesque period, and found throughout the Arezzo region.

The examples in this exhibition are highly indicative of this kind of artistic production but we should not forget some of the important masterpieces of metalworking in the Arezzo province which owing to their great preciousness, rarity and fragility it has not been possible to bring here. Of these we must mention the rarest and most precious, as regards the Middle Age: this is the so-called Holy Cross or Cross of Fra Mansueto. This splendid and very rare reliquary cross, made of delicate filigree in silver gilt, precious stones, pearls and rare French «champslevé» enamels and created to contain a fragment of the True Cross was given in 1258 by the French king, St. Louis, to a follower of St. Francis, Fra Mansueto, being then in France as an apostolic legate. This magnificent work dates from the beginning of the thirteenth century and is of French workmanship and provenance. It forms part of the outstanding collection in the Pinacoteca Comunale in Castiglion Fiorentino. Recently renovated, this museum without doubt occupies a position of great importance for the exceptional quality of the objects it contains.
Also of Northern European provenance is the astonishing image of St. Ursula, profoundly disturbing for the fixity of its rapt gaze. The Saint, represented with a crown, was a noble Breton princess who was martyred together with the 11,000 virgins, thereby saving the city of Cologne. This extraordinary reliquary bust in silver gilt with translucent enamel, quartz, glass paste and pearls, is without doubt the most notable work in the Castiglion Fiorentino museum. It is the work of a craftsman of great skill, both from an artistic and a technical point of view; he was presumably from the Upper Rhine. To the base of the figure he applied a series of delightfully delicate plaquettes in translucent enamel. The workmanship is typically French and is datable to the third decade of the fourteenth century.
Although it has not been possible to send these two masterpieces to this exhibition, three other very valuable liturgical objects have been included: two mostrances with attractive enamelling and a reliquary arm from the fifteenth century.
Another famous reliquary bust represents Arezzo's patron, St. Donatus, and is to be found in the Pieve di S. Maria Assunta, Arezzo. This priceless example of the art of metalworking is of silver and translucent enamel. It was made, so the inscription informs us, in 1346 by two Arezzo goldsmiths, «Pietro and Paolo Aretini». The Saint wears a bishop's gown with mitre and cope. From the mitre, decorated by an arrangement of four-sided translucent enamel plaques hang the infulae. Enamel was also applied to the delicately engraved cope and embellished with precious stones. This, too, is a work of very high quality and it communicates a deep spirituality, emphasised by the stiff, archaizing form of the youthful face, rendered more austere and noble by the uniformity of the silver surface and, unlike the St. Ursula bust, left unadorned and without polychromy.
Staying with the fourteenth century, we should mention the astonishing monumental reliquary in copper, silver and enamel; it is in the form of a tree and is, in fact, known as «The

Tree of Lucignano». From the trunk extend six branches, each ending in a mounted casket with, on one side, translucent enamel and, on the other, painted parchment behind a glass pane. Tiny branches of red coral embellish the caskets and, inserted along the trunk, the spaces between the six branches. The tree is surmounted by a crucifix, the original of which is unfortunately missing following a theft early this century and has been replaced by a modern version. The tree is inserted into a base which has the form of a small Gothic Temple and this in turn rests on a broad polygonal base on which, before they too were stolen, were enamel plaques. A long inscription, placed on the pedestal at the time of its completion in 1471, tells us that the reliquary was begun in 1350, but does not give the name of its maker or makers. It clearly belongs to the Arezzo-Sienese school, to which it owes its conception and a great deal of the execution in a severely Gothic style. It was completed in 1471 by Gabriello di Antonio, at which date half-length figures of Prophets in miniature were substituted beneath the glass panes. They were painted by a well-known miniaturist of the circle of Piero della Francesca. This great work was contained in a cabinet painted by Luca Signorelli, who received the commission in Lucca on 16th October 1482. The cabinet, kept in the church of S. Francesco, was destroyed; forming part of it, perhaps, was a lunette depicting «St. Francis receiving the Stigmata». The reliquary is now in the recently reorganized Museo Comunale, next to the church. In the main room of the museum, decorated with attractive fifteenth century frescos, one can today admire the extraordinary and original masterpiece of Tuscan metalworking.
Moving on Cortona and the Museo Diocesano, rich in work of great distinction both in the field of painting (pictures by Pietro Lorenzetti, Fra Angelico, with a famous Annunciation, Sassetta, Bartolomeo Della Gatta, Signorelli etc.) and other arts, we find another reliquary of large dimensions and exquisite workmanship, and a splendid example of Renaissance metalworking. This is the «Vagnucci Reliquary» so named because it was commissioned for Cortona Cathedral by the Bishop of Perugia, Jacopo Vagnucci, in order to hold a precious relic which he had been presented by Pope Nicholas V, and which Nicholas himself had been given by Gregory, the Patriarch of Constantinople. The work is signed by the goldsmith Giusto da Firenze and dates from 1457-8. The style of the base is dependent on the Gothic tradition but becomes wholly Renaissance in the rich intricacy of its enamelling and in the Florentine style and taste of the two rounded figures supported by the two branches, figures probably depicting the Pope and the Patriarch of Constantinople.
Of the numerous examples of the goldsmith's art which constitute the remarkable patrimony of Arezzo Cathedral, and today kept in the Museo del Duomo, we should at least mention one of the most famous: the so called «Peace of Siena». It is of gold embellished on both sides with enamel, pearls and precious stones. Of Franco-Flemish workmanship from the early fifteenth century it represents the dead Christ supported on one side by an angel and

on the other by the Virgin Mary and St. John. It was the priceless gift of Pope Pius II Piccolomini to the Cathedral of Siena and it came to Arezzo Cathedral at the end of the eighteenth century. The high quality and wonderful skill of its workmanship reveal characteristics of the French tradition and in particular, that of Paris, renowned for the sophisticated elaborateness of the enamelling technique known as «en ronde bosse». It was later inserted into an elegant reliquary, made by Giuseppe III di Spagna in 1815.The veneration of the two protomartyrs of Arezzo is related to one of the most important examples of metalworking in the Museo del Duomo: the Urn of SS. Lorentino and Pergentino. It is of chased copper, silver plated and gilded, surmounted by a Madonna of the Misericordia and with the Stories of the two Saints embossed in low-relief. Begun in 1498, the Urn is the work of a certain Master Niccolò of Borgo Sansepolcro who, according to Salmi, executed the stories of the Saints after designs by Bartolomeo Della Gatta.
We ought to mention on final, precious example of fifteenth century metalworking in the museum, this time of a profane character. This is the rare Crest from a tournament helmet. It has the form of a dragon and displays singular skill and verve in its workmanship.
With the sixteenth century, however, let us move on to Montevarchi where, as a part of the rich collection of the Collegiate Church of S. Lorenzo, and displayed next door in the Museum, is a large silver cross, ornately and delicately embossed and included in this exhibition. Its preciousness and splendid workmanship has resulted in its being popularly known as the «Cellini Cross», although we know it to be, in fact, the work of Piero di Martino Spigliati from the years 1551-52. He depicted scenes from the Old and New Testaments on it and in a style described as «grandiloquent with echoes of Michelangelo». One cannot, however, dispute its great imagination and liveliness nor the skill with which this pupil and follower of Benvenuto Cellini has executed the typically Mannerist small figures with characteristic borrowings from Michelangelo's art.
Among the remarkable number of ecclesiastical treasures in the Province of Arezzo those of Sansepolcro Cathedral are certainly worthy of note. They are now displayed in the Museo Civico to which they were consigned at the time when the collection was being reorganised and enlarged. It contains many important examples of the art of metalworking and owes its existence mainly to Bishop Costaguti, the famous great preacher who lived from the second half of the eighteenth to the beginning of the nineteenth century. He was Bishop of Sansepolcro from 1778 to 1818. The fame of Monsignor Roberto Costaguti spread far beyond the city, to the extent that in 1779 he was summoned to the Court of Empress Maria Teresa of Austria in order to deliver a series of sermons.
Acclaimed and petted by the Empress and her daughters he returned home laden with precious gifts. Among these was the grand, austere pontificial tapestry in blue silk brocade woven with silver thread, apparently embroidered, by the Princesses themselves. There were also

many sacred vessels in silver, the work of illustrious silversmiths, as well as a few reliquaries. Among these, and of particular rarity and interest are a pair of reliquaries in the form of miniature altars for which reason they were called «ad altarolo». They are of incised ebony on which there is a profusion of tiny decorative details in silver guilt, wrought silver and pearls, together with innumerable tiny figure which reproduce on a much-reduced scale the monumental sculpture characteristic of Northern European Mannerism.

A study of these singular works, unusual and foreign to typically Italian work, has enabled this writer firstly to identify their maker as the renowned German goldsmith, Matheus Walbaum who headed a large and very active workshop in Augsburg, where he worked from 1579, and, secondly, to establish that the two little altars were in fact made in Augsburg between the end of the sixteenth century and the early part of the seventeenth century. They are works of great delicacy and refinement, created by an artist used to working for the court, using rare and expensive materials and creating works of superb inventiveness and skill, as, for example, the famous mechanical figures in which Walbaum specialised.

From the Sansepolcro museum and exhibited here are a Mediaeval pectoral cross (encolpian), a «Pace» from the fifteenth century in silver, and a statuette of the Madonna of the Rosary from the sixteenth century.

It is clear that, given the vast output of goldsmiths in Italy and in Tuscany in particular, what has been presented here is only a general survey, but we hope that the works in this exhibition will be sufficient to form an introduction to an important aspect of Italian art during the period of its greatest output, from the Middle Age to the Renaissance and Baroque periods and the eighteenth century.

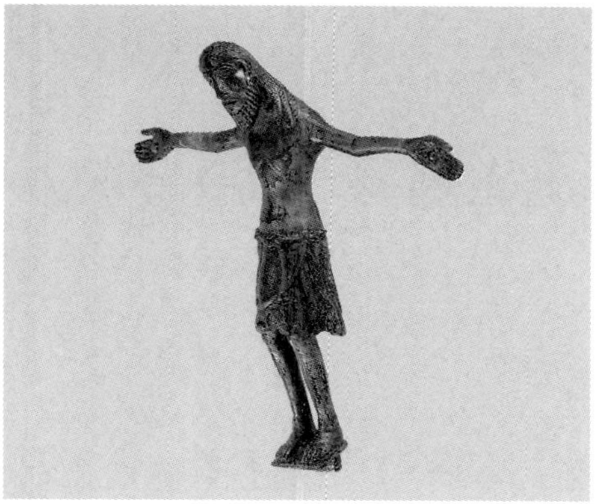

96. CRUCIFIX
Cathedral Museum, Arezzo
From S. Piero in Frassino (Ortignano-Raggiolo)
Aretine (?) metal craftswork of 12th cent.
18 cm. x 16 cm.
Gilt and engraved bronze.

The Christ, without his cross, is dressed in a long loincloth with oblique folds reaching to the knee and held up by a double-knotted ribbon which thus forms two girdles terminating in a tassel. The type of iconography of the «*Christus triumphans*» is blended with that of the «*Christus patiens*» as can be seen in the expression of the wide-open eyes and in the position of the head, barely inclined forwards to the right. The legs, slightly flexed, are parted and are supported on a step. The arms are outstretched (the right one has been restored), the stomach flat and the chest is barely sketched with two lines which model the muscle formation slightly. The face, emitting serene composure, is rendered with skill and expertise and displays hair which is finely engraved and which, flowing from a median line, is gathered into three plaits on each side, terminating on the chest. The stupendous firegilding creates a fine, overall, plastic effect which confers a great monumentality to the bronze.

Similar examples of this sculpture, which stylistically could be collocated in the so-called «late Ottonian» current of the Rhine workshop of Roger of Helmershausen, can be found very nearby in the Aretine Valdarno and in the *Museo Statale d'Arte Medioevale e Moderna* in Arezzo, but the sculptural prototype which could have inspired the goldsmith is the crucifix in the Cathedral Museum of Arezzo which originally (indeed up until the mid 13th century) was clad in gold plate to the extent that it was considered the work of a goldsmith. The slightly wavy outline and the overall structure (especially of the receding, barely-modelled chest) strongly call to mind the huge crucifix which may have been source of inspiration for the artists of applied art. The considerable documentation on bronze casting works, the close, friendly contacts with the Emperors, the presence of master craftsmen in the Pieve workshops, and, last of all, the quite significant number of these bronzes in Aretine territory (some even being of the 13th century), justify the hypothesis that a casting tradition was operative in this area. It must also be pointed out that some examples preserved in the Siena province are actually in the parish area of Arezzo, and it is known from boundary disputes that these parishes were certainly more attached to Arezzo than to Siena. Artistically at that time, the Aretine culture was autonomous as various miniatures and sculptures amply demonstrate. Finally, an important fact not to be overlooked is the presence of the «*Studium Generale*» in the city of Arezzo.

Arte Aurea Aretina II, p. 58, n° 14, with ref.

G.C. and G.R.

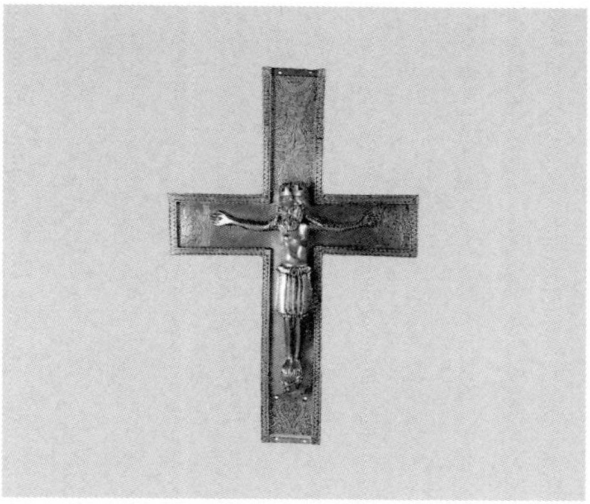

97. PROCESSIONAL CROSS
Museo Statale d'Arte Medioevale e Moderna, Arezzo
Inv. Lay Fraternity 15109
23 x 24.5 cm.; Christ: 15 x 7 cm.
Engraved and chiselled gilt copper. Christ in cast bronze
Tuscan manufacture from 12th cent.

The Cross is bordered on the outline with a projecting fillet with serpentine incisions. The background is hammered with a burin and engraved at the top of the main arm with an Angel bearing incense and descending from heaven. At the sides of the smaller arm there are half figures of the Virgin and St John. Christ, in full relief, is of the «*Triumphans*» type, with a tripartite crown, eyes wide open and head erect and slightly inclined forwards, though not rigid. The loincloth drops to the knee and is held up by a ribbon tied at the centre with a double knot to form two lappets which hang down along the central folds, where originally a stone was set. On the back, similar to the front in its ornamentation, Evangelical symbols are portrayed: an eagle and an Angel on the vertical arm, a lion and an ox on the horizontal one. At the centre is the Agnus Dei, inside a circular medallion. That the Christ belongs to monumental sculpture seems beyond doubt. The solemnity of the Nazarene figure is above all in the serene glance and the composure of the bearing, which together create an imposing, evocative effect. The head, which does not have the triangular form still frequent in many Romanesque sculptures (particularly those from the North), is firmly placed on the torso where the vigorous forms, which at the same time seem rather meagre, are rendered with a nobleness rather unusual for this type of craftswork. These characteristics lead one to suppose that this Cross is of Italian make, indeed, it is certainly Tuscan. Similarities with the figure of Christ can be found

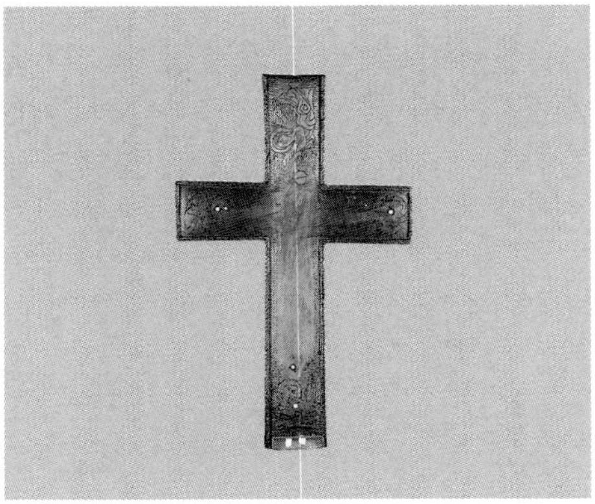

in the Umbro-Tuscan sculpture production from the second half of the 12th century. This ornament is therefore nothing if not an eloquent testimony to the reflection of a particular phase in Tuscan plasticity in small-scale metal sculptures.

Galoppi Nappini, 1987, p. 178 with ref.; *Gioielli e Ornamenti Preziosi*, n° 154.

D.G.N.

98. PROCESSIONAL CROSS
Museo Statale d'Arte Medioevale e Moderna, Arezzo
Inv. Lay Fraternity 15107
22 x 14.5 cm.
Engraved and chiselled gilt copper
Aretine (?) manufacture from 12th cent.

The Cross exhibits, on both sides, a dotted decoration applied with a burin and the outline has a frame engraved in spirals. On the *mutilated* back of the crucifix, we find the images of the Madonna, St John, an unidentified saint and, at the top of the main arm, an incense-bearing Angel descending from heaven. At the back we can read the Evangelical symbols and, in the lower part of the main arm, the full figure of an Angel who is holding up a scroll. At the centre, inside a circular medallion, there is the mystic Lamb with a chalice. Similar in typology to the other cross (n° 21), it exhibits analogies in the treatment of the metal and the ornamentation, principally in the dotted background rendered with a burin.

The iconography of these Crosses from the Romanesque period up until the 14th century varies little, especially on the backs, where we generally find the Cross-bearing Lamb or the Redeemer blessing at the centre, while the symbols of the Evangelists are on the four lateral panels, following the customary vision of the Apopcalypse. On the back, a Crucifix stands out in the centre, to the right there constantly finds place the Virgin, while on the left there is usually St John the Baptist. The upper panels vary between an Angel and a Saint, while below there is almost always Adam's skull with Golgotha in the background.

The Cross, the typology of which can be assimilated with that of the previous Cross analysed (cfr. item n° 2) and with that of another one in the *Museo Diocesano* at Cortona, can perhaps be included among the local goldsmith's craft from the 12th century, which was not without Romanesque influence from over the Alps, specifically connected with the production of the Belgo-Rhenish goldsmith Godefroy De Claire, the interpreter of a sculptural language set on plastic values of a clearly Romanesque flavour. In the instance of these Crosses, certain values have been filtered down to a more modest lexis, connected to a more provincial cultural area.

Galoppi Nappini, 1987, p. 179; *Gioielli e Ornamenti Preziosi*, n° 155.

D.G.N.

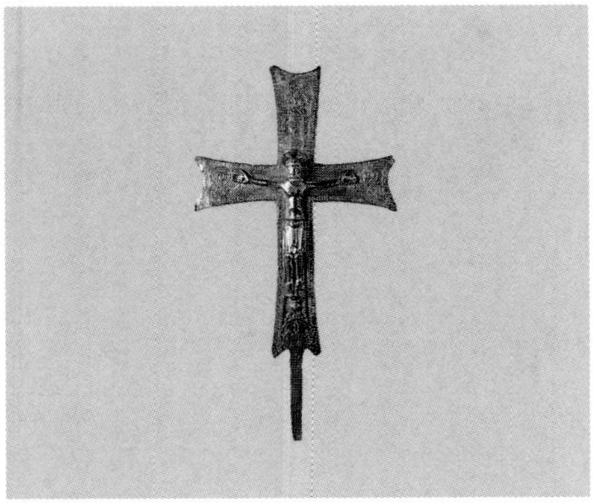

99. PROCESSIONAL CROSS
Radda in Chianti (Si), Pieve di Santa Maria Novella
cm. 41 x 20
Gilded and engraved, cast bronze Cross
Tuscan workshop, XII century.

A few years ago the Cross was completely restored by the Opificio delle Pietre Dure of Florence. In addition to having brought back to light the piece's original "hot-work" silver plating, a fact that makes this artifact unique vis-a-vis all the other examples available in the Sienese Chianti area, this extremely accurate restoration has fixed the exact collocation of the Christ which, long ago, had been erroneously placed on the back of the Cross.
The Cross's arm endings, whose corners originally held small spheres, present a hollowed circle arch form, and both sides bear an engraved decoration. The front bears an incision of the cross with a halo, with above the "titulus" (IC XC) and St. Michael the Archangel. On the lateral extremities are the grieving figures of the Virgin and St. John the Evangelist. The "tugurium" of the Basilica dell'Anastasi, with the symbolic representation of the Resurrection, according to the iconography in use at the end of XII century, is represented below. The dead Christ is in the center of the reverse side, with the "titulus", and the arms' extremities bearing the figures of the four Evangelists.
The "triumphans" type figure of Christ in relief, with feet resting on a "suppedameum", can be attributed to the so called «romanesque» current. The stylistic origins of this current in Italy can be found in the Crosses of Casalmonferrato, of Spilamberto in Modena, and the bronze reliefs on the San Zeno portal in Verona. Parallel to this current, which during the XII century, with the imposing Crucifix of Mirabella Eclano (Avellino), spread «from Alvernia» and «from Aquitania» to the South of Italy, we find the Cross of Santa Maria Novella. This cross's firm structure of the Christ, its expressiveness, now set free from the classic and byzantine formulas, and the still archaic style of its incisions, fix its dating to not later than the thirteenth century and its attribution as the first Chianti area specimen comparable to the «romanesque» style grouping.

C. Alessi in *Oreficeria Sacra nel Chianti Senese* (XII century), catalog of the San Gusmè exhibition, Siena 1985, pgs. 26, 27, n° 3 w/bibl.

C.A.

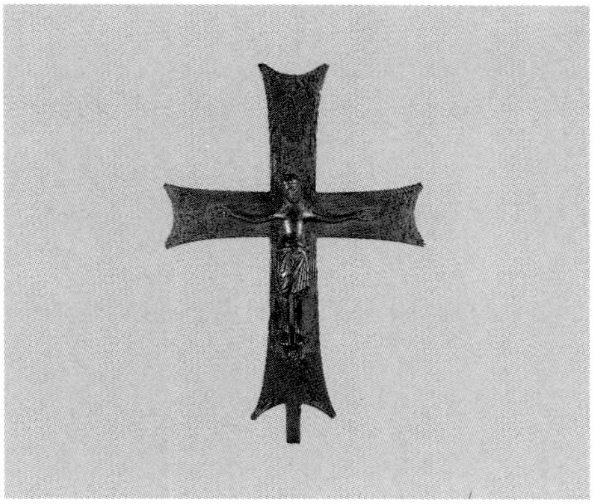

100. PROCESSIONAL CROSS
From the Parish Church of S. Giovanni Battista - Cavriglia
Cross: 35 x 26 cm.; Crucifix: 17 x 16.8 cm.
Engraved and gilt copper; bronze. Mediocre. Gilding deteriorated, dirty
Crucifix 12th cent.; cross 13th cent.

A Latin processional cross with the arms terminating in swallow tails. At the end of each arm, the half figure of the Saviour is portrayed at the top, with on the right the three-quarter figure of St John the Baptist and on the left that of the Madonna, while Mount Golgotha is stylized below. The back also exhibits an engraved cross with a nimbus at the crossing of the arms. The Crucifix takes after the typology of the still-alive, wide-eyed «*Christus Triumphans*», nailed to the Cross. The arms are slightly flexed with open palms and fingers close together, and the chest is smooth. He is covered with a long loincloth to the knee. Legs and feet are represented parallel and supported on a suppedaneum. The verse on the Cross carries the engraved Evangelists' symbols: the Eagle, the Lion, the Ox and the Angel, and on the surface there is a cross designed with the image of a «*dolente*» Christ.
The splendid crucifix, of great historical interest in the art world, has Christ clad in a long loincloth which, already in the 9th century, had replaced the tunic. Furthermore, it is from the 12th century onwards that elements of Eastern origin such as the reclining head of the «*Christus patiens*», are found cast together with elements of ancient Western tradition, such as the wide- open eyes of the «*Christus triumphans*». This chronological attribution is confirmed also through the stylistic comparison between this specimen from Cavriglia and a series of crosses of the so-called «late Ottonian» period, which go back to models produced in Rhenish circles by the workshop of Roger of

Helmershausen. Precise similarities have also been identified in liturgical bronze rings and wooden monumental sculptures. In fact, a parallel can be found between this crucifix and the wooden one in the Arezzo Cathedral, datable from the second half of 1100 and also influenced by «Ottonian bronzes».

The Cross, on the other hand, seems to be more recent to the Crucifix, and I suggest it dates from the 13th century. This is on account of a series of formal links with some crosses from the Umbro-Tuscan area which can be dated from 1200.

The precious ornaments from Cavriglia lead us to assume that the work was done by local craftsmen who were inspired by sculptoral models of the Rhine area. They were therefore easily transportable and represented important cultural vehicles for the spreading of a common sculptural lexis.

Arte Aurea Aretina, p. 70, n° 17, with bibl.; *Gioielli e Ornamenti Preziosi*, n° 196.

M.G.C.G.

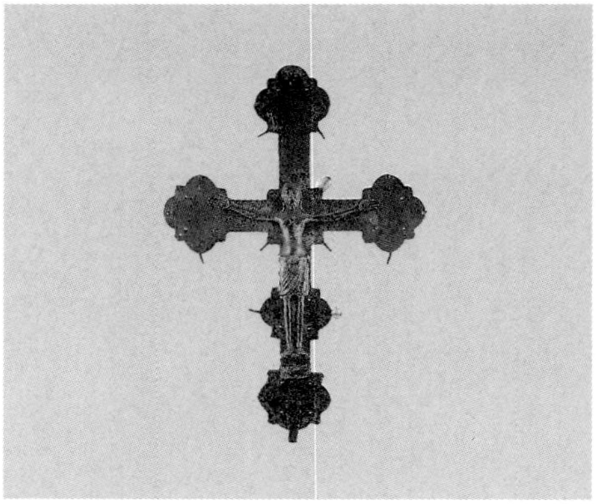

101. PROCESSIONAL CROSS
Arezzo. Palazzo Vescovile, from Pontenano di Sotto, Pieve di S. Paolo (Talla)
Cross: 37 x 26 cm.; Crucifix: 19 x 17.5 cm.
Engraved and gilt copper; bronze. Aretine metal craftswork: Cross 14th cent.; Crucifix 12th cent.

The cross is decorated by engraving with geometrical and foliated motifs. The finials which had once been applied are missing (the rivet holes can be seen) and only two spheroidal buttons in rock crystal which once decorated the ends still exist. The Agnus Dei which once had been applied on the intersection of the arms is also missing. This work is very close, on consideration of the engraving and ideation, to the handcrafts conserved on Aretine territory of the 14th and 15th centuries. The crucifix, in flask cast bronze with a chisel finish and fire-gilded, is part of the iconography of the «*Christus triumphans*». Indeed, he stands up on his own, supported without any flexion of the legs. The arms are outstretched and slightly turned upwards. The face is erect and the eyes open. He is raised up on the cross, exalted by the cross, not yet dead. The loincloth is held by a belt which is draped around, creating very plastic chiaroscuro effects. The manufacture seems to stem from that current which was defined «Romanesque» which has its prototypes in the Rhenish goldsmith, Godefroy De Claire.

It must be emphasized that this type of manufacture which is found in the area of Italy, may be the work of local goldsmiths who worked along the lines of small-scale sculptural models of Rhenish production, easy to transport, and which constituted a cultural vehicle for the spreading of a common sculptural lexis.

Arte Aurea Aretina II, p. 58, n° 15, with bibl..

G.C. and G.R.

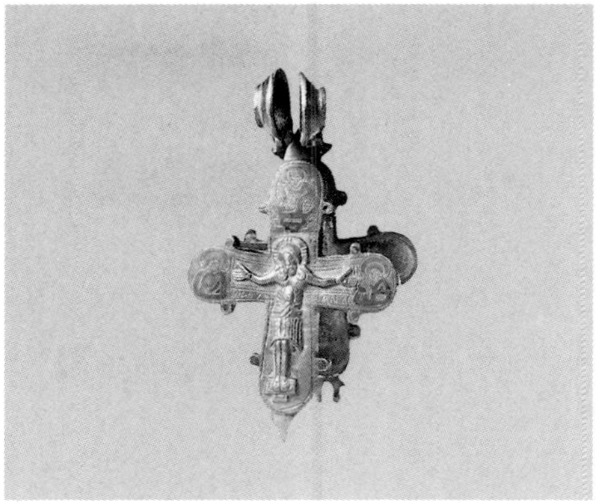

102. ENKOLPION
Museo Civico, Sansepolcro
13 x 7.5 cm.
Damascene and silver-plated bronze, embossed and chisel-engraved
Oriental manufacture from the first half of the 13th cent.

Cross reliquary worn around the neck, with webbed profile, on the back of which Christ Crucified is portrayed with long hair falling onto the shoulders, whiskers and a beard. The head is slightly bent, his expression solemn. The loincloth uncovers the knees. The legs are joined, rigidly vertical and parallel, while the feet, pierced by nails (like the hands), rest on the suppedaneum. Outlined at the ends of the three upper arms of the cross are St John, the Madonna and the Redeemer, with the addition of a damask in silver. At the sides of Christ an inscription in Greek, rather difficult to interpret, is engraved. On the back, a roughly-embossed, standing Madonna and Child in a long dress; in the arm borders, within damascene circles, there are three unidentified saints.

The popular origin of the object is confirmed by the writing. The work is rather crude and tries to imitate more refined and prized examples. The object reflects oriental influence, but the iconography of Christ in the frontal stance, with a slightly bent head, an expression of suffering and a thick beard, leads us to compare it to Western specimens which could be dated from the beginning of the thirteenth century. The rather sketchy work makes it still more difficult to define the geographical area. We tend towards giving credit to a Syrian influence.

Galoppi Nappini, 1988, p. 158; *Gioielli e Ornamenti Preziosi*, n° 190.

D.G.N.

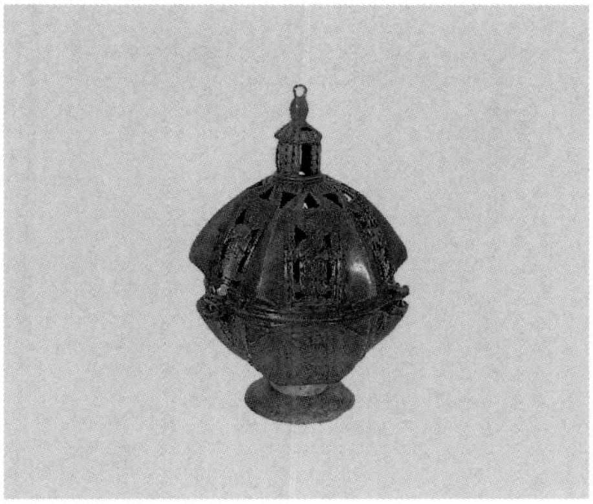

103. THURIBLE
Cathedral Museum, Arezzo
From Ponte a Caliano - Capolona
20 x 11 cm.; Base, 6 cm.
Cast bronze
Aretine workshop from 13th cent.

The thurible, spheroidal in shape, has a round, smooth base and a bowl designed with six ribs separating six plant motifs.
The upper part faithfully repeats the lower part, and instead of the floreated decorations, it exhibits six whole figures of Saints of a Byzantine flavour, skilfully inserted among triangular open work. The lid ends in a small circular lantern (it appears to be a hut) decorated with closely-packed grooves. In the Romanesque period, the thurible had a low foot and a hemispheric bowl; even the lid was often a half-sphere, or else an oval, as can be seen in the thuribles of the pictures in the lower church of S. Clemente in Rome (11th century). The open work on the lid was tondi or rosettes or leaves intermingled with animals. Towards the end of the 11th century and the successive one, the lid began to take on the form of a tower, beginning a slow transformation until it became an actual piece of architecture. The Byzantine influence evident in this object can be explained by the presence in Arezzo (precisely in the Duomo Vecchio of Pionta) of master craftsmen from Ravenna, who, under the direction of Maginardo, had transformed the Cathedral profoundly. The cultural presence of Ravenna was strongly pronounced and, starting from Arezzo, passed through San Veriano, Palazzo del Pero, Anghiari, Città di Castello, right into Romagna towards the Exarchate. In this case, therefore, there was an evident lingering in the applied arts of influences which the major arts had absorbed a long time previously.

Arte Aurea Aretina II, p. 59, n° 18, with bibl.; *Gioielli e Ornamenti Preziosi*, n° 177.

G.C. and G.R.

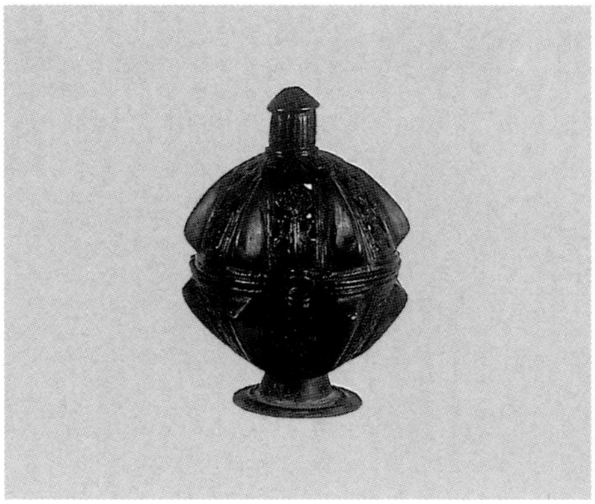

104. THURIBLE
Museo Statale d'Arte Medioevale e Moderna, Arezzo
Inv. Lay Fraternity 19214
From the Church of S. Margherita at Taena - Arezzo
16 x diam. base 36 cm.
Cast bronze with open work
Aretine manufacture from 13th cent.

On a round, smooth base, the object is spheroidal in shape, with six beaten, projecting ribs alternating with an open work motif with circular and plant ornamentation, inserted into a rectangle with a burin-engraved frame. The upper part faithfully repeats the lower part. The lid ends in a small, grooved, cylindrical lantern with four openings where the chain had once been applied. This cylindrical lantern is similar to that of other thuribles of the period which are in the Cathedral Museum at Arezzo. This leads one to suppose that the provenance of the objects was the same workshop which operated in that period at Arezzo.
Although based on typologies of the 12th century, certain decorative and morphological details, such as the ornamentation and the beating, place it chronologically towards the first half of the 13th century.

Galoppi Nappini, 1988, p. 181; *Gioielli e Ornamenti Preziosi*, n° 156.

D.G.N.

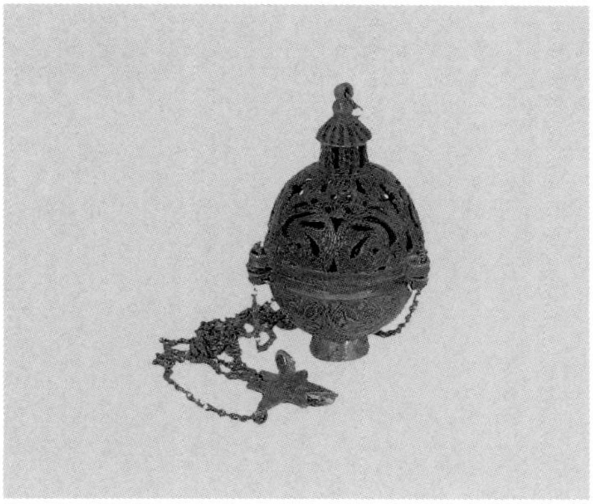

105. THURIBLE
Cathedral Museum, Arezzo
From Anciolina - Loro Ciuffena
17 x 9 cm. Base; 4 cm.
Cast bronze
Aretine metal craftswork from the 13th cent.

The bowl is decorated with floreal racemes in the shape of counterposed volutes. The upper part repeats similar motifs carried out, however, in open work and terminating with a cylindrical lantern which is slightly grooved. This type of lantern is found precisely in two other thuribles in the Cathedral Museum and also in one conserved in the Mediaeval and Modern Museum of Arezzo, all of them from the 13th century. It is likely that these articles all came from the same workshop. The starry grip is original. It should be remembered that the ornamentation consisting of plant racemes and volutes, represents, besides Man's struggle between good and evil, also the fruit of his work. At this stage we are, in fact, at the height of agricultural progress and the vine tendrils, the cycle of the seasons, and the scenes from life on the land are a constant in Romanesque art, mainly owing to the rebirth of the countryside in this period.

Arte Aurea Aretina II, p. 59, n° 16, with bibl.; *Gioielli e Ornamenti Preziosi*, n° 179.

G.C. and G.R.

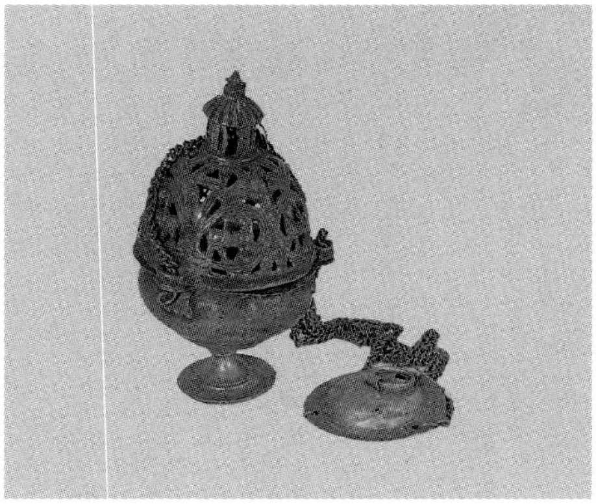

106. THURIBLE
Cathedral Museum, Arezzo
From Calbi - Arezzo
16 x 9 cm.
Cast bronze
Aretine metal craftswork from the 13th cent.

The object has a smooth bowl and a round base which was redone in the late Renaissance. Its original state must therefore be looked for in the upper part which has zoomorphic insertions and plant motifs in the open work. The round lantern is similar to the other thuribles of the same period. This leads one to suppose that they all came from the same Aretine foundry in operation at that time. It is to be remembered that the foundry art of Arezzo has not been studied sufficiently. It enjoyed a period of splendour, without fluctuating, from the 12th to the 15th centuries. There is a considerable quantity of bells signed and dated by Aretines and citizens of Cortona which can still be found on the territory.

Arte Aurea Aretina II, p. 59, n° 17, with bibl.; *Gioielli e Ornamenti Preziosi*, n° 178.

G.C. and G.R.

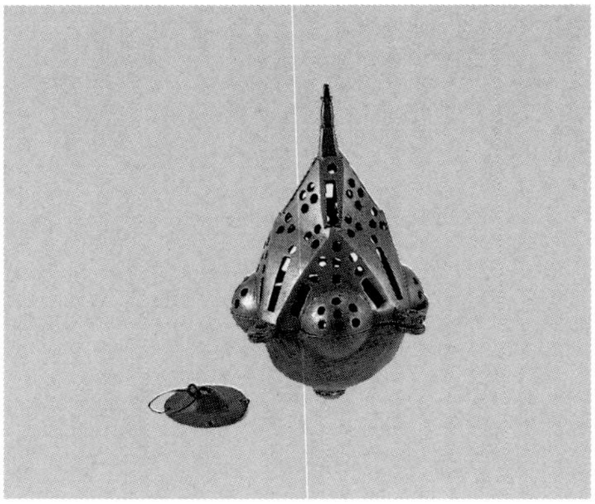

107. THURIBLE [censer]
Arezzo, Museo del Duomo
Cm. 20 x 14
Cast bronze
Aretine Workshop - early XIV century.

The foot is missing from this thurible which has a spheric cup with a four-foiled perimeter. The base of the highly geometrized cover, which repeats the cup's perimeter, develops its structure into a high gothic-like architectural form distinguished by the circular and rectangular fretwork that imparts to it great originality.
This artwork is remarkably creative and significant because similar pieces of this type are very rare. Specimens considered somewhat similar to this one can be found in the Pinacoteca Comunale of Castiglion Fiorentino, in the Museo Taglieschi of Anghiari, and in the Museo Diocesiano of the Città di Castello.

Arte Aurea Aretina II, pg. 60, n.20.
Gioielli e Ornamenti Preziosi, n. 180.

G.C.

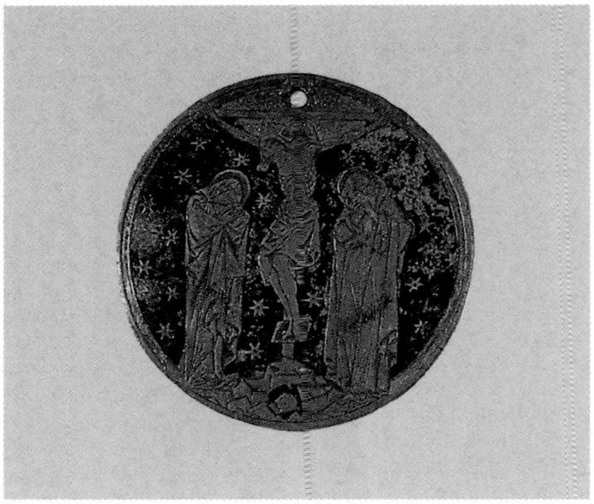

108. MEDALLION
Arezzo, Private Collection
Diam. cm. 8
Copper, traces of gold-leafing, blue and red enamel
Sienese goldsmith of the early XIV century (ca.1320): Tondino di Guerrino?

This medallion was, without a doubt, made in the area of Siena during that exceptional period that begun with the manufacture of the chalice by Guccio di Mannaia, donated to Assisi by Niccolò IV (1288-1292) and ended in the early decades of the XIV century. In fact, the medallion (or plaquette), depicting the «Crocifisso fra dolenti», [«Crucifix among the Suffering»] has extremely significant stylistic affinities with the crucifix on the plaquette situated on the foot of the aforementioned chalice by Guccio. Thus, our medallion, too, partakes of that culture and rightfully belongs within the artistic climate established by Guccio, the great goldsmith that anticipated the gothic style related to the great French miniating tradition and with the affreschi of Assisi.
This rare enamelled incision takes us, as A. Bagnoli pleasantly suggests, within the artistic context of Tondino di Guerrrino. Therefore, it dates back to the year 1320, also because of its close relationship with the crucifix that Pietro Lorenzetti painted in fresco in the transept of the lower Basilica of Assisi. The great technical ability and skill displayed in the quality of the incision «a figure risparmiate», a technique that allows the enamel to penetrate into the carvings, made the Sienese gothic goldsmiths famous for they were able to distribute and connect the parts to be enamelled with exceptional acumen and sensitivity. It is well known that by leaving large areas to be later covered with the enamel, open there is great danger of chipping, even if the object were to be only very lightly bumped. With exceptional skill, our goldsmith/enameler placed the little stars that connect the enamels on

the medallion's background. These served to accentuate the high spirituality of the depicted heaven but they also involved an unusual enamelling operation: because the enamel turns red when it comes into contact with the base metal, in order to obtain the glaring purple, which is barely perceptible today, the color blue was superimposed over the red. The red color is visible in very limited areas around the border. The poor state of preservation of the enamel, partly chipped and erased, and the loss of a great deal of gold-liefing do not diminish the exceptional quality of our medallion. Incidentally, we do not know its function, (perhaps a mantle clasp, a belt decoration, a plaquette for a reliquary bust, a peace?). The hole in the uppper section was without doubt made later.

Gioielli e Ornamenti Preziosi, n.200.

G.C.

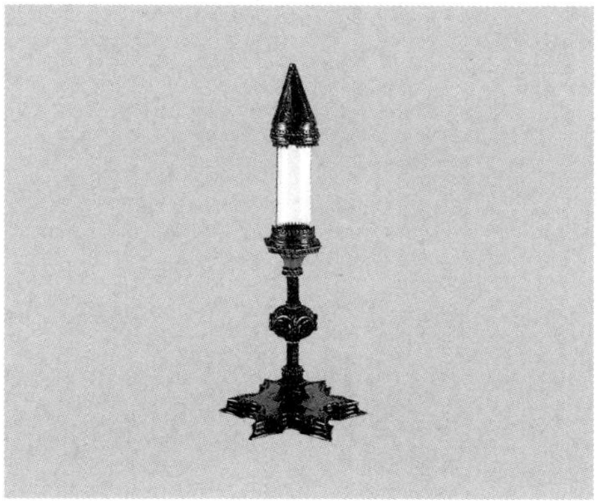

109. RELIQUARY
Arezzo, Private Collection
Cm. 15 x 34
Gilded copper, embossed, chiselled, engraved; enamelled tondi in the knot; engraved and enamelled silver.
Sienese manufacture of the mid-XIV century.

Architectural reliquary with a six point star-shaped foot, elevated by a moulded and beaded frame. The points on the star-like foot bear checkerboard style incisions; the two portions of the hexagonal stem divided by the knot, are decorated with blue and green colored enamel skillfully applied in hollowed incisions that form lozenge-shaped and cross-shaped decorations. The round knot with flattened poles is embellished with embossed and engraved acanthus leaves, and set with six silver tondi whose finely engraved figures (crucifix among the suffering and the saints) are covered by blue, red, green, purple and yellow translucent enamels, producing a whole of rare beauty and exceptional worth. Over the stem sits the cylindrical glass theca with moulded base, set into a frame of little lance-shaped leaves, a motif that is repeated in the exquisitely decorated cone-shaped cover. The cone-shaped cover and the cylindrical theca project the elegant architectural structure of a minaret.
The exceptional quality of the translucent enamels and the structural elegance of this artwork are without doubt attributable to a Sienese workshop operating around the middle of the XIV century.

Gioielli e Ornamenti Preziosi, n. 201.

G.C.

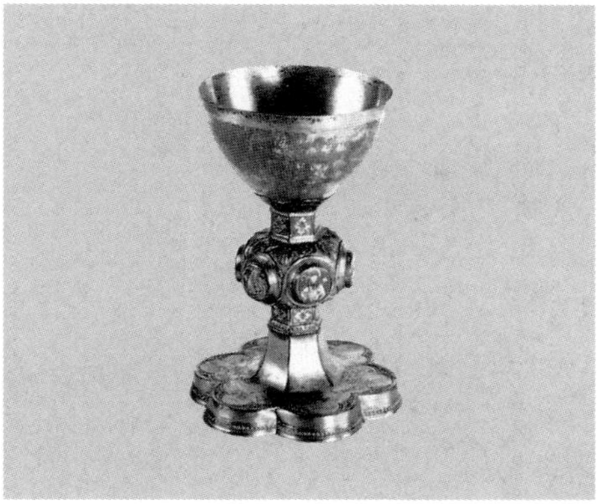

110. CHALICE
Arezzo, Museum of Medieval and Modern Art
Cm. 15 x diam. base cm. 36
Gilded copper, engraved; translucent enamels.
Aretine manufacture of the XIV century.

The chalice's base is multifoiled, surrounded by a beaded frame. Three-foiled arch motifs are engraved on its flat surface; the hexagonal stem is adorned in its two connecting elements with a floral decoration on each front. The knot in the center is embossed with leaf-shaped decorations and it is set with six tondi that contain enamelled medallions bearing the immages of the Crucifixed Christ, St. John, St. Donato, the Virgin with the Child, the Grieving Madonna, and a not too well defined Saint, perhaps St. Firmina. The corolla is multifoiled and decorated with arches intertwined with flowers.
The type of object and its stylistic profile reveal a marked local character, a fact which is easily verifiable in other artworks that have been recovered within the Aretine Diocese. The quality of the enamels, above all of the Crucifixed Christ, indicate a goldsmith with good technical and design skills. In spite of the small dimensions, all the figures have been outlined with a sure hand, with the anatomical details and folds in the vestments masterfully and attentively executed.

Oggetti e Ornamenti Preziosi, n. 157.
Arte Aurea Aretina, pg. 54; Galoppi Nappini, 1987, pg. 183.

D.G.N.

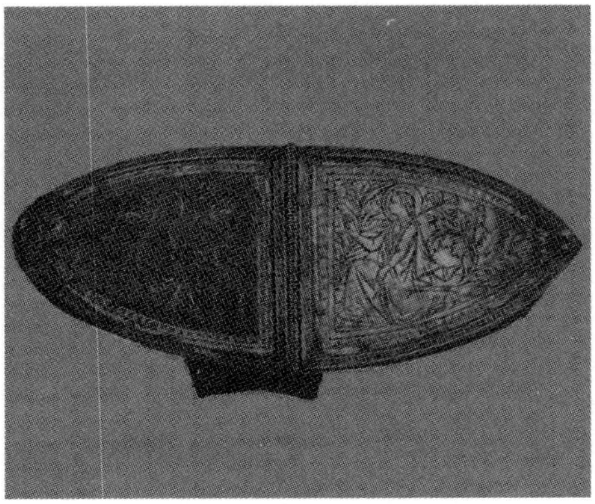

111. NAVICELLA
Arezzo, Museo del Duomo from the Parochial Church of Subbiano
Cm. 4 x 16
Engraved and gilded copper
First half of the XIV century.

The navicella's plain, star-shaped base has six points. The upper portion of the navicella is composed of two parts united in the center by a hinge. On these parts two half-length figures are engraved representing the Virgin and the Angel.
The poor state of preservation of this object, whose workmanship is fairly modest, makes a determination of its style difficult. However, the simple and delicate design seems to mirror, in the poverty of the metal and in the parsimony of its composition, a definite Aretine style.

Arte Aurea Aretina, p. 58.
Gioielli e Ornamenti Preziosi, n. 181.

G.C., D.G.N., G.R.

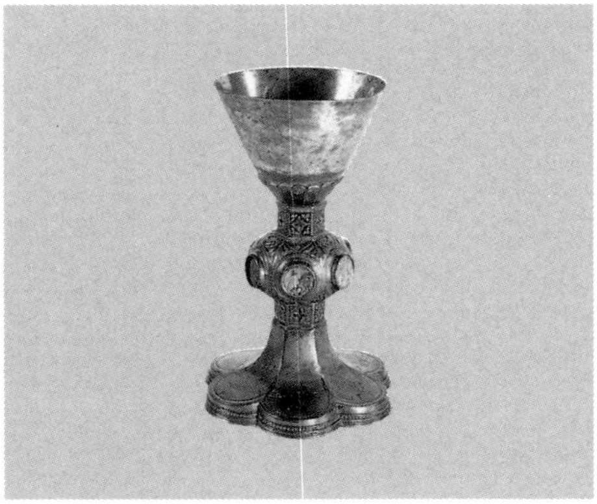

112. CHALICE
Arezzo, Museum of Medieval and Modern Art
Cm. 15 x 13,5
Engraved and gilded copper; vitrous pastes
Aretine manufacture of the XIV century.

The flat, six-lobed base of the chalice is decorated with arches and lilies. The hexagonally divided stem is adorned by geometrical type decorations in opaque blue, red and white enamel. The knot is decorated with embossed leaves motifs and by six tondi at one time adorned by translucent enamels; of these enamels, only two specimens remain and they represent the half-length figures of the Virgin and an unidentified Saint (part of the vitrous paste has fallen off). The corolla and perhaps the cup were part of a remake added later.
Although the loss of the four enameled plaquettes has seriously deformed the artwork, the excellent workmanship is evident in the two remaining medallions.

Arte Aurea Aretina II, pg. 60, no.21.
Galoppi Nappini 1987, pg. 184.
Oggetti e Ornamenti Preziosi,n. 158.

D.G.N.

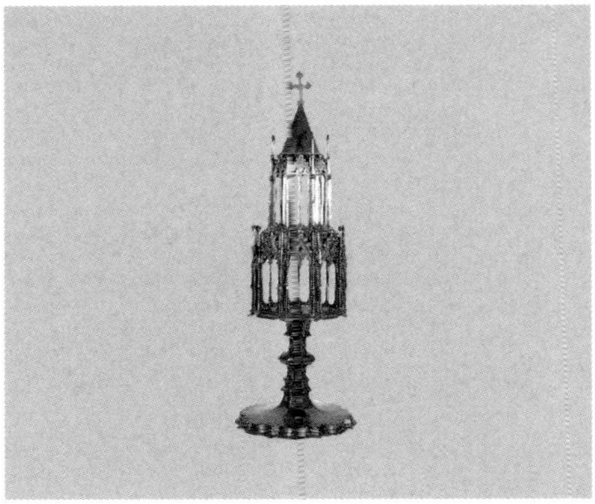

113. RELIQUARY
From the Convento della Verna
Cm. 75 x 27
Gilded copper and vitrous pastes, engraved, decorated with fretwork
Second half of the XIV century.

The reliquary rests on a mixtilinear eight-lobed base with eight points, engraved on the surface with lobe motifs; on the intermediate angles there are decorations ending in lily-shaped motifs. The octagonal stem is interspaced by frames, one of which is notched. One of these frames bears the following inscription in enamelled gothic characters: HOC OPUS FECIT FIERI FRATER LODOVICUS DE BIBBIENA. The flattened and faceted knob is placed between two enamelled octagon blocks depicting wild birds of prey. The shape of the reliquary is that of an octagonal two tiered temple-like structure with each section separated from the other by small columns resting on pillars. On the first tier each section bears a two-light mullioned window decorated on the front by a small central rosette; slender pyramid-like cusps rise along the columns while the upper tier is made of still smaller two-light mullioned windows with pyramid-like cusps and fronts. A three-foiled cross terminates the octagonal shaped cupola.
The complex architectural structure of this artwork recalls other Sienese examples of this type, such as the reliquary of San Savino in the Orvieto Museum.

Arte Aurea Aretina, pg. 59.
Gioielli e Ornamenti Preziosi, n. 197.

G.C., D.G.N., G.R.

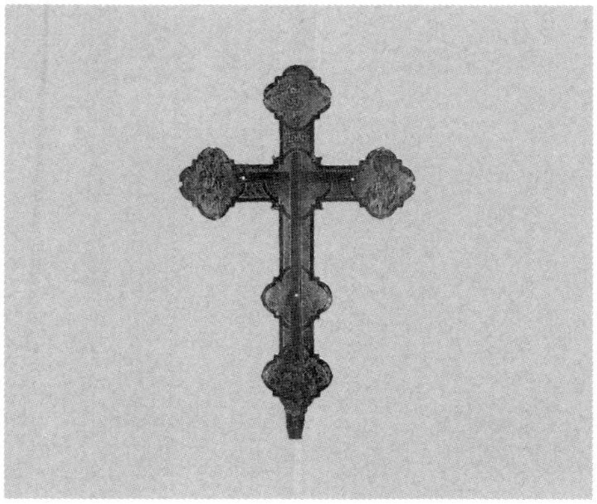

114. PROCESSIONAL CROSS
Arezzo, Museum of Medieval and Modern Art
Inv. Fraternita dei Laici 15110
Cm. 37,5 x 24
Engraved and gilded copper
Tuscan manufacture of the XIV-XV centuries.

Mixtilinear framed panels are set on the front of the arm endings. In these panels the following figures are represented: the Virgin, St. John, the Pelican feeding its young, and Adam's skull in the Golgotha background. The full relief figure of the Crucified Christ, whose past presence here is suggested by the engraving of the cross in the background, the INRI inscription, and by the holes obviously intended for attaching the figure, is missing. The upper portion of the back of the cross bears the half-length figure of the Evangelists, Luke and John with their symbols. The central panel depicts the mystic Lamb with the tormented vexillum. In the lower part of the main arm, we find St. Matthew with the Angel and lower still St. Mark with the lion. The cross's background is grained with floral decorations. In addition to the Crucifix, all the small spherodial elements that normally decorate this type of artwork are missing. On the whole, this cross is distinguished by the delicate outline of its incisions. Its artistic and architectural profile is assumed to be Florentine, as are the thick, full-bodied figures wrapped in ample drapings. This type of church ornament was widely diffused between the end of the XIV century and the early part of the XV around Florence and within the Aretine area close to Florence.

Galoppi Nappini, 1987, pg. 184.
Oggetti e Ornamenti Preziosi, n. 159.

D.G.N.

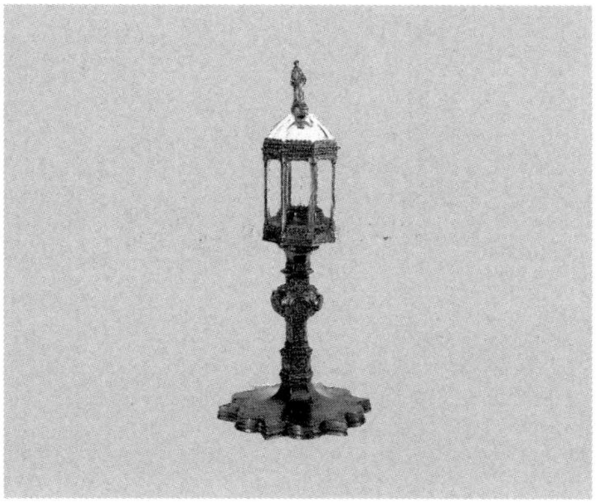

115. RELIQUARY
Arezzo,Private Collection
Cm. 16 x 36,50
Gilded copper, embossed and engraved; engraved cast silver; rock crystal
Florentine workshop
Foot and stem: end of XIV century
Theca with dome cupola in rock crystal: XV century.

Architectural reliquary with a high edged, six-foiled mixtilinear foot whose border frames a cross-beaded knurled motif; simple incisins decorate the onten edge of the foot. The polygonous sectins of the stem are decorated with lozenge-shaped motifs and include a circular knot with six silver tondi bearing the once enamelled, engraved figures of Christ in Piety with the Madonna and St. John, and three Saints. A small collar above the knot, connects the octagonal shaped theca. The theca is divided by little silver pillars that meet the frames decorated with a minute, lance-shaped leaves motif. The precious cover in rock crystal is shaped like a small flattened dome cupola divided in eight segments and mounted on a frame decorated with a lance-shaped leaves motif. The statuette standing on the peak of the dome (perhaps a friar) is mould casted. The cover is connected to the theca with a hinge that allows it to open.
The artwork, whose lower portion (base and stem) recalls gothic style features, dates back to between the end of the XIV century and the beginning of XV; even from a stylistic point of view, this lower portion of the reliquary is considerably distant from the XV century dating of the theca. The crystal rock cover (which may have been manufactured in Venice and mounted in Florence), as well as the architectural profile of the theca and the statuette of the Saint, all reflect Renaissance period styling.

Gioielli e Ornamenti Preziosi, n. 202

G.C.

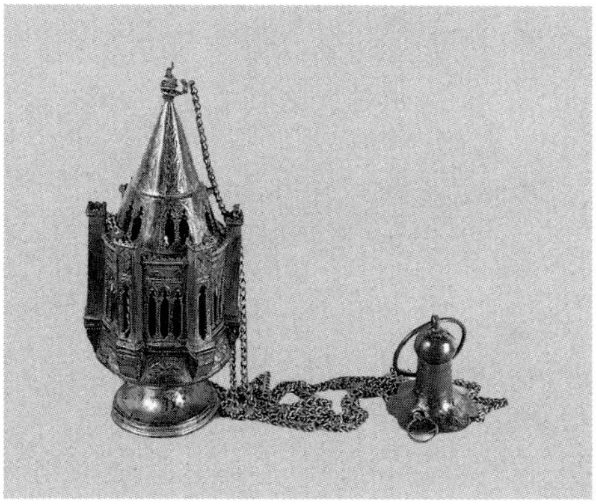

116. THURIBLE [censer]
Castelnuovo Berardenga (Siena), Chiesa di San Giovanni Evangelista a Cerreto
Cm. 26,5 high; base diameter cm. 7,5
Gilded Copper with engraved decorations
Sienese Shop, end of the XIV - beginning of XV century.

This thurible has the architectural form of a towered castle, a form that was widely used for this type of object during the fourteenth and fifteenth centuries. The cup, or brazier, engraved with a repeated motif of a stylized four-leaf clover, sits on the round base. The two tiered cover, on which the four leaf clover motif is repeated, is composed of: arched (two-light and three-light) mullioned openings; of little towers on the corners' edges; and of a cusp with a leaves pattern engraving. The cover is topped off by a bud on which a non-original chain is attached. Underneath the cup, the following words are inscribed in capital letters: «HIONNES. EQUITIS. HOSTILI. DE GUELFIS. ANNO 1623». Without a doubt, and as the inscription indicates, the thurible became the property of the church, together with the navicella (previously described) when its owner the Sienese nobleman Giovanni dé Guelfi donated it, in the year 1623.
The thurible of San Giovanni a Cerreto is very similar to other thuribles still present in the Sienese area.

C. Alessi, in *Oreficeria Sacra nel Chianti Senese* (XII-XIV century), catalog of the San Gusmè exhibition, Siena 1985, pgs. 41-42, n° 10 with previous bibliography.
M. Collareta, in *Oreficeria Sacra Italiana*, Museo Nazionale del Bargello, Florence 1990, pgs. 10-11,92-92, nos. 4 and 23.

C.A.

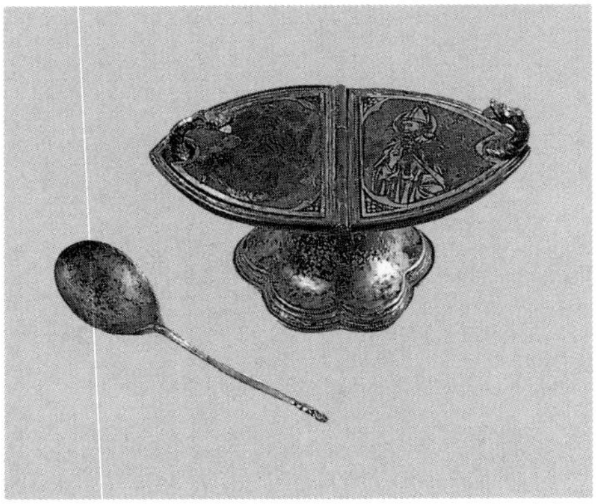

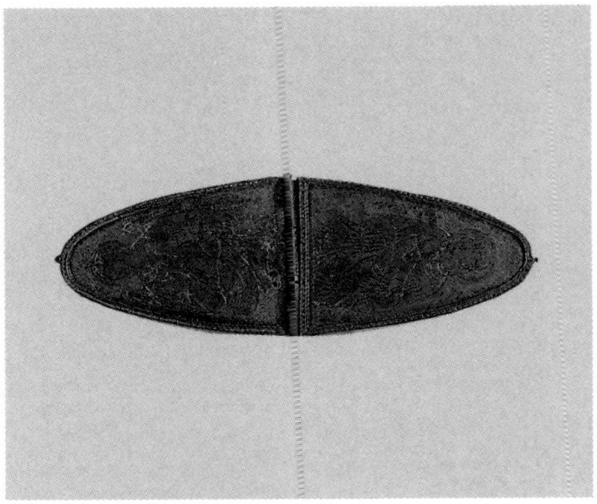

117. NAVICELLA [sail boat]
Castelnuovo Berardenga (Siena), Chiesa di San Giovanni a Cerreto
Cm. 16x14; teaspoon cm. 13
Cast Copper, embossed, engraved and gilded; enamels
SIENESE GOLDSMITH, first quarter of the fifteenth century.

This Navicella is quite rare due to the very few antique pieces of its kind that have survived. It is in excellent condition, especially its enamels which, in specimens of this sort, are usually worn out or lost.
The structure of this rather small piece of artwork is simple and recalls fourteen century style patterns. Compared to examples of the preceding century, the foot's multifoiled form is enriched by a moulded step, while the long and narrow cup, closed by two decorated wings with dragon heads, sits on a short cylindrical stem.
The following words, inscribed under the foot: HIONNES EQUITIS. HOSTILII DE GUELPHIS. ANNO DOMINI. 1623, probably refer to the donor and the year of the donation to the Chiesa di San Giovanni. The figure of the Assunta [Madonna] surrounded by cherubs, and a Holy Bishop who appears to be St. Augustine in the act of blessing, are depicted on the navicella's cover with opaque enamel. In spite of the rather arcaic enamelling technique utilized in representing these figures, the so called «a figure risparmiate» technique, a Tuscan variant on the «champlevé» method utilized in Siena during the thirteenth and fourteenth century, the type of object, the analysis of the style expressed in depicting the figures and the obvious relationship with pictorial texts of the end of the fourteenth century and the beginning of the following one, place the execution of this navicella during that period. There is an affinity, in fact, between the navicella and the products coming out of the shop of Goro di Ser Neroccio (Siena 1382-1456?); this is particularly true with the representation of the Assunta whose image is very close to the Assunta on the mantle clasp displayed in the Museo dell'Opera del Duomo which has been attributed to this Sienese goldsmith. Here, we are probably dealing with a craftsman trained in the shop of Goro di Ser Neroccio.

Oreficeria Sacra nel Chianti Senese (XII-XV century), catalog of the San Gusmé exhibition, Siena 1985, n° 9, pgs. 39-40, w/bibl.

L.M.

118. NAVICELLA [sail boat]
Arezzo, Museum of Medieval and Modern Art
Inv. Fraternita dei Laici 15159
Cm. 20,5 x 7 x 5
Engraved and gilded copper
Attr. Parri Spinelli (1387-1453) XV century (1400 ca).

The navicella rests on a circular base; hull-shaped, its wide and oblong cover consists of two wings joined together by a hinge. The surface is engraved with two elegant half-length figures. The Virgin's face is turned three-quarters toward the right and her slender hands hold a book. Viewed in perspective, the Archangel is depicted unrolling a scroll bearing the following invocation in gothic style characters: «Ave Gratia P.». The object's structure is very simple and its narrow and oblong shaped hull gives it the customary XIV/XV century style classification. The object's well-defined designs, which are partly worn off unfortunately, are visible however in the minute details of the drapings and in the size of its monument-like figures. The marked engravings of the folds and of other areas indicate that these were originally enamelled. The background is thickly engraved in a cross-like motif in order to make the enamel stick better on the vast surface.
In 1916, Salmi indicated that this navicella was probably the work of Parri Spinelli, the son of the painter Spinello Aritino. The figures' oblong proportions and the ample drapings depicted in the two skillfully executed engravings are features that identify Parri's entire artistic production. Furthermore, we can make two direct comparisons with a fresco painting, in the church of St. Francis in Arezzo. In the represention of the Announciation in this fresco, particularly in the image of the Madonna, we find, a precise resemblance with the Virgin in our navicella. Still attributable to Parri Spinelli is a cross from the church of S. Salvatore al Vescovo

in Florence, in gilded and silver plated copper, dating back to the year 1415 ca., when according to Vasari, Parri was probably working in Ghiberti's Florentine workshop.

M. Salmi, *L'Oreficeria Medievale nell'Aretino, Rassegna d'Arte* XVI, 1916, pg. 239. *Arte Aurea Aretina*, pg. 65. Galoppi Nappini 1987, pg. 88. *Oggetti e Ornamenti Preziosi*, n° 160.

D.G.N.

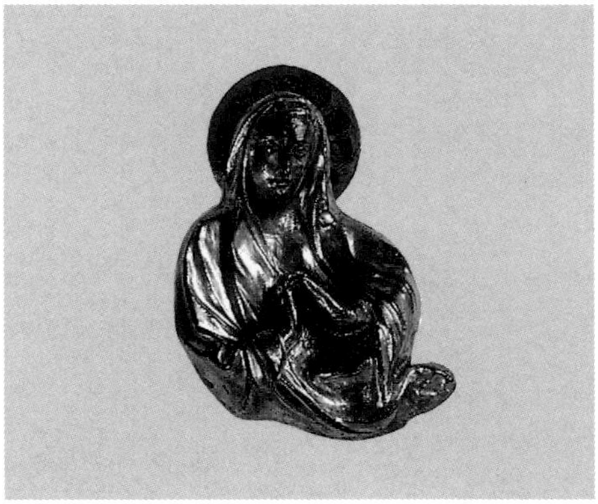

119. ALTORILIEVO [high relief] representing «The Virgin»
Arezzo, Museum of Medieval and Modern Art
Inv. Fraternita dei Laici 15118
Cm. 7
Gilded copper, embossed and chiselled with opaque enamel
Tuscan manufacture of the second half of the XV century.

A remarkable piece of altorilievo representing a bust of the Virgin with hands joined in the act of prayer. The aureole behind the head is radiated with traces of red enamel.
Expertly modeled, this small metal sculpture was probably the companion of the one of San Giovanni (also part of this exhibit) on a large processional cross which, considering the elegant features of these two plaquettes, must have been exceptionally beautiful.
The stylistic connotations of these slender, gracefully modeled figures strongly evoke Parri Spinelli's thin, elongated figures. Thus, in seeking the origin of the artwork that accommodated these works originally, we must look to Arezzo and Florence, the areas where this painter spent significant periods of time.

Galoppi Nappini, 1987, pg. 190. *Oggetti e Ornamenti Preziosi*, n° 161.

D.G.N.

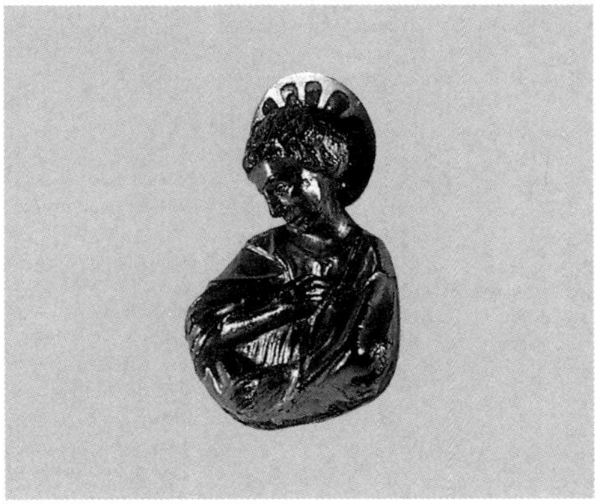

120. ALTORILIEVO [high relief] representing «St. John»
Arezzo, Museum of Medieval and Modern Art
Inv. Fraternita dei Laici 15119
Cm. 7
Gilded copper, embossed and chiselled with opaque enamel
Tuscan manufacture of the second half of the XV century.

This altorilievo represents a bust of St.John, with his head inclined in reverence, and with a hand holding his garment. The aureole behind the head is radiated with traces of opaque red enamel.
The elongated face, the waves in the garment and the thin, slender hands have been skillfully treated by the artist who makes us regret the loss of the processional cross that surely accommodated this sculpture, together with the one of the Virgin (also part of this exhibit). Following a pattern that is typical of the international Gothic style, worthy of Parri Spinelli's production, both these figures display a sinuous treatment of the folds in the garments.

Galoppi Nappini, 1987, pg. 190. *Oggetti e Ornamenti Preziosi*, n° 162.

D.G.N.

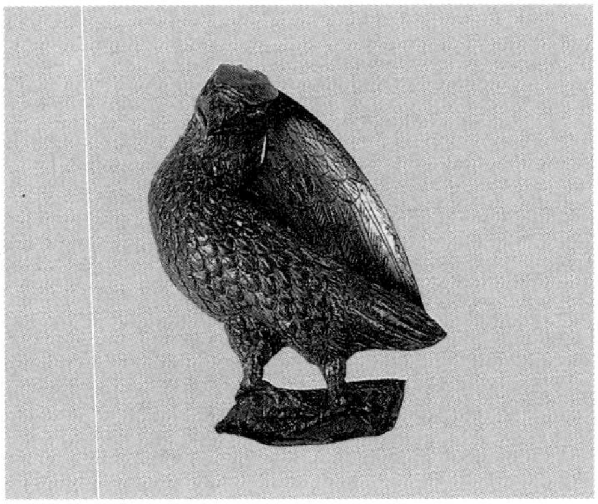

121. ALTORILIEVO [high relief] representing an «Eagle»
Arezzo, Museum of Medieval and Modern Art
Inv. Fraternita dei Laici 15113
Cm. 9
Gilded copper, embossed and chiselled
Tuscan manufacture of the XV century.

This altorilievo of an eagle, the Evangelist symbol of St. John, has been skillfully executed, especially the treatment of the feathers and the claws. A large version of this plaquette, together with the one representing the lion, St. Mark's Evangelist symbol (also exhibited here), was to be part of the furnishings of a large XV century lithurgical interior.

Galoppi Nappini, 1987, pg. 189. *Gioielli e Ornamenti Preziosi*, n° 164.

D.G.N.

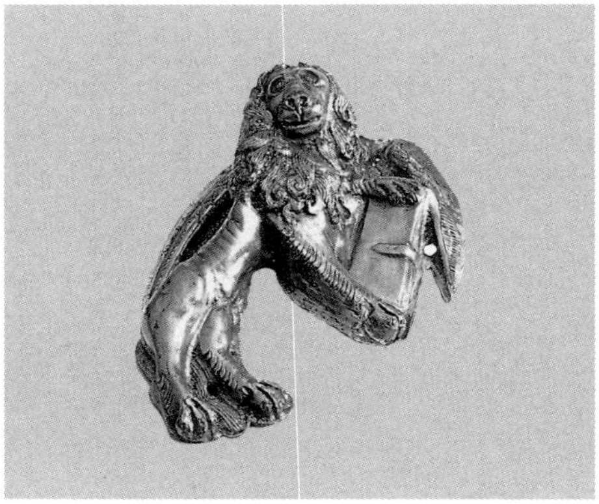

122. ALTORILIEVO [high relief] representing a «Winged Lion with Book»
Arezzo, Museum of Medieval and Modern Art
Inv. Fraternita dei Laici 15112
Cm. 9
Gilded copper, embossed and chiselled
Tuscan manufacture of the XV century.

This altorilievo of a winged lion holding a book with his front legs, is the Evangelist symbol of St. Mark.
A large version of this small metal sculpture, with the skillfully engraved lion's mane, was to be part of a large XV century lithurgical interior, together with the other altorilievo representing the eagle (also exhibited here).

Galoppi Nappini, 1987, pg. 189. *Gioielli e Ornamenti Preziosi*, n° 163.

D.G.N.

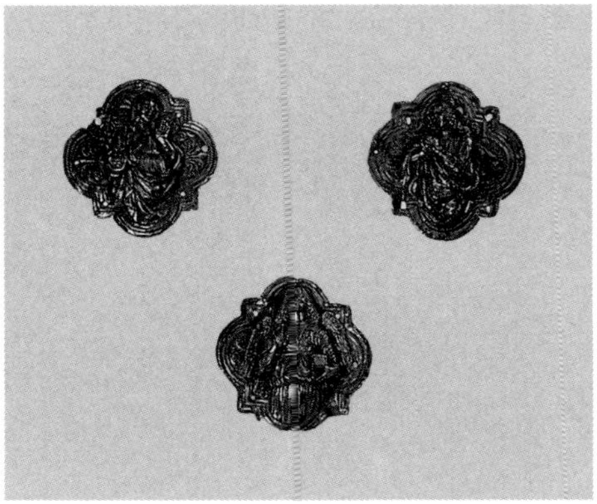

123. 3 PLAQUETTES (for cross's terminals)
Arezzo, Museo del Duomo
Cm. 6x6
Embossed copper, engraved and gilded
Aretine goldsmithery workshop (?) mid-XV century.

Once serving as cross endings these three plaquettes, depict the Virgin, the Announcing Angel and St. John the Evangelist. The figures enclosed in the classic quatrefoil are embossed and engraved. The relief's background is richly decorated with an excellently embossed and engraved leaves motif. Following the patterns of advanced fifteen century styling, these figures, too, are excellently executed and evoke memories of Ghiberti, as filtered and executed perhaps by an Aretine goldsmith.

Arte Aurea Aretina II, pg. 54, n° 35. *Gioielli e Ornamenti Preziosi*, n° 182.

G.C., G.R.

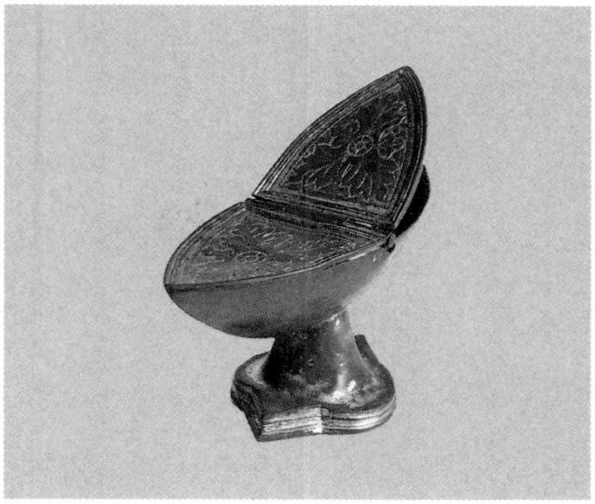

124. THURIBLE and NAVICELLA
Arezzo, Museo del Duomo
Thurible: Cm.21 x 7; Navicella: cm. 16,5 x 8
Embossed Copper, engraved and gilded
XV century.

The thurible's architectural form is hexagonal, and its plain, circular base, (which perhaps is no longer the original) is embossed. The under-cup bears engraved Kufic style decorations that are alternated by applied corbels sustaining the small towers with three-foiled windows and engraved decorations that rise upwards. There are three-light mullioned window openings topped by engraved, intertwining arches between the counterforts. On the thurible's cone shaped cusp, whose style is rather oriental, there are leaves-shaped engravings whose quality is not particularly noteworthy. The thurible still preserves some of its gilding and on the whole it is a product of fair workmanship, at least as far as its architectural framework is concerned, where some of its elements are rather unique, especially the little round towers.

The navicella, with its embossed and tiered mixtilinear base, has a careened cup obtained in the process of embossing. The hinged cover bears incisions of framed acanthus leaves. The design of the leaves indicates a certain culture of transition, from the pointed Gothic style leaf to the rounded leaf pattern typical of the Renaissance. It is with confidence, therefore, that we attribute these locally produced pieces to the XV century.

Arte Aurea Aretina, pg. 60. *Gioielli e Ornamenti Preziosi*, n° 185.

G.C, D.G.N., G.R.

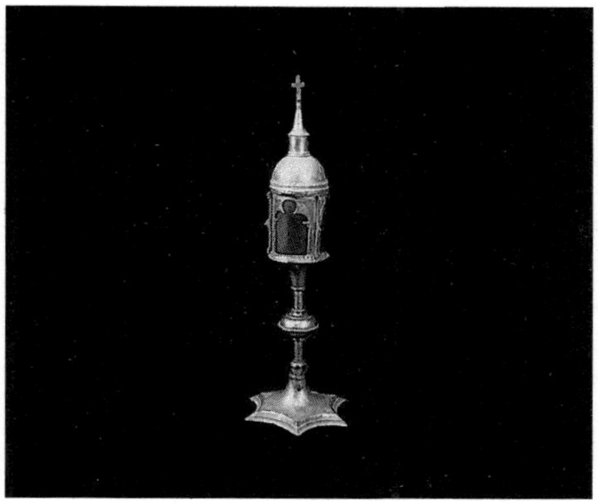

125. RELIQUARY
Arezzo, Museo del Duomo
From the Chiesa della Pieve - Arezzo
Cm. 38x14
Embossed copper, engraved and gilded
XV century.

The reliquary has a star-shaped base with six points. Its frame is decorated by a fine beaded motif. The stem contains a plain flattened knot with central moulding. The theca takes the form of a round-based, small trabea-covered temple that encloses a glass cylinder. On the surface of the temple there are six trabea-arched windows engraved with leaves motifs and subdivided by column-like strips. The theca is sealed by a miniature engraved temple topped by a cross.

The Renaissance styled reliquary has only slight touches that recall the archaic era; such is the case of the star-shaped base which does not, however, in any way change the overall structure of the artwork. The piece is a handsome specimen of local manufacture, simple in is form, yet not lacking in elegance. It is typical of the territory's ecclesiastical production that still portrays a certain amount of XIV century styling. The fact is that these sacred art objects remained bound to tradition for a longer period of time than others. The reason for this was twofold: on the one hand, the nature itself of the object left little room for innovative change, and secondly, the entities who commissioned these works were, for obvious reasons, strictly bound to well defined canons of stylistic formulations.

Arte Aurea Aretina, pg. 62. *Gioielli e Ornamenti Preziosi*, n° 186.

G.A., D.G.N., G.R.

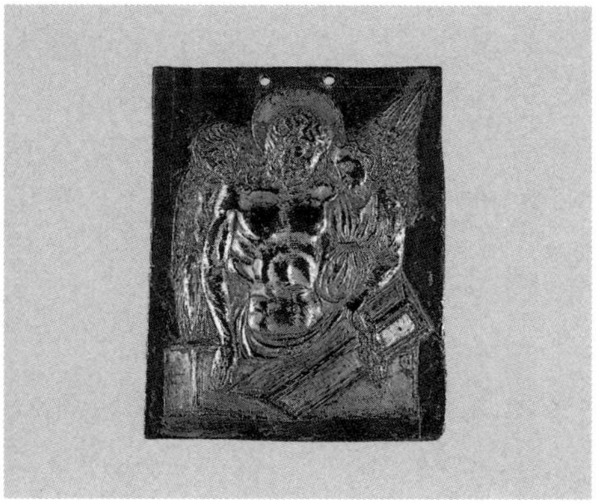

126. PLAQUETTE (depicting «La Pietà»)
Arezzo, Museum of Medieval and Modern Art
Inv. 15143
Cm.11,5 x 8,8
Bronze with gilded parts in relief
Anonymous Tuscan of the XV century.

Rectangular plaquette depicting the half-length figure of Christ, with a cruciferous halo, emerging from the uncovered sarcophagus sustained by two angels. A piece of Christ's garment, held by the angel on the right, falls on the edge of the sarcophagus's obliquely placed cover. One of the wings of this same angel is unfolded and is pointing upwards. There are two holes on the plaquette's upper edge. The hand of a skilled artist is evident in the treatment of the head of Christ and of the angels. There are no references on this plaquette in literature, the figures' style and the layout of the scene induces us to attribute this work to Tuscany's sacred art production of the XV century. While in the upper part of the scene the anonymous artist has been influenced by patterns typical of the Donatello school, as for example the face of Christ and the form of the angel's wing, in the rest of the scene the quality level is not as excellent, as for example the execution of Christ's arm and the sarcophagus' cover. It is quite probable that the artist was inspired by a model that did not include the whole sarcophagus.

Vannel Toderi, 1987, pg. 141. *Gioielli e Ornamenti Preziosi*, n° 165.

F.V.T.

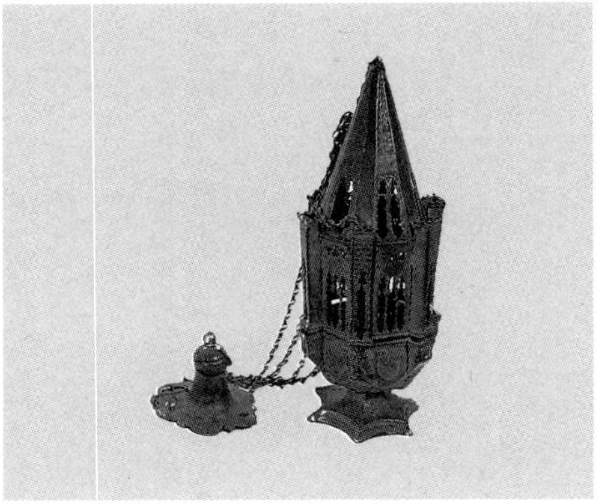

127. THURIBLE
Arezzo, Museo del Duomo
From Bagno di Chio - Castiglion Fiorentino
Cm. 22 x 8 - Foot: cm. 8
Embossed and engraved copper
Aretine workshop of the XV century.

The reliquary's round cup, with six rectangular corbels, sits on the star-shaped hexagonal foot. The cup is decorated with embossed and engraved motifs that include rosettes and lunettes framing the acanthus leaves. The reliquary's upper portion is shaped like a temple; the little towers, which are positioned above the cup's corbels, separate the oblong three-foiled, three lights, mullioned windows. The dodecagonal pyramid-shaped cusp that terminates the structure is decorated with three-foiled, two lights, mullioned windows decorated with lance-shaped leaves' motifs. The hexagonal hook appears to be an original of the period.
The oject is decidedly very beautiful and well proportioned. On the matter of style, we must point out that while the cup is definitely Renaissance, the overall architectural framework, the rather oblong three-foiled windows, the cusp and the star-shaped base still reflect the Gothic style.

Arte Aurea Aretina, II, pg. 62, n° 28, w/bibl. *Gioielli e Ornamenti Preziosi*, n° 184.

G.C., G.R.

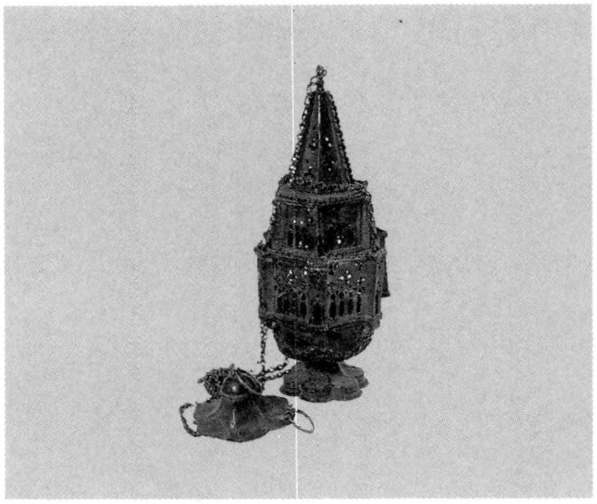

128. THURIBLE Arezzo, Museo del Duomo
Cm. 28 x 12
Embossed and engraved copper with traces of gilding
Aretine workshop of the mid-XV century.

The object is formed like a temple with an engraved hexagonal tiered base. The cup is embossed, and engraved with a radiated acanthus cluster motif; consoles alternate the emblem of the coat of arms of the S.S. Annunziata (perhaps it is there to indicate the object's origins) and Christ's monogram. The three tiered cover is decorated by six little towers and by arches that intertwine to form a preciously complicated pattern of architectural fretwork. In place of the towers, the tapered second level has acanthus leaves spirals that separate the three-foiled windows with fretworked tympanum, and connect to each other by a rounded arch obtained through the engraving process. A Gothic style pinnacle, shaped like a hexagonal pyramid, richly decorated with lacy motifs on the ribs and with cross-shaped fretwork on the flat surfaces, completes the structure. This thurible can be attributed to an Aretine goldsmithery workshop of the second half of the XV century, whose work was inspired by Florentine cultural models.

Arte Aurea Aretina, II, pg. 62, n° 29. *Gioielli e Ornamenti Preziosi*, n° 183.

G.C, G.R.

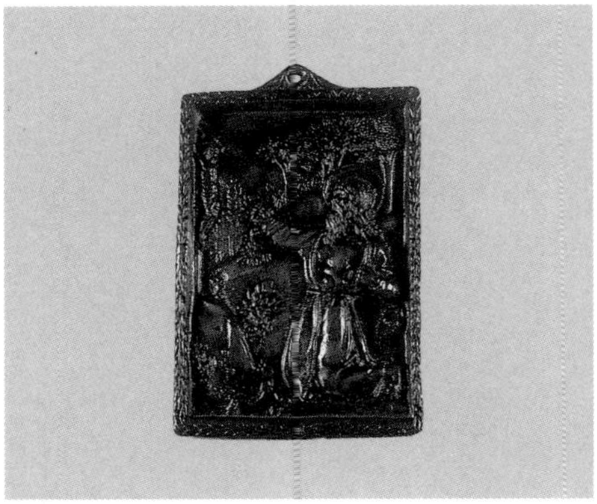

129. PLAQUETTE (depicting «San Gerolamo»)
Arezzo, Museum of Medieval and Modern Art
Inv. 15153
Cm. 12,3 x 8
Bronze
Cerchia del Filarete
XV century.

Rectangular plaquette depicting the haloed saint on his knees in front of a crucifix in the act of beating his chest with a stone. A serpent lies at his feet and around him, among the rocks, the heads of two bears and two lions are visible. In the background, a mountainous landscape with trees is depicted. A laurel motif makes up the border, on the upper portion of which the following inscription appears: S.HIERONIMVS. A small triangle centered above the border is decorated with leaves and bears a hole for hanging.
The plaquette was initially attributed to the Padova school and its dating fluctuated between the XV to the first half of the XVI century. According to more recent studies, the piece is to be attributed instead to Filarete or to someone within his group, and its dating placed within the XV century.
Antonio Averulino, called «il Filarete» (1400-1469), was a Florentine sculptor and architect, who worked in Florence, Rome, Venice, Bergamo and in Milan where he was recommended to Francesco Sforza by Piero de' Medici. We lack definite news about him after the year 1465.

Vannel Toderi, 1987, pg. 141 w/bibl. *Gioielli e Ornamenti Preziosi*, n° 166

F.V.T.

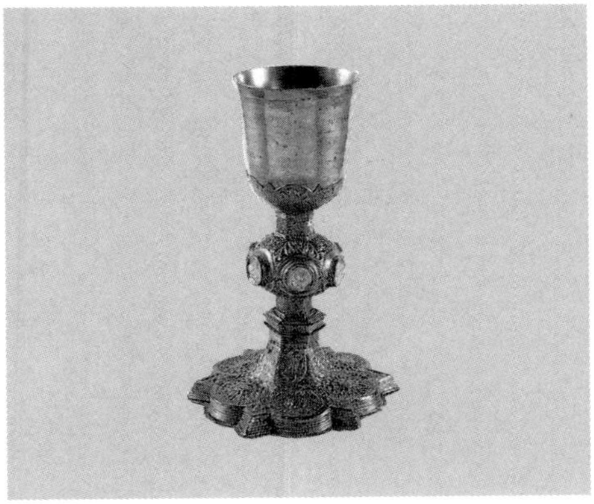

130. CHALICE
Arezzo, Museum of Medieval and Modern Art
Inv. Funghini 960
Cm. 19,5 x 12,5
Gilded copper, engraved, translucent enamels
Aretine manufacture of the first half of the XV century.

The chalice's base is mixtilinear with six lobes and six points; it is decorated by rich floral and plant motifs and it is bordered by a beaded pattern. The hexagonal-shaped stem is composed of a knot and two connecting elements decorated with geometric motifs in blue, red and white opaque enamel. The knot includes six plaquettes, at one time decorated with translucent enamel of which only traces now remain. Depicted in the six tondi are the head and shoulder figures of the Madonna, of St. John, of Christ in Piety, and of other unidentified saints. The knot is decorated with leaf motifs. The undercup is engraved with floral motifs and bears the same six-lobe and-six points mixtilinear motif decorating the base. The cup's shape is cylindrical. There are many objects of this type and style in the territory encompassing the Aretine diocese.
The author of this piece utilized XIV century style norms in the composition of the chalice's knot and in the enamelling, and he added a richly embossed ornamentation to the base in order to improve its rather expeditious execution.

Arte Aurea Aretina II, pg. 61, n° 24 w/bibl. Galoppi Nappini 1987, pg. 186. *Gioielli e Ornamenti Preziosi*, n° 168.

D.G.N.

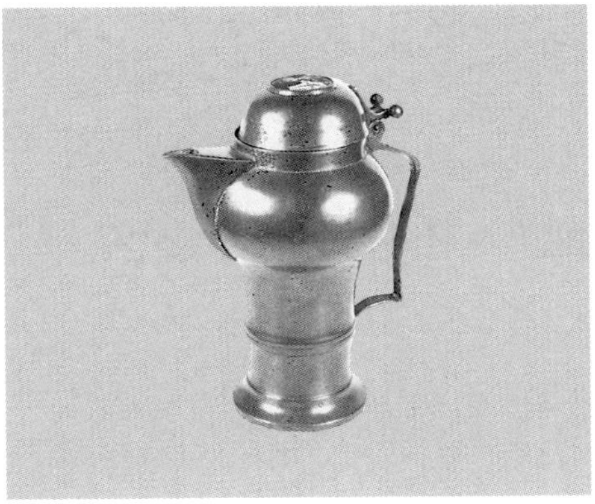

131. WATER JUG
Arezzo, Museum of Medieval and Modern Art
Inv. Fraternita dei Laici 15384
Cm. 22 x base diam. cm. 8
Brass and translucent enamels
Florentine manufacture of the XV century.

Circular based brass water jug whose plain container sustains the rounded upper body with spout. On the jug's cover there is an excellently executed medallion bearing a Florentine coat of arms. A long handle moves down from the jug's cover to the container's moulding close the jug's base.
We know from documented illustrations that this object was a widely used, everyday water container in Florentine households of the XV century.

Galoppi Nappini 1987, pg. 187. *Gioielli e Ornamenti Preziosi*, n° 167.

D.G.N.

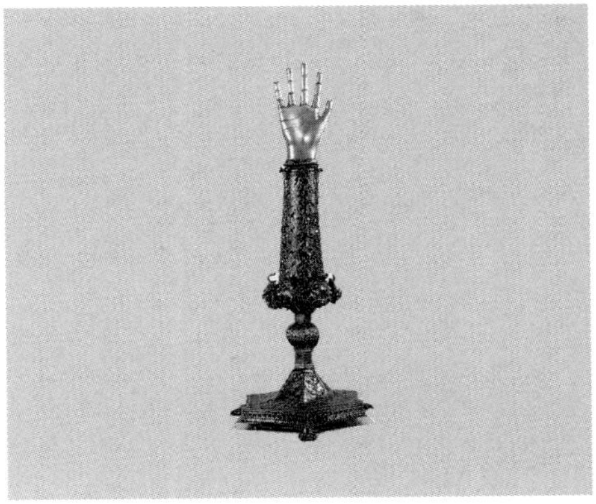

132. RELIQUARY ARM (of Santa Margherita)
Castiglion Fiorentino, Pinacoteca Comunale
From the Chiesa di San Francesco - Castiglion Fiorentino
Cm. 57 high
Engraved, gilded and silver plated copper
Aretine manufacture (?) of the XV century.

This arm-shaped reliquary sits on a hexagonal, six-point base above three lion paws. The six surface segments of this base have been engraved with acanthus leaves; one of the segments depicts the kneeling donor. On the decoration that goes around the base's border, a rather worn out inscription in Gothic characters reads: «HOC OPUSFECIT FIERI FRATER PAULUSDE CASTEGLIONE ARTINO DUM PREDICABAT IN ARIMINO».
The edge of the base is decorated with a fretwork motif. The hexagonal knot on the stem bears the same leaves engraving that appears on the base. The cylindrical theca, which contains the relic of Santa Margherita, rises from a corolla of richly moulded and engraved open leaves. The theca is covered by fretwork and subdivided in six bands which are decorated alternatively with flower and leaf motifs. The reliquary terminates with an open silver hand, on whose pertinence we have some doubts.
Although the inscription would place the object in the Romagna area, its style patterns and decorations, especially the wide acanthus leaves motif, which we find in other pieces from the Aretine area, suggest that it is probably a product manufactured in this area during the XV century.

Arte Aurea Aretina II, pg. 63, n° 31 w/bibl. *Gioielli e Ornamenti Preziosi*, n° 193.

D.G.N.

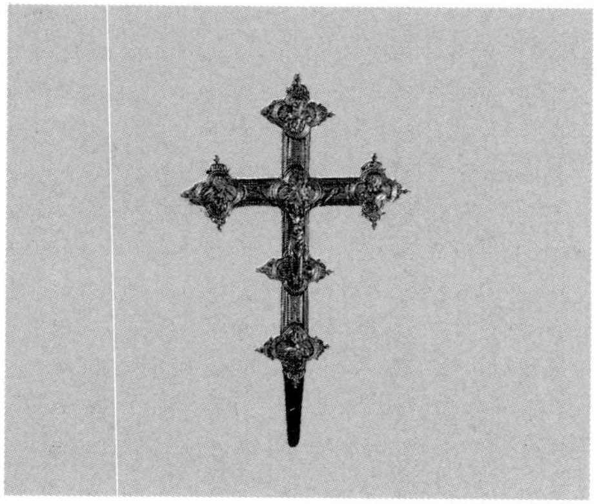

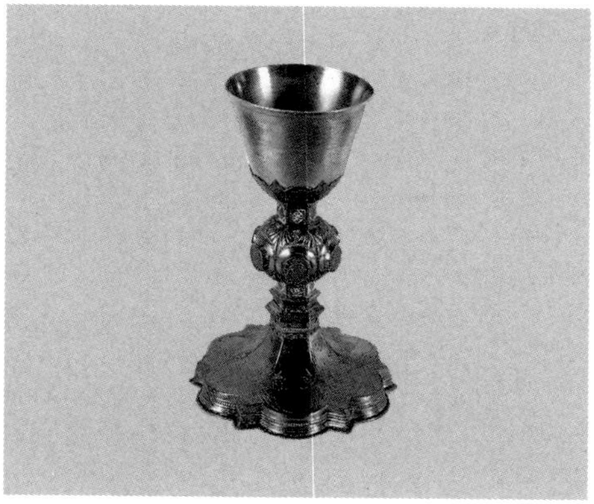

133. PROCESSIONAL CROSS
Castellina in Chianti (Si), Chiesa di San Martino a Cispiano
Cm. 45,5x28
Gilded bronze, embossed, engraved, with copper plaquettes on the cross's front; gilded and engraved on the back. The Crucifix is in cast bronze
Sienese goldsmith, second half of the XV century.

This type of Cross was already in use during the fourteenth century and it continued to be used in the fifteenth and sixteenth centuries. On the front of the Cross, we have the Crucifix, in full relief and gilded, and six embossed and four-foiled plaquettes depicting: God the Father (top), the Virgin and St. John Evangelist (at the extreme ends of the horizontal arm) and St. Agnes (below); then, where the arms cross over, the pelican, symbol of the Resurrection is depicted, while lower still is the sun and the moon. Rectangular shaped copper plaquettes engraved with floral motifs are inserted on the arms' surfaces.
On the back of the Cross there are five engraved plaquettes that depict the four Evangelists and in the center the mystic Lamb with the banner of grief. Five cherubs are engraved along the surface of the arms. The following words are inscribed below: «Questa Croce ha fatto la Compagnia di Sancta Agniesa». [«This Cross made for the Society of St. Agnes»]. Even though it was executed for a small and rather marginal lay confraternity, this Croce di San Martino a Cispiano has remarkable artistic merit that must be attributed to a Sienese goldsmith operating during the second half of the fifteenth century. Not far from the methods utilized by the Sienese goldsmith Francesco d'Antonio (known from 1440 to 1477), the author of this Cross displays singular analogies with the author of the reliquary bust of Santa Cristina, still preserved in the Spedale di Santa Maria della Scala in Siena.

C. Alessi, in *Oreficeria Sacra nel Chianti Senese*, catalog of the exhibition (San Gusmè), Siena 1985, pgs. 46-48, n° 14, w/bibl.

C.A.

134. CHALICE
Castelnuovo Berardenga (Siena), Chiesa di San Giovanni a Cerreto
Cm. 21,5 high; base diameter cm. 14,5
Engraved and gilded copper, enamels
SIENESE GOLDSMITH, first half of the XIV century.

Chalice on multifoiled and mixtilinear foot with beaded frame on the step, engraved with three-foiled arches which are separated by rosettes and acanthus leaves. On the hexagonally sectioned stem the following inscription appears in gothic characters and in *champlevé* enamel: AVE MARIA GRATIA PLENA. Directly above, there are only traces of the red enamelled rosettes that once decorated the engraved panels. The knot is decorated with leaf motifs and on the six plaquettes, whose light blue opaque enamel is practically all worn off, the following subjects appear: the *Crucifixion*, the *Madonna*, *St. John the Evangelist*, *St. Michael the Archangel*, and a holy *Bishop*. One enamel has been substituted. On the under-cup there are flower and rosette engravings.
Like numerous examples of chalices of this type present in the Sienese area, or preserved in Italian and foreign museums, this chalice is difficult to date. In fact, the structure of this lithurgical piece — characterized by the mixtilinear foot, by the geometric enamel decorations on the stem, and by the knot decorated with translucent or *champlevé* enamels — underwent only slight changes during the fourteenth and fifteenth centuries. A stylistic examination of the figures in the enamels leads one to anticipate the dating of this chalice's execution to the first half of the fourteenth century. In addition, even the method of using recessed enamel «a figure risparmiate», [with figures saved] a common technique in Siena since the beginnings of the fourteenth century, speaks in favor of an early dating. The method consisted in scooping out the bottom of the copper plate and filling it with blue enamel; in so doing, the contours of the figures, of the decorations, of the folds in the garments and of other details would be deeply engraved. These incisions would then be filled with melted vitreous paste so that the surface, «risparmiata» [saved] from the metal, once gilded, would stand out.
The enamelled tondi or nails on the stem's knot, recall the work of the goldsmiths Tondino di Guerrino and Andrea Riguardi and the important Sienese goldsmithery pieces of the early fourteenth century. In particular, the figures' curled hairdressings, the bowed heads, the characterization of the faces, particularly the accentuation of the eyes and noses, recall the «saved» enamels of the Pastorale di San Galgano (Siena, Museo dell'Opera del Duomo), while the Crucifix, although remindful of the wooden crucifixes by Giovanni Pisano, recalls the enamels attributed to Tondino di Guerrino.
The more cursive style as well as the greater rigidity of the forms, compared to the works by the Sienese goldsmith, leads us to think of the work as a product of a shop, or at the very least of an artist strongly inspired by Tondino di Guerrino. It might very well be that the work is by Andrea Riguardi, an artist who is still not well known but who signed, together with Tondino di Guerrino, the chalice in the British Museum in London.

L. Martini in *Oreficeria Sacra nel Chianti Senese* (XII-XV century), catalog of the San Gusmé exhibition, Siena 1985, n° 5, pgs. 32-35, with previous bibliography.

L.M.

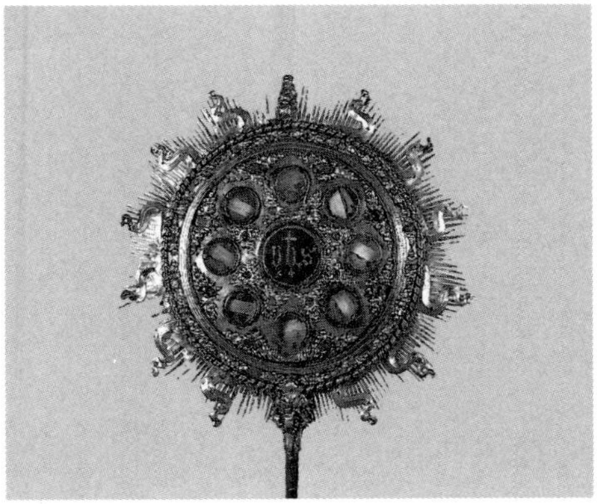

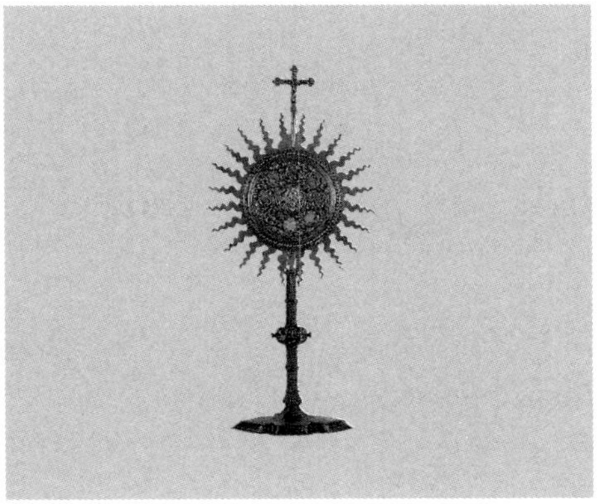

135. RELIQUARY
Castiglion Fiorentino, Pinacoteca Comunale
From the Chiesa di San Francesco - Castiglion Fiorentino
Cm. 40
Gilded copper, embossed and engraved, enamels, semi-precious stones
Aretine art, second half of the XV century.

Disc type reliquary with Bernardinian sunburst that recalls the tablets that St. Bernardino used to leave as a memento of his sermons. In the center, inside a tondo, San Francesco is depicted receiving the stigmata. Surrounding the central figure, there are eight medallions in relief depicting four Saints, while the alternating four plaquettes enamelled with opaque enamels depict the Resurrection, the Announciation (which appears upside down) and St. Michael the Archangel.
The medallions are enclosed in embossed and engraved acanthus clusters set in the center with a semi-precious stone. The richly composed frame has both plain and knurled motifs, a string of acanthus leaves with a central semi- precious stone, and a spiral of moulded lamina from which the sunburst rises. The sunburst is composed of rigid rays alternated by serpent-shaped ones. An acanthus leaves cluster in richly embossed and engraved lamina, connects the sunburst disc to the (missing) stem. The same leaves motif is repeated on the disc's upper portion where there was once a cross, now missing. The back of the reliquary is a faithful replica of the front. The central tondo contains the Bernardinian symbol enamelled in red, and the remaining tondi contain the relics. While the piece's quality level is good, the incisions covered by translucent enamels are remarkable; particularly impressive is the tondo of the Resurrection which appears to be inspired by the models of Pier Francesco. Noteworthy too are the acanthus clusters, which have been masterfully modeled and set.

Arte Aurea Aretina II, pg. 64, n° 36 w/bibl. *Gioielli e Ornamenti Preziosi*, n° 195.

G.C., G.R.

136. RELIQUARY
Castiglion Fiorentino, Pinacoteca Comunale
From the Chiesa di San Francesco - Castiglion Fiorentino
Sunburst: cm. 70 x 35. Foot: cm. 25 x 13
Gilded copper, enamels
Tuscan workshop - Foot: XIV century; Sunburst: XV century.

The reliquary's foot has a mixtilinear and oblong quatrefoiled base that rests on a moulded step and connects to the hexagonal stem with four ribs that separate the acanthus leaves engraved on the lobes. The stem is interrupted in the center by a knot decorated by two strings of bean-shaped decorations, crystals and semi-precious. stones. Four additional knobs give the stem form and elegance. The theca for the relics is an elegantly framed circular disc. On the front, a six-lobe central circle frames an engraved lamina covered by translucent enamel depicting the «Madonna Assunta» enclosed in a mandorla; all around eight minor six-lobe circles enclose an equal number of relics. All the circles are connected by clusters of embossed and engraved leaves. On the back of the cross the following inscription appears: REX VENIT INPA (on the horizontal arm) XPVS XPVS DEUSOHOF (on the vertical arm). The back of the reliquary is a faithful replica of the front with the exception of the central circle, the one that corresponds with the front's «Madonna Assunta», which contains the unframed Bernardinian monogram, enamelled in opaque blue. The other lobed circles have inscriptions and are connected, as they are in the front, by groups of embossed and engraved leaves. The Gothic-like foot is probably the result of a separate assembly. The quality level of the plaquette treated with translucent enamelling is remarkable and it allows one to see the extremely fine incisions of the Assunta sustained by the six angels. With the blue, green, yellow and sky-blue colored enamels, we enter the sphere of Tuscan art, just as we do when we view the representation of the «Madonna della Mandorla» in the door of the same name within the Florentine Cathedral Duomo.

Arte Aurea Aretina, 1987, pg. 88-89, n° 30 w/bibl. *Gioielli e Ornamenti Preziosi*, n° 184.

G.C.

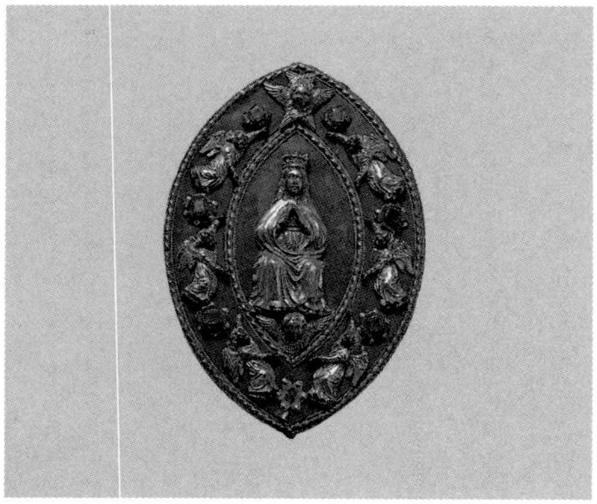

137. MANTLE CLASP
Church of St. Augustine - Castiglion Fiorentino
Cm. 16x11
Silver, gilded silver and stones; applied on a wooden support
Second half of the XV century.

The clasp, shaped like an almond, is in silver leaf with embossed and engraved gilded silver figures. The brooch's backside bears an engraving of the Visconti family's coat of arms and the following inscription: LAURENTIA FECIT FIERI. The crowned Virgin, resting on a cherub, is in the center of the frame. The frame surrounding the Madonna depicts six flying angels, alternated by embossed and engraved flowers set with precious stones. The gems are square-cut (carré) and rectangular (baguettes).
As the coat of arms and family name on the piece indicate, the work was commissioned by the same Lorenza Visconti who had also ordered from Bartolomeo della Gatta the St. Michael panel, now located in the Museum of Castiglion Fiorentino.

Arte Aurea Aretina II, pgs. 65-66, n° 39, w/bibl; *Gioielli e Ornamenti Preziosi*, n° 198.

G.C. and G.R.

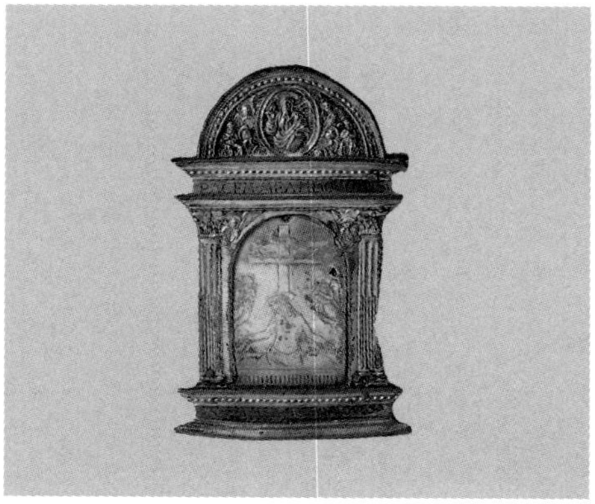

138. PEACE
Sansepolcro Civic Museum
From the art treasures of the Cathedral of Sansepolcro
Cm. 18x9
Silver, gilded copper, embossed and engraved artwork
Florentine manufacture of the second half of the XV century.

Shaped as an architectural facade, the object acts as a frame for an arched plaquette depicting a lightly embossed engraving of Christ, emerging from the Sepulchre, flanked by two Angels, with a cross in the background. Rising from the base of the object, which bears the inscription PACEM MEAM REGNO VOS, are two fluted pilaster strips topped by Composite capitals and two winged cherubs. Above the architrave on which the words PACEM MEAM DO VOBIS are inscribed, there is a round arched lunette. Within the lunette, an almond shaped mandorla depicts God the Father in the act of blessing, flanked by two kneeling Saints and the faces of winged cherubs. On the back of the piece, the original overturned handle serves to grip the artwork.
Various elements and features of this artwork are typical of the Renaissance period. Due to its poor architectural execution, the piece is thought to be of the type produced in «series» in one of the many Florentine shops of the second half of the XV century.

Gioielli e Ornamenti Preziosi, n° 191.

D.G.N.

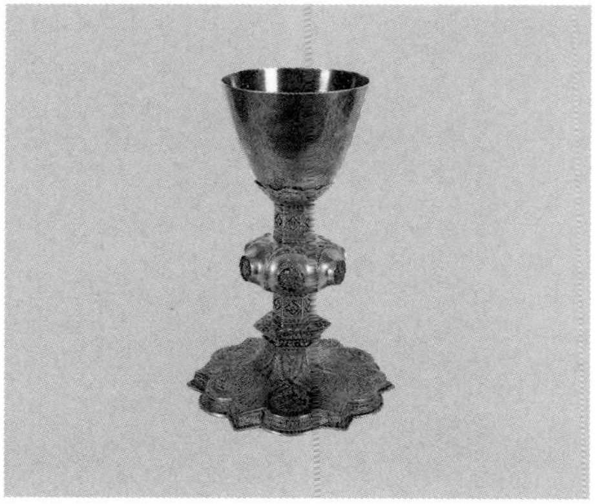

139. CHALICE
Arezzo, Private Collection
Cm. 15x22
Gilded copper, engraved, embossed and chiselled, enamels; partly gilded silver cup, with engraved tondi on the silver knot that bear traces of enamelling
Florentine manufacture of the second half of the XV century.

The chalice's mixtilineal hexagonal foot rests on a high moulded and beaded step. The foot is composed of a complex leaf motif, with strips that depict evangelist symbols, a dragon topped by a bird (a heraldic symbol perhaps) and a rosette motif. The hexagonal stem's engravings are in red and blue enamel with rosette motifs. The large knot around the stem is set with six protruding silver tondi with engravings of the Madonna, St. John, a holy bishop, two saints, and a coat of arms, all bearing traces of enamelling. The juncture where the foot is attached to the stem is accented by a protruding frame composed of chiselled leaves.
The cup and under-cup portions of the chalice are products of a restoration, perhaps conducted in the 17th century, and it was probably then that the tondo depicting the coat of arms was included in the silver knot as replacement of a missing one.

Gioielli e Ornamenti Preziosi, n° 203.

G.C.

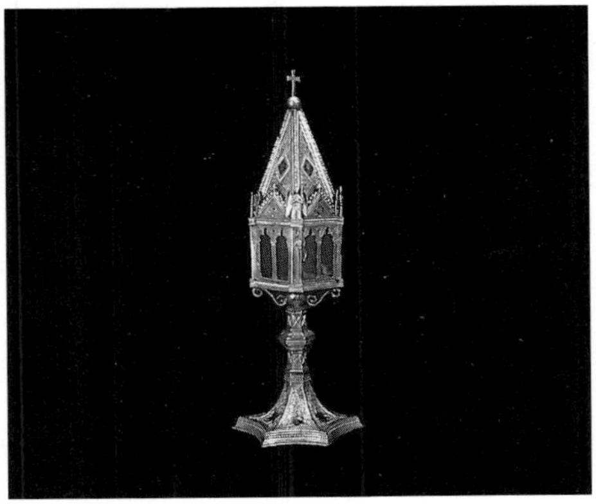

140. RELIQUARY OF THE CROSS
Arezzo, Duomo Museum
Cm. 18x15
Gilded copper, embossed and engraved, nielli, embossed and engraved silver
End of XV century.

The reliquary's hexagonal base is decorated with lozenges and divided in six concave segments. The segments, which are decorated with embossed and engraved floreal motifs, are enriched by six nielli which twice depict the figures of St. Donato, St. Stefano, and the initials of the Opera del Duomo. The stem is composed of a flattened and tiered knot; the high part of the small temple is attached to the stem by a sphere and by four spirals. The small temple has a square base with three-foiled mullioned windows topped by pinnacles and angular pilaster strips, in turn topped by four kneeling Angels. The architectural structure is completed by a spire decorated in the same syle as the foot, with embossed and engraved floreal motifs and with four lozenges. The globe with cross now situated on the spire's summit, replaces a former statue of St. Donato, stolen during the XVIII century. The reliquary probably comes from the Old Duomo, and as documents from the Archives seem to attest, it was constructed in the year 1496.

Arte Aurea Aretina, pg. 64,w/bibl.; *Gioielli e Ornamenti Preziosi*, n° 187.

G.C., D.G.N., G.R.

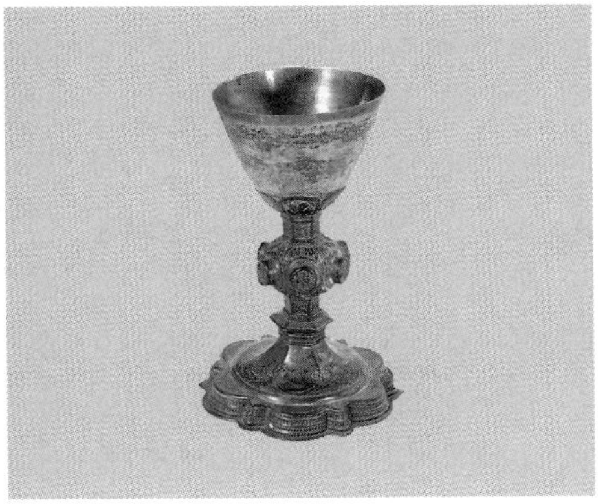

141. CHALICE
Arezzo, Duomo Museum
Da Montione - Arezzo
Cm. 17x11
Gilded copper, embossed and engraved; enamels
Aretine manufacture of XV century.

The chalice's mixtilineal hexagonal base has a tiered and beaded base. Two blocks engraved with floreal motifs support the embossed and engraved knot decorated with six tondi depicting the Christ in Pietá, the Virgin, the Saints, all gilded on a blue colored enamelled background. The under-cup, which is engraved with plant motifs, supports a flaring cup. On the whole, the object's under-cup engraving is not very detailed, but nonetheless the convexity of the foot displays a certain originality.

Arte Aurea Aretina II, p. 62m n° 26 w/bibl.

G.C. and G.R.

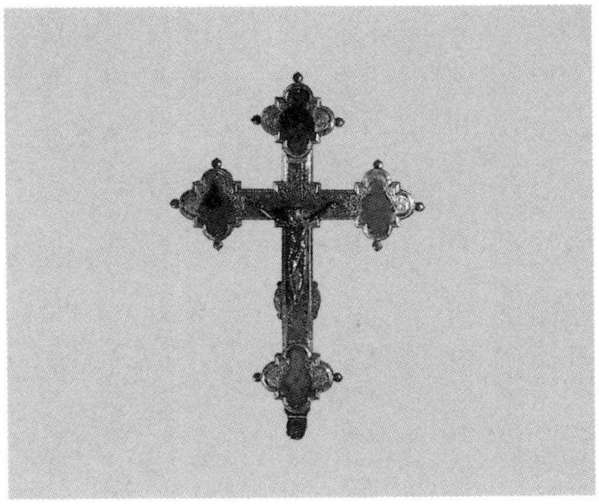

142. PROCESSIONAL CROSS
Arezzo, Museum of Medieval and Modern Art
Inv. Funghini 1291
Cm. 51x36. Christ cm. 13x12
Gilded and silver plated copper leaf on a wooden interior with intaglio enamels
Aretine manufacture of the XV-XVI century.

The interior structure of the cross is made of wood. The wood is covered by copper leaf that has been gilded, silver plated and engraved. The shape is that of a latin cross with four-foiled arm extremities. On the summits of the external lobes there are eleven metallic spherules. The cross is outlined by a moulded, beaded and gilded frame. According to the usual medieval iconography of the Crucifixion, the back panels were meant to house high reliefs depicting the Madonna, St. John, and the Eternal Father; unfortunately only the oxidized impressions of these remain in the background. A well constructed Crucifix, probably originating from another artwork of a later date, is positioned in the cross's center. The remaining surface is entirely covered by elegant leaf motifs, vine shoots and spirals. On the back of the cross there are three red enamelled panels (those on the top and in the center of the cross have been lost). In the final plaquettes of the minor arm there are head and shoulder images of St. Eugenia and St. Firmina, as we read in the abbreviated inscriptions. The lower panel of the major arm bears the following enamelled inscription: PLEBS/BALNEI/AUREI (DONO DEDIT). The wide grooves which have been engraved in all three panels have been filled with red enamel. The good design quality of the panels was probably inspired by the «Pierfrancesco» school, as witnessed by certain anatomical details in the figures depicted, such as the long and slender necks, the sense of weight and essentiality portrayed in the design of the vestments.

GALOPPI NAPPINI 1987, pg. 193. *Gioielli e Ornamenti Preziosi*, n° 169.

D.G.N.

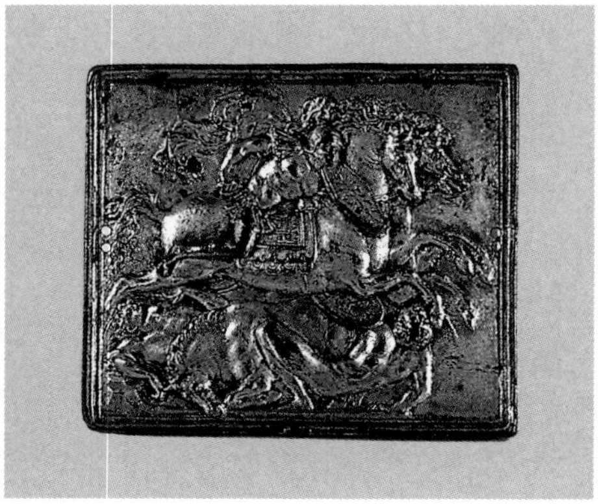

143. PLAQUETTE
Arezzo, Museum of Medieval and Modern Art
Inv. 15317
Cm. 4,6x5,4
Gilded Bronze
Moderno: end of XV, beginning of the XVI century.

Rectangular plaquette with moulded frame depicting, on the right, two riding cavaliers in antique armour who run over two fallen warriors and a horse.
The plaquette can be attributed to Moderno rather than to one of his followers. In addition to the rectangular form, there is also a round plaquette of the same type that bears the inscription «DVBIA FORTVNA». The rationale behind its attribution to Moderno is the fact that the last two letters «NA» stand apart from the others and are joined together so as to form the letter «M» which is Moderno's initial. If this attribution is accepted, the plaquette would be placed within Moderno's Roman period, that is the year 1507, when having transferred himself to Rome, the artist became more influenced by classic models.

VANNEL TODERI, 1987, pg. 144 w/bibl. *Gioielli e Ornamenti Preziosi*, n° 170.

F.V.T.

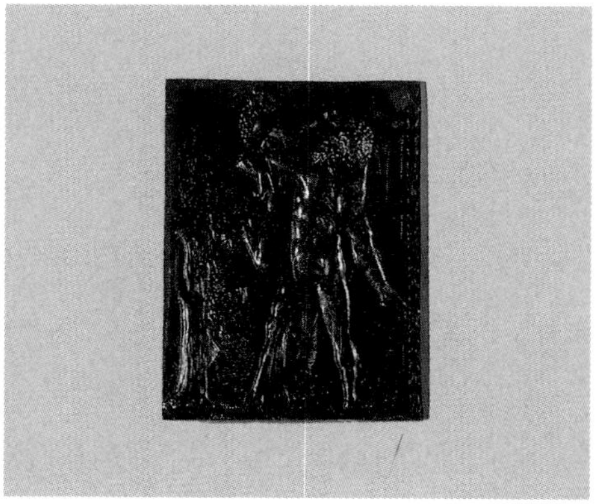

144. PLAQUETTE with «Ercole and Anteo»
Arezzo, Museum of Medieval and Modern Art
Inv. 15306
Cm. 9,8x7,7
Bronze
Moderno: end of XV, beginning of the XVI century.

Rectangular plaquette with moulded frame depicting the back side of a nude Ercole with legs spread apart, in the act of lifting and squeezing Anteo's body to death. Depicted on the left, hanging on a tree branch, are the skin of a lion, an arch, and a quiver.
The plaquette is a work by Moderno and is part of a series which includes similiarly styled plaquettes, of the same form and period, some of which depict Ercole's feats. The scene of the battle between Ercole and the giant Anteo is taken from an original classic.

VANNEL TODERI 1987, pg. 143 w/bibl. *Gioielli e Ornamenti Preziosi*, 171.

F.V.T.

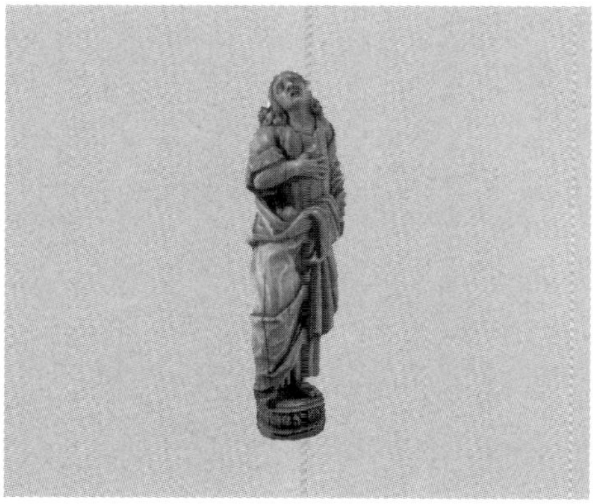

145. STATUETTE
Arezzo, Duomo Museum
Height: cm. 16
Carved Ivory
Northern Europe: end of XV, beginning of the XVI century.

The small statue is a representation of St. John standing on a tiered base The base is adorned by a band decorated with stylized leaves. The Apostle is dressed in a tunic and his left hand holds the drape that falls from his shoulder. The other hand is placed on his chest in a gesture of sorrow. The head leans slightly backwards. The figure is placed on a round wooden base.
The statue is without doubt St. John the Evangelist who, according to traditional iconography, is here represented in his youth, beardless and with a full head of hair, as part of a «Crucifixion» scene. As his pose suggests, the Saint stood at the right of the Cross, while the opposite side should have been occupied by the Virgin, which unfortunately was stolen.
The details of this work bring to mind Flemish artworks. The work, in fact, displays a nordic, fifteen-sixteen century inspired sensitivity that still draws on certain late-gothic stylistic features. Evidence of this is the subject's dramatically accented expression: eyes lifted upwards toward heaven while the lips droop downwards.
It is very probable that the model for the composition of this figure may have been taken from one of the numerous incisions of the «Crucifixion». These were widely diffused, beginning with the first half of the XV century, as a source of inspiration. Consider, too, the Dürer or the Lucas Cranach xylographies which at times come very close to resembling Flemish impressions.

Arte Aurea Aretina, 1987, pg. 94, n° 40.

B.T.

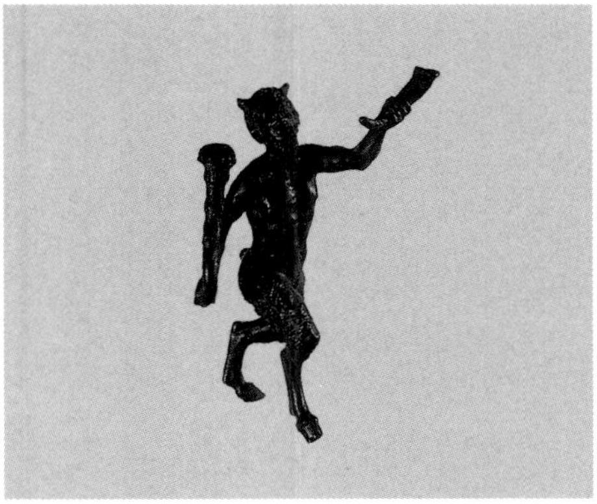

146.-147.-148.-149.-150.-151. SMALL BRONZES
Arezzo, Museum of Medieval and Modern Art
Heights: From cm. 10 to cm. 32
Bronze Mould Cast
Andrea Briosco, called «Il Riccio»: beginning of the XV century.

The pieces are part of a collection of small Renaissance bronzes from the Aretine Museum. The collection includes a series of small statues depicting «Fauns» by Andrea Briosco from Padova, called «Il Riccio», (beginning XVI century), the most famous artist for this type of work, whose fame won him great fortunes during the Renaissance and seventeenth century. The collection also includes a series of classically inspired «Venuses» in the style of Giambologna. Among these, a delightful «Venere Inginocchiata» [Kneeling Venus] that draws on a Greek-Hellenistic model on the order of the Venus by Doidalsas, an artist that inspired Gianbologna as well. The same is true of a «Neptune» and of a small «Venus di Milo».

MHAETZKE, 1987, pg. 224 *Gioielli e Ornamenti Preziosi*, n° 172.

A.M.M.

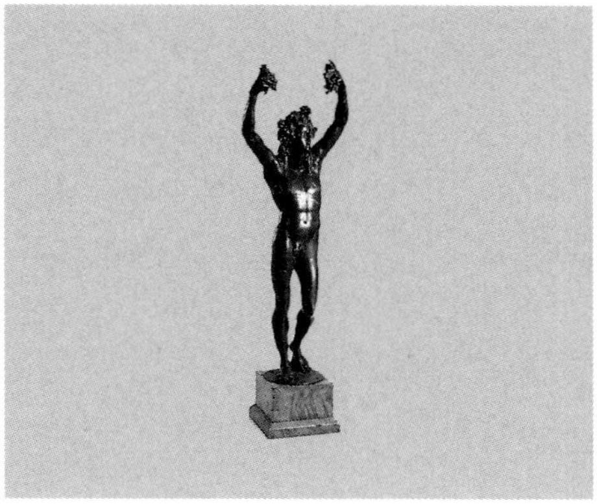

152. STATUETTE of BACCHUS
Museo Archeologico, Florence
Inv. 2287 (Previously in the Uffizi Gallery, n° 304.)
Ht. 38 cm.
«Cire perdue» cast bronze
1st cent. A.D.

Only the torso is antique, the limbs and head having been added during a restoration attributed to Benvenuto Cellini (16th cent.). The base is modern. Restoration work was carried out on a fragment consisting of the nude torso with traces of locks of hair flowing onto the shoulders, in order to reconstruct the upraised arms, together with clusters of grapes in the hands. The head is crowned with trails of vine leaves.

M. Cristofani, in *Palazzo Vecchio: committenza e collezionismo medicei, 1537-1610*, Exhibition catalogue, Florence 1980, p. 38, with bibl.; *Gioielli e Ornamenti Preziosi*, n° 52.

E.P.

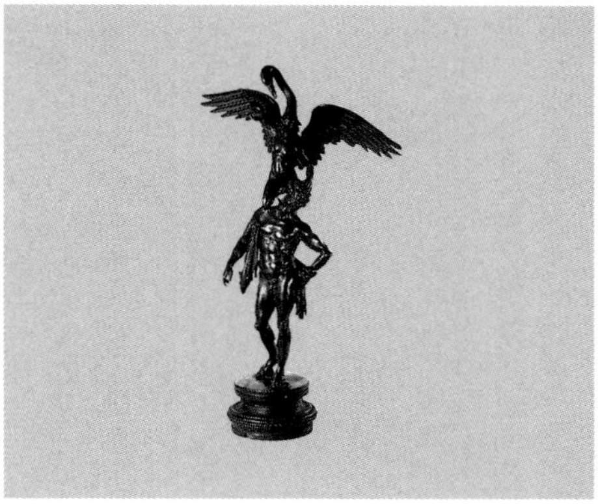

153. STATUETTE of SATYR AND CHERUB (?)
Museo Archeologico, Florence
Inv. 547 (Previously in the Uffizi Gallery, n° 301.)
Ht. 38.5 cm.; ht. of base 6.3 cm.
Full-cast bronze
Probably a work of the modern age (16th cent.?).

Recomposed from several fragments; the base, too, pertains.
The nude youth, with a ram's fleece on the right arm, is identifiable with a dancing Satyr. On the right shoulder he supports a nude child, with large spread wings and a head covering ending in a swan's head; with the right arm he holds an oenochoe from which he pours a drink for the Satyr.
Previously attributed to Etruscan production, the bronze group finds no equivalent in the Etruscan iconographic tradition or in that which the Romans derived from Greek models. The Satyr's head recalls statuary types created by the Greek sculptor Lysippus, active in the second half of the 4th century B.C.

M. Martelli, in *Palazzo Vecchio: committenza e collezionismo medicei*, 1537-1610, Exhibition catalogue, Florence 1980, p. 35, n° 44, with bibl.; *Gioielli e Ornamenti Preziosi*, n° 53.

E.P.

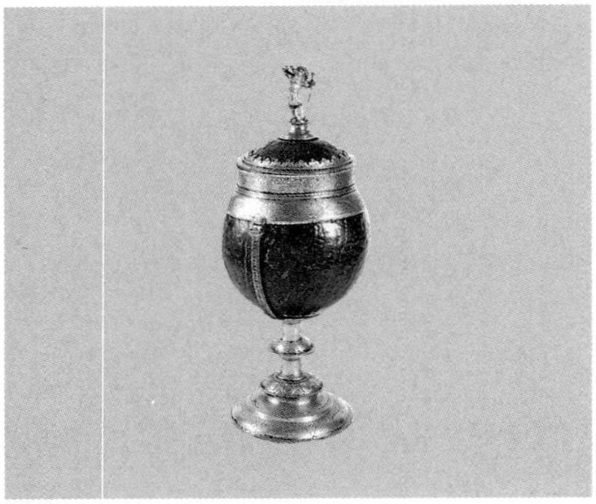

154. GOBLET WITH COVER
Arezzo, Museum of Medieval and Modern Art
Inv. Fraternita dei Laici, 15160
Cm. 21,5
Gilded copper, engraved, coconut shell
Florentine manufacture of the XVI century.

Gilded copper goblet on a two tiered circular base. The base is engraved with lily motifs and it is connected to a flattened knot decorated with egg-shaped ornamentations. The stem bears another flattened knot which is subdivided by a central moulding. Reaching up from the under-cup's palmette decoration, the three arms that support the coconut join the golden band decorated with semi-circled engravings. The coconut cover with its tapered and notched golden border rests on the upper gold band decorated with lily and spiral motifs. Standing on the very top of the goblet's cover, centered on a spool-shaped base, is the small statue of a shepherd holding a stick and drinking from a jug. In recalling the ovoidal shape of the nut, this exquisite piece of artwork sets an example of sober equilibrium and bizarre luxury.

GALOPPI NAPPII, 1987, pg. 195. *Gioielli e Ornamenti Preziosi*, n° 174.

D.G.N.

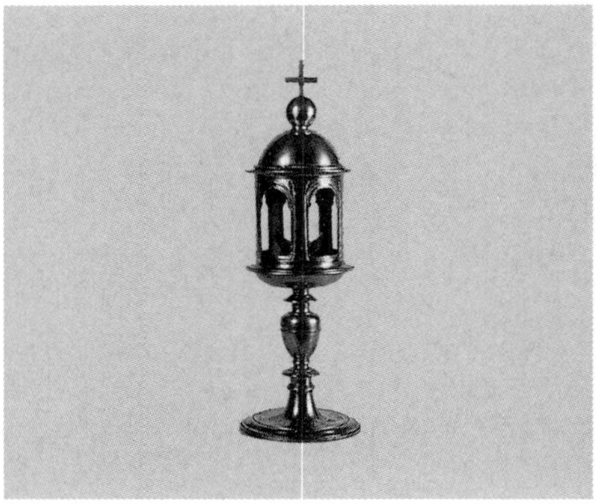

155. SMALL TEMPLE OSTENSORIUM
Arezzo, Museum of Medieval and Modern Art
Inv. Funghini 961
Cm. 25
Gilded metal
Aretine manufacture of the XVI century.

Ostensorium with a smooth, round base, and a stem composed of a pear-shaped knot enclosed within two discoidal junctures. The theca, whose construction resembles a small temple, consists of four small round arches resting on slender engraved columns. The lunule is inside. Circular mouldings introduce the semi-spheric cupola dome on whose top a sphere and a cross are set.
Although simple in its form, the artwork is rather elegant. Its shape recalls the conventional patterns widely utilized in the Florentine and Aretine territories during the XVI century. *Arte Aurea Aretina* II, pg. 66, n. 41.

GALOPPI NAPPINI, 1987, Pg. 195. *Gioielli e Ornamenti Preziosi*, n. 175.

D.G.N.

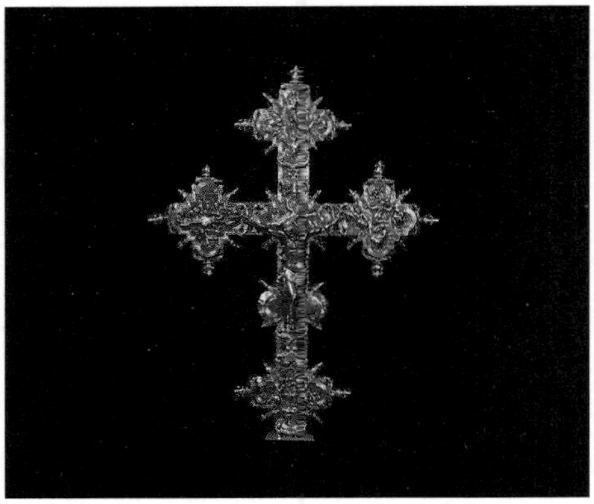

156. PROCESSIONAL CROSS
Montevarchi, Museo della Collegiata
Cm. 58,4x32,1
Silver, gilded silver. Cross: Embossed and engraved lamine. Christ and endings of the Cross : mould cast and chiselled; engravings
Piero di Martino Spigliati. XVI century (1551-1552).

Latin processional cross with arm endings composed of four-foiled panels, embellished by a decoration motif of small pine cones and flowers on acanthus spirals. On the back of the cross, in the center of each panel, a story from the Old Testament is depicted: (top panel) the Creation of Adam and Eve; (left panel) the Temptation and Original Sin; (center panel) Human Work and Eva's Maternity; (right panel) Cain killing Abel; (bottom panel) the Sacrifice of Isaac. In addition, the Cross bears an incision that depicts the coat of arms of the city of Montevarchi. On the front of the cross, depicted in the center of the arm endings, starting from the bottom and moving toward the left: a story from the New Testament, the Nativity, the Last Supper, the Prayer in the Olive Garden, the Resurrection and the Creation of the World in the center. The lower panel bears the following inscription: «F./RAT./ERNITA/D (I) SANC/TA MARIA DEL (L) ACTE DI MONTE VARCHI». The figure on the Crucifix is in keeping with the «Christus dolens» type, with the head leaning downwards, the bearded face and the eyes closed. The cross was commissioned by the Confraternita del Latte di Montevarchi [the Milk Confraternity of Montevarchi] and it was executed between the years 1551 and 1552 by the Florentine goldsmith Piero di Martino Spigliati.
From the memories recorded in the books of the Fraternita della Collegiata di Montevarchi, we learn that the Cross was restored by the Florentine goldsmith Simone Pignoni during the early years of the XVII century.

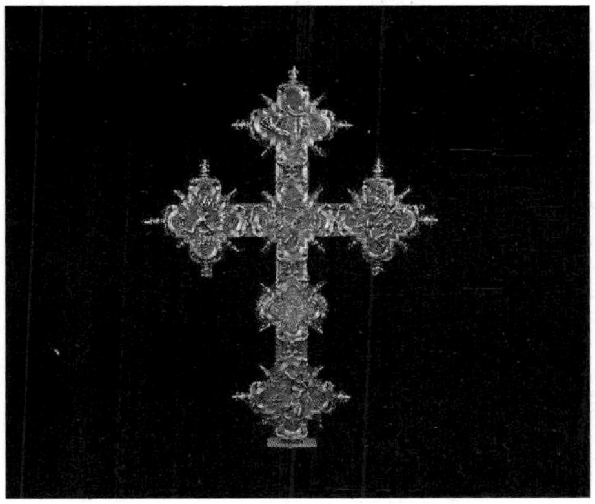

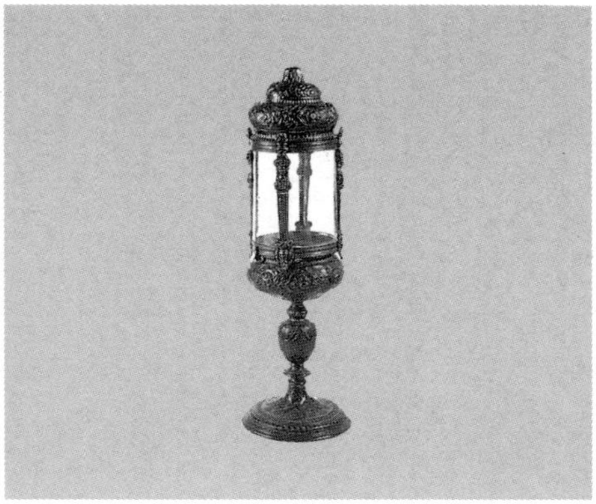

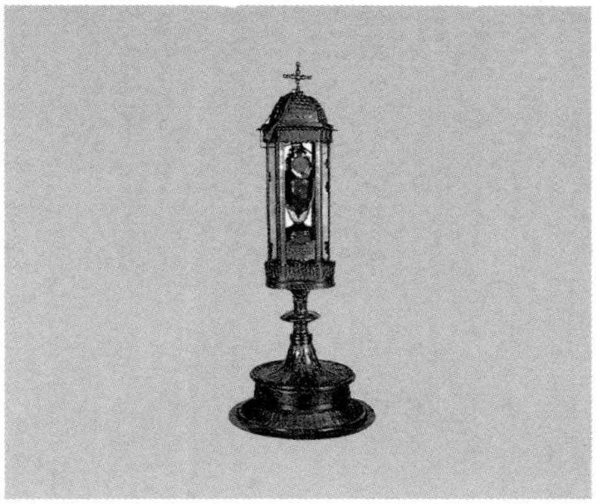

As far as its formal styling is concerned, this precious cross remains faithful to fifteen century design patterns. The changes it has undergone primarily concern the decorative details. These were enriched during the course of the XVI century with significant emphasis on plastic ornamentation. One of the principal characteristics of this Cross, which also sets it apart from examples of a later period, and makes it so unique and valuable, is the fact that contrary to the crosses that bear a single figure, usually an Evangelist or a Saint, its panels tell a story, they are decorated and depict scenes from the Old and New Testament. Noteworthy, too, is the marked naturalistic gusto with which the vegetation and the animals are depicted in the panels' background. On the other hand, the nudes depicted on the back of the Cross exhibit a more vivid plastic sense, with an obvious reference to Michelangelo. There are stylistic references recalling Raffaello, especially if we observe certain scenes depicted on the Cross, as for example The Last Supper.
It is not clear whether this precious artwork is a processional cross or a cross-shaped reliquary or a staurotheca that can be opened along its borders and that contains the relics inside.

Arte Aurea Aretina, 1987, pgs. 96-97, n° 43 w/bibl.; *Gioielli e Ornamenti Preziosi*, n° 199.

M.G.C.G.

157. RELIQUARY
Arezzo, Museum of Medieval and Modern Art
Inv. Funghini 962
Cm. 33 x base diameter cm. 11
Gilded Copper, embossed and engraved
Italian manufacture of the XVI-XVII centuries.

The reliquary has a circular base decorated with palmette engravings, winged cherubs and flowers. The stem, which is composed of a pear shaped knot set between two junctions, one spool and the other bud shaped, is engraved with a leaf motif design and the faces of winged cherubs. The theca rests on a cup decorated with an embossed ornamentation of flowers and winged angels. The base of the little temple that forms the theca is circular with six openings scanned by ridged pilaster strips. The same ornamentation found under the theca. is repeated on the two tiered cupola dome cove. The object was probably meant to be an ostensorium but it lacks the lunule which is generally found inside the theca.
Set in a classically Renaissance pattern, the piece is attributable to Florentine manufacture between the end of the XVI century and the first years of the following century. The piece's stylistic approach, however, appears to be Venetian in origin.

GALOPPI NAPPINI, 1987, pg. 196. *Gioielli e Ornamenti Preziosi*, n° 176.

D.G.N.

158. RELIQUARY
Arezzo, Private Collection
Cm. 22x51
Gilded Copper, carved, embossed, engraved
Aretine manufacture (?) beginning of the XVI century.

A circular based architectural reliquary on a high foot, whose decoration, starting from the base consist of: a band of vertical notches, with an inclined strip of chiselled plant leaves, then a second band of vertical notches that frame the chiselled plant volutes, and finally by a strip of embossed and engraved laurel leaves that join the foot to the base of the stem. The base of the hexagonally sectioned reliquary, with the two wide fronts and with the frames made of small chiselled leaves, decorated with fretwork, is set on this stem base, which is, in effect, a flattened knot divided into segments.
The architectural form of the reliquary is given by the six small, moderately engraved pillars. The trabeation repeats the leaves motif found at the base. The artwork is topped by an irregularly shaped, original hexagonal dome, divided into segments by vault ribs that separate an embossed and chiselled pelta decoration. A small apical cross with coil-like arms completes the artwork.
The reliquary contains the relic of St. Ubaldo Adimari, of the Order of the Servi di Maria, in a rock crystal vial and still preserves the identification seals of the Aretine bishop Agostino Albergotti (1802-1825). This leads one to believe that this reliquary is part of a series of 265 reliquaries that up to the last century were preserved in the church of St. Catherine of Arezzo. The most precious of these reliquaries were sold by the Albergotti family around the year 1900. The presence of the Servite religious order in Arezzo and bishop Agostino's seal lead one to believe that the artwork originates in Arezzo and that it might have even been manufactured in an Aretine shop.

Gioielli e Ornamenti Preziosi, n° 204.

G.C.

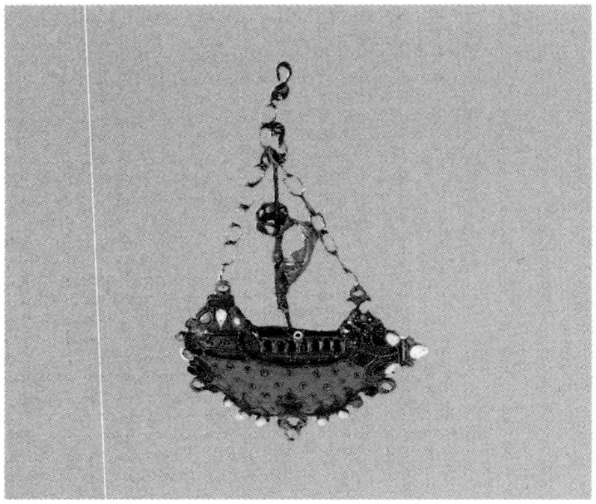

159. PENDANT
Arezzo, Capitolo della Cattedrale
Cm. 6,5x4
Gold and Enamel
Second half of the XVI century.

This precious jewel was part of a votive offering to the Madonna delle Lacrime [Madonna of the Tears] who is worshipped in the Aretine church of the S.S. Annunziata. The pendant, whose shape is that of a sailing ship, is also known as a «navicella». The piece is in full relief, and richly decorated with precious enamels. The structure is complete of chains that are fastened to the ship's extremities and then hooked up to the top of the ship's mast. This piece is part of a wide series of jewels produced in Venice, perhaps also in Florence and in England. The jewel speaks eloquently of the goldsmith's skill and refinement in observing even the smallest of details in spite of the object's small dimensions.

Arte Aurea Aretina II, Pg. 67, n° 45. *Gioielli e Ornamenti Preziosi*, n° 188.

G.C.

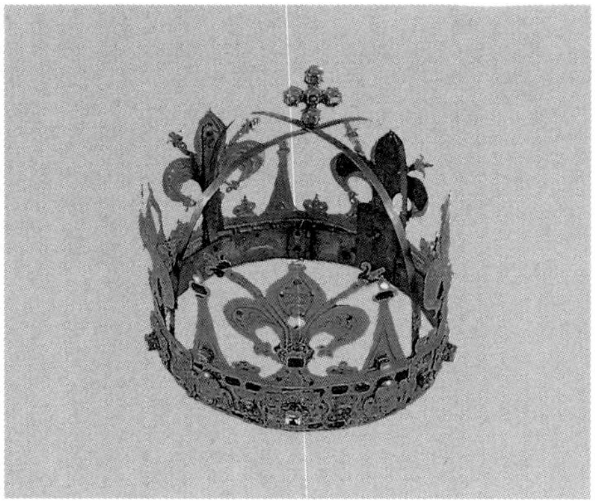

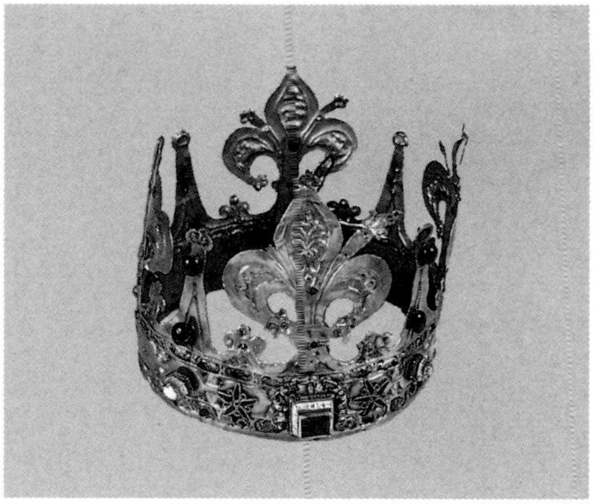

160.-161. (2) CROWNS
Arezzo, From the Church of the S.S. Annunziata
Large crown: cm. 17,5x17,5. Small crown: cm. 9x10,5
Gold leaf, metal support, embossed, chiselled, enamels and precious stones
Bastiano Lamberti (Aretine goldsmith): 1601.

The two crowns are made up of a base band and of an upper portion mounted à jour with lilies, alternated by embossed and engraved pinnacles. The interior of both crowns is reinforced with iron plates. In the large crown, two bands of gilded metal meet to sustain a small Rennaissance style cross set with rubies. This same crown is divided in three parts by hinges (which are not meant to act as openings since the metal structure is riveted by gold lamina) and it is decorated with five embossed and chiselled cherubs positioned to coincide with the base band pinnacles. Both crowns are decorated with opaque and translucent enamels and enriched with a variety of precious stones such as: differently colored quartz, almandine type garnets (with ruby-like colorings), turquoises, emeralds, oriental pearls and rubies. Since the settings are not homogeneous (nearly all are riveted), we can presume that these stones were votive offerings, of the sixteenth century, added later to the crowns. We learn this from the cabochon garnet ring situated on the large crown, with its stem sawed in half, but whose setting is richly engraved with floral motifs accentuated by precious enamels. A brooch has also been added to the small crown and its large quartz stone is surrounded by bands, some of which are enamelled, a clear indication of Renaissance style taste.

The two crowns belong to the Madonna del Bambino, o delle Lacrime [Madonna with Child, otherwise known as the Madonna of Tears] group which is worshipped in the church of the S.S. Annunziata in Arezzo. They were executed by the Aretine goldsmith Bastiano Lamberti in the year 1601. The fact that the two crowns are typical products of the local area is suggested by their rather provincial execution and by some inaccuracies in the engraving. On the other hand, some of the settings are exquisitely refined. The remarkable engravings and embossed decorations on these crowns denote a style whose origins lie in other centers, such as Florence, (a Cellini style is evident). The Aretine goldsmith confined his work to simple «adaptations».

Arte Aurea Aretina, pg. 69. *Gioielli e Ornamenti Preziosi*, n° 189. S. PIERI, *La S.S. Annunziata di Arezzo*, Compagnia. *Santuario, Parrocchie*, Cortona 1991, pg. 30.

G.C., D.G.N., G.R.

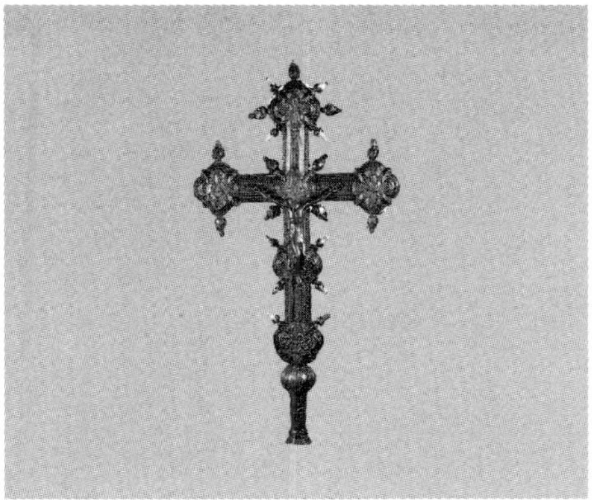

162. PROCESSIONAL CROSS
Arezzo, Museum of Medieval and Modern Art
Inv. Funghini 1270
Cross: cm. 62x32; Crucifix: cm. 14x12,5
Gilded and silver plated copper leaf on a wooden interior, embossed and chiselled. White and light blue majolica buds, bronze Christ obtained through a mould cast. Florentine manufacture of the XVI century.

The cross's extremities are three-foiled. The point were the arms meet is strengthened by four angulations. The lower portion of the major arm is strengthened by a lobe and two angulations per side. Rising on the summit of the external lobes and at the intersection angles of the arms, are twenty-one white and light blue majolica buds, decorated at the base with small golden stars, and gathered within acanthus leaves. The arms of the cross are adorned with floral decorations. Starting from the interior, moulded frames and a bean-shaped motif make up the gilded copper profiles. On the front of the work, at the four-foiled points of the cross, there are embossed and chiselled silver plated copper plaquettes in alto-relievo. These plaquettes depict on the summit the Eternal Father, on the lateral arms St. Mark (on the left) and St. John (on the right), and at the intersection of the arms, the pelican that feeds its young (behind the head of Christ). Proceeding toward the lower part, there is St.Luke (behind the legs of Christ) and St. Matthew.
The little statue of Christ is not an original, though it is well modelled, with the head leaning toward the right. A thin textured loin-cloith is knotted on the hip. The crossed feet are pierced by a nail. The Christ has been placed on what originally was the backside of the work, without considering the usual iconography of the Crucifixion. Furthermore, this type of cross, so conceived, probably did not bear a Crucifix but merely depicted a story with figures.
On the back side of the cross the following head and shoulder portraits are depicted: St. John (on the right), the Virgin (on the left), St. Francis of Assisi and the Wolf (high above), and in the center the Agnus Dei with the tormented vexillum. Below, along the lower end of the major arm, there is Magdalene and then, too, St. Peter.
The cross is clearly from the 16th century as both its style and iconography and decorating details indicate. The well constructed Crucifix presents clear references to Giambologna models. The inspiration for the embossed figures is probably taken from a more valuable example The Tuscan, almost surely Florentine manufacture of the piece is evident from the characteristics of its embossed figures and its general typology, as references to other precious artworks of the area seem to indicate.

GALOPPI NAPPINI, 1987, pg. 194. *Gioielli e Ornamenti Preziosi*, n° 173.

D.G.N.

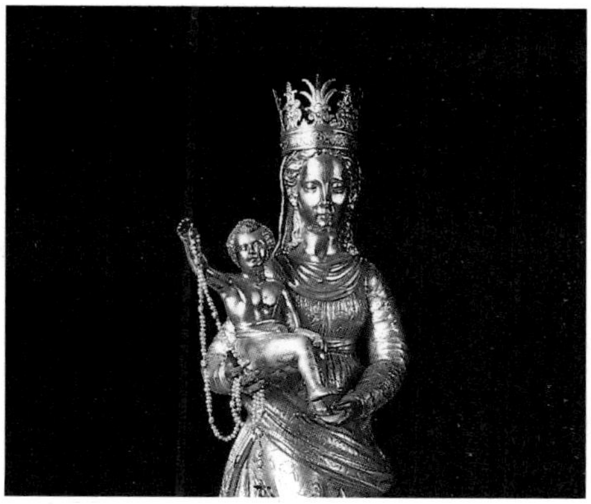

163. RELIQUARY STATUETTE of the Madonna del Rosario
Sansepolcro, Museo Civico
From the Cathedral
Silver leaf, gilded copper, chiselled and embossed, gilded ornaments with gilded glass paste
Central Italian manufacture with nordic influences; end of the XVI century - beginning of the XVII century.

Reliquary statuette depicting a standing Virgin with the Child sitting on the right arm. The Madonna's face and hands are in silver; the hair is covered by a veil that falls down covering her shoulders; the high silver crown on her head is decorated with leaf and cross-shaped motifs. The body is wrapped in a gown, with a rich mantle in gilded silver that emanates remarkable chiaro-scuro effects. The garment, which has deep folds and lays very close to the body, is decorated with large clusters of damask motifs, flowers and leaves, with medallions inside oval frames.
The Madonna's leg is bent and rests on the base's platform. The Child, made entirely of silver, holds in his right hand a rosary made of blister pearls with gilded granules, a mother-of-pearl cross, and a large medallion in silver filigree. The face is well defined, and the hair is finely chiselled to form thick clusters of curls. The statue stands on a reliquary pedestal whose shape is that of a parallelepiped, decorated on the four fronts with a variety of ornaments, scrolls and shells. Through the center of these fronts, which are four openings covered by glass, one is afforded the view of the relics and of the small jewelry pieces made of gold and of gilded glass pastes. On the whole, the piece exemplifies a very high level of goldsmithery artistry, probably commissioned for some princely treasure.
The figure's severe and composed attitude, as well as the unit's near column-like appearance, seem to indicate a Central Italian manufacture, particularly

influenced by German or otherwise trans-alpine taste considerations. Because these reliquary statuettes were widely diffused not only in Italy but also within foreign schools, and since we lack elements of comparison, we are unable to provide a more precise indication of where they were produced.

Arte Aurea Aretina, 1987, pg. 99, n° 48.

D. GALOPPI NAPPINI - Il Museo Civico di Sansepolcro; Il Tesoro della Cattedrale; Firenze, 1988 Gioielli e Ornamenti Preziosi, n° 192.

D.G.N.

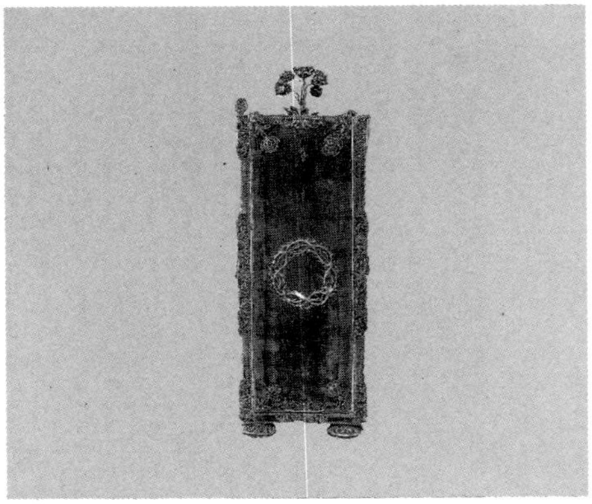

164. RELIQUARY with Case
Monte S. Savino, Tesoretto from the Church of S. Augustine
Compagnia dei Bianchi
Reliquary: cm. 30x8,5. Case: cm. 43x14,3
Reliquary: Embossed and engraved lamina, mould casted and engraved stem and balustrades, mould casted cross.
Case: Wood covering of crimson silk velvet with silver filigree decorations; mould casted and engraved silver crown of thorns; the coat of arms composed of engraved silver lamina.
Florentine manufacture, 1694.

Round reliquary, (which is not been shown duringe this exhibition), as a plain step base and a bombé frame decorated in a bean-shaped motif surrounding the central structure. The stem is composed of a pear-shaped knot whose upper half is decorated with vertical profiles and set within two plain spool-shaped knots. From the moulded frame on the cup's brim four balustrades reach up to form the architectural theca. The balustrades are hinged to the reliquary's cover, which is very high and decorated on its summit with bean-shaped decorations and a small cross.

The reliquary's case is a small closet-like structure entirely covered by crimson red silk velvet and decorated with floral themes and filigreed leaves; the crown of thorns on the central wall door is an allusion to the Sacred Thorn that is contained within. A scroll and the Noceti coat of arms are nailed on the opposite wall. The remaining two walls are decorated with flowers at the corners and a large central rosette is framed by a filigreed flower and leaf motif. A bouquet of flowers sits above.

As we learn from the inscription on the cartella: «AB HAC SACRATISSIMA SPIA MENTE ET CORDE TRANSFIXUS COMES FRANCISCUS: NOCETUS COMMISSARIUS F.F. ANNO DNI MDCXCIV» the piece was commissioned by Count Francesco Noceti, the Commissioner of Monte San Savino (on behalf of the Grand Duchess Vittoria della Rovere, then Princess of Monte San Savino) between 1692 and 1694. The relic contained inside must be identified as the one mentioned by the local historian Fortunio, as having been donated by a jew, who later became a christian, to the Compagnia dei Bianchi in the year 1406. We can deduct that during Fortunio's time the relic was preserved in another reliquary and that the Noceti family had the reliquary remade in the year 1694. However, the stylistic dissonance between the lower portion of the reliquary, which appears to be more antique and still in keeping with Renaissance patterns, and the higher portion, more akin to seventeenth century modes, could lead us to suppose that the goldsmith perhaps used a more antique sacred vase (in this case the lower part of our piece appears to be a small ciborium) which he may have had available in his shop.

The Compagnia dei Bianchi [Society of the Whites] originated in the 1300's as the Compagnia dei Disciplinati [Society of the Disciplined] and their purpose was to do penance, excercize mercy and do prayer in order to stop the wars. They held their services in a small church which was torn down in the year 1785, during the time of Leopold's suppression, in order to expand the local theater «Sansovino».

Arte Aurea Aretina, 1987, pgs. 104-106, n° 52, w/bibl.

G.C.

THE COIN AS AN ARTISTIC CREATION
by *Franca Maria Vanni*

A singular chapter in the history of ancient imitations during the Renaissance is dedicated to pseudo-coins.
Vasari writes that different artists imitated Roman and Greek coins impelled by the desire of enriching their knowledge of the Ancient World (*Le Vite*, II, pg. 223) the first amongst these is Ghiberti: «... but amusing himself much more in the art of sculpture and drawing, he occasionally worked with colours and rarely cast small bronze figurines ... still delighted in counterfeiting minting dies of antique medallions (*Le Vite*, II, pg. 232).The creation of pseudo-coins was mainly encouraged by humanistic studies, since some coinings were directly suggested by humanists with the aim of producing evidence for their hypothesis, and also by iconographical researches which began with the collection of *Imagines* by Andrea Fulvio dedicated to Pontiff Leone X in 1517.
Evemero's doctrines, which during the Graeco-Roman world had found an exceptionally favourable climate, were the subject of renewed interest in the courts of the Cinquecento. Philosophers' speculations and historical events had created the circumstances for believing that the gods might have been of human origin. Furthermore, Evemerism revealed to be a precious tool for historical research in an attempt to give a chronological order, in historical annuals, to those men who later became gods.
The revival of ethnic legends, in which mythological characters assumed the role of founders of a people, concludes the historicizing of these characters and creates the assumptions for the artist to freely create the faces of the past on metal.
The apex of this iconographical research is represented by the PROMTUARIUM ICONUM INSIGNORUM A SAECULO HOMINUM by Guillaume Rouille, published in 1553 where an apparently precise chronological picture of gods, heroes, prophets and patriarches, philosophers and Caesars is introduced.
In this work, Rouille states that in his attempt to reproduce the faces of ancient characters, of which no material evidence was available, he referred to physiognomical principles. This scientific principle supported the theory that a correlation between parts of the body and inclination of the spirit existed. Thus, deducing the nature of the character from the information given by ancient authors one can always reproduce the character's basic somatic features. In Rouille's Promptuarium one can find numerous faces, the prototype of which is verifiable against the series of noble men attributed to Valerio Balli known as Vicentino. The mould of the «coin» portraying Labieno (N. 177 C) was attributed to this author, who represented the art of engraving at its peak in the sixteenth Century.
The false coins of the Renaissance filled in the missing ones of the collections that were being formed at that time.
Probably around the sixteenth Century a real and proper pseudo-coin industry was developing. In fact, Enea Vico argued against Rouille's Promptuarium and shortly after Agostini

expressed in his «Dialogues of Medals» his own doubts on the authenticity of those representations of characters who had never been portrayed on coins, warning scholars against using these examples as historical documents.
It is not by chance that these coin-shaped creations belong to the first half of the sixteenth century; they are, in fact, an expression of an era where research into the ancients, pushed to extreme limits, had induced scholars to find a place in history even for those men who had been products of the imagination.
Having reached the second half of the century, scholars' attitude towards the Classical world had changed and lead them to doubt the real historical contribution of these works.
In the last part of this section of the exhibition, dedicated to numismatics, we display a series of gold coins minted in the first half of the sixteenth century, contemporary with the aforementioned pseudo-coins aforementioned, in order to demonstrate the diversity which is immediately perceptible between art creations and legal currency, tied to precise themes. We have chosen some coins which were minted in the cities of Lucca, Pisa and Siena before they became part of the Medici State.
During the Early Renaissance the few republics which still maintained their independence had preserved in their currency — aboveall for the fame and diffusion of certain coins — the old medieval typologies, for instance the large foiliated S of Siena or the Virgin Mary and child on the coins of Pisa.
During the transitional phase towards Renaissance forms the relationship, which has always linked the coin to political power, is reproposed in different forms of aesthetic value. On the coins minted in these centres one can observe on the one hand the recovery of the classical repertory — see the image of the she-wolf with twins (N. 165 C) which appears for the first time on the coins from Siena of 1511, referring to the legend concerning the foundation of the city by Senius — and on the other hand the persistence of the themes taken from religious iconography especially when tied to the city, for instance, the image of the «Volto Santo» on the coins of Lucca or the image of Our Lady of the Assumption on the currency of the city of Siena when the population, having retreated to Montalcino, were making their last attempt to save their own independence.
When the importance of art, for personal prestige, induced the sovereigns to employ famous craftsmen to make moulds for their coins and to put their portrait on them, which has always been the authorities' greatest form of propaganda, this engraving technique became widely spread. A form of art which until then was not considered as such and which produced great masterpieces in the art of engraving.

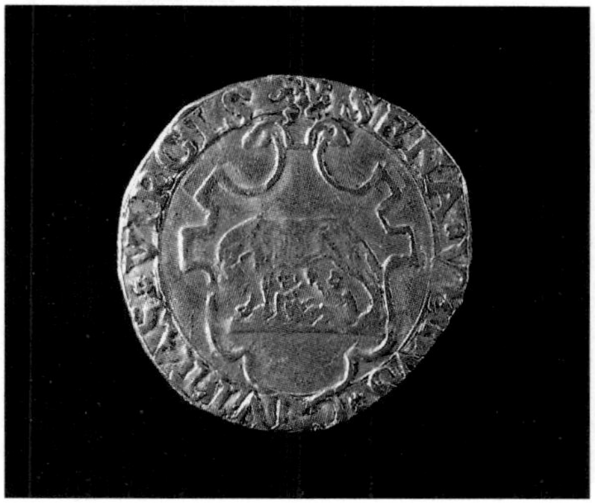

SIENA MINT
165. Scudo d'Oro del Sole [Gold scudo of the sun]
Inv. 2112
Gold
Gr. 3,29
1533-1548
F/sign of the sun SENA VETVS CIVITAS VIRGIS - wolf with twins; in the field,
(59 CNI)
B/ ALPHA.ET. .PRINCIPIV ET FI - foiled cross

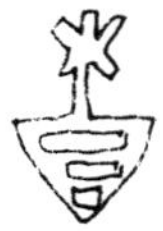

The coin was minted between the years 1533 and 1548 when it became common practice to indicate the year of minting on the coins. The engraving of a little sun precedes the legend, on the front of the coin and this, according to Promis, was the sign that identified the quality level of the gold in 917 thousands. The typology of the wolf with the twins on the front perhaps symbolizes the legend, which was widespread during the Renaissance, that the city's founder was Senio, the son of Romolo.

CNI, XI, Toscana, pg. 397, n° 235.

F.M.V.

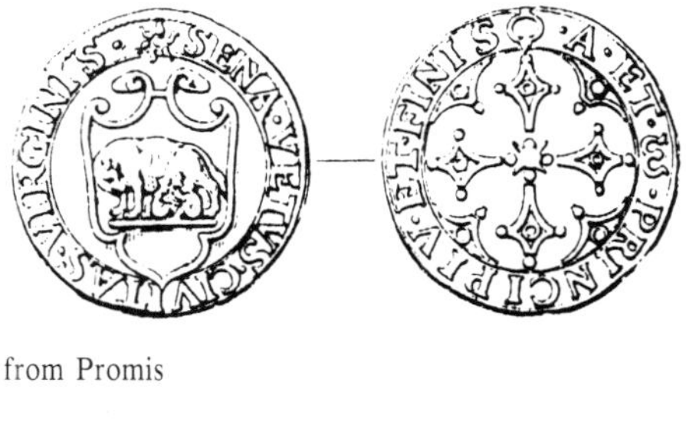

from Promis

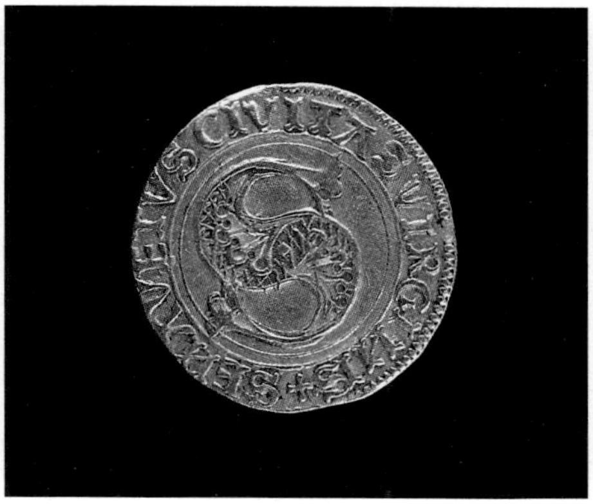

166. Ducato senese [Sienese ducat]
Inv. 2093
Gold
Gr. 3,49
XV century
F/S.CIVITAS VIRGINIS SENA VETVS - large foiled «s»
B/ALFA ET O PRINCIPIVM FINIS
(50 or 73 CNI) - cross.

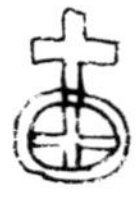

The minting of this coin had its beginning in the second half of the XV century. It differs from the preceding Sienese coinings of the mid 1400's because of a variant introduced in the legend on the reverse side: after the name of the first letter of the Greek alphabet, Alfa, in Latin characters, the Latin O is engraved in place of the traditional symbol.

CNI, XI, Toscana, pg. 376, n° 46.

F.M.V.

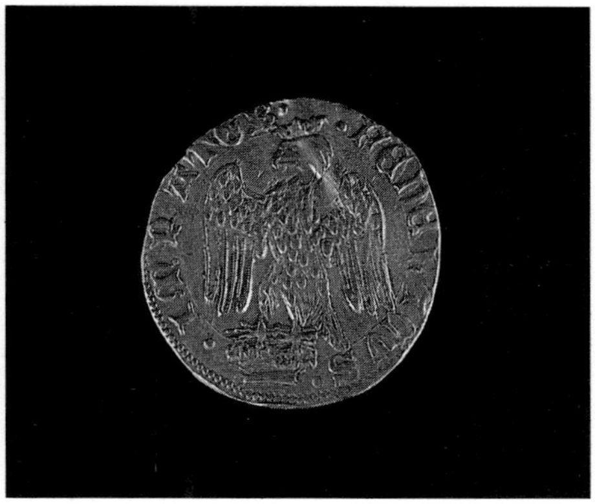

PISA MINT
167. Zecchino
Inv. 1919
Gr. 3,48
Gold
XV century
F/ FEDERICVS IMPATOR - crowned eagle with spreaded wings, with head turned in S position on capital.
B/ PTERIGE.VI RGO.PIS - the haloed blessed Virgin with veil, seated in perspective ; the Child is seated on her left arm; the Child has his right hand raised in the act of blessing; the sign of the minter, «S», in the field; two branches joined to the stem.

Up until the year 1495, the Pisans continued to mint independent coins, even in gold, with the name of Emperor Federick II, from whom they had received important jurisdictions and privileges in the Orient.

CNI, XI, Toscana, pg. 302.

F.M.V.

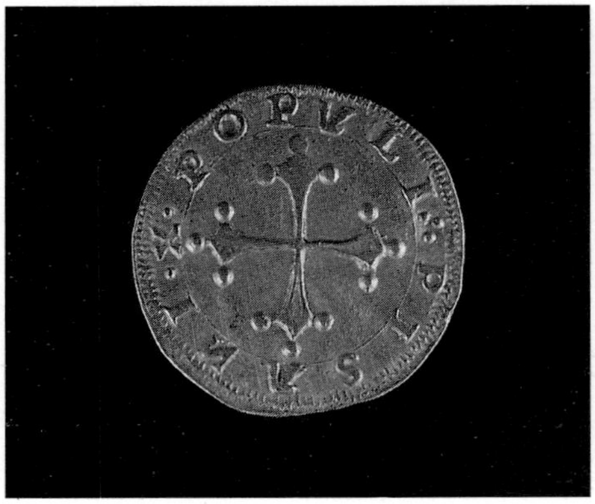

168. Zecchino, Second Republic
Inv. 81921
Gr. 3,45
Gold
1495-1509
F/ POPVLI PISANI - Pisan cross.
B/ PTEGE.V IRGO.PIS - the blessed Virgin with a linear limbo, crown and veil, is seated in front; the Child sits on her knees.

After Charles VIII's return to France, the city of Pisa became once again a Municipality and, as such, continued to mint it own coins until the year 1509 when it lost its independence.

CNI, XI, Toscana, pg. 316.

F.M.V.

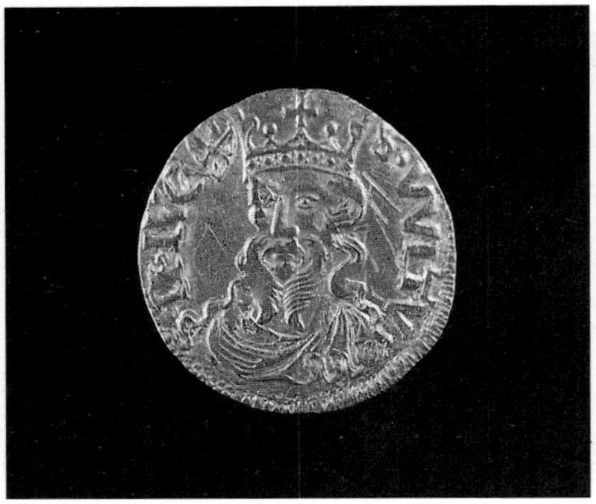

169. Zecchino [Fine gold]
Inv. 76737
Gr. 3,45
Gold
XVI century
F/S.VVLT DE LVCA - perspective of The Holy Face with open crown; in the field, emblem of the minter.
Dal Portico 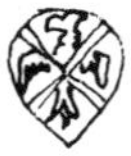

B/s. MARTINVS - St. Martin on a horse with a poor man.

Because of the extensive business relations entertained by the people of Lucca in the wool and silk sectors, in 1572 a new gold coin was created, the zecchino, to substitute the scudo d'oro. The large ducat, which had preceded the scudo d'oro in the 1400's, served as a model for the new coin. The minting die for the coin was cut by the minter Agnolo di Nicolò Fraschini who signed his works with the initial «A» inside a circle. The typology is the same as that of the quattro-scudi coin, also in gold, but since the size of the punch on the reverse side was larger than the planchet, the legend was divided in three parts.

CNI, XI Toscana, pgs. 101, 161.

F.M.V.

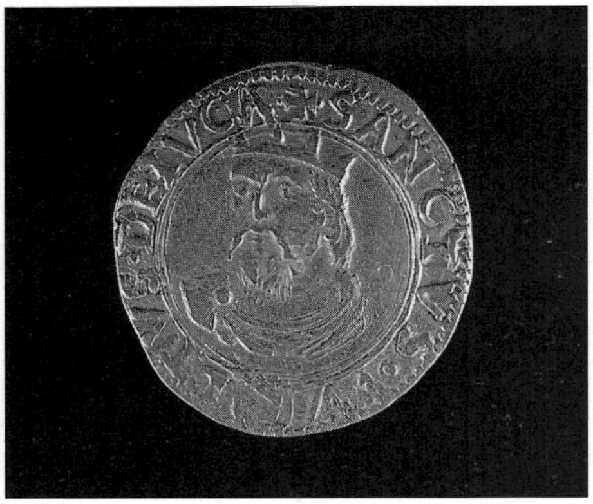

LUCCA MINT
170. Scudo d'Oro del Sole [Gold Scudo of the Sun]
Inv. 76738
Gr. 3,29
Gold
1552
FRONT: S.VVLTVS DE LVCA - perspective of The Holy Face with crown.
BACK: CAROLVS. IMPERATOR - 15 small sun 52 - inside Samnite scudo LIBERTAS.

The Republic of Lucca coined the "scudo d'oro" for the first time in 1535. The R / CAROLVS IMPERATOR legend on the scudo is to commemorate the privilege of monetization granted by Charles V to the city of Lucca.
Widely circulated because it was readily accepted in all markets, the scudo d'oro was frequently recoined, especially during the period 1552-1576. During the course of every recoining, the scudo was subjected to some change, such as the little emblem of the sun depicted on the back of this specimen, which resembles the coins minted in France by Louis XI.

CNI, XI, Toscana, pg. 120, n° 332 variant.

F.M.V.

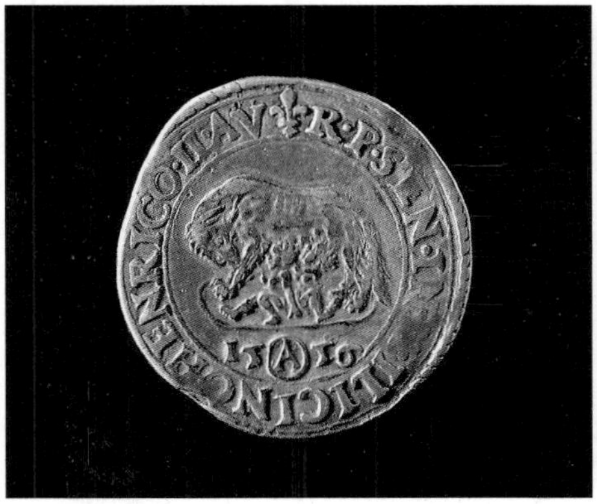

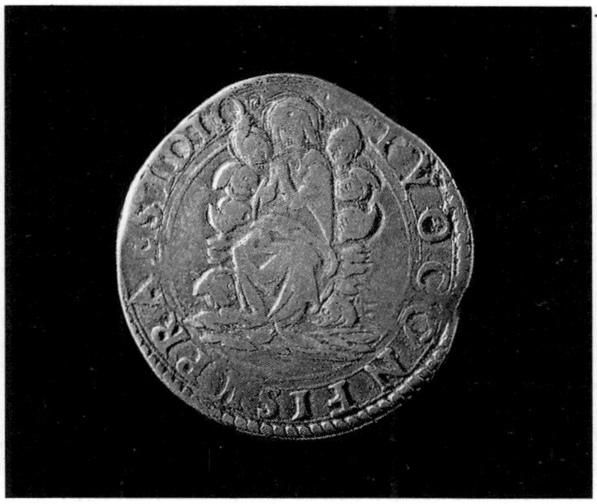

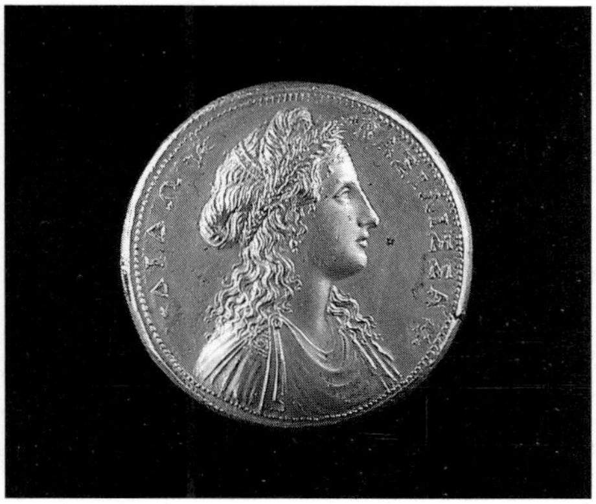

MONTALCINO MINT
171. Testone
Inv. 2120
Gr. 9,14
Silver
F/R.P. SEN.IN.ILICINO.HENRICO.II.AV lily; a standing. Roman female wolf, on the left, breast-feeding the twins; below 15 to 56
B/ TVO CON FISI PRAESIDIO - the haloed and veiled blessed Virgin, seated on the clouds, in perspective, with hands joined in prayer, surrounded by eight heads of angels, four on each side.

In the year 1555 Siena was attacked and forced to surrender to Charles V who then turned the city over to Cosimo dei Medici. As soon as the arms suspension pact preceding the surrender was published, 252 noble families and 435 common ones, led by Mario Bandini, Captain of the People, left the city and with what was left of Henry II's French military forces, repaired to Montalcino, where for a few years they preserved the old form of government. Here they even opened a coining workshop whose activity lasted for four years from 1555 to 1559. During this last year, after the battle of St. Quintino, Henry II was forced to sign a peace treaty with Philip II and as part of the agreement he withdrew his troops from Tuscany. Thus, the Sienese were forced to sign the surrender, in Florence, and in so doing, Montalcino was reunited with the rest of Tuscany, under the domain of the Medici.

CNI, XI, Toscana, pg. 256.

F.M.V.

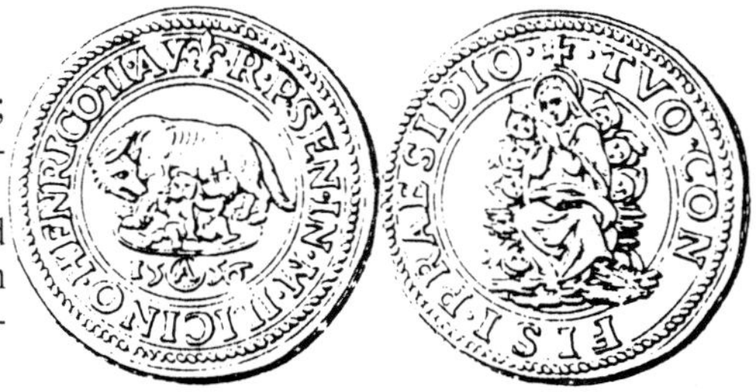

from Promis

172. Gold plated Silver
Inv. 148579
Gr. 64,3 - mm. 4,3
Front/right: Bust of Didone ΔΙΔΟ ΒΑΣΙΛΙΣΣΑ
Back/a view of the city of Carthage inside the walls; on the upper left ΚΑΡΧΗΛΩΝ background; in the forefront 3 boats in the water symbolize the maritime character of the city.

On the back of the specimen, the only clue, beyond the legend, that indicates the city of Carthage is the figure of Hercules, the protector of the Fenicians, in the little temple in the center of the city's walls. A careful examination of the buildings that compose the city's panorama, and here we note an amphitheater, an arch of triumph, a circular construction that immediately brings to mind the Pantheon dell'Urbe, and the obelisks, clearly indicates that the artist was inspired by Renaissance Rome and it provides, too, a tacit yet evident declaration of the piece's modernity. The image of Didone acts as affirmation of Evemero's doctrines calling for the humanization of ancient pagan gods, and for the artist's right to express his fantasy and creativity, to create, in metal, the faces of illustrious personalities from the past. The coinage of this pseudo-coin is attributed to Alessandro Cesati called «il Grechetto».

F.M.V.

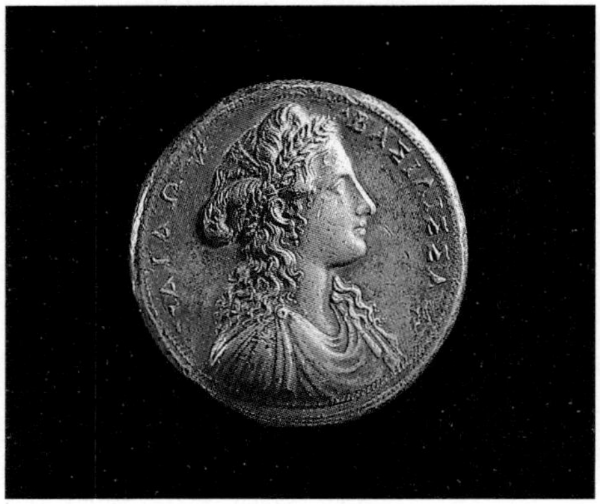

173. Silver
Inv. 148580
Gr. 83 - mm. 4,3
Front/as the preceding
Back/as the preceding
Silver version of number 172.

F.M.V.

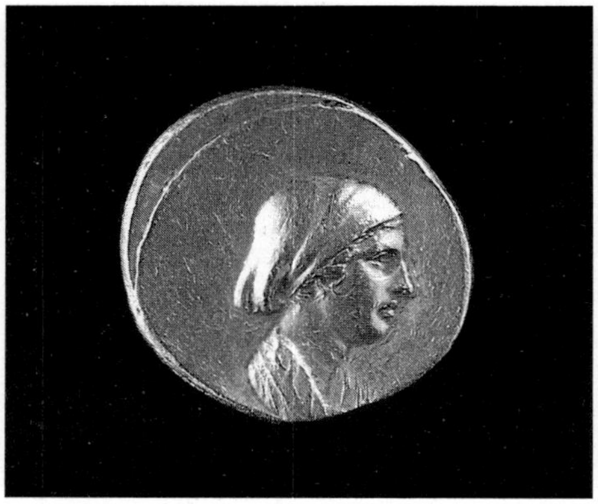

174. Gold
Inv. 148586
Gr. 17,3 - mm. 2,6x2,4
Front/right: Female head with "sacchos"
Back/Hercules resting over the lion's cast-off skin; in his right hand he holds a "scyphum" and in his left a club; ΤΩ ΝΙΑΤΑΝ

In 1576 Goltz published a specimen that was analogous to the Florentine one but in a better state of conservation, or more accurately coined. In Goltz's design, in fact, the liquid flowing out of the "scyphum" in Hercules' hand is quite evident, while the specimen in the Medicean museum does not show this detail, perhaps due to an imperfection or to the deterioration of the piece. On the back, the image of Hercules recalls the passage in Diodoro Siculo's text (Biblioth. Hist. Lib. IV, pg. 161), narrating that Hercules, in Crotone as a guest of that city's founder, was inadvertently killed by him. The specimen's typology corresponds with the authentic emissions of that city (GARRUCCI, Crotone tav. CIX, 36), while the female head on the front is the counterfeiter's fantasy creation. This latter image is interpreted by Gori as being the image of the city's protectress.

GORI, II pg. 20, XI; TONDO, 1986, pg. 663; per confronto GOLTZ 1576, tav. XXVIII, IX.

F.M.V.

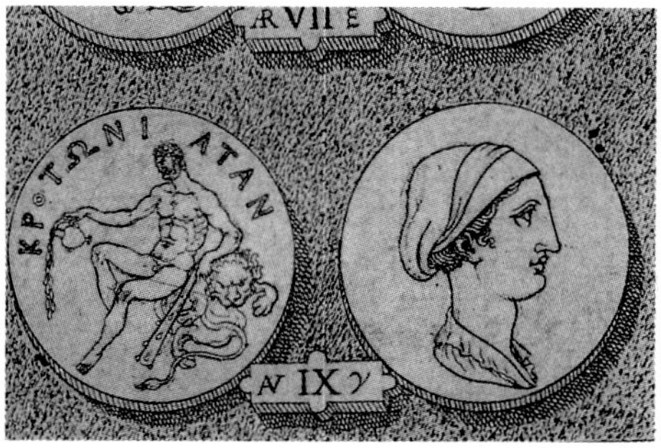

from Goltz

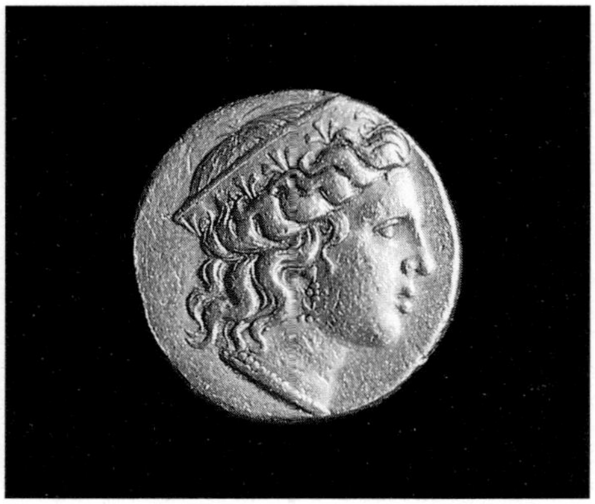

175. Gold
Inv. 148587
Gr. 13,4 - mm. 1,9
Front/right: Female bust with "stephanos" and floral ornaments
Back/cyst from which a serpent exits; on the exergue

During the first half of the 1700's, Scipione Maffei published, in the *Verona Illustrata*, a coin that was entirely identical to the one in the Florentine numismatic collection, part of the Bianchini collection, suggesting that, on the basis of the legend and of the serpent, the piece was to be interpreted and attributed to the city of Iaso. Already catalogued as doubtful by Eckhel in *Doctrina Numorum veterum*, the coin was definitely eliminated from the Iasos emissions by Sestini who described it in the *Lettere di Continuazione* (VIII, table 1, 7).

TONDO 1990, p. 184 w/bibl., 1985 p. 166; 1986, p. 669.

F.M.V.

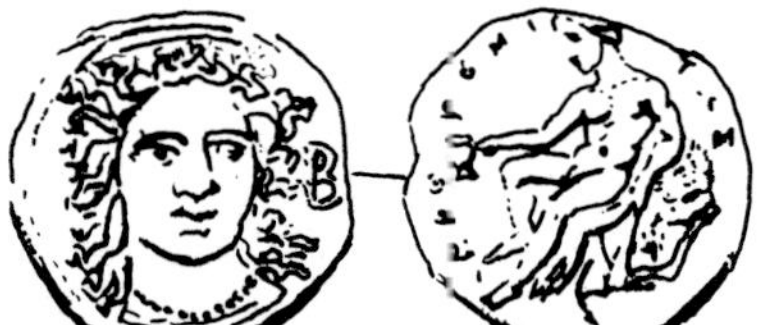

from Sarrucci

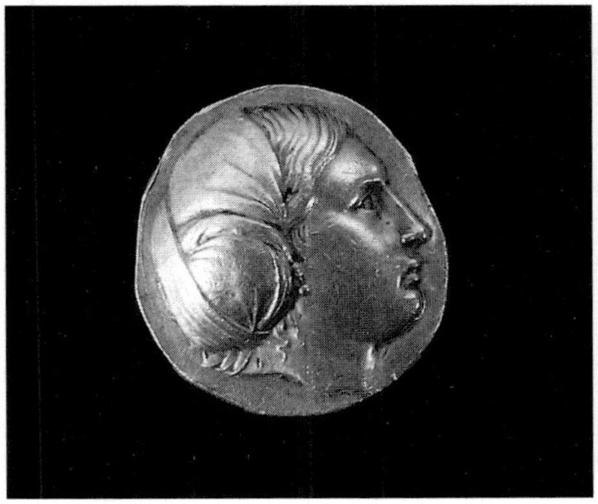

176. Gold
Inv. 148589
Gr. 25,5 - mm. 2,9
Front/right: Female bust with "sacchos" and floral ornaments
Back/polyp;

In the first edition of *Classes Generales*, Domenico Sestini's interpretation of the symbols on the back of the specimen led him to suggest, although with some perplexity, that the coin be attributed to Siponto according to Strabone (C.V.). That the coin belongs, in fact, to the sixteenth century is clearly indicated by the fact that the face of the woman on the front is reproduced in a design in *Imagines* by Fulvio Orsini wherein the author recognized the image of Saffo. The representation of the polyp on the back of the specimen is taken from the Sicilian litres, already known at the end of the 1500's. The intertwining of the animal's tentacles appears to have been taken from a coin with a EU monogram, whose coinage is to be attributed to Eukleidas or Euainetos.

BALDWIN BRETT, 1974, p. 55 e tav. 22, 406; GORI, III, pg. 16-17; TONDO 1990, pgs. 182-183.

F.M.V.

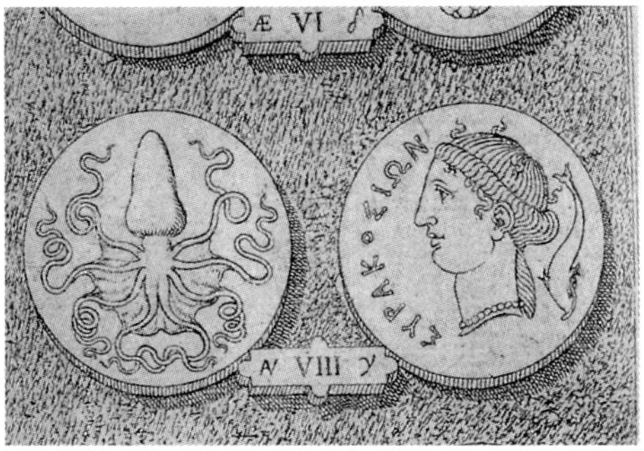

from Goltz

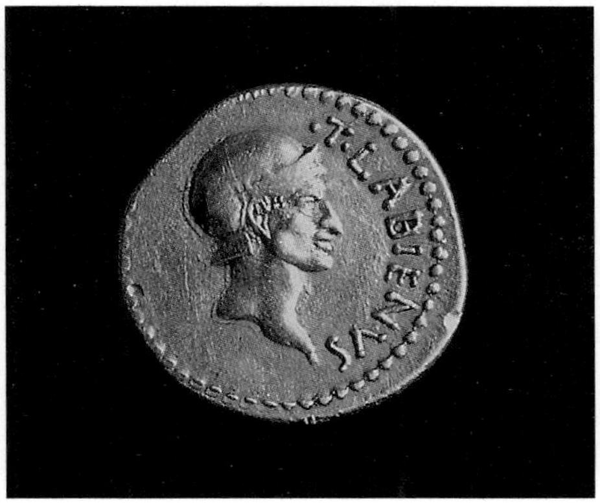

177. Gold
Inv. 148581
Gr. 7,0 - mm. 2,0
Front/Bust of Labienus with helmet on the right; in the circle T.LABIENVS.
Back/CINGVLVM - a view of the city inside the walls.

Believing this coin to be authentic, CUMANO published a silver specimen of it in the year 1867 (Rev. Num. p. 314). But his argumentations must not have been too convincing because in spite of its historical appeal, the denarius was immediately considered false. In part, the reason why this coin was suspect was that it would have been the only emission of a heretofore unknown minter, Titus Labienus. Titus Labienus was the father of Quinctus Atius Labienus Particus, a minter in the year 40 B.C. (BABELON, p. 224). After abandoning Caesar's party, this emission by Titus Labienus was to commemorate the founding of the city of Cingulum in Picenum.
In reality, the coin was created during the first half of the 1500's and it is attributed to Valerio Belli, called «il Vicentino». The reverse of the coin recalls a coin which Goltz believed to belong to the Crotone mint, wherein the image of the emitting city, excluding the subjects on the sides of the city's gates, is analogous to that of Cingulum. The first publication of this type by Gorlaeus (*Thesaurus numismatum Rom*, Amsterdam, 1608) dates back to the year 1608.

TONDO, 1986 pg. 664.

F.M.V.

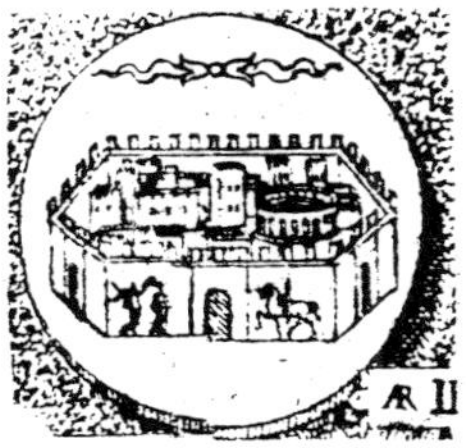

from Gorbalus

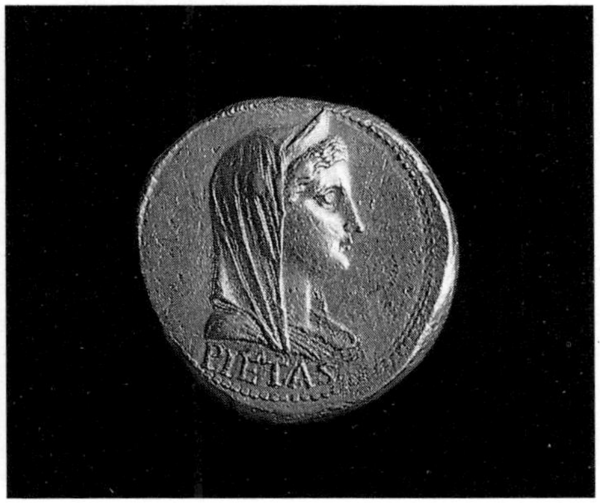

178. Gold
Inv. 148582
Gr. 35,2 - mm. 3,0
Front/Right: Veiled Bust of Livia, draped and with diadem; below PIETAS.
Back/Vesta, veiled and draped, seated on the left with Palladio on the right, and with a long transversal scepter on the left; s.c. on the exergue VESTA;

The coin is a hybrid creation that utilizes the typology of the back's dupondius, minted by Tiberio on behalf of Druso Cesare, on the front, with a bust of Livia, and the dupondius of an emission in bronze emitted by Tito on behalf of his daughter Giulia represented as Vesta, on the back. Both dupondiuses were among the coins already known during the 1500's and they were correctly attributed to Tiberio and Giulia Augusta.

GORI, II, pg. 21, XII.

F.M.V.

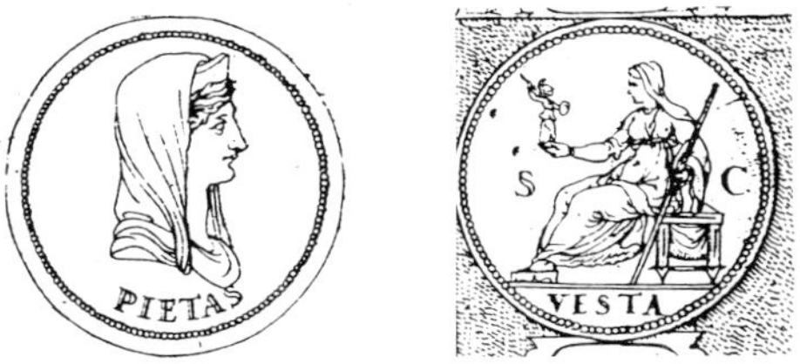

from E. Vico: a, 1548; b, 1557

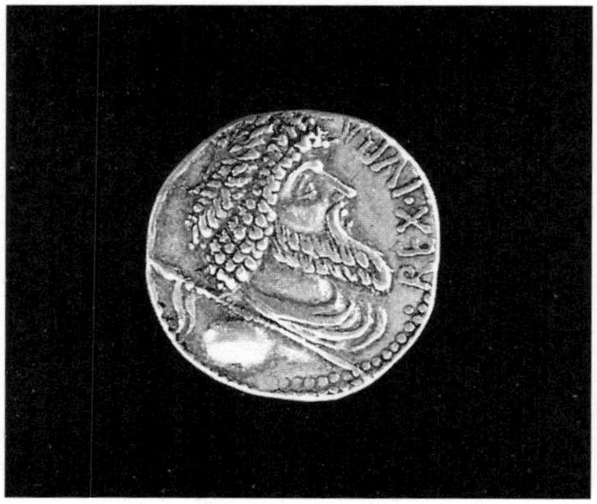

179. Gold
Inv. 148588
Gr. 6,9 - mm. 2,0
Front/Right: Bust of king Juba I, with beard; the king's hair is curled and bound by a diadem; he wears an armour and a regal mantle. In front of the right shoulder is a scepter Ͻ·ϯ(Y)XXℓ
Back/prospective of an octostyle temple with a globe in the middle of the field. (HMMLKT) = king Juba.

The specimen imitates the silver emission of Giuba I, king of Numidia, dating back to the middle of the first century b.C. The legend, which the original bears on the right side, is missing here. There are other known gold specimens that have already been declared false, Cabinet des Medailles, Paris. Visconti (Icon. gr. pl. L.V., I) and declared false by Lenormant (num. des rois gr.; p. 171 and tav. XC, 4).

F.M.V.

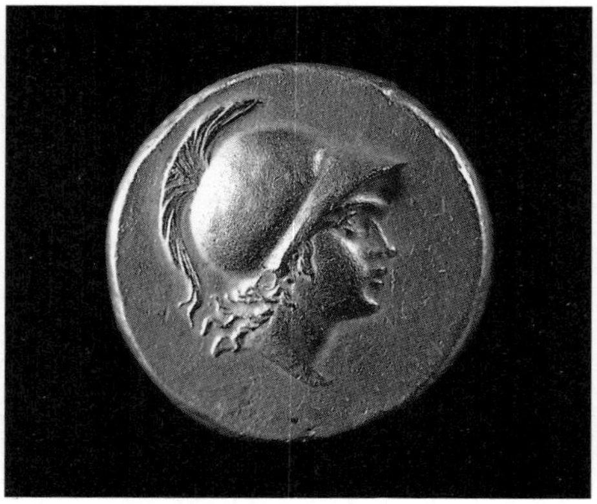

180. Gold
Inv. 148584
Gr. 56 - mm. 3,4
Front/Achilles' head with helmet
Back/Teti with head turned to the right; in his hand is Achilles' helmet and armour; left background MH/TPOZ; right. background ΠΗ/ΛΕΙ/ΔΟΥ

For centuries, coins created during the Renaissance were held to be true. In fact, when the coin could not be considered contemporary with the figure it represented, rather than consider it false, an attempt was made, through a search of ancient authors, to find a likely emitting authority who might have had some sort of connection with the subject represented on the specimen. Such is the case of this coin which, in the year 1700, was held to be from the age of Alexander: «Alexander, uti a Velleio memoriae proditum (Histor. Lib. I, VI) iure materni generis, Achille auctore, paterni Ercule gloriatus est...» «Igitur rarissimum hoc aureum numisma altera facies Achillis, altera Thetidis imagines praeferat donec viri docti meliora depromant, facile crediderim pertinere ad ipsum Alexandrum Magnum...» (GORI).

GORI, II, pg. 11, II.

F.M.V.

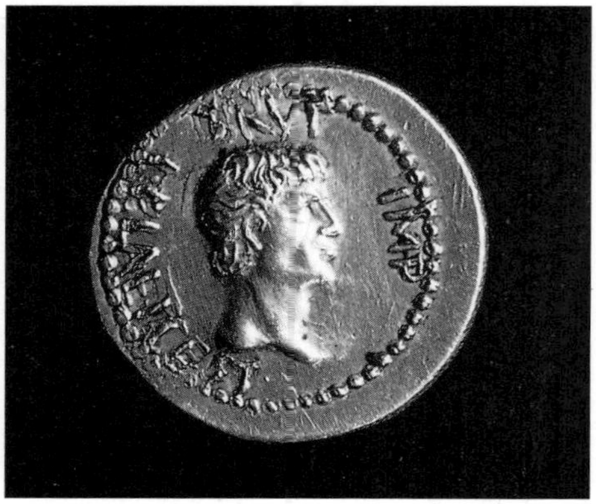

181. Gold
Inv. 148585
Gr. 7,1 - mm. 2,1
Front/BRVT IMP L PLAET CEST - male head on the right Back/two daggers at the sides of a "pileus"; on the exergue (E) ID MAR

A gold remake of the most interesting denarius coined by Marcus Giunius Brutus in the year 43 b.C. It celebrates the assassination of Caesar on the ides of March in the year 44 B.C.
First made public by Poliziano in the *Prima* Centuria *Miscellanea* at the end of the 1400's, and published several times during the century that followed, the coin becomes the emblem of a people's regained freedom. It is perhaps in this spirit that Cavino reproduced the back of this coin on a medal for Lorenzino dei Medici when he celebrated the assassination of Alexander in 1537.

POLLARD, 489; JOHNSON-MARTINI, 1989, 1176; POLIZIANO I Centuria; CHOUL, 1558; AGOSTINI, Dialog I; TONDO, 1986 pg. 664.

F.M.V.

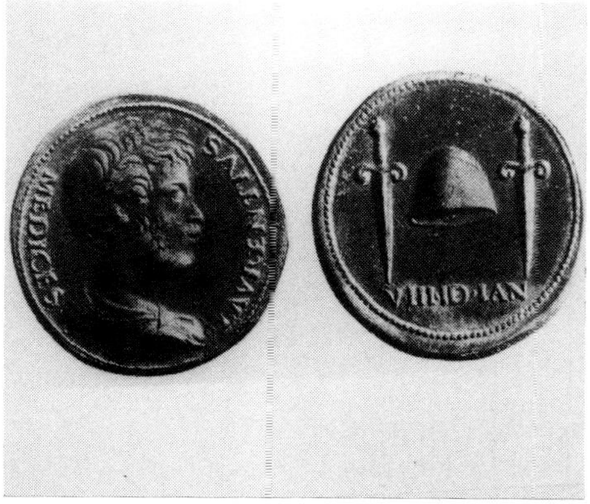

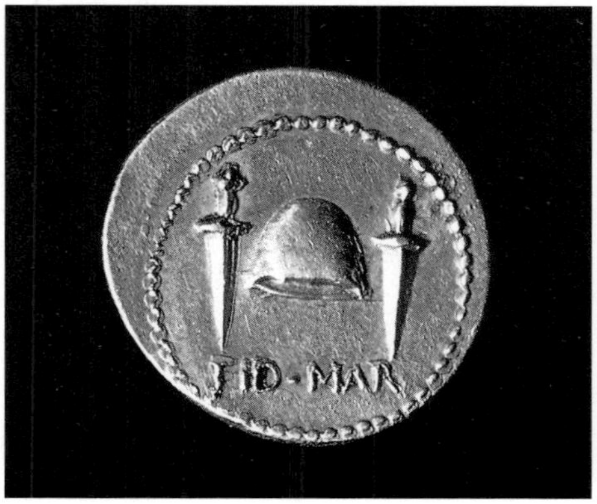

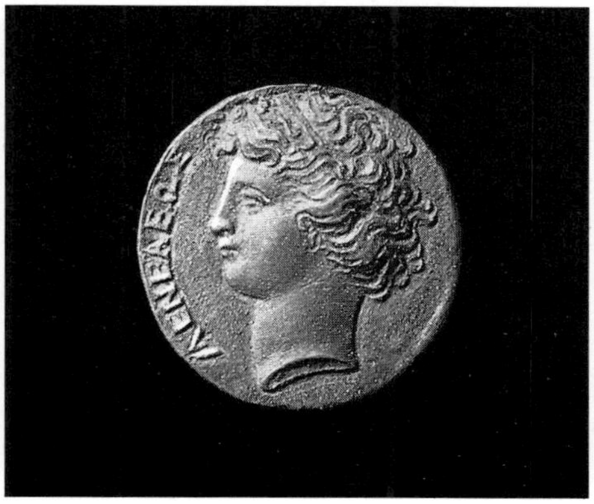

182. Bronze
Inv. 148583
Gr. 7,9 - mm. 2,0
Front/left: head with short curly hair
ΑΙΝΕΑΕΩΣ
Back/Troy's horse under whose legs, Achilles drags Hector's body; in the center of the animal's body, there is opening out of which the Greek soldiers exit; in the field, the city's buildings; in field
ΕΜ / ΙΩ
One of the effects of Evemero's medieval doctrine, which in spite of renewals continued, even during the period of the Renaissance, is the search of a hero or a demigod from whom an entire people can descend. This is how many widely spread ethnic legends in literature as well as in art were born. The favours afforded by these mythological beliefs is on the one hand explained by considerations of prestige and on the other hand by the ideological support they could provide in the exercise of power. A typical example is the legend of Troy with which, in observance of the Virgil tradition, the Franchi and before them the Roman descendants of Enea were connected (SEZNEC p. 19).
The back is represented in the placchetta of Museum Brescia, attributed to Valerio Belli (ROSSI p. 70, 97b).

F.M.V.

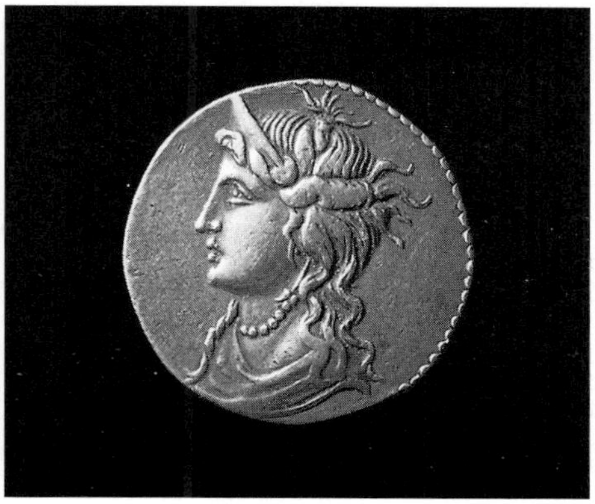

183. Silver
Inv. 148591
Gr. 10,2 - mm. 2,4
Front/left: Female head with a diadem and long hair
Back/labyrinth with lightening on the sides and a lit altar; a star above; in exergue
ΚΝΩΣΙΩΝ
A pseudo-coinage inspired by the Greek mint of Cnosses on the island of Crete. In fact, the more ancient emissions from this city represent the square form of a labyrinth as for example in a stater dating back to 300 b.C. The labyrinth depicted in the Florentine specimen, according to its most ancient diagram, is connected to the legend of Teseo and Arianna, whose idealized features are depicted on the front of the coin, whereas in authentic coinages the head of Hera appears. In 1553 Giullaume Rouille had the *Proptuarium iconum insigniorum a saeculo hominum* printed, and convinced as he was of the validity of physiognomic science, he declared in this work that one of his specific objectives was that of reconstructing the faces from the past on which there was no material testimony. In fact, if one accepts the theory that there is a correlation between body parts and the soul's inclinations, and if information on the subject's personality is available from the texts of ancient authors, the person's characteristic somatic features can always be represented. Even though they represent people who are far apart, both in terms of space as well as time, some of the pseudo-coins which Rouille illustrates in his work, in fact, prove these correlations to be true.

F.M.V.

THE RENAISSANCE GLYPTIC: ANOTHER VIEW OF ANTIQUITY
by *Franca Maria Vanni*

The art of engraving precious and semi-precious stones, dates back to the IV millenium B.C. and was practised by the craftsman of ancient civilizations such as Assyrian-Babylonian, Egyptian, Cretan, Mycene and Phoenician. The earliest examples of engraved stones were the seals created for proof of ownership and bore «negative images» of symbols or figures peculiar to the objects's owner.

During the Greco-Roman period, glyptic art became extremely widespread, as demonstrated by the large number of carved gemstones uncovered during excavations. It was used for typically ornamental purposes such as cameos, or the engraved gems — no longer used for their original purpose — could be deciphered or read «directly» rather than from their imprint.

During the High Middle Age, the art of gem carving attained great peaks, especially during the Carolingian period (IX century) when craftsmen demonstrated considerable skills. The *Museo Archeologico* in Florence owns one specimen that combines the rarity of both the gem and the material: it is an agate intaglio with an engraving of a male bust and the inscription *Norpertus* which may have been the owner's name(1).

This minor art gradually declined over the years and it was only during the Renaissance that the glyptic enjoyed another moment of splendor which derived from renewed interest in ancient Greek and Roman culture which typified the era.

In this climate of revived artistic fervor and admiration for the great masters of the past, groups of artists were formed in the great Renaissance glyptic centers such as Venice, Rome, Florence and Milan. These artists raised the craft of engraving semi-precious stones to levels of perfection worthy of antiquity. In fact, their greatest ambition was to create objects that could be mistaken for ancient pieces.

In Florence, during the second half of the sixteenth century, the Grand Duke Francesco I (1574-1587) opened the Grand Ducal workshops in the *Casino di San Marco*, home of Lorenzo the Magnificent's mythical *Accademia*, which under Ferdinando, Cardinal and Grand Duke were to comprise the *Opificio delle pietre dure*. This was where semi-precious and gemstones were collected from all parts of the world and where craftsmen sought to develop new engraving methods that could repeat the ancient techniques. And it was probably in these workshops that the cameo depicting the Allegory of the Great Mother Earth, on exhibit (n. 199 C) was made.

In his chapter on Vellano da Padova Vasari captured the attitude of Renaissance artists regarding the fashion of the XV and XVI centuries, that of imitating ancient objects. «So great is the passion for counterfeiting some things that most of the time, the manner is so well imitated... that the thing which imitates is so similar to that which is imitated that unless one has an exceptionally good eye, it is impossible to discern any difference between the two».

And again from Vasari's *Lives of the Artists* we learn that in Florence, Lorenzo Ghiberti had dedicated a special study to ancient art: «...was, indeed, the first to imitate the works of the ancient Romans, which he studied very carefully... he engraved stones and cameos». Since the really great craftsmen who were capable of imitating the ancients and sometimes, in the opinion of their contemporaries, surpassing them, were rare indeed, pressure from patrons transformed them into roving artists at the service of whoever appreciated them more. For this reason it is difficult to identify specific workshops or schools as references. In addition to the famous artists who excelled in glyptic art and engraving during the Renaissance, such as Valerio Belli(2), Matteo del Massaro and Giovanni Bernardi da Castelbolognese(3), many gem carvers worked for the Medici court. One of these, of whom Vasari had a very high opinion was the Pisan Giovanni delle Corniole who was summoned to Florence by Lorenzo the Magnificent in order to learn the technique of engraving gems. «Pier Maria Serbaldi of Pescia was defined as an «imitator of ancient things»; the aptness of the famous Tuscan's definition of this artist is borne out by a gem depicting Polyhymnia in Paris and a cornelian with scenes of a Bacchanal in Paris(4).

In addition to Florence, artists skilled in engraving gemstones also worked in Rome, Venice and Milan. Since those cities lacked a chronicler like Vasari, to describe their works, these artists have remained anonymous. However, their production must have been copious and certainly contributed to spreading the fashion of cameos and carved gemstones beyond the noble court collections.

The greatest concern that preoccupied anyone who owned a dactyliotheca was conserving the stones, not so much for the fact that they were relics from antiquity, but rather because — in case of need — they provided an enormous financial reserve. In fact, that is precisely how Sixtus IV viewed the collection of his predecessor, Paul II, when he pawned it at the Medici bank to obtain substantial loans(5).

Ensuring proper conservation often required the skills of specialized craftsmen. Sometimes, however, fragments of ancient gems had to be restored or reintegrated in order to make them whole and increase their value. One examle of this is the famous cameo with a charioteer, most of which was reconstructed in gold by Benvenuto Cellini (n. 184 C) and the chalcedony intaglio of a man's head by an unknown, but certainly gifted artist whose skill is evident in the gold reconstruction of the missing part of the skull from the gem (n. 194 C).

The distance between restoration and copying is so short that it is not always easy to distinguish the ancient pieces from the more recent ones derived from them.

Artists are attracted by style, by the refinement of Hellenstic and Roman specimens, and it is this style, this elegance of execution that they tried to copy. But imitators view antiques through the features that appeal to their contemporary minds and it is for this reason that the copy often captures the signs of the past better than the original. For Renaissance men the iconography of the figure and the scene was of prime importance because it gave them the opportunity of reconstructing their own idea of antiquity(6). This is the concept that gave rise to the need for

reconstructing the missing parts of a particularly beautiful or significant fragment. The lure of Ancient Greece and Rome that exerted itself not only on the major arts, but also on glyptics that were inspired by antiquity, led to results that were so perfect that even today there are doubts as to whether some gems, such as the cornelian with the portrait of Nerone (n. 186 C) from Lorenzo the Magnificent's collection, are acheological treasures or Renaissance fakes.
Lorenzo is credited with having restored glyptic art to its former splendor. And although one should not underestimate the contribution of his patronage to this art, it is important to remember that there is evidence of fine engravings on gemstones from earlier periods.
Before it became part of the Medici collection the above mentioned cornelian with Nero's portrait belonged to the collection of Pietro Barbo who was to become Pope Paul II. Documents from the archives reveal that the prelate had ordered many pieces from the Roman engraver Giuliano di Scipio Amici(7). According to Pannuti(8)the stone was almost certainly engraved around the middle of the XV century. Therefore, it is probable that the «false» antiques in Lorenzo's collection date from the era of Pope Paul II(9).
For this exhibit we have selected a group of stones engraved during the Renaissance; the subjects come from the classic repertory, but are depicted according to the then contemporary «manner» of viewing the ancient world. We do not know the artist to whom these works should be attributed they reveal consummate technique and a more a less direct knowledge of Greek and Roman masterpieces. During the Renaissance, as in the ancient world, it was not customary — with a few exceptions-to put the engraver's name on the stone. We can only say that these works were made possible thanks to educated customers with an eye for beauty, and who, especially in the XVI century, gave rise to that system of patronage which was one of the greatest incentives for the development of Renaissance art.

NOTES

1. The «mirror»-type engraving proves that the stone was used as a seal. Florence, Museo Archeologico, inv. n. 15060. cfr. L. TONDO-F.M. VANNI, *Le gemme dei Medici e dei Lorena nel Museo Archeologico di Firenze*, Florence, 1990, p. 177, 145 and also G.A. KORNBLUTH, *Carolingian Treasure Engraved Gems of the Ninth and Tenth Centuries*, Chapel Hill, 1986.

2. A. BALLARIN, *Valerio Belli e la glittica del '500*, Vicenza, 1973.

3. For the biography and *corpus* of this artist's works cfr. V. DONATI, *Pietre dure e medaglie del Rinascimento. Giovanni da Castel Bolognese*, Varese, 1989.

4. Idem pag. 33.

5. For a description of the still unclear circumstances in which the Cardinal Pietro Barbo's gems were transferred to Medici ownership, cfr. N. DACOS *La fortuna delle gemme medicee nel Rinascimento*, in A.V. *Il tesoro di Lorenzo il Magnifico*, Florence, 1980, p. 88-89.

6. Regarding the relationship between antiquity and the Renaissance, cfr. E. Kris *Meister und Meisterwerke der Steinschneidekunst in der italienischen Renaissance*, Vienna, 1929; for Renaissance works copied from antiquities, L. COURAJOD, *L'imitation et la contrefaçon des objet d'art antiques au XV et XVI siècles*, Paris, 1889.

7. E. MUNTZ, *Les arts à la Cour des Papes pendant le XV e le XVI siècle*, Paris, 1879, II. p. 114 ff.

8. U. PANNUTI, «Catalogo delle gemme che non recano l'iscrizione LAV.R.ME ma provenienti dal tesoro di Lorenzo de' Medici in *A.V. Il tesoro*, cit. p. 80, 61.

9. The matter of fakes in the group of gems marked with Lorenzo's initials was dealt with by E.R. CURTIUS, *Europäische Literatur und lateinisches Mittelalter*, Berne, 1954; according to the author 15 pieces are modern. Interesting reading on counterfeits in general can be found in the catalogue of the exhibition «*Vrai ou Faux?*», Paris, 1991.

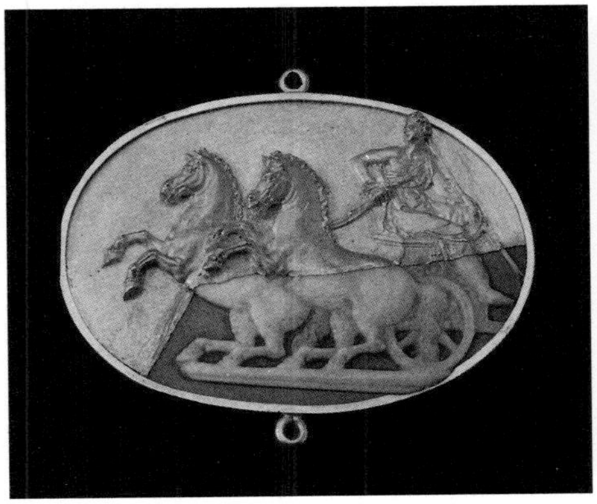

184. CAMEO
Chalcedony (fragmented)
Inv. 14475
Set in gold during the Renaissance period, the scene depicts, on the left, a male figure seated on a two-horse chariot
Hellenistic Period?

From the 1799 inventory: «Onyx. Fragment of a chariot. The rear part of the horse, the wheels, the legs and the extremities of the figure sitting on the chariot are antique and magnificently sculptured in a very beautiful compact white over a light sardonyx background. The remaining surface is filled in with gold, and although the work does not follow the antique style, it has been executed with such skill and mastery that no one but Benvenuto Cellini, to whom the work is generally attributed, could have executed this restoration.» (P. 1336, 40). The artist of the *Vita* (I, chapter 27) tells us that around the year 1523 he worked on many antique gems for the purpose of increasing their worth.

GIULIANO, n° 108 w/bibl.; TONDO-VANNI, p. 35, n° 1

F.M.V.

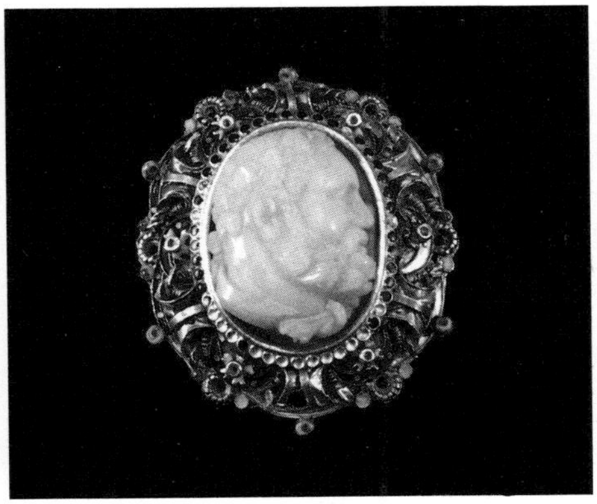

185. CAMEO
Chalcedony
Inv. 14626
Set in gold with enamels and hard stones
The head of Hercules with a crown of poplar leaves on the right; the hero wears a 'leontè' tied around the neck
XVI century.

The figure of this mythical hero enjoyed great interest during the Renaissance, particularly within the court of Cosimo, for the grand-duke held very dear the legend that the city of Florence had been founded by Hercules.

GIULIANO, n° 87; TONDO-VANNI, pg. 40, n° 88.

F.M.V.

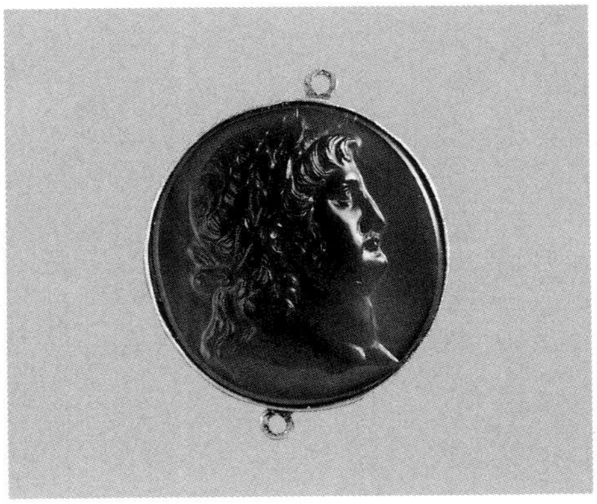

186. CAMEO
Cornelian
Inv. 14541
Double link gold line
Profile of the head of Nerone on the right, a portrait during his youth. The emperor's hair is short and a cluster of curls frames his face; the crown of laurel on his head is held on the back by a knotted tenia; signs of an incipient beard on his cheeks.
Mid-XV century.

According to the 1799 inventory (pg. 1477, 106) the gem was assumed to belong to Cosimo il Vecchio [Cosimo the Elder], but the gem can also be verified in the description provided in the Barbo Inventory of 1457; if we are to believe the above assumption, the piece would have gone into the medicean collection during the XV century. The cameo was inspired by prototypes of coins representing the emperor Nerone, particularly in a sestertius dating back to between the years 64 and 68 A.D. (RIC, I, pg. 160, 238).

Gioielli e Ornamenti, n° 185; GIULIANO, n° 170 w/bibl.; TONDO-VANNI, pg. 48, n° 252.

F.M.V.

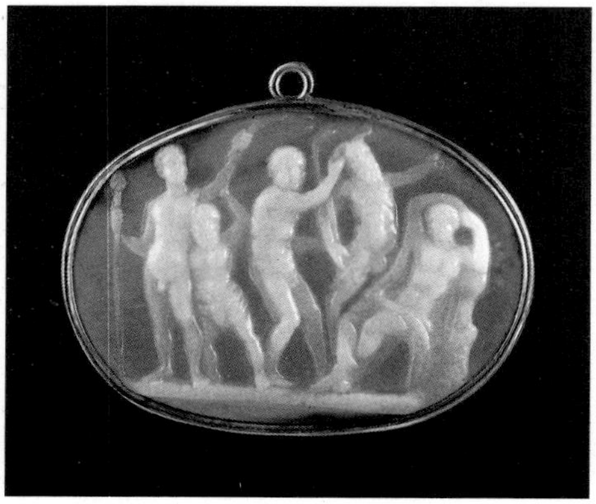

187. ENGRAVING
Chalcedony
Inv. 14455
Single link gold line
On one side Arianna, semi-nude, is sleeping on a rock; on the other side, Bacchus, with a thysus and a torch, supported by a silenus. Between them, a young bacchant is holding back the Pan god.
XVI century.

The not so perfect workmanship of the gem, the greater prominence given to the central character of the scene, the bacchant holding back the Pan god, and the scene's general layout suggest a Renaissance rather than an ancient creation. The elliptic form of the stone, widely used by authors of metallic plaquettes toward the end of the XV century, which appears to condition the entire layout of the scene, brings us once again to that era in which, thanks to Lorenzo the Magnificent, glyptic art was once again revived.

GIULIANO, n° 59 w/bibl. TONDO-VANNI, pg. 41, n° 105.

F.M.V.

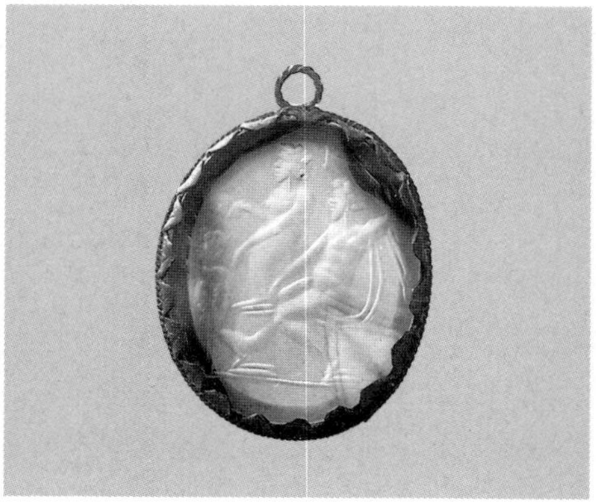

188. ENGRAVING
Zoned Light Agate
Inv. M. 1447
Single link silver line, notched, with a plant motif decoration
Vulcano is seated in front of an anvil which he is beating with a hammer; the female figure behind the anvil on the left is to be interpreted as Venus, with a cupid in front of her.
XVI century.

The scene refers to the Eneide episode (VIII,370) in which Venus asks Vulcano new arms for Enea.

F.M.V.

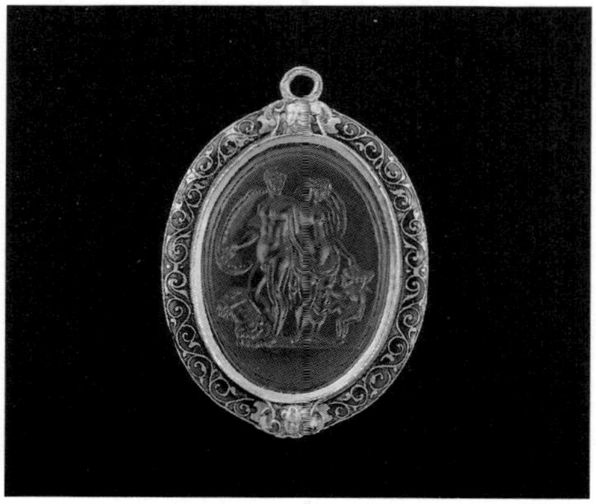

189. ENGRAVING
Cornelian
Inv. M. 14721
The setting is decorated with blue colored enamel plant spirals; at the extremities of the linked frame, at a point which is diametrically opposite to it, there are small heads in four different poses. The lower part of the reverse side is chipped.
Renaissance period.

A nude Mars, on the left, is depicted in the act of departing; he holds a shield in his right hand and his armour is at his feet; he turns to a semi-nude Venus, who is busy listening to Amore, who appears to want to lift himself up into his mother's arms.

TONDO-VANNI, pg. 170, n° 60.

F.M.V.

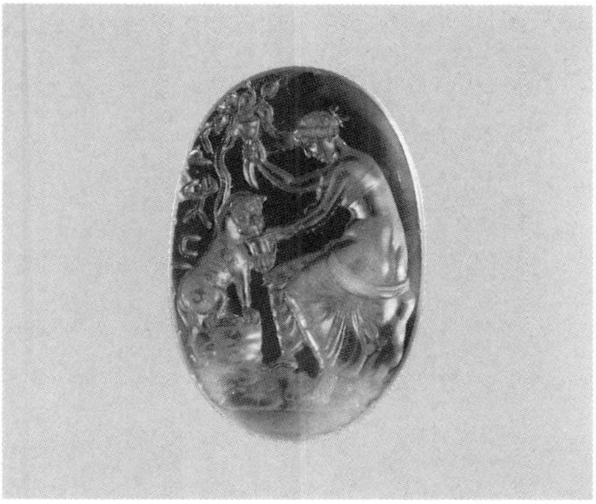

190. ENGRAVING
Cornelian
Inv. M. 14744
Menade, seated on a rock, offers a drink to a panther with a kantaros; in her right hand she holds a cup; behind the panther a bush, of ivy?; on the side, cabalistic characters between the animal and the bush.
XVI century.

TONDO-VANNI, pg. 167, n° 31.

F.M.V.

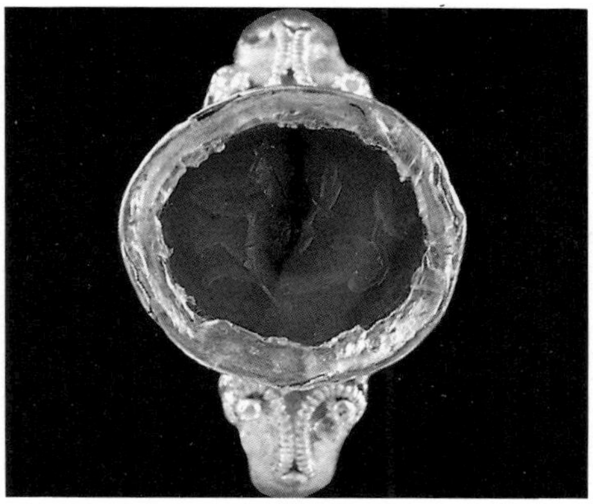

191. ENGRAVING
Cornelian
Inv. M. 1369
The stone is mounted on a gold ring with decorations on the sides; the stone is raised by a modius shaped mounting.
XV or XVI century.

Tritone playing a marine trumpet and holding a rudder in his right hand; the mythological figure's forelegs are those of a horse.

Gioielli e Ornamenti Preziosi, n° 85.

F.M.V.

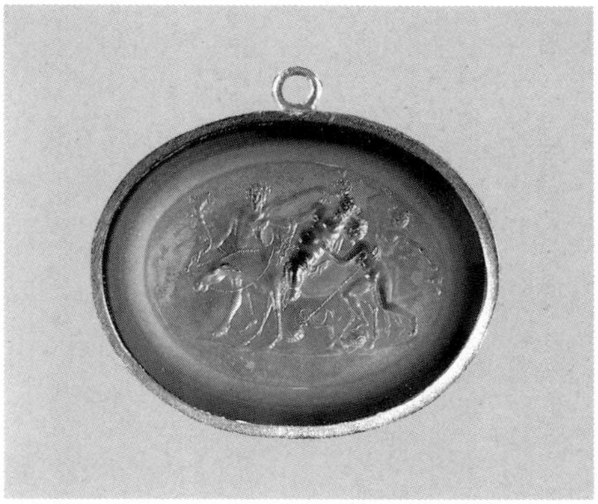

192. ENGRAVING
Onyx
Inv. 14773
Composed of three layers; a sky-blue colored layer between two sardonyx ones. Gold mounting.
XVI century.

The scene depicts a drunken Sileno on a donkey. The figure holds a cup in his right hand, and rests the other hand on the shoulders of a beardless nude bacchant who comes to his aid. A bearded nude faun, with an ivory decorated drinking horn in his right hand precedes him and turns to the left to crown him. Another young faun, holding a torch and a kantaros, is behind the donkey.

ZANNONI, V, table 35, 4.

F.M.V.

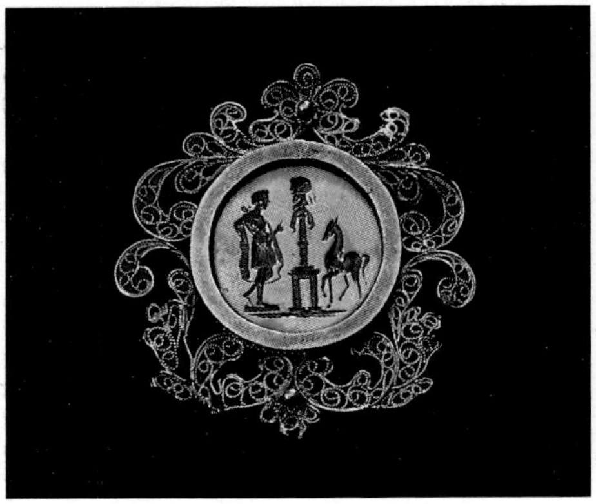

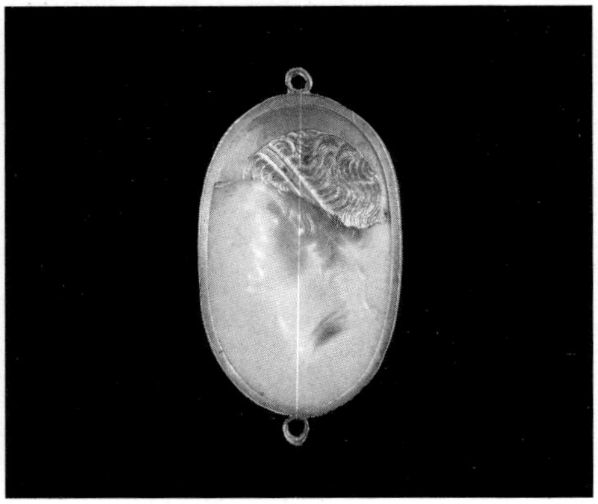

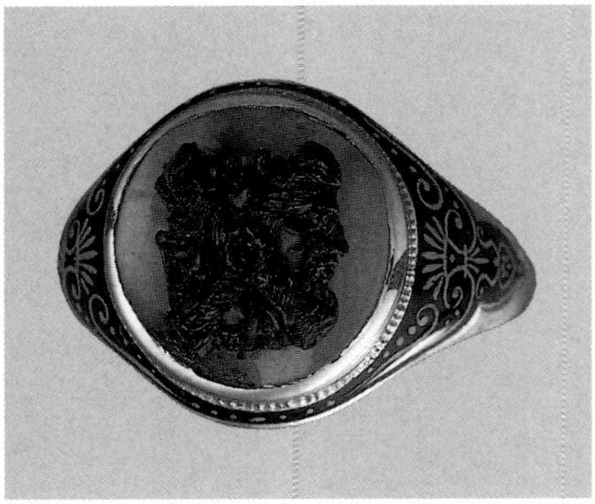

193. . ENGRAVING
Cornelian (two colored layers)
Inv. M. 2368
The stone is set on a filigree gold mounting Renaissance period.
Profile of a soldier on the right, in front of a column above a pedestal; above, a bearded head, crowned with laureate. On the other side of the column a horse without harness.

Gioielli e Ornamenti Preziosi, n° 88.

F.M.V.

194. ENGRAVING
Chalcedony Sapphirine
Inv. 15001
Gold restoration on head's summit. The gem is set in a gold mounting lined with copper
Left profile of beardless male, with the head adorned by a diadem
Hellenistic age; restored mid XVI century.

The refinement of the incision and the elegance of the features date this fragment back to the hellenistic age. The gold restoration must have occurred around the middle of the XVI century when it was common to reconstruct a gem's missing pieces in order to make the piece whole again. As far as the identity of the figure represented is concerned, Gori felt the features resembled certain Syrian kings.

TONDO-VANNI, pg. 174, n° 106 w/bibl.

F.M.V.

195. CAMEO
Onyx
Inv. 15214
Composed of two layers, the higher of which is black colored. The cameo, fragmented in the background, is mounted on a gold ring and enamelled with white decorations on a blue background. The four bearded heads of Jupiter are gathered together according to the four cardinal points.
End of the XVI century.

The ring that houses the cameo was without doubt manufactured after the gem, probably in the eighteen century. This can be seen not only from the style of the mounting, but also from the presence of a scratch on the border which the new collocation was unable to conceal.

Gioielli e Ornamenti Preziosi, n° 90.

F.M.V.

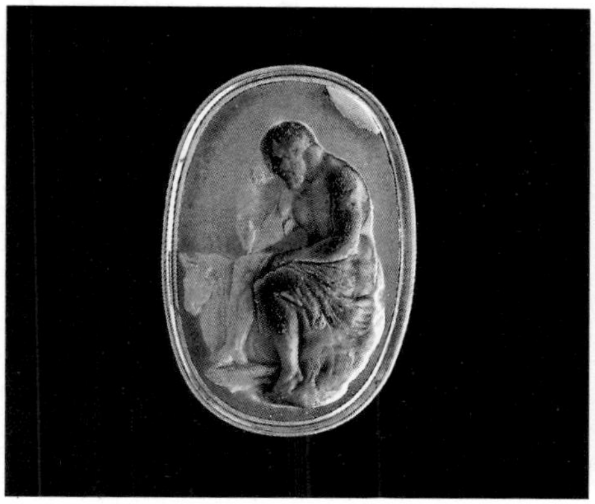

196. CAMEO
Chalcedony (three layers)
Inv. 15159
Small fracture on top restored in gold. The gem is set in a gold ring mounted á jour.
Male figure seated on the left; with his right hand he holds his head as well as a sword (barely visible because of the fracture in the cameo); the head of an ox appears below.
XVI century.

The scene represents the Aiace episode, the Greek hero who having been denied Achilles' weapons, became insane and in a moment of fury killed the herds and then having regained his senses, contemplated suicide. The iconographic image is inspired by the famous painting by Timomachos.

Gioielli e Ornamenti Preziosi, n° 91.

F.M.V.

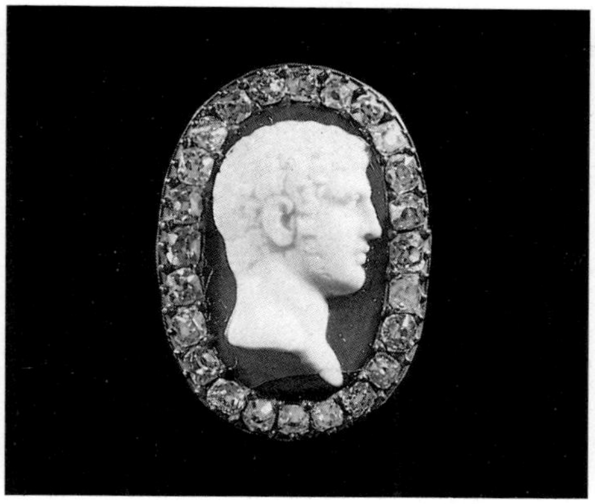

197. CAMEO
Chalcedony (white on a burnt brown layer)
Inv. 15170
Fractured at the base of the neck. The cameo is mounted on a brooch surrounded by 24 diamonds.
Nude head of young man with curly hair on the right; two long side whiskers on the cheeks frame the face.
XVI century.

The portrait is inspired by the famous aquamarine head of Hercules by Gnaios at the British Museum in London.

,*Gioielli e Ornamenti Preziosi*, n° 94.

F.M.V.

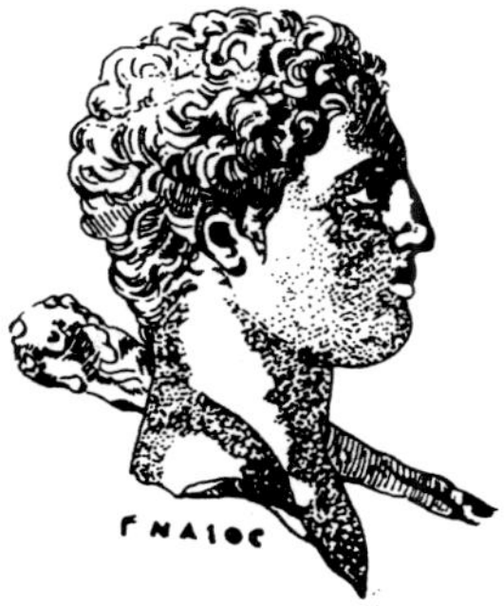

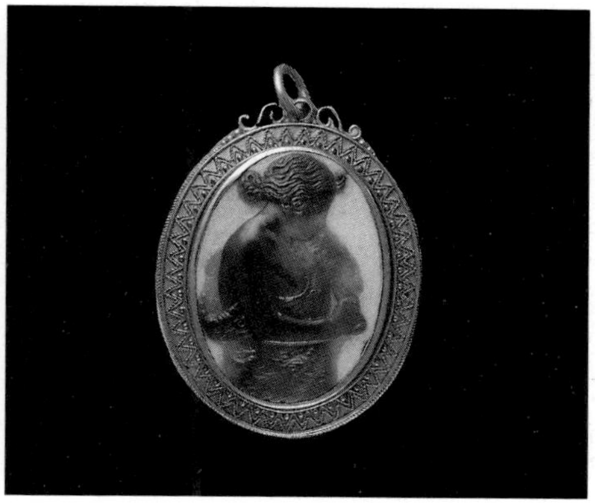

198. CAMEO
Chalcedony Agate (on a sky blue background)
Inv. 15215
The cameo is set in a gold medallion
Second half of the XVI century.

On the right, the half-length figure of a young girl in a pensive pose; she is holding her head with her right hand; in her left hand she holds a knife. She is dressed in a tunic made of animal skin. Lucretia?

Gioielli e Ornamenti Preziosi, n° 96.

F.M.V.

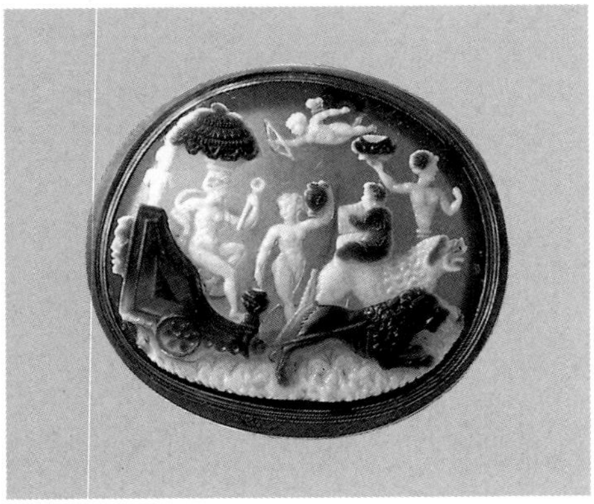

199. CAMEO
Chalcedony Sardonyx (three layered: transparent, white and burnt)
Inv. 15266
The cameo is mounted, á jour, in a gold ring
The scene depicts a cart pulled by two lions moving toward the right; the cart appears to be covered by a canopy supported by a herm. A cupid holding an arch descends from above; the cart is preceded by two nude figures carrying vases; between them, seated on a white lion, is an older female figure playing a large syrinx.
Florentine manufacture: second half of the XVI century.

The scene could be interpreted as an allegorical representation of a great Mother Earth on a cart surrounded by her retinue. Cartari described the deity in 1556 in the following terms: «The Earth's cart is pulled by lions, which indicates, according to some, that the earth hangs in the air, supported by the wheels, because the sky-blue spheres of the Continuum surround her, as the ferocious and impetuous lions indicate, for such is the nature of the Heavens surrounding the earth's sustaining air» (pg. 116). Then, in another passage he completes the description by saying: «.....on her head is a crown made of towers because the earth's environs, like the crown, are filled with cities, castles and villages......she holds a sceptre in her hand, which means that the earth holds everyone's kingdoms» (pg. 122).

F.M.V.

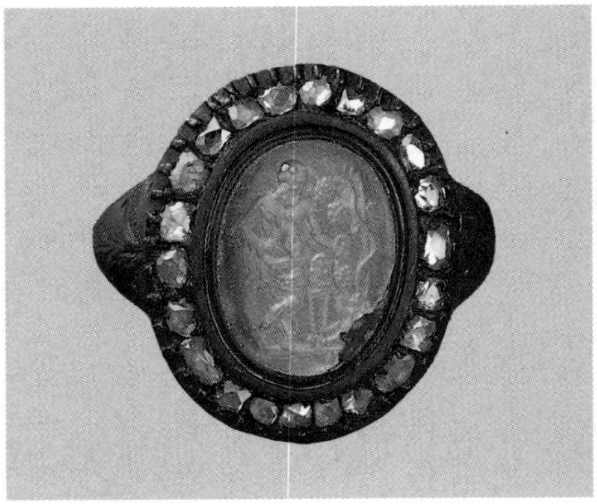

200. CAMEO
Amethyst
Inv. 15456
The gem is set in a silver ring and surrounded by 24 zircons; the ring's shoulders are decorated with graffito designs of plants
Second half of the XVI century.

The scene depicts a faun, on the right, seated on the ground over animal skins, in the act of showing hornpipes; on the side, a vine-shoot.

Gioielli e Ornamenti Preziosi, n° 105.

F.M.V.

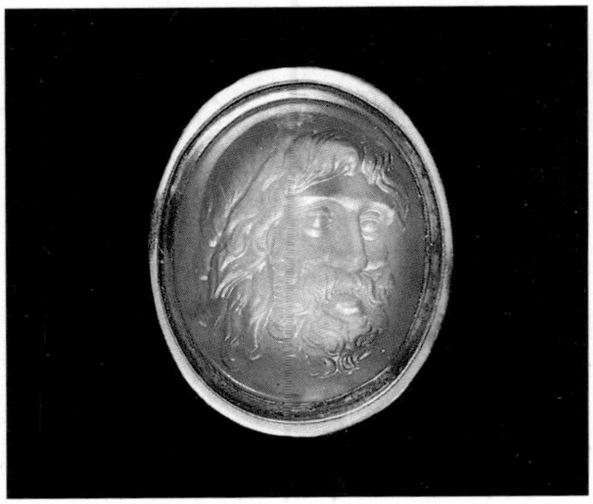

201. CAMEO
Green Chalcedony
Inv. 15408
The gem is mounted, á jour, in a gold ring
XVI or XVII century.

The head of Jupiter is turned three-quarters toward the right.

Gioielli e Ornamenti Preziosi, n° 110.

F.M.V.

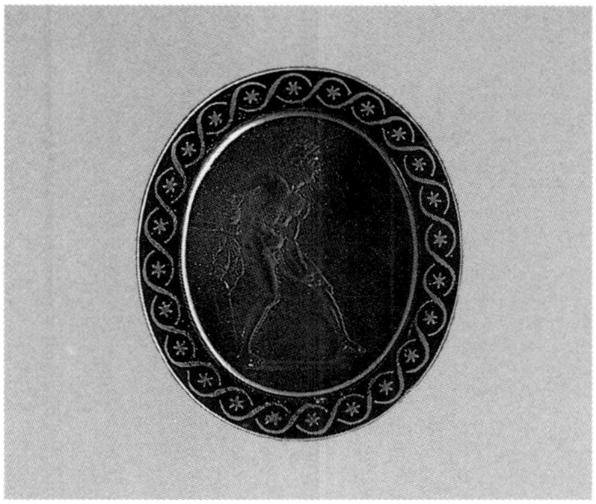

202. CAMEO
Green Chalcedony
Inv. 15461
The gem is mounted on a ring with enamelled festoon decorations
XVI century.

Young hero, nude, turned to the right; he is holding a short sword in his hand and a folded mantle lays over his arm; the other hand is lowered seemingly pointing toward something.

Gioielli e Ornamenti Preziosi, n° 114.

F.M.V.

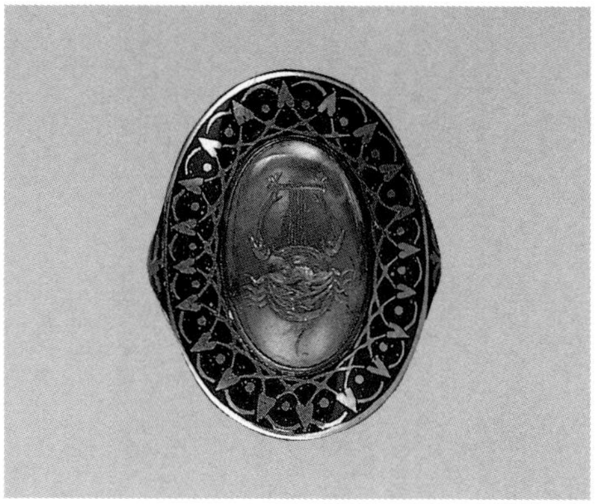

203. CAMEO
Amethyst
Inv. 15277
The gem is set in a gold ring with black enamel decorations of intertwined leaves
XVI or XVII century.

The lyre, a musical instrument, in an upright position,is forged to resemble a crab.

Gioielli e Ornamenti Preziosi, n° 116.

F.M.V.

SMALL GEMSTONE AND PRECIOUS METAL ARTIFACTS FROM THE MEDICI COLLECTIONS
by *Anna Maria Massinelli*

The selection of items on display does not make any pretext at philological reconstructions of any particular contest. We do believe, however, that it can recreate that sense of variety and curiosity of the gemstone items collected in the *Tribuna degli Uffizi* during the course of two centuries. They document a less known aspect which, albeit in the background, judging from the quantities that have been traced and carefuly described in the inventories, must have been anything but a secondary part of the Medici collections. These were the curios that astounded visitors to the Uffizi who were drawn to the treasure in the *Tribuna*. We can understand the satisfaction, of knowing that he owned a unique piece, with which the Grand Duke could show objects such as the chalcedony hand that already had a broken pinky by the mid-eighteenth century[23], or the orange crystal that was artificially colored by a special heat treatment (*Museo di Mineralogia*, inv. 13200) or the piece with the chalcedony bust of Hercules (*Museo degli Argenti*), inv. 783) which probably dates from the era of Cosimo I de' Medici[24]. This list of princely curios could continue with hundreds of pieces made of the finest materials and depicting the most unusual subjects.
Towards the end of the XVI century the palaces of Florentine collectors included Galleries filled with sculptures, paintings, medals and precious stones. The *Casa Gaddi* and the *Casa Salviati*, described by Agostino del Riccio between 1595 and 1598[1] seem to mirror the Grand Ducal models: the *Galleria del Palazzo del Casino di San Marco* and the Uffizi Gallery, both established on the basis of Francesco I de' Medici's (1541-1587) wide-ranging and unusual interests. The amount of the items displayed in the Gallery of the *Palazzo del Casino di San Marco* can be verified through the inventory that was drawn up in 1587, the year of Francesco's death[2].
Here, amidst numerous small marble, bronze and even silver statues the predominating items are those whose value derives from the rarity of the material, unusuality of form or exotic origins. Thus, the entire span was articulated by a sequence of small objects that were probably more suitable for a glass cabinet in a small studio.
Francesco's intentions, however, went beyond this: he envisioned having the masterpieces of the family collections housed in one place, the Uffizi Gallery. The fulcrum of the Gallery was to have comprised the octagonal *Tribuna* designed by Bernardo Buontalenti[3]and completed in 1584 as a sort of sanctuary to house the treasure. It was Francesco who ordered the *studiolo* in Palazzo Vecchio to be dismantled and the all the objects that had previously been kept in that little room to be transferred to the *Tribuna*[4]. Other items from the *Palazzo del Casino di San Marco* were also destined for the *Tribuna*, but Francesco's sudden death in October 1587 prevented him from completing his project. The general inventory of the *Tribuna* was made in 1589[5], by his brother Ferdinando during the second year of the Grand Duchy.
Eighteenth century views of the *Tribuna degli Uffizi*: the painting by Johann Zoffany, dated

1773, like the drawings prepared by Giuseppe Magni for the Gallery's drawing portfolio, curated by Benedetto de Greyes, show some changes with respect to the original arrangements, although the situation had not been completely modified[6]. We can still see the shelves that ran along the walls at about shoulder height. Here marble, gemstone and bronze busts and statuettes follow upon each other in no specifically elaborate order, but according to an arrangement that is nearly confirmed by the inventory of the *Tribuna* which dates from 1769. The original arrangement of the items that crowded the shelves in the late fifteeneighties can be reconstructed through the first general inventory of the *Tribuna* dated 1589.
Most of the semi-precious stone vases, the large ones and those with particularly valuable mountings were kept in two cabinets: 84 in the first and 77 in the second[7].
Other miscellaneous small objects and medals were in the drawers of the chests: the *tempietto* built for Francesco I to drawings by Buontalenti was overflowing with gold and silver medals. It was removed quite quickly to be replaced by Ferdinando's piece also designed by the same architect[8]. The drawers of the monumental *studiolo* contained vases and carved gems such as rubies, sapphires, topazes, emeralds and opals. Many of these can be found today in the *Museo degli Argenti* and in the *Museo di Mineralogia* (Silver Museum and Mineralogy Museum).
Of the remaining loose stones, there is an astounding number of smoked crystals also known as Bohemian topaz, and hyaline crystals in such different shapes and facets it is impossible to find two identical stones.
A particularly large Bohemian topaz was used for the coat of arms on Ferdinando's chest[8a], but it seems that up to the time of Cosimo III the court artisans were busy cutting crystals. At the beginning of the eighteenth century the Grand Duke enjoyed himself by taking handful of gems from these drawers, arousing the admiration of the King of Denmark who came to Florence in 1708: «And we cannot pass over this in silence, but must describe the great quantity of precious jewels that the Grand Duke had spread on table covered with green velvet cloth. The diamonds, emeralds and rubies, in different sizes, formed three rows of over twohundred, and the collection of onyx, topazes and chalcedonies was something fabulous... diamonds of different sizes were here and there in papers, and the Grand Duke was particularly knowledgable about the topazes that he himself had collected and ordered cut by skilled artisans»[8b].
The various trinkets in the drawers of the chest included animal heads carved in gemstones that had previously belonged to Cosimo I de' Medici and which can now be found in the *Museo di Mineralogia* (a dog's head in onyx and another in amethyst, belived to be Mexican and a chalcedony boar's head), and in the *Museo degli Argenti* (*Inv. Gemme*, 846), an amethyst bird's head, considered Mexican[9] and finally the «new» bear's and dog's head which are on display. The group was described as in the *Tribuna* up to 1769; in 1781 along

with a significant number of gemstones it was delivered to the Grand Duke's private secretary[10]. The drawers also contained the panther and jasper cut with the gilded silver fawn[11] that belongs to the *Museo di Mineralogia*.
Other items were distributed on the shelves that are still visible in the above-mentioned eighteenth century views of the *Tribuna* and which contained a continuous row of small drawers. From the 1589 inventory it would seem that they contained miniature paintings as well as tiny bronzes, small gemstone busts, small jars and vases, many ornamental knives and daggers in precious metal with gems; here the inventory specified the origins, German (*germani*) or Moslem (*dommaschino*). For example, the listing for the «fourteenth shelf», reads: «An antique silver figurine of Jupiter with a flame in one hand a spear in the other/An agate vase with gilded silver lid and feet/an ebony square miniated in gold with a tondo miniature of the *Torre di Nembrotte*, with silver border by Giorgio (...) / A German or Damascus knife with a rock crystal hilt and enamelled gilded silver ferrule and black leather sheath with/tip and 3 enameled and gilded silver ferrules with silver chain/an open ebony box with brass border containing a portrait/ of the Grand Duchess Cristina attached with a silver chain by the hand of Costantino de' Servi...[12].
The solution adopted for arranging the items along the wall-shelves is quite interesting: the visitor's eye was meant to be struck by the encyclopedic variety of the materials, the techniques and the categories of objects in the collection. Perhaps it was Buontalenti himself who had conceived of the spire-shaped units made of wood enhanced with gold, with niches for small figurines or precious vases. Each of the eighteen spires was topped by a considerably large bronze sculpture. The sequence was interrupted by six arches, also made of gilded wood, with «steps» for smaller items. At the top of the arches were silver groups depicting the Labors of Hercules by Giambologna[13]. For example, the eleventh spire was described as follows «a gilded wood spire with steps and niches containing four ancient bronze figurines, two agate and jasper vases with gilded silver lids, handles and feet/An ancient bronze female nude with one hand at her thigh and in the other a bunch of flowers about b. 2/3 high is atop the spire.»[14]
One of the six arches, «the fourth» contained: «an arch of gilded miniated wood on which the following figures stood: four ancient bronze figures/an ancient bronze head of Bacchus, with gilded silver cloth, resting on a stand of mixed stones/a small, antique chalcedony cat sits atop a wooden cube/a chalcedony dolphin straddled by a small *putto* stands on a black bone pedestal (*Museo degli Argenti, inv. Gemme* 811)/A silver Hercules with a boar and stick on his shoulders by Giambologna about 3/4b high/Two small ancient bronze figurines stand on the shelf below the arch/A chalcedony head with alabaster bust, gilded silver draping on a black wood stand/A vase of half an ostrich egg engraved with grotesques by Marchionni with gilded silver and borders and a crab that serves as a stand/A bronze

figurine of a baboon, with a cape rests on a wooden cube/A bronze figure of Capitoline Jupiter, with one hand raised, stands on a base of the same metal, 1/2 b. high.

Each structure, therefore served as a visual and conceptual link between a group of objects that differed as to materials, periods and subjects, forming a unitary complex which, in the eye of the observer, was a sort of microcosm, a mirror of artistic creativity and the variety of materials found in nature. The same purpose was pursued in other areas, the so-called «*monti di miniera*», consisted of blocks of uncut minerals resting on silver bowls with bronze or silver figurines — generally of sacred subjects (even though there was one of Hercules with the Lion) — fastened to them. Perhaps the best example of the taste expressed by these compositions is the one described in the 1589 inventory: «a "*monte di miniera*" of silver and more, with several figures working the mines, rests on a gilded silver cup, about 2/3 b. high with a glass lid».

During the XVII century, the collection of bases and other small semi-precious stone items grew even larger. A separate nucleus came from part of Cristina di Lorena's dowry which is now in the *Sala di Madama* in the Uffizi[16].

In the years to follow gifts provided other occasions for enriching the collection such as a precious jasper vase that arrived from Saxony slightly before 1670, or a serpentine Chinese cup (*Museo degli Argenti, Inv. Gemme* 745), or an entire group of vases and dishes in turned black stone[17] still recognizable in a group of serpentine vases from Saxony now in the *Museo di Mineralogia*[18]. These are items of various origins which make the already diversified panorama of the collection even more interesting. Another example can be found in the two fine Chinese jade bowls that Prince Galitzine sent from Moscow in the early eighteenth century: «two Oriental chalcedony bowls decorated with branches and flowers in relief, each made of a single piece in China and given to H.R.H. by Prince Gallicene Moscovita (*sic.*)[19]. These pieces can also be recognized in the *Museo di Mineralogia* (inv. 13633-13634).

The last additions, by a member of the Medici family, date from Prince Ferdinando a fine collector of *Wunderkammer* items. The inventory prepared upon his death in 1713 lists a considerable number of crystal and chalcedony vases and «trays» with elaborate silver filigrée and precious gem trimmings[20].

Some attempts at collecting various gemstone items in the *Tribuna* were still being made in the latter half of the XVIII century and immediately preceded the definitive dispersal of the collection. In 1770, for example, Giuseppe Querci, director of the Gallery, when reviewing items scattered throughout the residences recognized as «worthy of being chosen» many small gemstone items found on some of the mezzanines in *Palazzo Pitti*. Between 1771 and 1780 they remained in the cabinets and drawers of the chest in the *Tribuna*[21].

The list, prepared when the items were turned over to the Uffizi, describes a considerable number of vases and bowls in different stones, either plain or trimmed, but interesting because of the variety of the stones.

Many jars or small vases have very unusual shapes: barrels, columns, half a grooved ball, hearts, octagons, boatshaped, octagonal acorn-shaped pyramid, buckets, baskets, a pear-shaped agate drop that opens in two, bound in gilded silver». One of the most unusual is the «small coffee pot with agate body and foot, handle, spout and lid in silver filigrée» on display. But the variety of objects is such that it includes a lapislazuli toothpick with gold inlay, dagger hilts, bat handles, crowns, about one hundred «*Belzuar stones*» with filigrée mountings; spoons such as the one in oriental agate with a similar handle and cornelian at the end with gilded silver binding» that can be found in the *Museo degli Argenti, Inv. Gemme* 1116). There is also a rounded agate column with base and capital in gilded metal leaf, decorated with garnets and turquoise» from the *Museo di Mineralogia* (inv. n. 13328) or the two oval heliotropes embedded in gilded silver that is partly enameled with festoons, and four feet with the agates at the ends forming two tables, also in the *Museo degli Argenti* (*Inv. Gemme*, 720, 727).

In the general sorting of the Gallery's treasure that took place during the early seventeen eighties, following the establishment of the *Real Museo di Fisica e Storia Naturale*, the items deemed to be of scientific and mineralogical interest were selected for the new museum. The Uffizi kept all those items considered to be of particular antiquarian, historical-artistic value such as the cameos and large semi-precious stone vases. It was an aribitrary selection made according to rather unclear criteria which ultimately penalized — for exampe — the large crystal vases in natural shapes made by Milanese craftsmen during the latter half of the XVI century[22].

NOTES

1. cfr. C. Acidini, «Niccolò Gaddi collezionista e dilettante del Cinquecento», in *Paragone*, 359-361. 1980, pp. 141-175; A. Del Riccio, «Delle lodi delle pietre», in: P. Barocchi, *Scritti d'arte del Cinquecento*, II, 1973, p. 1250.

2. Archivio di Stato di Firenze, Guardaroba Medicea 138, cc. 154-168, cfr. A.M. Massinelli-F. Tuena, *Il tesoro dei Medici*, Milan 1992, pp. 230-233. Cfr. also A.S.F., G.M. 126 «Inventario della Guardaroba del fu Granduca Francesco I che dalla consegna del di lui Guardaroba Giovanni Battista da Cerreto passa nella consegna di Benedetto Fedini Guardaroba del nuovo Granduca Ferdinando I».

3. A. Biancalani; S. Rudolph, «Mostra Storica della Tribuna degli Uffizi, Florence, 1979, Uffizi, General Catalogue 1980 pp. 23; L. Berti *Profilo di storia degli Uffizi*.

4. Cfr. «L'ambiente veniva riscoperto e ricostruito agli inizi del '900», cfr. G. Poggi, «Lo studiolo di Francesco in Palazzo Vecchio», in: Il Marzocco, XV, 1910, p. 1; A. Lenzi, Palazzo Vecchio, Milan-Rome 1929, pp. 231-241; L. Berti, Il Principe dello Studiolo, Florence, 1967.

5. Florence, Uffizi Library, Manuscript 70.

6. O. Millar, Zoffani and his Tribuna, London 1967, for the views by Giuseppe Magni cfr. ibidem, tables 17/19.

7. These are the most significant vases as regards both size and mountings currently, and almost entirely, conserved in the *Museo degli Argenti*, cfr. inv. 1921 in: K. Aschengreen Piacenti, *Il Museo degli Argenti a Firenze*, Florence 1968 pp. 131-144. Many of these items have been the object of specific studies regarding both the stone and goldsmithing work, with considerable contributions regarding the identification of the craftsmen, especially from Milan, cfr. *Palazzo Vecchio, Committenza e Collezionismo Medicei*, exhibition catalogue, Florence 1980, pp. 215-236 with bibl. For eighteenth century tampering with these vases cfr. P. Barocchi-G. Gaeta Bertel, «Danni e furti di Giuseppe Bianchi in Galleria, in: Labyrinthos 13/16, 1990, pp. 321-337.

8. A.M. Massinelli, Magnificenze Medicee: gli stipi della Tribuna degli Uffizi, in: Antologia di Belle Arti, 1990 p. 111, with bibl.

8a. *Splendori di Pietre Dure*, exhibition catalogue, Florence 1988, p.   (Topaz coat of arms).

8b. P.F. Covoni, Visita del Re di Danimarca a Firenze nel 1708, Florence 1886, in: K. Aschengreen Piacenti, Collectors and Princes, in: Apollo, September 1977, pp. 206-207.

9. A.M. Massinelli, «*Bronzi e anticaglie della Guardaroba di Cosimo I de' Medici*», exhibition catalogue, Florence 1991, p. 14, 17 with bibl.

10. Uffizi Library, inv. 1769, c. 312.

11. The list of items in the drawers of the chest today comes from the 1704 Gallery inventory published in Massinelli 1990, op. cit. pp. 111-134.

12. Uffizi Library, ms. 80, c. 10.

13. For the groups of the Labors of Hercules by Giambologna cfr. A Radcliffe, Giambologna's Twelve Labours of Hercules, in The Connoisseur CIC 1978, pp. 12-19; C.W. Fock, The Original Silver Casts of Giambologna's Labours of Hercules in: Studien zum europaeischen Kunsthandwerk. Festschrift Yvonne Hackenbroch, Munich 1983, pp. 141-145. The data on the eighteenth century vicissitudes of the silver groups in the Tribuna, up to the time of their disappearance were traced by the author and published in: A.M. Massinelli, F. Tuena, Il tesoro dei Medici, Milan 1992, pp. 70-71, the documents are quoted on p. 235. In 1726 ivories were placed atop the cabinet (Archivio di Stato di Firenze, Guardaroba Medicea 1292, c. 241 v. Uffizi Library, inv. 1753, nn. 882, 883, 884/92. In 1790 they were «whitened», the latest information dates from 1797 when they were sent to the Guardaroba (Uffizi Library, inv. 1784, c. 314, Filza XXVIII, fas. 40).

14. Uffizi Library, ms. 70, cc. 25-26.

15. ibidem, c. 22.

16. cfr. *Palazzo Vecchio, Committenza e Collezionismo Medicei*, exhibition catalogue, Florence 1980 pp. 218-220, 223-225-232-235.

17. K. Aschengreen Piacenti, Note su due vasi del Museo degli Argenti, in: Scritti in onore di Ugo Procacci, II, Milano 1977, pp. 567-570.

18. Florence, *Museo di Mineralogia*, inv. nn. 13671/74; 13738/40.

19. Uffizi Library, inv., 1704, n. 1032.

20. cfr. K. Aschengreen Piacenti, Collectors and Princes, in: Apollo, September 1977, pp. 206-207.

21. Florence, Uffizi Library, Filza IV, fasc. 25.

22. These items were returned to the Museo del Bargello at the end of the XIX century and then transferred to the Museo degli Argenti in 1926.

23. Uffizi Library, inv. 1794 n. 1078; inv. 1753, n. 2335; inv. 1769 n. 1572.

24. The small statuette could possibly be identified with the «Termine di marmo co' mantello di 1/4» sent to the Scrittoio di Calliope in Palazzo Vecchio in 1559, cfr. Massinelli 1991, cit. p. 14. It is possible that the person who wrote the inventory took the material for marble, on the other hand, similar pieces of such dimensions do not, to my knowledge, come from the Medici collections.

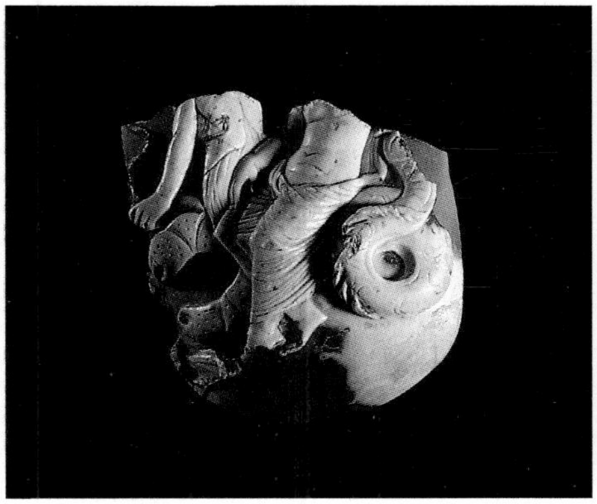

204. FRAGMENT OF A CAMEO
Inv. Gems 1921, n° 1040
Height 6.2 x 5.9 cm.
Light Breccia
Roman period.

Representing Nereid on the back of Triton. Both heads and an arm are missing from the figures.

An.M.M.

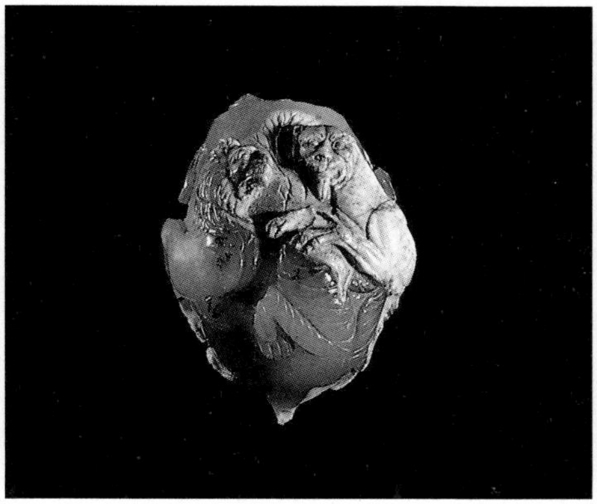

205. CAMEO
Inv. O.d.A. 1911, n° 1089
Height 5.6 cm.; diameter 4.2 cm.
Chalcedony of Egypt
Roman period.

Oval fragment with figures of a lion, a tiger and a man in relief.

An.M.M.

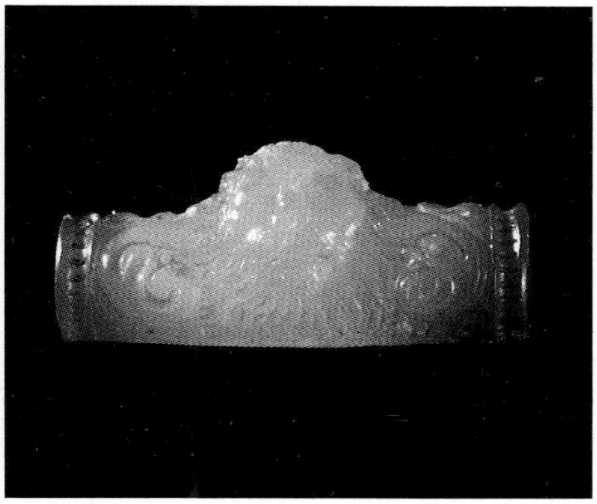

206. SEAL
Inv. Gems 1921, n° 348
Length 3.7 cm.
Cornelian
XVI century.

Cylinder, decorated in relief representing two lion heads; the two engravings at the extremities represent the Medici coat of arms and a male head crowned with laurel.

An.M.M.

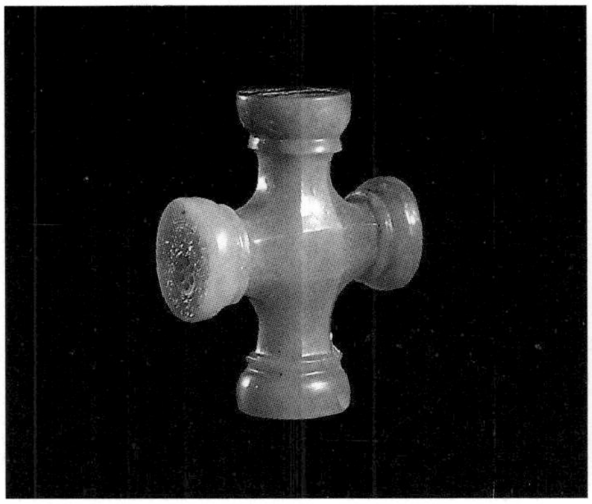

207. SEAL
Inv. Gems 1921, n° 349
Height 4.7 x 5.5 cm.
Agate
XVI century.

Cross shaped seal with four engravings at the extremities representing the Medici coat of arms, intertwined monogram, crucifixion; inscription «VITA EXORDIUM MORTIS INITIUM».

An.M.M.

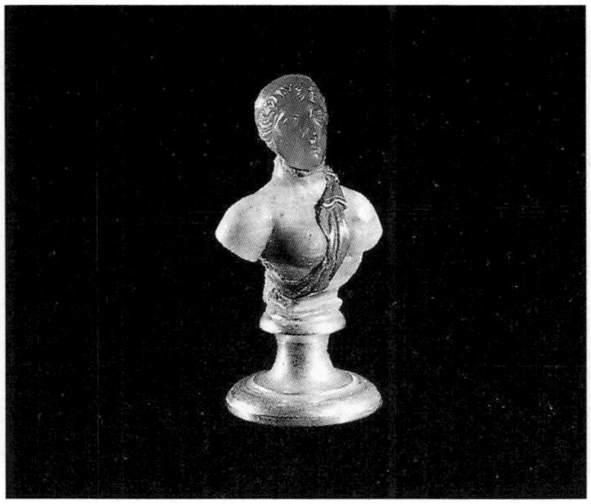

208. BUST
Inv. Gems 1921, n° 466
Height 5.7 cm.
Oriental alabaster and sardonyx, silver
XVI century.

Female bust with silver chlamys. Gilded metal foot.

An.M.M.

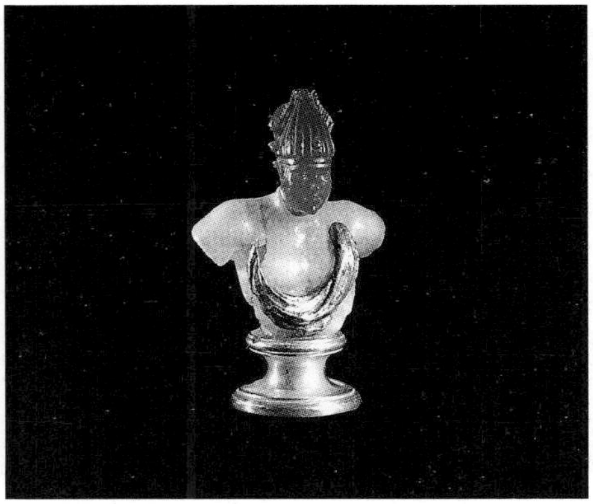

209. BUST
Inv. Gems 1921, n° 468
Height 6.3 cm.
Oriental alabaster and oriental sardonyx, silver
XVI century.

Bust of Priest of ancient Egypt, a fragment of chlamys in silver gilt; gilded metal foot.

An.M.M.

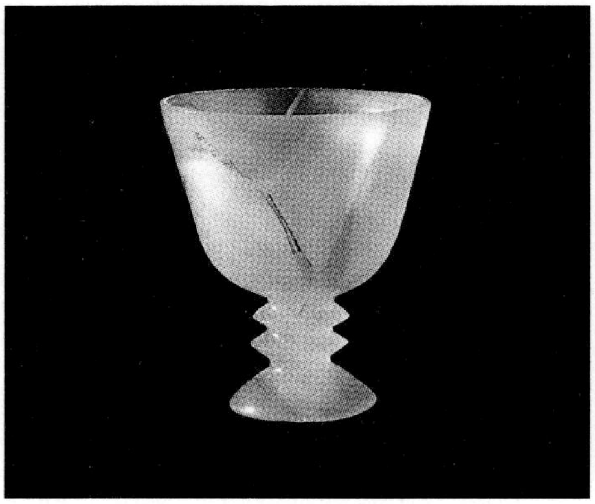

210. CHALICE
Inv. Gems 1921, n° 459
Height 5.5 cm.; diameter 4.8 cm.
Oriental chalcedony
XVI century.

An.M.M.

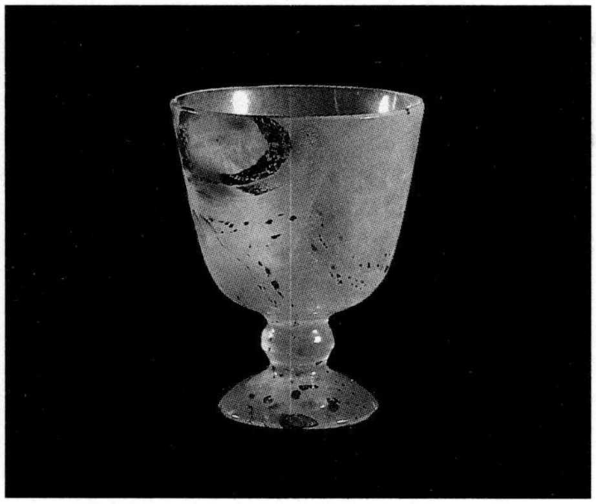

211. CHALICE
Inv. Gems 1921, n° 472
Height 5.6 cm.; diameter 4.5 cm.
Oriental chalcedony
XVI century.

Chalices carved out of one sole piece of material.

An.M.M.

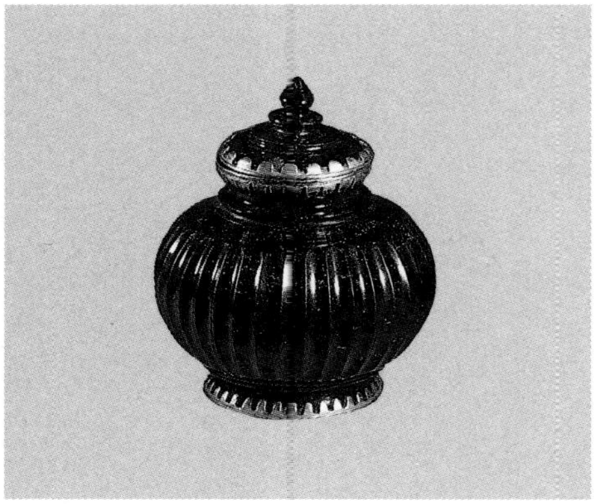

212. POT
Inv. Gems 1921, n° 445
Height 6.5 cm.; diameter 5.9 cm.
Blood-red jasper and silver
XVI century.

Round shape pot with lid, *baccellato*, with silver gilt setting.

An.M.M.

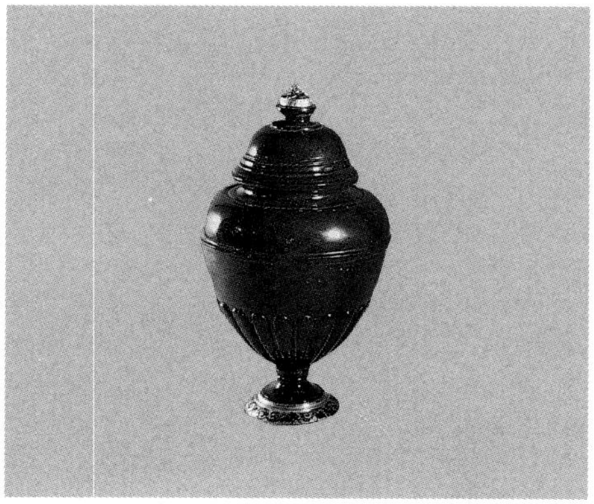

213. POT
Inv. Gems 1921, n° 446
Height 9.4 cm.; diameter 5.6 cm.
Blood-red jasper and gold
XVI century.

Pot with lid, *baccellato* on the lower part of the body; enamelled gold foot.

An.M.M.

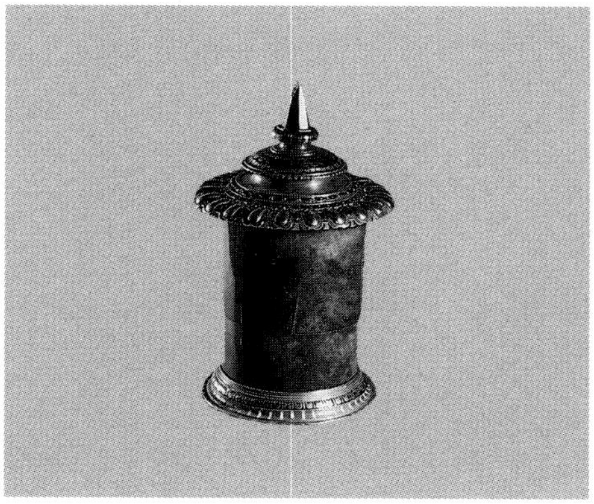

214. VESSEL
Inv. Gems 1921, n° 790
Height 7.8 cm.; diameter 3.6 cm.; lid: diameter 5 cm.
Blood-red jasper and gold
XVI century.

Two-piece cylinder; enamelled gold foot and lid.

An.M.M.

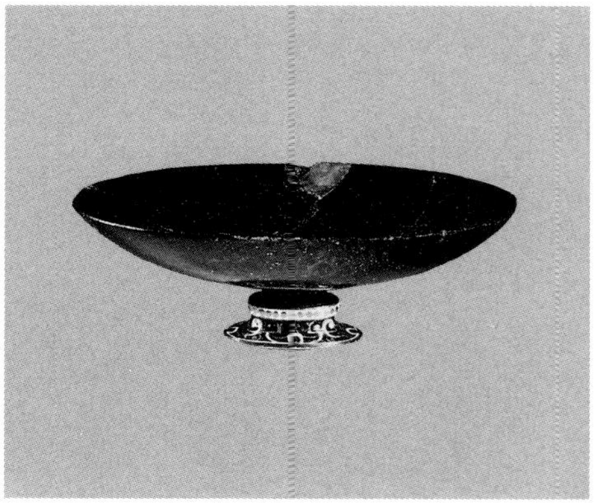

215.-216. TWO BOWLS
Inv. Gems 1921, n° 574-575
Height 3.1 cm.; width 6 x 9.6 cm.
Lapislazuli
XVI century.

Oval shaped bowls with enamelled gold foot.

An.M.M.

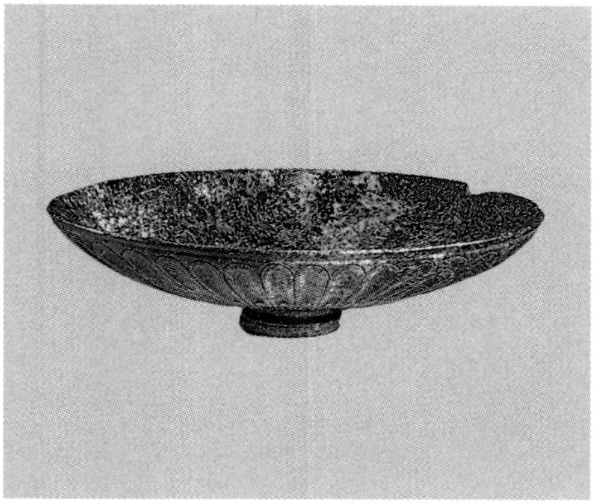

217. BOWL
Inv. Gems 1921, n° 577
Height 2.6 cm.; width 5.9 x 10 cm.
Lapislazuli
XVI century.

Oval shaped bowl - one sole *baccellato* piece.

An.M.M.

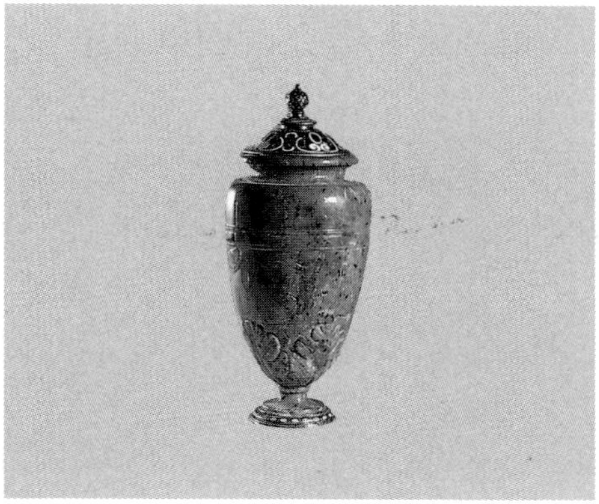

218. POT
Inv. Gems 1921, n° 718
Height 9 cm.; diameter 4.1 cm.
Emerald plasma
XVI century.

Urn shaped pot with engraved silver acanthus leaves on the body and small circle at the foot with enamelled gold lid.

An.M.M.

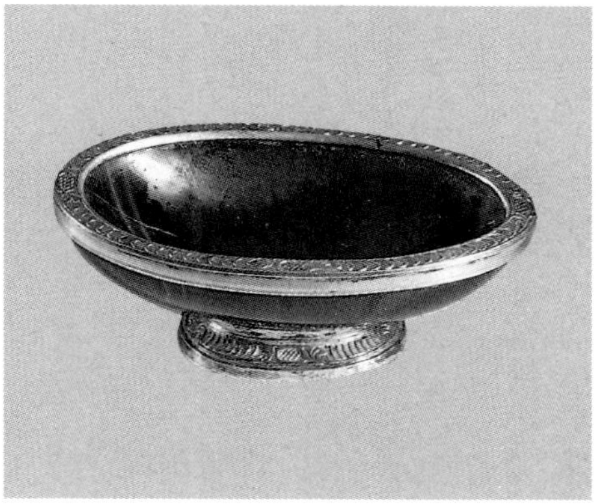

219. SMALL BOWL
Inv. Gems 1921, n° 734
Height 2.1 cm.; width 3.4 x 6 cm.
Oriental sardonyx and silver
XVI century.

Oval shaped bowl with gilded and enamelled silver setting.

An.M.M.

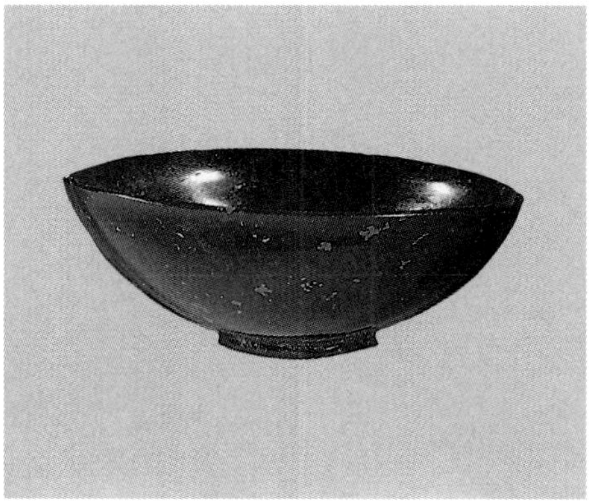

220. BOWL
Inv. Gems 1921, n° 762
Height 3.5 cm.; width 5.7 x 9 cm.
Blood-red jasper
XVI century.

Oval shaped bowl - carved out of one sole piece of material.

An.M.M.

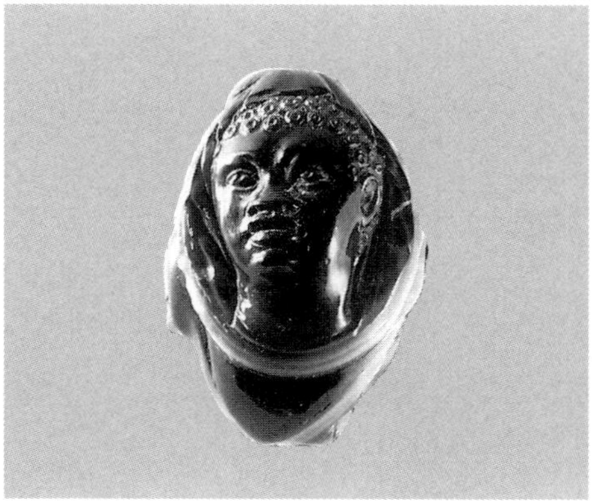

221. CARVED STONE
Inv. Gems 1921, n° 1034
Height 2.9 x 2.1 cm.
Agate
XVI century.

Oval in shape, vertically pierced, with three heads of Moors, cameo engraved.

An.M.M.

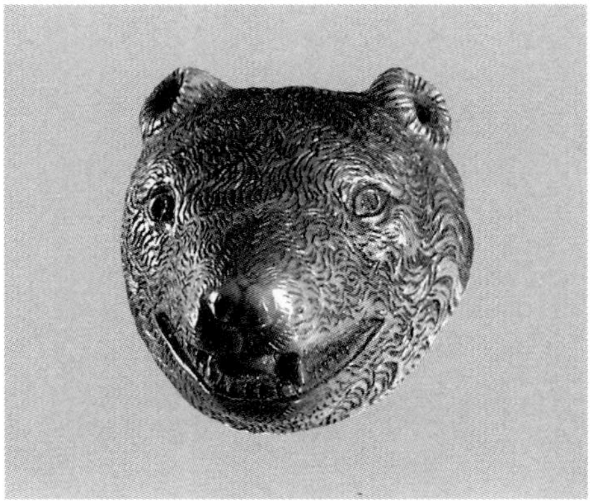

222. HEAD OF A BEAR
Inv. O.d.A. 1911, n° 1114
Length 2.6 cm.
Agate
XVI century, later assimilated into the Genius Familiaris.

Small head of a bear with a hole at the neck-join.

An.M.M.

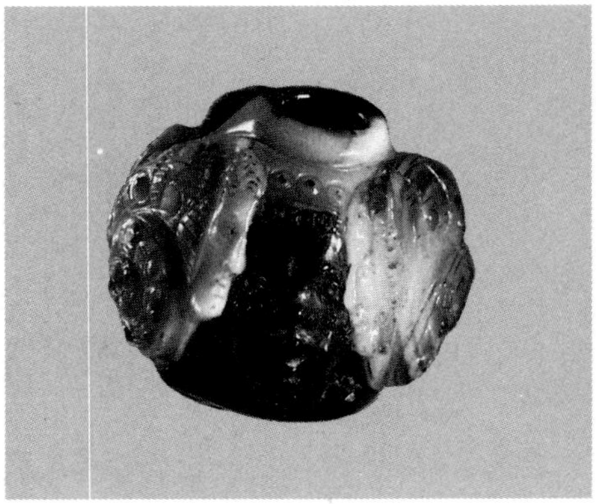

223. CARVED STONE
Inv. Gems 1921, n° 1033
diameter 2.2 cm.
Agate
XVI century.

Round in shape, vertically pierced, with three heads,two are cameo engraved, and one - representing a Medusa- is cameo applied.

An.M.M.

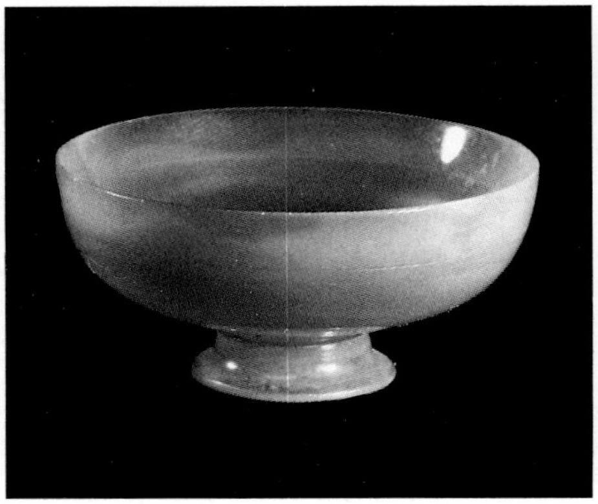

224. BOWL
Inv. Gems 1921, n° 511
Height 1.9 cm.; diameter 4 cm.
Cornelian
XVI century.

Round in shape -carved out of one sole piece of material.

An.M.M.

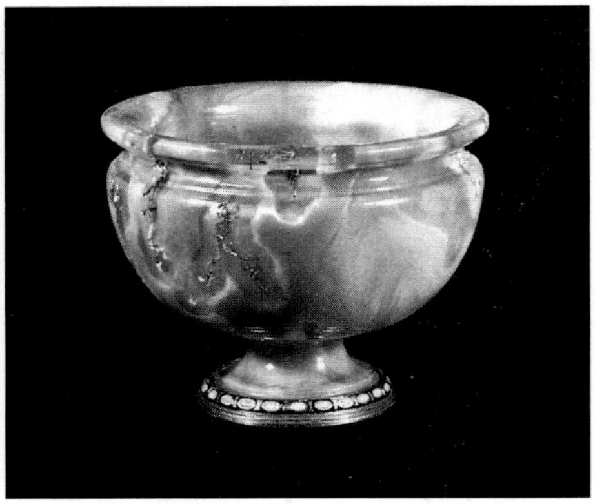

225. BOWL
Inv. Gems 1921, n° 534
Height 3.9 cm.; diameter 5 cm.
Oriental chalcedony and gold
XVI century.

Round in shape, carved out of one sole piece of material with enamelled gold setting.

An.M.M.

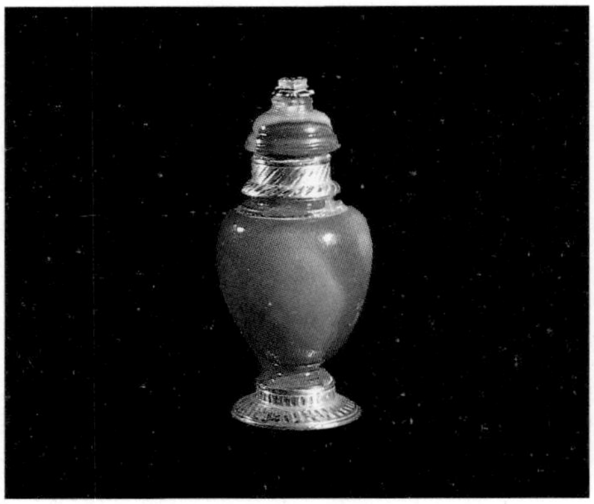

226. POT
Inv. Gems 1921, n° 810
Height 4.8 cm.; diameter 2.2 cm.
Oriental Agate and silver
XVI century.

Pot similar to numbers 628-629, 732 with enamelled gold and emerald bands.

An.M.M.

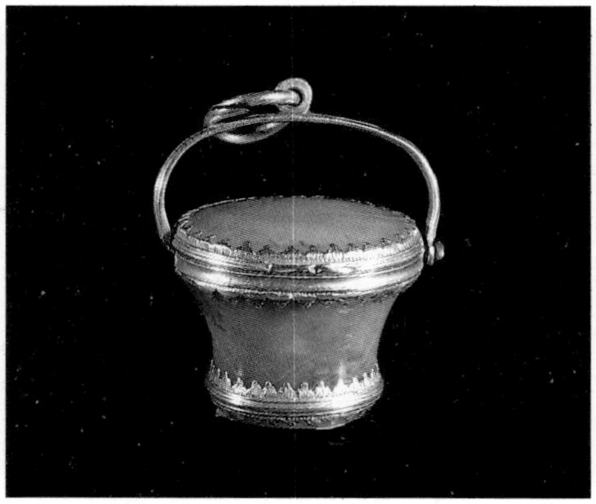

227. BASKET
Inv. Gems 1921, n° 394
Height 1.9 cm.; width 2.3 x 2.2 cm.
Agate, gold and copper
XVI century.

Basket with gold lid and setting; lined with copper.

An.M.M.

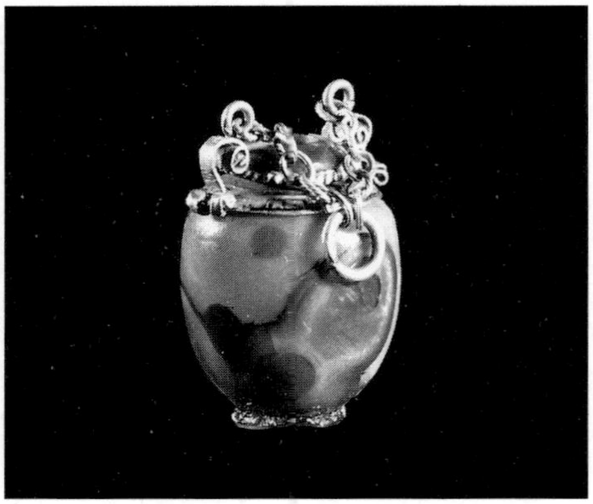

228. POT
Inv. O.d.A. 1911, n° 1111
Height 2.8 cm. with handles 3.2 cm.
Agate and gold
XVI century.

Urn shaped pot with enamelled gold setting and chain.

An.M.M.

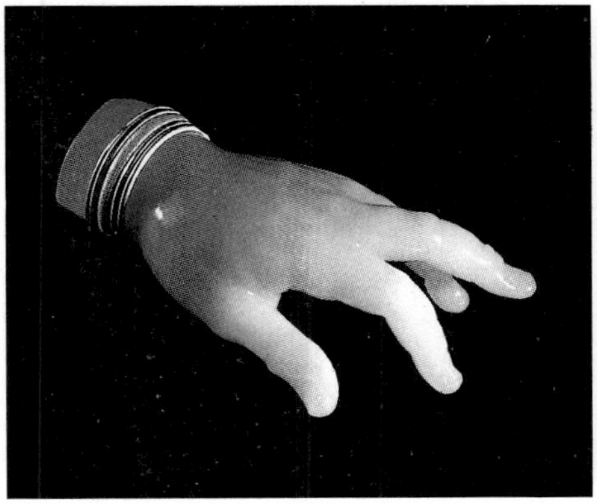

229. LEFT HAND
Inv. Gems 1921, n° 826
Length 7.3 cm.
Chalcedony and silver
XVI century.

The little finger was already broken in 1769, according to the inventory.

An.M.M.

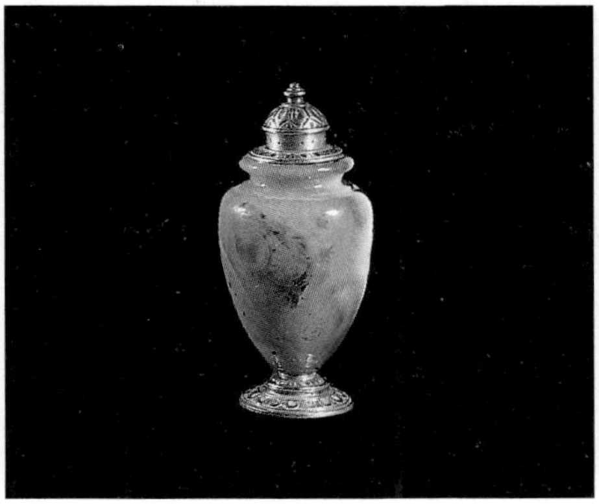

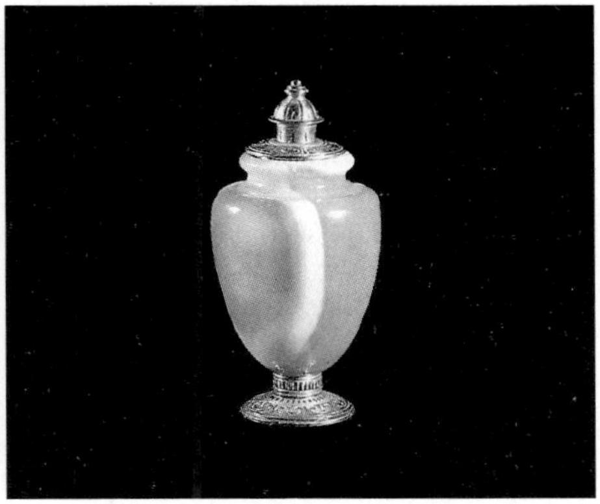

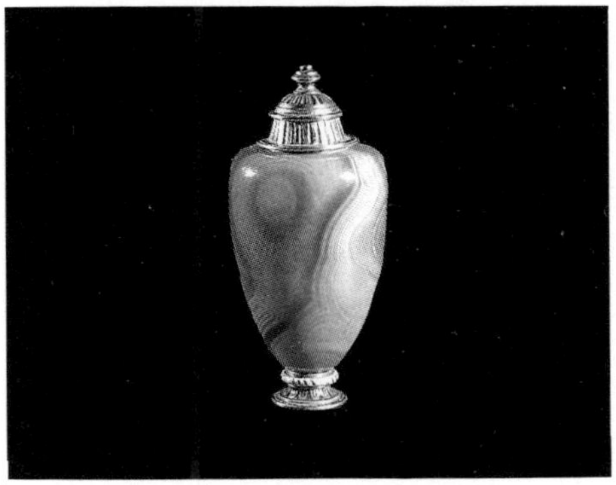

230.-231.-232. THREE POTS
Inv. Gems 1921, n° 628-629, 732
Height 5.5 cm.; diameter 2.7 cm.
Oriental agate and silver
XVI century.

Urn shaped pots with enamelled silver foot and lid.

An.M.M.

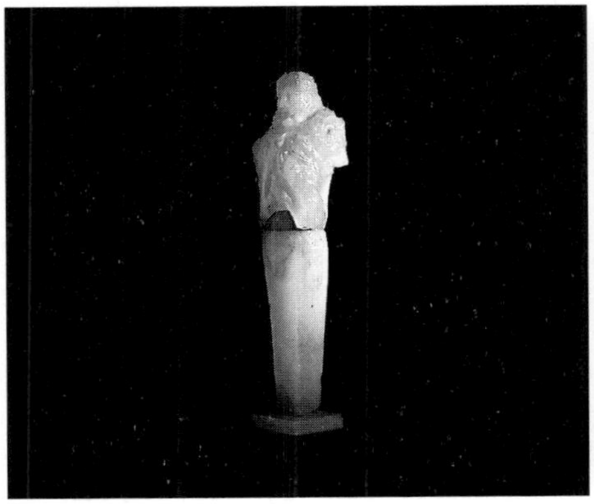

233. HERM
Inv. Gems 1921, n° 783
Height 14.7 cm.
Oriental chalcedony
XVI century.

Element with bust of Hercules with beard wrapped in lion's skin.

An.M.M.

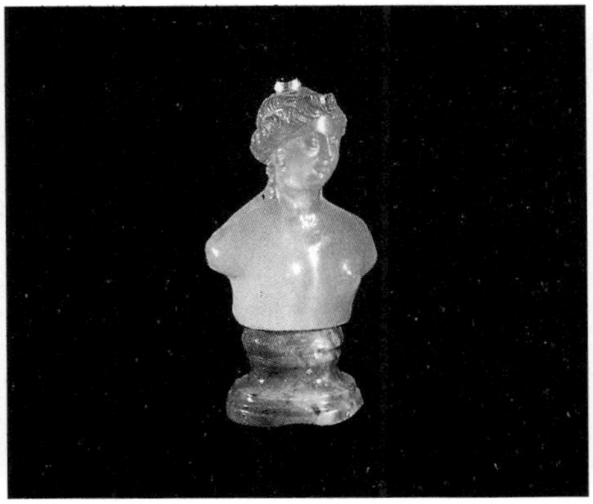

234. BUST
Inv. Gems 1921, n° 834
Height 3.1 cm.
Agate, gold, garnet
XVI century.

Female bust on jasper base with gold pin surmounted by garnet.

An.M.M.

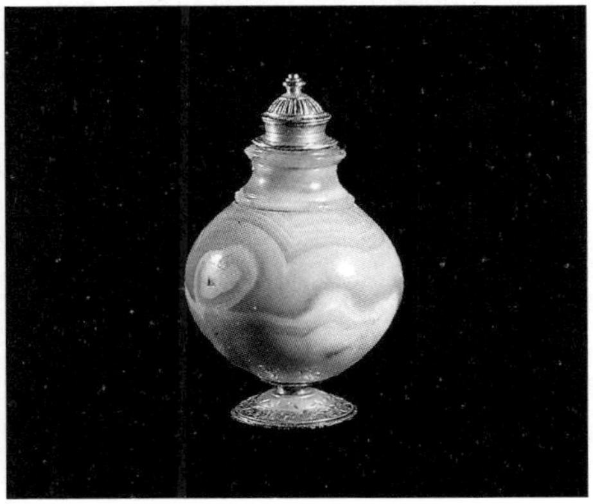

235. POT
Inv. Gems 1921, n° 630
Height 6.7 cm.; diameter 4.3 cm.
Oriental agate and silver
XVI century.

Olla shaped pot with enamelled silver foot and lid.

An.M.M.

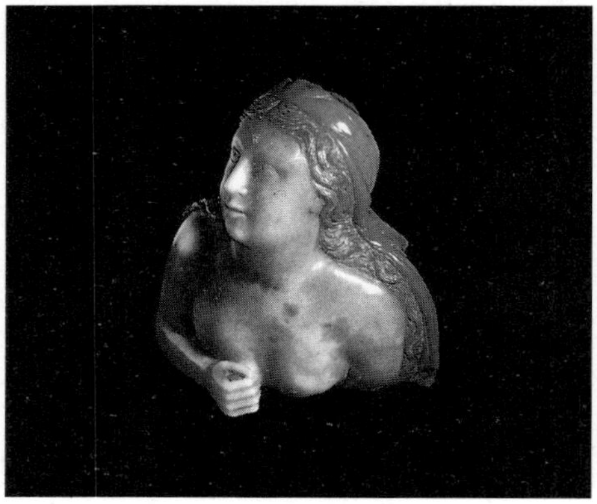

236. BUST
Inv. O.d.A. 1911, n° 1076
Height 5 cm.
Chalcedony
XVI century.
Female Bust. (Lucretia?)

An.M.M.

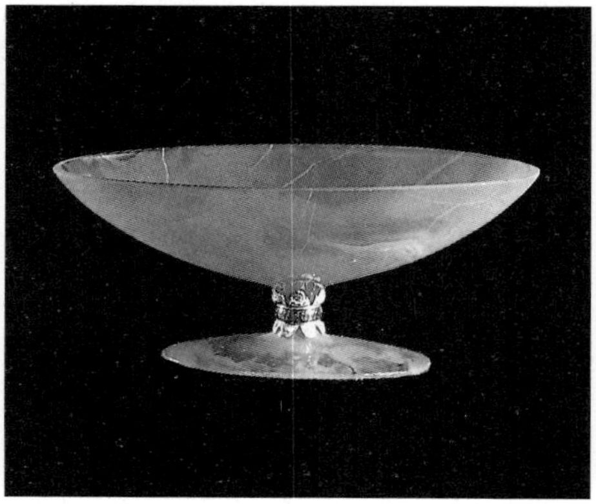

237. CUP
Inv. Gems 1921, n° 477
Height 3.8 cm.; width 4.7 x 9.5 cm.
Oriental chalcedony and gold
XVI century.
Oval shape cup with enamelled gold setting.

An.M.M.

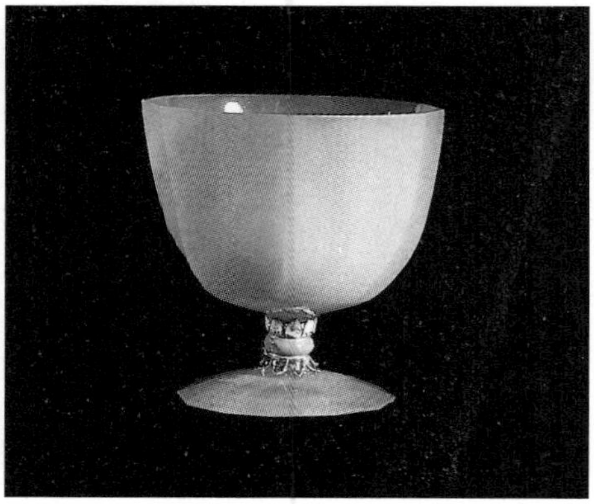

238. CUP
Inv. Gems 1921, n° 649
Height 6.5 cm.; width 5.3 x 6.6 cm.
Oriental chalcedony and gold
XVI century.
Dodecagon oval shaped cup with enamelled gold setting.

An.M.M.

239. VESSEL
Inv. Gems 1921, n° 788
Height 9.7 cm.; diameter 4.4 cm.
Oriental chalcedony and gold
XVI century.
Box shaped vessel with lid, mounted at the foot in enamelled gold.

An.M.M.

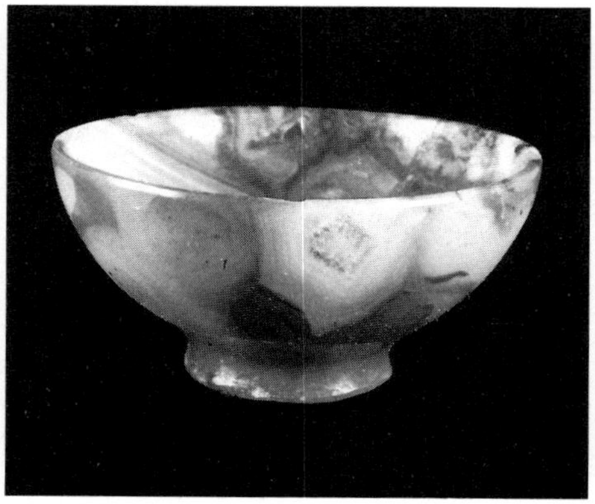

240. BOWL
Inv. Gems 1921, n° 546
Height 2.9 cm.; diameter 5.9 cm.
Cornelian breccia
XVI century.
Round in shape - carved out of one sole piece of material.

An.M.M.

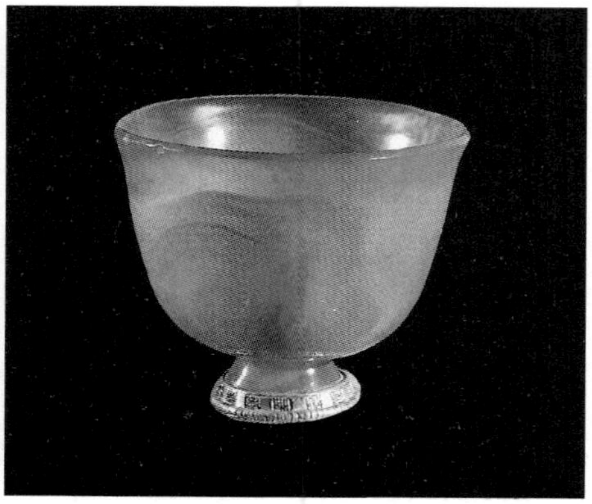

241. SMALL BOWL
Inv. Gems 1921, n° 677
Height 3.7 cm.; diameter 4.7 cm.
Oriental chalcedony and silver
XVI century.
Cup with enamelled silver gilt setting.

An.M.M.

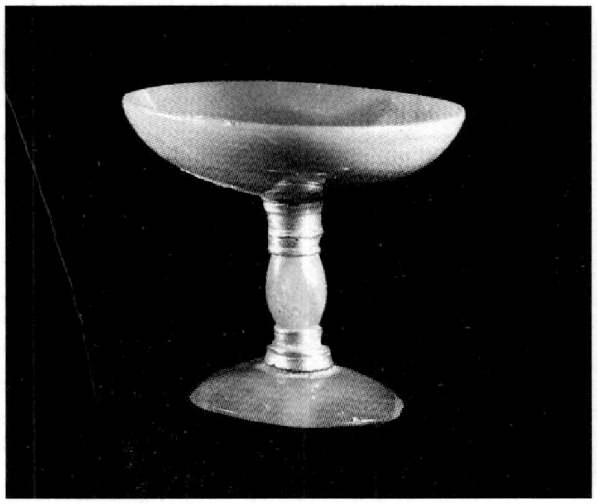

242. CUP
Inv. O.d.A. 1911, n° 1102
Height 4.8 cm.; width 4.5 x 5.6 cm.
Agate and silver
XVI century.

Oval in shape made out of three pieces with silver gilt setting.

An.M.M.

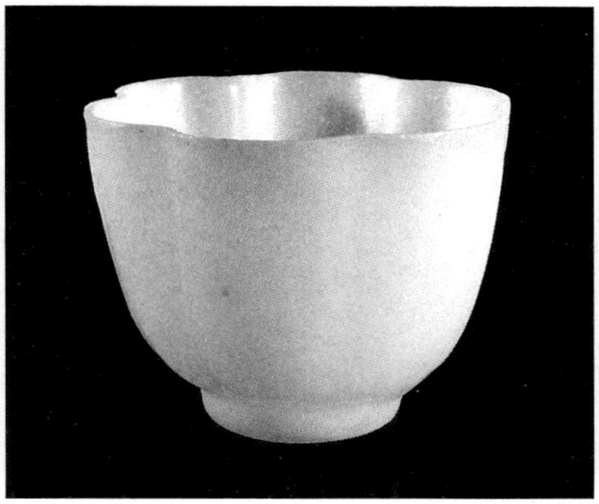

243. CUP
Inv. O.d.A. 1911, n° 1100
Height 3.9 cm.; diameter 5.1
Jade (?)
XVI century.

Round in shape, faceted, carved out of one sole piece of material.

An.M.M.

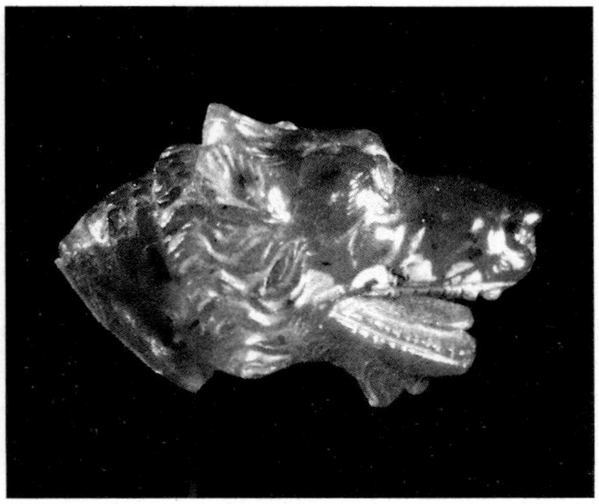

244. HEAD OF A DOG
Inv. O.d.A. 1911, n° 1113
Length 2.8 cm.
Emerald plasma
XVI century.

Small head of a dog.

An.M.M.

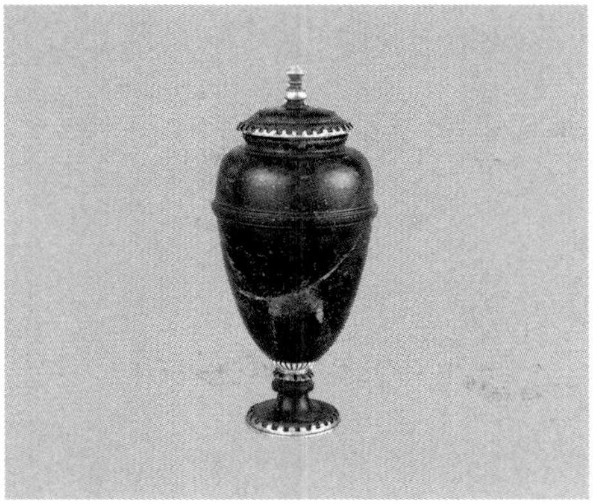

245. URN STYLE VASE
Florence, Museo degli Argenti
Inv. Gemme 1921, n. 658
From the Tribuna degli Uffizi
Cm. 13 high.
Lapislazuli and gilded and enamelled silver
Florentine manufacture of the end of the XVI century.

Pear-shaped urn in lapislazuli with a horizontal band sculptured on its shoulder. The urn rests on a low step bordered by a small gilded silver band connected to the urn's body by a double gilded and enamelled silver ring. The cover is made of lapislazuli and the cuspidate knob is made of gilded silver. The original mounting has been partly tampered with.

Gioielli e Ornamenti Preziosi, n° 211.

An.M.M.

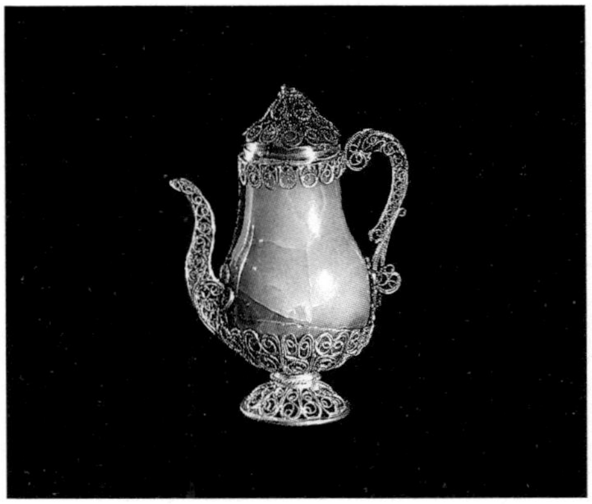

246. COFFEE-POT
Inv. Gems 1921, n° 591
Height 6.6 cm.; diameter 3 cm.
Oriental agate and silver
XVI century.

Vessel mounted in the shape of a coffee-pot in silver filigree.

An.M.M.

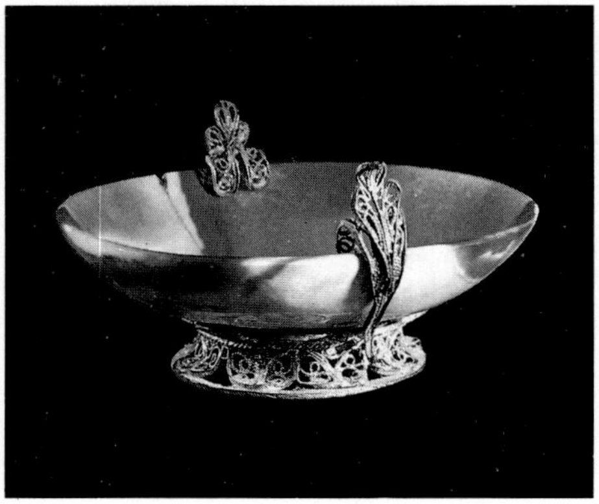

247. BOWL
Inv. Gems 1921, n° 684
Height 3.8 cm.; width 7.6 x 7.7 cm.
Oriental Agate and silver
XVII century.

Oval bowl with silver filigree setting.

An.M.M.

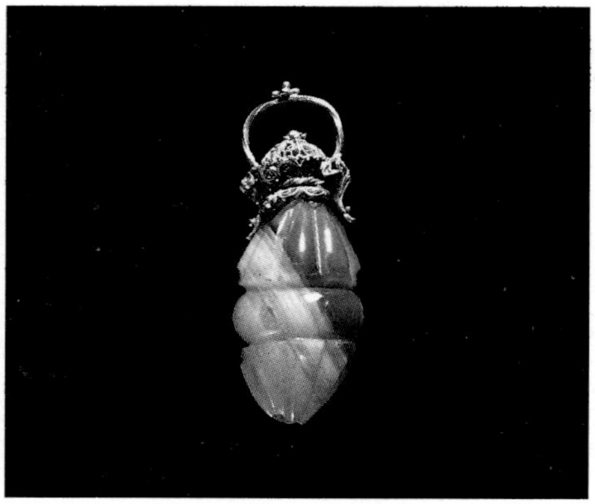

248. SMALL BOTTLE
Inv. O.d.A. 1911, n° 1112
Height 3.6 cm.; diameter 1.3 cm.
Chalcedony
XVII century.

Engraved stone, with loop-hole, with small lid and handle in gold filigree.

An.M.M.

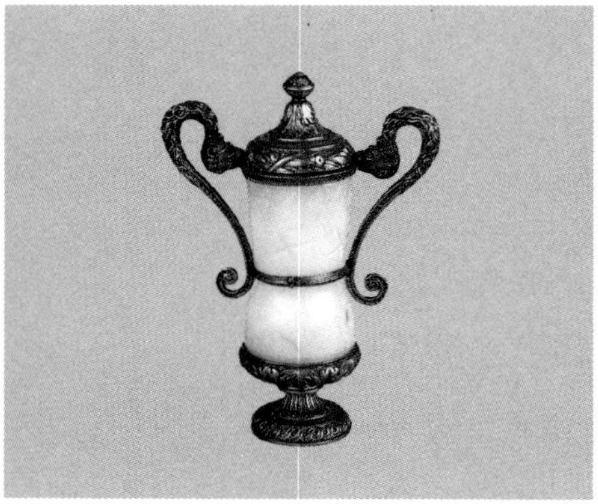

249. CYLINDRICAL STYLE VASE
Florence, Museo degli Argenti
Inv. Gemme 1921, n° 494
From the Tribuna degli Uffizi
Cm. 14,5 high.
Oriental agate, gilded silver, embossed and engraved
Antique vase mounting: Florentine craftsmanship of the XVII century.

Cylindrical vase made of oriental agate with geometric intagli on its upper half. The piece rests on a base of gilded silver, embossed along the border with a plaited pattern and on the pedestal with a bean-shaped motif. The raised spiral-like handles are made of gilded silver, and are attached to the rim of the vase's border by small lion heads and to the band situated below, midway down the vase.
The base of the vase is coated in gilded silver with an embossed and engraved leaves' motif. The pointed cover is coated with gilded silver, has a scalloped edge and an acanthus leaves motif on the cusp and on the knob.

Gioielli e Ornamenti Preziosi, n° 212.

An.M.M.

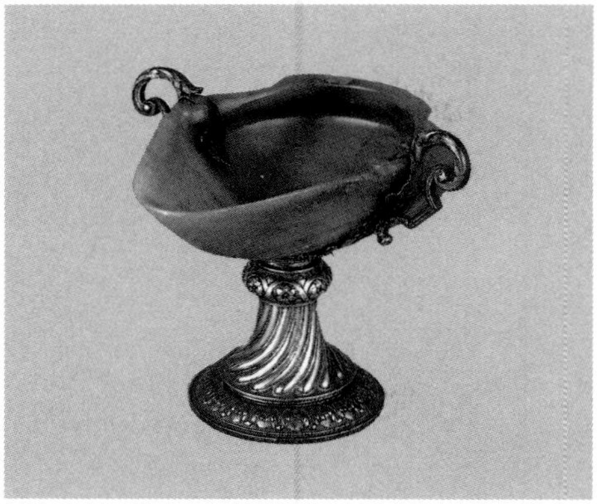

250. BOWL
Florence, Museo degli Argenti
Inv. Gemme 1921, n° 695
From the inheritance of the Grand Prince Ferdinand who died in the year 1713
Cm. 4,7 high; with handles cm. 7,7
Jasper, amethyst and crystal, gilded silver.
Bowl: Florentine craftsmanship of the second half of the XVII century.
Mounting: Sicilian craftsmanship of the second half of the XVII century.

Oval shaped arched bowl made of jasper. The raised handles are made of gilded silver filigree, with eight crystals and octagonal-shaped faceted amethysts set on the highest points of the handles. The bowl rests on a low pedestal made of gilded silver lamina.

Gioielli e Ornamenti Preziosi, n° 213.

An.M.M.

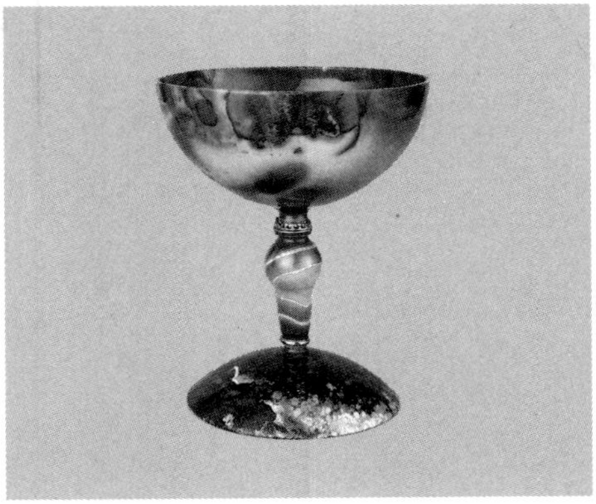

251. CUP
Florence, Museo degli Argenti
Inv. Gemme 1921, n° 667
From Palazzo Pitti, sent to the Uffizi Gallery in 1771
Cm. 19x15
Agate, gilded silver
Florentine manufacture of the XVII century.

Cup made of agate on a high balustrade pedestal connected to a round base by two bands of gilded silver.

Gioielli e Ornamenti Preziosi, n° 214.

An.M.M.

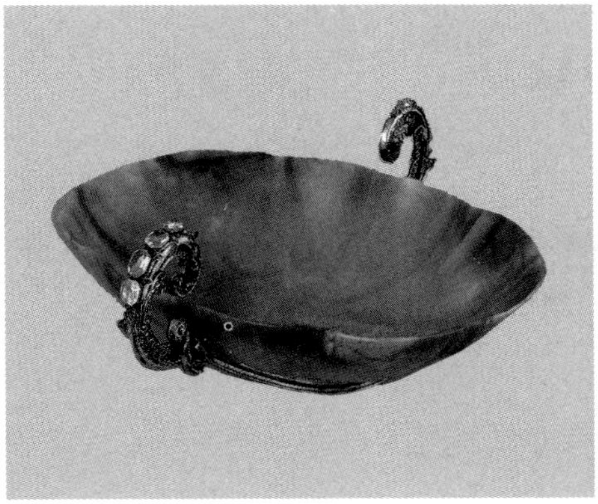

252. Shell-Type BOWL
Florence, Museo degli Argenti
Inv. Gemme 1921, n° 476
From Palazzo Pitti, sent to the Uffizi Gallery in 1771
Cm. 11 high; with handles cm. 11,7
Jasper, gilded silver and rosettes
Florentine manufacture of the first half of the XVII century.

Oblong shaped bowl made of jasper. Bean-shaped motifs are engraved over half of the piece while the other half is decorated with a spiral pattern. The piece rests on a high gilded silver base. The border of the foot is decorated with a leaf motif; a bean-shaped spiral decoration adorns the pedestal, while rosettes decorate the knot situated at the bowl juncture. The handles are made of gilded silver.

Gioielli e Ornamenti Preziosi, n° 215.

An.M.M.

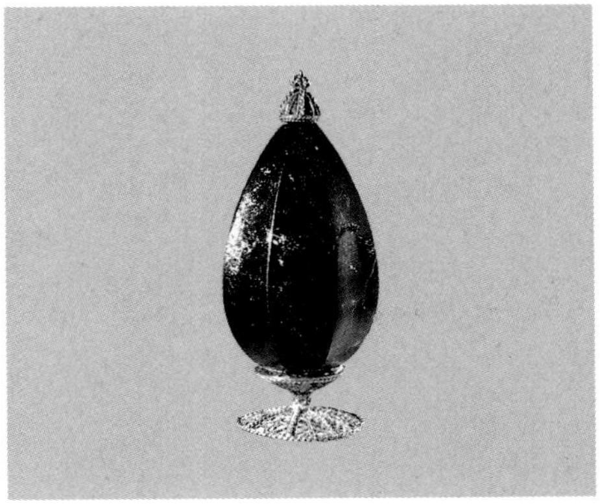

253. SCENT BOTTLE
Inv. Gems 1921, n° 700
Height 8.7 cm.; diameter 4.1 cm.
Lapislazuli and gold
XVII century.

Faceted drop-shaped pot with lid and foot in gold.

An.M.M.

THE ANCIENT PERIOD
GLOSSARY OF TERMS

ACERRA [—]	Type of turibolo (thurible, or metal container) shown in ancient illustrations in the priestesses' hands.
ALABASTRON [—]	Small, cylindrical-shaped flask with a short neck used as containers for perfumed oils and unctions. The name derives from the material of which they were originally made (alabaster), even though they were later made of clay, glass or metal.
ARDIGLIONE	see FIBULA
ARCO	see FIBULA
ARIBALLOS [—]	Small, round or oval-shaped vessel used for perfume or oil, with a narrow neck and a single handle, particularly diffused in Greece in archaic times (9th-7th century B.C.).
ARMILLA [—]	Gold bracelet that the Romans gave to warriors as a reward for acts of valour.
BACCELLATURA [—]	Decorative piece typically found in classical architecture made of kidney-shaped ornaments in relief.
BALTEO	Belt worn «across the shoulders» by Roman soldiers from which they hung their daggers.
BORCHIA [STUD]	Small metal disc crafted in various ways as an ornament for clothes, furniture, etc.
BULLA [—]	Round, medallion similar to a «borchia» worn as an amulet by children until they reach adulthood.
BULINO [SCALPEL]	Steel tool, similar to a scalpel for engraving metals.
CADUCEO [—]	Rod with two, symmetrically entwined snakes and two wings at the top, symbol of Mercury, representing prosperity and peace.
CAMMEO [MULTI LAYERED STONE]	Work in relief using complementary colours and different thichnesses in order to emphasize the polycromy and fullbody of the surface.
CATENA [CHAIN NECKLACE]	Technique by which gold and silver was worked which involved bending a round wire to form single rings closed by soldering, which formed a curve and were linked together.

CHIMERA
[CHIMERA]
Horrific monster which caused disaster and tragedy that was invincible. Born of the union between Typhoeus and Echidna. It was a beast taking three forms, with the front of a lion, the middle of a wild goat and the back of a dragon. From its mouth came flames and poison. It was finally defeated by Bellerophon on his famous horse, Pegasus.

CISTA
[CIST]
Box used to contain female toilette items.

CORNUCOPIA [—]
The horn of plenty. Horn-shaped vessel overflowing with fruit or flowers. Symbol of fertility.

CRATERE [—]
Large vessel where water and wine was mixed during banquets. Taking various styles in the development of its base, bowl, rim and handles.

DITTICO [—]
Double, waxed writing-tablet that could be doubled over, used as an almanac.

ELMO
[HELMET]
Iron, metal or leather piece of armour with crest or visor, which covered the head and part of the neck.

FIBULA
[BROOCH]
Decorative brooch in the form of a safety-pin, usually made of bronze. Its name derives from the thin, sharp, shin-bone which was used in more ancient times as a brooch.

FIORINO
[FLORIN]
Gold coin introduced by the Republic in 1252 in Florence. The name comes from the flower or lily depicted on it.

FUSAIOLO [—]
A heavy ring that is placed round a notch at the base of a spindle to enable it to spin at a constant speed.

KLINE [—]
A single or double bed on which guests could lie, propped up with cushions so as to remain sitting up during banquets.

IPOGEO
[HYPOGEUM]
Underground tomb.

INTAGLIO
[CARVING]
Precious or hard stone on which figures are obtained using a deep, negative relief.

LARARIUM [—]
Part of a Roman house reserved for worship constisting of a shrine. An essential part of this was

	a painting of the family spirit, found between the two «Lari». Below the altar or «ara» one, or two snakes were represented with offerings. Apart from the painting on the «larcurio» there were also sacred relics and votive gifts.
MODONATURA [—]	These rose up from the ground and reinforced the cornices giving them proportion.
OIONICHE [—]	Wine jug with body of varying roundness, three-lobed rim and upright handle.
OLPE [—]	Long, rather thin wine jug with round rim.
ORIENTALIZZANTE [—]	This term refers to the widespread imitation of oriental objects and designs in western Mediterranean countries, particularly Greece and Italy. This phenomena occurred between the 8th and the 6th centuries.
PASTICHE [—]	A mixture of various styles and periods.
PATERA [—]	Small, bowl-shaped cup without handles, used to offer libations to the gods.
PISSIDE [PYX]	Small, round vessel with lid.
SCARABEO [BEETLE]	Hard stone crafted into shape of beetle on undersurface. These figures were used as personal seals and were pierced from one side to another and threaded onto rings where they could be rotated.
SCIFO [—]	Drinking cup with cut-off cone shape and two, small handles.
SFINGE [SPHINX]	Monster with winged lion's body and woman's head which, standing on the top of a rock, would stop travellers and ask them a very difficult riddle. If the unfortunate wayfarer failed to solve the puzzle, he was thrown over the precipice. Edipus was to defeat her.
SITULA [—]	Cut-off cone-shaped container with narrow base.
STIPE [—]	Latin term meaning votive offering, used in archeology to refer to the group of votive offerings discovered in store rooms and utility cupboards in various sacred sites. What's more, these pieces have been found on waste heaps, thrown there in ancient times when they became too many.

TENIA [—]	Headband used by priests and wound round the head of the winner of a race or competion. It represented divine protection.
TRIPODE [TRIPOD]	Three-legged, bronze stool where Azia sat and gave forth in the sanctuary at Delphi.
TUMULO [TUMULUS]	Low, round or oval hill rising above one or more graves. This was often surrounded by a ditch with remains either buried underground, or in a burial chamber.
UNGUENTARIO [—]	Small vessel used to contain ointment or other pharmaceutical preparations.
ZECCA [MINT]	State-owned workshop where coins are issued.

THE MIDDLE AGES AND THE RENAISSANCE
GLOSSARY OF TERMS

CALICE
[GOBLET]

Sacred vessel of primary importance in Christian liturgy in which wine is consecrated during the service.

Used until the beginning of Christianity as a drinking vessel of glass, wood or bone. In Italy, probably the oldest to be inherited by us are those dated 6th century B.C. The silver treasures of (Cathedral Museum, Città di Castello) and the treasures of Galognano (near Poggibonsi, but in storage at the Fine Arts Commission in Siena).

In Venice there are examples of Byzantine traditions dated between the 9th and the 12th century, with cups made of gemstone and set in precious metal. The sacred vessels, according to liturgical prescriptions, had to be made of a substance which didn't absorb liquid. Metal was therefore used and if the metal wasn't noble or silver the cup was gold plated on the inside.

CORONE PER IMMAGINE SACRE
[CROWNS FOR SACRED IMAGES]

Ornaments of circular shape to adorn sacred images, particularly statues of the Madonna and Child. The custom to crown images of the Madonna is ancient (8th Century) and is documented throughout the Middle Ages and the Renaissance and very widespread in the 17th century.

The crowns were generally made of precious metal. Those made of base metal contain gold and silver plating and are made using techniques of embossment, engraving, lightened with perforations and enriched with enamelled precious stones and simple glass.

CROCE ASTILE

A processional cross generally fixed on a pole using its extendable vertical shaft.

The oldest ones didn't have a pole and were carried by hand (as can be seen in the saints by Margarito on the covering cloth of the Madonna of Glory, at Monte San Savino).

The image of the crucifix appeared around the 9th century.

By the 13th century the angular crosses or those

with reinforced endings gave way to a richer style with three or more metal, crystal or precious stone spheres set into the extremities.
During the 12th and 13th centuries gold-plated bronze crosses were widespread, whilst in the 14th century crosses with translucent enamels became common and were to last for subsequent centuries.
During the Renaissance there followed a high-quality output with the contribution of famous artists (the Pollaiolo cross and the Luca della Robbia), later, after the Counter Reformation the decorative patterns diminished and subsequently took new, spectacular forms in the Baroque style.

ENCOLPIO

A Small cross of base metal (apart from rare exceptions) with a double valve and a hinge with a pin at the top to allow for vertical extension.
The surfaces generally portray images of Jesus and Mary.
It was worn around the neck on a cord by pilgrims coming back from the Holy Lands. The «encolpio» which is in reality a religious shrine, could, also contain, small, internal cavities in which relics and offerings from sacred places were put. They were generally made in Palestine to be sold to pilgrims. Its wide diffusion suggests it was a product for the people and were found throughout Italy especially in the 11th and 12th centuries.

FERMAGLIO DA PIVIALE
[CLASP FOR A CEREMONIAL CLOAK]

A clasp, generally made of precious metal which closed a ceremonial cope (cloak) at the breast.
It was the privilege of Bishops, Cardinals and the Pope to wear it around the 10th century.

NAVICELLA
[INCENSE-BOAT]

A metal container in the shape of a Small ship used to hold grains of incense to burn in the thurible.
It was used mainly in the 14th century but it seems that it also existed previously in the form of a simple container.
There are also very valuable models decorated with enamel, engravings, and rare combinations of enamelling and chasing.
In the 14th and 15th centuries the structure was very

simple and elegants — in profile it was almost a half moon but successive baroque models assumed a heavier, more elaborate style, taking on the shape of a galleon ship.

OSTENSORIO
[MONSTRANCE]

A receptacle in which the consecrated Most is exposed for adoration.
The custom of exposing the Eucharist originated at the beginning of the 13th century and became practised custom when the celebration of Corpus Christi began in the middle of the same century.
The receptacle derived its shape from the surrounding shrine and ciborium. It became widely used in the 17th century and hept its original form in the following centuries. From the middle of the 17th century a type of receptacle with a decorated stem in place of the simple one was quite common (figure of an angel, a saint or a cardinal virtue).
The parts, which fixed the Host and its rest for display, were generally made of gold or gold plated metal.

PACE
[PAX]

Liturgical object generally a tablet with a holy image which was used to offer the «Kiss of peace» before Communion. It appeared in England in the 12th century and then spread to France, Germany and soon afterwards to Spain.
The «pax» were generally made of metal and various other models were reproduced from a prototype mold. Here we refer to those with illustrated figures and bas-relief. There are also valuable ones in enamel, with engravings and niello. S. Carlo Borromeo gave indications that the «pax» was probably made of gold or silver and metal showing the dead body of Christ supported by the Virgin Mary. As a matter of fact this iconography is seen more frequently but models with illustrations of the Resurrection, the deposition of Christ from the Cross, the Crucifixion and other figurations have also been found. Today this object is no longer in use.

PISSIDE [CIBORIUM]

A goblet-shaped lidded vessel used to hold consecrated Wafers in Holy Communion.
Containers used for this purpose were in existence from the beginning of Christianity. The oldest ciboriums were tower-shaped, mostly cylindrical with a hinged lid. They could be made of wood, bone, ivory, or metal. Those made of metal and decorated with enamel were in widespread use during the 12th and 13th centuries.
The adoption of ciboriums which rested on a stem and feet in the 13th century led to the disappearance of the tower-shaped vessels.
Later on, the shape of the ciborium slowly began to resemble the chalice with a larger cup and a small cross on the top of the lid.
During the Counter Reformation this typology was established definitively and in following centuries the only variation was in terms of volume, and stylistic changes with decorations adhering to the era.

RELIQUIARIO [RELIQUARY]

The reliquary is a casing which preserves and exhibits sacred relics. The relics consisted of mortal remains of Saints and items ascribed to them, including those which traditionally related to the Madonna and Christ.
The custom of venerating relics originated with Christianity and is derived from the worship of the Martyrs.
Reliquaries were divided into very diverse typologies, from those called «capselle» in use by the 4th century which were placed inside the altar, to those exposed for adoration. The latest of these in the Pre-Romanic age, with the comeback of crafting in gold, were also made with valuable materials and very rare gems.
At the same time that these small reliquary cases were in use there were also «anthropomorphous» variations alluding to the relics (such as an arm, foot or head etc.) which were housed in them, and more so than the boxes, caskets and other types of

reliquary, they acknowledged the high spirituality of the Middle Ages.
Other types of reliquary were made in the form of crosses; «zoomorphous» (with animals linked to Christian symbolism) «phytomorphous» (plant remains) and «encolpio» (small crosses).
During the Gothic period the typology of the «bust» and «architectonic» reliquaries were the most common and continued to be so for the whole of the Renaissance.
During the Baroque period all churches had an extraordinary number of reliquaries but by the 19th century the fervor had died out.

TURIBOLO
[THURIBILE]

A metal receptacle for burning incense.
In catholic liturgy it was in use by the 4th century and from the 9th century onwards it was used as an incense burner during Mass.
Primitive thuribiles were boxes, either round or hexagonal, resting on three feet or upright chains.
Handmade thuribiles in Medieval times assumed a spheroid shape and consisted of a cup and a lid with four chains joined to a ring. Later on architectonic styles were infused with obvious symbolic reference to the «building ideals of Celestial Jerusalem».
In the 14th century, the form of thuribiles became decisively architectonic, taking on architectural style analogous with the times (elongated shapes with towers and pinnacles). They lasted throughout the Renaissance period, aligning themselves with the new concepts of «proportion». The reference to miniaturized architecture was lost in the 17th century, being replaced by decorative floral patterns which transformed it into a «flaming vessel».
The thuribile is a cup-shaped metal receptacle resting on a base which contains a carbon burner on which the grains at incense are placed. The container is closed with a perforated lid to allow burning which nourishes the air and the release of fragrance.

GLOSSARY OF TECHNIQUES

Ancient goldsmiths, when making ornamental pieces, used a variety of techniques and tools which differed according to the effect desired.

AGEMINAZIONE

This form of decoration was obtained by inlaying metals of different colors in special dovetailed grooves on a base made of a harder metal. The inlay was fixed by hammening the gold, silver and copper wires into place. Subsequently the surface was filed to remove rough edges and polished.

CATENE [CHAINS]

The most common type of gold and silver chain was called «fiocco in fiocco». The rounded wire was bent to form single rings which were soldered together, shaped to form a cuve and then hooked one to another. This base could be made more sophisticated by doubling or tripling the rings or links and combining them with different chains to form strings of chains. When this stage was completed, the chain was slightly flattened using a hammer which gave it a plaited look. The ends were covered with small foil tubes.

DORATURA [GOLD-PLATING]

Gold-plating silver and bronze objects was a common feature of ancient gold craftwork. Plating consisted of hammering gold leaf onto the object and alternating this with annealing until red hot which restored the original molecular structure of the metals. Intricate brooches could not be hammered in this way and so a thicker sheet of gold was bent into place and fixed on using clips.

This technique of gold-plating using mercury as an amalgam, as it was originally employed remains a mystery, even though the Etruscans were most probably familiar with this liquid metal because it existed in the metal-bearing hills of the Maremma region of Italy.

Today industrial gold-plating is done using electroplating. The objects to be plated are galvanized with gold in a salt solution.

FILI [WIRE-DRAWING]

Wires of various sizes were made from thin sheets. These were rounded using hammers and then

passed through threading dies made of hard stone, bronze or iron (a technique that is still used today), or, move commonly, twisted to make round wires that were largely regular inshape.
Another example of finishing off gold thread or wire was knurling which was carried out by applying pressure with a tool equipped with several blades which gave remarkable decorative effects.

FILIGRANA
[FILIGREE]

Widespread in Mesopotamia from the 3rd century B.C., this technique of using gold threads to create decorative designs was very common in Etruscan gold craftwork during the «orientalizzante» period. Twisted threads of varying thickness (in an «armilla» found in Vetulonia these were a mere two-tenths of a millimetre thick) were soldered onto a piece of foil or plate giving life and texture to the flat surface.
More commonly, the Etruscans preferred a technique called «a giorno» which involved molding the thread into various twists and curves inside an empty frame set in a sheet of gold. The parts were then soldered together and onto the supporting structure.

FUSIONE
[FUSION]

The first objects made using the fusion process were found in Mesopotamia and date back to 3,500 years B.C. These were made using a simple method called «open fusion», which consisted of filling a hollow mold made of hard stone or clay with a stream of fused metal. Once the metal was cold and had taken the form of the hollow space, it was deburred and finished off using a chisel.
This method was only effective with flat pieces, it did not allow for rounded pieces or oblique angles and so the methed called lost wax casting (cire perdue) was adopted. An object modelled in wax had a cone-shaped attachment to it and was then immersed in a thick coating of clay. When this dried the little attachment wsa pierced, the piece was turned upside down and heated so as to melt the wax and harden the clay mold. Before it cooled the molten metal was poured into the hollow through

the attachment hole. When this solidified, the whole thing was plunged into cold liquid to shatter the mould and free the object inside This was then filed and chiselled to perfection.
Nowadays a technique called «microfusion» is used which repeats the old process of lost was casting with some variations and new techniques. The original technique fascinated Cellini so much that he described his casting of Perseus with great enthusiam and anxiety. Today mercury can be used instead of wax (solidified by freezing), and the casing is made in a vacuum to avoid the little bubbles that frequently form (which then show up as little spots on the finished model). What's more the molten metal is inserted using a centrifuge to speed up the process and obtain improved compactness and adherence to the model's surface.

GRANULAZIONE
[GRANULATION]

This technique was used from the 3rd century B.C. by peoples in Asia, Egypt, the Aegean Islands and Greece. It entered Etruria as a result of Phoenician influence in the 7th century B.C. and was developed to produce highly refined and sophisticated works. It fell into disuse in Roman times and after, inspite of sporadic attempts to revive it, it dropped out of use.
This technique consisted of placing tiny, gold spheres on a sheet of gold, soldering them into place and to each other, and so creating a wide variety of decorative designs.
The tiny spheres or grains were obtained by cutting threads of gold leaf into pieces, which were then placed in layers of carbon powder with added flux in a crucible. This was heated until the gold's point of fusion was reached, at which time the little pieces of thread and foil melted forming spheres.

INCISIONE
[ENGRAVING]

Engraving is a completely different process from chasing although they are sometimes confused with each other. The difference is that the chisel used in chasing dents the metal without removing any, while the burin and the «ciappola» with their sharp tip remove a shaving of the metal.

Some Egyptian jewellery dated 2000 B.C. have engraved parts believed to have been done using sharpened tools made of precious stones. The technique of engraving with a burin wasn't used on a wide scale until the advent of iron and steel tools.

There are several methods of engraving: the «aquaforte» or «strong water» as it used to be called, employed nitric acid to eat away the metal surface; engravings were produced on an industrial level with the help of mechanized instruments such as the pantograph, the *diamantatrici*, and the «guilloche» (the latter being an old technique used in the 19th century by Fabergé while serving the Tzars); currently photogravure is common as well as the latest technique of electro-erosion, also used to manufacture stamps and dies.

NIELLO
[NIELLO]

The name derives from the latin «nigellum», which means «blackish» and in fact consists of a sulphur mix containing lead, copper and silver sulphides which are black in colour.

This mixture used to be applied predominant to silver that had previously been engraved so as to emphasize the relief effect.

The finely ground niello powder was mixed with gum and painted on the engraved parts. This was left to dry and then heated to 100°C in a kiln or by blowtorch, which melted the mixture allowing it to spread along the incisions. After cooling, the surfaces were filed down to the metal underneath in parts to highlight the contrast with the black engravings.

SBALZO E CESELLO
[EMBOSSMENT AND CHASING]

Embossment is one of the oldest and most refined techniques of crafting gold, and is carried out on sheets of metal that have previously been fixed to blocks of hot pitch. The design is then traced onto the sheet and the outline and details to be embossed are pricked onto the surface. Then, using mostly wide, round, smooth pieces of iron, called embossment irons, and a special hammer, the sheet is beaten. The pitch, which contains animal fats and bees' wax, absorbs the blows, allowing the metal to bulge yet protecting it with its elasticity. Thus the metal is distorted like plastic, taking the form of the design and produces buckles or «sbalzi» from which the technique derives its Italian name «lo sbalzo».

This process is done in negative relief from underneath.

The metal is alternately embossed and annealed (or reheated) to avoid ruptures when hardening. Annealing establishes the metal's original structure. Once the embossing stage is finished, the molded sheet or panel is removed from the pitch and, after any hollows created by the negative embossment have been filled up with pitch once more, the topside is finished off.

The final stage is done using thin, blunt irons called «ceselli» (chisels). These are used to accentuate outlines blurred by the embossment; to pick out the different designs; to accentuate oblique cavities and to add subtle and refined decorative details. Chasing or chiselling is therefore a valued and sophisticated way of finishing off the top surface of pieces.

SMALTO [ENAMELLING]

Enamel decorations are done by a technique which adds metal oxides to glass powder to obtain various colors. The mixture, with the addition of water is applied to the metal to be decorated using a paintbrush. Various metals and alloys can be decorated this way: gold, silver, copper, bronze and brass. Iron is rarely used and it is impossible to enamel platinum because the glass powder will not adhere to it. Once the powder has been applied to the metal it is baked in the oven, bearing in mind that the enamels' metting points vary according to the metal oxide utilized. For this reason the enamels with the highest melting points are baked first.

An extremely shiny finish can be achieved by applying very thin layers of enamel and baking repeatedly.
The major processes and methods of enamelling were recorded in the 11th century by the monk Theophilus. One was the «champlevé» method by which grooves cut in the metal base vere filled in with enamed colors, and the other, the «cloisonné» in which metal strips or wires were placed on edge on the base and then filled up with enamel.
In the Gothic period the «translucent» type became widespread. Here, a thin layer of enamel was applied to a previously engraved metal surface which accentuated the design according to the depth of the grooves.
Both French and Sienese workshops became famous for their use of this technique.
The use of enamels and glass powder dates back to ancient times. Examples have been found in Caucasus graves belonging the first millenium B.C. The oldest remains originate in the East (bracelets found in Oxus' treasure are important examples and are dated 7th century B.C.).
The fusing of enamels in filigree settings was common in ancient Greece and particularly widespread in Asia Minor, and amongst Shiitic and Etrurian civilisations and hence in Rome.
As the adoption of coloured semi-precious stones became common, enamels were forgotten for a centuries until they were revived in the period of the Byzanthine Empire and the Middle Ages. In Gothic times, Sienese enamellists were to influence artists and their paintings.

STAMPO
[STAMPING]

If it was necessary to produce a decoration repeatedly, punches were used to beat the panel using the embossing process.

BIBLIOGRAPHY

AGDS II	*Antike Gemmen in Deutschen Sammlungen. Staatliche Museen Preussischer Kulturbesitz Antikenabteilung Berlin*, München, 1969.
AGOSTINI	A. AGOSTINI, *Dialoghi delle Medaglie*, Roma 1592.
AG. WIEN II	*Die antiken Gemmen des Kunsthistorischen Museums in Wien*, München, 1979.
AREZZO 1987	*Il Museo Archeologico Nazionale G.C. Mecenate in Arezzo*, Firenze 1987.
ARTE AUREA ARETINA	*Arte Aurea Aretina. Oreficeria aretina attraverso i secoli, Catalogo della Mostra - Arezzo*, Firenze 1985.
ARTE AUREA ARETINA II	*Arte Aurea Aretina II - Oreficeria aretina attraverso i secoli, Catalogo della Mostra - Arezzo*, Firenze 1988.
ARTE AUREA ARETINA 1987	*Arte Aurea Aretina. Manifatture Europee in terra di Arezzo, Catalogo della Mostra - Arezzo*, Firenze 1987.
BABELON	E. BABELON, *Description Historique et chronologique des, Monnaies de la Republique Romaine*, Paris-London, 1885-1886 vol. I.
BALDWIN	A. BALDWIN BRETT, *Catalogue of the Greek Coins. Museum of Fine Arts Boston*, New York, 1974.
BMC	*British Museum Catalogue of Greek Coins. Crete and Argian Islands*, London, 1886.
CARTARI	*Le imagini con la sposizione de i dei degli antichi raccolta per Vincenzo Cartari*, Venezia, 1556.
CENTO PREZIOSI ETRUSCHI	*Cento Preziosi Etruschi, Catalogo della Mostra - Arezzo*, Firenze 1984.
CHOUL	G. CHOUL, *Discorso della religione antica dei Romani Lyon*, 1558.
CNI	*Corpus Numimorum Italicorum*, XI, Toscana, secche minori, Milano, 1929.
CRAWFORD	M.H. CRAWFORD, *Roman Republic Coinage*, Cambridge, 1975.
DAVID	M. DAVID, *Le Museum de Florence I*, VIII, Paris, 1799-1802.
DONATI	V. DONATI, *Pietre dure e medaglie del Rinascimento. Giovanni da Castel Bolognese*, Ferrara, 1989.
ETRUSKER IN DER TOSKANA	*Etrusker in der Toskana. Etruskische Gräber der Frünzeit, Katalog der Ausstellung - Hamburg*, Firenze, 1987.
GALOPPI NAPPINI 1987	D. GALOPPI NAPPINI, in *Il Museo Statale d'Arte Medievale e Moderna in Arezzo. Le oreficerie*, Firenze 1987.
GARRUCCI	R. GARRUCCI, *Le monete dell'Italia antica*, Roma, 1885.
GIOIELLI E ORNAMENTI	*Gioielli e Ornamenti dagli Egizi all'Alto Medioevo, Catalogo della Mostra - Arezzo*, Firenze, 1988.
GIOIELLI E ORNAMENTI PREZIOSI	*Tesori dei Musei Toscani, Gioielli e Ornamenti Preziosi dagli Etruschi al Rinascimento, Catalogo della Mostra - Tokyo*, Tokyo, 1991.
GIULIANO	A. GIULIANO, *I Cammei della Collezione Medicea del Museo Archeologico di Firenze*, Roma, 1989.
GOLTZ	H. GOLTZ, *Historia Siciliae et Magnae Greciae*, Bruges, 1576.
GORI	A.F. GORI, *Museum Florentinum exhibens insigniora vetustatis monumenta quae Florentiae sunt in thesauro mediceo. Gemmas antiquaé ex thesauro mediceo et privatorum dactyliothecis Florentiae*, Florentiae, 1731-1732.
HAGUE	M. Maaskant-Kleibrink, *Catalogue of the Engraved gems in the Royal Coin Cabinet. The Hague*. The Hague, 1978.
HENIG	H. Henig, *A Corpus of Roman Engraved Gemstones from British Site*, 1978.
JOHNSON	C. JOHNSON, R. MARTINI, *Milano Civiche Raccolte Numismatiche. Medaglie sec. XVI.* A.V. - CAVALLERINO *Bollettino di Numismatica. Monografie*, Roma, 1988.
JOHNSON	C. JOHNSON, R. MARTINI, *Milano, Civiche Raccolte Numismatiche. Medaglie sec. XVI*, Cavino. *Bollettino di Numismatica. Monografia*, Roma, 1989.
L'ORO DEGLI ETRUSCHI	*L'Oro degli Etruschi*, Novara, 1983.
LANZI	L. LANZI, *La Real Galleria di Firenze accresciuta e riordinata per comando di s. a.r. l'arciduca gran duca di Toscana' in Giornale de' letterati*, XLVII, Pisa, 1782.
LAZZARESCHI	V. LAZZARESCHI, *Le monete in: I palazzi dei mercanti nella libera Lucca del 1500. Immagine di una città stato al tempo dei Medici*, Lucca, 1980.
LIPPOLD, Gemmen und Kameen	G. Lippold, *Gemmen und Kameen des Altertums und der Neuzeit*, Stuttgart, 1922.
MAA SKANT, EG	M. MAASKANT - KLEIBRINK, *The engraved gems. Description of the collection in the rijks Museum G.M. Kam at Nijmegen*, Nijmegen, 1986.

MAETZKE — A.M. MAETZKE, in *Il Museo Statale d'Arte Medievale e Moderna in Arezzo*, Firenze, 1987.

MAZARD — J. MAZARD, *Corpus Nummorum Numidiae Mauretanieque Paris*, 1955.

MILANI, Mus. Arch. — A. MILANI, *Museo Archeologico di Firenze*, Firenze, 1912.

MÜLLER — *Numismatique de l'ancienne Afrique Copenhagen*, 1862, vol. III.

OREFICERIA SACRA NEL CHIANTI SENESE — *Oreficeria Sacra nel Chianti Senese* (XII-XV sec.), *Catalogo della Mostra di S. Gusmè*, Siena, 1985. A cura di Cecilia Alessi e Laura Martini.

ORI E ARGENTI — *Ori e Argenti, Ori e Argenti nelle Collezioni del Museo Archeologico di Firenze*, Firenze, 1990.

PANNUTI — U. PANNUTI, *Catalogo delle Gemme che non recano l'iscrizione LAU. R. MED. ma provenienti dal tesoro di Lorenzo De' Medici in AA.VV., Il Tesoro di Lorenzo il Magnifico*, Firenze, 1980.

POLLARD — J.G. POLLARD, *Medaglie Italiane del Rinascimento*, Firenze, 1985.

PROMIS — D. PROMIS, *Monete della repubblica di Siena*, Torino, 1868.

RIC — H. MATTINGLY E.A. Sydenham, *The Roman Imperial Coinage*, London, 1923-1966.

ROSSI — F. ROSSI, *Placchette secolo XV-XIX, Musei Civici di Brescia*, Vicenza, 1974.

SCHÄTZE DER ETRUSKER — *Schätze der Etrusker, Ausstellungskatalog - Saarbrücken*, Firenze, 1986.

SEZNEC — J. SEZNEC, *La sopravvivenza degli antichi dei*, Parigi, 1980, ed. italiana.

SUNDWALL — J. SUNDWALL, *Die Alteren Italischen Fibeln*, Berlin, 1943.

TONDO — L. TONDO, *La scoperta della monetazione di Iasos negli studi numismatici in Bollettino d'Arte.* Supplemento: *Studi su Iasos di Caria*, Roma, 1985.

TONDO — L. TONDO, *Imitazioni di monete antiche dal nucleo cinquecentesco del Medagliere di Firenze in Procedings of the 10th International Congress of Numismatics*, 1986.

TONDO — L. TONDO, *Domenico Sestini e il Medagliere Mediceo*, Firenze, 1990.

TONDO — L. TONDO, *I Cammei*, in *Le Gemme dei Medici e dei Lorena nel Museo Archeologico di Firenze*, Firenze, 1990.

TONDO — L. TONDO, F.M. VANNI, *Le Gemme dei Medici e dei Lorena nel Museo Archeologico di Firenze*, Firenze, 1990.

VANNEL TODERI — F. VANNEL TODERI, in *Il Museo Statale d'Arte Medievale e Moderna in Arezzo. Placchette*, Firenze, 1987.

VON O. HESSEN 1975 — O. VON HESSEN, *Secondo contributo all'archeologica longobarda in Toscana, reperti isolati e di provenienza incerta*, in *Studi dell'Accademia Toscana di Scienze e Lettere La Colombaria* XLI, 1975.

VICO 1557 — E. VICO, *Le imagini delle donne auguste intagliate in istampe di rame; con le vite et isposizioni di E. Vico sopra i riversi delle loro medaglie antiche*, in Vinegia, 1557, libr. I.

VICO 1548 — E. VICO, *Le immagini con tutti i riversi trovati et le vite de li imperatori tratte dalle medaglie et dalle Historie de gli antichi*, Venezia, 1548, libr. I.

VISCONTI — E.Q. VISCONTI, *Opere varie II*, 1829 Milano, III, 1830.

WEBER — F. WEBER, M.D. PARKES, *Medals of Priam, Augustus... attributed to Alessandro Cesati*, in *Numismatic Chronicle*, serie III, XVII, 314 essc.

ZANNONI — *Reale Galleria di Firenze illustrata, serie V. Cammei ed Intagli*, Firenze, vol. I, 1824; vol. II, 1831.

SUMMARY

Printed in Florence - Italy
on June 1992
by Nuova Grafica Fiorentina

In collaboration with

MONTE DEI PASCHI DI SIENA

MPS

BANK ESTABLISHED 1472